Microsoft Press

Inside
COM+
Base Services

Guy Eddon
Henry Eddon

PUBLISHED BY
Microsoft Press
A Division of Microsoft Corporation
One Microsoft Way
Redmond, Washington 98052-6399

Library of Congress Cataloging-in-Publication Data
Eddon, Guy, 1974–
    Inside COM+ Base Services / Guy Eddon, Henry Eddon.
      p.   cm.
    Includes index.
    ISBN 0-7356-0728-1
    1. COM (Computer architecture)   I. Eddon, Henry, 1945–   .
  II. Title.
  QA76.9.A73E33   1999
  005.2'76--dc21   99-40455
                                     CIP

Printed and bound in the United States of America.

1 2 3 4 5 6 7 8 9 WCWC 4 3 2 1 0 9

Distributed in Canada by Penguin Books Canada Limited.

A CIP catalogue record for this book is available from the British Library.

Microsoft Press books are available through booksellers and distributors worldwide. For further
information about international editions, contact your local Microsoft Corporation office or
contact Microsoft Press International directly at fax (425) 936-7329. Visit our Web site at
mspress.microsoft.com.

Intel is a registered trademark of Intel Corporation. Active Directory, ActiveX, DirectX,
Microsoft, Microsoft Press, MS-DOS, Visual Basic, Visual C++, Visual FoxPro, Visual InterDev,
Visual J++, Visual Studio, Win32, Windows, and Windows NT are either registered trademarks
or trademarks of Microsoft Corporation in the United States and/or other countries. Other
product and company names mentioned herein may be the trademarks of their respective owners.

The example companies, organizations, products, people, and events depicted herein are
fictitious. No association with any real company, organization, product, person, or event is
intended or should be inferred.

Acquisitions Editor: Eric Stroo
Project Editor: Alice Turner
Technical Editor: Marc Young
Manuscript Editor: Ina Chang

CONTENTS

Foreword xiii

Preface xv

PART I: FUNDAMENTAL
PROGRAMMING ARCHITECTURE

CHAPTER ONE

Component Software   **3**

From Object-Oriented Programming to Component Software 6

Object-Oriented Programming 7

Code Sharing and Reuse 8

Component Software 9

The Evolution of COM+ 11

From OLE to COM+ 12

RPC and COM+ 15

From COM to COM+ 16

Windows DNA: A Three-Tier Approach 18

Component Services 20

CHAPTER TWO

The *IUnknown* Interface   **29**

Interface Definition Language 31

The Client 36

The *CoInitializeEx* Function 36

The *CoCreateInstance* Function 36

The Methods of *IUnknown* 39

The *CoUninitialize* Function 42

The V-Table Situation 43

Building the Client Project 46

The Component 48

Implementing the *AddRef* and *Release* Methods 49

Implementing the *IUnknown::QueryInterface* Method 50

The *ISum::Sum* Method (Finally) 57

The *IClassFactory* Interface 57

Exported DLL Functions 63

The *CoCreateInstance* Function Revisited 67

Building the Component Project 70

Component Registration 74

Merging Object Identity 81

Containment 83

Aggregation 85

CHAPTER THREE

Language Integration   **91**

Type Libraries 92

Using Type Libraries 92

Building a Type Library 93

Registering a Type Library 96

An Easy C++ Client 101

C++ Templates (A Quick Introduction) 102

Namespaces 110

The Active Template Library 111

The ATL COM AppWizard 112

The ATL Object Wizard 113

Adding Methods and Properties to an Interface Using ATL 115

Building a Simple COM+ Object Using ATL 116

COM+ Programming in Visual Basic 118

QueryInterface: The Visual Basic Way 119

Building a Client in Visual Basic 122

Implementing COM+ Interfaces in Visual Basic 122

Building a Component in Visual Basic 124

COM+ Programming in Java 126

Calling a COM+ Object from Java 132

Implementing COM+ Objects in Java 136

ActiveX Controls and JavaBeans Integration 141

The Sandbox Model 142

CHAPTER FOUR

Apartments   **145**

A Quick Review of Threads 146

Apartment Types 147

    Single-Threaded Apartments 149

    Multithreaded Apartments 157

    Marshaling Interface Pointers Between Apartments 158

    How to Choose a Threading Model 162

Threading Models for In-Process Components 165

    Apartment Interactions 166

    Objects That Support the MTA Model 169

    Objects That Support All Apartment Models 170

    The Free-Threaded Marshaler 172

    Neutral Apartments 181

    Comparing the Apartment Models 183

    Writing Thread-Safe Components 185

Apartments and Language Integration 187

    Threading Options for Visual Basic Components 188

    Threading Options for Java Components 192

The Ten Threading Commandments 193

PART II: BASE FACILITIES

CHAPTER FIVE

Automation   **197**

The *IDispatch* Interface 199

    Automation Types 200

Implementing *IDispatch* 212

    Designing a Pure Dispinterface 212

    Designing a Dual Interface 213

    Implementation Techniques 217

    Properties 225

    Collections 227

    The (New and Improved) *IDispatchEx* Interface 229

Building Automation Clients 235

    Building Automation Clients in C++ 235

    Building Automation Clients in Visual Basic 240

Scripting 242

    Building Automation Clients in Script 243

    Scriptlets 245

CHAPTER SIX

Exceptions **249**

Error Codes 250

    FACILITY_ITF Error Codes 251

    Helper Macros 251

Rich Error Information 252

    The *ISupportErrorInfo* Interface 253

    The *ICreateErrorInfo* Interface 253

    Obtaining Error Information 255

    The *IErrorInfo* Interface 256

CHAPTER SEVEN

Component Categories **259**

Standard Component Categories 261

    Default Components 262

Registering a Component Category 265

    The *ICatRegister* Interface 265

Obtaining Component Category Information 268

    The *ICatInformation* Interface 268

CHAPTER EIGHT

Connection Points **271**

A Simple Connectable Object 272

    The Source Interface 272

    The *IConnectionPoint* Interface 273

    The *IConnectionPointContainer* Interface 276

    Implementing a Sink in C++ 279

    A Visual Basic Sink 283

    A Java Sink 289

A Complete Connectable Object 291

    Enumerators 292

    When to Use Connection Points 297

CHAPTER NINE

Type Information **301**

Creating a Type Library 302

    Adding Type Information 305

Obtaining Type Information 318

    The *ITypeLib* Interface 319

The *ITypeInfo* Interface 321

The *ITypeComp* Interface 325

Reading Type Information Using High-Level Languages 326

CHAPTER TEN

Persistence **329**

The *IPersist* Interface Family 329

The *IStream* Interface 331

Persisting an Object 333

Implementing a Persistable Object 335

Building Persistable Objects in Visual Basic 339

Building Persistable Objects in Java 344

Structured Storage 346

The *IStorage* and *IStream* Interfaces 347

The *IPropertySetStorage* and *IPropertyStorage* Interfaces 349

CHAPTER ELEVEN

Monikers **355**

Initializing Objects 355

Class Objects 357

Custom Activation Interfaces 357

More on Monikers 358

The *IMoniker* Interface 359

The *MkParseDisplayName* Function 364

The Class Moniker 367

The Marvelous Moniker: Improving the Class Moniker 370

The New Moniker 377

The Java Moniker 378

The Running Object Table 379

PART III: REMOTING ARCHITECTURE

CHAPTER TWELVE

Surrogates **385**

DLL Surrogates 386

Running In-Process Components Locally 386

Running Components Remotely 388

Custom Surrogates 391

A Custom DLL Surrogate: *DllNanny* 391

An Introduction to Marshaling 394

Standard Marshaling 396

Type Library Marshaling 398

Custom Marshaling 399

CHAPTER THIRTEEN

Executable Components   **401**

Building an Executable Component 403

Registering the Class Objects 407

Remote Instantiation 409

Integrating the Marshaling Code 411

Managing the Lifetime of an Executable Component 414

Race Conditions 415

Executable Component Shutdown 417

Custom Activation Interfaces 420

Singletons 424

CHAPTER FOURTEEN

Custom Marshaling   **427**

Marshaling Interface Pointers: An Overview 428

Re-Creating an Interface's V-Table 429

Interprocess Communication 430

Will That Be Custom or Standard Marshaling? 431

Can You Say "Custom Marshaling"? 435

Pardon Me, What Is the CLSID of Your Proxy Object? 437

How Big Did You Say Your Interface Is? 438

Unmarshaling the Interface Pointer 444

Marshal-by-Value 450

CHAPTER FIFTEEN

Standard Marshaling   **455**

The Standard Marshaling Architecture 456

The Standard Marshaling Interfaces 460

Registering the Proxy/Stub DLL 475

Converting Marshaled Interface Pointers to Strings 476

The OBJREF Moniker 478

Handler Marshaling 479

CHAPTER SIXTEEN

Interface Definition Language **485**

Types 485
    Enumerated Types 487
Directional Attributes 487
Arrays 491
    Fixed Arrays 492
    Conformant Arrays 492
    Varying Arrays 495
    Open Arrays 496
    Character Arrays 498
    Multidimensional Arrays 501
    Passing Arrays of User-Defined Types from Visual Basic 502
Pointers 503
    Full Pointers 504
    Unique Pointers..504
    Reference Pointers 505
    Interface Pointers 505
Interface Design Recommendations 509

CHAPTER SEVENTEEN

Asynchronous Calls **511**

Making Asynchronous Calls 511
    Defining Asynchronous Interfaces 512
    Calling Asynchronous Interfaces 513
    Implementing Asynchronous Interfaces 516
    Interoperability 518
Call Cancellation 519
    Requesting Method Call Cancellation 520
    Terminating the Method 522
Pipes 523

CHAPTER EIGHTEEN

Security **527**

The Windows Distributed Security Model 527
    The COM+ Security Model 528
    COM+ Security Packages 531

Declarative Security: The Registry 532

    Default Security 533

    Configuring Default Access and Launch Permissions 537

    Configuring Component Security: The AppID Key 539

    The *IAccessControl* Interface 541

    Configuring Component Identity 547

Programmatic Security 550

    The *CoInitializeSecurity* Function 551

    Using the *IAccessControl* Interface with *CoInitializeSecurity* 560

    Activation Credentials: The COAUTHINFO Structure 563

    The *IServerSecurity* Interface 566

    Cloaking 570

    The *IClientSecurity* Interface 572

CHAPTER NINETEEN

The Network Protocol   575

Spying on the Network Protocol 577

    Running Network Monitor 580

    Remote Activation 581

Internet Services 583

Calling All Remote Objects 586

    The ORPCTHIS and ORPCTHAT Structures 588

Marshaled Interface Pointers 590

    The Standard Object Reference 592

    The DUALSTRINGARRAY Structure 593

    The *IRemUnknown* Interface 595

    The *IRemUnknown2* Interface 600

The OXID Resolver 600

Garbage Collection 604

    A Remote Method Call 607

Channel Hooks 608

    A Useful Channel Hook: Obtaining the Client's Name 611

APPENDIX

Remote Procedure Calls   617

The Design and Purpose of RPC 617

    Interface Definition Language 618

    Binding 619

Location Transparency 619

Handles 620

The Prime Application 621

Client Initialization 622

Client Computation 625

The Prime Server 625

Context Rundown 626

Debugging 627

Distributed Computation 627

Bibliography 629

Index 631

FOREWORD

Well, it's been over a decade since I started writing applications for Microsoft Windows. Back then, it was easy for someone to say that they really understood Windows and all of its subsystems. Each of these subsystems exposed only a few hundred functions: in Windows 2.11, Kernel had 283, User had 141, and GDI had 213, for a grand total of 637 functions. How hard could it be to understand what these few functions did?

Over the past 10 years, Microsoft has greatly extended these modules and has added numerous subsystems to Windows: telephony, remote access, print spoolers, 3-D graphics, Internet access, security, registry, services, multimedia, networking, and so on. It is now impossible for any individual to fully understand the entire operating system. For this reason, I've advised developers to pick certain components of the system, study them, learn them, and become specialists in them. This is not to say that you should ignore other parts of the system—I've specialized in Kernel and User, but I've also dabbled in GDI, networking, and lots of other areas.

At Microsoft, different teams develop each of these subsystems and each team develops its own "philosophy." For example, I know that the registry functions all start with a *Reg* prefix and return an error code. But I also know that most Kernel functions have no special prefix and return *FALSE* if they fail; in these cases, I have to call *GetLastError* to see the reason for the failure. This inconsistent behavior among subsystems is one of the reasons that Windows programming has had a reputation for being difficult to learn.

By now, it is obvious to everyone that Microsoft is firmly committed to Windows for the present and for the foreseeable future. To achieve this end, it has needed a plan that allows new subsystems to be added without steepening the developer's learning curve too much. In other words, there must be consistency in using the various subsystems (or components). The technology to address this need is COM+.

Microsoft exposes new technologies by implementing each new subsystem as a COM+ object. You can easily see this design when you use directory services (Active Directory), transaction services (Microsoft Distributed Transaction Coordinator), graphics (DirectX), shell extensions, controls (ActiveX controls), data (OLE DB), scripting (ActiveX scripting), and on and on. COM+ is now *the* way to interact with these subsystems. In fact, in an effort to reduce the Windows learning curve for new developers, Microsoft is going back to older subsystems and exposing those systems as COM+ objects.

It is now imperative that Windows developers understand the core infrastructure of COM+. With this understanding, you can easily take advantage of these new subsystems as well as more easily expose your own subsystems. Distributed computing is a massive undertaking that requires addressing many difficult problems, such as data transfer, incompatible computer architectures, disparate network architectures, timing issues, and so on. Fortunately, Microsoft has teams of developers working to solve these problems and to make things easier for the rest of us. Windows 2000 offers the first enterprise-level release of COM+.

With Microsoft firmly behind it, COM+ will undoubtedly be the best way to interact with subsystems, not only on a single machine but also on any computer anywhere in the world (and possibly beyond). *Inside COM+ Base Services* is our guidebook. Let's keep our fingers crossed and hope that it is translated into Martian.

Jeffrey Richter

PREFACE

COM+ is not a radical departure from COM—it is the next stage of evolution of the COM programming model. COM was originally designed as a minimalist's component architecture. With the advent of the three-tier programming model, applications have become more complex. To help developers who work in this new world, COM+ offers a richer set of services than was available in COM. These services evolved from the technology previously known as Microsoft Transaction Server (MTS) and include features such as automatic transactions, role-based security, load balancing, object pooling, queued components, the in-memory database, and an external publish-and-subscribe event model.

COM+ offers many powerful and useful run-time services that save you the effort of building similar services yourself. While working on this book, we came to realize that it is impossible to explain these services without first explaining the fundamental component model at the heart of COM+. Whether or not you use these services in your components—for some developers, COM+ services offer little advantage[1]—you must understand the fundamental COM+ programming architecture before you can use COM+ effectively.

Inside COM+ Base Services describes the fundamental component model at the core of COM+. Once you understand the issues involved in building software components, you'll be able to decide where and how to use the COM+ component services effectively. *Inside COM+ Component Services* (forthcoming from Microsoft Press) covers these services in detail, along with issues involved in building multitier enterprise applications.

In this book, we make two assumptions—that you're interested in learning about COM+ and that you're familiar with a modern programming language such as C++, Microsoft Visual Basic, or Java. One of the central tenets of COM+ is the concept of language neutrality, so we've structured *Inside COM+ Base Services* around that idea. Although you can build COM+ components in a wide variety of development environments, we focus on the most popular trio: C++, Visual Basic, and Java. Visual Basic and Java developers will learn a lot from this book even though these languages hide a large part of the COM+ infrastructure.

---

1. For example, DirectX, a set of specialized components for graphics programming in Microsoft Windows, does not use any COM+ component services because of its critical performance requirements.

In many cases, we present examples in C++ and then show how components written in higher-level languages can tie into the same functionality. However, you must understand the fundamentals of C++ in order to use many of the sample programs.

Remember the Sojourner rover that roamed the surface of Mars during the summer of 1997? It ran on an 8-bit Intel 80C85 processor containing only 6500 transistors (compared with 5.5 million transistors in a Pentium). It had a radio modem capable of 9600 bps and was powered by solar energy and nonrechargeable lithium D-cell batteries. It was a feat of modern engineering achieved with the most basic components. In a less dramatic way, COM+ is like that—it consists of a fundamental set of ideas that can give rise to some amazingly powerful systems.

System Requirements for the Companion CD

To run the code on the companion CD, you will need Microsoft Visual Studio 6.0 and Microsoft Windows 98 or Microsoft Windows NT 4.0. (Microsoft Windows 2000 is required for some chapters.)

Acknowledgments

Thanks to Eric Stroo, our acquisitions editor, for guiding yet another book to a successful conclusion. Mary Kirtland and Saji Abraham of Microsoft Corporation supported us throughout this project by answering many questions. Thanks to Eric Maffei and the rest of the MSJ gang. Thanks to Alice Turner, the project editor; Marc Young, the technical editor; and Ina Chang, the manuscript editor, for their hard work and dedication to this book.

Guy Eddon
Henry Eddon
http://www.guyeddon.com

PART I

FUNDAMENTAL PROGRAMMING ARCHITECTURE

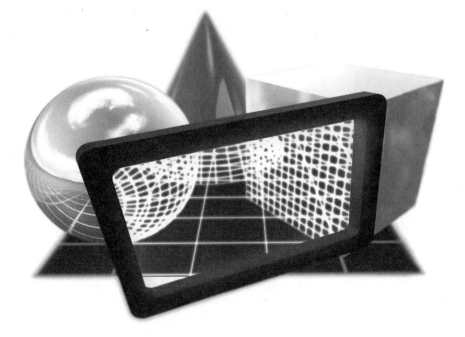

CHAPTER ONE

Component Software

For as long as personal computers have existed, the industry has provided increasingly powerful hardware for CPU-hungry software. Companies such as Intel have upgraded their processors from 8 to 16 to 32 bits and have increased their clock speed from 4.77 to over 550 megahertz (MHz). Under development are 64-bit processors that will run at still higher clock speeds. Yet the cost of developing a new processor is so prohibitive that only the largest corporations can afford the expense of upgrading. And we might someday run into the law of diminishing returns, making the expense of development outweigh the possible improvements.

Many other ways have been suggested for improving overall processing speed. Foremost has been the concept of *parallel processing*. Parallel processing holds that in an ideal environment, if one CPU can do x amount of work in a certain amount of time, 10 CPUs can do $10x$ work in the same time. Parallel processing can be implemented in two major ways: *symmetric multiprocessing (SMP)* and *distributed computing*.

With SMP, several (or several hundred) CPUs are placed inside a single computer. The host operating system must support multithreading so that different threads can be scheduled to run on different CPUs concurrently. Implementing SMP requires special software support. Microsoft Windows NT, for example, was one of the first PC operating systems capable of supporting SMP. Today, Microsoft Windows 2000 can quite flexibly support up to 16 processors.

For our purposes, we will define distributed computing as a system in which computers are interconnected for the purpose of sharing CPU power and appear to users as a single application. The definition is rather vague when it comes to how the computers are interconnected. (According to this definition, sending a document to a remote color printer by copying the document from your computer to a floppy disk, walking to the computer connected to the color printer, inserting the disk, and printing the document qualifies as an example of distributed computing.) In theory, the exact manner in which computers are interconnected is irrelevant. Perhaps the more important issue is the throughput provided by the information conduit. A distributed system connected by a 100-megabits-per-second, Ethernet-based local area network (LAN) will yield very different performance from a system connected by a 56 Kbps modem.

Before expanding on our definition of distributed computing, let's explore a realistic, albeit hypothetical, distributed system. A large bank has branch offices all over the world. The bank used to have a mainframe-based computing center at its world headquarters, and all branch offices used terminals connected to that mainframe. All account and customer information was therefore stored in one place. The bank then decided to retire the mainframe computer and replace it with a distributed system. Each branch office now has a master computer that stores local accounts and handles local transactions. In addition, each computer is connected with all the other branch computers via a global area network. If transactions can be performed without regard to where the customer actually is or where the customer's account data is actually stored, and if the users cannot tell the difference between the new system and the centralized mainframe-based system it replaced, this is a successful distributed system.

What would cause the bank to replace the centralized system with a distributed system? Cost is the chief factor driving the industrywide push toward distributed systems. It can be much more economical to purchase and administer hundreds or even thousands of PCs than to purchase and maintain a single mainframe computer. But price alone is not the reason. A well-designed distributed system yields better performance for the same amount of money.

Another factor that might influence the bank's decision is that a distributed system can outperform any mainframe. Current technology makes it possible to build a network of 5,000 Intel Pentium-based PCs, each running at about 200 million instructions per second (MIPS), yielding a total performance of 1 million MIPS. A single CPU producing that kind of performance would need to execute one instruction every 10^{-12} seconds. Even assuming that electricity could travel at the speed of light (300,000 kilometers per second), only a distance of 0.3 millimeter would be covered in 10^{-12} seconds. To build a CPU with that sort of performance in a 0.3-millimeter cube would truly be a feat of modern engineering. (The CPU would generate so much heat that it would spontaneously combust.)

Reliability is both a major concern and a goal of any distributed system. A well-designed distributed system can realize much higher overall reliability than a comparable centralized system. For example, if we conclude that a particular centralized system has a failure rate of only 2 percent, we can expect users to experience 2 percent system downtime. During that downtime, all work grinds to a halt. In a distributed system, we might evaluate each node as having a 5 percent failure rate. (The difference in failure rates can be attributed to the fact that most mainframe computers are kept in specially cooled and dust-free rooms with an around-the-clock team of trained operators, while PCs are often locked in a closet and forgotten.) Ideally, fewer than 5 percent of the machines are down at any one moment, which translates into only a 5 percent degradation of total system performance—not total system failure. For mission-critical applications, such as control of nuclear reactors or spaceship navigation systems, in which reliability and redundancy are of paramount importance, a distributed system introduces an extra degree of reliability.

In the following formula, P is the probability of occurrence of the two unrelated events A and B:

$$P(A \cap B) = PA \times PB$$

The more general case is shown here:

$$P_{c,n} = c^n \times 10^{-2n}$$

$P_{c,n}$ is the probability that if there are n unrelated events and each one has a c percent probability of failure, all events will fail simultaneously. Thus, even with a 5 percent rate of failure per node, users of a system with 100 nodes will experience only a 20^{-100} percent chance of any downtime whatsoever. (This case is rather extreme since it is highly unlikely that 100 out of 100 computers would fail simultaneously.) Let's use the logic shown above to evaluate the risk of several computers failing at the same time.

Figure 1-1 shows the likelihood of simultaneous failure for between 1 and 5 computers out of a total of 10.

Distributed systems do not need to be taken off line for upgrade or maintenance work. Several servers can be taken off line at one time or additional servers can be added, all without unduly inconveniencing users or jeopardizing the company's main business. Capacity planning can also be done in a more sane and logical manner because there is little incentive to purchase extra processing power in advance of need.

5

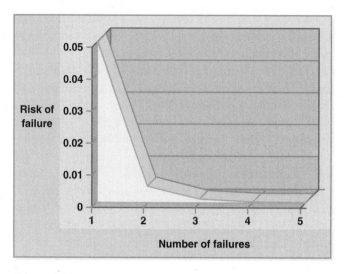

Figure 1-1.
Risk of multiple simultaneous failures in a system of 10 nodes.

In recent years, there has been much talk about migrating enterprise-wide systems from the two-tier paradigm called the client/server model to a three-tier architecture. The surging popularity of the Internet, the advent of the Java programming language, and the advent of the network computer have all spurred interest in the concept of three-tier system architecture. Later in this chapter, we'll take a look at the three-tier solution and examine how COM+ fits in with this architecture.

From Object-Oriented Programming to Component Software

Software development processes have not really changed much over the years. Most software development efforts are beleaguered by cost and time overruns, and the results are often bug-ridden and impossible to maintain. Over the years, a number of paradigms and methodologies, from flowchart creation to object orientation, have been offered and sometimes accepted for varying lengths of time as a panacea for these problems. Over time, all of these purported solutions have failed to meet expectations, and no reliable substitute has been found for what can be achieved by small groups of individuals, working on one project at a time. This is not to say that flowcharts are unhelpful or that object-oriented designs are flawed, but simply that they do not reduce software development to a formula that guarantees results. Perhaps these paradigms have been over-sold, or perhaps users have expected too much of them. The time has come to realize that software development is inherently difficult and fraught with many problems that have no single solution.

Object-Oriented Programming

Object-oriented programming is one of the more recent paradigms to enjoy a long and somewhat favorable reception by the software industry. This acceptance is reflected in the popularity of object-oriented programming languages such as Ada, Smalltalk, Java, and C++. Each of these languages carries the object-oriented flag at varying heights, depending on the original areas of expertise of their designers, the problems they set out to solve, and the limitations they faced. Smalltalk is an example of what happens when object-oriented ideas are carried to an extreme. C++, on the other hand, takes a pragmatic view of object-oriented programming, although this can be traced mostly to its roots in C and its stringent compatibility requirements with that language. And although Microsoft Visual Basic is not fully object-oriented, object-oriented ideas have permeated its design as it has evolved.

In a nutshell, the goal of object-oriented programming techniques is not to facilitate programming in a procedural manner that mimics the logic of a computer, but to allow developers to write software that deals with the way individuals think in the real world. Most software attempts to model, or "virtualize," things that we work with every day. Object-oriented programming languages allow developers to better express the existence of objects directly in the code. Disciples of the object-oriented school of programming believe that these techniques lead to more expressive code that is easier to develop and less costly to maintain.

Most object-oriented programming languages make an important distinction between an *object* and a *class*. A class is a template that defines its members. An object is an instance of a particular class and can actually do things. This relationship can be illustrated with the following example. Compare a cookie cutter and a cookie. A cookie cutter is a template (class) that defines various attributes of cookies, such as shape and size. A cookie, on the other hand, is analogous to an object because the cookie is created based on the cookie cutter.

7

To help programmers make better use of the object-oriented paradigm, most object-oriented programming languages provide support for the following three concepts:

- **Encapsulation**—the hiding of an object's implementation details

- **Inheritance**—the ability to reuse existing objects in the creation of new, more specialized objects

- **Polymorphism**—the ability of code to exhibit multiple behaviors depending on the object being used

Code Sharing and Reuse

Object-oriented programming became as popular as it did largely because it allowed developers to share code among entirely different projects. As mentioned, the redevelopment of similar code and algorithms occurs all the time, resulting in an incredible waste of time, effort, and money. While code sharing and reuse is considered a primary benefit of a well-implemented object-oriented design, the percentage of code actually being shared is still small. Until recently, even applications in suites such as Microsoft Office had different code to implement standard features such as toolbars, status bars, and spell checkers. Many of these standard graphical user interface (GUI) controls have been built into recent versions of Windows, allowing all applications to share them. If you think about it, an operating system is a great (but not tremendously flexible) example of code reuse.

Code reuse is one of those things that everyone assumed would happen spontaneously. This turned out to be wishful thinking, since code reuse needs to be planned for and its implications carefully thought through. If you write some code and then give it to friends so that they can use it, is that code reuse? What about code libraries that programmers link to their applications? While these are examples of code reuse, each has its problems. If you give your code to your friends and they don't like some aspects of it, they might go into your source code and make modifications. This tinkering is not in keeping with the idea of code reuse. Modifying someone else's source code is like breaking a figurine in a china store—the hapless browser becomes the proud new owner. If something doesn't work after someone changes your code, you are no longer obliged to support it. In addition, when you later update your own code and then make available the new version, your friends have to go through it and integrate their own changes anew. The code is then manifestly not reusable. If you purchase a class library and you don't like the way it works, that's too bad unless you also buy the source code so you can alter it, and that brings you back to the previous problem.

To better understand code reuse, we need a more solid definition. True code reusability means that the code must be written in a general enough manner for reuse to build something larger, while still being customizable in the way that the code works and what it does. Another problem with most types of code reuse is that they normally require the original developer and the person who wants to reuse the code to work in the same programming language. If a class library is written in C++, for example, it is basically impossible to reuse that code in an application written in any other language. By the same token, a Java class can be used only in a Java program. So although you often get more software reuse using an object-oriented programming language than if you don't, you still face limitations. How, then, can we apply code sharing and reuse to practical, real-life programming? While object-oriented programming has long been advanced as a solution to the problems at hand, it has yet to fulfill this promise.

Component Software

The breakdown of a project into its logical components is the essence of object-oriented analysis and design. That's also the basis for component software, which is composed of reusable pieces of software in binary form (as opposed to source code) that can be plugged into components from other vendors with relatively little effort. It is important to realize that a component-based approach to software development does not dictate the structure of an application. Rather, it is a model that makes possible the programming, use, and independent evolution of binary software components. Components are independent of the applications that use them as well as the programming languages used to create them.

Software components can be divided into a variety of categories, including visual components, such as buttons or list boxes, and functional components, such as ones that add printing or spell checking capability. For example, a component-based architecture might enable spell checker components from multiple vendors to be plugged into a single word processing program from another vendor. This would hold many advantages for the end user. A user might love the word processor produced by company A but hate the spell checker it comes with. If the word processor was designed so that the spell checker component can be replaced, the user can purchase a spell checker from company B, which specializes in creating spell checkers. Component software enables software developers to specialize in what they do best.

A good analogy for component software can be found in the automobile industry, in which car manufacturers often buy individual car parts, such as engines and transmissions, from various manufacturers and then assemble cars from these components. With component software, the pieces can be used as they are—they don't need to be recompiled, you don't need the source code, and you aren't restricted to one programming language. The term for this process is *binary reuse,* because it is based on interfaces rather than on reuse at the source code level. While the software components must adhere to the agreed upon interface, their internal implementation is completely autonomous. For this reason, you can build the components using procedural languages as well as object-oriented languages.

One of the main goals of a component-based programming model is to promote *interoperability.* Interoperability is one of those buzzwords in the computer field that means different things to different people. In the context of component software, interoperability simply means the ability of components to work together. When you examine a project and notice areas in which software seems to be forced together unnaturally, the application should be divided into components.

Let's use the example of controls. In the good old days of Windows programming, if your program needed a toolbar, you simply wrote the toolbar code directly into the main part of the application. This approach had two inherent problems. First, your goal was probably not to create a cool toolbar but to create a great application with a toolbar. Second, after you consumed many precious hours developing a toolbar, if other developers in your company wanted to use that toolbar in their projects, they couldn't easily reuse it if the code was sprinkled throughout the program, responding to *WM_CREATE, WM_PAINT,* and *WM_LBUTTONDOWN* messages.

A component-based approach to this problem would make the toolbar into a separate component. The problem then becomes how the toolbar component and the application should interact—the whole issue of interoperability. The component software paradigm mandates that all components define an interface that exposes the functionality available in that component. As long as the component implements the interface and the client applications abide by it, interoperability results. In the toolbar example, the application developers could simply purchase the toolbar component from some other developer who specializes in toolbars, thus saving development, debugging, and maintenance time.

In the software world, there is no better example of the impact of components than that of ActiveX controls. An ActiveX control is a type of COM+ component that is typically placed on a form, where it can interact with the user.

The user perceives the ActiveX control and the form as a single application, even though the two pieces of software were developed independently, perhaps even in different programming languages, and are not compiled together. The control and the form work together through interfaces. The form interrogates the control to learn what interfaces it supports, and the control does the same to the form. You can use object-oriented programming concepts in conjunction with a component-based approach to build flexible and powerful objects that can easily be reused by other developers.

One important principle of object-oriented programming, mentioned earlier, is encapsulation. Encapsulation hides the implementation of an object from users of the object. The users of an object have access only to the object's interface. Developers who use prebuilt objects in their projects are interested only in the "contract"—the promised behavior that the object supports. Component software formalizes the notion of a contract between an object and a client. Each object declares what it is capable of by implementing certain interfaces. The only way to access the services of an object is through the interfaces that it supports. Such a contract is the basis for interoperability.

Interfaces

An interface is actually a very simple thing—a semantically related set of methods grouped together under one name. For now, this will be our working definition of an interface. For example, the Win32 API is an interface to the functionality of the Windows operating system. With component software, not only can operating systems make an interface available, but so can software components built by us ordinary folk. An interface is a strongly typed contract between a software component and its clients; it is an articulation of an expected behavior and expected responsibilities, and it gives programmers and designers a concrete entity to use when referring to the component. Two objects that implement the same interfaces are said to be polymorphs. Although not a strict requirement of the model, you should factor interfaces in so that they can be reused in a variety of contexts.

The Evolution of COM+

As is the case with most significant technologies, COM+ was not invented overnight by a lone caffeine-crazed developer. It is the result of multiple paths of technological evolution, as shown in Figure 1-2. To better understand the underpinnings of COM+, let's examine the technologies from which it evolved.

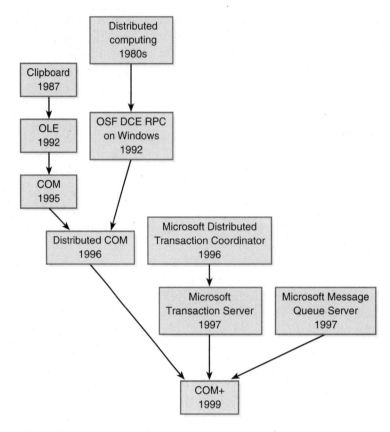

Figure 1-2.
The evolution of COM+.

From OLE to COM+

Microsoft's MS-DOS operating system was developed for a very limited computer (by today's standards). As Intel advanced with more powerful CPUs, such as the 80286 and 80386, Microsoft began to envision the possibilities of running multiple applications concurrently. Then, with the advent of the cooperatively multitasking Windows environment, Microsoft realized that users wanted to exchange data among various applications. The clipboard and Dynamic Data Exchange (DDE) initiatives were two of the first interprocess communication facilities that Microsoft incorporated into Windows. DDE was a message-passing service designed for use by developers to incorporate data exchange facilities into their applications. However, DDE was a rather complex protocol to follow, and consequently few applications aside from Microsoft Excel implemented it successfully.

The clipboard provided users with a primitive but easily understood paradigm of cut, copy, and paste operations. You could use it to create compound documents—documents containing different types of content. (For example, a word processing document could contain text, bitmaps, charts, and sound clips.) Suppose that you wanted to create the 1992 annual report for your company using one of the first versions of Microsoft Word for Windows. First you probably would have written the text describing the state of the company and the progress made over the prior year. Then you might have loaded Excel to create a spreadsheet with figures on the company's performance. Finally, you might have selected some cells in the spreadsheet, copied them to the clipboard, and pasted them into your Word document. Without the clipboard, you might have had to print your Word document and Excel spreadsheet separately and then literally cut and paste them using scissors and glue.

The fact that the clipboard service was both easy to implement from the developer's perspective and easy for the user to control made it an immediate hit. The clipboard continues to be popular in today's Windows applications. Nevertheless, the shortcomings of the clipboard quickly became apparent. The basic problem with the clipboard as a means of creating compound documents was the lack of intelligence involved in the data transfer. For example, after you created your company's annual report using the clipboard, you might have discovered a need to update some of the figures in the Excel spreadsheet. This required that you once more select, copy, and paste new figures into your Word document.

The original concept of object linking and embedding (OLE) grew out of Microsoft's effort to address this problem. OLE was first released with Microsoft Windows 3.1 in 1992. The original idea of OLE was to provide an improved mechanism for dealing with compound documents. For example, a smart compound document could either embed the Excel spreadsheet data in or link it with the Word document. Whenever linked figures were updated in the spreadsheet, the new data automatically found its way to the Word document. Also, you could open and edit the linked or embedded figure in Excel by double-clicking it in Word. This capability was a great boon to users, although few understood how it operated. In fact, DDE was used internally by the first release of OLE as the interprocess communication protocol. OLE contained some very interesting ideas, foremost of which was the concept that compound document objects supported by different applications could work together in the creation of a "super-document." The OLE designers continued to broaden and refine their ideas until they began to view compound document objects as software components—small, self-contained software objects that could be plugged into an application, thereby extending its functionality.

OLE 2, released in 1993, further refined the linking and embedding capabilities and extended them with *in-place activation*. In-place activation, sometimes called *visual editing,* allows one application to take on the appearance of another, enabling the user to edit all of the data contained in a compound document without leaving the context of a single window. Although most developers did not realize it at that time, or for a long while after, the architecture of OLE 2 was built around the revolutionary idea of component-based software. In the long run, this has proved to be by far the most important contribution of OLE 2. Over the years, OLE has faded into the background while COM has taken center stage.

Most software projects are still designed around the idea of producing a behemoth that encompasses every feature any user might conceivably desire. The trouble with this model of software development is that applications become more fragile as they grow. If it is difficult to have a complete understanding of an application containing 100,000 lines of code, it is all but impossible with 1,000,000 lines. Even a small modification in an application of that size requires extensive retesting of the entire system. Often what appears to be an innocuous modification in one section of code does damage in many other locations.

COM acts as the "glue" between components, enabling unrelated software objects to connect and interact in meaningful ways. These components can then be reused in many environments on both the client and the server. For example, a particular business component can be used in a desktop application as well as by a Web application running in Microsoft Internet Information Server (IIS). COM lets you group objects into distinct components so that your applications consist of replaceable pieces that provide specific functionality.

Building a system based on interoperable components doesn't mean that the user can't have an icon on the desktop to launch the application. Even applications built from components must give the user the illusion that the application is a single unit. For example, let's examine the architecture of Microsoft Internet Explorer. The shell is a simple ActiveX document host, and the actual parsing and rendering of HTML is done by an ActiveX document component that is loaded whenever the user navigates to a Web site. If the Web site contains an ActiveX control, the control is downloaded and installed. This component-based architecture keeps every part of the application focused on a specific job. COM enables different teams of developers, perhaps using different programming languages, to develop components for one application. The components work together seamlessly so long as everyone plays by the rules of COM.

Let's review some of the challenges faced by the software industry that led Microsoft to develop COM. The continuous evolution of computer hardware and software has brought an increasing number of sophisticated applications to users' desktops and to networks. Such complex software has created a commensurate number of problems for developers:

- ■ Modern software applications are large and complex—they are time-consuming to develop, difficult and costly to maintain, and risky to extend with additional functionality.

- ■ Applications continue to be developed in a monolithic style—they come prepackaged with a range of static features, none of which can be added, removed, upgraded independently, or replaced with alternatives.

- ■ Applications do not lend themselves to integration—neither the data nor the functionality of one program is readily available to another program.

- ■ Programming models reflect the provider's upbringing—they vary widely depending on whether the service is coming from a provider in the same address space, in another address space on the same machine, in another machine running across the network, or in the operating system.

Does COM fix all of these problems? As the nature of the difficulties described here suggests, no one idea can single-handedly address all of these issues. But as you'll see in the following sections, software that follows the COM architecture can better meet these challenges. COM+ itself has evolved from a combination of classic COM and Microsoft Transaction Server (MTS), which is described later in this chapter[1]. For the time being, COM+ embodies the glorious culmination of a long evolution of ideas that began with OLE.

RPC and COM+

Back in the 1980s, simply connecting several computers together over a LAN was a major achievement. For the PC to be accepted in mission-critical applications there needed to be a distributed support system analogous to that of a centralized operating system. This approach, however, would not go anywhere unless industry groups cooperated on the creation of standards. In the world of mainframe computers, standards were a nonissue; software was written for specific hardware. (In those days, IBM's computers were not expected to talk to other companies' computers.)

---

1. With the release of Windows NT 4.0 in 1996, COM gained the functionality necessary to invoke components that ran on remote computers connected via a network. This technology, at first called Distributed COM, is now an integral part of COM+ itself.

In the late 1980s, various industry groups tried to get enough companies to define standards and then agree to abide by them. One of the groups, the Open Software Foundation (OSF), became an industrywide consortium with a mandate for defining standards in a broad spectrum of areas. The OSF members decided to address the issue of distributed computing. Out of this effort grew the specifications for the Distributed Computing Environment (DCE), an environment for creating distributed systems. To this end, DCE began designing a comprehensive and integrated set of tools and services to support the creation of distributed applications, in a manner analogous to the support offered by the operating system in a centralized environment.

One outcome of the DCE effort was a specification for communicating between computers. This specification, known as Remote Procedure Calls (RPCs), allows applications on different computers to communicate. COM+ uses RPCs for its intercomputer communication.

From COM to COM+

COM+ currently encompasses two areas of functionality: a fundamental programming architecture for building software components (which was first defined by the original COM specification), plus an integrated suite of component services with an associated run-time environment for building sophisticated software components. Components that execute within this environment are called configured components. Components that do not take advantage of this environment are called unconfigured components; they play by the standard rules of COM. While you can use the COM+ programming model without the component services and run-time model, much of the power of COM+ is realized when these two parts are used together.

The COM+ programming architecture described so far provides a model for creating component software. For many developers, however, this is insufficient. In the typical corporation, for example, developers build business components that operate as part of a larger application, often using a client/server or three-tier approach. Developers expend a great deal of effort to build the simplest of components. Even if the goals of a business component are relatively modest, developers must create a robust and secure housing for it. If many clients connect to the component simultaneously, developers must ensure that only clients with the proper authorization can perform certain privileged operations using the component. Scalability is another concern if the component might be accessed by a large number of clients simultaneously.

Large systems need to anticipate client failures in the midst of complex operations involving the database server. The client might have been storing data locally and then updating data on the database server based on some local information. If the client fails in the middle of this type of operation, you cannot be sure of the integrity of the database without implementing some sort of transaction protocol. Finally, if the internal data structures of the component become corrupted, this corruption must be detected before the integrity of the database itself is compromised. You can see that a major problem with the basic model for component software is that developers are left to implement an enormous amount of functionality themselves—functionality that has little to do with the goals of the application itself.

Microsoft has realized that writing robust server-side systems requires intensive work. Threading and concurrency, security and administration, robustness, and the like are crucial to any distributed system, and developing software with these features seamlessly integrated requires tremendous effort. This effort is also completely unrelated to the actual processing done by the system. Microsoft SQL Server, for example, is a database server that deals with these issues in addition to its bread-and-butter work of processing SQL queries.

Out of this realization, Microsoft developed Microsoft Transaction Server (MTS), the first Windows-based implementation of a run-time environment that provides these services for software components. The run-time environment and component services offered by COM+ have evolved from ideas that originated with MTS. COM+ provides a robust run-time environment that deals with most of the issues facing developers of server-side systems and enables them to develop simple, in-process COM+ components containing the actual business-related functionality.

Although any in-process COM+ component can run in the COM+ run-time environment, in-process components not designed specifically for execution within that environment—executable components, for example—cannot take full advantage of the services offered by COM+.

The fundamental architecture of COM+ imposes minimal overhead, but Microsoft realized that many developers of customized corporate applications could benefit from a standard set of application services. For example, developers are often confronted with similar challenges when building line-of-business applications, such as security, reliability, concurrency, and scalability. Instead of forcing developers to create their own solutions to these problems for each application, COM+ offers these built-in services to components at run time. Not all components need or want these services. In specialized applications where performance is of the utmost importance, the run-time overhead imposed by these services causes developers to reject them. In many standard applications, however, these services offer tremendous value to both the developer and the overall stability of the entire project.

Windows DNA: A Three-Tier Approach

Many new enterprise information systems are being developed to run on Windows 2000. To help developers take better advantage of the application services offered by Windows 2000, Microsoft coined the term Windows DNA—Windows Distributed interNet Applications Architecture. Windows DNA is the application development model for the Windows platform. Basically, Windows DNA offers a three-tier architecture based on COM+, as shown in Figure 1-3. Because Windows DNA provides a comprehensive and integrated set of services on the Windows platform, developers are free from the burden of building or assembling the required infrastructure for distributed applications and can focus on delivering business solutions. The goal of the three-tier approach is to separate the business logic from a client/server system by moving it to a middle tier that runs on Windows 2000. The resulting three-tier architecture consists of a presentation layer, business logic components, and the data services layer.

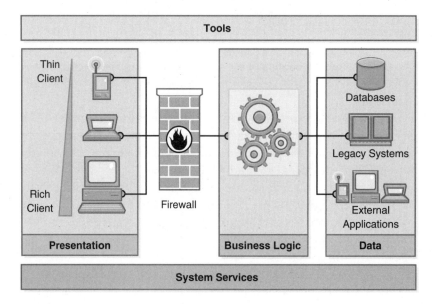

Figure 1-3.
The Windows DNA Architecture.

Presentation

The client side of a client/server system typically encompasses the functionality of both the user interface and the business logic that drives the system, leaving only the database on the server side. This design leads to heavyweight client-side applications that tend to be tied to a particular operating system and can be difficult to deploy and support. In a three-tier architecture, the client is designed to be as lightweight as possible, normally handling only the user interface. Such a thin client might consist of forms designed in Visual Basic or perhaps only of HTML pages designed to run in a Web browser such as Internet Explorer.

Developing client-side applications composed solely of HTML pages is alluring to many corporations because of their platform independence and ease of distribution. Developers of applications that require a user interface richer than the one possible purely with HTML might consider using Dynamic HTML or scripting code (Internet Explorer supports both VBScript and JScript) or including ActiveX controls or Java applets in their Web pages. Like HTML, Java applets are platform-independent, and both Java applets and ActiveX controls offer automated distribution. Applications requiring an even more robust presentation layer can be built with full-fledged programming languages including Visual Basic, Java, and C++. While client programs built in HTML use the Hypertext Transfer Protocol (HTTP) to communicate with the Web server, applications built in Visual Basic, Java, or C++ typically make direct method calls to the business components running in the COM+ environment.

Business Logic

While the client/server architecture is relatively fixed on deploying the client-side and the server-side components on different computers, the business logic component of a three-tier design can lead to more flexible solutions. For example, the business logic of an application might be implemented as an in-process COM+ component designed to run in the process of the client application on the client side or in the process of a Web server on the server side. Alternatively, the business logic component might run in the COM+ environment on a third machine that is separate from both the client and the database server.

Data

The data tier of the Windows DNA model consists of SQL servers such as SQL Server, Oracle, Sybase, DB2, or any other database server that supports OLE DB or Open Database Connectivity (ODBC). Typically, COM+ components running in the middle tier use ActiveX Data Objects (ADO, the COM+ component that provides a high-level wrapper for OLE DB) to connect with and query the database. OLE DB makes it possible to access data from a wide variety of database servers, including legacy systems.

Component Services

Microsoft found that developers spend too much of their time writing housekeeping code—as much as 30 percent of the total time they spend building COM+ components. COM+ component services provide a standard implementation of services that are frequently needed by component developers, thereby freeing developers to concentrate on the business problem at hand. This should bring the ideas originating in COM+ to an even wider audience, which is important if COM+ is to fulfill its goal of becoming the component object technology of the future for Windows services. Figure 1-4 shows the evolution of services from COM to COM+.

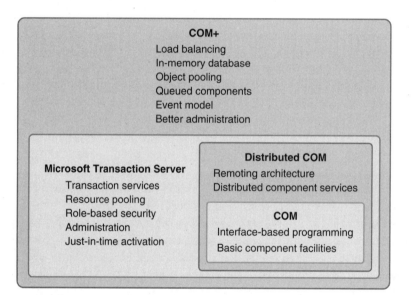

Figure 1-4.
The evolution of component services from COM to COM+.

Just-In-Time Activation

Although COM+ makes certain demands of your components, it also offers them much in the way of functionality. One major feature of COM+ is its ability to scale middle-tier components so that they can support hundreds or even thousands of simultaneous clients. A client that attempts to instantiate a COM+ object running in a COM+ environment receives a reference to a context object implemented by COM+—not a reference to the component's object (as shown in Figure 1-5). Only when the client later makes a method call into the component does COM+ finally instantiate the actual object. This technique, known as *just-in-time activation*, lets client programs obtain references to objects that they might not intend to use immediately, without incurring unnecessary overhead.

When implementing complex business logic components, one component can access other components, and those components can invoke still other components. Managing this chain reaction properly is a complex task. In COM+, the system-created context object that shadows each user object contains information that helps manage these complex relationships.

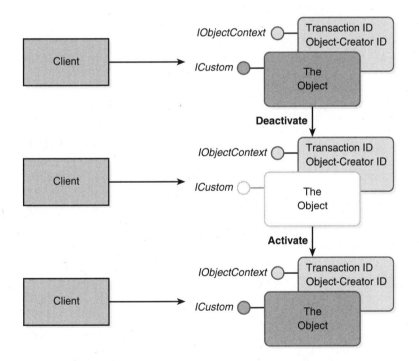

Figure 1-5.
A client application using a configured COM+ component while it is transparently activated and deactivated.

COM+ also extends the COM model to allow early deactivation of an object. COM+ can deactivate a component even while client programs maintain valid references to that component. It does this by releasing all references to the object. This in turn causes properly built COM+ components to be destroyed when their internal reference count reaches zero. If the client requests services from an object that has been deactivated by COM+, that object is transparently reactivated. So while it might appear to a client process that it is using a single object from the time of creation until the time it releases the object, the client might in fact be working with many different instances of the same class. This ensures that the semantics of COM are not violated.

Just-in-time activation is a powerful resource-sharing concept because it enables COM+ to share the resources of the server more equitably among the active components. Imagine that a client process spends 10 percent of its time requesting services from a particular object. With the automated deactivation of objects running in COM+, the object is instantiated only 10 percent of the time instead of 90 percent. This can make a server machine far more scalable than if all objects remain active for the entire duration of their clients.

Object Pooling

To enhance the overall scalability of a distributed application, COM+ supports object pooling. When a client application releases an object that supports object pooling, instead of destroying the object, COM+ recycles it for later use by the same or another client. When a client later attempts to access the same kind of object, COM+ obtains an object from the pool if one is available. COM+ automatically instantiates a new object when the pool of recycled objects is empty. Objects that support pooling are required to restore their state to that of a newly manufactured object.

You should decide whether or not to support recycling of an object by weighing the expense of creating new objects against the cost of holding the resources of that object while it is stored in the object pool. An object that takes a long time to create but does not hold many resources when deactivated is a good candidate for recycling. Imagine an object that creates a complex memory structure on startup. If this type of object supports pooling, it can simply reinitialize the structure when deactivated and thereby increase performance at run time because the structure need not be re-created at each activation. With other objects, recycling might not be advantageous. For example, an object that is cheap to create and stores a lot of state for each client is not a good candidate for recycling because its state is not reusable by other clients.

Load Balancing

A distributed COM+ application can potentially have thousands of clients. In such cases, the just-in-time activation and object pooling features can fall short of providing the required application scalability. Therefore, the client workload should be distributed among multiple servers in a network. In COM+, load balancing is implemented at the component level. This means that a client application requesting a specific component first contacts a load balancing router. The router contains information about a cluster of machines belonging to the distributed application and balances the workload among these servers. Once the desired object has been instantiated on one of the servers in the application cluster, the client receives a reference directly to the component on the particular server. Any future requests by the client go directly to the component. While many load balancing algorithms have been devised, COM+ uses a simple response-time analysis algorithm to load balance servers. (In the future, COM+ might enable other load balancing algorithms to be installed.)

Load balancing is also important in a failure scenario. If a client has a reference to a component on a server that goes down, COM+ automatically routes a client request from the server to another server in the application cluster. This failover support helps provide uninterrupted client service, increasing the overall stability of the system. Since the load balancing router itself represents a single critical failure point, you can use the Windows 2000 clustering service to set up one or more backup routers to be used in the event of a failure.

In-Memory Database

The In-Memory Database (IMDB), another powerful COM+ service, is a transient, transactional database-style cache that enhances the performance of distributed applications. Implemented as an OLE DB provider, the IMDB provides extremely fast access to data on the local machine. Client applications use high-level data access components such as the ADO to create and access indexed, tabular data. These cached databases can be generated dynamically by the COM+ application or loaded from a persistent data store.

Queued Components

Queued components are a key feature of COM+ based on the Microsoft Message Queue Server (MSMQ) infrastructure included with Windows 2000. Using queued components, a client can easily execute method calls against a COM+ component, even if that component is off line or otherwise unavailable. The MSMQ system records and queues the method calls and automatically replays them whenever the component becomes available. Figure 1-6 illustrates how MSMQ is used to transfer data between the client and component.

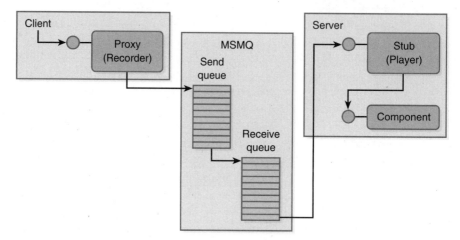

Figure 1-6.
A client application accessing an object via MSMQ.

Transactions

Using COM+, you can build components that automatically can participate in a distributed transaction. While transaction processing is one of its important features, COM+ actually enlists the help of the Microsoft Distributed Transaction Coordinator (DTC) to perform the transaction management. Microsoft originally designed OLE Transactions, an object-oriented, two-phase commit protocol based on COM, and then it implemented the specification in MS DTC, a transaction manager originally bundled with Microsoft SQL Server. (The OLE Transactions specification defines four fundamental interfaces: *ITransaction*, *ITransactionDispenser*, *ITransactionOptions*, and *ITransactionOutcomeEvents*.) However, Microsoft did not design the transaction management services provided by MS DTC solely for use by SQL Server. MS DTC is now an integrated service in Windows 2000, where its functionality is available to a wide variety of applications that require transaction management services.

In addition to the OLE Transactions specification, COM+ also supports the X/Open DTP XA standard. XA is the two-phase commit protocol defined by the X/Open DTP group. To allow COM+ to work with XA-compliant resource managers, the COM+ Software Development Kit (SDK) provides a special component that maps OLE Transactions to the XA standard. This makes it relatively straightforward for XA-compliant resource managers to provide resource dispensers that accept OLE Transactions from COM+ and then carry out the transaction with XA.

A transaction is typically initiated when an application is to perform some critical operation. The application initiates the transaction by notifying a transaction manager such as MS DTC. It then enlists the help of various resource managers to perform the work. (A resource manager is any service that supports the OLE Transactions specification, such as SQL Server.) Resource managers work in cooperation with MS DTC so that when the client application calls various resource dispensers, it carries with it information identifying the current transaction. (Resource dispensers are similar to resource managers, but without the guarantee of durability.)

Typically, transaction processing is most often applied to database access because of the crucial nature of the information stored there. However, transaction processing is not limited to the database management system (DBMS) domain. COM+, for example, also provides two resource dispensers: the ODBC Driver Manager and the Shared Property Manager. The ODBC Driver Manager is a resource dispenser that manages pools of database connections for COM+ components. You can also develop add-on resource dispensers using the COM+ SDK.

A resource manager enlisted to perform work on behalf of the client application also registers itself with the transaction manager. The transaction manager then keeps track of that resource manager throughout the remainder of the transaction. In transaction processing parlance, a transaction ends when the client application either commits or aborts the transaction. An abort operation causes the transaction manager to notify all resource managers involved in the transaction to roll back any operations performed as part of that transaction. A rollback can be likened to a humongous undo operation. If the client application fails before committing or aborting the transaction, MS DTC automatically aborts the transaction.

If everything goes well and the client application requests that the transaction be committed, MS DTC executes a two-phase commit protocol to commit the operations performed within the transaction. (A two-phase commit protocol ensures that transactions that apply to more than one server are completed on all servers or none at all.) The two-phase commit protocol results from coordination between MS DTC and supported resource managers. First, MS DTC queries each resource manager enlisted in the transaction to determine whether they agree to the commit operation. The vote must be unanimous; if any resource manager fails to respond or votes to abort the transaction, MS DTC notifies all the resource managers that the transaction is aborted and their operations must be rolled back. Only if all resource managers agree in the first phase of the protocol does MS DTC broadcast a second commit message, thereby completing the transaction successfully. A client application using transactions must be guaranteed that concurrent transactions are atomic and consistent, that they have proper isolation, and that once committed, the changes are durable. These conditions are sometimes referred to as the *ACID (atomic, consistent, isolated,* and *durable)* properties of transactions.

Each object running in the context of COM+ can be set to one of four levels of transaction support. A component can declare that it requires a transaction, requires a new transaction, supports transactions, or does not support transactions. The context objects of components that do not support transactions are created without a transaction, regardless of whether their client is running in the scope of a transaction. Unless the component developer or system administrator specifies otherwise, this setting is the default. Components that do not support transactions cannot take advantage of many features of COM+, including just-in-time activation. (Such components are never deactivated while clients hold valid references because COM+ does not have enough information about their current state.) Thus the default value is not recommended and is primarily intended to support components not originally designed for use with COM+.

Most COM+ objects are declared as either requiring a transaction or supporting transactions. Objects that support transactions can participate in the outcome of the transaction if their client is running in the scope of a transaction. If the client is not executing within a transaction, no transaction is available for the COM+ object. Objects that require a transaction either inherit the transaction of the client or have a transaction created for them if the client doesn't have one. Objects that require a new transaction never inherit the client's transaction; COM+ automatically initiates a fresh transaction regardless of whether the client has one.

Role-Based Security

As discussed, COM+ was designed to save developers from having to code a robust server-side process for every component that runs in the middle tier of a three-tier architecture. To this end, COM+ automatically helps components manage threading, concurrency, scalability, transactions, and security. The COM+ security model leverages that of Windows 2000. However, to simplify security issues, it offers two types of security, declarative and programmatic. You can use both when you design a COM+ object.

The key to understanding COM+ security is to understand the simple but powerful concept of roles. Roles are central to the flexible, declarative security model employed by most COM+ objects. A role is a symbolic name that abstracts and identifies a logical group of users—similar to the idea of a user group in Windows 2000. When a COM+ object is deployed, the administrator can create certain roles and then bind those roles to specific users and user groups. For example, a banking application might define roles and permissions for tellers and for managers. During deployment, the administrator can assign users Fred and Jane to the role of tellers and assign executive management to the role of managers. Fred and Jane can access certain components in the banking package, while executive managers can access all components. You can even configure role-based security on a per-interface, rather than a per-component, basis. The administrator can completely configure declarative security without help from the component developer. This is infinitely simpler than the low-level COM security model.

Sometimes, however, you might want to configure certain parameters to limit the access of users in particular roles. Perhaps you want tellers to be able to authorize withdrawals and transfers of up to $5,000, but only a manager should be able to authorize those above $5,000. Declarative security as configured by the administrator does not offer the fine degree of control you need. When you develop a COM+ object, you can use roles to program specific security logic that either grants or denies certain permissions.

Events

Distributed applications use COM+ events to advertise and deliver information to other components or applications without prior knowledge of the identity of the components or applications. Event models can be categorized as either internal or external. With internal event models, the event semantic is completely contained within the scope of the publisher and subscriber. This generally requires that the publisher and subscriber run simultaneously. (Connection points are an example of this type of event model.)

The COM+ event service implements an external event model. This model removes as much of the event semantics as possible from the publisher and subscriber. The subscriptions are maintained outside the publisher and the subscriber and are retrieved when needed. The publisher and subscriber are thus greatly simplified. In particular, the subscriber need not contain any logic for building subscriptions. In fact, an events subscriber is any component that implements a given event class interface. Anyone can build an event subscriber with no additional work. In a world where subscribers greatly outnumber publishers, this is a big advantage. Plus, because of the removal of the subscription logic from the subscriber, a third party such as an administrator can build subscriptions between publishers and subscribers that were built and sold independently.

Another benefit of maintaining subscriptions outside the publisher is that the subscription's lifecycle need not match that of either the publisher or the subscriber. You can build subscriptions before either the publisher or the subscriber is up and running. This type of subscription, known as a *persistent subscription*, allows publishers to activate subscribers prior to calling them. (In this unusual relationship, the lines between clients and components are blurred.)

CHAPTER TWO

The *IUnknown* Interface

This chapter focuses on the fundamentals of the COM+ programming model: defining custom interfaces in the Interface Definition Language (IDL) and then implementing those interfaces using any programming language. Our example in this chapter will develop a complete in-process component and a matching client. Creating this sample component requires an in-depth understanding of the two most fundamental COM+ interfaces: *00000000-0000-0000-C000-000000000046* and *00000001-0000-0000-C000-000000000046,* otherwise known as *IUnknown* and *IClassFactory.* Along the way, we'll encounter IDL, the starting point for programming with COM+.

Let's begin by defining a custom interface, *ISum,* that our in-process component will implement. Interfaces defined by Microsoft, such as *IUnknown* and *IClassFactory,* are called *standard interfaces;* interfaces that you define yourself are known as *custom interfaces.* In this chapter, the C++ declaration of the *ISum* interface is defined as follows:

```
class ISum : public IUnknown
{
public:
    virtual HRESULT __stdcall Sum(int x, int y, int* retval)=0;
}
```

As you can see, the class *ISum* has only one public member function, *Sum,* which is declared as a pure virtual function. The *virtual* keyword indicates that the member function can be redefined in a derived class. When you refer to a derived class using a pointer of the type of the base class, a call to one of the base class's virtual functions executes the derived class's version of that function. (An object's ability to exhibit multiple behaviors is called *polymorphism,* as discussed in Chapter 1.) The C++ compiler inserts the address of each virtual function into a special table called a *virtual function table,* or *v-table* (sometimes abbreviated as *vtbl*). This binary structure implements polymorphism in C++;

it also forms the basis of COM+ interfaces. At run time, every interface actually exists in memory as a v-table, as demonstrated by the following equation:

COM+ interface = C++ virtual function table

We specify the *pure* attribute of our *Sum* function by placing *=0* at the end of the function declaration. The *pure* attribute tells the compiler that no implementation for this function is provided. A class containing one or more pure virtual functions is known as an *abstract base class*. An abstract base class cannot be instantiated; it can be used as a base class only when you declare other classes that will derive from it and implement its methods. Normally, an abstract base class is used to enforce a certain protocol of methods. For example, *IUnknown* is defined in C++ as an abstract base class; it ensures that all its methods are implemented before any classes deriving from it are instantiated.

The *Sum* method in this interface is also declared as __*stdcall*, replacing the Pascal[1] calling convention used in bygone days of traditional Windows programming. These days, __*stdcall* is used by the Win32 API functions as well as COM+ interfaces. It pushes parameters onto the stack from right to left, but as in the Pascal calling convention, the called function pops its own arguments from the stack before returning. Functions that pop their own arguments from the stack cannot support a variable number of arguments, so the compiler automatically switches to the __*cdecl* calling convention (the default for C and C++ programs) for any functions with variable argument lists. The __*cdecl* calling convention is similar to __*stdcall* in that parameters are passed from right to left, but instead of the called function popping its own arguments from the stack, the calling function cleans up the stack after the function call returns. Because the function call must include stack cleanup code, the __*cdecl* calling convention creates larger executables than __*stdcall*.

The *Sum* function takes two integer arguments and returns their sum. To be exact, the function's return value is an *HRESULT* value indicating the success or failure of the call. The actual summation is returned as the function's third parameter, a pointer to an integer. Most interface methods return *HRESULT* values and provide their return values as pointer arguments. All COM+ errors are handled in the form of a 32-bit *HRESULT* value beginning with *0x8000xxxx*. To interpret *HRESULT* values, you can either consult the winerror.h system header file or call the Win32 API function *FormatMessage*, which provides a string that explains the error value. (Chapter 6 discusses *HRESULT*s and COM+ exception handling mechanisms.)

---

1. This calling convention specifies that parameters are pushed onto the stack from left to right and that the called function pops its own arguments from the stack before returning.

Finally, notice that *ISum* publicly inherits the *IUnknown* interface. As you know, all COM+ objects must implement the *IUnknown* interface, so any object that implements the *ISum* interface must implement *IUnknown* as well. The following equation clarifies the relationship between a C++ object and a COM+ object:

C++ object + *IUnknown* = COM+ object

From this examination of *ISum*, you can see that a COM+ interface is simply a contract that requires all implementations of an interface to adhere to the defined specifications. A COM+ interface does not contain any code. A *COM+ class* (coclass) is a named implementation of one or more interfaces. In C++, a coclass is usually implemented as a C++ class, although the two are not synonymous. In Microsoft Visual Basic, a coclass is implemented as a Visual Basic class module. One or more coclasses are contained in a *component*. A component is a sort of housing for coclasses that can be built as either a DLL or an EXE.

Interface Definition Language

One important aspect of COM+ is its language neutrality. A COM+ component can be written in any language and then seamlessly called from any other language. In the previous section, we defined the *ISum* interface using C++ code. In Java, the same *ISum* interface would look like this:

```
public interface ISum extends com.ms.com.IUnknown
{
    public abstract int Sum(int x, int y);
}
```

In Visual Basic, *ISum* would look like this:

```
VERSION 1.0 CLASS
BEGIN
    MultiUse = -1  'True
END
Attribute VB_Name = "ISum


Attribute VB_Exposed = True
Attribute VB_Creatable = True
Public Function Sum(x As Long, y As Long) As Long

End Function
```

These three language-based definitions expose the fallacy of our assumptions. How can we claim to have a language-neutral architecture and then define a single interface differently in every programming language? This would lead to chaos, since a single interface could have multiple correct definitions. The answer to this problem lies in IDL. (We'll introduce IDL in this chapter but provide more details in Chapter 16.)

The Open Software Foundation (OSF) originally developed IDL for the Remote Procedure Call (RPC) package of its Distributed Computing Environment (DCE). IDL helps RPC programmers ensure that both the client and server sides of a project adhere to the same interface. It is important to realize that IDL is not a programming language—it is a language used only to define interfaces.[2] For this reason, Microsoft decided to adopt IDL for use in defining COM+ interfaces. Standardizing on one special language for defining interfaces eliminates the confusion generated by having multiple languages define the same interface differently. You can code the implementation of an interface defined in IDL in any language you want. Today, all COM+ programming should begin in IDL. The interface definition for *ISum* written in IDL is shown in Listing 2-1.

component.idl

```
import "unknwn.idl";

[ object, uuid(10000001-0000-0000-0000-000000000001) ]
interface ISum : IUnknown
{
    HRESULT Sum([in] int x, [in] int y, [out, retval] int* retval);
};
```

Listing 2-1.
The interface definition for the ISum *interface expressed in IDL.*

The IDL file quickly betrays its roots in C. A cursory examination reveals a construct rather like a header file, which provides forward declarations for functions. Several aspects of this interface definition immediately attract attention. First, the definition begins with the *object* attribute, a Microsoft extension to IDL that identifies a COM+ interface. Any interface definition that doesn't begin with the *object* attribute describes an RPC interface, not a COM+ interface.

---

2. IDL plays an important role in the development of COM+ objects, but it is not part of COM+. IDL is simply a tool used to help programmers define interfaces.

After the *object* attribute comes the interface's *universally unique identifier (UUID)*, which distinguishes it from all other interfaces. A UUID is a 128-bit number, usually represented in hexadecimal, that is guaranteed to be unique across space and time. Two different developers might define an interface named *ISum*, but so long as both interfaces have different UUIDs, no confusion will result. The *ISum* interface as defined in the IDL file derives from *IUnknown*, the root of all COM+ objects. The interface definition of *IUnknown* itself is imported from the unknwn.idl file, where it is defined as follows:

```
[
  local,
  object,
  uuid(00000000-0000-0000-C000-000000000046),
  pointer_default(unique)
]

interface IUnknown
{
    typedef [unique] IUnknown *LPUNKNOWN;

    HRESULT QueryInterface(
        [in] REFIID riid,
        [out, iid_is(riid)] void** ppvObject);
    ULONG AddRef();
    ULONG Release();
}
```

Notice in the *ISum* interface definition that each argument of the *Sum* method is preceded by a directional attribute, *[in]* or *[out]*. Since the interface defines the communication between a client and a component, which might end up running on separate machines, the interface definition specifies the direction in which each parameter must travel. Directional attributes in IDL are optimizations that reduce the data transmitted between the client and the component. In this case, the first two parameters of the *Sum* function must be passed only to the component; they do not need to be passed back to the client because their value will not have changed. The third parameter is flagged with the *[out, retval]* attributes, indicating that the parameter is a return value and thus needs only to be passed back from the component to the client. Some languages such as Visual Basic and Java that insulate the developer from the returned *HRESULT* value transparently make the *[out, retval]* parameter appear to be the value returned by the function. Note that the *[in]* attribute is not required because it is applied to a parameter by default when no directional parameter attribute is specified.

Globally Unique Identifiers

A UUID is equivalent to a *globally unique identifier (GUID),* the term more commonly used in COM+. Normally, GUIDs are created interactively using the guidgen.exe utility. A GUID can also be generated at run time by calling the *CoCreateGuid* function. Visual Basic uses this method to dynamically generate the GUIDs applied to components.

You might wonder why a simple 32-bit value can't be used to identify interfaces. After all, a 32-bit value gives us 2^{32}, or 4,294,967,296, possible unique identifiers. However, the issue is not so much the total number of possible interfaces but how that space is divided to guarantee uniqueness. Witness the problems encountered with Internet Protocol (IP) addresses that also use 32-bit identifiers. There are not yet more than 4 billion computers connected to the Internet (maybe next year), but a lot of the addresses are wasted due to the allocation method.

The 128-bit interface identifier used by COM+ provides the theoretical possibility of creating a huge number of unique interfaces—approximately 340,282,366,920,900,000,000,000,000,000,000,000,000. That's enough to create one trillion new interfaces every second for the next 10,782,897,524,560,000,000 years.[3] In reality, the algorithm used to generate GUIDs limits the total number to significantly fewer unique interfaces, but still plenty for the foreseeable future.

Once you define an interface in IDL, you can use the Microsoft IDL (midl.exe) compiler to translate the interface into several C/C++ language source files. For now, we will focus on the header file generated by the MIDL compiler, which contains a C++ version of the interfaces defined in IDL. (For more information about the files generated by the MIDL compiler, see the section titled "Interprocess Communication" in Chapter 14.) For example, after compiling the component.idl file containing the *ISum* interface discussed above, the MIDL compiler generated a header file named component.h that includes the following code:

```
MIDL_INTERFACE("10000001-0000-0000-0000-000000000001")
    ISum : public IUnknown
```

---

3. The sun is expected to last only another 4.5 billion years, after which COM+ might lose some of its universal appeal.

```
{
public:
    virtual HRESULT STDMETHODCALLTYPE Sum(
        /* [in] */ int x,
        /* [in] */ int y,
        /* [retval][out] */ int __RPC_FAR *retval) = 0;
};
```

This code looks a lot like the C++ interface definition presented earlier; the only difference is the use of the *MIDL_INTERFACE* rather than the *class* keyword and the addition of the *STDMETHODCALLTYPE* macro. (In the basetyps.h system header file, *STDMETHODCALLTYPE* is defined as _ _*stdcall*.) In the rpcndr.h system header file, the *MIDL_INTERFACE* macro is defined as follows:

```
#define MIDL_INTERFACE(x)    struct __declspec(uuid(x)) __declspec(novtable)
```

In C++, a *struct* is equivalent to a class whose members are public by default. You can use _ _*declspec(uuid ("xxxxxxxx-xxxx-xxxx-xxxx-xxxxxxxxxxxx"))*, a Microsoft extension to C++, to attach a GUID directly to a class or structure. This GUID can later be retrieved using another Microsoft extension: _ _*uuidof(x)*. (The ability to have the compiler be aware of the GUID assigned to a class and be able to retrieve that GUID will prove useful later in this chapter.) The extension _ _*declspec(novtable)* tells the compiler not to generate code that initializes the virtual function pointer in the constructor(s) and destructor of the class. This significantly reduces code size. You should apply this option only to abstract base classes such as interface definitions.

We have discussed the problems involved in defining interfaces in a specific programming language, and we have learned how to use IDL to define interfaces in a manner independent of any individual programming language. We have also used MIDL to generate C/C++ code, bringing us back to a language-specific interface definition, the point at which we began. If MIDL could generate Visual Basic and Java code in addition to C++ code, language-dependent interface definitions generated from IDL code would be acceptable. However, you would be wrong to assume that MIDL contains some magic command-line parameter to generate anything other than C/C++ code. To avoid having to update MIDL's code generation engine for every new language that comes along, Microsoft looked for a more extensible mechanism—a way for MIDL to generate interface definitions in a single, universal format that all languages—including Visual Basic, Java, and C++ (arguably a broad spectrum of languages with quite different goals)—can understand. While you ponder the possibilities, let's turn to the client project.

The Client

Now that we have defined the *ISum* interface in IDL, let's write the code to create a client application that uses this interface, assuming for the time being that we already have an implementation of the *ISum* interface. For starters, we'll create the client in C++, since this language forces us to understand and to work closely with the underlying COM+ mechanisms. In Chapter 3, we'll branch out into Visual Basic and Java, where the same principles apply but the details are often hidden from view.

The *CoInitializeEx* Function

All COM+ applications begin with a call to *CoInitializeEx*, which initializes the COM+ library. (*CoInitialize* is an obsolete function that calls *CoInitializeEx* with the COINIT_APARTMENTTHREADED flag.) You must call this function before you can use any other COM+ services except certain COM+ memory allocation calls.[4] You could use *OleInitialize*, which calls *CoInitializeEx* internally, but this is done only when an application specifically intends to use the compound document features of OLE.

The first parameter of *CoInitializeEx* must be *NULL*.[5] The second parameter indicates the desired threading model, as shown in the following code fragment. (For more information about threading models, see Chapter 4.)

```
hr = CoInitializeEx(NULL, COINIT_APARTMENTTHREADED);
if(FAILED(hr))
    cout << "CoInitializeEx failed." << endl;
```

Notice that all COM+ function names are prefixed with *Co*, indicating that they are part of the COM+ API.

The *CoCreateInstance* Function

After initializing the COM+ library using *CoInitializeEx*, you must give the client a way to instantiate the desired coclass containing an implementation of *ISum*. The *CoCreateInstance* call is the standard way to do this, as shown here. You can think of it as the COM+ equivalent to C++'s *new* operator:

---

4. These calls are *CoTaskMemAlloc*, *CoTaskMemFree*, *CoTaskMemRealloc*, and the *IMalloc* methods of the task allocator object returned by *CoGetMalloc*.

5. In early versions of OLE, applications could replace the default memory allocator by passing the address of a custom allocator object to *CoInitializeEx*. COM+ does not currently support applications replacing this allocator, and if the parameter is anything but *NULL*, *CoInitializeEx* returns an *E_INVALIDARG* error.

```
// {10000002-0000-0000-0000-000000000001}
const CLSID CLSID_InsideCOM = {0x10000002, 0x0000, 0x0000,
    {0x00, 0x00, 0x00, 0x00, 0x00, 0x00, 0x00, 0x01}};

hr = CoCreateInstance(CLSID_InsideCOM, NULL,
    CLSCTX_INPROC_SERVER, IID_IUnknown, (void**)&pUnknown);
if(FAILED(hr))
    cout << "CoCreateInstance failed." << endl;
```

The first parameter of *CoCreateInstance* is a *class identifier* (*CLSID*). A CLSID is a GUID that is associated with the coclass we want to instantiate. *CoCreateInstance* uses this CLSID to search for a match in the HKEY_CLASSES_ROOT\CLSID section of the registry[6] in order to locate the desired component. HKEY_CLASSES_ROOT\CLSID is undoubtedly the most fundamental COM+-related key in the registry. If an entry for the CLSID is found, the various subkeys provide COM+ with information about the component; *CoCreateInstance* fails if no match is found.

As you might know, a component can contain multiple coclasses. A component that supports multiple coclasses must register a unique CLSID for each supported coclass. The client must call *CoCreateInstance* once for each COM+ object it wants to create. If some of the objects coexist in the same component, that's all right with COM+. In the registry, each coclass is listed by its CLSID, and the entry contains information specifying the component containing that coclass. Figure 2-1 shows two calls to *CoCreateInstance* for two different coclasses that turn out to be housed in the same component. Using the CLSID, *CoCreateInstance* does a lookup in the registry; in this case, both *Object1* and *Object2* originate from the same component.

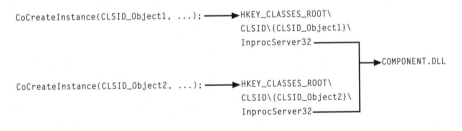

Figure 2-1.
Two coclasses that inhabit the same component.

---

6. The registry is a system-wide data store that contains information about the current user, machine configuration, application settings, and COM+ component information. You can view and edit the data in the registry with the registry editor utility, regedit.exe.

The second parameter of *CoCreateInstance* specifies whether this object will be part of an aggregate object. (Aggregation is covered later in this chapter.) Because this example does not use aggregation, we'll pass *NULL* for this parameter.

The third parameter specifies the context in which the component will run. COM+ provides support for calling in-process, local, and remote components. Sometimes a particular component is implemented in several flavors. (For example, it might be available in an in-process version and a local and remote version.) In such cases, you can select the version that best meets your needs. For each class context, you must use a different registry entry to specify that component type. The following table shows the available class contexts and the subkeys of HKEY_CLASSES_ROOT\CLSID\{*YourCLSID*} that identify the different component types available for a particular coclass. If you aren't particular about the component type, specify *CLSCTX_SERVER* to retrieve the first available in-process, local, or remote component, in that order. In our example, we'll access an in-process component, so we'll specify the *CLSCTX_INPROC_SERVER* class context.

Class Context Flags	Subkey	Description
CLSCTX_INPROC_SERVER	InprocServer32	Full path to a 32-bit in-process component.
CLSCTX_INPROC_HANDLER	InprocHandler32	Full path to a 32-bit DLL component handler.*
CLSCTX_LOCAL_SERVER	LocalServer32	Full path to a 32-bit executable component.
CLSCTX_REMOTE_SERVER	AppID	A GUID that references additional information for remote components. It is stored in the HKEY_CLASSES_ROOT\AppID\{*YourAppID*} section of the registry. (For more information, see the section titled "The *AppID* Registry Key" in Chapter 12.)

* The CLSCTX_INPROC_HANDLER class context is used by lightweight client-side handlers, a special type of COM+ in-process component that runs in the client process and implements certain client-side parts of the class. Instances of the actual class are accessed remotely. For more information, see Chapter 15.

Class Context Flags	Subkey	Description
CLSCTX_INPROC		Defined as a combination of the CLSCTX_INPROC_SERVER and CLSCTX_INPROC_HANDLER flags.
CLSCTX_SERVER		Defined as a combination of the CLSCTX_INPROC_SERVER, CLSCTX_LOCAL_SERVER, and CLSCTX_REMOTE_SERVER flags.
CLSCTX_ALL		Defined as a combination of the CLSCTX_INPROC_SERVER, CLSCTX_INPROC_HANDLER, CLSCTX_LOCAL_SERVER, and CLSCTX_REMOTE_SERVER flags.

When you instantiate a component using *CoCreateInstance*, you can use the fourth parameter to specify the interface identifier (IID) of the desired interface. (The IID is a 128-bit value composed in the same way as a GUID.) A pointer to this interface is returned in the fifth parameter. In this case, we are looking for a pointer to the *ISum* interface, so we could pass the *IID_ISum* value to *CoCreateInstance*. However, convention dictates that an application should normally get a pointer to the *IUnknown* interface first and then use the *QueryInterface* call to locate the other interfaces. Never ones to disregard convention, we'll pass *IID_IUnknown*.

The Methods of *IUnknown*

If all goes well, a pointer to the *IUnknown* interface of the requested COM+ object is returned in the fifth parameter of *CoCreateInstance*. The name *IUnknown* indicates that at this stage the true capabilities of the object are unknown. With this pointer, we can call any of the three *IUnknown* methods: *QueryInterface*, *AddRef*, or *Release*.

The *QueryInterface* Method

Every COM+ object is guaranteed to support the *IUnknown* interface, and a pointer to *IUnknown* can be obtained from *CoCreateInstance*. Aside from this rule, however, there are no guarantees. *QueryInterface* determines what other interfaces an object supports. We like to call this the "discovery phase" of the relationship between the client and the object, since the client calls *QueryInterface* to discover the capabilities of a particular object. In the following code, the *QueryInterface* method determines whether an object supports the *ISum* interface. If the object supports the desired interface, a pointer to that interface is returned in the second parameter of *QueryInterface*:

```
hr = pUnknown->QueryInterface(IID_ISum, (void**)&pSum);
if(FAILED(hr))
    cout << "The IID_ISum interface is not supported. " << endl;
```

The first parameter to *QueryInterface* is the IID of the interface being queried for. The *IID_ISum* value is declared in the component.h file and defined in the component_i.c file. The MIDL compiler generates both of these files based on the *ISum* interface definition contained in the component.idl file described previously. The component_i.c file contains the actual definitions for the GUIDs defined in the IDL file, as shown below:

```
// {10000001-0000-0000-0000-000000000001}
const IID IID_ISum = {0x10000001, 0x0000, 0x0000,
    {0x00, 0x00, 0x00, 0x00, 0x00, 0x00, 0x00, 0x01}};
```

The *AddRef* and *Release* Methods

The *AddRef* and *Release* methods perform reference counting, which is used to determine when an object can be freed from memory. For every interface pointer, you must call *AddRef* before calling any other methods, and you must call *Release* after you finish using the interface pointer. From the client's point of view, reference counting takes place on a per-interface basis. To make things more efficient, the objects themselves always call *AddRef* automatically before *QueryInterface* returns an interface pointer. For this reason, the client can skip the call to *AddRef* on interface pointers returned by the *QueryInterface* method or from the *CoCreateInstance* function.

Once we have a pointer to the desired interface, we no longer need the *IUnknown* pointer that was originally returned by *CoCreateInstance*. Accordingly, we can call the *IUnknown::Release* method to decrement the object's reference counter, as shown below. The value returned by the *Release* method is the interface's reference counter.

```
m_cRef = pUnknown->Release();
cout << "pUnknown->Release() reference count = " <<
    m_cRef << endl;
```

Note that calling *Release* on an interface pointer does not necessarily destroy the object providing the implementation. *Release* simply decrements the object's reference counter. An object is destroyed when its reference count falls to *0*. In the preceding code, we released the *IUnknown* interface pointer, but the object was not destroyed because the *ISum* interface pointer returned by *QueryInterface* caused the object's reference counter to be incremented via an implicit call to *AddRef.*

Since we don't have to worry about calling *AddRef* on the *ISum* pointer, we are ready to call the *Sum* method, as shown in the following code fragment. This, after all, is the goal of the entire sample project.

```
int sum;
hr = pSum->Sum(2, 3, &sum);
if(SUCCEEDED(hr))
    cout << "Sum(2, 3) = " << sum << endl;
```

Optimizing reference counting In the example above, we don't need to call the *AddRef* method on the *pSum* interface pointer because *AddRef* is automatically called on interface pointers returned by the *QueryInterface* method. Nevertheless, you must explicitly call the *AddRef* method whenever an interface pointer is aliased, as shown here:

```
IUnknown* pUnknown;
ISum* pSumOne;
ISum* pSumTwo;

// QueryInterface calls AddRef on pSumOne.
pUnknown->QueryInterface(IID_ISum, (void**)&pSumOne);

// Release IUnknown; we don't need it anymore.
pUnknown->Release();

// Copy a pointer.
pSumTwo = pSumOne;

// This requires an explicit AddRef.
pSumTwo->AddRef();

pSumOne->Sum(5, 3);
pSumTwo->Sum(4, 7);

// Now we've finished; call Release.
pSumTwo->Release();
pSumOne->Release();
```

Here the interface pointer *pSumOne* was copied to *pSumTwo*. This aliasing results in two interface pointers; therefore, we must call *AddRef* to increment the reference counter. In some cases, if you are certain that the reference count will remain above *0*, thus ensuring that the object is not freed, you can optimize away the extra *AddRef* and *Release* calls, as shown on the following page.

```
// QueryInterface calls AddRef on pSumOne.
pUnknown->QueryInterface(IID_ISum, (void**)&pSumOne);

// Release IUnknown; we don't need it anymore.
pUnknown->Release();

// Copy a pointer.
pSumTwo = pSumOne;

// Don't need this. Reference count is sure to be at least 1.
// pSumTwo->AddRef();

pSumOne->Sum(5, 3);
pSumTwo->Sum(4, 7);

// Matching AddRef commented out.
// pSumTwo->Release()

// Now we've finished; call Release.
pSumOne->Release();
```

In more complex code, it is often difficult to correctly remove the unnecessary *AddRef* and *Release* calls. Such code also becomes very fragile if someone modifies it without being aware of the reference counting assumptions made by the original developer. And in most cases, the performance improvement that comes from optimizing *AddRef* and *Release* calls is not significant. As we'll see in Chapter 19, the proxy caches *AddRef* and *Release* calls when you access remote objects so that each client call does not necessarily result in a remote call. All in all, *AddRef* and *Release* optimizations have been oversold.

The *CoUninitialize* Function

With the main job of the component complete, we'll execute some cleanup code. We need to call *IUnknown::Release* because we are finished with the *ISum* pointer. Note that this is the last open pointer to the object; therefore, the reference counter will be decremented to *0*, initiating the object's destruction. Then we'll call *CoUninitialize* to close the COM+ library, freeing any resources that it maintains and forcing all RPC connections to close, as shown here:

```
CoUninitialize();
```

Although our sample makes only one call to the *CoInitializeEx* function, more sophisticated applications might call it multiple times to support different threading requirements. (See Chapter 4 for more details about COM+ threading models.) In such cases, calls to the *CoInitializeEx* and *CoUninitialize* functions must be balanced—if there are multiple calls to *CoInitializeEx*, there must be the same number of calls to *CoUninitialize*. Only the *CoUninitialize* call corresponding to the *CoInitializeEx* call that initialized COM+ can close it.

The V-Table Situation

Figure 2-2 shows the mechanism through which a client program holding an interface pointer can call methods in a component.

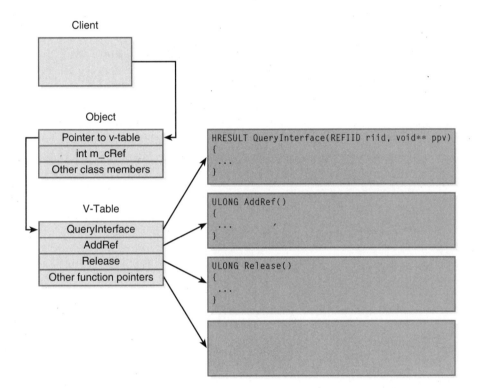

Figure 2-2.
An interface pointer is really a pointer to a pointer to a v-table containing function pointers.

You can see that for every C++ class containing virtual functions, the compiler automatically creates a v-table structure containing pointers to all of the class's virtual functions, including those declared in a base class. Note that a v-table is built on a per-class basis, not for each instance of the class. A pointer to the v-table itself is stored as the first member in the object's memory structure and is followed by the other members of the class. What we refer to as an *interface pointer* is actually a pointer to a pointer to a table of function pointers. Needless to say, this is a rather inconvenient way to describe the mechanism through which a client calls an object. C++ helps us forget about the extra level of indirection by implicitly converting *pUnknown->pVtbl->AddRef()* to *pUnknown>AddRef()*.

The indirection provided by a v-table can be compared with the software interrupts used by MS-DOS. An MS-DOS application requests service from the operating system by setting parameter values in various registers and then issuing software interrupt 21h. MS-DOS installs a pointer to an interrupt handler at vector 21h in the interrupt table and through it responds to the application's request. Although v-tables are based on direct function calls rather than on software interrupts, they provide a similar, well-known entry point for accessing an arbitrary service.

It is also important to realize that the function pointers in the v-table are stored in the order of declaration—that is, the first method declared in the IDL definition corresponds to the first function pointer in the v-table for that class. The v-table order of virtual functions that are declared in a base class and implemented in a derived class is determined by the order of the functions in the base class. Therefore, you cannot mess up a standard interface such as *IUnknown* simply by declaring its methods in the wrong order: the order of the *IUnknown* methods in your class's v-table is determined by their order in the system header file (unknwn.h), where *IUnknown* is declared.

When multiple inheritance is used to implement several interfaces in one class, the compiler concatenates the v-tables of the various interfaces. The order in which their entries appear in the class's memory layout is determined by the order in which the interfaces are inherited.

Problems with *QueryInterface*

In the system IDL file, unknwn.idl, the *IUnknown::QueryInterface* method is declared as follows:

```
HRESULT QueryInterface([in] REFIID riid,
    [out, iid_is(riid)] void** ppvObject);
```

The *iid_is* IDL attribute expresses the relationship between the first parameter and the second: *ppvObject* returns an interface pointer whose type is specified by *riid*. (For a complete discussion of the *iid_is* IDL attribute, see Chapter 16.) However, by the time the C++ compiler gets its hands on this interface in the unknwn.h system header file, the MIDL compiler has transformed the *QueryInterface* method to the following:

```
virtual HRESULT __stdcall QueryInterface(REFIID riid,
    void** ppvObject)=0;
```

This declaration is the source of much consternation and many bugs in COM+ clients and components. Figure 2-3 shows how the *QueryInterface* mechanism works when used correctly. Notice that COM+ objects are drawn with standard and custom interface "lollipops" extending from the left side of the object, while *IUnknown* is drawn separately on top of the object because all objects support this interface.

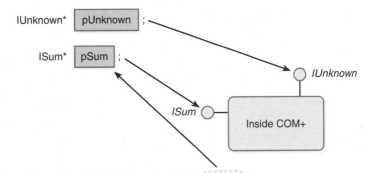

```
pUnknown->QueryInterface(IID_ISum, (void**) &pSum );
```

Figure 2-3.
Querying an object for its ISum *interface pointer.*

Because *QueryInterface* must be able to query for any interface (*IUnknown, ISum, IYouNameIt*), the second parameter is declared as a pointer to a pointer to pretty much anything (*void***). This very flexible declaration allows a programmer to do pretty much anything, including making pretty much any kind of mistake. Examine the following code to see whether you can find the insidious bug that the C++ compiler cannot:

```
hr = pUnknown->QueryInterface(IID_ISum, (void**)pSum);
```

The problem here is that the address-of (*&*) operator is missing before *pSum*. The compiler, blinded by the explicit *void*** cast, assumes that we know what we are doing and stuffs the retrieved pointer into any invalid location pointed to by *pSum*. The result is an immediate crash.

Another problem with *QueryInterface* relates to assigning a type of interface pointer to a pointer that was declared to point to a different type of interface. See if you can figure out what's wrong with this code:

```
ISum* pSum;
hr = pUnknown->QueryInterface(IID_IUnknown, (void**)&pSum);
int sum;
pSum->Sum(2, 3, &sum); // Uh-oh!
```

45

The *QueryInterface* call requests the *IUnknown* interface (*IID_IUnknown*), but it stores the pointer in *pSum*. The *pSum* function is a pointer to an interface of type *ISum*, not *IUnknown*, but the compiler thinks this is all right because *pSum* is explicitly cast to *void***. Because *pSum* is a pointer to an interface of type *ISum*, the compiler doesn't have any problem calling the *Sum* function. Of course, in this case *pSum* is only a pointer to *IUnknown* and might spontaneously combust when the *Sum* function is called.[7]

To make *QueryInterface* safer, Microsoft has overloaded the definition *IUnknown::QueryInterface* in the unknwn.h system header file. The new and improved version of *QueryInterface* that accepts only one argument is shown below:

```
template <class Q>
HRESULT STDMETHODCALLTYPE QueryInterface(Q** pp)
{
    return QueryInterface(__uuidof(Q), (void**)pp);
}
```

This alternative definition of the *QueryInterface* method is implemented as a function template and relies on the *__uuidof* operator, a Microsoft extension to C++ that aids in COM+ programming. (For more information about function templates, see the section titled "C++ Templates (A Quick Introduction)" in Chapter 3.) You can use the *__uuidof* operator to retrieve the GUID of an interface pointer as long as the GUID was supplied using another Microsoft extension, *__declspec(__uuid("xxxxxxxx-xxxx-xxxx-xxxx-xxxxxxxxxxxx"))*. Recall that the header files generated by the MIDL compiler use this extension, so this is the case for all interfaces defined in IDL. This technique makes calling *QueryInterface* even easier because you don't need to specify an IID—the correct one is obtained for you. Here is a sample that uses this modern form of *QueryInterface*:

```
ISum* pSum;
hr = pUnknown->QueryInterface(&pSum); // IID_ISum, (void**)&pSum
```

Building the Client Project

To build the client project, use the InProcess.dsw workspace file in the Samples\ The IUnknown Interface folder on the companion CD. When you build the projects in this workspace, Visual C++ automatically compiles the IDL file using

---

7. This code will run without complaint in this case because our implementation of *ISum* runs in-process with the client. However, changing the object's v-table slightly or running the component outside of the client process where it would depend on the marshaling infrastructure of COM+ would make this code deadly.

the MIDL compiler and then builds the client application. The complete client.cpp code is shown in Listing 2-2.

client.cpp

```
#define _WIN32_DCOM
#include <iostream.h>
#include "component.h" // Generated by MIDL

// {10000002-0000-0000-0000-000000000001}
const CLSID CLSID_InsideCOM = {0x10000002, 0x0000, 0x0000,
    {0x00, 0x00, 0x00, 0x00, 0x00, 0x00, 0x00, 0x01}};

void main()
{
    IUnknown* pUnknown;
    ISum* pSum;

    HRESULT hr = CoInitializeEx(NULL, COINIT_APARTMENTTHREADED);
    if(FAILED(hr))
        cout << "CoInitializeEx failed. " << endl;

    hr = CoCreateInstance(CLSID_InsideCOM, NULL,
        CLSCTX_INPROC_SERVER, IID_IUnknown, (void**)&pUnknown);
    if(FAILED(hr))
        cout << "CoCreateInstance failed. " << endl;

    hr = pUnknown->QueryInterface(IID_ISum, (void**)&pSum);
    if(FAILED(hr))
        cout << "IID_ISum not supported. " << endl;

    pUnknown->Release();

    int sum;
    hr = pSum->Sum(2, 3, &sum);

    if(SUCCEEDED(hr))
        cout << "Client: Calling Sum(2, 3) = " << sum << endl;
    pSum->Release();

    CoUninitialize();
}
```

Listing 2-2.
The complete client code.

The Component

Let's review the *ISum* interface definition we are attempting to implement in a coclass:

```
[ object, uuid(10000001-0000-0000-0000-000000000001) ]
interface ISum : IUnknown
{
    HRESULT Sum([in] int x, [in] int y, [out, retval] int* retval);
}
```

Although we can implement *ISum* using any language, such as Java or Visual Basic (we do both in Chapter 3), let's take this simple interface definition and implement it in C++. Recall the C++ definition of the *ISum* interface generated by MIDL in the component.h file:

```
MIDL_INTERFACE("10000001-0000-0000-0000-000000000001")
    ISum : public IUnknown
    {
    public:
        virtual HRESULT STDMETHODCALLTYPE Sum(
            /* [in] */ int x,
            /* [in] */ int y,
            /* [retval][out] */ int __RPC_FAR *retval) = 0;
    };
```

We call *ISum* an abstract base class because its four methods—three from *IUnknown* plus the *Sum* method declared above—are pure virtual functions, which means that they are unimplemented. To create a coclass in C++, the developer typically defines a C++ class deriving from the interfaces that the coclass will implement, as shown in the following code. Notice that the functions are no longer declared as *pure* (with the *=0* specifier) because the *CInsideCOM* class intends to implement these methods.

```
class CInsideCOM : public ISum
{
public:
    // IUnknown
    ULONG __stdcall AddRef();
    ULONG __stdcall Release();
    HRESULT __stdcall QueryInterface(REFIID riid, void** ppv);

    // ISum
    HRESULT __stdcall Sum(int x, int y, int* retval);

    CInsideCOM() : m_cRef(1) { g_cLocks++; }
    ~CInsideCOM() { g_cLocks--; }
```

```
private:
    ULONG m_cRef;  // The reference counting variable
};
```

Implementing the *AddRef* and *Release* Methods

Through reference counting, an object learns when it no longer has any clients and can therefore self-destruct. While the client sees reference counting as happening per-interface, objects use a single reference counter to keep track of all references regardless of what interface pointer is returned. To keep track of the current reference count, most COM+ objects maintain a private variable that is incremented and decremented by the *IUnknown::AddRef* and *IUnknown:: Release* methods.

The *IUnknown::AddRef* Method

The *CInsideCOM* class's implementation of the *AddRef* method is exceedingly simple; its only job is to increment the private variable *m_cRef*. This variable is the actual reference counter for *CInsideCOM* objects. Here is the entire implementation of *AddRef*:

```
ULONG CInsideCOM::AddRef()
{
    return ++m_cRef;
}
```

The *IUnknown::Release* Method

The component's implementation of the *IUnknown::Release* method obviously must decrement the *m_cRef* reference counter. However, the implementation is complicated by the fact that the reference counter might be decremented to *0*, indicating that no one is using the object. When the reference counter reaches *0*, the current instance of the *CInsideCOM* object is destroyed:

```
ULONG CInsideCOM::Release()
{
    if(--m_cRef != 0)
        return m_cRef;
    delete this;
    return 0;
}
```

Notice that both *AddRef* and *Release* return the resulting value of the reference counter, which should be used for diagnostic or testing purposes only. If the client needs to know that resources have been freed, you must provide an interface with higher-level semantics.

Implementing the *IUnknown::QueryInterface* Method

QueryInterface is the most interesting of all the *IUnknown* methods. Recall that *QueryInterface* is the method used to retrieve pointers to the other interfaces supported by the object. This technique is sometimes called a *sideways cast* because the interfaces returned by *QueryInterface* are not related through an inheritance hierarchy. Here is a typical implementation of the *IUnknown:: QueryInterface* method:

```
HRESULT CInsideCOM::QueryInterface(REFIID riid, void** ppv)
{
    if(riid == IID_IUnknown)
        *ppv = (IUnknown*)this;
    else if(riid == IID_ISum)
        *ppv = (ISum*)this;
    else
    {
        *ppv = NULL;
        return E_NOINTERFACE;
    }
    AddRef();
    return S_OK;
}
```

This implementation of *QueryInterface* simply compares the requested IID with every IID that the object supports. Because this object implements only *IUnknown* and *ISum*, only pointers to these interfaces can be returned. Notice that after the *this* reference has been cast to the requested interface pointer, the *AddRef* method is called. This optimization relieves the client from having to repeatedly call *AddRef* on each interface pointer obtained through *QueryInterface*. The client is required to call *AddRef* for every new copy of an interface pointer on a given object that is not obtained through *QueryInterface*.

It is interesting to note that the C++ comparison operator (==) is used to compare the IIDs. This comparison is possible because the objbase.h system header file overloads the comparison operator to perform the comparison using the *IsEqualGUID* function, as shown here:

```
__inline BOOL operator==(const GUID& guidOne, const GUID& guidOther)
{
    return IsEqualGUID(guidOne,guidOther);
}
```

Bridging the Gap: The C++ and COM+ Type Systems

As you know by now, a C++ class is not equivalent to a COM+ class. Before you build COM+ classes out of the basic construction material provided by C++, you should know about an important area of mismatch between C++ and COM+ that must be overcome, which relates to their type systems. The basic implementation of the *IUnknown::QueryInterface* method shown previously uses C-style casts to convert the *this* reference in C++ to a COM+ interface pointer. While this is acceptable, it is better to use C++ features to help bridge the gap between C++ and COM+ type systems. You can use the *static_cast* operator as a replacement for C-style casts in the *QueryInterface* method. Consider the following code fragment:

```
class CCar : public ICar
HRESULT CCar::QueryInterface(REFIID riid, void** ppv)
{
    if(riid == IID_IUnknown)
        *ppv = (IUnknown*)this;
    else if(riid == IID_ISum)
        *ppv = (ISum*)this;

    ⋮
```

In this fragment, *ISum* is not a base class of the *CCar* class, but the C++ type system does not flag an error; the compiler assumes that we know what we're doing because we have employed the explicit C-style cast.[8] By replacing the C-style cast with the *static_cast* operator, as shown below, the compiler helps us catch this error before it causes run-time havoc. The *static_cast* operator does the conversion based solely on the types present in the expression; no run-time type checking is involved.

```
class CCar : public ICar
HRESULT CCar::QueryInterface(REFIID riid, void** ppv)

{
    if(riid == IID_IUnknown)
        *ppv = (IUnknown*)this;
    else if(riid == IID_ISum)
        *ppv = static_cast<ISum*>(this); // Compile-time error

    ⋮
```

---

8. Actually, the compiler first converts this older C-style cast to a *static_cast*, but because that would cause an error in this case, the compiler silently demotes the cast to use the *reinterpret_cast* operator. The *reinterpret_cast* operator is a type-blind casting operator, which effectively is equivalent to the older C-style casts.

The Importance of Identity

The *IUnknown* interface is the most fundamental interface pointer you can have to an object; it establishes the identity of the object. This is important because in order for the remoting architecture of COM+ to be able to work its magic, the unique identity of each object must be preserved. As a consequence of the need to preserve identity in COM+, you must adhere to several rules regarding implementation of the *IUnknown::QueryInterface* method. While it might seem somewhat esoteric, understanding the implications of identity in COM+ will help you understand the entire architecture, which is based on the following fundamental ideas:

- Objects must support static interface sets.

- *IUnknown* must be unique.

- *QueryInterface* must be reflexive.

- *QueryInterface* must be symmetric.

- *QueryInterface* must be transitive.

Objects must support static interface sets The set of interfaces accessible through *QueryInterface* must be static, not dynamic. If a call to *QueryInterface* for a specific interface pointer succeeds the first time, it must succeed again, and if it fails the first time, it must fail on all subsequent attempts. Thus, given one object's *IUnknown* interface pointer named *pUnknown*, the following code must execute successfully:

```
ISum* pSum1 = 0;
ISum* pSum2 = 0;

// Ask the object (referenced by pUnknown) for any one
// interface pointer two times.
HRESULT hr1 = pUnknown->QueryInterface(IID_ISum, (void**)&pSum1);
HRESULT hr2 = pUnknown->QueryInterface(IID_ISum, (void**)&pSum2);

// Both attempts must either succeed or fail
if(!(SUCCEEDED(hr1) == SUCCEEDED(hr2)))
    cout << "Error: Objects must support a static set of interfaces."
    << endl;

// Release the references added by QueryInterface.
if(SUCCEEDED(hr1) && SUCCEEDED(hr2))
{
    pSum1->Release();
    pSum2->Release();
}
```

IUnknown must be unique *QueryInterface* must always return the exact same memory address for each client request for a pointer to the *IUnknown* interface.[9] This means that you can always determine whether two pointers are pointing to the same object simply by comparing their *IUnknown* interface pointers; if they both point to the same address, they refer to the same object. Thus, given one object's *IUnknown* interface pointer named *pUnknown*, the following code must execute successfully:

```
IUnknown* pUnknown1 = 0;
IUnknown* pUnknown2 = 0;

// Ask the object (referenced by pUnknown) for its IUnknown interface
// pointer two times.
HRESULT hr1 =
    pUnknown->QueryInterface(IID_IUnknown, (void**)&pUnknown1);
HRESULT hr2 =
    pUnknown->QueryInterface(IID_IUnknown, (void**)&pUnknown2);

// Both attempts must succeed.
if(FAILED(hr1) || FAILED(hr2))
    cout << "IUnknown must always be available." << endl;

// The two pointer values must be identical.
if(pUnknown1 != pUnknown2)
    cout << "Error: Object identity rules have been violated!"
    << endl;

// Release the references added by QueryInterface.
if(SUCCEEDED(hr1) && SUCCEEDED(hr2))
{
    pUnknown1->Release();
    pUnknown2->Release();
}
```

QueryInterface must be reflexive The reflexive rule requires that if a client holds a pointer to an interface and queries for that same interface, the call must succeed. Thus, given one object's *IUnknown* interface pointer named *pUnknown*, the following code must execute successfully:

```
ISum* pSum1 = 0;
ISum* pSum2 = 0;
```

(continued)

---

9. Only the *IUnknown* interface pointer must have the same address returned by every call to *QueryInterface*; other interfaces are not subject to this same restriction. You can exploit this little-known loophole to create tear-off interfaces that come and go dynamically.

```
// Ask the object for an interface pointer.
HRESULT hr1 =
    pUnknown->QueryInterface(IID_ISum, (void**)&pSum1);

if(SUCCEEDED(hr1))
{
    // Assuming that was successful, ask for the same interface
    // using the interface pointer retrieved above.
    HRESULT hr2 =
        pSum1->QueryInterface(IID_ISum, (void**)&pSum2);

    // The second request for the same interface must
    // also succeed.
    if(FAILED(hr2))
        cout << "Reflexive rule of QueryInterface violated." <<
            endl;

    // Release the references added by QueryInterface.
    pSum1->Release();
    if(SUCCEEDED(hr2))
        pSum2->Release();
}
```

***QueryInterface* must be symmetric** The symmetric rule requires that if a client holds a pointer to one interface and queries successfully for a second interface, then the client must be able to call *QueryInterface* through the second pointer for the first interface. Thus, given one object's *IUnknown* interface pointer named *pUnknown*, the following code must execute successfully:

```
IOne* pOneA = 0;

// Ask the object for an interface pointer.
HRESULT hr1 =
    pUnknown->QueryInterface(IID_IOne, (void**)&pOneA);

if(SUCCEEDED(hr1))
{
    ITwo* pTwo = 0;

    // Assuming that was successful, ask for another interface
    // using the interface pointer retrieved above.
    HRESULT hr2 =
        pOneA->QueryInterface(IID_ITwo, (void**)&pTwo);
```

```
    if(SUCCEEDED(hr2))
    {
        IOne* pOneB = 0;

        // Assuming that was successful, ask for the first
        // interface again using the interface retrieved in
        // the preceding step.
        HRESULT hr3 =
            pTwo->QueryInterface(IID_IOne, (void**)&pOneB);

        // The second request for the IOne interface
        // must succeed.
        if(FAILED(hr3))
            cout << "Symmetric rule of QueryInterface violated."
                << endl;

        // Release the references added by QueryInterface.
        pTwo->Release();
        if(SUCCEEDED(hr3))
            pOneB->Release();
    }

    pOneA->Release();
}
```

QueryInterface must be transitive   The transitive rule requires that if a client holds a pointer to one interface, queries successfully for a second interface, and through that pointer queries successfully for a third interface, then a query for the third interface through the pointer for the first interface must also succeed. Thus, given one object's *IUnknown* interface pointer named *pUnknown*, the following code must execute successfully:

```
IOne* pOne = 0;

// Ask the object for an interface pointer.
HRESULT hr1 = pUnknown->QueryInterface(IID_IOne, (void**)&pOne);

if(SUCCEEDED(hr1))
{
    ITwo* pTwo = 0;

    // Assuming that was successful, ask for a second interface
    // using interface pointer retrieved above.
    HRESULT hr2 = pOne->QueryInterface(IID_ITwo, (void**)&pTwo);
```

(continued)

```
if(SUCCEEDED(hr2))
{
    IThree* pThreeA = 0;

    // Assuming that was successful, ask for a third
    // interface using interface pointer retrieved in the
    // preceding step.
    HRESULT hr3 =
        pTwo->QueryInterface(IID_IThree, (void**)&pThreeA);

    if(SUCCEEDED(hr3))
    {
        IThree* pThreeB = 0;

        // Assuming that was successful, ask for the third
        // interface using interface pointer retrieved in
        // the first step.
        HRESULT hr4 = pOne->QueryInterface(IID_IThree,
            (void**)&pThreeB);

        // This request must succeed.
        if(FAILED(hr4))
            cout <<
                "Transitive rule of QueryInterface violated."
                << endl;

        // Release the references added by QueryInterface.
        if(SUCCEEDED(hr4))
            pThreeB->Release();
        pThreeA->Release();
    }

    pTwo->Release();
}

pOne->Release();
}
```

The sample implementation of the *IUnknown::QueryInterface* method shown previously meets all of the requirements. Figure 2-4 shows the effects of the symmetric, reflexive, and transitive rules of *QueryInterface*.

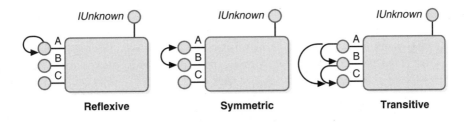

Figure 2-4.
The reflexive, symmetric, and transitive rules of QueryInterface.

The *ISum::Sum* Method (Finally)

The last method to be implemented is the *Sum* method, the sole method of the *ISum* interface. The implementation of this method should not cause any surprise:

```
HRESULT CInsideCOM::Sum(int x, int y, int* retval)
{
    *retval = x + y;
    return S_OK;
}
```

The *IClassFactory* Interface

Perhaps you're wondering what really happens when the client calls *CoCreate-Instance*. How does *CoCreateInstance* return that first pointer to an object's *IUnknown* implementation? This is an excellent question, but unfortunately the answer is a bit complicated. In our sample, *CoCreateInstance* needs only to create an instance of the *CInsideCOM* class that implements *ISum*. This could be as simple as using the C++ *new* operator, and in fact the *new* operator is ultimately used. But here is the place to recall that one of the central tenets of COM+ is the concept of *location transparency*, which states that clients should be able to reach objects easily, regardless of whether they are in-process, local, or remote components. Assuming that our object is running in-process, you could use the *new* operator simply to create an instance of the *CInsideCOM* class. But what if that component is running in a separate process address space or on a remote computer? The *new* operator is obviously not the whole answer.

COM+'s answer to this issue is *IClassFactory*, which is an interface implemented by COM+ objects that manufacture other COM+ objects. For this reason, the name *IClassFactory* is a misnomer; a much more descriptive name would be *IObjectFactory*. Be that as it may, most coclasses have an associated class factory that implements the *IClassFactory* interface. The class factory, in turn, enables clients to instantiate the desired coclass using a helper function such as *CoCreateInstance*; in fact, *CoCreateInstance* calls methods of the *IClassFactory* interface internally. The term *class factory* describes creation objects that implement the *IClassFactory* interface. The more general term for this type of object is a *class object*, which refers to any creation object regardless of what interfaces it might implement. Since most class objects implement the *IClassFactory* interface, this term is often used synonymously with *class factories*. Figure 2-5 shows how a coclass is instantiated by a class factory.

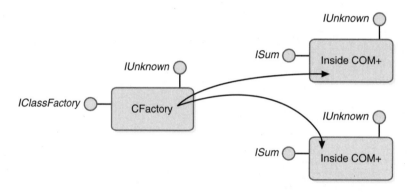

Figure 2-5.
A class factory creating instances of a coclass.

In the unknwn.idl file, *IClassFactory* is defined as follows:

```
interface IClassFactory : IUnknown
{
    HRESULT CreateInstance([in, unique] IUnknown* pUnkOuter,
        [in] REFIID riid,
        [out, iid_is(riid)] void** ppvObject);
    HRESULT LockServer([in] BOOL fLock);
}
```

As you can see, *IClassFactory* has two methods: *CreateInstance* and *LockServer*. The *CreateInstance* method actually instantiates a COM+ object; the *LockServer* method prevents the component from unloading while a client is still using one of its objects.

Here is the declaration of the C++ class *CFactory*, which implements the *IClassFactory* interface for the purpose of instantiating *CInsideCOM* objects:

```
class CFactory : public IClassFactory
{
public:
    // IUnknown
    ULONG __stdcall AddRef();
    ULONG __stdcall Release();
    HRESULT __stdcall QueryInterface(REFIID riid, void** ppv);

    // IClassFactory
    HRESULT __stdcall CreateInstance(IUnknown* pUnknownOuter,
        REFIID riid, void** ppv);
    HRESULT __stdcall LockServer(BOOL bLock);

    CFactory() : m_cRef(1) { g_cLocks++; }
    ~CFactory() { g_cLocks--; }

private:
    ULONG m_cRef;
};
```

IUnknown must be implemented again because all COM+ objects must support this interface. We won't bore you with the implementation of *AddRef* and *Release* because these simply increment and decrement the *m_cRef* reference counter. The *IUnknown::QueryInterface* method, shown below, is also implemented in the standard way; client requests for either the *IUnknown* or *IClassFactory* interfaces are honored with the desired interface pointer to the class object. Note that the object's reference counter is incremented via the *AddRef* method before any interface pointers are returned.

```
HRESULT CFactory::QueryInterface(REFIID riid, void** ppv)
{
    if(riid == IID_IUnknown)
        *ppv = (IUnknown*)this;
    if(riid == IID_IClassFactory)
        *ppv = (IClassFactory *)this;
    else
    {
        *ppv = NULL;
        return E_NOINTERFACE;
    }
    AddRef();
    return S_OK;
}
```

The *CreateInstance* Method

The *IClassFactory::CreateInstance* method is invoked when the client calls the *CoCreateInstance* function to instantiate an object. Here is a sample implementation of the *IClassFactory::CreateInstance* method:

```
HRESULT CFactory::CreateInstance(IUnknown *pUnknownOuter,
    REFIID riid, void** ppv)
{
    if(pUnknownOuter != NULL)
        return CLASS_E_NOAGGREGATION;

    CInsideCOM *pInsideCOM = new CInsideCOM;
    if(pInsideCOM == NULL)
        return E_OUTOFMEMORY;

    HRESULT hr = pInsideCOM->QueryInterface(riid, ppv);
    pInsideCOM->Release();    // In case QueryInterface fails
    return hr;
}
```

The first parameter to *CreateInstance* tells us whether the client is instantiating the object as part of an aggregate object. Recall that when the client code calls *CoCreateInstance*, its second parameter specifies aggregate information; this is where the value of the *pUnknownOuter* parameter of *IClassFactory:: CreateInstance* comes from. This particular component doesn't support aggregation, so to the client that wants to create the object as part of an aggregate, we return the error *CLASS_E_NOAGGREGATION*. (We'll discuss the identity tricks made possible by aggregate objects in the section titled "Aggregation" on page 85.)

CreateInstance actually manufactures a spanking new *CInsideCOM* object using the C++ *new* operator. *CreateInstance* knows which coclass to instantiate because every externally exposed coclass has its own associated class object. Assuming that all is well, we now call *CInsideCOM::QueryInterface* (not *CFactory::QueryInterface*) to get the interface requested by the client in the fourth parameter of *CoCreateInstance*. (This is provided to the component as the second parameter [*riid*] of the *IClassFactory::CreateInstance* method.) In the case of this class object, only the *IUnknown* and *IClassFactory* interfaces are supported. Recall that inside the *QueryInterface* method, *AddRef* is called to increment the reference counter, so the client doesn't need to call *AddRef* on the interface pointer returned by *CoCreateInstance*.

The phantom reference   The call to the *Release* method immediately following the *QueryInterface* call in the preceding code fragment might seem rather odd. If *QueryInterface* does us the favor of calling *AddRef*, why should we turn around and call *Release*? The reasoning behind this seemingly inexplicable behavior arises from the problem of what to do if the *QueryInterface* call fails. *QueryInterface* might fail simply because the client requested an interface not supported by the object. If that happens, *AddRef* is not called, but the component is left with an object that has no client, an object with a reference count of *0*, and an object that will never be destroyed. Obviously, this is not a good situation.

To handle this potential catastrophe, the object's constructor initializes the value of the reference counter variable, *m_cRef*, to *1*. This setting is artificial because at the time of construction, no client yet has a reference to the object. The counter is set to *1* so that if the *QueryInterface* call fails, the subsequent *Release* call in the *IClassFactory::CreateInstance* method will decrement the reference counter to *0*. The *Release* method's implementation will realize that the object has no remaining clients (*m_cRef* == 0) and will destroy the object. Although initially somewhat confusing, this defensive programming practice deals cleanly with the problem of a failed *QueryInterface* call with a minimum of overhead. When *QueryInterface* succeeds, the extra *Release* call does no damage because it simply undoes the phantom reference count set by the object's constructor.

Artificial reference counts   Another common defensive programming technique you can use when implementing or using COM+ objects is called *artificial reference counts*. If, while writing code that uses an object, you call a function and pass that object as a parameter, the function might *Release* the object, causing premature destruction of the object and failure of your code on return from the function. By inserting a call to *AddRef* before passing the object to the function, and then *Release* on its return, you artificially increment the object's reference counter, thereby ensuring that it will not be destroyed.

The *LockServer* Method

Although it is simple enough to implement the *IClassFactory::LockServer* method in in-process components, this method was designed primarily for executable components, which have an unusual cyclical reference counting problem with class objects. Executable components typically provide the COM+ marshaling infrastructure with a reference to their class objects on startup. (For information about how an executable component registers its class objects with COM+, see the section titled "Building an Executable Component" in Chapter 13.) An executable component that relies on the class object's reference counter, *m_cRef*, to determine when to unload will never exit because there will always be at least one outstanding reference to each of the component's class objects. To avoid this catch-22 situation, use the *IClassFactory::LockServer* method to lock an executable component in memory while outstanding references to the class objects are extant. (For more information about this method, see the section titled "Managing the Lifetime of an Executable Component" in Chapter 13.)

Because of the cyclical reference counting problem in executable components, developers did not bother to count client references for class objects in the modulewide lock counter (*g_cLocks*) that prevents components from unloading. Instead, they used the *IClassFactory::LockServer* method for this purpose when implementing both in-process and executable components. This was ineffective for both in-process and executable components because most clients never called the *IClassFactory::LockServer* method to begin with. This error was at least partly the fault of the documentation for the *IClassFactory::LockServer* method, which inaccurately claims that *LockServer* is "called by the client of a class object to keep a server open in memory, *allowing instances to be created more quickly*" [our italics]. *LockServer* was designed to meet the critical need for component lifetime management in COM+, not as an optimization that squeezes extra cycles from a component at run time.

The *LockServer* method was also subject to a particularly nasty race condition in early versions of COM+, which has been corrected for executable components. (For more about this race condition, see the section titled "Race Conditions" in Chapter 13.) In-process components are not vulnerable to this race condition, but they still do not need to rely on the *IClassFactory::LockServer* method. Taken together, these problems meant that components relying on the *IClassFactory::LockServer* method for lifetime management sometimes unloaded while a client held only a pointer to a component's class object; this was obviously unacceptable because if the client attempted to use this invalid pointer, an access violation resulted.

In-process components do not provide the COM+ marshaling infrastructure with a pointer to their class objects; such pointers are retrieved via the *DllGetClassObject* function (which is discussed in detail later in this chapter). Thus, in-process components can safely use the class object's reference counter, *m_cRef*, to determine when all the class objects have been freed, thereby allowing the component to unload without wreaking havoc on unsuspecting clients. This solution leaves in-process components with little need for the *IClassFactory::LockServer* method.

Although the previous discussion makes clear that the *LockServer* method is irrelevant to in-process components, the fact that the component implements the *IClassFactory* interface mandates that we implement this method. The implementation of the *LockServer* method is fairly straightforward. Based on the Boolean parameter *bLock*, this method either increments or decrements the modulewide lock counter variable named *g_cLocks*, as shown here:

```
long g_cLocks = 0;

HRESULT CFactory::LockServer(BOOL bLock)
{
    if(bLock)
        g_cLocks++;
    else
        g_cLocks--;
    return S_OK;
}
```

Exported DLL Functions

We've almost completed our journey through the code required to build a COM+ object. Before we go on, we need to decide how to package this object. Do we want to create an executable (EXE) component or an in-process (DLL) component? Executable components require a *main* or *WinMain* function; in-process components require two helper functions, *DllGetClassObject* and *DllCanUnloadNow*. For this first attempt at building a COM+ component, let's create an in-process component. (For information on building executable components, see Chapter 13.) Don't worry about having to implement those two extra functions—it's no big deal.

In Windows, DLLs are controlled by three primary functions: *LoadLibrary(Ex)*, *GetProcAddress*, and *FreeLibrary*. You use the Win32 API function *LoadLibrary(Ex)* to load a DLL into the caller's address space. You use *GetProcAddress* to retrieve pointers to the functions exported by the DLL, enabling clients to access its services. When a client has finished using the services offered by the DLL, the DLL is freed by a call to *FreeLibrary*. The *FreeLibrary* function decrements the library's usage counter, unloading the library when the counter reaches *0*.

The *DllGetClassObject* Function

COM+ helps you transition to an object-oriented world of components and work with them in a consistent manner. On some level, however, COM+ is just a shiny veneer that sits on top of Windows; an in-process COM+ component is just a fancy name for a Windows DLL. To call the methods of a COM+ object housed in a DLL, we need to obtain the address where it is loaded in memory. The *IUnknown::QueryInterface* method is designed to return interface pointers, but we can only call the *QueryInterface* method once we have an *IUnknown* interface pointer. How do we get that first pointer to *IUnknown*? This is where *DllGetClassObject* comes in. The *DllGetClassObject* function is not a method of any interface; it is a fossilized exported function that gives us that first pointer.

As you know, each class factory creates only one type of object, while a typical component might contain multiple coclasses, each of which requires its own class factory. The purpose of *DllGetClassObject* is to direct us to the correct class factory for the type of object we want to create. Since our sample component has only one supported coclass (*CLSID_InsideCOM*), our implementation of *DllGetClassObject* is rather rudimentary:

```
HRESULT __stdcall DllGetClassObject(REFCLSID clsid,
    REFIID riid, void** ppv)
{
    if(clsid != CLSID_InsideCOM)
        return CLASS_E_CLASSNOTAVAILABLE; // Tough luck!

    CFactory* pFactory = new CFactory;
    if(pFactory == NULL)
        return E_OUTOFMEMORY;

    // riid is probably IID_IClassFactory.
    HRESULT hr = pFactory->QueryInterface(riid, ppv);
    pFactory->Release();    // Just in case QueryInterface fails
    return hr;
}
```

DllGetClassObject first checks to see whether the client has requested the *CLSID_InsideCOM* coclass. If it hasn't, we simply return the error *CLASS_E_CLASSNOTAVAILABLE*. If the client requests a class object supported by this component, *DllGetClassObject* instantiates a class factory using the C++ *new* operator. After that, we call *QueryInterface* to ask the class factory for a pointer to its *IClassFactory* interface. The third parameter of *DllGetClassObject* returns the *IClassFactory* interface pointer back to the client.

Notice once again that the *Release* method is called immediately after the *QueryInterface* call. Remember that this call works to cleanly deallocate the *CFactory* object in case the *QueryInterface* call fails.

You might be wondering why *DllGetClassObject* even bothers with the *IID* parameter of the *IClassFactory* interface. After all, if all objects are instantiated by a class factory, why not simply hard-code *IID_IClassFactory* and rename the *DllGetClassObject* function *DllGetClassFactory*? The answer is that some objects might have special requirements not met by *IClassFactory* and might want to implement a custom activation interface. A custom activation interface is useful when a standard implementation of *IClassFactory* just won't do. For example, suppose you want to support licensing to restrict your component to machines on which it was properly installed. *IClassFactory* does not offer this functionality, but an improved version of the interface, *IClassFactory2*, does. The IDL definition of the *IClassFactory2* interface is shown below:

```
interface IClassFactory2 : IClassFactory
{
    typedef IClassFactory2* LPCLASSFACTORY2;

    typedef struct tagLICINFO {
        LONG cbLicInfo;
        BOOL fRuntimeKeyAvail;
        BOOL fLicVerified;
    } LICINFO;

    typedef struct tagLICINFO* LPLICINFO;

    // Fills a caller-allocated LICINFO structure with
    // information describing the licensing capabilities of
    // this class factory
    HRESULT GetLicInfo([out] LICINFO* pLicInfo);

    // Creates and returns a license key
    HRESULT RequestLicKey([in] DWORD dwReserved,
        [out] BSTR * pBstrKey);

    // Creates an instance of the object class supported by this
    // class factory, given a license key
    HRESULT CreateInstanceLic([in] IUnknown* pUnkOuter,
        [in] IUnknown* pUnkReserved, [in] REFIID riid,
        [in] BSTR bstrKey, [out, iid_is(riid)] PVOID* ppvObj);
}
```

In rare cases in which neither *IClassFactory* nor *IClassFactory2* is sufficient, a custom activation interface might be the only solution. (This advanced topic is covered in Chapter 11.) The client then passes the *IID* parameter of the custom activation interface to the *CoGetClassObject* function. Note that if a class object does not implement *IClassFactory*, clients cannot instantiate objects using *CoCreateInstance* because that function automatically queries for the *IClassFactory* interface.

The *DllCanUnloadNow* Function

The last function we need for our sample component is *DllCanUnloadNow*. This function determines whether the DLL is in use, based on the *g_cLocks* modulewide lock counter maintained by the component. This lock counter keeps track of the number of class objects, objects, and *IClassFactory::LockServer* calls. If the lock counter reaches *0*, the component does not have any valid clients, so *DllCanUnloadNow* returns *S_OK* and the caller can safely unload the DLL from memory.[10] Otherwise, it returns *S_FALSE* to indicate that the DLL should not be unloaded. A standard implementation of *DllCanUnloadNow* is shown below:

```
HRESULT __stdcall DllCanUnloadNow()
{
    if(g_cLocks == 0)
        return S_OK;
    else
        return S_FALSE;
}
```

Notice that you do not have to call *DllCanUnloadNow* directly—it is called by the *CoFreeUnusedLibraries* function. Client applications can occasionally call *CoFreeUnusedLibraries* to unload DLLs that are no longer in use. *CoFreeUnusedLibraries* walks an internal list of loaded in-process components and queries each DLL about its status by calling the *DllCanUnloadNow* function. If a component returns *S_OK*, *CoFreeUnusedLibraries* calls the *CoFreeLibrary* function to physically unload the DLL. In-process components that do not implement *DllCanUnloadNow* are unloaded only when the client process calls *CoUninitialize* (usually just before exiting). The *CoUninitialize* function unloads all in-process COM+ components.

---

10. Due to the potential for race conditions in multithreaded in-process components, COM+ might not immediately unload the DLL even if *S_OK* is returned by *DllCanUnloadNow*. For a discussion of this race condition, see the section, "*Making* DllGetClassObject *and* DllCanUnloadNow *Thread-Safe*," in Chapter 4.

The *CoCreateInstance* Function Revisited

You might wonder how the *CoCreateInstance* function actually works its magic. It actually calls another function, *CoGetClassObject*, which provides an interface pointer to the requested class object associated with a specified CLSID. The following code fragment shows the *CoGetClassObject* function in action. If necessary, *CoGetClassObject* dynamically loads the code required to obtain the class object interface pointer, even if that code happens to be on a remote machine. It checks the registry entries for the requested CLSID to learn where the component can be found.

```
hr = CoGetClassObject(CLSID_InsideCOM, CLSCTX_INPROC_SERVER,
    NULL, IID_IClassFactory, (void**)&pClassFactory);
if(FAILED(hr))
    cout << "CoGetClassObject failed. " << endl;
```

Normally, *CoGetClassObject* retrieves a pointer to an object's implementation of *IClassFactory*, although some other activation interface might be requested. *CoCreateInstance* retrieves the *IClassFactory* interface pointer so that it can call the *IClassFactory::CreateInstance* method to manufacture a COM+ object, as shown here:

```
hr = pClassFactory->CreateInstance(NULL, IID_IUnknown,
    (void**)&pUnknown);
if(FAILED(hr))
    cout << "pClassFactory->CreateInstance failed." << endl;
```

Once *CoCreateInstance* finishes creating the object using the class factory, the class factory can be released, as shown here:

```
pClassFactory->Release();
```

If you prefer, you can replace the call to *CoCreateInstance* in the client with equivalent code that uses *CoGetClassObject* directly. Is there a reason for doing this? Absolutely. *CoGetClassObject* provides greater control over how and when objects are instantiated and has lower overhead than multiple calls to *CoCreateInstance*. Since you can use *CoGetClassObject* to return a pointer to an object's *IClassFactory* implementation, clients that want to create several objects of the same coclass should use a single call to *CoGetClassObject* followed by multiple calls to the *IClassFactory::CreateInstance* method instead of multiple calls to *CoCreateInstance*. The code on the following page replaces *CoCreateInstance* in the client project with equivalent code that uses *CoGetClassObject*.

```
IClassFactory* pClassFactory;
CoGetClassObject(CLSID_InsideCOM, CLSCTX_INPROC_SERVER, NULL,
    IID_IClassFactory, (void**)&pClassFactory);
pClassFactory->CreateInstance(NULL, IID_IUnknown,
    (void**)&pUnknown);
pClassFactory->Release();
```

In fact, you can even instantiate and access an in-process COM+ object without using any COM+ functions. The following C++ code loads an in-process component, obtains a pointer to the *DllGetClassObject* function, and calls *IClassFactory::CreateInstance*—all without using a single COM+ API function.[11]

```
IUnknown* pUnknown;
IClassFactory* pClassFactory;

// Load the DLL.
HINSTANCE myDLL = LoadLibrary("C:\\component.dll");

// Declare a pointer to the DllGetClassObject function.
typedef HRESULT (__stdcall *PFNDLLGETCLASSOBJECT)(REFCLSID clsid,
    REFIID riid, void** ppv);

// Get a pointer to the component's DllGetClassObject function.
PFNDLLGETCLASSOBJECT DllGetClassObject =
    (PFNDLLGETCLASSOBJECT)GetProcAddress(myDLL,
        "DllGetClassObject");

// Call DllGetClassObject to get a pointer to the class factory.
DllGetClassObject(CLSID_InsideCOM, IID_IClassFactory,
    (void**)&pClassFactory);
// IClassFactory::CreateInstance and IUnknown::Release
pClassFactory->CreateInstance(NULL, IID_IUnknown,
    (void**)&pUnknown);
pClassFactory->Release();
```

When activating an in-process component, *CoGetClassObject* loads the DLL by calling the *CoLoadLibrary* function, which is just a wrapper around the standard Win32 *LoadLibrary* function. Then it calls *GetProcAddress* to retrieve the address of the *DllGetClassObject* function exported by the DLL. The address returned from *GetProcAddress* is used to call the *DllGetClassObject* function and retrieve an interface pointer to the class object, magically leading us into the world of COM+. Figure 2-6 puts in perspective the functions and the order in which they are called when activating an in-process component.

---

11. We are not suggesting that you actually write code like this, but it can be helpful to see that in the simple case of an in-process component, COM+ is not doing anything incredibly complex in *CoCreateInstance*.

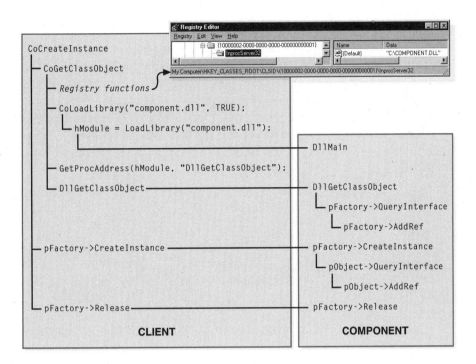

Figure 2-6.
A client calling CoCreateInstance *to instantiate an in-process COM+ object.*

The Service Control Manager

In reality, *CoGetClassObject* delegates the task of locating and loading the component to the Service Control Manager (SCM—pronounced "scum")[12] implemented by the rpcss.dll system process. After the SCM locates and loads the requested component, COM+ and the SCM drop out of the picture, allowing the client and the component to communicate directly. In the case of unconfigured COM+ components (which do not run in the COM+ run-time environment), COM+ does not insert a mediator between in-process components and their clients that could hurt performance; in-process components configured to execute in the COM+ run-time environment pay a price for the extra services provided. For executable and remote components, the COM+ marshaling infrastructure is used to transfer parameters and function invocations between the client and component. When an object is invoked on a remote machine, the SCM on the local machine contacts the SCM on the remote machine to request that it locate and load the component.

---

12. The COM+ SCM is often confused with the Windows 2000 Service Control Manager used to manage Win32 services.

Building the Component Project

Before we build the component, we must create a module definition (.def) file that lists the exported functions, as shown in Listing 2-3. The *DllGetClassObject* and *DllCanUnloadNow* functions are exported for use only by COM+. Placing them in the import library can lead to unusual behavior if a program linked to the library incorrectly makes calls to them. Therefore, we must use the optional *PRIVATE* keyword to prevent the function names from being placed in the import library generated by the linker; it has no effect on the export table in the DLL.

component.def

```
LIBRARY          component.dll
DESCRIPTION      '(c)1999 Guy Eddon'
EXPORTS

                 DllGetClassObject   @1    PRIVATE
                 DllCanUnloadNow     @2    PRIVATE
```

Listing 2-3.
The module definition file listing the exported functions DllGetClassObject *and* DllCanUnloadNow.

To build the component project, open the InProcess.dsw workspace file in the Samples\The IUnknown Interface folder on the companion CD. Then build the project named Component. The complete component.cpp code is shown in Listing 2-4.

component.cpp

```
#include "Component\component.h" // Generated by MIDL

// {10000002-0000-0000-0000-000000000001}
const CLSID CLSID_InsideCOM =
    {0x10000002,0x0000,0x0000,
    {0x00,0x00,0x00,0x00,0x00,0x00,0x00,0x01}};

long g_cLocks = 0;

class CInsideCOM : public ISum
```

Listing 2-4.
The complete component code.

```
{
public:
    // IUnknown
    ULONG __stdcall AddRef();
    ULONG __stdcall Release();
    HRESULT __stdcall QueryInterface(REFIID riid, void** ppv);

    // ISum
    HRESULT __stdcall Sum(int x, int y, int* retval);

    CInsideCOM() : m_cRef(1) { g_cLocks++; }
    ~CInsideCOM() { g_cLocks--; }

private:
    ULONG m_cRef;
};

ULONG CInsideCOM::AddRef()
{
    return ++m_cRef;
}

ULONG CInsideCOM::Release()
{
    if(--m_cRef != 0)
        return m_cRef;
    delete this;
    return 0;
}

HRESULT CInsideCOM::QueryInterface(REFIID riid, void** ppv)
{
    if(riid == IID_IUnknown)
        *ppv = (IUnknown*)this;
    else if(riid == IID_ISum)
        *ppv = (ISum*)this;
    else
    {
        *ppv = NULL;
        return E_NOINTERFACE;
    }
    AddRef();
    return S_OK;
}

HRESULT CInsideCOM::Sum(int x, int y, int* retval)
```

(continued)

component.cpp *continued*

```
{
    *retval = x + y;
    return S_OK;
}

class CFactory : public IClassFactory
{
public:
    // IUnknown
    ULONG __stdcall AddRef();
    ULONG __stdcall Release();
    HRESULT __stdcall QueryInterface(REFIID riid, void** ppv);

    // IClassFactory
    HRESULT __stdcall CreateInstance(IUnknown* pUnknownOuter,
        REFIID riid, void** ppv);
    HRESULT __stdcall LockServer(BOOL bLock);

    CFactory() : m_cRef(1) { g_cLocks++; }
    ~CFactory() { g_cLocks--; }

private:
    ULONG m_cRef;
};

ULONG CFactory::AddRef()
{
    return ++m_cRef;
}

ULONG CFactory::Release()
{
    if(--m_cRef != 0)
        return m_cRef;
    delete this;
    return 0;
}

HRESULT CFactory::QueryInterface(REFIID riid, void** ppv)
{
    if(riid == IID_IUnknown)
        *ppv = (IUnknown*)this;
    else if(riid == IID_IClassFactory)
        *ppv = (IClassFactory*)this;
```

```
    else
    {
        *ppv = NULL;
        return E_NOINTERFACE;
    }
    AddRef();
    return S_OK;
}

HRESULT CFactory::CreateInstance(IUnknown *pUnknownOuter,
    REFIID riid, void** ppv)
{
    if(pUnknownOuter != NULL)
        return CLASS_E_NOAGGREGATION;

    CInsideCOM *pInsideCOM = new CInsideCOM;
    if(pInsideCOM == NULL)
        return E_OUTOFMEMORY;

    HRESULT hr = pInsideCOM->QueryInterface(riid, ppv);
    pInsideCOM->Release();
    return hr;
}

HRESULT CFactory::LockServer(BOOL bLock)
{
    if(bLock)
        g_cLocks++;
    else
        g_cLocks --;
    return S_OK;
}

HRESULT __stdcall DllCanUnloadNow()
{
    if(g_cLocks == 0)
        return S_OK;
    else
        return S_FALSE;
}

HRESULT __stdcall DllGetClassObject(REFCLSID clsid, REFIID riid,
    void** ppv)
```

(continued)

component.cpp *continued*

```
{
    if(clsid != CLSID_InsideCOM)
        return CLASS_E_CLASSNOTAVAILABLE;

    CFactory* pFactory = new CFactory;
    if(pFactory == NULL)
        return E_OUTOFMEMORY;

    // riid is probably IID_IClassFactory.
    HRESULT hr = pFactory->QueryInterface(riid, ppv);
    pFactory->Release();
    return hr;
}
```

Component Registration

After we build the client and component, we are almost ready to run and test the code. First, however, the correct entries must be placed in the Windows registry so that the client can locate the component. The simplest way to arrange for the creation of registry entries is by using a registration (.reg) file, as shown in Listing 2-5.

component.reg

```
REGEDIT4

[HKEY_CLASSES_ROOT\CLSID\{10000002-0000-0000-0000-000000000001}]
@="Inside COM+: In Process Component"

[HKEY_CLASSES_ROOT\CLSID\{10000002-0000-0000-0000-000000000001}\
InprocServer32]
@="C:\\Component.dll"
```

Listing 2-5.
The component registration file.

The registry file shown here provides the entries necessary for the client to activate the component built in this chapter. You might need to adjust the path of the InprocServer32 key to the folder where your component.dll file was built. To add this information to the registry, simply double-click on the registration file or execute the following command at the command line:

```
C:\WINDOWS>regedit c:\component.reg
```

Self-Registering Components

Registration files are a useful and relatively easy way to automate the addition of items to the registry. Most commercial software vendors, however, prefer that their software packages have as few unneeded files as possible. Registration files are also not terribly flexible. They do not offer a ready-made solution if an application's setup program decides that due to the configuration of the user's computer, different registry settings should be created. A better way is to create a self-registering component, which does not rely on an external registration file to be properly registered. Like plug-and-play devices that carry with them all the necessary configuration information, self-registering components carry with them all the code required to create the necessary registry entries.

In-process components and executable components have slightly different self-registration mechanisms. For in-process components, self-registration means that the component must export two additional functions, *DllRegisterServer* and *DllUnregisterServer*. A setup program can load the DLL and call these functions to instruct the component to register itself. You can also use the RegSvr32.exe utility that comes with Windows to call these exported functions, as shown here:

```
C:\WINDOWS\SYSTEM>regsvr32 c:\component.dll
```

An alternative when you work in Visual C++ is to choose Register Control from the Tools menu. This feature uses the RegSvr32.exe utility to load the DLL and call its *DllRegisterServer* function.

Self-registering executable components do not export the *DllRegisterServer* and *DllUnregisterServer* functions; they examine their command-line parameters for the /RegServer or /UnregServer flags when they are executed. Some self-registering executable components automatically reregister themselves at startup. (For more on building self-registering executable components, see the section titled "Building an Executable Component" in Chapter 13.)

Adding Self-Registering Features to a Component

At run time, registry entries can be created using the Win32 API functions that manipulate the registry, including *RegCreateKeyEx*, *RegOpenKeyEx*, *RegEnumKeyEx*, *RegSetValueEx*, *RegCloseKey*, and *RegDeleteKey*.[13] To automate the rather dreary process of creating and removing the typically needed registry entries, we have written a module that makes the low-level calls to these registry functions. The registry.cpp file containing the C++ source code is on the companion CD.

---

13. These functions are part of the Win32 API, not COM+, and because their names are relatively descriptive, they will not be described here in detail. See the Win32 reference documentation for more information.

The registry.h file, shown in Listing 2-6, declares the four main functions of the module, *RegisterServer*, *UnregisterServer*, *RegisterServerEx*, and *Unregister-ServerEx*. These high-level functions can be called from any component to add and remove standard registry entries.

registry.h

```
// This function will register a component.
HRESULT RegisterServer(const char* szModuleName, REFCLSID clsid,
    const char* szFriendlyName, const char* szVerIndProgID,
    const char* szProgID, const char* szThreadingModel);

// This function will unregister a component.
HRESULT UnregisterServer(REFCLSID clsid,
    const char* szVerIndProgID, const char* szProgID);

struct REG_DATA
{
    const char* pszKey;
    const char* pszValue;
    const char* pszData;
};

// These functions will register and unregister a component
// based on data from a global array.
HRESULT RegisterServerEx(const REG_DATA regData[],
    const char* szModuleName);
HRESULT UnregisterServerEx(const REG_DATA regData[]);
```

Listing 2-6.
The registry.h file.

Several steps are required to replace the registration file used to register the component in the previous section. First, you must include the registry.h file containing forward declarations for the registration functions, and then you must write the *DllRegisterServer* and *DllUnregisterServer* functions, as shown here:

```
// component.cpp
#include "registry.h" // Add this!!!

// And these...
HRESULT __stdcall DllRegisterServer()
{
    return RegisterServer("component with registration.dll",
        CLSID_InsideCOM,
```

```
        "Inside COM+: In Process Component", "Component.InsideCOM",
        "Component.InsideCOM.1", NULL);
}


HRESULT __stdcall DllUnregisterServer()
{
    return UnregisterServer(CLSID_InsideCOM, "Component.InsideCOM"
        "Component.InsideCOM.1");
}
```

Notice that the *RegisterServer* and *UnregisterServer* functions both require certain pieces of information that will be entered into the registry. While this makes it easy to understand how they work, it also limits the flexibility of the registration code, because every new entry not supported by these functions must be added manually or else you must modify the implementation of the registry.cpp code. A newer and more flexible way to add registry entries is to define an array of registry data in the application and have the registration code insert this information into the registry for you.[14] So as an alternative to the *RegisterServer* and *UnregisterServer* functions, we have also written *RegisterServerEx* and *UnregisterServerEx*, which use this new method based on an array. The array containing the registry data is shown below:

```
const REG_DATA g_regData[] = {
    { "CLSID\\{10000002-0000-0000-0000-000000000001}", 0,
        "Inside COM+: In Process Component" },
    { "CLSID\\{10000002-0000-0000-0000-000000000001}"
        "\\InprocServer32", 0, (const char*)-1 },
    { "CLSID\\{10000002-0000-0000-0000-000000000001}\\ProgID",
        0, "Component.InsideCOM.1" },
    { "CLSID\\{10000002-0000-0000-0000-000000000001}"
        "\\VersionIndependentProgID", 0,
        "Component.InsideCOM" },
    { "Component.InsideCOM", 0,
        "Inside COM+: In Process Component" },
    { "Component.InsideCOM\\CLSID", 0,
        "{10000002-0000-0000-0000-000000000001}" },
    { "Component.InsideCOM\\CurVer", 0,
        "Component.InsideCOM.1" },
    { "Component.InsideCOM.1", 0,
        "Inside COM+: In Process Component" },
    { "Component.InsideCOM.1\\CLSID", 0,
        "{10000002-0000-0000-0000-000000000001}" },
    { 0, 0, 0 }
};
```

---

14. Incidentally, this is also how the Active Template Library (ATL) handles component registration needs.

Although this array looks a bit messy, it is more flexible because any registry settings that need to be added require only another entry in the array—you don't have to modify the actual registration functions. The array begins with the subkey name of *HKEY_CLASSES_ROOT*, followed by a named value (if any) and the actual data. If the named value is *0*, the data element is assigned to the default value. A named value of *−1* is a placeholder indicating that the fully qualified pathname of the component should be inserted. This is retrieved via a call to the Win32 API function *GetModuleFileName*. The last entry (*0, 0, 0*) indicates the end of the array.

Now the *DllRegisterServer* and *DllUnregisterServer* functions can be simplified, as shown below:

```
HINSTANCE g_hInstance; // Global hInstance of the DLL

HRESULT __stdcall DllRegisterServer()
{
    char DllPath[MAX_PATH];
    GetModuleFileName(g_hInstance, DllPath, sizeof(DllPath));
    return RegisterServerEx(g_regData, DllPath);
}

HRESULT __stdcall DllUnregisterServer()
{
    return UnregisterServerEx(g_regData);
}
```

The *GetModuleFileName* function, which retrieves the path and filename of the DLL, requires the instance handle (*hInstance*) of the DLL. This handle is passed to the *DllMain* function and is stored in the *g_hInstance* global variable when the DLL is loaded, as shown here:

```
BOOL WINAPI DllMain(HINSTANCE hInstance, DWORD dwReason,
    void* pv)
{
    g_hInstance = hInstance;
    return TRUE;
}
```

Regardless of which registration method you use, you must add the *DllRegisterServer* and *DllUnregisterServer* functions to the end of the exported function list in the module definition file, as shown in boldface in Listing 2-7:

component with registration.def

```
LIBRARY          component.dll
DESCRIPTION      '(c)1999 Guy Eddon'
EXPORTS

                 DllGetClassObject   @1      PRIVATE
                 DllCanUnloadNow     @2      PRIVATE
                 DllRegisterServer   @3      PRIVATE
                 DllUnregisterServer @4      PRIVATE
```

Listing 2-7.
The component with the registration.def file, which contains the exported functions DllRegisterServer *and* DllUnregisterServer.

The *OLESelfRegister* flag   Some developers consider the *OLESelfRegister* flag an anachronism in COM+, and don't bother including it in a component's version information resource. This is regrettable because the flag serves an important purpose: it tells a client whether a component supports self-registration. Without it, a potential client must load a component and attempt to activate its self-registration code. This is not such a problem for in-process components because a client can simply check for the existence of the *DllRegisterServer* function. If it exists in the DLL's export table, the component almost definitely supports self-registration. Still, the DLL must be loaded to make the determination, which can waste resources, unless the client wants to use knowledge of the Win32 DLL file format to check the export table for the *DllRegisterServer* function; this latter method is certainly not recommended. For executable components, the situation gets even worse: there is simply no way to determine whether an executable component supports self-registration. A client can only launch the executable with the */RegServer* command-line parameter and hope for the best. If self-registration is not supported, it is impossible to tell what the executable component might do.

One example of a service that uses the *OLESelfRegister* flag is Internet Component Download. Microsoft Internet Explorer uses this service to automatically download components such as ActiveX controls from a Web site. For security reasons, the .inf format used by the Internet Component Download service does not include syntax for changing registry information. Instead, the service looks inside .ocx, .dll, and .exe files for the *OLESelfRegister* flag in the version information resource. For components that are marked as self-registering, the service attempts to activate the self-registration code in the component. Components that are not marked in this way are not automatically registered. This setting can be overridden in the .inf file.

When you create a self-registering component, you should always indicate this feature by including the *OLESelfRegister* flag in the version information section of the resource script file. Visual Basic, for example, always includes the *OLESelfRegister* flag in all components built in that language. (Of course, Visual Basic also provides the self-registration code.) The *OLESelfRegister* flag is shown in boldface in Listing 2-8. A client program can read the version information resource out of an .ocx, .dll, or .exe file using the file installation library functions of the Win32 API.[15]

component.rc

```
VS_VERSION_INFO VERSIONINFO
  FILEVERSION 1,0,0,1
  PRODUCTVERSION 1,0,0,1
  FILEFLAGSMASK 0x3fL
#ifdef _DEBUG
  FILEFLAGS 0x1L
#else
  FILEFLAGS 0x0L
#endif
  FILEOS 0x10004L
  FILETYPE 0x1L
  FILESUBTYPE 0x0L
BEGIN
    BLOCK "StringFileInfo"
    BEGIN
        BLOCK "040904B0"
        BEGIN
            VALUE "CompanyName", "Microsoft Corporation\0"
            VALUE "FileDescription", "Inside COM+ Component\0"
            VALUE "FileVersion", "1, 0, 0, 1\0"
            VALUE "InternalName", "InsideCOM+\0"
            VALUE "LegalCopyright", "Copyright © 1999\0"
            VALUE "OriginalFilename", "component.dll\0"
            VALUE "ProductName", "Inside COM+\0"
            VALUE "ProductVersion", "2, 0, 0, 1\0"
            VALUE "OLESelfRegister", "\0"
        END
```

Listing 2-8.
A resource file that you can use to determine whether a component supports self-registration.

---

15. Specifically, the functions *GetFileVersionInfoSize*, *GetFileVersionInfo*, and *VerQueryValue* are used for this purpose. For sample code that uses these functions to check whether a component has the *OLESelfRegister* flag in its version information resource, see the CheckReg.dsw workspace file in the Samples\The IUnknown Interface\CheckReg folder on the companion CD.

```
          END
          BLOCK "VarFileInfo"
          BEGIN
               VALUE "Translation", 0x0409, 1200
          END
     END
```

To build the component that supports self-registration, open the InProcess.dsw workspace file in the Samples\The IUnknown Interface folder and build the Component with Registration project. Then use RegSvr32 to test the new functionality. You should see the message box shown in Figure 2-7.

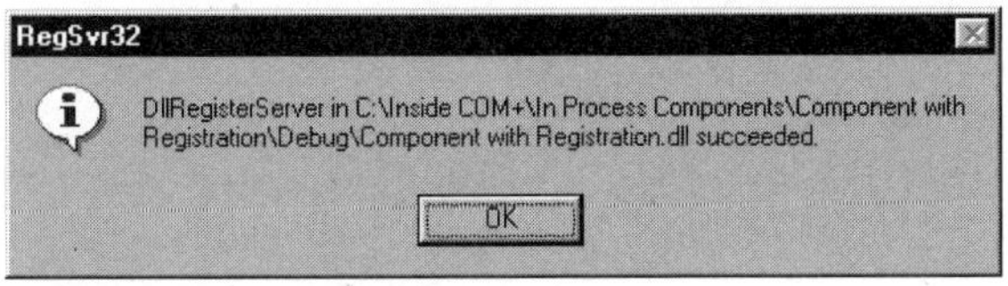

Figure 2-7.
The message box that appears when you register an in-process component using RegSvr32.exe.

Merging Object Identity

COM+ has been criticized for not supporting implementation inheritance. But inheritance is just one technique that enables code reuse—it is by no means the only technique. Language-based implementation inheritance often comes with many of its own problems; witness the fragile base class problem in C++. COM+ novices often claim that containment and aggregation serve as the reuse mechanisms of COM+. Nothing could be further from the truth. Code reuse in COM+ happens by factoring your functionality into interfaces that are implemented by objects, which can then be reused by any application, written in any language, running anywhere that COM+ is supported.

So what are containment and aggregation needed for? They are simply techniques for merging the identities of two or more objects. These techniques can be useful when you want to transparently add some services to an object without modifying its source code. Recall that the *IUnknown* interface pointer of every object defines its identity. This means that if you want to merge the functionality of two distinct objects, you must make sure that the new super-object represents only a single identity to the client. In other words, the object must adhere to the rules of identity we discussed previously.

- Objects must support static interface sets.

- *IUnknown* must be unique.

- *QueryInterface* must be reflexive, symmetric, and transitive.

Registration Using Context Menus

To make the self-registration of components even easier, you can add the following registry script to your registry. This script provides context menus for registering and unregistering components; you simply right-click on a .dll, .ocx, or .exe file and choose Register Component or Unregister Component. For in-process components, this script simply launches the RegSvr32 utility.

```
REGEDIT4

[HKEY_CLASSES_ROOT\.dll]
@="dllfile"

[HKEY_CLASSES_ROOT\dllfile\shell\Register Component\command]
@="regsvr32 \"%L\""

[HKEY_CLASSES_ROOT\dllfile\shell\Unregister Component\command]
@="regsvr32 /u \"%L\""

[HKEY_CLASSES_ROOT\.ocx]
@="ocxfile"

[HKEY_CLASSES_ROOT\ocxfile\shell\Register Component\command]
@="regsvr32 \"%L\""

[HKEY_CLASSES_ROOT\ocxfile\shell\Unregister Component\command]
@="regsvr32 /u \"%L\""

[HKEY_CLASSES_ROOT\.exe]
@="exefile"

[HKEY_CLASSES_ROOT\exefile\shell\Register Component\command]
@="\"%L\" /regserver"

[HKEY_CLASSES_ROOT\exefile\shell\Unregister Component\command]
@="\"%L\" /unregserver"
```

Containment

The basic idea of containment, in which one object completely reimplements the interfaces of another, is shown in Figure 2-8.

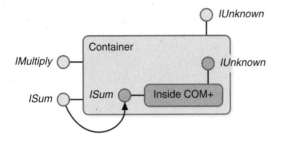

Figure 2-8.
Delegating method calls using containment.

The containment technique simply follows through on the idea that any COM+ object can be a client of another object; it requires no special support from COM+. Here we see that one object pretends to support an interface when it is really acting only as a mediator by passing along the client's request to a third party. Using multiple inheritance in C++, the container object implements both the *IMultiply* and *ISum* interfaces, as shown in the following class declaration:

```
class CContainer : public IMultiply, public ISum
{
    // Methods and data go here...
};
```

The *IMultiply* interface works similarly to the *ISum* interface except that instead of adding two numbers, it returns their product. Using IDL syntax, the *IMultiply* interface is expressed as follows:

```
[ object, uuid(10000011-0000-0000-0000-000000000001) ]
interface IMultiply : IUnknown
{
    HRESULT Multiply(int x, int y, [out, retval] int* retval);
}
```

In the usual fashion, the container object actually implements the *IMultiply* interface using its *Multiply* method. As part of its construction sequence, however, the container object also instantiates the *CLSID_InsideCOM* object, as shown in the code on the following page.

```
HRESULT CContainer::Init()
{
    return CoCreateInstance(CLSID_InsideCOM, NULL,
        CLSCTX_INPROC_SERVER, IID_ISum, (void**)&m_pSum);
}
```

There is never any danger that the identity laws of COM+ will be violated because the outer object never hands out a direct *ISum* interface pointer to the client. Instead, the outer object's *QueryInterface* method returns a pointer to its own implementation of *ISum*:

```
HRESULT CContainer::QueryInterface(REFIID riid, void** ppv)
{
    if(riid == IID_IUnknown)
        *ppv = (IMultiply*)this; // Choose left-most base
    else if(riid == IID_ISum)
        *ppv = (ISum*)this;
    else if(riid == IID_IMultiply)
        *ppv = (IMultiply*)this;
    else
    {
        *ppv = NULL;
        return E_NOINTERFACE;
    }
    AddRef();
    return S_OK;
}
```

Notice that the request for the *IUnknown* interface pointer in the code above is satisfied by casting the *this* pointer to an *IMultiply* interface pointer. This coercion is required because the *CContainer* class uses multiple inheritance to implement the *IMultiply* and *ISum* interfaces, as shown in Figure 2-9.

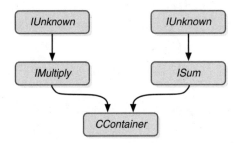

class CContainer : public IMultiply, public ISum

Figure 2-9.
Multiple inheritance in action.

Because *IMultiply* is derived from *IUnknown* and *ISum* is derived from *IUnknown*, we have run into one of the snags of multiple inheritance in C++. Luckily, since both interfaces are abstract base classes, we don't have to worry about duplicate function implementations. Nevertheless, the code that attempts to cast the *this* pointer into a pointer to *IUnknown*—a legal operation—runs afoul of the compiler's type checking. The cast is ambiguous because it is not clear whether we want *IMultiply*'s *IUnknown* or *ISum*'s *IUnknown*. The truth of the matter is that we couldn't care less, so casting the *this* pointer to either *IMultiply* or *ISum* will work fine.[16]

Now when the client calls the *ISum::Sum* method, the container object simply delegates the call to the *CLSID_InsideCOM* object, as shown here:

```
HRESULT CContainer::Sum(int x, int y, int* retval)
{
    // Delegate this call to our contained object.
    return m_pSum->Sum(x, y, retval);
}
```

This code demonstrates the simplest kind of containment—it does nothing besides delegate to another object. More sophisticated uses of containment might add code before and after delegating the call to the internal object, which might allow the container object to modify the behavior of the internal object in some way. The container object might even decide not to delegate to the internal object under some circumstances. In such cases, the container object is expected to provide the entire behavior necessary to satisfy the client request.

Aggregation

Aggregation is a specialized form of containment supported by COM+. Instead of requiring an object to provide stub methods that delegate to the actual object, as is the case with standard containment, aggregation allows the inner object's interfaces to be exposed directly as if they belong to the outer object (also called the aggregate object). Note that aggregation works only with in-process[17] components. The architecture of an aggregate object and its inner object is shown in Figure 2-10.

---

16. It is generally best to choose the leftmost base class when casting because some compilers, including Visual C++, place the leftmost base class at the top of the object layout and then do not require an adjustor thunk to manipulate the *this* pointer. This is why *IMultiply* is preferable to *ISum* for casting of the *IUnknown* interface pointer.

17. The limitation is actually even more stringent because you cannot use aggregation across apartment boundaries. For details about the apartment models, see Chapter 4.

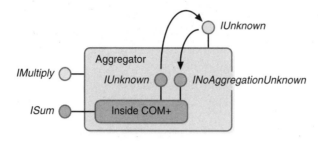

Figure 2-10.
A COM+ object being aggregated.

The outer object implements only the *IMultiply* interface, as shown in the following class declaration:

```
class CAggregator : public IMultiply
{
// Methods and data go here...
};
```

While the outer object is being initialized, the inner object is instantiated, as in the containment example in the previous section. In this case, however, the second parameter of the *CoCreateInstance* call made by the outer object is a pointer to the *IUnknown* interface of the outer object itself, as shown below. This parameter tells the InsideCOM object that it is being aggregated. On returning from *CoCreateInstance*, the outer object saves the *m_pUnknownInner* pointer returned by the inner object for later use in the *QueryInterface* method.

```
HRESULT CAggregator::Init()
{
    return CoCreateInstance(CLSID_InsideCOM,
        (IUnknown*)this, CLSCTX_INPROC_SERVER,
        IID_IUnknown, (void**)&m_pUnknownInner);
}
```

If the object does not support aggregation, it returns the *CLASS_E_NOAGGREGATION* error. If it does support aggregation, the first interface pointer requested by the outer object must be *IUnknown* or the *IClassFactory:: CreateInstance* method must return an error, as shown in the next code snippet. This is required because aggregatable objects have two implementations of the *IUnknown* interface: one for use solely by the outer object and another for use by clients of the outer object.

```
HRESULT CFactory::CreateInstance(IUnknown *pUnknownOuter,
    REFIID riid, void** ppv)
{
    if(pUnknownOuter != NULL && riid != IID_IUnknown)
        return CLASS_E_NOAGGREGATION;

    CInsideCOM* pInsideCOM = new CInsideCOM(pUnknownOuter);
    if(pInsideCOM == NULL)
        return E_OUTOFMEMORY;

    // riid is probably IID_IUnknown.
    HRESULT hr = pInsideCOM->
        QueryInterface_NoAggregation(riid, ppv);
    pInsideCOM->Release_NoAggregation();
    return hr;
}
```

Notice that in the code above, the *pUnknownOuter* parameter provided by the *CreateInstance* method is passed to the *CInsideCOM* class's constructor. In the constructor, the object determines whether it is being created as a stand-alone object or as part of an aggregate object, as shown in the following code. If the pointer to the outer object's *IUnknown* interface is NULL, the object is being created as a stand-alone object and thus sets the *m_pUnknownOuter* pointer to its own *IUnknown*. Otherwise, it sets *m_pUnknownOuter* to the outer object's *IUnknown*, also called the controlling unknown.

```
CInsideCOM::CInsideCOM(IUnknown* pUnknownOuter) : m_cRef(1)
{
    g_cObjects++;

    if(pUnknownOuter != NULL)
        // We're being aggregated.
        // No AddRef!
        m_pUnknownOuter = pUnknownOuter;
    else
        // Standard usage
        m_pUnknownOuter = (IUnknown*)(INoAggregationUnknown*)this;
}
```

The inner object saves the *m_pUnknownOuter* pointer without calling *AddRef*; this is normally prohibited by the reference counting rules governing *IUnknown*. If the inner object were to *AddRef* the outer object and the outer object were to *AddRef* the inner object, an unbreakable reference counting cycle would occur. With aggregation, the inner object holds a non-reference-counted interface pointer. This works because the outer object is responsible for destroying the inner object before it exits, so the *m_pUnknownOuter* pointer is always valid during the lifetime of the inner object.

Although the outer object does not implement the *ISum* interface, it exposes this interface via its *IUnknown::QueryInterface* method. If the client requests the *ISum* interface from the outer object, the *IUnknown::QueryInterface* call is simply delegated to the inner object, as shown in boldface in the following code. This technique allows the client to have a direct pointer to the inner object (without being aware of it) instead of having to go through a stub function as in the containment example. Of course, in the containment example, pre-delegation and post-delegation processing is possible. These types of processing are not available with aggregation.

```
HRESULT CAggregator::QueryInterface(REFIID riid, void** ppv)
{
    if(riid == IID_IUnknown)
        *ppv = (IUnknown*)this;
    else if(riid == IID_ISum)
        return m_pUnknownInner->QueryInterface(riid, ppv);
    else if(riid == IID_IMultiply)
        *ppv = (IMultiply*)this;
    else
    {
        *ppv = NULL;
        return E_NOINTERFACE;
    }
    AddRef();
    return S_OK;
}
```

One problem with aggregation is that it is easy to break the COM+ object identity rules. The whole point of aggregation is to make interfaces implemented by another object a part of your object's identity. The trick to pulling this off is to never let the client know that your component is melding two identities into one. For example, imagine a client that retrieves a pointer to the *IMultiply* interface of the object and then calls *QueryInterface* for the *ISum* interface. The outer object delegates the *QueryInterface* call to the inner object and then returns a direct pointer to the *ISum* interface—so far, so good. Using the *ISum* pointer, the client later calls *QueryInterface* again, this time to retrieve the *IMultiply* interface. This call fails because the inner object does not know about the *IMultiply* interface supported by the aggregate object.

This failure violates the symmetric rule of *QueryInterface*, which specifies that if a client holding a pointer to one interface queries successfully for another interface, the client must be able to call *QueryInterface* through the new pointer for the first interface. Thus, the client suddenly finds that what it thought was the single identity of a COM+ object actually has a split personality.

To solve this insidious problem, objects that support aggregation end up implementing two sets of *IUnknown* methods. One set simply delegates to the outer object's *IUnknown* interface, and the other set does the typical work of *IUnknown*. The delegating set of *IUnknown* methods, shown below, is used by all custom interfaces implemented by the inner object and is the only one seen by clients of the outer object. This ensures that, from the perspective of the client, the identity of the object is preserved.

```
ULONG CInsideCOM::AddRef()
{
    return m_pUnknownOuter->AddRef();
}

ULONG CInsideCOM::Release()
{
    return m_pUnknownOuter->Release();
}

HRESULT CInsideCOM::QueryInterface(REFIID riid, void** ppv)
{
    return m_pUnknownOuter->QueryInterface(riid, ppv);
}
```

The second, nondelegating, set of *IUnknown* methods is available only to the outer object for use in implementing its *QueryInterface* method. The only way for the outer object to obtain a pointer to the nondelegating version of *IUnknown* is through the initial call to *IClassFactory::CreateInstance*. This is why the outer object must request the *IUnknown* interface via the *CreateInstance* method.

You might expect that with two implementations of *IUnknown* in one object, naming collisions would occur. You can avoid this problem by giving the second implementation of *IUnknown* a new name: *INoAggregationUnknown*. Because COM+ is a binary standard, it is not concerned with the name given to an interface—only with its v-table layout. Therefore, the *INoAggregationUnknown* interface is defined with a v-table structure identical to that of the real *IUnknown*:

```
interface INoAggregationUnknown
{
    virtual HRESULT __stdcall QueryInterface_NoAggregation(
        REFIID riid, void** ppv)=0;
    virtual ULONG __stdcall AddRef_NoAggregation()=0;
    virtual ULONG __stdcall Release_NoAggregation()=0;
};
```

An aggregatable object can thus implement two versions of the *IUnknown* interface: one that delegates to the outer object's *IUnknown* interface and one that does the typical work of returning interface pointers and reference counting. When the object is not being aggregated, only the nondelegating *INoAggregationUnknown* interface is used, as shown below. Notice that the pointer returned by *QueryInterface* is cast to an *IUnknown* pointer, and then *AddRef* is called. This ensures that the correct version of *AddRef* is called for the specific interface pointer being returned: requests for the inner object's *IUnknown* interface invoke the nondelegating *AddRef*, while requests for the *ISum* interface invoke the delegating version of *AddRef*.

```
HRESULT CInsideCOM::QueryInterface_NoAggregation(REFIID riid, void**
ppv)
{
    if(riid == IID_IUnknown)
        *ppv = (INoAggregationUnknown*)this;
    else if(riid == IID_ISum)
        *ppv = (ISum*)this;
    else
    {
        *ppv = NULL;
        return E_NOINTERFACE;
    }
    ((IUnknown*)(*ppv))->AddRef();
    return S_OK;
}


ULONG CInsideCOM::AddRef_NoAggregation()
{
    return ++m_cRef;
}


ULONG CInsideCOM::Release_NoAggregation()
{
    if(--m_cRef != 0)
        return m_cRef;
    delete this;
    return 0;
}
```

CHAPTER THREE

Language Integration

Now that we've built an in-process component in C++ that implements the *ISum* interface and a matching C++ client, what is the next step? Let's find a way to make our component more accessible to a wider variety of developers. Consider this: If we decided to market this component, who would our customers be? Even discounting the fact that a component with the ability to add two numbers is of limited value, only developers with a good grasp of C++ and COM+ would have any use for the component. Perhaps we could broaden our potential market a bit if we made the component accessible to developers using Microsoft Visual Basic or Java, and maybe we could even make the component easier to use from C++. (Support for scripting languages is covered in Chapter 5.)

Recall that COM+ is a binary standard for building and integrating software components, so the language used to build or call COM+ objects is irrelevant. So why is anything special required to make a component accessible to developers using heterogeneous languages? Developers using C++ typically define their interfaces in the Interface Definition Language (IDL) and then use the Microsoft IDL (MIDL) compiler to translate those interface definitions into a header file that the C++ compiler can understand. Of course, neither Visual Basic nor even Java can read C/C++ header files, but those languages still require that the interface definitions be available.

To solve this problem, the COM+ designers developed type libraries. Type libraries facilitate language integration in COM+ by making a component's interface definitions available to programming languages other than C++. Visual Basic and Microsoft Visual J++ generally depend on type libraries for their COM+ integration features. In this chapter, we'll begin with a discussion of how type libraries facilitate language integration in COM+, and then we'll examine how using type libraries can make client-side COM+ programming in C++ easier. We'll also introduce the Active Template Library (ATL), which assists in building COM+ components in C++. Finally, we'll cover COM+ issues from the perspective of Visual Basic and Visual J++.

Type Libraries

You can think of a type library as a binary version of an IDL file. The type library contains a binary description of the interfaces exposed by the classes in a component and defines their methods, parameters, and return types. Many environments have built-in support for type libraries: Visual Basic, Visual J++, and Microsoft Visual C++, as well as Borland Delphi, Microsoft Visual FoxPro, and Visual Basic for Applications (VBA), the version of Visual Basic embedded in the Microsoft Office applications. Rumor has it that the next version of Microsoft (Visual) Macro Assembler might also support COM+ via type libraries.

Using Type Libraries

Microsoft has defined the COM+ interfaces for building type libraries—*ICreate-TypeLib(2)* and *ICreateTypeInfo(2)*—and for reading type libraries—*ITypeLib(2)* and *ITypeInfo(2)*. Microsoft also provides a standard implementation of these interfaces that is available to all applications as part of the system file oleaut32.dll. Few programs other than the MIDL compiler have any need for the interfaces used to build type libraries,[1] but Visual C++, Visual J++, and Visual Basic can all read type libraries. What is the advantage of describing your interfaces in a type library? Because a type library provides nearly complete[2] information about your interfaces to anyone who is interested, sophisticated modern programming tools can read this information and present it to programmers in an accessible format, making feasible the integration of COM+ components built in different programming languages.

One simple example of a use for type information can be seen in Visual Basic,[3] which has an automatic code completion feature that displays a drop-down list while you write code, as shown in Figure 3-1. The statement builder drop-down list makes code suggestions. To insert an item into your code, you simply double-click it or press the Tab key while it is selected. If the selected item is a method, Visual Basic displays all of its parameters and their types. It retrieves all of this information from the type libraries of preselected components. As you'll see, the profound importance of type libraries to language integration in COM+ extends far beyond this simple example.

---

1. Visual Basic and Visual J++ automatically generate type libraries for components built in those languages.
2. Not all IDL attributes are supported by the current implementation of type libraries in COM+. For details, see Chapter 16.
3. Both Visual C++ and Visual J++ offer a similar feature.

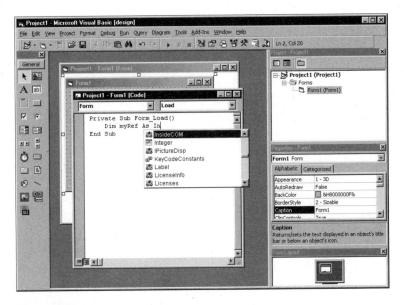

Figure 3-1.
The statement builder feature in Visual Basic.

Building a Type Library

While you can build a type library manually using the system implementations of the *ICreateTypeLib(2)* and *ICreateTypeInfo(2)* interfaces, it is much easier to use the MIDL compiler. With a few simple changes, you can compile the *ISum* interface definition presented in Chapter 2 into a binary type library (.tlb) file using the MIDL compiler. The improved IDL file that tells the MIDL compiler to generate a type library for our component is shown in Listing 3-1; the additions are shown in boldface.

component.idl

```
import "unknwn.idl";

[ object, uuid(10000001-0000-0000-0000-000000000001) ]
interface ISum : IUnknown
{
    HRESULT Sum(int x, int y, [out, retval] int* retval);
}
```

Listing 3-1. *(continued)*
The component.idl file from Chapter 2 expanded to include type library information.

component.idl *continued*

```
[ uuid(10000003-0000-0000-0000-000000000001),
  helpstring("Inside COM+ Component Type Library"),
  version(1.0) ]
library Component
{
    importlib("stdole32.tlb");
    interface ISum;

    [ uuid(10000002-0000-0000-0000-000000000001) ]
    coclass InsideCOM
    {
        interface ISum;
    }
};
```

To instruct MIDL to generate a type library, you must add the *library* keyword to the IDL file. Anything defined in the *library* section of the IDL file is added to the type library. The library has a universally unique identifier (UUID) defined for it and contains a coclass (COM+ class) statement that lists the interfaces supported by a COM+ class. In this case, the *InsideCOM* coclass supports only one interface: *ISum*. The *version* attribute specifies the version number of the type library only; it does not convey version information for the interface or the class. The system type library file, stdole32.tlb, provides definitions of the *IUnknown*, *IDispatch*, and *IEnumVARIANT* interfaces that are specially designed for use in high-level languages such as Visual Basic and Java that rely on type libraries for their COM+ integration features. The *importlib* IDL statement references this information in the new type library; all type libraries should bring in the base types defined in stdole32.tlb.

You can use the *helpstring* attribute to describe a type library, coclass, interface, method, or any other element in a type library. Applications often use this information to provide a user-friendly name for a component. Visual Basic, for example, uses these strings in the References dialog box, shown in Figure 3-2, to present the user with a selection of available components. Using this dialog box, you can set a reference to the type library stored inside a component. The type library provides Visual Basic with enough information to access the component.

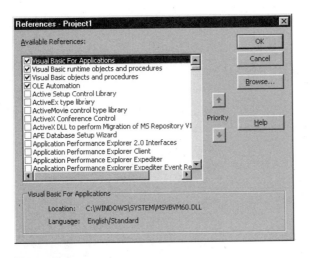

Figure 3-2.
The Visual Basic References dialog box.

Type Translation

Because COM+ provides a language-independent binary standard, it must play referee among all the different data types used in the languages that support COM+. For example, the 32-bit integer arguments used by the *Sum* method declared in Listing 3-1 (beginning on page 93) are treated as Long values by Visual Basic. The following table shows the type mappings between IDL types and the native C++, Visual Basic, and Java types. You'll see a blank if an IDL type cannot be automatically converted into a native type.

IDL Type	C++	Visual Basic	Java
signed char	signed char		byte
unsigned char	unsigned char	Byte	
wchar_t	wchar_t	Integer	char
signed short	short	Integer	short
unsigned short	unsigned short		
signed int	int	Long	int
unsigned int	unsigned int		
signed hyper	_ _int64		long

(continued)

continued

IDL Type	C++	Visual Basic	Java
float	float	Single	float
double	double	Double	double
BSTR	BSTR	String	java.lang.String
boolean	bool	Boolean	boolean
VARIANT	VARIANT	Variant	com.ms.com.Variant
DATE	DATE	Date	double
CY	CY	Currency	long
SAFEARRAY	SAFEARRAY	[] (a standard Visual Basic array)	com.ms.com.SafeArray
IUnknown*	IUnknown*	IUnknown	com.ms.com.IUnknown
IDispatch*	IDispatch*	Object	java.lang.Object

Embedding a Type Library in a Component

Instead of leaving a component's type library as a separate .tlb file, you can embed the type library in the component as a resource. This makes your component neater, because the file includes both the component and the type information that describes how to use it. To include a type library as a resource in a C++ component, you must first create a resource script (.rc) file, as shown in Listing 3-2. When the resource file is compiled, the type library will be added and then linked with the component file. Components written in Visual Basic and Visual J++ automatically have their type libraries embedded in the component file.

component.rc

```
1 TYPELIB "component.tlb"
```

Listing 3-2.
A resource script file that includes a type library in a component.

Registering a Type Library

Before an application can make use of a type library, the type library must be entered into the registry. Languages such as Visual Basic and Visual J++ scour the registry for components that contain type libraries. To register a type library, you insert the necessary entries under the HKEY_CLASSES_ROOT\TypeLib key in the registry. This key declares each type library installed on the system.

A library identifier (LIBID) consists of a globally unique identifier (GUID) that identifies each registered type library. The LIBID corresponds to the UUID defined by the *library* statement in the IDL. Every LIBID key in the registry contains several subkeys that specify the version number of the type library, the path to that library, several flags, and an optional path to a directory that contains help files with information about the contents of the type library.

As shown in Chapter 2, you can use a registration (.reg) file to create these registry entries. It is preferable, however, to integrate the type library registration with the component self-registration steps. Programmatically registering a type library is as easy as calling the *LoadTypeLibEx* function.[4] You can use this call to create all the necessary entries automatically. In addition to filling in a complete registry entry under the *TypeLib* key, the function adds entries for each of the Automation-compatible interfaces (including dual interfaces) defined in the type library. (Dual interfaces are described in Chapter 5.) This information is required for marshaling purposes. Note that *LoadTypeLibEx* and *RegisterTypeLib* do not register COM+ objects, only type libraries. That is, registry entries are created only in HKEY_CLASSES_ROOT\TypeLib and HKEY_CLASSES_ROOT\Interface—not in HKEY_CLASSES_ROOT\CLSID. Registering COM+ objects is the responsibility of the component self-registration code.

Two other utility functions can prove helpful when you work with type libraries. The *UnRegisterTypeLib* function removes the specified type library information from the registry. This function is typically called by setup programs during the uninstall phase. In-process components often call this function in the *DllUnregisterServer* function. The *QueryPathOfRegTypeLib* function returns the path of an already registered type library.

The HKEY_CLASSES_ROOT\Interface key contains information about each registered interface available on the system that has an interface identifier (IID). This section begins with *{00000000-0000-0000-C000-000000000046}*, the IID of the *IUnknown* interface, and then proceeds with some standard COM+ interfaces, such as *IClassFactory*, *IMalloc*, and *IMarshal*, before heading off into some of the more esoteric interfaces, such as *IExternalConnection*, and finally into custom interfaces. One IID subkey under HKEY_CLASSES_ROOT\Interface is required for each new interface your application defines. The IID subkey might contain additional subkeys; these are listed in the following table.

---

4. The *LoadTypeLib* function followed by *RegisterTypeLib* achieves the same result.

Subkeys of HKEY_CLASSES_ROOT\Interface\{*YourIID*}	Description
BaseInterface	Identifies the interface from which the current interface is derived
NumMethods	Specifies the number of methods in the associated interface
ProxyStubClsid32	Identifies the CLSID of the 32-bit proxy/stub DLL that knows how to marshal this interface
TypeLib	Specifies the LIBID associated with the type library in which the interface is described

The following code is an improved version of the self-registration code that calls *LoadTypeLibEx* to register the component's type library; changes are shown in boldface. The first parameter of the *LoadTypeLibEx* function is the path and filename of the DLL file retrieved by the call to *GetModuleFileName*. This assumes that the type library has been embedded in the DLL file using a resource, as discussed previously. Because all COM+ functions require Unicode character strings, the C run-time function *mbstowcs* (Multi-Byte String To Wide Character String) is called to convert the string to a corresponding sequence of wide characters; *OLECHAR* is defined as a *wchar_t* in the system IDL file wTypes.idl. The second parameter of *LoadTypeLibEx*, *REGKIND_REGISTER*, is a flag indicating that the type library should be registered as well as loaded. You can use another flag, *REGKIND_DEFAULT*, to load a type library without registering. If the call succeeds, an *ITypeLib* interface pointer to the loaded (and in this case registered) type library is returned in the third parameter of *LoadTypeLibEx*. In our case, the only reason for loading the type library is to register it, so we can immediately free the type library by calling the *Release* method:

```
HRESULT __stdcall DllRegisterServer()
{
    char DllPath[MAX_PATH];
    GetModuleFileName(g_hInstance, DllPath, sizeof(DllPath));

    // Convert DllPath to wide characters
    OLECHAR wDllPath[MAX_PATH];
    mbstowcs(wDllPath, DllPath, sizeof(wDllPath));
```

```
    ITypeLib* pTypeLib;
    HRESULT hr =
        LoadTypeLibEx(wDllPath, REGKIND_REGISTER, &pTypeLib);
    if(FAILED(hr))
        return hr;
    pTypeLib->Release();

    return RegisterServerEx(g_regData, DllPath);
}

HRESULT __stdcall DllUnregisterServer()
{
    UnRegisterTypeLib(LIBID_Component, 1, 0,
        LANG_NEUTRAL, SYS_WIN32);
    return UnregisterServerEx(g_regData);
}
```

To build the type library project, you use the Type Libraries.dsw workspace file in the Samples\Language Integration folder on the companion CD. Building the Create TypeLib project in this workspace automatically compiles the IDL file using the MIDL compiler, thereby producing the type library file (component.tlb). Then you embed the type library in the component.dll file using the resource script file component.rc. Finally, you register the component by choosing Register Control from the Tools menu in Visual C++. The component should self-register successfully; you can see several new entries in the aforementioned areas of the registry.

The OLE/COM Object Viewer (oleview.exe) utility that comes with Visual C++ is useful when you explore the registry and type libraries, either as .tlb files or embedded within components. It can function as an alternative to the registry editor because it is designed specifically for viewing the registry information that pertains to COM+ objects. Another nice feature is its ability to reverse-engineer type libraries into their original IDL source code.

RegTlb: A Utility for Registering Stand-Alone Type Libraries

It is quite easy to call *LoadTypeLibEx* programmatically, but it is a chore during the development process. To make this task easier, we have created a simple utility named RegTlb for registering any stand-alone type library file. The code for the regtlb.cpp file is shown on the following page.

regtlb.cpp

```cpp
#define _WIN32_DCOM
#include <windows.h>
#include <iostream.h>

void main(int argc, char** argv)
{
    if(argc < 2)
    {
        cout << "Usage: regtlb tlbfile.tlb" << endl;
        return;
    }

    CoInitializeEx(NULL, COINIT_APARTMENTTHREADED);

    OLECHAR psz[MAX_PATH];
    mbstowcs(psz, argv[1], sizeof(psz));

    ITypeLib* pTypeLib;
    HRESULT hr =
        LoadTypeLibEx(psz, REGKIND_REGISTER, &pTypeLib);
    if(FAILED(hr))
    {
        cout << "LoadTypeLibEx failed." << endl;
        return;
    }
    else
        cout << "Type library registered." << endl;

    pTypeLib->Release();

    CoUninitialize();
}
```

Once the program has been compiled, simply execute a command-line statement such as *RegTlb component.tlb* and all the necessary registry entries are created automatically. This is similar to the way that the RegSvr32 utility works (except that RegSvr32 does not register stand-alone type libraries). We'll leave it to you to improve RegTlb so that it also lets you unregister type libraries using the *UnRegisterTypeLib* function.

An Easy C++ Client

Let's see how we can use a type library to simplify the client application we built in Chapter 2. The easyclient.cpp application shown in Listing 3-3 uses the type library embedded in the component.dll file:

easyclient.cpp

```
#define _WIN32_DCOM
#import "component.dll" no_namespace

#include <iostream.h>

void main()
{
    CoInitializeEx(NULL, COINIT_APARTMENTTHREADED);
    ISumPtr myRef(__uuidof(InsideCOM));
    int result = myRef->Sum(5, 13);
    cout << "5 + 13 = " << result << endl;
    myRef = NULL;
    CoUninitialize();
}
```

Listing 3-3.
A C++ client that uses the type library embedded in component.dll.

The first immediately apparent simplification is in the layout of the program. We've gone from over 30 lines of code without a type library to 12 lines of code with a type library. More important, the user no longer has to be a C++ or COM+ expert. How did the type library perform this magic? If you look at the first line of code, you'll see the answer: the *#import* directive. This Microsoft language extension incorporates information from a type library. It instructs the compiler to process the designated type library, converting the contents to C++ code that describes the interfaces contained in the type library.

When the C++ compiler encounters the *#import* directive, it generates two header files that reconstruct the type library's contents in C++ source code. The primary header file has the same name as the type library plus the .tlh (type library header) extension. This file is similar to the header file produced by the MIDL compiler—it contains the abstract base class definitions for the interfaces.

The secondary header file, also with the same name as the type library but with the .tli (type library implementation) extension, contains the implementations of compiler-generated member functions and is included when you use the *#include* directive in the primary (.tlh) header file. Both header files are placed in the compiler's output directory. They are then read and compiled as if the .tlh file were named using a *#include* directive in the source code.

The most interesting aspect of these header files is their use of Microsoft's smart pointer template classes. But before we become engrossed in smart pointers, you should have a solid grounding in C++ template classes. If, like us, you struggle to keep up with the latest features of C++, Java, and Visual Basic, you might find the next section useful. If you are already a template guru, just skip to the section on smart pointers.

C++ Templates (A Quick Introduction)

In C++, *templates* (sometimes called *parameterized types*) generate code based on a parameter's type. Using templates, you can design a single class that operates on data of many types instead of having to create a separate class for each type. The classic example of a template creates a function that compares two values and returns the greater one. In C, you could accomplish this task with a macro, as shown here:

```
#define max(a, b) ((a > b) ? a : b)
```

Although macros of this sort are valid in C++, they are frowned upon because of their lack of type checking. For example, the compiler has no objection to code such as this:

```
max(60, 'b'); // Compiler says no problem!
```

Macros can also lead to more insidious bugs like this:

```
int x = 6;
cout << max(++x, 6) << endl; // Displays 8
```

The fact that this code prints the value *8* might seem odd—until you mentally expand the macro as the compiler does:

```
cout << ((++x, 6) ? ++x : 6) << endl;
```

Because the preprocessor expands macros by substitution, the variable *x* is incremented twice.

Templates were added to the C++ language to address some of these issues. The template version of the preceding macro is shown here:

```
template <class T>
T max(T a, T b)
{
    return (a > b) ? a : b;
}
```

Templates come in two basic types: *function templates* and *class templates.* A function template defines a function that can accept arguments of any type, as shown in the preceding example. A class template defines an entire class that can be generalized to work with any type. The *template* keyword begins the definition of the template and is followed by the type argument enclosed in angle brackets (< and >). The *class* keyword indicates a type argument to a template, even though the actual type argument can be any type—it need not be a class. This keyword is followed by the actual function template definition, with the argument *T* representing the type. You can think of this argument as a variable representing the type of the actual parameter. You can use this function template for any of the following types:

```
max(10, 12);          // int
max(10.8, 12.5);      // float
max('a', 'b');        // char
max(true, false);     // bool
```

Because no macro substitution is used, the following code works fine:

```
int x = 6
cout << max(++x, 6) << endl; // Displays 7
```

Type checking is also enforced, making this code illegal:

```
max(60, 'b'); // Compiler says big problem!
```

When a function template is first called for each type, the compiler creates an *instantiation,* or version, of the template function specialized for that type. This instantiation is called every time the function is used for the type. If you have several identical instantiations, even in different modules, only one copy of the instantiation ends up in the executable file. For example, *max(10, 12)* causes the compiler to generate the following code:

```
int max(int a, int b)
{
    return (a > b) ? a : b;
}
```

And *max('a', 'b')* generates this code:

```
char max(char a, char b)
{
    return (a > b) ? a : b;
}
```

Whereas macros have no overhead because the preprocessor expands them, you can minimize the overhead of templates using the *inline* keyword, which tells the compiler to insert a copy of the function body into each place the function is called. Inline functions can make a program faster because they eliminate the overhead associated with function calls (at the cost of making the resulting executable image larger because code is being duplicated in multiple places).

You can also override a template function to define special behavior for a specific type. Say you want to compare the lengths of two strings using the *max* function template. The standard version generated by the compiler would compare only the pointer addresses. The following code shows a function that overrides the compiler's default instantiation of the template to compare string lengths:

```
template<> char* max(char* a, char* b)
{
    return (strlen(a) > strlen(b)) ? a : b;
}
```

Now you can write code such as this:

```
cout << max("hello", "good-bye") << endl; // Displays good-bye.
```

You can use a class template to generalize an entire class so that it can work with any type. For example, a string class might need to work with single-byte characters as well as double-byte Unicode characters. Here is the definition of a rudimentary string template class:

```
template <class T> class String
{
    struct sRep;
    sRep* rep;
public:
    String();
    String(const T*);
    String(const String&);

    ⋮
};
```

You can instantiate this template class for the regular character and a Unicode character, as shown here:

```
String<char> cs;
String<wchar_t> ws;
```

This review of C++ templates should give you enough information to get started with smart pointers. We'll revisit C++ templates later in this chapter in the section titled "The Active Template Library."

Smart Pointers

A *smart pointer* is an object that looks, acts, and feels like a normal pointer but offers greater functionality. Smart pointers are generally designed to make programming safer and easier. In C++, they are implemented as template classes that encapsulate a pointer and override standard pointer operators. What do smart pointers have to do with COM+? Because COM+ programming in raw C++ can be difficult and can lead to errors, smart pointers can improve the programmer's odds of success. Let's look at three aspects of standard smart pointers, with an eye toward how they can improve client-side COM+ programming:

- Construction and destruction
- Copying and assignment
- Dereferencing

Constructing a smart interface pointer can be as simple as initializing the pointer to *NULL* or as complex as calling *CoCreateInstance(Ex)* to retrieve a pointer to the requested interface. Normally, a smart pointer class's constructor is overloaded to support all of these capabilities. The destructor of a smart interface pointer can automatically call *Release*. A smart pointer can overload the assignment operator (=) so that any attempt to copy the pointer results in an automatic *AddRef* call, relieving the programmer of the burden of reference counting. Finally, the smart pointer class can override the indirection operator (*) to perform some basic error checking, ensuring that the internal "dumb" pointer is not *NULL* or invalid in some other way.

IUnknown is what makes the smart pointer concept so appealing in COM+. Because *IUnknown* is supported by all COM+ objects and has a unique and clearly defined set of methods and associated semantics, a smart pointer that wraps COM+ interface pointers can provide a lot of built-in functionality. For the most part, smart pointer classes are implemented as template classes because otherwise they would be useful only with a specific pointer type. For example, you could build a well-designed smart pointer class for *IUnknown* interface pointers, but this class would be of limited value to someone who wanted to access the *ISum* custom interface. Because you can use template classes to create generic wrappers to encapsulate pointers of almost any type and since interface pointers share similar semantics, you can build a template version of the smart pointer class, allowing the smart pointer to be used with any interface pointer type.

A simple smart pointer   The idea of a smart pointer is relatively simple, and implementing its basic features is quite easy. However, building a commercial-grade smart pointer is a lot of work; you have to consider many subtle semantic conditions. Below is the Simple Smart Pointer (SSP) template class we built; you can use it in place of standard pointers in C++.

```
template <typename Q>
class SSP
{
    public:
        SSP(Q* pItf = 0) : m_pItf(pItf)
        {
            if(m_pItf)
                m_pItf->AddRef();
        }

        ~SSP()
        {
            if(m_pItf)
                m_pItf->Release();
        }

        Q* operator->()
        {
            return m_pItf;
        }

        operator Q*()
        {
            return m_pItf;
        }

        void** GetItfPointer()
```

```
    {
        if(m_pItf)
        {
            m_pItf->Release();
            m_pItf = 0;
        }
        return (void**)&m_pItf;
    }

private:
    Q* m_pItf;
};
```

Client code that uses this smart pointer is shown below. Note the conspicuous lack of a *Release* call before the function returns. Typically, this bug would leave the component thinking that it still has an outstanding reference. In this case, however, the smart pointer's destructor automatically calls *Release* when the pointer goes out of scope. The smart pointer also calls *AddRef* on the *IUnknown* interface pointer and then calls *Release* when the function returns.

```
void TestSSP(IUnknown* pUnknown)
{
    SSP<IUnknown> sspUnknown(pUnknown);
    SSP<ISum> sspSum;

    HRESULT hr = sspUnknown->QueryInterface(IID_ISum,
        sspSum.GetItfPointer());
    if(FAILED(hr))
        cout << "IID_ISum not supported" << endl;

    int sum;
    hr = sspSum->Sum(2, 3, &sum);
    if(SUCCEEDED(hr))
        cout << "Client: Calling Sum(2, 3) = " << sum << endl;
}
```

Built-in smart pointer support in Visual C++   Microsoft has defined a set of complex smart interface pointer classes as part of the Microsoft Foundation Classes (MFC), ATL, and the Visual C++ compiler's built-in support for COM+ in the header files comdef.h, comutil.h, and comip.h. Each of these smart interface pointers has unique quirks, which makes switching from one to another difficult. For the sake of this nonpartisan discussion, we'll examine the smart interface pointer provided with Visual C++.

The Visual C++ smart pointer template classes are used in the code generated by the compiler in response to the type library specified by the *#import* statement. The fundamental template class defined by Microsoft is *_com_ptr_t*. The *_com_ptr_t* template class is a smart pointer implementation that encapsulates interface pointers and eliminates the need to call the *AddRef, Release,* and *QueryInterface* methods of the *IUnknown* interface. In addition, it wraps the call to *CoCreateInstance(Ex)* when you instantiate a new COM+ object. The *_COM_SMARTPTR_TYPEDEF* macro establishes *typedef*s of COM+ interfaces as template specializations of the *_com_ptr_t* template class. For example, the following code

```
_COM_SMARTPTR_TYPEDEF(ISum, __uuidof(ISum));
```

is expanded by the compiler into:

```
typedef _com_ptr_t<_com_IIID<ISum, __uuidof(ISum)>> ISumPtr;
```

You can then use the *ISumPtr* type in place of the raw interface pointer *ISum**. To instantiate an object, you declare a variable of type *ISumPtr* and pass the CLSID of the coclass to the constructor, as shown here:

```
ISumPtr myRef(__uuidof(InsideCOM));
```

The smart pointer's constructor calls *CoCreateInstance(Ex)*, followed by *QueryInterface* for the *ISum* interface. Now you can use *myRef* to call methods of the *ISum* interface with code nearly identical to that used with dumb pointers:

```
int result = myRef->Sum(5, 13);
```

Notice that the value returned by the function is not an *HRESULT* but the actual sum previously returned via a pointer in the third parameter. The compiler notices that the parameter is marked as *[out, retval]* in the type library, and, as shown in the following code, it generates a wrapper function in the .tli file that provides the real return value:

```
int __inline ISum::Sum ( int x, int y ) {
    int _result;
    HRESULT _hr = raw_Sum(x, y, &_result);
    if (FAILED(_hr))
        _com_issue_errorex(_hr, this, __uuidof(this));
    return _result;
}
```

This code ends without calls to *AddRef* or *Release* since the smart pointer fully automates reference counting. Before you call *CoUninitialize*, however, it is important to set the smart pointer to *NULL*, as shown in the following code fragment, to force a call to *Release*. After *CoUninitialize*, any attempts by the smart pointer to call *Release* in the destructor will crash.

```
myRef = NULL;
CoUninitialize();
```

Here you can begin to see flaws in the smart pointer approach. Although the idea of smart interface pointers is initially appealing, in practice it is difficult to build a bulletproof smart pointer. And if you do build a smart pointer without any holes, it will probably be too restrictive for practical use. Using a smart pointer does not absolve you of the responsibility of understanding COM+'s lifetime reference counting rules. In fact, it requires that you become intimately familiar with the implementation details of the smart pointer in addition to understanding *IUnknown*.

If you like Microsoft's smart pointer template classes but are not keen to have the C++ compiler generate code based on a type library, you can use the smart pointer classes directly simply by including the comdef.h header file. The client application, shown in Listing 3-4, uses these header files to call the component we created in Chapter 2. Be sure to compile and link this file with the component_i.c file generated by the MIDL compiler.

smartpointerclient.cpp

```
#define _WIN32_DCOM
#include <comdef.h>      // Defines the smart pointer class
#include <iostream.h>
#include "component.h" // Generated by MIDL

void main()
{
    CoInitializeEx(NULL, COINIT_APARTMENTTHREADED);
    _COM_SMARTPTR_TYPEDEF(ISum, __uuidof(ISum));
    ISumPtr myRef(CLSID_InsideCOM);
    int result;
    myRef->Sum(5, 13, &result);
    cout << "Client: 5 + 13 = " << result << endl;
    myRef = NULL;
    CoUninitialize();
}
```

Listing 3-4.
A C++ client that uses the smart pointer template classes provided with Visual C++.

Namespaces

By default, the .tlh file generated by the compiler in response to the *#import* directive is enclosed in a namespace with its name lifted from the *library* statement in the original IDL file. A *namespace* is a declarative region that attaches an additional identifier to any names declared inside it. The additional identifier makes it less likely that a name will conflict with names declared elsewhere in the program. C++ provides a single global namespace by default, which can cause problems when global names clash. For example, you might want to import two different type libraries that contain identically named items into the same C++ source file. Normally, this is not a problem for COM+ since everything works based on GUIDs. The *#import* directive, however, enables COM+ objects to appear almost as standard C++ objects, with the GUIDs hidden in the compiler-generated code.

These two C++ header files illustrate the problem:

```
// one.h
class Math { ... };
```

```
// two.h
class Math { ... };
```

With these definitions, it is impossible to use both header files in a single program because the *Math* classes will clash. Namespaces in C++ address this problem. You can use the identical names in separate namespaces without conflict even if the names appear in the same translation unit. As long as the names are in separate namespaces, each will be unique because of the addition of the namespace identifier.

You use the C++ *namespace* keyword to declare a namespace, as in these examples:

```
// one.h
namespace one
{
    class Math { ... };
}
```

```
// two.h
namespace two
{
    class Math { ... };
}
```

Now the *Math* class names will not clash because they have become *one::Math* and *two::Math*.

Declarations made outside all namespaces are still members of the global namespace. You can use the names from a namespace by using an explicit qualification with the namespace name (*one::Math*) or by selecting a namespace using the *using* keyword, as shown here:

```
using namespace two;
Math x();    // Refers to two::Math
```

When you use the *#import* directive, you can suppress the generated namespace by specifying the *no_namespace* attribute, as shown here:

```
#import "component.dll" no_namespace
```

Be aware that suppressing the namespace can lead to name collisions if you import multiple type libraries from different components. This example uses only one component, so specifying the *no_namespace* attribute to avoid dealing with namespaces does not create a problem.

The Active Template Library

The *#import* directive and smart interface pointers help make client-side COM+ programming easier and more enjoyable. But these extensions do not help you build COM+ components themselves. To help you build COM+ components in C++, Microsoft offers the Active Template Library (ATL), which is a part of the Microsoft Foundation Classes and Templates (MFC&T). ATL is composed of C++ template classes that support the most common COM+ programming chores, such as implementing the *IUnknown*, *IClassFactory*, and *IDispatch* interfaces, as well as dealing with component registration issues. (*IDispatch* is covered in Chapter 5.)

The design of ATL is based loosely on that of the Standard Template Library (STL), originally developed by Hewlett-Packard and now part of the ANSI/ISO standards for C++. As their names imply, both libraries heavily leverage the template functionality in C++. Template libraries differ from traditional C++ class libraries in two important ways. First, you generally access the functionality of a template library by instantiating a class from a template rather than deriving from a base class. Because of this design difference, a class hierarchy does not necessarily define the relationships among the classes in a template library. Second, template libraries are typically supplied in source code form; they are often contained in header files and require little or no run-time DLL support.

The differences between traditional C++ class libraries and template libraries can be illustrated by comparing the MFC library to ATL. MFC is a heavy-duty library containing over 100,000 lines of code that does everything from support database functionality to create ActiveX controls (with the kitchen sink thrown in for good measure). This versatility makes MFC a great choice for developers working on standard double-clickable Windows-based applications who want as much prefabricated functionality as possible. Nevertheless, the 972 KB overhead of the mfc42.dll run-time file might be unacceptable to those working on small and (hopefully) lightweight COM+ components that can be downloaded over a low-bandwidth Internet connection. ATL, on the other hand, has a 57-KB DLL (atl.dll), and even that is optional. Of course, ATL has a much more limited scope than MFC: ATL lets you easily create most types of COM+ components, including ActiveX controls.

The ATL COM AppWizard

To make working with ATL easier, Microsoft provides the ATL COM AppWizard in Visual C++, shown in Figure 3-3. This simple wizard asks you to choose one of three types of components: DLL, EXE, or Win32 service. It even lets you specify that the proxy/stub interface marshaling code be merged with the main project rather than built as a separate DLL. Based on these few decisions, the wizard generates the source code for a component. For example, if you choose an in-process component, the wizard generates code for the standard DLL entry points, including *DllMain*, *DllGetClassObject*, *DllCanUnloadNow*, *DllRegisterServer*, and *DllUnregisterServer*.

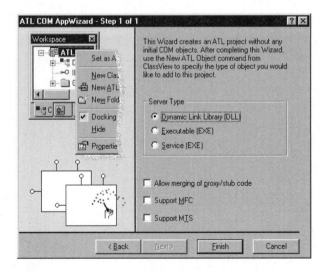

Figure 3-3.
The ATL COM AppWizard, which generates some of the framework code to create a COM+ component.

The ATL Object Wizard

Although the ATL COM AppWizard quickly generates the main housing for a component, it doesn't implement any coclasses. For this task, Microsoft provides the ATL Object Wizard, shown in Figure 3-4. This wizard lets you add several different types of coclasses to a component, from rudimentary COM+ objects to objects that can operate within the COM+ run-time environment. You can also create several types of ActiveX controls, such as basic controls that work with Microsoft Internet Explorer and full controls that work with almost any container, including Visual Basic.

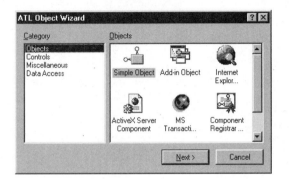

Figure 3-4.
The ATL Object Wizard, which helps you create a COM+ object based on ATL.

The simplest type of object, aptly named *simple object,* does not provide automatic support of any standard COM+ interfaces besides *IUnknown* and *IClassFactory* and thus often is the best choice when you are planning to implement custom interfaces. The interfaces implemented automatically for some of the other available object types are listed in the following table.

Object Type	Implemented Interfaces	Description
Simple Object	*IUnknown*	A minimal COM+ object
Add-in Object	*IDSAddIn*	A Visual C++ extension object
Internet Explorer Object	*IObjectWithSite*	An object that works with Internet Explorer, but without a user interface
Active Server Component	*IDispatch*	An object that can work with Active Server Pages in Internet Information Server

(continued)

continued

Object Type	Implemented Interfaces	Description
MS Transaction Server Component	*IObjectControl*	An object designed to work with Microsoft Transaction Server
MMC SnapIn	*IComponent, IComponentData, ISnapinAbout*	A Microsoft Management Console snap-in object
Lite Control	*IPersistStreamInit, IOleControl, IOleObject, IOleInPlaceActiveObject, IViewObjectEx, IOleInPlaceObject-Windowless*	An object that supports the interfaces needed by Internet Explorer, including support for a user interface
Full Control	All of the lite control interfaces, plus *IPersistStorage, ISpecifyPropertyPages, IQuickActivate, IDataObject, IProvideClassInfo2*	An object that supports the interfaces for all ActiveX control containers
Composite Control	Same as full control	A control that can host other controls
HTML Control	All of the full control interfaces, plus *IDispatch*	A control with DHTML functionality that displays an HTML Web page in its user interface
Lite HTML Control	Same as lite control, plus *IDispatch*	A control with DHTML functionality that displays an HTML Web page in its user interface but supports only the interfaces needed by Internet Explorer
Lite Composite Control	Same as lite control	A composite control that can host other controls but supports only the interfaces needed by Internet Explorer
Property Page	*IPropertyPage*	An object that implements a property page

Based on the object type you choose, the ATL Object Wizard presents options that let you select the threading model supported by the object, specify whether a custom interface should include support for *IDispatch*, and specify whether the object supports aggregation. Figure 3-5 shows the most common options presented for a simple object.

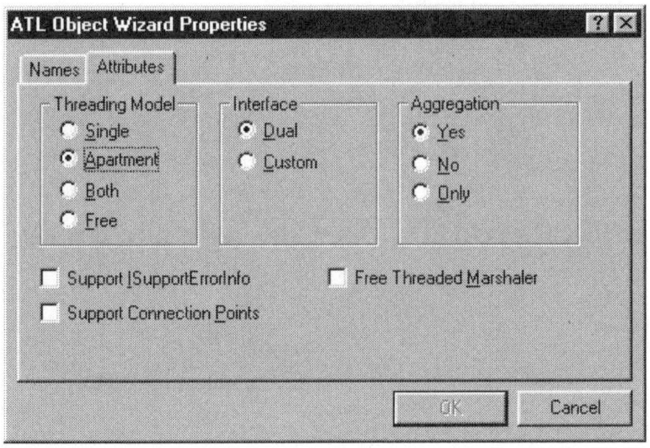

Figure 3-5.
Options for the simple object in the ATL Object Wizard.

Adding Methods and Properties to an Interface Using ATL

The next step after adding a COM+ object to an ATL project is to add the desired methods and properties to the interface. The simplest way to do this is to use the wizard-like dialog boxes provided by Visual C++. Figure 3-6 shows the Add Method To Interface dialog box.

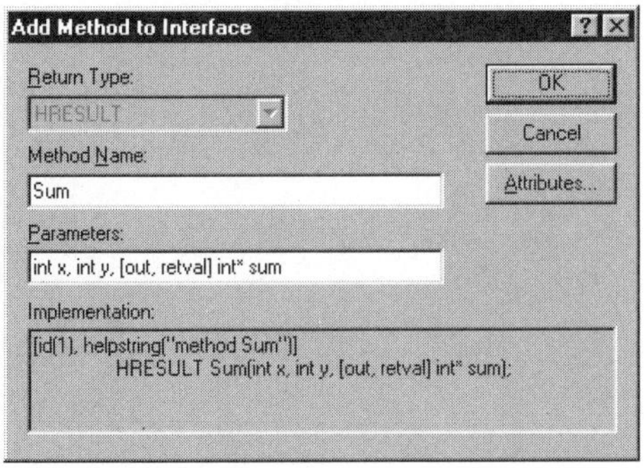

Figure 3-6.
The Add Method To Interface dialog box.

Once you add interfaces and methods to an ATL-based component, your implementation work is complete. There is no need to mess with *IUnknown*, *IClassFactory*, or even registration functions because ATL provides all of this default functionality. It provides the module definition (.def) file containing the DLL exports and the resource script (.rc) file that references the type library. MIDL even generates the IDL file and then compiles it as an automated part of the build process.

Figure 3-7 shows the fundamental ATL classes used to implement a COM+ object.

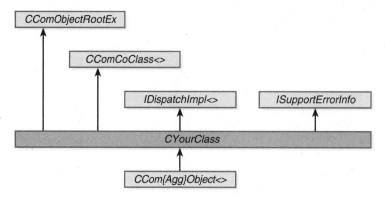

Figure 3-7.
The ATL object model.

CComObjectRootEx is the essential ATL class. It provides the default table-driven *QueryInterface* mechanism and is a required part of every ATL object. The *CComCoClass* class defines the default class factory and aggregation model for an object. For objects supporting a dual interface, you can use *IDispatchImpl* to provide a default implementation of the *IDispatch* interface. The *ISupportErrorInfo* interface must be supported if you use the *IErrorInfo* interface to report errors back to the client. This interface is easy to implement using the *ISupportErrorInfoImpl* template class.

Building a Simple COM+ Object Using ATL

You can take the following steps to build a simple COM+ object using ATL:

1. Open Visual C++.

2. Choose File/New and click the Projects tab.

3. Select ATL COM AppWizard, enter the project name *TestATL*, and then click OK.

4. When the ATL COM AppWizard appears, click Finish.

5. The wizard will provide some information about what it is about to do. Click OK.

6. Choose Insert/New ATL Object.

7. When the ATL Object Wizard appears, click the Simple Object icon, and then click Next.

8. In the Short Name text box, type *InsideCOM*, and in the Interface text box, type *ISum*. Then click OK.

9. Right-click the *ISum* interface in *ClassView*, and select Add Method.

10. In the Method Name text box, type *Sum*, and in the Parameters text box, type *int x, int y, [out, retval] int* sum*. Then click OK.

11. Now expand the *ISum* interface within the *CInsideCOM* class in *ClassView*, as shown in Figure 3-8, and double-click the *Sum* method.

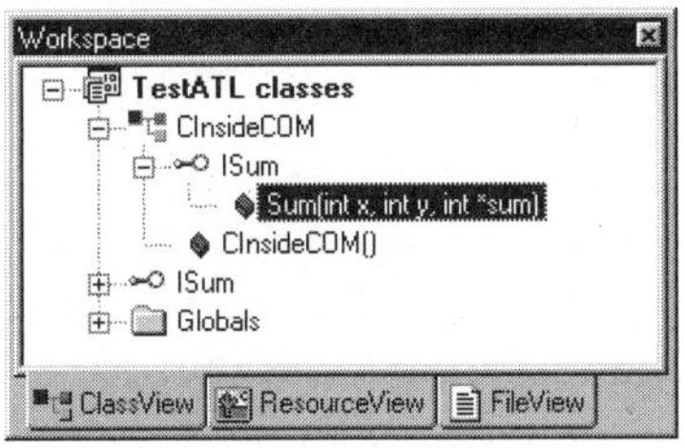

Figure 3-8.
The ISum::Sum *method shown in the Visual C++ Workspace window.*

12. Add the line of code shown here in boldface:

```
STDMETHODIMP CInsideCOM::Sum(int x, int y, int * sum)
{
    // TODO: Add your implementation code here
    *sum = x + y;
    return S_OK;
}
```

13. Choose Build/Build TestATL.dll.

You can test this ATL-based component using any language that supports COM+. To create a test program in Visual Basic, simply create a Standard EXE project and set a reference to the TestATL 1.0 Type Library in the References dialog box, which you can open by choosing References from the Project menu. Then type the code shown here in boldface in the *Form_Load* procedure:

```
Private Sub Form_Load()
    Dim x As New InsideCOM
    MsgBox x.Sum(6, 3)
End Sub
```

COM+ Programming in Visual Basic

You can develop COM+ components quite successfully in Visual Basic. Visual Basic is perhaps best at creating the more complex varieties of COM+ components, namely ActiveX controls and ActiveX documents. Developing such components in raw C++ can be quite an undertaking. Visual Basic is also surprisingly flexible and easy to use when it comes to providing the fundamental aspects of COM+ programming.

Visual Basic automatically calls *CoInitializeEx* and *CoUninitialize*—without any intervention from the programmer. The *New* keyword in Visual Basic replaces *CoCreateInstance(Ex)* as the object instantiator. Visual Basic's automatic garbage collection algorithm calls *IUnknown::Release* on object references that go out of scope. You can also explicitly call *Release* by setting an object reference to *Nothing*, as shown here:

```
Set myRef = Nothing
```

While you can use the *New* keyword to instantiate coclasses in Visual Basic, its use is somewhat limited. First, if you use *New* to instantiate classes defined within the active project, Visual Basic does not use *CoCreateInstance*. Instead, it uses an internal object creation mechanism that does not involve COM+. Therefore, you should not instantiate such classes using the *New* keyword. Also, *New* instantiates only COM+ objects running on the local machine, unless specified otherwise by the registry settings.

To overcome these limitations, Visual Basic offers the *CreateObject* function as an alternative to the *New* keyword. This function always uses COM+ to instantiate the object. The first parameter of *CreateObject* specifies the name of the coclass to be instantiated. (Visual Basic retrieves the object's CLSID from the registry by passing its name to the *CLSIDFromProgID* function.) In addition, the *CreateObject* function takes an optional second argument called *servername*, which dynamically specifies the name of a remote machine where the object should be instantiated. You can set the *servername* parameter to the computer name of the remote machine or the IP (Internet Protocol) address, such as *199.34.57.30*. When you specify a *servername* parameter, Visual Basic calls the *CoCreateInstanceEx* function to instantiate the object. (The *CoCreateInstanceEx* function is discussed further in Chapter 13.) A sample use of the *CreateObject* function is shown in boldface below:

```
Private Sub Form_Click()
    Dim myRef As Object
```

```
    ' Create object based on a ProgID.
    Set myRef = CreateObject("TestATL.InsideCOM", "MyServer")

    MsgBox myRef.Sum(5, 3)
End Sub
```

QueryInterface: **The Visual Basic Way**

Although a COM+ class can support multiple interfaces, Visual Basic tries to simplify things by assuming that the programmer wants access to the default interface; it therefore automatically calls *QueryInterface* to request that interface. This simplification makes sense, since most classes have a primary interface through which most operations are performed. Unfortunately, Visual Basic also hides the name of the default interface! If a default interface named *IMyDefault* is implemented by a COM+ class named *MyClass*, Visual Basic uses the name *MyClass* as an alias for the *IMyDefault* interface. This technique seems to work acceptably when you access a COM+ object from Visual Basic, but it can be rather confusing when you are trying to implement a COM+ interface in Visual Basic.

Using the *Implements* keyword, a Visual Basic class module can implement any COM+ interface described in a type library. When the desired interface happens to be the default, the code that implements the COM+ class instead of the desired interface can look mighty strange. If you need access to the other (nondefault) interfaces supported by an object, you can execute a *QueryInterface* using the *Set* statement. If needed, the *Set* statement calls the *IUnknown::QueryInterface* method to cast the *rvalue* interface pointer to the type of the *lvalue* reference. For example, the following code snippet shows two references—*MyRef1* and *MyRef2*. *MyRef1* is declared as an *IUnknown* interface pointer; *MyRef2* is a pointer to the *IMyInterface* interface. When *MyRef2* is set to *MyRef1*, a *QueryInterface* call that requests the *IMyInterface* interface pointer from the object pointed to by *MyRef1* takes place.

```
Dim MyRef1 As IUnknown
Set MyRef1 = New MyObject

Dim MyRef2 As IMyInterface
Set MyRef2 = MyRef1 ' QueryInterface executed!
```

In the preceding code, *MyRef1* is declared *As IUnknown*. This declaration might look odd to a Visual Basic programmer, but it is actually much more efficient than declaring references *As Object*. *As Object* actually uses the *IDispatch* (Automation) interface, which is much less efficient than a normal v-table-based interface.

In an IDL file, you indicate the default interface using the *[default]* attribute, shown below in boldface. If no interface in a *coclass* statement is declared as the default, the first interface listed is treated as the default. Here is an IDL file containing multiple interfaces that can be compiled into a type library and implemented in Visual Basic:

```
import "unknwn.idl";

[ object, uuid(00000000-0000-0000-0000-000000000001) ]
interface IDefaultInterface : IUnknown
{
    HRESULT ThingOne();
}


[ object, uuid(00000000-0000-0000-0000-000000000002) ]
interface ISecondaryInterface : IUnknown
{
    HRESULT ThingTwo();
}


[ uuid(00000000-0000-0000-0000-000000000003) ]
library Component
{
    importlib("stdole32.tlb");
    interface IDefaultInterface;
    interface ISecondaryInterface;

    [ uuid(00000000-0000-0000-0000-000000000004) ]
    coclass TheClass
    {
        [default] interface IDefaultInterface;
        interface ISecondaryInterface;
    }
};
```

The following Visual Basic code uses the previously defined type library, accompanied by C++-style pseudocode comments that explain what the code does in COM+ terms. Notice that the *IDefaultInterface* interface is hidden from the Visual Basic programmer and is instead referred to by the coclass name as *TheClass*.

```
Private Sub Command1_Click()
    ' IDefaultInterface* myRef1;
    ' CoCreateInstance(CLSID_TheClass, NULL,
    '     CLSCTX_INPROC_SERVER, IID_IDefaultInterface,
    '     (void**)&myRef1);
    Dim myRef1 As New Component.TheClass

    ' ISecondaryInterface* myRef2;
    Dim myRef2 As Component.ISecondaryInterface

    ' myRef1->ThingOne();
    myRef1.ThingOne

    ' myRef1->QueryInterface(IID_ISecondaryInterface,
    '     (void**)&myRef2);
    Set myRef2 = myRef1

    ' myRef2->ThingTwo();
    myRef2.ThingTwo

    ' myRef1->Release();
    Set myRef1 = Nothing

    ' Garbage collector calls myRef2->Release();
End Sub
```

One solution to the hidden default interface problem in Visual Basic is to make *IUnknown* the default interface of a coclass in the IDL file, as shown in boldface in the following code. This technique tricks Visual Basic into showing all interfaces of a coclass; when Visual Basic thinks it is hiding the default interface from you, it is really hiding only *IUnknown*!

```
[ uuid(00000000-0000-0000-0000-000000000003) ]
library Component
{
    importlib("stdole32.tlb");
    interface IDefaultInterface;
    interface ISecondaryInterface;

    [ uuid(00000000-0000-0000-0000-000000000004) ]
    coclass TheClass
    {
        [default] IUnknown;     // IUnknown will be hidden.
        interface IDefaultInterface;
        interface ISecondaryInterface;
    }
};
```

Building a Client in Visual Basic

Earlier in the chapter, we built a COM+ component in C++ that contains a type library. Because the type library enables language integration in COM+, you can easily use this component from most other programming environments. Here are the steps required to build a client in Visual Basic:

1. Open Visual Basic.

2. Select the Standard EXE project, and click OK.

3. Choose Project/References, and then select Inside COM+ Component Type Library.

4. Click OK.

5. Place a CommandButton control on Form1.

6. Choose View/Code.

7. From the Object list box, select Command1.

8. Enter the following code shown in boldface:

```
Private Sub Command1_Click()
    Dim myRef As New Component.InsideCOM
    MsgBox "myRef.Sum(5, 6) returns " & myRef.Sum(5, 6)
End Sub
```

9. Choose Run/Start.

10. Test the component by clicking the Command1 button.

Implementing COM+ Interfaces in Visual Basic

In addition to creating client applications in Visual Basic, you can also use Visual Basic to build COM+ components. Visual Basic can produce in-process or executable components as well as components that run in the COM+ run-time environment. By default, the following interfaces are implemented automatically by in-process components built in Visual Basic:

Interface	Description
IUnknown	The Visual Basic Virtual Machine (VM) handles *QueryInterface* and reference counting for all COM+ objects. See Chapter 2.
IDispatch	Provides Automation support. See Chapter 5.
IProvideClassInfo	Provides a single method of accessing the type information for an object's coclass entry in its type library. See Chapter 9.
ISupportErrorInfo	Ensures that error information can be correctly propagated up the call chain. See Chapter 6.
IConnectionPoint and *IConnectionPointContainer*	Supports connection points for connectable objects. See Chapter 8.
IExternalConnection	Manages an object's count of marshaled (external) references, enabling the object to detect when it has no external connections so it can shut down properly. See Chapter 13.

For each coclass, the Visual Basic Virtual Machine (msvbvm60.dll) automatically provides a class object that implements the *IClassFactory* interface so you can create instances of the coclass using standard mechanisms such as *CoCreateInstance(Ex)*. Unfortunately, you cannot aggregate objects built in Visual Basic, nor can you aggregate another object from Visual Basic. For in-process components, Visual Basic exports the standard COM+ functions: *DllGet-ClassObject*, *DllCanUnloadNow*, *DllRegisterServer*, and *DllUnregisterServer*. The implementations of *DllRegisterServer* and *DllUnregisterServer* automatically provide all the code needed for the component to support self-registration. The project name supplied in the Project Properties dialog box in Visual Basic is combined with the *Name* property of a class module to produce the program identifier (ProgID). For example, a project named Zoo containing a class named *Dog* would be registered with a ProgID of Zoo.Dog.

To implement a COM+ interface in Visual Basic, you do not need interface definitions written in IDL because Visual Basic deduces the interface definition and creates the necessary type information automatically. If needed, however, you can use Visual Basic to implement a specific interface described in a type library. This technique is useful when you want to create a component in Visual Basic that will interoperate with a client that demands support for a particular custom interface with a well-known IID.

While each class module in Visual Basic defines only one class, a single class can implement multiple interfaces. The public properties, methods, and events of the class module define the default interface of the class. You can use the *Implements* keyword to implement additional interfaces in a class module. For example, a *Math* class might implement several different interfaces, as shown here:

```
Implements IArithmetic
Implements IGeometry

Private Function IArithmetic_Add(x As Integer, _
    y As Integer) As Integer
    ' Code here...
End Function
Private Function IArithmetic_Subtract(x As Integer, _
    y As Integer) As Integer
    ' Code here...
End Function

Private Function IGeometry_TriangleArea(base As Integer, _
    height As Integer) As Integer
    ' Code here...
End Function
```

A client program written in C++ would navigate among these interfaces using the *IUnknown::QueryInterface* method; in contrast, a Visual Basic client would use the *Set* keyword to perform the typecast, as described earlier in the section titled "*QueryInterface*: The Visual Basic Way." Notice that the name of each class module becomes the name of the coclass, but the name of the default interface defined by the class module is the class name prefixed with an underscore. For example, a Visual Basic class module named *Math* becomes a coclass named *Math* with a default interface named *_Math*.

Building a Component in Visual Basic

Earlier, we built a simple C++ client that uses a type library via the *#import* statement to invoke a component that supports the *ISum* interface. Now let's use Visual Basic to create a component that implements the *ISum* interface and is called by the C++ client. To do so, follow these steps:

1. Open Visual Basic.

2. Select the ActiveX DLL project, and click OK.

3. Choose Project/References, and select Inside COM+ Component Type Library.

4. Click OK.

5. In the Code window, type *Implements InsideCOM* and press Enter.

6. From the Object list box, select InsideCOM.

7. In the code window, enter the following code shown in boldface:

```
Private Function InsideCOM_Sum(ByVal x As Long, _
    ByVal y As Long) As Long
    InsideCOM_Sum = x + y
End Function
```

8. In the Properties window, set the *Name* property to *VBInsideCOM*.

9. Choose Project/Project1 Properties.

10. In the Project Name text box, type *VBComponent*.

11. In the Project Description text box, type *The VBInsideCOM Component*.

12. Select Apartment Threaded in the Threading Model section. This marks your component as *ThreadingModel=Apartment* in the registry. (For more on apartment threading, see Chapter 4.)

13. Click OK to close the Project Properties dialog box.

14. Choose File/Make VBComponent.dll, specify a folder for the DLL, and then click OK.

15. Choose File/Save Project, and accept all the default names.

16. Choose File/Exit.

To test this Visual Basic component from C++, use the easyclient.cpp program in Listing 3-3 on page 101 as a starting point or use the code shown in Listing 3-5 below. Be sure to include the component.h file that was generated by the MIDL compiler in previous exercises so that the compiler can find the definition of *ISum*.

vbclient.cpp

```cpp
#import "VBComponent.dll" no_namespace
#import "component.dll" no_namespace
#include <iostream.h>

void main()
{
    CoInitialize(NULL);
    ISumPtr myRef(__uuidof(VBInsideCOM));
    int result = myRef->Sum(5, 13);
    cout << "5 + 13 = " << result << endl;
    myRef = NULL;
    CoUninitialize();
}
```

Listing 3-5.
A C++ client that uses a component created in Visual Basic.

COM+ Programming in Java

Although one major goal of COM+ is to be programming-language neutral, COM+ programming has until recently been almost exclusively the domain of C++. As you know, COM+ programming in C++ is not for the faint of heart. Many developers who do COM+ programming use Visual C++, its wizards, and MFC. Although this makes COM+ programming significantly easier, it also means you have to wade through thousands of lines of code you didn't write and don't understand. Although you can use Visual Basic to build COM+ components, some developers don't consider Visual Basic a serious contender in the COM+ programming arena. Instead, they often use Visual Basic as a "glue" language to combine components created in lower-level languages such as C++.

Microsoft realized that with some decent development tools, Java would make a great programming language for building and using COM+ components. Visual J++ is Microsoft's answer to both of these ideas; it is a great Integrated Development Environment (IDE) for Java development and provides Java with access to COM+ capabilities.

What is it about Java that makes it so great for COM+ programming? The following table shows that although Java and COM+ were developed completely independently, they are complementary technologies. COM+ is an architecture for building components, while Java is a great programming language for building and using those components. You might be surprised to see COM+ described as simple. The original ideas of COM+ certainly are simple, but its implementation and use from languages such as C++ makes people think it's complicated. Once you start programming COM+ in Java, you'll see why COM+ is simple.

Characteristic	Java	COM+
Programming language	Yes	No
Language-independent component architecture	No	Yes
Virtual machine	Yes	No
Simple	Yes	Yes
Robust	Yes	Yes
Object-oriented	Yes	Yes
Platform-independent	Yes	Yes
General-purpose	Yes	Yes
Multithreaded	Yes	Yes
Distributed	No (but Java 1.1 supports Remote Method Invocation [RMI])	Yes

In computing, diametrically opposed technologies are often forced to co-exist. As you'll see, Microsoft has integrated COM+ and Java very cleanly, in a manner that does not conflict with the spirit of Java in any way and does not add any new keywords or constructs to Java. Java already has the necessary constructs for implementing and using COM+ objects. Most of the changes that Microsoft has made to support the Java/COM+ integration model have been in Microsoft's Java Virtual Machine (msjava.dll). A Java Virtual Machine is a module that translates binary .class[5] files from Java bytecode into native op-codes for execution on a particular platform.

To access COM+ objects from a Java application, you simply open a project in Visual J++ and choose Project/Add COM Wrapper. Visual J++ then goes through the HKEY_CLASSES_ROOT\TypeLib key in the registry looking for all components containing valid type library information. This information is displayed in the COM Wrappers dialog box, shown in Figure 3-9. Each entry is shown with the user-friendly name found in the version number key for the type library settings—normally the *helpstring* parameter for the library found in the IDL file.

---

5. In Java, source files are saved with the .java extension; files compiled to binary Java bytecode are saved with the .class extension.

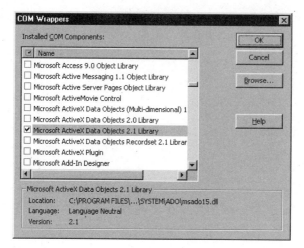

Figure 3-9.
The COM Wrappers dialog box enables Java applications to call COM+ components.

It is important to understand that Java support for COM+ is based on type libraries—a Java program can call any COM+ object for which type library information is available. This information might be available as a .tlb file or might be embedded as a resource within the component.

Let's say that you want to call a particular component from a program written in Java. The first step is to use the COM Wrappers dialog box to create Java class wrappers for the COM+ classes in the component. You simply add a check mark next to the components you want to use and then click OK. Visual J++ automatically converts the type library information to Java source files.[6] If you think about it, this is rather amazing: Visual J++ inputs the information contained in a type library and spits out Java source files—one for each class and interface described by the type library. By default, these source files are placed in a new subdirectory with the same name as the type library.

Each Java file generated by Visual J++ contains special Javadoc-style comments identifying it as a wrapper for a coclass. The comments take the form of /** @com and so are often referred to as @com comments. Listing 3-6 on page 130 shows the isum.java file produced when Visual J++ generates wrappers for the Inside COM+ Component Type Library we built in Chapter 2. The Visual J++ compiler recognizes the special @com Javadoc-style syntax and emits .class files containing special attributes that indicate that the application is invoking

---

6. Actually, Visual J++ invokes a separate helper utility named jactivex.exe to read the type library and generate the Java to COM+ wrappers.

COM+ objects. Typically, you don't need to code the @com directives yourself because Visual J++ contains wizards that generate these wrappers based on the information contained in a type library. However, to better understand the Java/COM+ integration model, let's examine the COM+ directives supported by Visual J++, which are shown in the following table:

Directive	Description
@com.class(GUID, security, casting)	Specifies that the Java class represents a coclass with the given GUID, casting support, and Java security requirements.
@com.interface(GUID, thread, type)	Indicates that the Java interface represents a COM+ interface with the specified GUID, threading model, and types.
@com.method(dispid, vtable, ...)	Marks the Java method as a COM+ interface method, which should be exposed in the object's v-table, dispatch table, or neither.
@com.parameters	Specifies which parameters are in, out, or a return value and how they should be mapped to COM+ and from COM+ to Java.
@com.typeinfo	Specifies additional information from the type library that represents this coclass.
@com.transaction	Specifies the transaction support required of the COM+ run-time environment.
@com.struct	Specifies that the Java class is a Java-Callable Data Wrapper (JCDW). (JCDWs are proxies for external data structures, such as structs, unions, and arrays.)
@com.structmap	Indicates how the field in a JCDW should map to COM+ and from COM+ back to this field in Java. You can also use this directive to custom marshal the data between Java and COM+ and to specify the data's offset from the beginning of the JCDW.

You might wonder how a program can cross the bridge from Java bytecode to a COM+ object. Well, when the Microsoft Java VM sees these special COM+ attributes in a class, it translates all Java method invocations on the class into calls to the specified coclass. So the Microsoft Java VM is actually the bridge between Java and COM+. For this reason, Java programs that use COM+ components work only on platforms supported by the Microsoft Java VM (at least for now).

isum.java

```
//
// Auto-generated using JActiveX.EXE 5.00.2918
//   ("C:\PROGRAM FILES\MICROSOFT VISUAL STUDIO\
//   VJ98\jactivex.exe" /wfc  /w /xi /X:rkc /l
//   "C:\WINDOWS\TEMP\jvc12F4.TMP" /nologo /d
//   "C:\My Documents\Visual Studio Projects\JavaClient"
//   "C:\COMPONENT.DLL")
//
// WARNING: Do not remove the comments that include "@com"
// directives. This source file must be compiled by a @com-aware
// compiler. If you are using the Microsoft Visual J++ compiler,
// you must use version 1.02.3920 or later. Previous versions
// will not issue an error but will not generate COM-enabled
// class files.
//

package component;

import com.ms.com.*;
import com.ms.com.IUnknown;
import com.ms.com.Variant;

// VTable-only interface ISum
/** @com.interface(iid=10000001-0000-0000-0000-000000000001,
    thread=AUTO) */
public interface ISum extends IUnknown
{
    /** @com.method(vtoffset=0, addFlagsVtable=4)
        @com.parameters([in,type=I4] x, [in,type=I4] y,
        [type=I4] return) */
    public int Sum(int x, int y);


    public static final com.ms.com._Guid iid = new
        com.ms.com._Guid((int)0x10000001, (short)0x0,
        (short)0x0, (byte)0x0, (byte)0x0, (byte)0x0, (byte)0x0,
        (byte)0x0, (byte)0x0, (byte)0x0, (byte)0x1);
}
```

Listing 3-6.
The COM+ wrapper for the ISum *interface generated by Visual J++ when a Java
application imports the type library of the component created in Chapter 2.*

Several items are worth noting about the generated wrapper files. The *ISum* interface defined in the isum.java source file *extends* (Java lingo for "derives from") the *IUnknown* interface. At last, our friend *IUnknown*! The *InsideCOM* class declared in the insidecom.java wrapper file, shown in Listing 3-7, *implements* the *IUnknown* and *ISum* interfaces. In Java, the *extends* keyword enables single inheritance among classes or interfaces, while the *implements* keyword enables a class to support multiple interfaces—which is crucial for supporting COM+. The GUIDs for the *ISum* interface and the *InsideCOM* coclass are also declared in the wrapper files, both in the @com Javadoc comments and as constants in the class and interface definitions.

insidecom.java

```
//
// Auto-generated using JActiveX.EXE 5.00.2918
//   ("C:\PROGRAM FILES\MICROSOFT VISUAL STUDIO\
//   VJ98\jactivex.exe" /wfc  /w /xi /X:rkc /1
//   "C:\WINDOWS\TEMP\jvc4120.TMP" /nologo /d
//   "C:\My Documents\Visual Studio Projects\JavaClient"
//   "C:\COMPONENT.DLL")
//
// WARNING: Do not remove the comments that include "@com"
// directives. This source file must be compiled by a
// @com-aware compiler. If you are using the Microsoft Visual
// J++ compiler you must use version 1.02.3920 or later.
// Previous versions will not issue an error but will not
// generate COM-enabled class files.
//

package component;

import com.ms.com.*;
import com.ms.com.IUnknown;
import com.ms.com.Variant;

/** @com.class(classid=10000002-0000-0000-0000-000000000001,
    DynamicCasts)
    @com.interface(iid=10000001-0000-0000-0000-000000000001,
    thread=AUTO) */
public class InsideCOM implements IUnknown,
    com.ms.com.NoAutoScripting, component.ISum
```

Listing 3-7. *(continued)*

The COM+ wrapper for the InsideCOM *coclass generated by Visual J++ when a Java application imports the type library of the component created in Chapter 2.*

insidecom.java *continued*

```
{
    /** @com.method(vtoffset=0, addFlagsVtable=4)
        @com.parameters([in,type=I4] x, [in,type=I4] y,
        [type=I4] return) */
    public native int Sum(int x, int y);


    public static final com.ms.com._Guid iid = new
        com.ms.com._Guid((int)0x10000001, (short)0x0, (short)0x0,
        (byte)0x0, (byte)0x0, (byte)0x0, (byte)0x0, (byte)0x0,
        (byte)0x0, (byte)0x0, (byte)0x1);

    public static final com.ms.com._Guid clsid = new
        com.ms.com._Guid((int)0x10000002, (short)0x0,
        (short)0x0, (byte)0x0, (byte)0x0, (byte)0x0, (byte)0x0,
        (byte)0x0, (byte)0x0, (byte)0x0, (byte)0x1);
}
```

Calling a COM+ Object from Java

When you use the Java-callable wrappers for COM+ objects, you must always invoke methods through an interface, not through the class itself (just as COM+ objects are always called through an interface in C++). Listing 3-8 shows a simple Java program that instantiates the *InsideCOM* coclass and then invokes methods of the *ISum* interface.

javaclient.java

```
/**
 * This class can take a variable number of parameters on the
 * command line. Program execution begins with the main()
 * method. The class constructor is not invoked unless an
 * object of type 'Class1' created in the main() method.
 */

import component.*;

public class JavaClient
```

Listing 3-8.
A Java client application that invokes the InsideCOM *coclass implemented in* C++.

javaclient.java

```
{
    /**
     * The main entry point for the application.
     *
     * @param args Array of parameters passed to the application
     * via the command line.
     */
    public static void main (String[] args)
    {
        // TODO: Add initialization code here
        ISum myRef = (ISum)new InsideCOM();
        int result = myRef.Sum(5, 4);
        System.out.println(
            "Java client: myRef.Sum(5, 4) returns "
            + result);
    }
}
```

As in the Visual Basic code presented earlier, you won't recognize any COM+ function calls in this code—no *CoInitializeEx*, no *CoCreateInstance(Ex)*, and no *IUnknown* methods such as *QueryInterface*. The *import* statement makes accessible the compiled version of the generated COM+ wrapper files in the *component* subfolder. Note that this statement is not analogous to the C++ *#import* directive that generates code based on the contents of a type library—although the name of the C++ directive was inspired by the Java statement. In Java, you can reference any class using its fully qualified name (for example, *component.InsideCOM*) if the class can be found in the *classpath* (the path the compiler uses to find packages referenced in a Java application). The *import* statement simply lets you refer to the class using its short name (such as *InsideCOM*). If the class name is qualified by the package name (*component.InsideCOM*), the *import* statement is not needed.

Java's *new* keyword instantiates the *InsideCOM* class. This instantiation leads the Microsoft Java VM into the insidecom.class file generated by Visual J++, where the Microsoft Java VM encounters special attributes indicating that this is a coclass wrapper. The generated .class file also contains the CLSID of the coclass. The Microsoft Java VM then uses that CLSID to call *CoCreateInstance(Ex)*. The *IUnknown* pointer returned by *CoCreateInstance(Ex)* is then cast by the Java code to *ISum*, as shown here:

```
ISum myRef = (ISum)new InsideCOM();
```

Hidden from view is the call to the *IUnknown::QueryInterface* function that lets clients choose among an object's supported interfaces. The simple typecast from the *InsideCOM* class to the *ISum* interface forces the Microsoft Java VM to call the object's *QueryInterface* function to request a pointer to *ISum*. In this manner, a Java program can retrieve an interface pointer to any interface supported by a COM+ object. Simply casting the object to the appropriate interface yields correct results.

If the object does not implement the requested interface and the *QueryInterface* call fails, an exception of type *java.lang.ClassCastException* is thrown when you attempt the cast. One option is simply to catch this exception using Java's exception handling mechanism. To determine whether an object implements the desired interface before casting, you can use the *instanceof* operator, as shown in the following code:

```
IUnknown myRef = new InsideCOM();
if(myRef instanceof ISum)
{
    // Now we know that InsideCOM implements ISum.
    // It is safe to cast (ISum)myRef.
}
```

To instantiate an object on a remote machine, client applications can rely on the *RemoteServerName* registry setting to specify the name of the machine on which the object should be created. (This setting is described in detail in Chapter 12.) Alternatively, Java applications can directly invoke the *CoCreateInstanceEx* function using J/Direct, the facility that Java developers can use to make direct calls to functions exported by DLLs. A client application using *CoCreateInstanceEx* has much greater flexibility than that permitted by the registry settings. The code fragment below shows how to call *CoCreateInstanceEx* from Java:

```
int HRESULT = 0;

// Set up the CoServerInfo structure to specify the
// machine name and security info
com.ms.com.COSERVERINFO ServerInfo =
    new com.ms.com.COSERVERINFO();
ser.pwszName = "ServerMachine";

// Set up the MULTI_QI structure to request certain interfaces
com.ms.com.MULTI_QI qi = new com.ms.com.MULTI_QI();
qi.pIID =
    com.ms.com.ComLib.getGuidOf(com.ms.com.IUnknown.class);
```

```
// Call CoCreateInstanceEx
HRESULT = com.ms.win32.Ole32.CoCreateInstanceEx(
    new com.ms.com._Guid(CLSID_InsideCOM), null,
    com.ms.win32.win.CLSCTX_REMOTE_SERVER, ServerInfo, 1,
    new com.ms.com.MULTI_QI[]{qi});
```

Reference counting, another painful COM+ chore, is handled automatically in Java. As with the smart interface pointers in Visual C++, you do not need to call *IUnknown::AddRef* when you create a new reference to an object, nor do you need to call *IUnknown::Release* when you finish using a reference to an object. As it does for native Java objects, the garbage collector performs reference counting automatically and calls the *Release* method on object references that go out of scope. Setting an interface reference to *null*, as shown below, can trigger Java's garbage collection algorithm:

```
myRef = null;
```

The Java garbage collection mechanism is not guaranteed because many COM+ objects can be called only on the thread on which they were created. Because garbage collection can occur at unpredictable times, the required thread might have expired by the time garbage-collection reclaims the object; this can result in memory leaks and tie up other system resources. You should therefore explicitly free COM+ objects in a timely and predictable fashion. You can use the *com.ms.com.ComLib.release* method to force Java to release all its reference counts on a COM+ object, as shown here:

```
ComLib.release(myRef);
```

Building a Client in Java

To build a COM+ client program in Java, follow these steps:

1. Open Visual J++.

2. Choose File/New Project.

3. Click the New tab, and then select the Applications folder and the Console Application project type.

4. In the Name text box, type *TestCOM*, and click Open.

5. Choose Project/Add COM Wrapper.

6. Select the Inside COM+ Component Type Library check box, and click OK.

7. Open the class1.java source file.

8. Modify the class template by adding the code shown here in boldface:

```
/**
 * This class can take a variable number of parameters on
 * the command line. Program execution begins with the main()
 * method. The class constructor is not invoked unless an
 * object of type 'Class1' created in the main() method.
 */
import component.*;

public class Class1
{
    /**
     * The main entry point for the application.
     *
     * @param args Array of parameters passed to the
     * application via the command line.
     */
    public static void main (String[] args)
    {
        // TODO: Add initialization code here
        ISum myRef = (ISum)new InsideCOM();
        int result = myRef.Sum(5, 4);
        System.out.println(
            "Java client: myRef.Sum(5, 4) returns "
            + result);
    }
}
```

9. Choose Debug/Start to run the application.

Implementing COM+ Objects in Java

Up to now, we have examined how to call COM+ objects built in C++ from Java. You can also implement COM+ objects in Java. These components can be called from languages such as C++ and Visual Basic as well as from Java itself. Like the rest of the Java/COM+ integration model, this functionality has been implemented cleanly. Let's say you want to implement the *ISum* interface in Java. The steps involved are shown below:

1. Define the interfaces and coclasses in IDL.

2. Convert the IDL file into a type library using the MIDL compiler.

3. Generate Java wrappers for the interfaces and coclasses defined in the type library.

4. Build Java classes that implement the desired interfaces.

Recall that all COM+ programming should begin in IDL. When you implement COM+ interfaces in Java, you must first define the interfaces in IDL. For the Java project, you can reuse the component.idl file created for the C++ component and presented earlier in Listing 3-1 beginning on page 93. Then you implement the *ISum* interface in Java, as shown in Listing 3-9. Notice that the class and the *Sum* method are declared as *public* so that they are accessible from outside the package.

class1.java

```
/**
 * @com.register ( clsid=FDDA9DC0-B472-11D2-BB50-006097B5EAFC,
 *     typelib=FDDA9DC1-B472-11D2-BB50-006097B5EAFC )
 */
public class Class1 implements component.ISum
{
    public int Sum(int x, int y)
    {
        return x + y;
    }
}
```

Listing 3-9.
A Java implementation of the ISum *interface.*

In order for a client to invoke a Java class via COM+, the Microsoft Java VM must dynamically create a COM+ callable wrapper object that exposes the functionality of the Java class. The Microsoft Java VM contains what is essentially a generic COM+ object with a virtual function table that is constructed dynamically to support several standard COM+ interfaces as well as any COM+ interfaces implemented by the Java class. (For more on how virtual function tables can be constructed dynamically, see Chapter 8.) The COM+ callable wrapper object implemented by the Microsoft Java VM also supports aggregation, which means that any COM+ object written in Java can be aggregated, although COM+ objects written in Java cannot aggregate other COM+ objects. The Microsoft Java VM provides default implementations of the following interfaces for COM+ components written in Java:

Interface	Description
IUnknown	Handles *QueryInterface* and reference counting for all COM+ objects. See Chapter 2
IDispatch and *IDispatchEx*	Provides Automation support. See Chapter 5.
IProvideClassInfo and *IProvideClassInfo2*	Provides a method for accessing the type information for an object's coclass entry in its type library. See Chapter 9.
ISupportErrorInfo	Ensures that error information can be correctly propagated up the call chain. See Chapter 6.
IConnectionPointContainer	Supports connection points for connectable objects. See Chapter 8.
IExternalConnection	Manages an object's count of marshaled (external) references, enabling the object to detect when it has no external connections so that it can shut down properly. See Chapter 13.
IMarshal	Specifies how a COM+ object can be marshaled between processes and computers. See Chapter 14.

With Visual Basic, developers are basically stuck with the default implementations of these standard interfaces provided by the Visual Basic VM. Java developers, in contrast, can provide custom implementations for most[7] of these interfaces simply by implementing them. Like Visual Basic, the Microsoft Java VM also provides class objects for each coclass. These class objects implement the *IClassFactory* interface and support standard *IClassFactory::CreateInstance* semantics.

Packaging and Registering Java Components

The binary files produced by Java compilers containing Java bytecode are saved with the .class file extension. However, this is not necessarily the best medium for distributing a Java application. Typically, the collection of .class files that make up an application or component are packaged together. Visual J++ offers several packaging options, which are shown in the following table:

---

7. The Microsoft Java VM's implementation of *IUnknown*, *IExternalConnection*, and *ISupportErrorInfo* cannot be overridden. However, Microsoft allows Java components to implement the *IExternalConnectionSink* interface, which notifies you when external connections are added and released.

Packaging Type	Description
COM DLL (.dll)	A COM+ in-process component.
Windows EXE (.exe)	A standard Win32 application in Portable Executable (PE) file format.
Cab Archive (.cab)	A cabinet file, which is an efficient way to package multiple files to ensure efficient download and installation of Java packages and classes executed on (or behind) HTML in Internet Explorer.
Self-extracting Setup (.exe)	A self-extracting setup executable file, which provides a mechanism to distribute a stand-alone application to users. The setup also includes an uninstalling program.
Zip Archive (.zip)	A file that packages multiple files (such as Java packages and classes) in a single, uncompressed file that is compatible with Internet Explorer and other browsers.

When you build a COM+ component in Visual J++, the .class files that make up that component are packaged together inside one .dll file, and the component generated automatically supports the standard COM+ exported functions, including built-in self-registration via the *DllRegisterServer* and *DllUnregisterServer* functions. As expected, after registration the InprocServer32 entry in the HKEY_CLASSES_ROOT\CLSID section of the registry points to the component built in Visual J++. You'll find it helpful, however, to turn off the packaging feature of Visual J++ and view the raw registry entries created for the .class files built in Java.

Shown below are the most interesting registry entries created during the build process when packaging has been disabled. Notice that the *InprocServer32* key for the *JavaComponent* component is listed as msjava.dll—the Microsoft Java VM! Because Java code is compiled into bytecode, it can't be called directly from a language such as C++. Instead, the Microsoft Java VM provides the COM+ support for your Java programs. Client applications think they are working directly with your component, but they are actually working with msjava.dll, which actually runs your Java code. When packaged as a COM+ DLL, the same basic mechanism is at work, but the .class files are wrapped in a .dll file that simply loads the Microsoft Java VM and proceeds as usual.

```
[HKEY_CLASSES_ROOT\CLSID\{FDDA9DC0-B472-11D2-BB50-006097B5EAFC}\
    InprocServer32]
@="C:\WINDOWS\SYSTEM\MSJAVA.DLL"
"CodeBase"="file:C:\My Documents\JavaComponent\"
"JavaClass"="Class1"
"ThreadingModel"="Both"
```

The *JavaClass* value names the Java class that is to be exposed as a COM+ object. The *CodeBase* value specifies a path that should be added to the classpath when the object is created. This helps ensure that the class named by the *JavaClass* value can be located and accessed.

Building a Component in Java

To build a COM+ component in Java, follow these steps:

1. Open Visual J++.

2. Create a new component project by selecting COM DLL in the Components folder on the New tab of the New Project dialog box. Name the project JavaComponent and click Open.

3. Choose Project/Add COM Wrapper.

4. Select the Inside COM+ Component Type Library item, and click OK.

5. Modify the class1.java file so that it looks as follows. (The changes are shown in boldface.)

```
/**
 * This class is designed to be packaged with a COM DLL
 * output format. The class has no standard entry points,
 * other than the constructor. Public methods will be exposed
 * as methods on the default COM interface.
 * @com.register ( clsid=FDDA9DC0-B472-11D2-BB50-006097B5EAFC,
        typelib=FDDA9DC1-B472-11D2-BB50-006097B5EAFC )
 */
public class Class1 implements component.ISum
{
    // TODO: Add additional methods and code here
    public int Sum(int x, int y)
       {
            return x + y;
       }

    /**
     * NOTE: To add auto-registration code, refer to the
     * documentation on the following method
     *   public static void onCOMRegister(boolean unRegister) {}
     */
}
```

Choose File/Save Class1.java.

Choose Build/Build.

To test this Visual J++ component from C++, you can use the easyclient.cpp program in Listing 3-3 on page 101 as a starting point or enter the code shown in Listing 3-10. Otherwise, you can use Visual Basic or Java itself to build a client for this component.

jclient.cpp

```
#import "JavaComponent.dll" no_namespace
#import "component.dll" no_namespace
#include <iostream.h>

void main()
{
    CoInitialize(NULL);
    ISumPtr myRef(__uuidof(Class1));
    int result = myRef->Sum(5, 13);
    cout << "5 + 13 = " << result << endl;
    myRef = NULL;
    CoUninitialize();
}
```

Listing 3-10.
A C++ client that uses the COM+ component created in Java.

ActiveX Controls and JavaBeans Integration

To enable Java developers to use the thousands of commercially available ActiveX controls, Microsoft has extended its Microsoft Java VM so that ActiveX controls can be hosted in a Java applet or application. The Microsoft Java VM also lets you expose JavaBeans components as ActiveX controls. These components, which are designed for Java, might eventually compete with ActiveX controls in the marketplace of reusable components. As compelling JavaBeans components become commercially available, they will immediately be usable by the large number of ActiveX control containers such as Visual Basic, Visual C++, Borland Delphi, and Powersoft PowerBuilder.

Thus, an ActiveX control appears as a JavaBeans component to a Java programmer, and a JavaBeans component appears as an ActiveX control to a developer using any of the wide array of development tools that support COM+. The Microsoft Java VM is the bridge that makes this bidirectional support possible. Developers can work in the environment with which they are most familiar and still take advantage of all available components, regardless of the development tools or platforms used to build them.

Exposing an existing JavaBeans component as an ActiveX control is as simple as running the JavaReg utility to register the control and generate a type library that describes its properties, methods, and events. After you run JavaReg, the JavaBeans component looks and functions just like a native ActiveX control in any control container. For example, a Visual Basic application can take advantage of a JavaBeans component that has been turned into an ActiveX control.

The Sandbox Model

Because a user can automatically download Java applets from Web sites, security is a big concern. To prevent Java applets from potentially damaging the user's system, applets typically run in a *sandbox*—a carefully delimited execution environment that prevents applets from posing a security threat. Local file access, for example, is off limits. COM+ services are also not available to applets running in the sandbox. Note that the sandbox restriction applies only to applets; standard Java applications do not run in the sandbox and therefore might use COM+ services. Running applets in the sandbox is a necessary for security reasons, but the restrictions imposed by the sandbox prevent applets from doing many useful and interesting things, such as accessing COM+ services. To overcome this limitation, the Microsoft Java VM categorizes applets as either *trusted* or *untrusted*.

Untrusted applets run within the sandbox and cannot use COM+ services, as is the norm for untrusted applets. All .class files that aren't loaded from the class path—including those downloaded from the Internet—are considered untrusted. Trusted .class files are those that are either loaded from the class path or extracted from a cabinet (.cab) file that has a digital signature. By using .cab files, you can designate Java applets downloaded from the Internet as trusted. Trusted applets run outside of the security sandbox; they can therefore read and write files and use COM+ services.

Four path-related registry values are relevant to the security of Java applets. These values are stored in the HKEY_LOCAL_MACHINE\SOFTWARE \Microsoft\Java VM key. The names and typical values are shown here:

```
Classpath = "C:\WINDOWS\java\classes;."
LibsDirectory = "C:\WINDOWS\java\lib"
TrustedClasspath = ""
TrustedLibsDirectory = "C:\WINDOWS\java\trustlib"
```

During development in Visual J++, all .class files are considered trusted, so you don't have to worry about security issues. If you want to distribute a Java applet that uses COM+ services over the Internet, you must ensure that your applet runs outside of the sandbox on the user's machine. To do so, you can create digitally signed .cab files for your Java classes using the cabinet and code signing tools in the Platform SDK. In addition to enabling applets to run outside the sandbox, using .cab files for your classes speeds up downloading and makes installation more secure. Windows applications and COM+ components written in Java that do not run in a Web browser and are not downloaded over the Internet are automatically executed outside the sandbox and can therefore use COM+ services.

CHAPTER FOUR

Apartments

Both COM and its predecessor, OLE, were developed at a time when Microsoft Windows did not support multithreading, so COM initially provided no support for multithreaded components. Later, as threading became ubiquitous in Windows, COM was extended to include threading support. Today, COM+ provides support and interoperability for components that use threads to varying degrees, from old-fashioned single-threaded objects to objects that can be called on any thread.

COM+ supports two primary threading models: one for user-driven graphical user interface (GUI) applications and another for worker components that do not display a user interface, both of which use the threading infrastructure provided by the operating system. The threading model designed for GUI applications is synchronized with the message queues used by Windows, making it much easier for user-driven applications to work with COM+ robustly. The threading model designed for worker components, on the other hand, does not use window messages to deliver COM+ method calls—this model works well for components that need the best possible performance and that don't have to worry about synchronizing COM+ calls with a user interface.

Both models are and will continue to be important. Unfortunately, the details of these threading models and the implications of the ways in which they can be combined can be overwhelming at first. Luckily, in most cases a deep understanding of these threading models is not crucial to the success of a project, and reading this chapter once to obtain an overview of the issues involved will be sufficient. If you design a system that makes heavy use of threads, however, you might want to work through this chapter carefully to ensure that you fully understand the implications of your design decisions.

A Quick Review of Threads

A *thread* is a path of execution through a process. Every process has one or more threads of execution. As part of the Win32 process-creation function *CreateProcess*, an initial thread is automatically created. This initial thread begins execution at the *main* function (for console applications), *WinMain* function (for GUI applications), or *ServiceMain* function (for services). To create additional threads, a process can call the Win32 *CreateThread* function. Note that the system executes threads only, never processes. Threads enable an application to perform (or appear to perform) several tasks concurrently, which can lead to greater functionality in an application and improved responsiveness in the user interface. On machines with multiple processors, different threads can execute concurrently on different processors, yielding improved overall performance.

Normal function calls are *synchronous,* meaning that the caller must wait for the function to finish executing before it can proceed, as shown in the following code fragment:

```
// Some code here...
MyFunc();    // Call MyFunc.
// Some more code here...
// Code here executes only when MyFunc has finished.
```

The *CreateThread* function enables functions to execute asynchronously, meaning that the caller does not have to wait for the called function to finish executing, as shown in this code fragment:

```
// Some code here...
CreateThread(..., MyFunc, ...);    // Call MyFunc.
// Some more code here...
// Code here executes immediately;
// MyFunc is executing concurrently.
```

When a thread eventually finishes executing, you can call the *GetExitCode-Thread* function to retrieve the thread's return value. A thread (*MyFunc* in the preceding code) terminates when it returns from the main thread function or when it explicitly calls *ExitThread*. (You can also use the Win32 *TerminateThread* function to kill a misbehaving thread, but this is not recommended.)

All kernel objects, including threads, have an associated usage counter. For threads, this usage counter is initially set to *2*. When a thread terminates, its usage counter is implicitly decremented. The thread's creator should also decrement its usage counter using the Win32 *CloseHandle* function. In this way, the thread object's usage counter will reach *0* and the system will automatically destroy the thread object.

Priority values are assigned to each process and thread. The kernel's thread scheduler uses these values as part of its algorithm to determine the order in which threads should be scheduled for execution. You can adjust the priority value assigned to a process by calling the *SetPriorityClass* function, and you can call *SetThreadPriority* to control the priority of a thread. The two values are combined to arrive at the actual priority value of a thread, called the thread's *base priority.* You can call the corresponding *GetPriorityClass* and *GetThreadPriority* functions at any time to obtain the current settings.

One of the biggest challenges associated with the safe use of threads is synchronization. Any unprotected access to data shared by multiple threads is an access violation waiting to happen. For example, if two threads manipulate an unprotected data structure, data is likely to become corrupted. It is easy to envision a scenario in which one thread might begin to read some data only to be preempted by the scheduler, which might execute another thread that begins to modify the data in the shared structure. When execution focus eventually returns to the first thread, the data might no longer be consistent. This scenario will likely end in an exception.

This type of synchronization problem is difficult to correct because it can happen infrequently and seemingly at random, making it difficult to reproduce. Win32 offers several options for thread synchronization: events, critical sections, semaphores, and mutual exclusion (mutex) objects. Since data itself cannot be protected against concurrent access by different threads, you must write intelligent code that prevents this from happening. You can use the Win32 thread synchronization objects to guarantee that only one thread at a time executes a particular section of crucial code. Note that only data shared by multiple threads are at risk. Automatic variables located on the stack of a thread pose no difficulties because they are allocated on a per-thread basis; the same is true of thread local storage (TLS). Windows also provides support for fibers—lightweight, usermode threads that must be manually scheduled—but these have little bearing on COM+, and so are not covered here.

Apartment Types

Over the past decade, Windows has evolved from a cooperatively multitasked 16-bit environment into a preemptively multitasked 32-bit operating system. In the process, threads have slowly but surely found their way into nearly all aspects of the operating system, from the C run-time library to the Microsoft Foundation Class (MFC) library. This transition has at times been painful, but the advantages have far outweighed the temporary inconveniences caused by the integration of threading. Because COM entered the threading game rather late, developers have experienced more than a little consternation as threading support has been added.

Around the time that multithreading support was added to COM, many of Microsoft's design decisions were affected by the amount of existing thread-unsafe legacy code.[1] Microsoft felt that it was crucial to enable existing thread-unsafe components to interoperate seamlessly with the new multithreaded components. Thus, it defined several levels, called *threading models*, of thread safety. The basic unit of thread safety in COM+ is called an *apartment*. An apartment is a set of threading rules shared by a group of objects. As such, an apartment cannot be compared with a Win32 object such as a process or a thread. Instead, the apartment concept serves only to clarify the threading rules applied to a COM+ object; these rules differ by apartment type.

The three types of apartments are single-threaded apartments (STAs), neutral apartments (NAs), and multithreaded apartments (MTAs). STAs can have only one thread executing per apartment, while NAs and MTAs can have multiple threads executing per apartment. Method calls to objects in an STA are automatically synchronized and dispatched using window message queues, while method calls to objects in an MTA or NA are not. Not all platforms that support COM+ support all apartment types. The Windows CE operating system, for instance, currently supports only the MTA model.

Immediately to the right of Java Man on the evolutionary time line stands OLE 1, a compound document architecture that originally used Dynamic Data Exchange (DDE) messages for its interprocess communication. Until the advent of the MTA model, COM had not entirely shed its seedy, message-based past. In fact, to this day the STA model notifies an object of method calls by posting messages to a window message queue. That's right: any component[2] that supports the STA model must contain a message loop such as the one shown below or nothing will happen:

```
// Bet you thought you'd never see another one of these!
MSG msg;
while(GetMessage(&msg, 0, 0, 0))
    DispatchMessage(&msg);
```

---

1. The first version of COM to be multithreading was released in Microsoft Windows NT 3.51.

2. Only executable STA components require a message loop; in-process components do not have message loops because the client application is responsible for processing window messages.

Why, you ask in disbelief, does a component architecture with as much finesse as COM+ rely on window message queues? By relying on message queues to dispense method calls, COM+ effectively has hooks into every object in an STA. Since messages are processed sequentially, method calls to objects in an STA are automatically synchronized to ensure that thread safety is not compromised. The MTA model does not rely on message queues because COM+ does not have to provide thread synchronization for such objects.

In the past, the combinations of STAs and MTAs in a single process have been dubbed single-threading, apartment-threading, free-threading, and mixed-threading models. You should avoid this terminology because it simply causes additional confusion, even though some documentation might still refer to COM+ threading models using these obsolete names. A good way to think of these threading models is to remember that they all rely on the basic unit of an apartment. Some of those apartments can have only a single thread (STAs); others support multiple threads (MTAs and NAs). Note that all three apartment types can be combined in a single process; a process can contain zero or more STAs but at most one MTA and one NA.

The threading models in COM+ allow clients and components that use different threading architectures to work together. From the perspective of a client, all objects appear to use the client's threading model. Likewise, from the perspective of an object, all clients appear to support the object's threading model. Clients and components have different responsibilities in relation to the threading models. Clients can use the Win32 *CreateThread* function to launch new threads of execution and can access COM+ objects from these new threads. This technique is often used to improve the responsiveness of an application or to enable the application to access several different objects concurrently. Components, on the other hand, rarely call the *CreateThread* function, and doing so is strongly discouraged. Instead, a component simply declares its threading model at start-up and then lets COM+ handle the concurrency requirements mandated by the particular situation.

Single-Threaded Apartments

The current STA model is descended from the original thread-oblivious model used by OLE. In the latter model, objects could be accessed only from a single thread in the process. The modern STA model evolved to overcome this limitation; it allows a single process to contain multiple STAs. Since each STA has one and only one thread associated with it, the ability of multiple STAs to exist in a single process means that several threads can use different COM+ objects concurrently—a big improvement. Legacy components written prior to the advent of the COM+ threading models actually run in a single STA, called the main STA.

A particular thread of execution declares its support for a threading model by calling *CoInitializeEx*. The second parameter of *CoInitializeEx* specifies whether the thread supports the STA (*COINIT_APARTMENTTHREADED*) model or the MTA (*COINIT_MULTITHREADED*) model. The obsolete function, *CoInitialize*, calls the *CoInitializeEx* function with the *COINIT_APARTMENTTHREADED* flag, as shown in the following code fragment. In part because these two calls are equivalent, legacy components are considered to support the main STA model.

```
// Single-threaded apartment (STA)
// This code is equivalent to CoInitialize(NULL).
CoInitializeEx(NULL, COINIT_APARTMENTTHREADED);
```

The STA model owns any COM+ objects instantiated by its thread, so all method calls on the object are executed by the thread that created the object. The fact that the same thread that created an object is always used to execute its methods is important to objects that have thread affinity; an object that requires thread affinity must be executed by a particular thread. For example, some objects use thread local storage (TLS) to associate data with a specific thread. An object using TLS expects that the same thread will be used to execute all of its methods. If a different thread executes a method, any attempt to access TLS data will fail. Because objects running in the MTA or NA model can be executed on a variety of different threads, they cannot use TLS. Only objects running in an STA may have thread affinity.

As in the original thread-oblivious model, method calls on objects running in an STA are dispatched using window message queues. This does not mean that a component must display a user interface or even create a window. The first call to *CoInitializeEx* with the *COINIT_APARTMENTTHREADED* flag in a process calls the Win32 function *RegisterClass* to register the *OleMainThreadWndClass* window class. During this and every subsequent call to *CoInitializeEx* with the *COINIT_APARTMENTTHREADED* flag, the system automatically calls the Win32 function *CreateWindowEx* to create a hidden window of the *OleMainThreadWndClass* window class for each STA. The message queue of this hidden window is used to synchronize and dispatch COM+ method calls on this object. For this reason, the thread associated with an STA must retrieve and dispatch window messages using *GetMessage* and *DispatchMessage* or similar functions.

You can display the hidden window using a utility such as Microsoft Spy++, which comes with Microsoft Visual C++, as shown in Figure 4-1. A method call is received as a message to this hidden window. When the component retrieves the message (*GetMessage*) and then dispatches it (*DispatchMessage*), the hidden window's window procedure (*wndproc*) receives the message. This window procedure, implemented as part of COM+, then calls the corresponding interface method of the object.

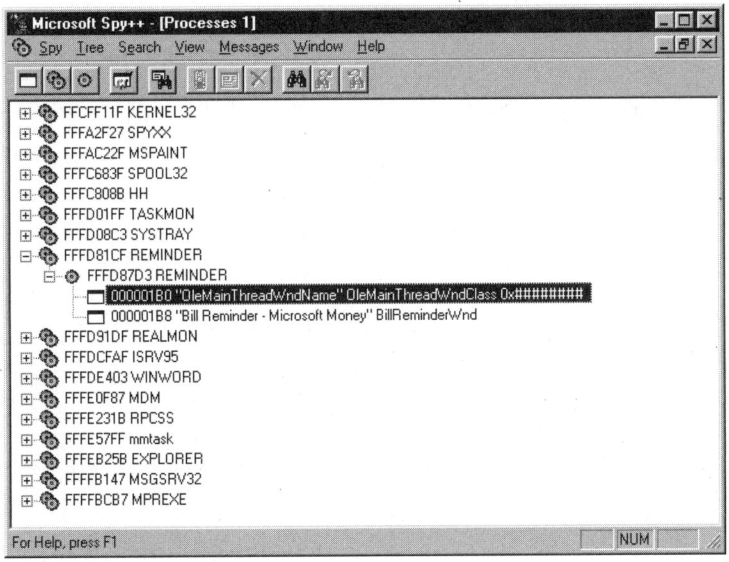

Figure 4-1.
The hidden STA window created by COM+ and uncovered using Microsoft Spy++.

This message-queuing architecture solves the problem of multiple clients making concurrent calls to an object running in an STA. Since all the calls are submitted as window messages posted to a message queue, the calls are serialized automatically. The object receives method calls in an orderly fashion when the message loop retrieves and dispatches the messages in the queue. Because COM+ serializes the calls in this manner, the object's methods do not need to provide synchronization. Note that the dispatched method calls are always made on the thread that instantiated the object. You can easily verify this using the Win32 *GetCurrentThreadId* function or the *CoGetCurrentProcess*[3] function to retrieve the thread identifier in each method of an object. The thread identifier is always the same for all objects running in one STA.

---

3. *CoGetCurrentProcess* is recommended because it always returns a unique value identifying the current thread. The thread identifiers returned by the *GetCurrentThreadId* function can be reused as threads are created and destroyed.

In some circumstances, an object can be reentered by the same thread, similar to the way in which a window procedure can be reentered. If a method of the object processes window messages, another call to a method might be dispatched. You can easily avoid this problem by not processing window messages during a method call. An object might also be reentered if a method makes an outgoing call and the outgoing method then calls back into the object, perhaps via a mechanism such as connection points. (For more on connection points, see Chapter 8.) COM+ does not prevent these types of reentrancy; it guarantees only that the calls will not execute concurrently.

An STA's message-based method invocation mechanism is used even when the client and component are separated by a network. Figure 4-2 shows how the STA model works. Each number indicates a separate thread of execution. In the first thread, the client calls the proxy, which in turn calls the channel. (The COM+ channel is basically a wrapper around the RPC marshaling infrastructure.) Then a second thread is created to block while sending the data across the network using an RPC. Meanwhile, the first thread sits in a message loop waiting for incoming calls and other window messages. This message loop operates until the RPC call made by the second thread notifies it that a response has been received.

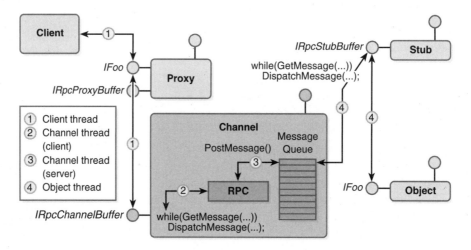

Figure 4-2.
The inner workings of the STA model.

Across the network, a server-side thread takes the received data packet and posts a message containing the client request to the message queue of the hidden window. Another message loop is then needed to take messages from the queue and dispatch them back to the channel's internal window procedure, which in turn calls the stub using the object's thread. Finally, the stub unpacks the parameters and calls the desired method in the object. The process of packing parameters for transmission is called *marshaling* and is basically repeated in reverse order once the method has finished executing. (For more on marshaling and the *IRpcProxyBuffer*, *IRpcChannelBuffer*, and *IRpcStubBuffer* interfaces, see Chapter 15.)

Note that four threads—two on the client side and two on the component side—are required to make the STA model work. An internal optimization of the STA model is possible when the client and the component both execute on the same machine. In such cases, COM+ automatically uses only two threads—one in the client process and one in the component. In this case, the reentrancy requirements of the STA model are met using a system supplied callback function to the RPC transport that retrieves and dispatches window messages.

Message Filters

An executable component can implement the *IMessageFilter* interface in each STA to control aspects of the call delivery mechanism employed by COM+. Building a custom message filter allows an application that uses STAs to better integrate COM+ calls with UI-driven threads. You can use this technique to abort a lengthy method call if the user gets tired of waiting. Note that since message filters work only with the STA model, they do not offer a generic way to cancel method invocations. COM+ also supports a generic call cancellation facility for all apartment types; see Chapter 17 for details.

An application that supplies a custom message filter must provide COM+ with a pointer to its implementation of the *IMessageFilter* interface via the *CoRegisterMessageFilter* function, as shown here:

```
IMessageFilter* pMF = new CMessageFilter;
IMessageFilter* pOldMF;

CoRegisterMessageFilter(pMF, &pOldMF);
```

CoRegisterMessageFilter installs the new message filter and returns a pointer to the previous message filter, enabling the caller to restore the previous message filter (if any) at a later time. (Since COM+ provides a default message filter for STAs, it is unlikely that the pointer to the previous message filter will be NULL unless you have purposely passed a null pointer to the *CoRegisterMessageFilter* function.) The IDL definition of the *IMessageFilter* interface is shown on the following page.

```
interface IMessageFilter : IUnknown
{
    // Called in a component to notify it of an incoming
    // method call
    DWORD HandleInComingCall(
        [in] DWORD dwCallType,    // Type of incoming call
        [in] HTASK htaskCaller,   // HTASK of the calling task
        [in] DWORD dwTickCount,   // Elapsed time since call
                                  //   was made
        [in] LPINTERFACEINFO lpInterfaceInfo); // More info
                                               // (see below)

    // Called in a client to notify it that the component has
    // rejected or postponed a call
    DWORD RetryRejectedCall(
        [in] HTASK htaskCallee,   // Server task handle
        [in] DWORD dwTickCount,   // Elapsed tick count
        [in] DWORD dwRejectType); // Returned rejected message

    // Called in a client when a window message is received
    // while a method call is pending
    DWORD MessagePending(
        [in] HTASK htaskCallee,   // Called application's
                                  //   task handle
        [in] DWORD dwTickCount,   // Elapsed tick count
        [in] DWORD dwPendingType); // Call type
}
```

An object's implementation of the *IMessageFilter::HandleInComingCall* method is called by COM+ when an incoming method invocation is received, giving the apartment the opportunity to accept, reject, or postpone the call. The first parameter of the *HandleInComingCall* method specifies the nature of the call made by the client; it can be one of the following values:

```
// Call types used by IMessageFilter::HandleInComingCall
typedef enum tagCALLTYPE
{
    CALLTYPE_TOPLEVEL = 1,   // Top-level call -- no outgoing call
    CALLTYPE_NESTED   = 2,   // Callback on behalf of previous
                             //   outgoing call -- should
                             //   always handle
    CALLTYPE_ASYNC    = 3,   // Async call -- cannot be rejected
    CALLTYPE_TOPLEVEL_CALLPENDING = 4,  // New top-level call
                                        //   with a new logical
                                        //   thread ID
    CALLTYPE_ASYNC_CALLPENDING   = 5    // Async call -- cannot
                                        //   be rejected
} CALLTYPE;
```

The *CALLTYPE_NESTED* flag indicates that a reentrant call is being made while the apartment is involved in executing some other method on behalf of the same client; the *CALLTYPE_TOPLEVEL* flag indicates that no other active calls are pending in the apartment. The fourth parameter of the *IMessageFilter:: HandleInComingCall* method provides a pointer to an *INTERFACEINFO* structure, shown below. The *INTERFACEINFO* structure tells the message filter which object is receiving a call, the IID of the interface implemented by that object, and the method number in the interface.

```
// Additional interface information about the incoming call
typedef struct tagINTERFACEINFO
{
    IUnknown    *pUnk;      // The pointer to the object
    IID         iid;        // Interface id
    WORD        wMethod;    // Interface method
} INTERFACEINFO, *LPINTERFACEINFO;
```

Based on the information provided, the message filter's implementation of the *IMessageFilter::HandleInComingCall* method can return one of the three values shown in the enumeration shown below. Basically, the method should return *SERVERCALL_ISHANDLED* if it wants to accept the call, *SERVERCALL_ REJECTED* if it cannot process the request, or *SERVERCALL_RETRYLATER* if the object cannot handle the request currently but might be able to later.

```
// Values returned by IMessageFilter::HandleInComingCall and
// passed to the IMessageFilter::RetryRejectedCall method on
// the client
typedef enum tagSERVERCALL
{
    SERVERCALL_ISHANDLED    = 0, // Process the call
    SERVERCALL_REJECTED     = 1, // Reject the call
    SERVERCALL_RETRYLATER   = 2  // Tell the caller to try
                                 //    back later
} SERVERCALL;
```

If a message filter rejects or postpones a call by returning the value *SERVERCALL_REJECTED* or *SERVERCALL_RETRYLATER* from the *IMessageFilter::HandleInComingCall* method, the system immediately calls the *IMessageFilter::RetryRejectedCall* method on the client's implementation of the *IMessageFilter* interface. The third parameter of the *RetryRejectedCall* method indicates the value returned by the object's message filter from the *HandleInComingCall* method; this is either *SERVERCALL_REJECTED* or *SERVERCALL_RETRYLATER*.

Typically, a client application silently retries calls that have failed with the *SERVERCALL_RETRYLATER* flag. If, after a reasonable period of time, the call still does not go through, it is reasonable to inform the user and cancel the request. The COM+ channel uses the value returned from the *IMessageFilter:: RetryRejectedCall* method to determine what action to take. A value of *−1* indicates that the call should be canceled, causing the proxy to return the value *RPC_E_CALL_REJECTED* from the canceled method. This is the action that the default COM+ message filter takes. If the *RetryRejectedCall* method returns a value greater than *−1* but smaller than *100*, COM+ retries the call immediately. A value equal to or greater than *100* causes the system to wait the specified number of milliseconds and then retry the call.

The system calls the *IMessageFilter::MessagePending* method in client applications if a window message appears in the application's message queue while an outstanding method call is pending. The default message filter allows certain window messages (such as WM_PAINT) to be dispatched while a call is pending. This avoids freezing the UI and giving the impression that the application has crashed. Input messages, such as messages originating from the mouse and keyboard, are generally discarded so the user does not begin another operation while the call is pending. The third parameter of the *MessagePending* method can specify one of the following values to indicate whether the pending call is a top-level or nested call.

```
// Pending type indicates the level of nesting
typedef enum tagPENDINGTYPE
{
    PENDINGTYPE_TOPLEVEL = 1, // Top-level call
    PENDINGTYPE_NESTED   = 2  // Nested call
} PENDINGTYPE;
```

The *IMessageFilter::MessagePending* method should return one of the values shown in the following *PENDINGMSG* enumeration. Returning the value *PENDINGMSG_CANCELCALL* cancels the outstanding method call, causing the outstanding method call to fail with the value *RPC_E_CALL_CANCELLED*. *PENDINGMSG_WAITDEFPROCESS* defers processing the message until the outstanding method call completes. *PENDINGMSG_WAITNOPROCESS* discards the message and waits for the pending method to return. Note that the client apartment's message filter can display the standard busy dialog box to the user by calling the *OleUIBusy* function. A sample implementation of the *IMessageFilter* interface is available on the companion CD in the Samples\ Apartments\Message Filters folder.

```
// Return values of MessagePending
typedef enum tagPENDINGMSG
{
    PENDINGMSG_CANCELCALL = 0,        // Cancel the outgoing call
    PENDINGMSG_WAITNOPROCESS = 1,     // Wait for the return and
                                      //   don't dispatch the message
    PENDINGMSG_WAITDEFPROCESS = 2     // Wait and dispatch the message
} PENDINGMSG;
```

Multithreaded Apartments

A thread enters the MTA model by calling *CoInitializeEx(NULL, COINIT_ MULTITHREADED)*, as shown in the code fragment below. Because only one MTA is ever created in a process, only the first thread to call the *CoInitializeEx* function using the *COINIT_MULTITHREADED* flag creates the MTA. Every subsequent thread that calls the *CoInitializeEx* function using this flag joins the existing MTA.[4]

```
// Enter the MTA.
CoInitializeEx(NULL, COINIT_MULTITHREADED);
```

Threads running in the MTA do not need to retrieve or dispatch window messages because COM+ does not use messages to deliver method calls on objects running in the MTA. Since method calls are made directly through a v-table, COM+ does not impose any synchronization on objects running in the MTA. Therefore, these objects must provide their own synchronization using critical sections, events, mutexes, semaphores, or other mechanisms as dictated by their synchronization requirements.

Multiple clients can concurrently execute an object's methods from different threads, and thus threads of an MTA cannot use TLS or have any other thread affinity whatsoever. An object running in the MTA receives calls through a pool of COM+-allocated threads[5] belonging to the object's process. The system creates these threads at run time and reuses them as appropriate. Since the system automatically spawns threads as necessary to enable concurrent access to the component, you should avoid calling the Win32 *CreateThread* function.

---

4. Some documentation incorrectly states that only the initial thread must call *CoInitializeEx* with the *COINIT_MULTITHREADED* flag, and that all other threads implicitly join the MTA. This technique might work in some cases, but it is not considered legal COM+ code.

5. Actually, the MTA uses threads from the thread pool created and maintained by the RPC runtime libraries.

In fact, calling *CreateThread* to enable concurrency in a component is strongly discouraged because in most cases this will interfere with the system's threading pooling algorithm. A utility such as Process Viewer (pview.exe), included with Visual C++, can be useful for dynamically spying on the threads created by COM+.

Marshaling Interface Pointers Between Apartments

As you know, client applications bind threads to apartments by calling the *CoInitializeEx* function. Any objects instantiated by those threads become members of the apartment to which the thread belongs. The client can call the *CreateThread* function to spawn additional threads, and each thread that wants to access COM+ objects must declare its apartment type by calling *CoInitializeEx*. The following code fragment shows how a thread in the client process creates an STA and instantiates a coclass:

```
void __stdcall ThreadRoutine(void)
{
    CoInitializeEx(NULL, COINIT_APARTMENTTHREADED);

    IUnknown* pUnknown;
    HRESULT hr = CoCreateInstance(CLSID_InsideCOM, NULL,
        CLSCTX_INPROC_SERVER, IID_IUnknown, (void**)&pUnknown);

    pUnknown->Release();
    CoUninitialize();
}
```

The *IUnknown* pointer returned by the *CoCreateInstance* call in the preceding code can be used only in this apartment. For example, if this pointer were passed through a global variable to the thread of another apartment and then used to call a method, an *RPC_E_WRONG_THREAD* error could result. This error is returned by the interface proxy if the client attempts to use an interface pointer that was not marshaled for use in a different apartment.

Remember that interface pointers in COM+ are apartment-relative—that is, they cannot be used by a thread in another apartment unless special precautions are taken. If COM+ were to allow the sharing of raw interface pointers, it would have no way of guaranteeing the synchronization required by the different apartment models because the object could be called directly from other apartments on other threads. Instead, the system provides the *CoMarshalInterThreadInterfaceInStream* and *CoGetInterfaceAndReleaseStream* functions to enable the marshaling of an interface pointer from one apartment to another. *CoMarshalInterThreadInterfaceInStream* marshals the apartment-neutral representation of an interface pointer into a stream object; its declaration is as follows.

```
WINOLEAPI CoMarshalInterThreadInterfaceInStream(IN REFIID riid,
    IN LPUNKNOWN pUnk, OUT LPSTREAM *ppStm);
```

Let's say that the thread of an STA—let's call it STA1—wants to pass an interface pointer to the thread of another STA, which we'll call STA2. STA1 first calls *CoMarshalInterThreadInterfaceInStream* to obtain an apartment-neutral interface representation stored in a stream object. The first parameter of *CoMarshalInterThreadInterfaceInStream* is the IID of the interface that is being marshaled, and the second parameter is a pointer to the object that implements that interface. The resultant *IStream* pointer returned in the third parameter can then be stored in a global variable accessible to STA2. STA2 passes this *IStream* pointer to the *CoGetInterfaceAndReleaseStream* function to unmarshal the stream and obtain an apartment-relative interface pointer to a proxy that is appropriate for use in STA2. Any calls made by the STA2 thread to the object in STA1 are now made through the proxy that was loaded in STA2 when the interface pointer was unmarshaled, as illustrated in Figure 4-3. The declaration of the *CoGetInterfaceAndReleaseStream* function is shown below:

```
WINOLEAPI CoGetInterfaceAndReleaseStream(IN LPSTREAM pStm,
    IN REFIID iid, OUT LPVOID FAR* ppv);
```

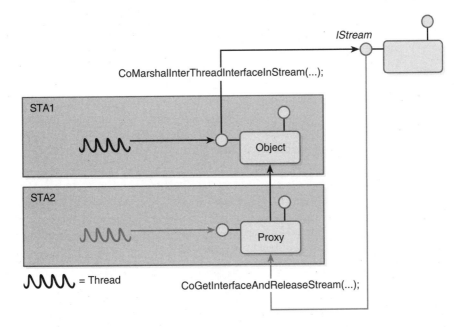

Figure 4-3.
The thread of one STA passing an interface pointer to another STA.

As shown in the following client-side code, the thread in STA1 instantiates a COM+ object and then calls *CoMarshalInterThreadInterfaceInStream* (shown in boldface) to marshal that interface pointer into an apartment-neutral representation. The resultant *IStream* pointer is then passed as an argument to a newly spawned thread. STA1 can now continue to use its interface pointer, and when it finishes working, it can release the pointer without danger. Notice that the *IStream* pointer is not released in this code; it is released by the receiving thread.

```
// STA1

IMyInterface* pMyInterface;
hr = CoCreateInstance(CLSID_MyCOMClass, NULL,
    CLSCTX_LOCAL_SERVER, IID_IMyInterface,
    (void**)&pMyInterface);

// Marshal interface pointer to stream.
IStream* pStream;
hr = CoMarshalInterThreadInterfaceInStream(IID_IMyInterface,
    pMyInterface, &pStream);

// Spawn new thread;
// pass pStream to new thread.
DWORD threadId;
CreateThread(NULL, 0, (LPTHREAD_START_ROUTINE)ThreadRoutine,
    pStream, 0, &threadId);

// Do other work...

pMyInterface->Release();
```

The new thread begins execution at the *ThreadRoutine* function. Its only argument is the *IStream* pointer containing the marshaled interface pointer to the object it wants to call, as shown in the following code. This code first creates a new STA, STA2, by calling *CoInitializeEx*, and then it unmarshals the stream object by calling *CoGetInterfaceAndReleaseStream* (shown in boldface). This has the effect of returning an apartment-relative interface pointer usable by STA2 and automatically releasing the stream. When it finishes using the interface pointer, STA2 must release it. Any method calls invoked on the interface pointer returned by *CoGetInterfaceAndReleaseStream* are marshaled back to the actual object in STA1 by the proxy loaded in STA2.

```
void __stdcall ThreadRoutine(IStream* pStream)
{
    // Create STA2.
    hr = CoInitializeEx(NULL, COINIT_APARTMENTTHREADED);

    // Unmarshal interface pointer from stream.
    IMyInterface* pMyInterface;
    hr = CoGetInterfaceAndReleaseStream(pStream,
        IID_IMyInterface, (void**)&pMyInterface);
    // Do work with pMyInterface...

    pMyInterface->Release();

    CoUninitialize();
}
```

Their long and sophisticated-sounding names notwithstanding, *CoMarshal-InterThreadInterfaceInStream* and *CoGetInterfaceAndReleaseStream* are basically wrapper functions for *CoMarshalInterface* and *CoUnmarshalInterface*. Interestingly, the *CoMarshalInterThreadInterfaceInStream* function calls *CoMarshalInterface* with the *MSHCTX_INPROC* flag. This flag was added to *CoMarshalInterface*[6] to indicate that the unmarshaling will be performed in another apartment of the same process. The following pseudocode shows the internals of *CoMarshalInterThreadInterfaceInStream* and *CoGetInterfaceAnd-ReleaseStream*:

```
HRESULT MyMarshalInterThreadInterfaceInStream(REFIID riid,
    IUnknown* pUnknown, IStream** pStream)
{
    CreateStreamOnHGlobal(NULL, TRUE, pStream);
    return CoMarshalInterface(*pStream, riid, pUnknown,
        MSHCTX_INPROC, NULL, MSHLFLAGS_NORMAL);
}

HRESULT MyGetInterfaceAndReleaseStream(IStream* pStream,
    REFIID riid, void** ppv)
{
    HRESULT hr = CoUnmarshalInterface(pStream, riid, ppv);
    pStream->Release();
    return hr;
}
```

---

6. *CoMarshalInterface* is discussed further in Chapter 15.

Passing Interface Pointers Between Threads in the MTA

As shown in Figure 4-4, interface pointers can be passed directly between threads running in the MTA; they do not need to be marshaled using the *CoMarshalInterThreadInterfaceInStream* and *CoGetInterfaceAndReleaseStream* functions. Of course, any attempt to pass an interface pointer from an MTA to an STA thread must be marshaled using the *CoMarshalInterThreadInterface-InStream* and *CoGetInterfaceAndReleaseStream* functions. In addition, message filters implementing the *IMessageFilter* interface cannot be used in the MTA model.

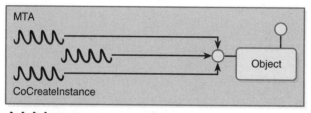

Figure 4-4.
Interface pointers passed directly between threads in an MTA.

How to Choose a Threading Model

Which threading model is right for you? Generally speaking, threads that interact directly with the user interface should use the STA model, while components that run without a significant user interface usually do best with the MTA model. Remember that in the STA model, window message queues are used to invoke methods in COM+ objects. Since any application that displays a window already has a message loop, the STA model is a natural fit. You can also use a combination of STAs, an NA, and an MTA in a single process when you need various threading models for different purposes in the same application. The following table compares the features of STAs, MTAs, and NAs.

If you are designing a new component without a significant user interface, the MTA model might seem like the obvious choice. This model is faster because the system does not need to synchronize calls into free-threaded objects. When you use the MTA model, however, the object must implement its own synchronization or fall prey to the thread synchronization problems discussed earlier.

Feature	STA	MTA	NA
Synchronization provided by COM+	Yes	No	No
Can have multiple threads executing in one apartment	No	Yes	Yes
Must marshal interface pointers between threads of different apartments	Yes	Yes	Yes
Must marshal interface pointers between threads in the same apartment	Not applicable; an STA has only one thread.	No	Not applicable; the NA has no resident threads.
Uses window message queues	Yes	No	Depends. Yes if an STA thread is executing in the NA; no if it is executing on an MTA thread.
Must call *CoInitializeEx* in every thread that uses COM+ services	Yes	Yes	Not applicable; there are only STA threads and MTA threads.
In-process calls are always invoked on the caller's thread	No	No (unless the object aggregates the Free-Threaded Marshaler).	Yes
Can use TLS	Yes	No	No

If you don't feel like dealing with thread synchronization issues, you can have the system do the work for you by selecting the STA model. In this model, COM+ synchronizes access to a component at the method level—in other words, it ensures that two different threads cannot call into an STA concurrently. You can simulate this behavior in an MTA by using a Win32 critical section, as shown in the following code. However, instead of building locks around entire methods as the STA does, a component that supports the MTA model normally uses locks only around small portions of the critical code within a method, resulting in improved concurrency.

```
class CMyClass
{
public:
    CMyClass::CMyClass()
    {
        // Create the critical section.
        InitializeCriticalSection(&m_cs);
    }

    CMyClass::~CMyClass()
    {
        // Before exiting, free the critical section.
        DeleteCriticalSection(&m_cs);
    }

    HRESULT __stdcall CMyClass::MyMethod(int MyParameter)
    {
        // Verify that no other method in the object is
        // being called.
        EnterCriticalSection(&m_cs);

        // Write your code here...

        // Leave the critical section, enabling another method
        // to execute.
        LeaveCriticalSection(&m_cs);
        return S_OK;
    }

    HRESULT __stdcall CMyClass::MyOtherMethod(int MyParameter)
    {
        EnterCriticalSection(&m_cs);

        // Write your code here...

        LeaveCriticalSection(&m_cs);
        return S_OK;
    }

private:
    // The critical section data structure
    CRITICAL_SECTION m_cs;
};
```

Threading Models for In-Process Components

In-process components work differently than executable components in that they do not call *CoInitializeEx* on start-up because their client thread will already have initialized COM+ by the time they are loaded. Instead, in-process components declare their supported threading model using registry settings. In the component's CLSID\InprocServer32 registry key, the *ThreadingModel* named value can be set to *Apartment*, *Neutral*, *Free*, or *Both* to indicate support for the various threading models; the table below translates these names into modern STA, NA, and MTA terminology.

ThreadingModel Values	Description
Not present	Single-threaded legacy component that runs only in the main STA
Apartment	STA
Neutral	NA
Free	MTA
Both	Supports the STA, NA, and MTA models

If no *ThreadingModel* value is specified, the in-process component is assumed to be a thread-oblivious legacy component. It is legal for different coclasses provided by a single in-process component to have different *ThreadingModel* values—in other words, the *ThreadingModel* value is set on a per-CLSID basis, not a per-DLL basis. The *RegisterServer* function we used in Chapter 2 to perform component self-registration can be used to set the *ThreadingModel* value in the registry. The last parameter of this function should contain one of the four strings from the preceding table. For example, the following statement registers a coclass, and the last parameter (shown in boldface) specifies that it supports the STA model:

```
RegisterServer("component.dll", CLSID_InsideCOM,
    "Inside COM+ Component", "Component.InsideCOM",
    "Component.InsideCOM.1", "Apartment");
```

If you are using the alternative table-driven version of the registration code (*RegisterServerEx*), you should add an extra entry for the *ThreadingModel* value, as shown in boldface in the following code.

```
const REG_DATA g_regData[] = {
    { "CLSID\\{10000002-0000-0000-0000-000000000001}", 0,
        "Inside COM+ Component" },
    { "CLSID\\{10000002-0000-0000-0000-000000000001}\\"
        "InprocServer32", 0, (const char*)-1 },
    { "CLSID\\{10000002-0000-0000-0000-000000000001}\\"
        "InprocServer32", "ThreadingModel", "Apartment" },
    { "CLSID\\{10000002-0000-0000-0000-000000000001}\\ProgID",
        0, "Component.InsideCOM.1" },
    { "CLSID\\{10000002-0000-0000-0000-000000000001}\\"
        "VersionIndependentProgID", 0,
        "Component.InsideCOM" },
    { "Component.InsideCOM", 0,
        "Inside COM+ Component" },
    { "Component.InsideCOM\\CLSID", 0,
        "{10000002-0000-0000-0000-000000000001}" },
    { "Component.InsideCOM\\CurVer", 0,
        "Component.InsideCOM.1" },
    { "Component.InsideCOM.1", 0,
        "Inside COM+ Component" },
    { "Component.InsideCOM.1\\CLSID", 0,
        "{10000002-0000-0000-0000-000000000001}" },
    { 0, 0, 0 }
};
```

Apartment Interactions

In this section, we'll look at how COM+ is able to support interoperability among all possible combinations of components, even when those components use different threading models. To recapitulate, here are the basic principles through which components create apartments and declare their supported threading model:

- Threads create or enter apartments that will be used to house objects or their proxies by calling *CoInitializeEx* with the *COINIT_APARTMENTTHREADED* (STA) or *COINIT_MULTITHREADED* (MTA) flag.

- In-process components declare the threading model(s) they support with one of the following registry entries: *Apartment* (STA), *Neutral* (NA), *Free* (MTA), or *Both* (STA, NA, and MTA).

The interaction of clients and components is relatively straightforward when both parties use the same threading models. When a client instantiates an object, COM+ compares the threading models supported by the client and the object. In the ideal case in which the two parties support the same threading model, COM+ allows direct calls from the client to the object; this yields the best performance for a given model. Obviously, executable components and in-process components running in a surrogate require marshaling code for use during cross-process or remote method calls. If both parties do not support the same threading models, however, COM+ must interpose itself between the client and the object—even if everything is running in the same process—to ensure that none of the threading rules for each party's apartment type is violated. It does this with a proxy/stub pair: the client makes calls through a proxy, which uses COM+ to deliver method calls to the stub; the stub in turn calls the actual object. As part of the marshaling process, a thread switch from the caller's thread to a thread in the object's apartment occurs.

Imagine that a client thread running in an MTA invokes an in-process component supporting the STA model. COM+ cannot allow the client's calls to proceed directly to the STA-based in-process object because concurrent access might occur. In such cases, when the interface pointer of the object is marshaled back to the client, COM+ loads the proxy/stub pair and provides the client with a pointer to the proxy. For this reason, even in-process components must provide marshaling code (usually in the form of a proxy/stub DLL) for any custom interfaces they implement if they are to support interoperability among apartment types.

As you've learned, in-process objects that do not have a *ThreadingModel* value in the registry are considered legacy components written prior to the advent of apartments in COM+. Such objects expect that the client will have only a single thread of execution, from which the object will be created and accessed. To ensure that these components continue to operate correctly, COM+ deals with thread-oblivious objects by creating them in the main STA of the client process, regardless of which thread instantiates the coclass. The main STA is a special designation awarded to the first STA created in a process. Calls from all other apartments, be they STAs, an NA, or an MTA, are marshaled to the thread belonging to the main STA; only then can a call be executed. Such calls are received by the proxy of one apartment and sent to the stub in the main STA via interapartment marshaling before being delivered to the object.

Compared with direct calls, interapartment marshaling is slow; therefore you should rewrite legacy in-process components to support the STA model. Another partial solution to the performance problem is to access legacy in-process components from the main STA only. The thread of the main STA can access the legacy component directly, thereby avoiding the interapartment marshaling performance penalty. Figure 4-5 shows a legacy component being called by two STA threads—one is the main STA, so it can access the object directly, while the auxiliary STA thread must be content to access the object through a proxy.

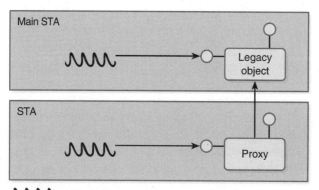

= Thread

Figure 4-5.
Two STA threads accessing an in-process object that does not have a
ThreadingModel *value specified.*

If you have no alternative but to use legacy in-process components, you should create the main STA in the main thread of the client process because once the main STA terminates, all in-process objects created there are destroyed. If the client carelessly spawns several threads, each of which calls *CoInitializeEx* with the *COINIT_APARTMENTTHREADED* flag, without first explicitly creating the main STA, one of those threads will randomly become the main STA through which all calls to legacy in-process objects will be marshaled.

The danger here is that the thread running the main STA might terminate at some point, taking with it all the objects created there. Another difficulty arises when an MTA-based client that does not have an STA instantiates a coclass from an in-process component that supports the STA model. In such cases, COM+ automatically creates the main STA by spawning a new thread and calling *CoInitializeEx(NULL, COINIT_APARTMENTTHREADED)* in that thread. The object is then created in the newly created host STA, and the interface pointer is marshaled back to the client thread in the MTA. Note that the term *host STA* describes an STA created automatically by the system; the main STA and the host STA might be one and the same when COM+ creates the first STA in a process.

Objects That Support the MTA Model

In-process objects that support the MTA model (*ThreadingModel = Free*) implement their own synchronization and are designed for use from an MTA only. MTA-based client threads that instantiate an object can use the object directly; this yields superior performance compared with the STA model. Initially, it might seem that any object supporting the MTA model can also be run safely in an STA. After all, the idea is to protect STA-based objects from concurrent access, and that is obviously not a concern for objects that support the MTA. Unfortunately, things get a bit more complicated. Imagine that a client thread belonging to an STA instantiates an object supporting the MTA model. One or more STAs present no threat to an object that supports the MTA because it manages its own synchronization. However, even in this deceptively simple case, the system must still perform thread synchronization.

This time, it is not the component but the client that needs protection. Although the component has declared its thread independence, the client has not. Pure clients and components are a rare phenomenon; it is much more common for clients and components to have a two-way conversation using connection points or some other private callback interface. In such cases, an MTA object might feel justified in calling the client back from any thread at any time. In effect, a component supporting the MTA model declares, "You can call me from any thread, so I can call you right back from any other thread." The hapless client, which created the object from an STA, is totally unprepared for this turn of events (pun intended). The possibility of multiple concurrent calls into an STA violates STA rules and would probably result in errors. For this reason, even when an STA-based client calls an object designed for MTA access, COM+ creates the object in the MTA and marshals all calls into and out of it.

Figure 4-6 shows how an in-process object designed for use from an MTA is created in the MTA even if it is instantiated by an STA-based thread. The result is that MTA-based threads can call directly into the object, while the STA-based thread that instantiated the object must make its calls via a proxy. Perhaps you are wondering how COM+ can create the object in an MTA if the client instantiates the object from an STA-based thread. If no MTA exists, COM+ first creates one by calling *CoInitializeEx(NULL, COINIT_MULTITHREADED)*. However, if the MTA already exists in the client process when the MTA-supporting object is instantiated, COM+ creates the object there. All calls to and from the object are marshaled from the MTA back to the STA-based client thread.

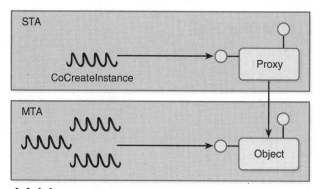

Figure 4-6.
When an STA-based thread instantiates an object designed for execution in the MTA, COM+ creates the MTA if necessary and instantiates the object there.

Objects That Support All Apartment Models

If even an in-process object designed for MTA access incurs the overhead of interapartment marshaling when accessed by an STA-based client thread, what's a conscientious developer to do? Well, to avoid the wrath of COM+, an in-process component can declare that it supports all apartment models (*Threading-Model = Both*). (The term *Both* is an anachronism that dates back to the time when only two threading models were available.) COM+ permits this type of object to be instantiated directly in an STA, the NA, or the MTA, resulting in a big performance advantage over MTA-only components called from an STA. Like MTA-only objects, an object that supports all the apartment models must provide its own synchronization because it can be accessed concurrently by multiple client threads.

In return for the privilege of being instantiated directly in any apartment, an in-process component supporting all three threading models must not make direct calls back to a client on any thread. Instead, it can only call the client back on the thread that received the interface pointer to the callback object. So the implicit promise made by every object supporting the three apartment models to all clients is: "You can call me from any thread, but I will call you back only on the one thread that received the interface pointer to the callback object." This is a component that would make any developer proud.

Although a coclass can support all the apartment types, at run time each object is still instantiated in an STA, the NA, or the MTA—not all three. If an object marked *ThreadingModel = Both* is instantiated by an STA thread, it belongs to that STA and all calls by the threads of other apartments must still be marshaled, as shown in Figure 4-7. Another option is to instantiate the object in the MTA, enabling all threads of the MTA to access the object directly but requiring that STAs access the object through a proxy. Finally, if an object marked *ThreadingModel = Both* is instantiated by an object in the NA, the new object will also be created in the NA.

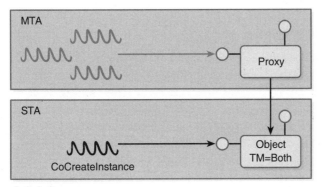

Figure 4-7.
Calls to an in-process object in a different apartment, even one registered with ThreadingModel = Both, *must still be marshaled.*

In-process objects that support the three threading models (*Threading-Model = Both*) never know whether they'll be created in an STA, the NA, or the MTA. However, it might be useful for the object to determine which threading model is in operation at run time. You can use the *isMTA* function, shown in the following code, to obtain this information. The *isMTA* function returns *true* if it is called from an MTA thread, *false* if the code is running in an STA thread. Note that although a coclass registered as *ThreadingModel = Both* can be instantiated in the NA, it is always executed on either an STA or MTA thread, depending on the threading model of the calling thread.

```
bool isMTA()
{
    HRESULT hr = CoInitializeEx(NULL, COINIT_MULTITHREADED);
    if(hr == RPC_E_CHANGED_MODE)
        return false;
    else
        CoUninitialize();
    return true;
}
```

It is also interesting to note that proxy/stub DLLs generated by the MIDL compiler support the three apartment models and therefore register themselves using the *Both* value for *ThreadingModel*. This is done because proxies must always be instantiated in the apartment of the creator so that calls can be made directly. If the proxy were created in another apartment, the caller would need a proxy to talk to the proxy!

The Free-Threaded Marshaler

In-process objects declared as *ThreadingModel = Both* are designed to be instantiated in any type of apartment; at run time, they are always instantiated in the apartment of the creator. This guarantees that the creating thread, as well as any other threads in the creating thread's apartment, can make direct calls to the object without having to go through a proxy/stub mechanism. Unfortunately, in order for the threads of other apartments in the process to call the object, the marshaling infrastructure must still be invoked.

Since in-process objects declared as *ThreadingModel = Both* are designed to handle concurrent access by multiple clients, it might seem that the client need not marshal the object's interface pointers between apartments. For example, if an object that supports all threading models is instantiated by an MTA thread, the object is created in the MTA. This means that all threads in the MTA can access the object directly. The client, however, must follow the threading rules of COM+ and always marshal interface pointers between the threads of different apartments. So any STA threads in the process still need to have the object's interface pointers marshaled for use in their apartment. The STA threads will then access the object via a proxy even though the object itself is perfectly capable of accepting the direct STA call with no danger to the STA thread. In this example, the need for client threads to remain independent of an object's internal threading model comes into conflict with the developer's desire to achieve the best performance.

The *free-threaded marshaler* (FTM) is an optimization technique designed for just such occasions. The FTM enables an in-process object to pass a direct pointer into any client apartment. When an object uses the FTM, all client threads, regardless of whether they are STA or MTA threads, call the object directly instead of through a proxy. Figure 4-8 shows an STA thread (STA1) that instantiates an in-process object that supports all the threading models. STA1 calls *CoMarshalInterThreadInterfaceInStream* to marshal the interface pointer to another STA thread (STA2). STA2 then calls the *CoGetInterfaceAnd-ReleaseStream* function to obtain an apartment-relative interface pointer for use in calling the object.

Normally, STA2 now has a pointer to a proxy that marshals calls to the thread of STA1 before the object is called. However, if the object in question uses the FTM, STA2 receives a direct pointer to the object from the *CoGet-InterfaceAndReleaseStream* function. Any threads running in the MTA also have direct access to the object. In this example, the decision to have STA1 instantiate the object is an arbitrary one. A thread belonging to any apartment in the process could instantiate the object; the result is nearly identical: all in-process calls are direct regardless of the calling thread's apartment type. The only difference is the apartment in which the object is actually created. But this is immaterial if all client calls can be made directly, irrespective of their apartment.

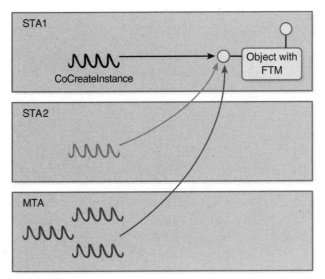

 = Thread

Figure 4-8.
An object that uses the FTM allows threads in different apartments but in the same process to access the object directly.

Notice that the situation shown in Figure 4-8 is fundamentally illegal: STA1, which is legally permitted to have only one thread executing its objects, now has multiple threads from STA2 and the MTA making direct calls to the object. In the pursuit of improved performance, the FTM enables us to break the threading rules of COM+. To use the FTM safely, you must completely understand the COM+ threading models as well as all the situations from which your object might be called. It is easy to crash the process through careless use of the FTM.

How the FTM Works

The FTM works by providing an implementation of the *IMarshal*[7] interface that the object exposes as its own via aggregation, as shown in Figure 4-9. When a client thread marshals an interface pointer using *CoMarshalInterThreadInterfaceIn-Stream*, the system queries the object for the *IMarshal* interface. If the object aggregates the FTM, the FTM's implementation of the *IMarshal* interface is returned. The FTM's implementation of *IMarshal* first checks to see what type of marshaling is taking place.

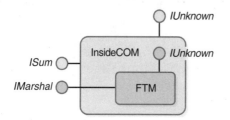

Figure 4-9.
The InsideCOM *object aggregating the FTM.*

If marshaling takes place between apartments or contexts[8] of a single process (defined by the marshal context flags *MSHCTX_INPROC* or *MSHCTX_CROSSCTX*, passed to *CoMarshalInterface*), the FTM simply copies the object's actual interface pointer into the marshaling stream. When a different client thread in another apartment later unmarshals the interface pointer by calling *CoGet-InterfaceAndReleaseStream*, instead of receiving a pointer to an interface proxy,

---

7. *IMarshal* is the custom marshaling interface defined by COM+; it is covered in detail in Chapter 15.

8. Contexts are a construct used primarily to distinguish between configured COM+ components that require different runtime services. They are covered later in this chapter.

the FTM simply retrieves the interface pointer to the real object that was placed in the stream. The second client thread can now make direct calls to the object regardless of the fact that it is running in a different apartment.

If the marshaling context is not *MSHCTX_INPROC* or *MSHCTX_CROSSCTX*, this indicates that marshaling is taking place between processes or possibly even between computers, so the FTM delegates the marshaling work to the standard marshaler obtained by calling *CoGetStandardMarshal*. The standard marshaler loads the appropriate interface proxy and stub[9] and returns a pointer to the proxy object to the client thread. The equivalent pseudocode for the main portion of the FTM is shown here:

```
HRESULT CFreeThreadedMarshaler::MarshalInterface(
    IStream* pStream, REFIID riid, void* pv,
    DWORD dwDestContext, void* pvDestContext, DWORD dwFlags)
{
    // If cross-apartment or cross-context marshaling,...
    if(dwDestContext == MSHCTX_INPROC ||
        dwDestContext == MSHCTX_CROSSCTX)
        // simply store the pointer directly in the stream.
        return pStream->Write(this, sizeof(this), 0);

    // Otherwise, delegate the work to the standard marshaler.
    IMarshal* pMarshal = 0;
    CoGetStandardMarshal(riid, pv, dwDestContext, pvDestContext,
        dwFlags, &pMarshal);
    HRESULT hr = pMarshal->MarshalInterface(pStream, riid, pv,
        dwDestContext, pvDestContext, dwFlags);
    pMarshal->Release();
    return hr;
}
```

Aggregating the FTM

The FTM is an object implemented as part of COM+; you instantiate it by calling the *CoCreateFreeThreadedMarshaler* function. The first parameter of the *CoCreateFreeThreadedMarshaler* function takes a pointer to the controlling object's *IUnknown* interface pointer, and the second parameter returns a pointer to the FTM's implementation of *IUnknown*. The FTM is usually aggregated in an object's constructor, as shown in boldface on the following page.

---

9. In Windows NT 4.0, the stubs of objects that aggregate the FTM are created in the apartment of the thread that marshaled the object out-of-process. This can cause an identity problem when the object is represented by multiple stubs in different apartments. In Windows 2000, the stubs of objects that aggregate the FTM are always created in the NA, which solves the identity problem. Since objects that aggregate the FTM are apartment-neutral, it doesn't matter which thread the call arrives on.

```
CInsideCOM::CInsideCOM() : m_cRef(1)
{
    InterlockedIncrement(&g_cComponents);
    CoCreateFreeThreadedMarshaler(this, &m_pFTM);
}
```

The pointer to the FTM returned by the *CoCreateFreeThreadedMarshaler* function is stored here as *m_pFTM*. This pointer is required in the object's implementation of *IUnknown::QueryInterface*, which must delegate any requests for the *IMarshal* interface to the FTM. COM+ automatically calls *Query-Interface* to request the *IMarshal* interface when an interface pointer on this object is marshaled or unmarshaled—for example, when the client calls *CoMarshal-InterThreadInterfaceInStream* or *CoGetInterfaceAndReleaseStream*. Most objects normally return *E_NOINTERFACE*, causing COM+ to default to its own standard marshaler. In this case, however, we intercept the request for the *IMarshal* interface and forward it to the FTM. The FTM then returns a pointer to its implementation of *IMarshal*, which has the special behavior discussed previously. Here's how the object's implementation of *IUnknown::QueryInterface* should look; the additions are shown in boldface:

```
HRESULT CInsideCOM::QueryInterface(REFIID riid, void** ppv)
{
    if(riid == IID_IUnknown)
        *ppv = (IUnknown*)this;
    else if(riid == IID_ISum)
        *ppv = (ISum*)this;
    else if(riid == IID_IMarshal)
        return m_pFTM->QueryInterface(riid, ppv);
    else
    {
        *ppv = NULL;
        return E_NOINTERFACE;
    }
    AddRef();
    return S_OK;
}
```

Before the object is destroyed, the FTM must be released as well. This call is typically made in the object's destructor, as shown here in boldface:

```
CInsideCOM::~CInsideCOM()
{
    InterlockedDecrement(&g_cComponents);
    m_pFTM->Release();
}
```

Problems with the FTM

Because the FTM enables threads in different apartments of a process to share direct interface pointers rather than use pointers to proxies—a calculated violation of the COM+ threading rules—an object that uses the FTM must abide by certain restrictions to ensure that the application doesn't crash:

■ An object that uses the FTM cannot hold direct interface pointers to an object that does not aggregate the FTM as part of its state. Regular objects are not as "apartment-agile" as objects that use the FTM and thus cannot be called under the same conditions.

■ An object that uses the FTM cannot hold references to proxies to objects in other apartments. Proxies are sensitive to the threading model and can return the error code *RPC_E_WRONG_THREAD* if called from the wrong thread.

Imagine an in-process object (OBJ1) that supports all the threading models (*ThreadingModel = Both*), aggregates the FTM,[10] and holds a pointer to some other object (OBJ2). This is a recipe for disaster because objects that aggregate the FTM are not permitted to hold apartment-relative resources such as object references. If a client thread running in an STA (STA1) marshals an interface pointer to OBJ1 to another apartment (STA2), the FTM, as expected, sees to it that a direct interface pointer is received by STA2.

Here's the problem: if STA2 calls a method of OBJ1 and that method in turn calls a method of OBJ2, this breaks the threading semantics expected by OBJ2. Unless OBJ2 also happens to aggregate the FTM, it cannot be called directly from STA2 without first being marshaled for use in that apartment. Any attempt to do this would probably result in random program faults or, if OBJ2 were only a proxy in STA1 to an out-of-process object, the infamous *RPC_E_ WRONG_THREAD* error. Figure 4-10 shows that the threads of STA1 and STA2 can access OBJ1 directly, but only the thread of STA1 can access OBJ2.

---

10. Although the FTM is typically used by objects marked *ThreadingModel = Both*, this is in no way a requirement. The *ThreadingModel* setting basically determines only from which apartment your *DllGetClassObject* function is called.

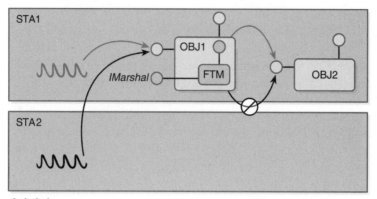

 = Thread

Figure 4-10.
COM+ threading rules are violated if STA2 calls OBJ1 and then OBJ1 calls OBJ2 directly.

The problem presented in Figure 4-10 is typical, but it is not easy to solve. One possible solution is to call *CoMarshalInterThreadInterfaceInStream* after you instantiate OBJ2. This call returns a stream-based, apartment-neutral representation of the OBJ2 interface pointer that can later be unmarshaled using the *CoGetInterfaceAndReleaseStream* function to obtain a valid interface pointer for use in STA2. The problem with this approach, however, is that *CoGetInterfaceAndReleaseStream* unmarshals the interface pointer and frees the stream object containing the apartment-neutral representation of the interface pointer, which means that the interface pointer can be unmarshaled from the stream only once! All future attempts to unmarshal the interface pointer from the stream will fail because it has already been released.

The Global Interface Table to the Rescue

The Global Interface Table (GIT) is a processwide holding table for interface pointers. Interface pointers can be checked into the GIT, where they are available to any apartment in the process. When a thread requests an interface pointer from the GIT, the interface pointer supplied is guaranteed to be usable by that thread. If necessary, the GIT automatically performs the necessary interapartment marshaling. Because the GIT permits an interface pointer to be unmarshaled as many times as desired, it can help solve problems that arise in objects that use the FTM.

The system-provided GIT is accessed through the *IGlobalInterfaceTable* interface, shown here in IDL notation:

```
interface IGlobalInterfaceTable : IUnknown
{
    // Voluntarily check an interface pointer into the GIT.
    HRESULT RegisterInterfaceInGlobal
    (
        [in]  IUnknown* pUnk,
        [in]  REFIID    riid,
        [out] DWORD*    pdwCookie
    );

    // Remove an interface pointer from the GIT.
    HRESULT RevokeInterfaceFromGlobal
    (
        [in] DWORD      dwCookie
    );

    // Unmarshal an interface pointer from the GIT to the
    // caller's apartment.
    HRESULT GetInterfaceFromGlobal
    (
        [in]  DWORD               dwCookie,
        [in]  REFIID              riid,
        [out, iid_is(riid)] void** ppv
    );
};
```

The GIT provides a perfectly adequate implementation of *IGlobalInterface-Table*, so there is really no need to implement this interface yourself. To instantiate the GIT, you call *CoCreateInstance* with the CLSID parameter set to *CLSID_StdGlobalInterfaceTable*, as shown in the following code. Only one instance of the GIT exists per process, so multiple calls to this function return the same instance. (This type of object is known as a singleton, and is discussed further in Chapter 13.)

```
IGlobalInterfaceTable* m_pGIT;
CoCreateInstance(CLSID_StdGlobalInterfaceTable, NULL,
    CLSCTX_INPROC_SERVER, IID_IGlobalInterfaceTable,
    (void**)&m_pGIT);
```

You check interface pointers into the GIT by calling the *IGlobalInterface-Table::RegisterInterfaceInGlobal* method. This method stores an apartment-neutral object reference in the GIT and returns a processwide cookie value that any apartment can use to obtain this interface pointer, as shown here:

```
DWORD m_cookie;
m_pGIT->RegisterInterfaceInGlobal(pMyInterface,
    IID_IMyInterface, &m_cookie);
```

You call the *IGlobalInterfaceTable::GetInterfaceFromGlobal* method in the thread of another apartment to retrieve an apartment-relative interface pointer from a cookie returned previously by *RegisterInterfaceInGlobal*, as shown in Figure 4-11. The interface pointer must also be released later, as shown in the code below, but any apartment in the process that wants to obtain an interface pointer can reuse the cookie. Thus, the GIT overcomes the limitation of the *CoMarshalInterThreadInterfaceInStream* and *CoGetInterfaceAndReleaseStream* pair, which allow unmarshaling to occur only once.

```
// Possibly called by a client thread in another apartment
m_pGIT->GetInterfaceFromGlobal(m_cookie, IID_IMyInterface,
    (void**)&pMyInterface);

// Use pMyInterface here.

pMyInterface->Release();
```

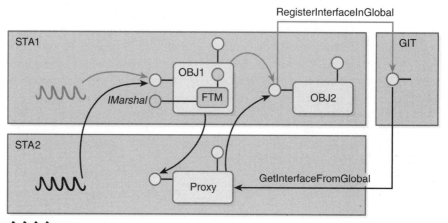

= Thread

Figure 4-11.
Using the GIT allows an object that aggregates the FTM to hold apartment-neutral object references across method invocations.

One problem with the GIT, however, is that each method invoked by the client must call *IGlobalInterfaceTable::GetInterfaceFromGlobal* to obtain the interface pointer and then *IUnknown::Release* to release it before returning to the client, because the object is not allowed to hold apartment-relative resources across method calls since it never knows which thread will call it. Unmarshaling interface pointers from the GIT can be a slow process, resulting in impaired performance if it is done often.

Before exiting, you should remove the interface pointer from the GIT by calling the *IGlobalInterfaceTable::RevokeInterfaceFromGlobal* method, as shown in the following code. There are no restrictions on which threads in the process can call this method. Remember to release the GIT object itself after you finish using it.

```
m_pGIT->RevokeInterfaceFromGlobal(m_cookie);

// Now release the GIT.
m_pGIT->Release();
```

Note that the application is responsible for coordinating access to the GIT in such a way that no thread in the process will call *RevokeInterfaceFromGlobal* while another is calling *GetInterfaceFromGlobal* for the same cookie; the GIT does not automatically provide this type of synchronization.

In addition to solving the problems commonly associated with objects that aggregate the FTM, the GIT offers an easier way for client applications to marshal interface pointers between the threads of different apartments. The GIT can replace calls to the *CoMarshalInterThreadInterfaceInStream* and *CoGetInterfaceAndReleaseStream* functions in components that do not make use of the FTM.

Neutral Apartments

Developers have toiled long and hard in their quest to build apartment-neutral objects that achieve the best performance for whatever threading model the client employs. As you've seen, marking your in-process coclasses *ThreadingModel = Both*, aggregating with the FTM, and using the GIT is a difficult way to achieve this goal. The NA was designed to make it easier for developers to create objects that can be called directly from any thread of any apartment in a process. Instead of breaking the rules, the NA offers a legal way to achieve the goals of objects that are marked *ThreadingModel = Both*, that aggregate the FTM, and that use the GIT. The advantages of using the NA model are so compelling that this is now the recommended model for nonvisual components in COM+.

Unlike an STA, which has only one thread, or the MTA, which can have multiple threads, the NA does not have any resident threads. Instead, STA threads (synchronized by window message queues) and MTA threads (unsynchronized) always make direct calls to objects running in the NA, as shown in Figure 4-12. In other words, objects instantiated in the NA are always executed on their caller's thread. Although the NA provides no built-in synchronization, when running on an STA thread, synchronization is provided via the modal message loop built into the STA model; when called from an MTA thread then no synchronization is provided. Also note that like the MTA, only one NA exists in a process. All objects marked *ThreadingModel = Neutral* that are instantiated in a process share the NA.

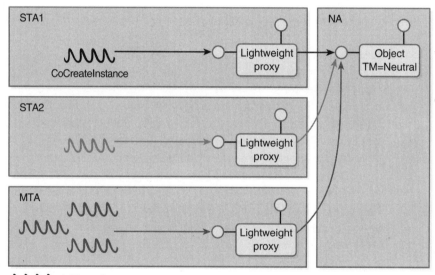

Figure 4-12.
Threads belonging to any apartment can call objects running in the NA without a thread switch.

The *CoInitializeEx* function is used only to bind threads to a particular threading model, either STA or MTA; it cannot be used to create the NA. The only way to instantiate an object in the NA is to call *CoGetClassObject* or *CoCreateInstance(Ex)* for a coclass that is marked in the registry as *ThreadingModel = Neutral*. As with objects running in the MTA, objects running in the NA are not permitted to have thread affinity because different threads might be used to execute their code. However, objects running in the NA are apartment-relative; that is, they belong to an apartment (the NA) and can hold apartment-relative resources such as object references as part of their state. In this way, they differ from objects that aggregate the FTM and must use the GIT to hold apartment-neutral object references across method invocations; objects running in the NA have no need for the FTM or the GIT.

This all sounds good, but perhaps you're wondering how to actually build objects that run in the NA. The first step in preparing an object for execution in the NA is to have the self-registration code set the *ThreadingModel* value to *Neutral*. The NA, like the other two COM+ apartment types, has some rules that govern the code you write. Fundamentally, objects designed to execute in the NA have similar implementation issues as objects that are marked *ThreadingModel = Both*. This means that the object must be prepared to deal with concurrent access by multiple threads. It also means that the object cannot use TLS or have any other form of thread affinity.

Contexts

Contexts are used in COM+ to keep track of the run-time properties (such as an object's transaction requirements) associated with configured components that take advantage of COM+ component services. Contexts and component services are covered in volume 2 of *Inside COM+*. Unconfigured components, the type covered by this book, normally run in the default context of every apartment unless they are created by a configured component, in which case they run in the context of the caller. When you consider the issue of contexts, the difference between objects that are marked *ThreadingModel = Both*, that aggregate the FTM, and that use the GIT and objects that run in the NA (*ThreadingModel = Neutral*) becomes clearer. Objects that aggregate the FTM can be called directly from any context of any apartment on any thread in the process. Objects that run in the NA can be called directly (without a thread switch) from any thread of any apartment in the process, but they are subject to the COM+ rules on apartments and contexts.

Comparing the Apartment Models

Although a variety of complex situations can arise when clients and in-process components of different threading models attempt to play together, COM+ handles all of these situations with aplomb. While the system enables all forms of interoperability using any combination of threading models between clients and components, a performance penalty results when the threading models of the two parties do not match. In most cases, you can circumvent this overhead with a little creative thinking. Imagine a situation in which an MTA thread accesses an object that supports only the STA model. In this case, COM+ has little choice but to introduce synchronization into the equation to protect the object. If you are aware that the coclass supports only the STA model, however, it makes sense for the client to create an STA from which to call this object. When an STA-based client calls an object that also supports the STA model, less overhead results.

How can the client determine which threading model is supported by a component? For in-process components, you need only examine the object's *ThreadingModel* registry entry to obtain this information. For executable components , you cannot determine programmatically what threading model is supported. It is generally less important for clients and executable components to use the same threading model because COM+ must load a proxy/stub pair for cross-process marshaling purposes in any case. The table below shows the variety of threading models that can be supported by clients and in-process components and describes how COM+ handles each unique situation; the first column on the left shows the creator's apartment type; the top row shows the *Threading-Model* value for the coclass that is being instantiated.

	Not Specified	Apartment	Free	Both	Neutral
Main STA	Created in the main STA. Direct access.	Created in the main STA. Direct access.	Created in the MTA. The MTA is created by the system if necessary. Proxy access.	Created in the main STA. Direct access.	Created in the NA. Lightweight proxy access —no thread switch.
STA	Created in the main STA. Proxy access.	Created in the caller's STA. Direct access.	Created in the MTA. The MTA is created by the system if necessary. Proxy access.	Created in the caller's STA. Direct access.	Created in the NA. Lightweight proxy access —no thread switch.

	Not Specified	Apartment	Free	Both	Neutral
MTA	Created in the main STA. The main STA is created by the system if necessary. Proxy access.	Created in a host STA. Proxy access.	Created in the MTA. Direct access.	Created in the MTA. Direct access.	Created in the NA. Lightweight proxy access —no thread switch.
Neutral (on an STA thread)	Created in the main STA. Proxy access.	Created in the caller's STA. Lightweight proxy access —no thread switch.	Created in the MTA. The MTA is created by the system if necessary. Proxy access.	Created in the NA. Direct access.	Created in the NA. Direct access.
Neutral (on an MTA thread)	Created in the main STA. Proxy access.	Created in a host STA. Proxy access.	Created in the MTA. Lightweight proxy access—no thread switch.	Created in the NA. Direct access.	Created in the NA. Direct access.

Writing Thread-Safe Components

Now that you have a thorough grounding in the theory behind the COM+ apartment models, let's translate this knowledge into something more concrete. This section presents the coding techniques required to make in-process components thread-safe; issues unique to creating thread-safe executable components are covered in Chapter 13. Several samples that demonstrate these techniques are available on the companion CD in the Samples\Apartments folder.

In-process objects that support the STA model (*ThreadingModel = Apartment*) expect to be accessed by the same client thread that created the object; this is similar to the way thread-oblivious components work. However, objects that support the STA model can be created in multiple STAs of the client process, while objects of a legacy component are always created in the main STA. Because multiple threads might access different objects in the component simultaneously, a component that supports the STA model must code its *DllGetClassObject* and *DllCanUnloadNow* entry points to allow for the possibility of concurrent access by multiple client STAs.

Making *DllGetClassObject* and *DllCanUnloadNow* Thread-Safe

Let's assume that two different STAs in the client process create instances of the same class simultaneously. It follows that the *DllGetClassObject* function might be called concurrently by two different threads. Fortunately, most typical implementations of *DllGetClassObject*, such as the one shown in the following code, are inherently thread-safe since a new class factory is instantiated for each caller and no global or static data is accessed. If your component is not a typical implementation, you must rewrite the *DllGetClassObject* function to be thread-safe.

```
HRESULT __stdcall DllGetClassObject(REFCLSID clsid,
    REFIID riid, void** ppv)
{
    if(clsid != CLSID_InsideCOM)
        return CLASS_E_CLASSNOTAVAILABLE;

    CFactory* pFactory = new CFactory;
    if(pFactory == NULL)
        return E_OUTOFMEMORY;

    HRESULT hr = pFactory->QueryInterface(riid, ppv);
    pFactory->Release();
    return hr;
}
```

DllCanUnloadNow can also be the root cause of a particularly nasty race condition. Since in-process components do not manage their own lifetimes, the *DllCanUnloadNow* function is designed to enable a client to determine whether the DLL can be unloaded. If *DllCanUnloadNow* returns *S_OK*, the DLL can be unloaded; if it returns *S_FALSE*, the DLL should not be unloaded at that point. The *DllCanUnloadNow* function is called by the *CoFreeUnusedLibraries* function, which is designed to be invoked by clients in their spare time. Here is a typical implementation of *DllCanUnloadNow*:

```
HRESULT __stdcall DllCanUnloadNow()
{
    if(g_cServerLocks == 0 && g_cComponents == 0)
        return S_OK;
    else
        return S_FALSE;
}
```

Now the client can call the *IUnknown::Release* method, as shown here, decrementing the usage counter to *0* and thus destroying the object (shown in boldface):

```
ULONG CInsideCOM::Release()
{
    if(--m_cRef != 0)
        return m_cRef;
    delete this;
    return 0;
}
```

As part of its cleanup duties, the destructor decrements the *g_cComponents* global variable, as shown in the code below. If this is the last object to be destroyed, *g_cComponents* is decremented to *0*. The object unwittingly enters a deadly race to exit the destructor before *DllCanUnloadNow* is called. If another thread in the client process calls *CoFreeUnusedLibraries*, *DllCanUnloadNow* returns *S_OK*, leading COM+ to believe that it can unload the DLL. However, unloading the DLL while the destructor's cleanup code is still executing results in a fault.

```
CInsideCOM::~CInsideCOM()
{
    g_cComponents--;
    // Pray nobody calls CoFreeUnusedLibraries now...
    // Some other cleanup code here...
}
```

To fix this race condition, Microsoft has modified the implementation of the *CoFreeUnusedLibraries* function. Instead of immediately unloading a DLL when *DllCanUnloadNow* returns *S_OK*, *CoFreeUnusedLibraries* waits about 10 minutes. If *CoFreeUnusedLibraries* is called again after 10 minutes and *DllCanUnloadNow* again returns *S_OK*, then and only then is the DLL unloaded. This heuristic approach, while not foolproof, works very well. After all, how many destructors do you know of that take 10 minutes to execute?

Apartments and Language Integration

While components written in C++ have the greatest flexibility and control over the apartment models in COM+, high-level programming languages such as Microsoft Visual Basic and Java have also been extended to support the evolving COM+ threading models. As you might expect, Visual Basic is currently the most limited environment in terms of threading models. Besides the legacy thread-oblivious model, Visual Basic provides support only for the COM+ multiple-STA model. The Microsoft Java VM, on the other hand, offers much better support for the apartment models. By default, components built in Java are marked *ThreadingModel = Both* in the registry, and the Microsoft Java VM automatically aggregates the FTM.

Threading Options for Visual Basic Components

Visual Basic was originally designed as a purely single-threaded environment. As threading has become pervasive in Windows, Visual Basic has been slow to adapt. Perhaps this is because Visual Basic has historically been so focused on creating GUI applications, so threading has seemed an unnecessary complexity. Now that Visual Basic has become a powerful component development tool, however, its limitations in the apartment department are more glaring. Recent versions of Visual Basic have allowed COM+ components to support either the legacy thread-oblivious model or the more modern STA model; currently, components built in Visual Basic cannot support the MTA or NA models. This means that serialization is a fact of life for COM+ components built in Visual Basic.

When multiple clients concurrently request the services of a single object, the requests are handled on a first-come, first-served basis. Recall that the STA model is synchronized with window messages, so method invocations are posted on the message queue and then processed sequentially. Actually, since objects implemented in Visual Basic run in the STA, serialization occurs at the apartment level. This means that if multiple objects are instantiated in one STA, a call to any one of the objects prevents all other objects in the apartment from executing concurrently.

One solution to this problem is to create an executable component and set its class *Instancing* property to *SingleUse*. This causes a new copy of the executable component to be launched for each new object instantiated. Since each object will run in a separate process, and therefore in a separate apartment, the objects can execute concurrently. Obviously, this is very inefficient use of system resources and does not scale well when a large number of objects are created. More typically, an in-process or executable component will set a class's *Instancing*[11] property to *MultiUse*. This provides the standard behavior in which each instance of a coclass is created in the parent process and concurrent access of an object by multiple clients results in serialization. The possible values for the *Instancing* property are shown in the following table:

---

11. In-process components cannot set the *Instancing* property to *SingleUse* because multiple copies of a DLL cannot be loaded in a client's address space.

Instancing Property Value	Description	In-Process Components	Executable Components
Private	The class cannot be accessed by external clients.	X	X
PublicNotCreatable	The class can be accessed by external clients, but only if first instantiated by the component.	X	X
SingleUse	Every instance of the class launches a new process.		X
GlobalSingleUse	Like *SingleUse*, but the methods and properties of the class are global.		X
MultiUse	Multiple instances of the class are created in one process.	X	X
GlobalMultiUse	Like *MultiUse*, but the methods and properties of the class are global.	X	X

Aside from the *SingleUse* option, the only way for a component written in Visual Basic to avoid the serialization imposed by the STA model is to make sure that each object runs in a separate STA. Since in-process components are not responsible for creating their own apartments, they have no control over the apartments in which their objects are instantiated. The best a Visual Basic–built in-process component can do is set its *ThreadingModel* value to *Apartment* and hope that the client will instantiate each object in a separate STA. Client applications written in Visual Basic instantiate all objects from one STA, but more sophisticated clients such as Microsoft Internet Explorer and Microsoft Internet Information Server have been optimized to run STA-based components in multiple STAs.

To specify the threading model used by an in-process component written in Visual Basic, choose Properties from the Project menu and then make your selection from the Project Properties dialog box, as shown in Figure 4-13. The default value is Apartment Threaded, and Visual Basic automatically sets the *ThreadingModel* registry value to *Apartment* for in-process components that support this model. Components that use the Single Threaded option are considered thread-oblivious, and therefore all objects exposed by such a component run in a single STA, regardless of how many STAs a client application might create. In-process components, especially ActiveX controls, that run in the legacy single-threaded mode do not work well with clients such as Internet Explorer or Visual Basic itself.

Another useful setting for in-process components created in Visual Basic is Unattended Execution. Selecting this check box tells Visual Basic that your component is a nonvisual component that should not display a user interface. Any statements such as *MsgBox* that attempt to display a UI are instead written to the Windows event log. This guarantees that the component will not freeze because of a modal dialog box that has been invoked by mistake.

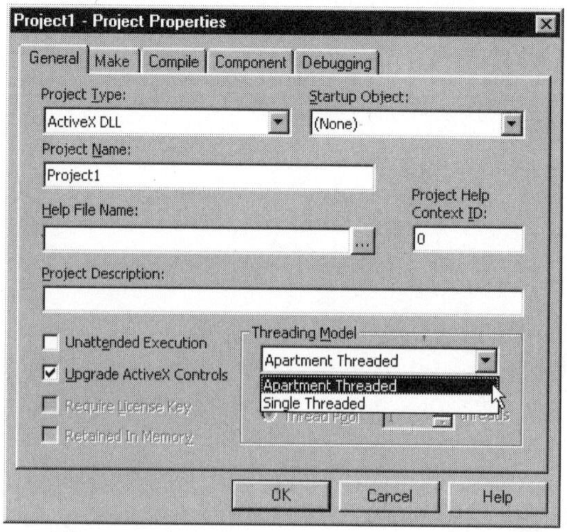

Figure 4-13.
The General tab of the Project Properties dialog box, showing the Threading Model drop-down list for an ActiveX DLL project.

Executable components built in Visual Basic have slightly different options available in the Project Properties dialog box, as shown in Figure 4-14. If you select the Thread Per Object option, each new object is created on a new thread (a new STA). The problem with the one-thread-per-object approach is that the component might get overwhelmed by a lot of clients connecting simultaneously. Another threading option available to executable components, Thread Pool, limits the component to a fixed maximum number of threads. This sets the maximum number of STAs that can be created to satisfy client demand. A thread pool size of one puts the component in the legacy single-threaded mode; a larger thread pool means that the component can support multiple STAs. The objects instantiated on behalf of clients are allocated based on a round-robin algorithm. As clients request objects, Visual Basic creates each object on the next thread in the pool. After the specified maximum number of STAs have been created, Visual Basic simply starts over with the first thread. (The round-robin algorithm does not attempt any form of load balancing. For example, if one STA contains few objects while other STAs are more heavily loaded, Visual Basic does not attempt to assign new objects to the underutilized STA. Instead, the algorithm simply proceeds sequentially.)

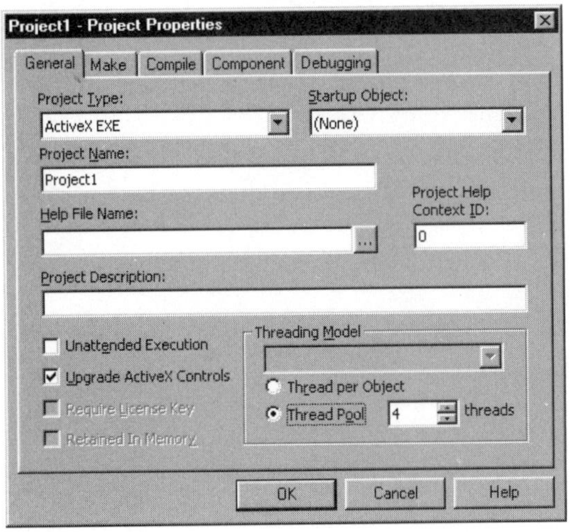

Figure 4-14.
The General tab of the Project Properties dialog box, showing the Threading Model options for an ActiveX EXE project.

The multiple-STA-based threading model offered by Visual Basic is vulnerable to certain problems relating to global data in application. Since the multiple-STA model enables multiple threads to execute code concurrently inside a single component, any access by the objects in that component to global variables can lead to data corruption unless some form of processwide synchronization was used to limit such access. Since Visual Basic does not currently offer any thread synchronization primitives, Microsoft has not taken this approach. Instead, a copy of any global variables is made for each apartment. For example, say that a project contains the following declaration:

```
Public X As Integer
```

If two apartments are currently running in the executable component, two independent integers are named X—one for each STA, as shown in Figure 4-15. Needless to say, this considerably alters the semantics of global variables and can be confusing. Perhaps they should be known as apartment variables rather than global variables! To help initialize the global variables for each new apartment, Visual Basic calls the *Sub Main* procedure (if one exists) once for each new apartment. To find out what thread is executing the code, you can check the Win32 thread identifier for the current thread using the *App.ThreadID* property.

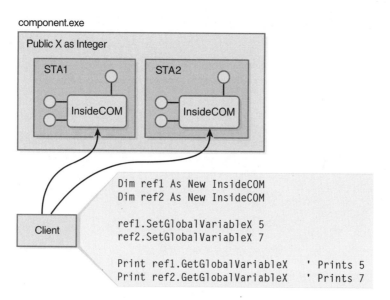

Figure 4-15.
Each apartment receives its own copy of global data.

Threading Options for Java Components

COM+ components built in Java are executed by the Microsoft Java VM (msjava.dll). In the registry, components built in Java have their *ThreadingModel* value set to *Both*. Thus, COM+ components built in Java implicitly support the STA and MTA models. In addition, the Microsoft Java VM automatically aggregates the FTM. In order to disable this functionality, you implement the *com.ms.com.NoAutoMarshaling* interface, an empty interface that simply acts as a flag to the VM.

Since most ordinary threads in a Java application do not have a message loop, by default the Microsoft Java VM does not instantiate STA model coclasses on the current thread. Instead, it instantiates STA-based classes on a special thread that it owns. This can be problematic because any Java-based calls to that object will result in a thread switch, which can hurt performance. By calling the *com.ms.com.ComLib.declareMessagePumpThread* method, an application can inform the Java VM that the thread will pump messages if necessary. The code fragment shown below calls *declareMessagePumpThread* and then enters a message loop using the *GetMessage*, *TranslateMessage*, and *DispatchMessage* method calls exposed by the *com.ms.win32.User32* class. This technique allows an STA-based Java thread to make direct calls to an STA-based object instantiated on the same thread without being marshaled to the Java VM's STA.

```
private Object comObject = null;

public void run()
{
    com.ms.com.ComLib.declareMessagePumpThread();
    comObject = new component.InsideCOM();
    com.ms.win32.MSG msg = new com.ms.win32.MSG();
    while (com.ms.win32.User32.GetMessage(msg, 0, 0, 0))
    {
        com.ms.win32.User32.TranslateMessage(msg);
        com.ms.win32.User32.DispatchMessage(msg);
    }
}
```

You can use the *com.ms.com.ComLib.threadStartMTA* method to explicitly create a new thread running the MTA. This method calls *CoInitializeEx* with the *COINIT_MULTITHREADED* flag. In contrast, the standard *java.lang.Thread.start* method always calls the older *CoInitialize* function to create an STA-based thread.

The Ten Threading Commandments

As you've seen, apartments are a far-reaching and important concept in COM+. Understanding how apartments work and how code running in different apartments interacts is important for every component developer. With single-threaded and multithreaded apartments, COM+ offers the best of both worlds: the performance and scalability of the multithreaded apartment, which has no extra overhead for thread switching or synchronization, and the ease of use of the single-threaded apartment, which guarantees that the state of your object will not be trampled by another thread. The following threading rules will keep you safe as you travel through the land of COM+:

1. Each STA can have only one thread.

2. Components that use STA threads must retrieve and dispatch window messages.

3. Always remember to marshal interface pointers between threads running in different apartments.

4. Call *CoInitializeEx* from every thread that uses COM+ services in order to declare the supported threading model.

5. Each object is associated with one and only one apartment, but an apartment can contain multiple objects.

6. The main STA is created by the first thread to call *CoInitialize* or *CoInitializeEx(NULL, COINIT_APARTMENTTHREADED)* within a process.

7. The main STA should remain alive until the process has completed all COM+ work with legacy components.

8. A process can have any number of STAs but at most one MTA and one NA.

9. Always define the *ThreadingModel* value in the registry for in-process objects.

10. Build nonvisual in-process objects that support the NA model (*ThreadingModel = Neutral*).

BASE FACILITIES

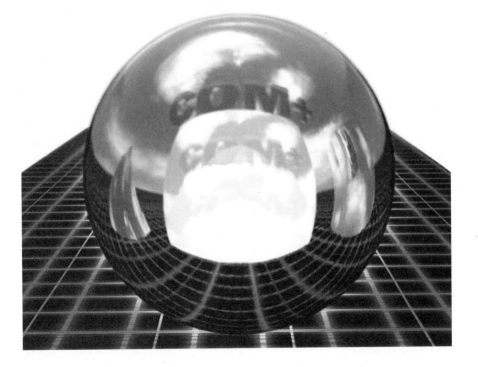

CHAPTER FIVE

Automation

Automation, the popular name for the *IDispatch* interface, was originally designed by the Visual Basic group at Microsoft. The Automation facility allows applications to expose their functionality for use by other programs. For example, full-featured applications such as Microsoft Word can expose a hierarchy of objects through Automation. Each object supports specific properties, methods, and events, enabling client programs to take advantage of the rich features offered in such applications by automating their use. An application that is normally driven by the end-user can thus be controlled by another program without any user involvement.[1]

Imagine developing a business application that performs standard data entry and reporting. It would be nice if the program could create graphs of the data as well. Rather than writing the code to produce the graphs, you can use the Automation objects exposed by Microsoft Excel to send the data to Excel and then ask Excel to print some fancy-looking graphs; the user never even has to see Excel on the screen. This type of integration is something that programmers only dreamed of a few years ago.

You might wonder why you need a specific facility such as Automation to expose the functionality of an application to other programs. After all, isn't that exactly the type of integration and reuse that was envisioned by the designers of COM+? Certainly an application can expose its capabilities via custom interfaces. But with this approach, each component typically defines its own set of custom interfaces. This is not a real problem for most applications, since each client program is typically designed to work with a certain set of interfaces germane to the data being processed. However, certain generic programs such as

---

1. Automation has supplanted Dynamic Data Exchange (DDE), an earlier message-based protocol sometimes used for the same purpose.

Microsoft Visual Basic and the Microsoft Java VM must deal with a wide variety of components, many of which might implement custom interfaces that did not even exist when those programs were written. In such cases, it can be difficult, if not impossible, for a client application to access a custom interface about which it has no prior knowledge.

So in addition to allowing applications to expose their functionality in a standard way, Automation was also developed to enable high-level languages such as Visual Basic to access components. Before the advent of type libraries, it was difficult for high-level environments to gain access to custom interfaces about which they had no information, whereas support for the standard *IDispatch* interface could be programmed into an environment by its developers. The environment could then work with any component that supported *IDispatch*, regardless of what services the component provided.

Over time, however, it became apparent that languages like Visual Basic could access components directly via custom interfaces as long as some information about the interfaces implemented by the component was available. This requirement was satisfied with the development of type libraries; type libraries have in turn diminished the importance of the *IDispatch* interface. It might seem obvious that a generic development environment such as Visual Basic can learn about an unknown custom interface by reading the component's type library. Visual Basic assumes that type information describing the custom interface is available, but this might not always be the case. Besides, the Automation facility was designed before type information was prevalent.

Automation has since been refashioned for use by interpreted scripting languages such as Visual Basic Scripting Edition (VBScript) and JScript that run in environments such as Microsoft Internet Explorer, Microsoft Internet Information Server (IIS), and the Microsoft Windows Scripting Host. These environments continue to rely only on Automation and have only limited support for type information. (Scripting languages can reference only the constants defined in a component's type library.) So implementing *IDispatch* remains a requirement for components to be accessed from these languages. Recently, the Automation facility was extended with the definition of the *IDispatchEx* interface, which supports more dynamic objects, whose properties and methods can change at run time. Thus Automation remains an important facility of COM+ that brings an extra level of interoperability to the system.

The *IDispatch* Interface

The *IDispatch* interface was defined so that a single, standard interface[2] could be used by all components wanting to expose their functionality to interested clients. This interface, and the marshaling code built for it, are now known as the Automation facility. You might wonder how a single interface can expose the functionality of any application. After all, how could the designers of *IDispatch* imagine every possible object, property, method, and event that an application might want to expose? The *IDispatch* interface would have to contain an infinite number of methods. In fact, the genius of *IDispatch* is that it was defined using just four methods—*GetTypeInfoCount*, *GetTypeInfo*, *GetIDsOfNames*, and *Invoke*. Here is the *IDispatch* interface defined in Interface Definition Language (IDL) notation:

```
interface IDispatch : IUnknown
{
    // Do you support type information?
    HRESULT GetTypeInfoCount(
        [out] UINT* pctinfo);

    // Gimme a pointer to your object's type information.
    HRESULT GetTypeInfo(
        [in] UINT iTInfo,
        [in] LCID lcid,
        [out] ITypeInfo** ppTInfo);

    // Gimme a DISPID of a method or parameters.
    HRESULT GetIDsOfNames(
        [in] REFIID riid,
        [in, size_is(cNames)] LPOLESTR* rgszNames,
        [in] UINT cNames,
        [in] LCID lcid,
        [out, size_is(cNames)] DISPID* rgDispId);
```

(continued)

---

2. *IDispatch* is called a standard interface because Microsoft defined it as part of COM+. The proxy-stub code needed to marshal the *IDispatch* interface is contained in the oleaut32.dll file; this is important because it means that applications implementing the *IDispatch* interface don't have to provide their own marshaling code.

```
// Call that method.
HRESULT Invoke(
    [in] DISPID dispIdMember,
    [in] REFIID riid,
    [in] LCID lcid,
    [in] WORD wFlags,
    [in, out] DISPPARAMS* pDispParams,
    [out] VARIANT* pVarResult,
    [out] EXCEPINFO* pExcepInfo,
    [out] UINT* puArgErr);
};
```

To better understand how the *IDispatch* interface works, it is helpful to think of it as a kind of surrogate interface. *IDispatch* doesn't offer any functionality of its own; it acts only as a standard conduit between a client and a component's functionality. The central *IDispatch* method is *IDispatch::Invoke*, which a client calls to invoke a particular method in the component. A unique number, called a dispatch identifier (DISPID), identifies each method. The *Invoke* method also takes a pointer to a DISPPARAMS structure containing the actual parameters to be passed to the method being called. Because the *IDispatch* marshaler knows how to marshal a pointer to the DISPPARAMS structure, it can marshal any Automation-based interface.

Automation Types

While *IDispatch* is not our favorite interface, we love the marshaler that Microsoft wrote for it. Usually called the type library marshaler because it performs marshaling based on the contents of a type library, this marshaler (contained in oleaut32.dll) can be used not only for *IDispatch*-based interfaces but also for custom interfaces that restrict themselves to Automation-compatible types.

To use the type library marshaler, you include the *oleautomation* attribute in the IDL file.[3] When you call *RegisterTypeLib* or *LoadTypeLibEx* to register a type library, the function checks the type library for the *oleautomation* attribute. If the flag is present, the ProxyStubClsid32 key in the registry is automatically set to point to the type library marshaler. This feature saves you from always having to build and register a proxy/stub DLL for any custom interfaces. Of course, because the Automation marshaler is general, it cannot match the performance of a standard proxy/stub DLL built from the code generated by

---

3. When compiling the IDL file, MIDL will insert the flag *TYPEFLAG_FOLEAUTOMATION* in the type library file for each interface that has the *oleautomation* attribute. This flag is recognized by the *RegisterTypeLib* and *LoadTypeLibEx* functions.

Microsoft IDL (MIDL). Nevertheless, in many situations the advantages of not having to build and register a proxy/stub DLL might outweigh the slight loss in performance from using the type library marshaler. (For more information about marshaling, see Chapters 14 and 15.)

The Automation-compatible types are described in the following table along with the equivalent native types in C++, Visual Basic, and Java. Most of the types are relatively self-explanatory; several, such as variants, safe arrays, BSTRs, and user-defined types, require special treatment and are described in detail in the sections that follow.

Automation-Compatible IDL Types	C++	Visual Basic	Java
boolean	Bool	Boolean	boolean
double	Double	Double	double
float	Float	Single	float
signed int	int/long	Long	int
signed short	Short	Integer	short
enum	Enum	Enum	com.ms.wfc.core.Enum
BSTR	BSTR	String	java.lang.String
CY	CY	Currency	long
DATE	DATE	Date	double
IDispatch*	IDispatch*	Object	java.lang.Object
IUnknown*	IUnknown*	IUnknown	com.ms.com.IUnknown
SAFEARRAY	SAFEARRAY	[] (A standard Visual Basic array)	com.ms.com.SafeArray
VARIANT	VARIANT	Variant	com.ms.com.Variant

Variants

All method parameters accessed via the *IDispatch* interface are dealt with as variants. A variant is defined by the VARIANT structure declared in the oaidl.idl system IDL file. The VARIANT structure, shown on the following page, is basically a giant union of all Automation-compatible types. Variants can contain strings, scalars, object references, or arrays. Each variant contains a VARTYPE member (defined as an *unsigned short* in wtypes.idl file) named *vt* that indicates the type of data currently stored by the variant. This member should be set to the correct *VT_* prefixed constant.[4]

```
struct tagVARIANT {
    union {
        struct __tagVariant {
            VARTYPE vt;
            WORD wReserved1;
            WORD wReserved2;
            WORD wReserved3;
            union {
                LONG lVal;                  // VT_I4
                BYTE bVal;                  // VT_UI1
                SHORT iVal;                 // VT_I2
                FLOAT fltVal;               // VT_R4
                DOUBLE dblVal;              // VT_R8
                VARIANT_BOOL boolVal;       // VT_BOOL
                SCODE scode;                // VT_ERROR
                CY cyVal;                   // VT_CY
                DATE date;                  // VT_DATE
                BSTR bstrVal;               // VT_BSTR
                IUnknown *punkVal;          // VT_UNKNOWN
                IDispatch *pdispVal;        // VT_DISPATCH
                SAFEARRAY *parray;          // VT_ARRAY
                BYTE *pbVal;                // VT_BYREF|VT_UI1
                SHORT *piVal;               // VT_BYREF|VT_I2
                LONG *plVal;                // VT_BYREF|VT_I4
                FLOAT *pfltVal;             // VT_BYREF|VT_R4
                DOUBLE *pdblVal;            // VT_BYREF|VT_R8
                VARIANT_BOOL *pboolVal;     // VT_BYREF|VT_BOOL
                SCODE *pscode;              // VT_BYREF|VT_ERROR
                CY *pcyVal;                 // VT_BYREF|VT_CY
                DATE *pdate;                // VT_BYREF|VT_DATE
                BSTR *pbstrVal;             // VT_BYREF|VT_BSTR
                IUnknown **ppunkVal;        // VT_BYREF|VT_UNKNOWN
                IDispatch **ppdispVal;      // VT_BYREF|VT_DISPATCH
                SAFEARRAY **pparray;        // VT_BYREF|VT_ARRAY
                VARIANT *pvarVal;           // VT_BYREF|VT_VARIANT
                PVOID byref;                // VT_BYREF
                CHAR cVal;                  // VT_I1
                USHORT uiVal;               // VT_UI2
                ULONG ulVal;                // VT_UI4
```

4. The correct *VT_* prefixed constant is listed in the comment to the right of the types in the VARIANT structure.

```
            INT intVal;                 // VT_INT
            UINT uintVal;               // VT_UINT
            DECIMAL *pdecVal;           // VT_BYREF|VT_DECIMAL
            CHAR *pcVal;                // VT_BYREF|VT_I1
            USHORT *puiVal;             // VT_BYREF|VT_UI2
            ULONG pulVal;               // VT_BYREF|VT_UI4
            INT *pintVal;               // VT_BYREF|VT_INT
            UINT *puintVal;             // VT_BYREF|VT_UINT
            struct __tagBRECORD {
                PVOID pvRecord;
                IRecordInfo* pRecInfo;
            }; __VARIANT_NAME_4;        // VT_RECORD
        } __VARIANT_NAME_3;
    } __VARIANT_NAME_2;
    DECIMAL decVal;
} __VARIANT_NAME_1;
};
```

Several helper functions make working with the VARIANT type easier; these are described in the table below. You can manipulate the VARIANT structure directly in C++, but you should use the helper functions instead because doing so ensures uniformity across applications that deal with variants. The most important and error-prone aspect of working with variants is the type conversion and coercion rules. Although a method of an *IDispatch*-based interface can be defined as expecting a string parameter, a client might choose to provide a numeric value instead. The Visual Basic statement *Form1.Caption = 123* illustrates this. Conversely, a client might pass a variant containing a string to a method expecting a floating-point value, as in the Visual Basic statement *Form1.Left = "132.4"*.

Function	Description
VariantChangeType(Ex)	Converts a variant from one type to another
VariantClear	Clears a variant
VariantCopy	Frees the destination variant and makes a copy of the source variant
VariantCopyInd	Frees the destination variant and makes a copy of the source variant, performing the necessary indirection if the source is specified to be *VT_BYREF*
VariantInit	Initializes a variant

The *VariantChangeType(Ex)* function is the primary function used to convert variants from one type to another. Typically, the implementation of the *IDispatch:: Invoke* method converts each variant parameter to the desired type using the *VariantChangeType(Ex)* function. If unsuccessful, *VariantChangeType(Ex)* returns the value *DISP_E_TYPEMISMATCH*; this error should be returned to the client application by the *Invoke* method. The code fragment below illustrates the use of the several variant helper functions, including *VariantChangeType*:

```
// Declare two variants.
VARIANT v1;
VARIANT v2;

// Initialize both of them.
VariantInit(&v1);
VariantInit(&v2);

// v1 = A long with the value of 5
v1.vt = VT_I4;
v1.lVal = 5;

// Convert v1 to a string and store the result in v2.
HRESULT hr = VariantChangeType(&v2, &v1, 0, VT_BSTR);
if(SUCCEEDED(hr))
    wprintf(L"%s\n", v2.bstrVal); // Displays 5

// Free the string in v2.
VariantClear(&v2);
```

BSTRs

Most programming languages have their own notion of what a string is and how to store one in memory. C++ stores strings as an array of ASCII or Unicode characters with a null terminator; Visual Basic stores strings as an array of ASCII characters and prefixes the string with a value indicating its length; Java stores strings as an array of Unicode characters with a null terminator. All COM+ API functions that accept string arguments require null-terminated Unicode strings. To enable components built in different languages to exchange strings, Microsoft defined a new type of string: the BASIC string (BSTR). A BSTR is basically a length-prefixed, null-terminated array of Unicode characters. In C++, you can treat a BSTR and an array of OLECHARs almost identically. But because the BSTR is prefixed by its length, it might contain embedded null characters. Figure 5-1 shows the in-memory representation of a BSTR containing the string "*Hello*":

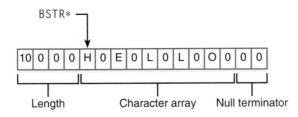

Figure 5-1.
The memory layout of a BSTR.

Because of the support built into the Visual Basic and Java virtual machines, BSTRs automatically map onto the native string formats of these languages. C++ developers, however, must use special helper functions that deal with BSTRs, as described in the table on the next page. The functions that create and delete BSTRs cache memory to improve the performance of those functions. For example, when a BSTR is freed, that memory is put into a cache. If the application later allocates another BSTR, it might get the free block from the cache. The code fragment below shows the use of several popular BSTR routines:

```
// Declare a BSTR.
BSTR b1;

// Allocate a new BSTR containing some text.
b1 = SysAllocString(L"Testing BSTRs");

// Display the BSTR.
wprintf(L"%s\n", b1);

// Display the number of bytes (2 bytes per ANSI character).
wprintf(L"%d bytes\n", SysStringByteLen(b1));

// Display the number of characters.
wprintf(L"%d characters\n", SysStringLen(b1));

// Free the BSTR.
SysFreeString(b1);
```

Function	Description
SysAllocString	Allocates a BSTR and copies a string into it
SysAllocStringByteLen	Takes an ANSI input string and returns a BSTR
SysAllocStringLen	Allocates a new BSTR, copies a specified number of characters into it, and then appends a null character
SysFreeString	Frees a BSTR
SysReAllocString	Allocates a new BSTR, copies the passed string into it, and then frees the old BSTR
SysReAllocStringLen	Creates a new BSTR containing a specified number of characters from an old BSTR, and then frees the old BSTR
SysStringByteLen	Returns the length (in bytes) of a BSTR
SysStringLen	Returns the length of a BSTR

Safe Arrays

The SAFEARRAY type is important because it makes array manipulation safer in high-level languages such as Visual Basic. Unlike standard vectors in C++, a SAFEARRAY contains information about the number of dimensions and the current array bounds. You can also use safe arrays to pass arrays in variant parameters used by *IDispatch*-based interfaces. The array descriptor that defines a safe array type is shown in Figure 5-2.

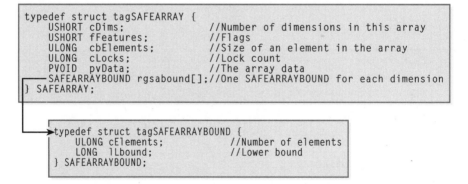

```
typedef struct tagSAFEARRAY {
    USHORT cDims;                    //Number of dimensions in this array
    USHORT fFeatures;                //Flags
    ULONG  cbElements;               //Size of an element in the array
    ULONG  cLocks;                   //Lock count
    PVOID  pvData;                   //The array data
    SAFEARRAYBOUND rgsabound[];      //One SAFEARRAYBOUND for each dimension
} SAFEARRAY;


typedef struct tagSAFEARRAYBOUND {
    ULONG cElements;                 //Number of elements
    LONG  lLbound;                   //Lower bound
} SAFEARRAYBOUND;
```

Figure 5-2.
The SAFEARRAY and SAFEARRAYBOUND structures.

A safe array can store a multidimensional array of data. In standard C++ notation, such an array might be defined as *long myArray[2][4]*. If defined in a safe array, this type of array would have two dimensions (*cDims*). For each dimension in a SAFEARRAY, a corresponding SAFEARRAYBOUND structure, shown in Figure 5-3 on page 215, is created and pointed to by the *rgsabound* member of the SAFEARRAY structure. Each SAFEARRAYBOUND defines the number of elements in that dimension and the starting index value of the dimension. In the sample array *long myArray[2][4]*, two SAFEARRAYBOUND structures are created, each with four elements (*cElements*) and a lower bound of *0* (*lLbound*).

While safe arrays are exposed as natural language-based arrays in Visual Basic, C++ developers must once again deal with special structures and helper functions when working with safe arrays. The safe array helper functions shown in the table below create, manipulate, and delete safe arrays in C++. *SafeArrayCreate(Ex)* and *SafeArrayDestroy* are the most basic. *SafeArrayCreateVector(Ex)* differs from *SafeArrayCreate(Ex)* in that it can be used only to create one-dimensional arrays.

Function	Description
SafeArrayAccessData	Increments the lock count of an array and returns a pointer to array data
SafeArrayAllocData	Allocates memory for a safe array based on a descriptor created with *SafeArrayAllocDescriptor*
SafeArrayAllocDescriptor(Ex)	Allocates memory for a safe array descriptor
SafeArrayCopy	Copies an existing array
SafeArrayCopyData	Copies a source array to a target array after releasing target resources
SafeArrayCreate(Ex)	Creates a new array descriptor
SafeArrayCreateVector(Ex)	Creates a one-dimensional array whose lower bound is always *0*
SafeArrayDestroy	Destroys an array descriptor
SafeArrayDestroyData	Frees memory used by the data elements in a safe array
SafeArrayDestroyDescriptor	Frees memory used by a safe array descriptor

(continued)

continued

Function	Description
SafeArrayGetDim	Returns the number of dimensions in an array
SafeArrayGetElement	Retrieves an element of an array
SafeArrayGetElemsize	Returns the size of an element
SafeArrayGetLBound	Retrieves the lower bound for a given dimension
SafeArrayGetUBound	Retrieves the upper bound for a given dimension
SafeArrayLock	Increments the lock count of an array
SafeArrayPtrOfIndex	Returns a pointer to an array element
SafeArrayPutElement	Assigns an element to an array
SafeArrayRedim	Resizes a safe array
SafeArrayUnaccessData	Frees a pointer to array data and decrements the lock count of the array
SafeArrayUnlock	Decrements the lock count of an array
SafeArraySetRecordInfo	Sets the *RecordInfo* stored in the given safe array
SafeArrayGetRecordInfo	Retrieves the *RecordInfo* of a safe array
SafeArraySetIID	Sets the GUID of the interface for the given safe array
SafeArrayGetIID	Returns the GUID of the interface for the given safe array
SafeArrayGetVartype	Returns the type stored in the given safe array

The code fragment below creates a two-dimensional safe array, with each dimension holding four *long* values:

```
// Create a SAFEARRAY of this type: long myArray[2][4];

SAFEARRAYBOUND pSab[2];
pSab[0].lLbound = 0;
pSab[0].cElements = 4;
pSab[1].lLbound = 0;
pSab[1].cElements = 4;

SAFEARRAY* pSa;
pSa = SafeArrayCreate(VT_I4, 2, pSab);
if(pSa == NULL)
    cout << "SafeArrayCreate failed" << endl;
```

You can use the *SafeArrayGetElement* and *SafeArrayPutElement* functions to read and write data in the array one value at a time. For example, the code fragment below assigns the value *3* to an element in the array using the *SafeArrayPutElement* function:

```
// long myArray[2][4];
// myArray[1][2] = 3; // leftmost dimension first (the standard way)

//     0   1   2   3
//    |---|---|---|---|
// 0  | x | x | x | x |
//    |---|---|---|---|
// 1  | x | x | 3 | x |
//    |---|---|---|---|

long index[2] = { 2, 1 }; // rightmost dimension first
long data = 3;
SafeArrayPutElement(pSa, index, &data);
```

The tricky part of the *SafeArrayPutElement* function is figuring out how to identify the desired element in the safe array. The second parameter of *SafeArrayPutElement* is a pointer to a vector of indexes for each dimension of the array. The rightmost (least significant) dimension is placed first in the vector *(index[0])*; the leftmost dimension is stored last *(index[pSa->cDims - 1])*. This is worth noting because it is exactly the opposite of how multidimensional arrays are accessed in C++. You can think of a two-dimensional array as a spreadsheet-style grid pattern, as shown in the code fragment above.

The obvious limitation of the *SafeArrayPutElement* and *SafeArrayGetElement* functions is that they manipulate only one value at a time. This can hurt performance when you do extensive work with safe arrays. As an alternative, you can call the *SafeArrayAccessData* and *SafeArrayUnaccessData* functions. *SafeArrayAccessData* locks the array in memory and returns a pointer to the data held by the safe array. This enables direct access to the data in the safe array. In the code fragment below, *SafeArrayAccessData* is called to obtain the array data. Then all the elements in the array are set directly via the pointer, after which *SafeArrayUnaccessData* is called to unlock the array. The *SafeArrayGetElement* function is then called to retrieve one element from the array to verify that the direct pointer access was successful. Finally the safe array is freed by calling the *SafeArrayDestroy* function.

```
// Lock the array get a pointer to its data.
long* pData;
SafeArrayAccessData(pSa, (void**)&pData);
```

(continued)

209

```
// Set or get any values in the array.
*pData = 4;
*(pData + 1) = 5;
*(pData + 2) = 6;
*(pData + 3) = 7;

*(pData + 4) = 8;
*(pData + 5) = 9;
*(pData + 6) = 10;
*(pData + 7) = 11;

// Unlock the array. (pData is no longer valid.)
SafeArrayUnaccessData(pSa);

// Now get one element by calling SafeArrayGetElement.
index[0] = 3;
index[1] = 1;
SafeArrayGetElement(pSa, index, &NewData);
cout << NewData << endl;      // Displays 11

// When finished, free the array.
SafeArrayDestroy(pSa);
```

When storing a safe array in a variant, you simply *OR* the variant type *(VARIANT.vt)* element with the *VT_ARRAY* flag, as shown below:

```
VARIANT v3;
VariantInit(&v3);

v1.vt = VT_I4|VT_ARRAY; // Array of 4 byte integers
v1.parray = pSa;
```

User-Defined Types

In the past, data structures could be passed to methods of v-table based interfaces, but only if those interfaces were marshaled by a proxy/stub DLL generated by the MIDL compiler. Interfaces that relied on type library marshaling, such as interfaces defined in Visual Basic or Java, could not accept structures as method arguments because the type library marshaler was not capable of handling these complex types. Since that time, the type library marshaler has been extended to support user-defined types (UDTs) and arrays of UDTs if they are passed using a safe array. To employ a UDT as a method argument, you define the structure in an IDL file, which is then compiled with MIDL to produce the type library. A sample UDT defined in IDL is shown on the next page; notice that the *typedef* IDL keyword is used to assign a GUID to the structure.

```
typedef [ uuid(10000099-0000-0000-0000-000000000001)]
    struct myDataType {
        int x;
        int y;
    } myDataType;
```

You can also pass UDTs as arguments to methods of a pure *IDispatch* interface using the variant type. A variant of the type *VT_RECORD* wraps a pointer to a *RecordInfo* object that contains the necessary information about the UDT. The system-provided *RecordInfo* object implements the *IRecordInfo* interface, as shown below in IDL notation:

```
interface IRecordInfo: IUnknown
{
    HRESULT RecordInit([out] PVOID pvNew);
    HRESULT RecordClear([in] PVOID pvExisting);
    HRESULT RecordCopy([in] PVOID pvExisting, [out] PVOID pvNew);
    HRESULT GetGuid([out] GUID* pguid);
    HRESULT GetName([out] BSTR* pbstrName);
    HRESULT GetSize([out] ULONG* pcbSize);
    HRESULT GetTypeInfo([out] ITypeInfo** ppTypeInfo);
    HRESULT GetField([in] PVOID pvData, [in] LPCOLESTR szFieldName,
        [out] VARIANT* pvarField);
    HRESULT GetFieldNoCopy([in] PVOID pvData, [in] LPCOLESTR szFieldName,
        [out] VARIANT* pvarField, [out] PVOID* ppvDataCArray);
    HRESULT PutField([in] ULONG wFlags, [in,out] PVOID pvData,
        [in] LPCOLESTR szFieldName, [in] VARIANT* pvarField);
    HRESULT PutFieldNoCopy([in] ULONG wFlags, [in,out] PVOID pvData,
        [in] LPCOLESTR szFieldName, [in] VARIANT* pvarField);
    HRESULT GetFieldNames([in,out] ULONG * pcNames,
        [out,size_is(*pcNames),length_is(*pcNames)] BSTR* rgBstrNames);
    BOOL IsMatchingType([in] IRecordInfo* pRecordInfo);
    PVOID RecordCreate();
    HRESULT RecordCreateCopy([in] PVOID pvSource, [out] PVOID* ppvDest);
    HRESULT RecordDestroy([in] PVOID pvRecord);
}
```

The *IRecordInfo* interface enables UDTs to be passed using variant types for *IDispatch*-based interfaces. At run time, a pointer to the system implementation of the *IRecordInfo* interface is obtained via a call to the *GetRecordInfoFromTypeInfo* or *GetRecordInfoFromGuids* function. The *GetRecordInfoFromTypeInfo* function retrieves the *RecordInfo* object for the UDT described in your type information. The code fragment on the following page loads the type library, gets the type information for the UDT, and then calls *GetRecordInfoFromTypeInfo*.

```
ITypeLib* pTypeLib = 0;
HRESULT hr = LoadTypeLibEx(L"component.exe", REGKIND_DEFAULT, &pTypeLib);

ITypeInfo* pTypeInfo = 0;
const GUID GUID_myDataType =
    {0x10000099,0x0000,0x0000,0x00,0x00,0x00,0x00,0x00,0x00,0x00,0x01};
hr = pTypeLib->GetTypeInfoOfGuid(GUID_myDataType, &pTypeInfo);
pTypeLib->Release();

IRecordInfo* pRecordInfo = 0;
hr = GetRecordInfoFromTypeInfo(pTypeInfo, &pRecordInfo);

pTypeInfo->Release();
pRecordInfo->Release();
```

Implementing *IDispatch*

The first step in any COM+ project is to define the interfaces in IDL. You use different IDL attributes depending on whether you are implementing a pure *IDispatch* interface or a dual interface. An interface based solely on *IDispatch* is called a *dispinterface*. The v-table of a dispinterface is identical to that of *IDispatch* itself. The methods and properties of the dispinterface are accessible only via the *IDispatch::Invoke* method. A dual interface is an *IDispatch*-based interface that also has v-table entries for the methods in the custom interface. This makes a dual interface accessible either via Automation or via the v-table.

Designing a Pure Dispinterface

You use the *dispinterface* statement shown here to design a pure *IDispatch*-based interface:

```
[ uuid(10000001-0000-0000-0000-000000000001) ]
dispinterface ISum
{
properties:
    [id(1)] int x;
    [id(2)] int y;

methods:
    [id(3)] int Sum(int x, int y);
};
```

The *dispinterface* statement is an alternative to the standard *interface* statement and has several interesting aspects. You do not need the *object* or the *oleautomation* attribute to indicate to MIDL that this interface uses only Automation-compatible types—this condition is obvious from the *dispinterface* statement. Notice that the *dispinterface* statement is not derived from *IUnknown* or *IDispatch*; *dispinterface* implicitly inherits the *IDispatch* interface.

The *Sum* method defined in the *dispinterface* statement returns an integer value rather than an *HRESULT*. Errors that occur during calls to methods in a dispinterface are returned by *IDispatch::Invoke*, thus freeing the method to return a real value. The method is assigned a unique number called a dispatch identifier, or DISPID. Notice that dispinterfaces can support properties as well as methods, while a regular interface supports only methods. This support is for the benefit of high-level languages, such as Visual Basic, which depend heavily on properties. Of course, all properties are actually implemented via the *IDispatch::Invoke* method.

Designing a Dual Interface

Using the *dispinterface* statement is not recommended because doing so restricts clients to using only the *IDispatch* interface to access an object. Instead of implementing a pure dispinterface, you can mark an object with the *dual* attribute. A coclass that sports a dual interface indicates that it allows clients to access its services via *IDispatch* or via direct access to its custom interface. Like other features of COM+, support for a dual interface sounds more complicated than it is. Figure 5-3 shows the v-table of a pure Automation-based component. The *IDispatch* interface is the only way to access the functionality of the object.

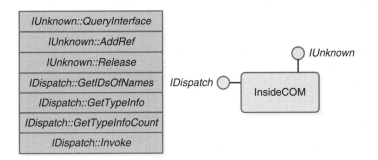

Figure 5-3.
The v-table of an object that implements a pure dispinterface.

With a dual interface, the v-table of the interface includes the *IDispatch* members plus any members of the custom interfaces supported by the object.

The object shown in Figure 5-4 supports the *ISum* custom interface in addition to *IDispatch*. The last entry in the object's v-table is the *Sum* method from the *ISum* interface. In this case, a client can choose whether to access the object via Automation or via the custom *ISum* interface.

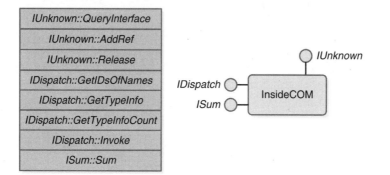

Figure 5-4.
An object that supports a dual interface, which includes a custom interface in addition to IDispatch.

Dual interfaces have been strongly hyped, but the advantages of supporting the *IDispatch* interface are limited. Since high-level environments such as Visual Basic and Microsoft Visual J++ can access custom interfaces directly, only scripting languages such as VBScript and JScript remain v-table-challenged; these scripting languages can access components only via the *IDispatch* interface. If you want developers working in a scripting language to access your component, *IDispatch* support is required.

Dual interfaces are one way to provide this functionality; by supporting a dual interface, you offer a choice to clients that need to access your component. Visual Basic, for example, always checks to see whether a component supports a dual interface. If it does, and if a type library describing the custom interface is available, Visual Basic uses the custom interface and completely bypasses Automation. If no type library is available or if the object supports only *IDispatch*, Visual Basic makes do with that interface.

One danger in using dual interfaces is that they force you to concentrate on issues relating to client access from a scripting language—not usually the primary market of a component. Focusing the design of an object on issues of client accessibility from scripting languages that don't have easy access to the *IUnknown::QueryInterface* method can lead you to develop an object that has only one interface with many methods. A one-interface-per-object design is not a good choice because you ignore the richness afforded by the *QueryInterface* method. Also, from a performance point of view, it can be quite limiting to restrict an interface to Automation-compatible types.

To get around the one-interface-per-object limitation, some developers have built hacks by which *QueryInterface*-style semantics can be built into a dispinterface or have suggested identity tricks that allow multiple *IDispatch* interfaces to be implemented by one object. However, none of these techniques has proved satisfactory in the long run. A better solution to the problems posed by dual interfaces is to simply not use them. Instead, you can use standard v-table interfaces and then design one additional *IDispatch*-based interface containing methods created specifically for use by scripting languages.[5] The Automation interface might even present a somewhat simplified view of the object's functionality to ease its use by scripts.

Regardless of which technique you choose, dual interfaces give clients a choice of how to access the services of a component, and they also ensure that the object is accessible to scripting languages such as VBScript. The IDL syntax required to indicate support for both *IDispatch* and a custom interface is shown here:

```
[ object, uuid(10000001-0000-0000-0000-000000000001),
  dual ]
interface ISum : IDispatch
{
    [id(1)] HRESULT Sum(int x, int y, [out, retval] int* retval);
}
```

Notice that in the IDL fragment, the syntax seems more standard. Now instead of deriving from *IUnknown*, the *ISum* interface derives from *IDispatch*, which is itself derived from *IUnknown*, so we still get the *QueryInterface*, *AddRef*, and *Release* methods added to the v-table. The interface header also includes the *dual* attribute to indicate a dual interface. Specifying a dual interface implies that the interface is Automation-compatible and that therefore, in the type library generated by MIDL, the interface has both the *TYPEFLAG_FDUAL* and *TYPEFLAG_FOLEAUTOMATION* flags set. When a component containing this type library calls *RegisterTypeLib*, this flag is detected and the HKEY_CLASSES_ROOT\Interface\{*YourIID*}\ProxyStubClsid32 registry entry is automatically set to the CLSID of the Automation marshaler (oleaut32.dll).

In the following example, we'll create a dual interface by implementing the four *IDispatch* methods. The class declaration for *CInsideCOM* after it has been modified to implement the *IDispatch* interface is shown on the following page.

---

5. For ease of implementation, the interface designed for scripting clients is usually built as a dual interface.

```
class CInsideCOM : public ISum
{
public:
    // IUnknown
    ULONG __stdcall AddRef();
    ULONG __stdcall Release();
    HRESULT __stdcall QueryInterface(REFIID iid, void** ppv);

    // IDispatch
    HRESULT __stdcall GetTypeInfoCount(UINT* pCountTypeInfo);
    HRESULT __stdcall GetTypeInfo(UINT iTypeInfo, LCID lcid,
        ITypeInfo** ppITypeInfo);
    HRESULT __stdcall GetIDsOfNames(REFIID riid,
        LPOLESTR* rgszNames, UINT cNames, LCID lcid,
        DISPID* rgDispId);
    HRESULT __stdcall Invoke(DISPID dispIdMember, REFIID riid,
        LCID lcid, WORD wFlags, DISPPARAMS* pDispParams,
        VARIANT* pVarResult, EXCEPINFO* pExcepInfo,
        UINT* puArgErr);

    // ISum
    HRESULT __stdcall Sum(int x, int y, int* retval);

    CInsideCOM() : m_cRef(1) { g_cComponents++; }
    ~CInsideCOM() { g_cComponents--; }
    bool Init(void);

private:
    ULONG m_cRef;
    ITypeInfo* m_pTypeInfo;
};
```

Notice that the class appears to derive only from *ISum* and not from *IDispatch*. In the component.h header file generated by MIDL, the *ISum* class has already been declared as inheriting from *IDispatch*, as shown in boldface in the following code fragment from component.h:

```
// Generated by MIDL in component.h
MIDL_INTERFACE("10000001-0000-0000-0000-000000000001")
ISum : public IDispatch
{
public:
    virtual /* [id] */ HRESULT STDMETHODCALLTYPE Sum(
        int x,
        int y,
        /* [retval][out] */ int __RPC_FAR *retval) = 0;

};
```

216

Implementation Techniques

You can implement the *IDispatch* interface in several ways. As with any other interface, you can implement *IDispatch* simply by writing the code for its four methods. This approach is quite difficult because of the complexity of the parameters that are passed to the *IDispatch::Invoke* method, the workhorse of the *IDispatch* interface. To simplify the process, Microsoft provides several helper functions, which are described in the table below.

These helper functions range from the primitive *DispGetParam* function, which simply helps to unpack VARIANT parameters from the DISPPARAMS array, to the *CreateStdDispatch* function, which in a single call provides a complete aggregatable implementation of the *IDispatch* interface. In between are the *DispInvoke* and *DispGetIDsOfNames* functions, both of which are trivial wrappers for the *ITypeInfo::Invoke* and *ITypeInfo::GetIDsOfNames* methods. You can use these functions to provide canned functionality for the *IDispatch::Invoke* and *IDispatch::GetIDsOfNames* methods.

IDispatch Helper Functions	Description
DispGetIDsOfNames	Automatic *ITypeInfo*-driven implementation of *IDispatch::GetIDsOfNames*.
DispGetParam	Retrieves a parameter from the DISPPARAMS structure, checking both named parameters and positional parameters, and coerces the parameter to the specified type. Helps implement the *IDispatch::Invoke* method.
DispInvoke	Automatic *ITypeInfo*-driven implementation of *IDispatch::Invoke*.
CreateStdDispatch	Creates an instance of the standard *ITypeInfo*-driven *IDispatch* implementation.
CreateDispTypeInfo	Constructs basic type information from an INTERFACEDATA description.

With this plethora of choices, it can be difficult to decide how to implement the *IDispatch* interface. If you're like us, you want to do the least amount of work to get a satisfactory implementation of *IDispatch* that will work with major client applications such as Visual Basic and scripting languages such as VBScript. The first determining factor is whether you intend to generate type information. The *CreateStdDispatch*, *DispInvoke*, and *DispGetIDsOfNames* helper functions all require type information in order to work their magic.

Of course, the easiest way to create type information is to run your IDL file through the MIDL compiler. Or you can call the *CreateDispTypeInfo* helper function to generate basic type information at run time. *CreateDispTypeInfo* requires that you fill out the INTERFACEDATA, METHODDATA, and PARAMDATA structures (shown in Figure 5-5) to describe every parameter of every method in the interface. Using MIDL to create type information is so easy, however, that the *CreateDispTypeInfo* function should only be used by specialized applications that require type information to be generated at run time.

```
typedef struct tagINTERFACEDATA {
    METHODDATA * cDims;    // Pointer to an array of METHODDATAs
    UINT         cMembers; // Count of members
} INTERFACEDATA, * LPINTERFACEDATA;

typedef struct tagMETHODDATA {
    OLECHAR   * szName;// Method name
    PARAMDATA * ppdata;// Pointer to an array of PARAMDATAs
    DISPID    dispid;  // Method ID
    UINT      iMeth;   // Method index
    CALLCONV  cc;      // Calling convention
    UINT      cArgs;   // Count of arguments
    WORD      wFlags;  // Same wFlags as on IDispatch::Invoke()
    VARTYPE   vtReturn;
} METHODDATA, * LPMETHODDATA;

typedef struct tagPARAMDATA {
    OLECHAR  * szName;  // Parameter name
    VARTYPE  vt;        // Parameter type
} PARAMDATA, * LPPARAMDATA;
```

Figure 5-5.
*The INTERFACEDATA, METHODDATA, and PARAMDATA
structures used by the* CreateDispTypeInfo *helper function.*

The *CreateStdDispatch* Function

The primary drawback to using *CreateStdDispatch* is that it supports only one national language. Even so, *CreateStdDispatch* is a good choice for components that are not hobbled by this restriction. To aggregate the standard dispatch object, you simply call the *CreateStdDispatch* function on startup, as shown in boldface in the following code:

```
HRESULT CInsideCOM::Init(void)
{
    ITypeLib* pTypeLib;
    if(FAILED(LoadRegTypeLib(LIBID_Component, 1, 0,
        LANG_NEUTRAL, &pTypeLib)))
        return E_FAIL;
```

```
HRESULT hr =
    pTypeLib->GetTypeInfoOfGuid(IID_ISum, &m_pTypeInfo);
pTypeLib->Release();
if(FAILED(hr))
    return hr;

return CreateStdDispatch(this, this, m_pTypeInfo,
    &m_pUnknownStdDisp);
}
```

When a client requests the *IDispatch* interface, you delegate the *Query-Interface* call to the dispatch object so the client application gets the standard dispatch object's *IDispatch* implementation, as shown in boldface in the code below. You should also release the standard dispatch object before destroying the *InsideCOM* object.

```
HRESULT CInsideCOM::QueryInterface(REFIID riid, void** ppv)
{
    if(riid == IID_IUnknown)
        *ppv = (IUnknown*)this;
    else if(riid == IID_ISum)
        *ppv = (ISum*)this;
    else if(riid == IID_IDispatch)
        return m_pUnknownStdDisp->
            QueryInterface(IID_IDispatch, ppv);
    else
    {
        *ppv = NULL;
        return E_NOINTERFACE;
    }
    AddRef();
    return S_OK;
}
```

The *IDispatch::GetTypeInfoCount* Method

If you opt for a slightly more hands-on approach to implementing the *IDispatch* interface, you'll probably decide to implement the four *IDispatch* methods yourself but delegate some of the more arduous work to COM+ helper functions. Here's how you do it. The *IDispatch::GetTypeInfoCount* function is called by the client to determine whether type information is available for the object. If the object provides type information, the integer pointed to by *pCountTypeInfo* should be set to *1*; otherwise, it should be set to *0*. Clients that want to determine whether to use early binding (which requires type information) or late binding when accessing the Automation component can call this function. A typical implementation of *GetTypeInfoCount* is shown on the next page.

```
HRESULT CInsideCOM::GetTypeInfoCount(UINT* pCountTypeInfo)
{
    *pCountTypeInfo = 1;
    return S_OK;
}
```

Implementing *IDispatch* using this approach requires type information. The component shown in the following code loads type information from the type library using the *LoadRegTypeLib* function. This function is invoked from the custom *Init* method called during object instantiation. Next the *ITypeLib:: GetTypeInfoOfGuid* method is called to retrieve the type information for the *ISum* interface. A pointer to this type information is stored in the member variable *m_pTypeInfo* for use by other methods of the *IDispatch* interface.

```
bool CInsideCOM::Init(void)
{
    // Load the type library.
    ITypeLib* pTypeLib;
    if(FAILED(LoadRegTypeLib(LIBID_Component, 1, 0,
        LANG_NEUTRAL, &pTypeLib)))
        return false;

    // Get the type info.
    HRESULT hr =
        pTypeLib->GetTypeInfoOfGuid(IID_ISum, &m_pTypeInfo);
    if(FAILED(hr))
        return false;

    // Release the type library.
    pTypeLib->Release();
    return true;
}
```

The *IDispatch::GetTypeInfo* Method

After determining that type information is available using the *GetTypeInfoCount* method, a client might call *IDispatch::GetTypeInfo*, as shown in the following code. This method returns a pointer to the type information provided by the object, which can then be used to get the type information for an interface. The first parameter of the *GetTypeInfo* method, *iTypeInfo*, specifies the index number of the interface for which the client is requesting type information. Since this is an *IDispatch* interface, only the index number *0*, which refers to *IDispatch*, is valid. If the client passes any other value, we simply return *DISP_E_BADINDEX*. The second parameter of *GetTypeInfo*, *lcid*, is a locale identifier. This parameter is important because some objects might want to return different type information based on the user's national language. Since our object does not support localized member names, this parameter is ignored. Before returning, *AddRef* must be called on the type information pointer in accordance with the reference counting rules in COM+.

```
HRESULT CInsideCOM::GetTypeInfo(UINT iTypeInfo, LCID lcid,
    ITypeInfo** ppITypeInfo)
{
    *ppITypeInfo = NULL;
    if(iTypeInfo != 0)
        return DISP_E_BADINDEX;
    m_pTypeInfo->AddRef();
    *ppITypeInfo = m_pTypeInfo;
    return S_OK;
}
```

The *IDispatch::GetIDsOfNames* Method

IDispatch::GetIDsOfNames is called by a client that has a method name (*Sum*, for example) and wants to get the DISPID associated with that method to call it via *IDispatch::Invoke*. The first parameter, *riid*, is unused and must be *IID_NULL*. The second parameter, *rgszNames*, points to an array of names for which the client is requesting DISPIDs. The third parameter, *cNames*, tells the component the number of names in the array, and the fourth parameter, *lcid*, specifies the locale identifier of the caller. Only one method or property can be mapped to a DISPID at a time. The other members of the array can be used to map the parameter names of methods into DISPIDs. This technique can be useful for sophisticated clients such as Visual Basic that allow developers to specify values for named arguments when calling methods.

The last parameter, *rgDispId*, is a pointer to an array in which the client wants to receive the requested DISPIDs. The implementation of *IDispatch:: GetIDsOfNames* shown in the following code simply delegates to the *DispGet-IDsOfNames* helper function, which does the actual work of mapping the requested names to DISPIDs based on the information in the type library. Of course, you could implement this functionality yourself, but with a function as easy to use as *DispGetIDsOfNames*, who would want to?

```
HRESULT CInsideCOM::GetIDsOfNames(REFIID riid,
    LPOLESTR* rgszNames, UINT cNames, LCID lcid,
    DISPID* rgDispId)
{
    if(riid != IID_NULL)
        return DISP_E_UNKNOWNINTERFACE;
    return DispGetIDsOfNames(m_pTypeInfo, rgszNames, cNames,
        rgDispId);
}
```

The *IDispatch::Invoke* Method

IDispatch::Invoke is used when the client is finally ready to call a method. The first parameter, *dispIdMember*, specifies the DISPID of the member you are invoking. This value can be obtained from a previous call to *IDispatch::GetIDsOfNames*. The second parameter, *riid*, is reserved and must be *IID_NULL*. The third parameter, *lcid*, specifies the locale identifier (LCID) of the client, and once more we will politely ignore this information. The fourth parameter, *wFlags*, can be chosen from the set of flags listed in the table below.

IDispatch::Invoke wFlags	Description
DISPATCH_METHOD	The member is invoked as a method. If a property has the same name, both this flag and the *DISPATCH_PROPERTYGET* flag can be set.
DISPATCH_PROPERTYGET	The member is retrieved as a property or data member.
DISPATCH_PROPERTYPUT	The member is changed as a property or data member.
DISPATCH_PROPERTYPUTREF	The member is changed by a reference assignment rather than by a value assignment. This flag is valid only when the property accepts a reference to an object.

The fifth parameter, *pDispParams*, is a pointer to a DISPPARAMS structure containing the actual parameters to be passed to this method. The sixth parameter, *pVarResult*, is a pointer to the return value that the client expects to receive after the completion of the method. The last two parameters, *pExcepInfo* and *puArgErr*, return extended error information to the caller. The EXCEPINFO structure, which is shown below, should be filled in by the *IDispatch::Invoke* method when an error occurs. If the HRESULT return code of the *Invoke* method is *DISP_E_EXCEPTION*, the client can retrieve the exception information pointed to by the *pExcepInfo* parameter.

```
typedef struct tagEXCEPINFO {
    WORD  wCode;            // An error code describing
                           //   the error
    WORD  wReserved;        // Should be 0
    BSTR  bstrSource;       // The source of the exception
```

```
    BSTR  bstrDescription;    // A description of the error
    BSTR  bstrHelpFile;       // Fully qualified filename for the
                              //   help file
    DWORD dwHelpContext;      // Help context ID of topic within
                              //   the help file
    ULONG pvReserved;         // Must be NULL
    ULONG pfnDeferredFillIn;  // Pointer to a function for
                              //   deferred fill in
    SCODE scode;              // Should be 0
} EXCEPINFO;
```

This technique works acceptably when you build a completely custom implementation of the *IDispatch::Invoke* method. If, however, you use the *DispInvoke* or *CreateStdDispatch* helper function to implement the *Invoke* method, client calls are automatically routed to the appropriate methods. These methods (the *ISum::Sum* methods) do not have a *pExcepInfo* parameter and therefore cannot take advantage of the Automation-based exception handling described here. The solution to this conundrum lies in more standard exception-handling techniques offered by COM+; exceptions are covered in Chapter 6. Basically, the solution is to use standard COM+ exception-handling techniques to generate the exception. The *DispInvoke* (or *CreateStdDispatch*) helper function then obtains this error information and automatically plugs it into the *pExcepInfo* parameter.

The *puArgErr* parameter helps the client application identify the first argument that has an error when the *IDispatch::Invoke* method returns *DISP_E_TYPEMISMATCH* or *DISP_E_PARAMNOTFOUND*. Since arguments are stored in *pDispParams->rgvarg* in reverse order, the first argument is the one with the highest index in the array.

The following code shows a simple implementation of *IDispatch::Invoke* that defaults to *DispInvoke*, another helper function provided in COM+. By deferring to the *ITypeInfo::Invoke* method, *DispInvoke* builds a stack frame, coerces parameters using the standard type conversion functions, pushes them onto the stack, and then calls the correct member function in the v-table. Keep in mind that you can use the *CreateStdDispatch* and *DispInvoke* helper functions only for dual interfaces. Pure dispinterfaces do not have method entries in their v-table and thus cannot make use of the services offered by *DispInvoke*. Components that implement a pure dispinterface implement *IDispatch::Invoke* by examining the *dispIdMember* parameter and directly calling the corresponding function.

```
HRESULT CInsideCOM::Invoke(DISPID dispIdMember, REFIID riid,
    LCID lcid, WORD wFlags, DISPPARAMS* pDispParams,
    VARIANT* pVarResult, EXCEPINFO* pExcepInfo, UINT* puArgErr)
```

(continued)

223

```
{
    if(riid != IID_NULL)
        return DISP_E_UNKNOWNINTERFACE;
    return DispInvoke(this, m_pTypeInfo, dispIdMember, wFlags,
        pDispParams, pVarResult, pExcepInfo, puArgErr);
}
```

A few minor changes remain to be made to the component's code. You must modify the object's *IUnknown::Release* method to release the type information before you exit, as shown here:

```
ULONG CInsideCOM::Release()
{
    if(--m_cRef != 0)
        return m_cRef;
    m_pTypeInfo->Release();
    delete this;
    return 0;
}
```

The *IUnknown::QueryInterface* function must be improved, as shown in the following code, so that clients requesting the *IDispatch* interface receive a valid pointer instead of being turned away with the *E_NOINTERFACE* return value:

```
HRESULT CInsideCOM::QueryInterface(REFIID riid, void** ppv)
{
    if(riid == IID_IUnknown)
        *ppv = (IUnknown*)this;
    else if(riid == IID_ISum)
        *ppv = (ISum*)this;
    else if(riid == IID_IDispatch)
        *ppv = (IDispatch*)this;
    else
    {
        *ppv = NULL;
        return E_NOINTERFACE;
    }
    AddRef();
    return S_OK;
}
```

Also, in the component's *IClassFactory::CreateInstance* method, the *Init* function must be called, as shown in the following code, to ensure that the type information is loaded from the type library:

```
HRESULT CFactory::CreateInstance(IUnknown *pUnknownOuter,
    REFIID iid, void** ppv)
```

```
{
    if(pUnknownOuter != NULL)
        return CLASS_E_NOAGGREGATION;

    CInsideCOM *pInsideCOM = new CInsideCOM;
    if(pInsideCOM == NULL)
        return E_OUTOFMEMORY;

    // Call the Init method to load the type information.
    pInsideCOM->Init();
    HRESULT hr = pInsideCOM->QueryInterface(iid, ppv);
    pInsideCOM->Release();
    return hr;
}
```

Since the *InsideCOM* object implements a dual interface, you can test the component using any of the standard client programs we built in previous chapters. To test the Automation capabilities of the component, you must build a new client that uses the *IDispatch* interface.

Properties

Although interfaces are made up of methods, Visual Basic distinguishes among method types, calling some properties and others events. Designing an *IDispatch*-based interface that contains properties is not difficult. To define properties, IDL provides the *propget*, *propput*, and *propputref* attributes. The last parameter of a method defined with the *propget* attribute must be a pointer type declared with the *out* and *retval* attributes. The last parameter of a method defined with the *propput* attribute must be an *in* parameter. For example, the IDL interface definition shown below contains two properties named *x* and *y*:

```
[ object, uuid(10000001-0000-0000-0000-000000000001), dual ]
interface ISum : IDispatch
{
    // The Sum method, now with optional parameters and
    // default values
    [id(1)] HRESULT Sum([optional, defaultvalue(-1)] int x,
        [optional, defaultvalue(-1)] int y,
        [out, retval] int* retvalue);

    // The x property
    [id(2), propget] HRESULT x([out, retval] int* retvalue);
    [id(2), propput] HRESULT x(int newvalue);

    // The y property
    [id(3), propget] HRESULT y([out, retval] int* retvalue);
    [id(3), propput] HRESULT y(int newvalue);
}
```

The interesting aspect of defining properties is that each property is defined as one, two, or even three distinct methods, depending on the property type. Standard properties are defined as a combination of two methods with the same name and DISPID; one method retrieves the property value, and the other sets it. The code fragment below shows the two methods used to implement the *x* property in C++. The name of every *propget* method is prefixed with *get_*, and the name of every *propput* method is prefixed with *put_*. Properties defined with the *propputref* attribute accept pointers and are implemented in methods prefixed with *putref_*.

```
// The propget method
HRESULT CInsideCOM::get_x(int* retvalue)
{
    *retvalue = m_x;
    return S_OK;
}

// The propput method
HRESULT CInsideCOM::put_x(int newvalue)
{
    m_x = newvalue;
    return S_OK;
}
```

Notice that in the *ISum* interface definition shown previously, the parameters of the *Sum* method were modified with the *optional* and *defaultvalue* attributes. The *optional* attribute indicates that the *Sum* method can be called without parameters; the *defaultvalue* attribute specifies the value to use when a client calls the *Sum* method without parameters. To adjust for this new definition of the *Sum* method, we'll modify the C++ implementation to check for the default values and use the property values instead:

```
HRESULT CInsideCOM::Sum(int x, int y, int* retval)
{
    // If the client did not specify parameters, then use
    // the property values.
    if(x == -1 && y == -1)
        *retval = m_x + m_y;
    else
        // Otherwise just add the numbers as usual.
        *retval = x + y;
    return S_OK;
}
```

Collections

In addition to supporting standard coclasses, Visual Basic also provides special support for a unique type of coclass called a collection. A collection is basically a Visual Basic–friendly technique for exposing an enumerator object. (Enumerator objects are described in Chapter 8.) Although a collection looks like an array, it is usually implemented internally as a linked-list data structure. This allows for items to be easily added and removed from anywhere in a collection. In addition, the *For Each...Next* statement in Visual Basic is a special language construct designed to work with collection objects. Collection objects generally expose several standard methods and properties, as described in the table below.

Member	Description	Required?
Add method	Adds an item to the collection	No
Count property	Read-only property that retrieves the number of items in the collection	Yes
Item method	Retrieves a specific item from the collection	Yes
_NewEnum property	Hidden read-only property that returns a pointer to the enumerator object that implements the *IEnumVARIANT* interface	Yes
Remove method	Removes an item in the collection	No

Of the items described in the table, the *_NewEnum* property is the most interesting. When you create a collection object, the *get__NewEnum* method that implements this *_NewEnum* property must return an *IUnknown* pointer to an enumerator object that implements the *IEnumVARIANT* interface. Visual Basic then queries for the *IEnumVARIANT* interface and uses the implementation of that interface to iterate the collection as required by the *For Each...Next* statement. The *IEnumVARIANT* interface follows the pattern of standard COM+ enumeration interfaces for VARIANT data types; the interface definition is shown below in IDL notation:

```
interface IEnumVARIANT : IUnknown
{
    // Return the next 0 or more items.
    HRESULT Next([in] ULONG celt,
        [out, size_is(celt), length_is(*pCeltFetched)]
            VARIANT* rgVar,
        [out] ULONG* pCeltFetched);
```

(continued)

```
    // Skip the next 0 or more items.
    HRESULT Skip([in] ULONG celt);

    // Reset the enumerator.
    HRESULT Reset();

    // Create a new enumerator with the identical state.
    HRESULT Clone([out] IEnumVARIANT ** ppEnum);
}
```

Because the _NewEnum_ property is designed for use by Visual Basic only,
it must be hidden from the programmer. To achieve this bit of subterfuge, you
use the _restricted_ IDL attribute to indicate that this property is not to be displayed to the user. Visual Basic also passes a special DISPID defined for the
NewEnum property, _DISPID_NEWENUM_ (–4), to _IDispatch::Invoke_ when
it requests an enumerator object. These attributes are shown below in the IDL
definition of the _INumbers_ interface, a sample interface implemented by a coclass
that defines a collection object:

```
[ object, uuid(10000001-0001-0000-0000-000000000001), dual ]
interface INumbers : IDispatch
{
    [propget, id(DISPID_NEWENUM), restricted] HRESULT _NewEnum(
        [out, retval] IUnknown** pVal);
    [propget] HRESULT Count([out, retval] long *pVal);
    [propget, id(DISPID_VALUE)] HRESULT Item(long index,
        [out, retval] long* pVal);
    HRESULT Add(long Val);
    HRESULT Remove(long index);
}
```

We won't bore you with the details of a linked-list implementation of the
INumbers interface or the enumerator object that implements _IEnumVARIANT_.[6]
You will, however, be pleasantly surprised by the client-side Visual Basic code
you can write that uses this collection object:

```
Dim Numbers As New InsideCOM

Print Numbers.Count    ' Prints 0

' Add items to the collection.
Numbers.Add 5
Numbers.Add 10
```

---

6. The sample is in the Samples\Automation\Collections folder on the companion CD.

```
Numbers.Add 15
Numbers.Add 20
Numbers.Add 25

Print Numbers.Count      ' Prints 5

' Remove items from the collection by index.
Numbers.Remove 2         ' Removes 10
Numbers.Remove 3         ' Removes 20

Print Numbers.Count      ' Prints 3

Dim Number As Variant

' Iterate through the collection and print each number (5, 15, 25).
For Each Number In Numbers
    Print "Number in the Numbers collection: " & Number
Next Number
```

The (New and Improved) *IDispatchEx* Interface

Recently, the *IDispatch* interface was extended through the definition of a new interface named *IDispatchEx*. The *IDispatchEx* interface derives from *IDispatch*, as you can see in the IDL definition below. In addition to the inherited *IDispatch* methods, *IDispatchEx* offers seven new methods that support the creation of dynamic objects (sometimes called "expando" objects) in which methods and properties can be added and removed at run time. In addition, unused parameters in the methods of *IDispatch* have been removed from *IDispatchEx*. For example, the unused interface identifier parameter passed to the *IDispatch::Invoke* and *IDispatch::GetIDsOfNames* methods has been removed from their respective methods in *IDispatchEx* (*IDispatchEx::InvokeEx* and *IDispatchEx::GetDispID*).[7]

```
interface IDispatchEx : IDispatch
{
    // Add a new member or get one DispID.
    HRESULT GetDispID(
        [in] BSTR bstrName,
        [in] DWORD grfdex,
        [out] DISPID *pid);
```

(continued)

---

7. This parameter is described in the documentation as reserved; only the *IID_NULL* value is permitted.

```
// Invoke a member using its DispID.
HRESULT InvokeEx(
    [in] DISPID id,
    [in] LCID lcid,
    [in] WORD wFlags,
    [in] DISPPARAMS *pdp,
    [out] VARIANT *pvarRes,
    [out] EXCEPINFO *pei,
    [in, unique] IServiceProvider *pspCaller);

// Remove a member using its name.
HRESULT DeleteMemberByName([in] BSTR bstrName,
    [in] DWORD grfdex);

// Remove a member using its DispID.
HRESULT DeleteMemberByDispID([in] DISPID id);

// Member type information is available here.
HRESULT GetMemberProperties(
    [in] DISPID id,
    [in] DWORD grfdexFetch,
    [out] DWORD *pgrfdex);

// Get the name of a member based on its DispID.
HRESULT GetMemberName(
    [in] DISPID id,
    [out] BSTR *pbstrName);

// Enumerate the DispIDs for the object.
HRESULT GetNextDispID(
    [in] DWORD grfdex,
    [in] DISPID id,
    [out] DISPID *pid);

// Some languages support namespaces.
HRESULT GetNameSpaceParent([out] IUnknown **ppunk);
};
```

The primary limitation of the *IDispatch* interface is that it assumes objects
are static. This means that the methods and properties offered by the object do
not change at run time. While custom v-table based interfaces are required to
offer a constant set of members, *IDispatchEx*-based interfaces are not. Instead,
IDispatchEx lets client applications dynamically add methods and properties at
run time that are not described by the static information in a type library. In fact,
you can even use the *IDispatch* interface in this dynamic way, although the

documentation seems to prohibit this by stating that "the member and parameter DISPIDs must remain constant for the lifetime of the object." One could
argue, however, that merely adding members to an object, as long as the assigned
DISPIDs remain valid, does not violate this rule.

One example of a component that makes use of this gray area is ActiveX
Data Objects (ADO). By setting the *Name* property of a *Command* object, you
enable that name to be used as a method of the *Connection* object to execute
the command, as shown in the code fragment below. The fascinating thing about
this code sample is that the *Hello* method (shown in boldface) does not exist
in the ADO type library, yet Visual Basic calls it without complaint. This becomes even more interesting when you realize that the *Connection* object is not
accessed via *IDispatch*; it is declared *As Connection*—not *As Object*. The explanation for this riddle is that in the case of dual interfaces, Visual Basic lets you
access methods and properties that are not in the type library. For these unknown
elements, Visual Basic has no choice but to resort to the *IDispatch* interface—
even if the object was not declared *As Object*.

```
' Set up the connection (not using IDispatch).
Dim cn As New Connection
cn.Open _
    "Provider=SQLOLEDB;Server=DatabaseServer;Database=Pubs;", _
    "sa"

' Create a command named Hello.
Dim cd As New Command
cd.Name = "Hello"
cd.CommandText = "select * from authors"
cd.ActiveConnection = cn

' Set up the recordset.
Dim rs As New Recordset

' Execute the Hello command as a method of the connection.
' Use IDispatch::GetIDsOfNames and IDispatch::Invoke because
' Hello is not in the type library
cn.Hello rs

' Display the records returned.
Do While Not rs.EOF
    Print rs(0), rs(1), rs(2)
    rs.MoveNext
Loop
```

Even though ADO proves that you can use the *IDispatch* interface to create dynamically expanding objects, *IDispatch* was definitely not designed to be used in this way. For example, you cannot delete members or get information about the nature of a member created at run time. The *IDispatchEx* interface was designed to formalize the idea of expandable objects and therefore adds methods to help support dynamic objects that might change at run time. Scripting languages such as VBScript and JScript offer more dynamic run-time models and therefore require a more flexible interface. The primary functionality offered by the new methods defined in *IDispatchEx* relates to adding, removing, and searching for members of an *IDispatchEx*-based interface.

Implementing *IDispatchEx*

Implementing the *IDispatchEx* interface is complicated because helper functions such as *DispInvoke* and *DispGetIDsOfNames* aren't provided for the methods of *IDispatchEx*. Remember that the *IDispatch* helper functions are based on type information, but since most objects that implement *IDispatchEx* generally do not update their type information at run time, helper functions that operate based on type information are not available. Since every object that implements *IDispatchEx* must also implement the methods of *IDispatch*, one relatively straightforward way to implement *IDispatchEx* is to delegate some *IDispatchEx* methods to their respective *IDispatch* methods. This works because most expandable objects have a steady core of methods defined by the interface's designer, on top of which the dynamic elements are added at run time.

For example, the simple implementation of the *IDispatchEx::GetDispID* method shown below delegates the call to *IDispatch::GetIDsOfNames*. Only if the *IDispatch::GetIDsOfNames* call fails with the return code *DISP_E_UNKNOWNNAME* does the *IDispatchEx::GetDispID* do any work. It first checks to see if the element name passed in by the client application is valid. In this case, a string comparison is done with a private member variable named *m_newsum*. If the *bstrName* string passed in by the client matches the *m_newsum* string, a new DISPID is returned to the client. In the sample implementation of *IDispatchEx::GetDispID*, the value of the DISPID returned has been hard-coded to *17*.[8]

```
HRESULT CInsideCOM::GetDispID(BSTR bstrName, DWORD grfdex,
    DISPID* pid)
```

---

8. A more realistic implementation of *IDispatchEx* would assign DISPIDs sequentially and keep track of those that had been assigned.

```
{
    // Try GetIDsOfNames. If that works, simply return.
    HRESULT hr = GetIDsOfNames(IID_NULL, &bstrName, 1,
        LOCALE_USER_DEFAULT, pid);

    // If GetIDsOfNames failed, then check the element name.
    if(hr == DISP_E_UNKNOWNNAME)

        // If the name is valid, assign a unique DispID
        // and return.
        if(wcscmp(bstrName, m_newsum) == 0)
        {
            *pid = 17;
            return S_OK;
        }
    return hr;
}
```

The *m_newsum* variable, declared as a BSTR, is obtained from the client in the *ISum::CreateNewSum* method shown below. This method is used by client applications to define new names for the *ISum::Sum* method. Note that no custom creation method is required to add elements to an object at run time. Instead, the client application can call the *IDispatchEx::GetDispID* method with the *fdexNameEnsure* flag in the second parameter to indicate that a new element is being added.

```
HRESULT CInsideCOM::CreateNewSum(BSTR name)
{
    m_newsum = SysAllocString(name);
    return S_OK;
}
```

The heart of the *IDispatchEx* interface is the *InvokeEx* method. Although it is not too different from its cousin the *IDispatch::Invoke* method, *InvokeEx* is the method called by the client to invoke elements created at run time. In the sample implementation of *IDispatchEx::InvokeEx* shown on the following page, the code first attempts to delegate the work to the *DispInvoke* helper function. If that succeeds, type information is available for the element invoked by the client and no special code is needed. If *DispInvoke* fails with the return code *DISP_E_MEMBER NOTFOUND*, no type information is available and so the client might request that an element be added at run time. The DISPID parameter is then checked, and if the value is *17* (the value returned by *GetDispID*), we know that the client is invoking the dynamic element. Since in this example the client request is only another name for the *Sum* method, the *DispInvoke* function is called with a DISPID of *1* (the DISPID of the *Sum* method).

233

```
HRESULT CInsideCOM::InvokeEx(DISPID id, LCID lcid, WORD wFlags,
    DISPPARAMS* pdp, VARIANT* pvarRes, EXCEPINFO* pei,
    IServiceProvider* pspCaller)
{
    ' Delegate to DispInvoke.
    HRESULT hr = DispInvoke(this, m_pTypeInfo, id, wFlags, pdp,
        pvarRes, pei, NULL);

    ' If that failed, then check if the DISPID is 17.
    if(hr == DISP_E_MEMBERNOTFOUND)
        if(id == 17)
        {
            ' Yes, so invoke the Sum method (DISPID of 1).
            HRESULT hr = DispInvoke(this, m_pTypeInfo, 1,
                wFlags, pdp, pvarRes, pei, NULL);
            return hr;
        }
    return hr;
}
```

The result of all this effort to create a dynamic object by implementing the *IDispatchEx* interface is that methods can be added to the *InsideCOM* coclass at run time. For example, the following VBScript code can be executed by the Windows Scripting Host. The *Hurray* method is added and then called using a reference to an *InsideCOM* object. The actual invocation of the *Hurray* method causes the Windows Scripting Host to get a pointer to the *IDispatchEx* implementation of the *InsideCOM* object using *QueryInterface* and then call *IDispatchEx::GetDispID* to get the DISPID of the *Hurray* method. Finally the *Hurray* method is invoked by calling *IDispatchEx::InvokeEx*, which eventually delegates the call to the *Sum* method.

```
Dim myRef
Set MyRef = CreateObject("Component.InsideCOM")
MsgBox "Sum(5, 3) = " & myRef.Sum(5, 3)

' Create a new method on the object.
myRef.CreateNewSum "Hurray"

' Execute the method added at run time.
' Calls IDispatchEx::GetDispID followed by
' IDispatchEx::InvokeEx.
MsgBox "Hurray(2, 8) = " & myRef.Hurray(2, 8)
```

Building Automation Clients

IDispatch has some problems that have made it somewhat unpopular with COM+ developers. The most serious of these problems is the performance of *IDispatch*-based components. Components using *IDispatch* can be accessed in two slightly different ways, known as *early binding* and *late binding*. Originally, *IDispatch* was designed so that every call to *IDispatch::Invoke* to invoke a method was preceded by a call to *IDispatch::GetIDsOfNames*. The client called *GetIDsOfNames* to get the DISPID of a particular method in the component. For example, if a client wanted to call the *Sum* method of an object, it would first call *GetIDsOfNames* to learn the DISPID of that method. This DISPID would then be passed as the first parameter to *IDispatch::Invoke* to actually call the *Sum* method. Subsequent calls to the *Sum* method could still call *GetIDsOfNames* to get the DISPID, or the client could cache the DISPID so that later calls to *Sum* could simply be made via a single call to *Invoke*.

This original way of using *IDispatch* is known as late binding. The main advantage of this technique is that a type library isn't required. The problem with late binding, however, is that two round-trips to the component are required for at least the first call to each method. With early binding, the component's type library is consulted to obtain the necessary DISPIDs, which are then hard-coded into the application so that at run time the client has to make only a single call to *IDispatch::Invoke*, omitting the call to *IDispatch::GetIDsOfNames*. This optimization is based on information from a type library and theoretically doubles the execution speed of each Automation-based method call compared with the late binding technique. However, not even early binding comes close to the performance of accessing an interface directly via its v-table, as is the case with custom interfaces.

Building Automation Clients in C++

Using the *IDispatch* interface from languages such as Visual Basic and VBScript couldn't be easier. These languages automatically make all the necessary calls to the four *IDispatch* methods. However, due to the flexibility and power of the *IDispatch* interface, creating Automation clients in C++ is more difficult than calling methods in a custom interface—another reason why Microsoft recommends that COM+ objects support dual interfaces. The *IDispatch* interface makes the object accessible to scripting languages such as VBScript; a custom interface makes the object easier for C++ developers to use.

Automation clients written in C++ follow a rather predictable series of steps. After initializing COM+ (*CoInitializeEx*) and instantiating a class (*CoCreateInstance*), the client calls *QueryInterface* for the *IDispatch* interface. If this is successful, the client has a pointer to the *IDispatch* interface and knows that it is dealing with an Automation object. Now we arrive at the fundamental step of calling the *IDispatch* methods, as shown in the following code. First *IDispatch::GetIDsOfNames* should be called to retrieve the DISPID of the desired method. Since our example component supports only a single *Sum* method with a known DISPID of *1*, we could skip this step and use early binding. For demonstration purposes, however, we'll show the call to *GetIDsOfNames*. Note that since all COM+ interfaces use Unicode strings, the string shown in this code fragment is prefixed with the letter *L*, indicating to the compiler that these are wide characters of the primitive type *wchar_t*.[9]

```
OLECHAR* name = L"Sum";
DISPID dispid;
pDispatch->GetIDsOfNames(IID_NULL, &name, 1,
    GetUserDefaultLCID(), &dispid);
```

IDispatch::GetIDsOfNames is called using the name of the *Sum* method and returns the DISPID of that method as the last parameter. In this example, the *dispid* variable should return the value *1*, which was defined as the DISPID in the IDL file. Although our *IDispatch* implementation ignores the locale information passed by *GetIDsOfNames*, it is still polite to provide the user's default LCID, which is retrieved by calling *GetUserDefaultLCID*. If in the future the component is upgraded to support localization, the information provided by the client will be correct.

After retrieving the DISPID, the client calls the specified method using *IDispatch::Invoke*. The hardest part about using the *Invoke* method is packing the DISPPARAMS structure with the required method parameters. The DISPPARAMS structure is shown below in IDL notation:

```
typedef struct tagDISPPARAMS {
    // Array of arguments
    [size_is(cArgs)] VARIANTARG* rgvarg;

    // Array of DISPIDs of named arguments
    [size_is(cNamedArgs)] DISPID* rgdispidNamedArgs;

    // Total number of arguments
    UINT cArgs;
```

---

9. In the system header files, *OLECHAR* is defined as *wchar_t*.

```
    // Number of named arguments
    UINT cNamedArgs;
} DISPPARAMS;
```

The first member of the DISPPARAMS structure is the actual pointer to an array of method arguments. It is declared as a VARIANTARG[10] pointer. Each VARIANTARG contains a *vt* member that indicates the data type. This member should be set to the appropriate *VT_** constant for the type of data stored in the VARIANTARG.

The second and fourth parameters are used for named arguments, and the third parameter specifies the total number of parameters. Thus, in the simplest case—a call to an Automation method with no parameters—the DISPPARAMS structure should be filled out as follows:

```
DISPPARAMS NoParams = { NULL, NULL, 0, 0 };
```

For methods such as *Sum* that expect to receive parameters, the arguments in the array should be arranged from last to first so that *rgvarg[0]* contains the last argument and *rgvarg[cArgs – 1]* contains the first argument. The following code packs two 4-byte integers into an array of two variants for the purposes of adding 2 and 7. The *VariantInit* function is called to initialize a new VARIANTARG to *VT_EMPTY*. Note that while the order of the *Sum* method's two parameters doesn't really matter (2 + 7 = 7 + 2), the order of the parameters in the example is 2, 7. This difference would of course be crucial in a method with different semantics.

```
VARIANTARG SumArgs[2];

VariantInit(&SumArgs[0]);
SumArgs[0].vt = VT_I4;
SumArgs[0].lVal = 7;

VariantInit(&SumArgs[1]);
SumArgs[1].vt = VT_I4;
SumArgs[1].lVal = 2;
```

Once you set the VARIANTARG's parameters, you must then create a DISPPARAMS structure that points to the array of parameters. As shown in Figure 5-6, the DISPPARAMS structure is initialized with a pointer to *SumArgs*, and the *cArgs* counter is set to *2*, indicating that there are two arguments in the array. Since no named parameters are used, the second and fourth parameters are ignored.

---

10. VARIANTARG is just another name for a VARIANT. The VARIANTARG type is used to pass parameters, while the VARIANT type carries the return value from a property or method call.

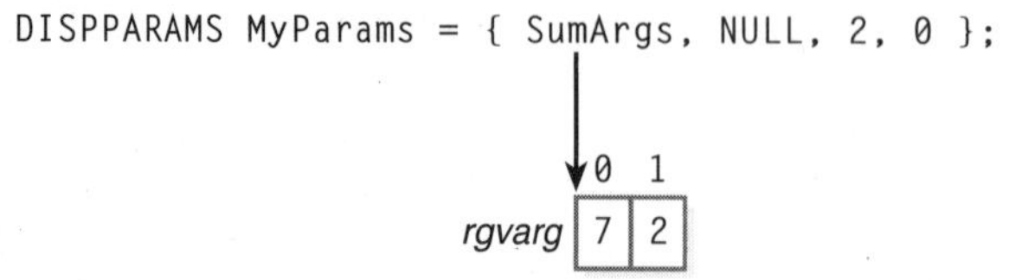

```
DISPPARAMS MyParams = { SumArgs, NULL, 2, 0 };
```

Figure 5-6.
The DISPPARAMS structure created for invoking the Sum *method with the parameters 2 and 7.*

Before *IDispatch::Invoke* is called, one final variant must be initialized in which the return value of the *Sum* method will be stored. After all this work, *Invoke* is finally called, as shown here:

```
VARIANT Result;
VariantInit(&Result);

HRESULT hr = pDispatch->Invoke(dispid, IID_NULL,
    GetUserDefaultLCID(), DISPATCH_METHOD, &MyParams,
    &Result, NULL, NULL);
if(FAILED(hr))
    cout << "pDispatch->Invoke() failed. " << endl;

cout << "2 + 7 = " << Result.lVal << endl;
pDispatch->Release();
```

You can use named parameters in addition to positional arguments when you invoke Automation-based methods. Actually, the term *named parameters* is a bit of a misnomer since the parameters are actually identified based on their DISPID value. Parameters are automatically assigned a DISPID value based on their position within the argument list. For example, the *Sum* method has three parameters that are implicitly assigned DISPIDs as follows:

```
HRESULT Sum([optional, defaultvalue(-1)] int x, // DISPID = 0
            [optional, defaultvalue(-1)] int y, // DISPID = 1
            [out, retval] int* retvalue);       // DISPID = 2
```

Therefore the *Sum* method can be invoked with the DISPPARAMS structure filled out as shown in Figure 5-7. This causes the *Sum* method to be called with the parameters *7, 2*; the Visual Basic equivalent is *Sum(y:=7, x:=2)*. The order of the named parameters in the array is not important, although they are generally passed in reverse order.

```
DISPPARAMS MyParams = { SumArgs, DispIds, 2, 2 };
```

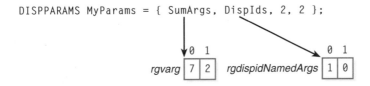

Figure 5-7.
The DISPPARAMS structure created for invoking the Sum *method with two named parameters.*

To omit an optional parameter when you use named arguments, you just don't pass it. For example, the declaration below calls the *Sum* method with only the *y* parameter:

```
VARIANTARG SumArg;
VariantInit(&SumArg);
SumArg.vt = VT_I4;
SumArg.lVal = 5;

DISPID DispId = 1; // The y parameter

DISPPARAMS Params = { &SumArg, &DispId, 1, 1 };

// Now IDispatch::Invoke calls ISum::Sum(-1, 5)
```

When you use position arguments, you must still define optional parameters. However, you should set the type to VT_ERROR and the value to DISP_E_PARAMNOTFOUND, indicating that the parameter is not actually being passed, as shown below:

```
VARIANTARG SumArgsOpt[2];

VariantInit(&SumArgsOpt[0]);
SumArgsOpt[0].vt = VT_ERROR;
SumArgsOpt[0].scode = DISP_E_PARAMNOTFOUND; // normally y

VariantInit(&SumArgsOpt[1]);
SumArgsOpt[1].vt = VT_I4;
SumArgsOpt[1].lVal = 3; // normally x

DISPPARAMS Params = { SumArgsOpt, NULL, 2, 0 };

// Now IDispatch::Invoke calls ISum::Sum(3, -1)
```

Building Automation Clients in Visual Basic

Working with Automation in C++ can be a trying experience, but in Visual Basic it's a breeze. In the following code, Visual Basic's *CreateObject* function instantiates the component based on a programmatic identifier. In the registry, under HKEY_CLASSES_ROOT, you'll find a ton of partially legible entries known as program identifiers (ProgIDs), organized alphabetically. Like a CLSID, a ProgID identifies a class, but with less precision. Since ProgIDs are not guaranteed to be unique, you can use them only where name collisions are manageable—for example, on a single machine. Every ProgID key should have a CLSID subkey containing the CLSID of the object. Given a ProgID, an application can use the *CLSIDFromProgID* function to retrieve the CLSID.

Most ProgIDs come in pairs. The version-independent ProgID is followed by the standard ProgID. The format of a version-independent ProgID is *Component.Class*; the two elements are separated by a period with no spaces, as in *Word.Document*. The format of the standard ProgID is identical, but with a version number at the end, as in *Word.Document.8*. The version-independent ProgID remains constant across all versions of a class. It is often used with high-level languages such as Visual Basic and always refers to the latest installed version of the application's class.

The *RegisterServer* function called in the component's self-registration code creates the ProgID registry entries, as shown in Figure 5-8.

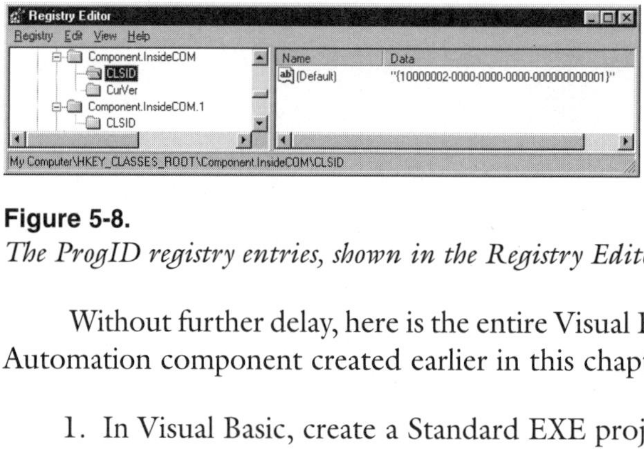

Figure 5-8.
The ProgID registry entries, shown in the Registry Editor.

Without further delay, here is the entire Visual Basic program that calls the Automation component created earlier in this chapter:

1. In Visual Basic, create a Standard EXE project.

2. Enter the following code on Form1:

```
Private Sub Form_Click()
    Dim myRef As Object
    Set myRef = CreateObject("Component.InsideCOM")
    Print "Sum(4, 6) = " & myRef.Sum(4, 6)
End Sub
```

3. Run the program, and click Form1 to test the component.

Because no design-time reference is set to a type library, the *CreateObject* method uses *IDispatch* via the late binding technique, meaning that *IDispatch:: GetIDsOfNames* is called before *IDispatch::Invoke*. If you want to use the early binding technique, you must set a reference to the component's type library by choosing References from the Project menu in Visual Basic and selecting the component. Visual Basic will obtain the DISPIDs for the interface method names at design time by using the information stored in the type library and thus needs to call only *IDispatch::Invoke* at run time.

Some people mistakenly assume that any object instantiated using the *CreateObject* function is always accessed via the *IDispatch* interface. Although *CreateObject* returns an *IDispatch* pointer, this pointer does not necessarily mean that you are stuck with that interface. The culprit is Visual Basic's *Object* type, which is the equivalent of an *IDispatch* pointer. Whenever a variable is declared *As Object*, the *IDispatch* interface is used. To overcome this limitation, you simply use the *IDispatch* pointer returned by *CreateObject* and call *IUnknown:: QueryInterface* to request some other interface pointer. As we saw in Chapter 3, a call to *QueryInterface* from Visual Basic is performed using the *Set* statement to cast one type to another. For example, the code shown below does not use the *IDispatch* interface at all, even though the *CreateObject* function is called. This is possible because Visual Basic reads the information stored in the component's type library.

```
Dim myRef As InsideCOM
Set myRef = CreateObject("Component.InsideCOM")
Print "Sum(4, 6) = " & myRef.Sum(4, 6)
```

The *Set* statement in the preceding code fragment calls *QueryInterface* on the *IDispatch* pointer returned by *CreateObject* to request a pointer to the *ISum* interface. When the *Sum* method is invoked, Visual Basic calls *ISum::Sum*—not *IDispatch::Invoke*. Since you can use *CreateObject* to instantiate an object that is not accessed through *IDispatch*, you might wonder what the difference is between the *CreateObject* function and the *New* keyword. The primary difference is that the *New* keyword uses the CLSID obtained from the type library, while *CreateObject* obtains the CLSID from the registry by calling the *CLSIDFromProgID* function. The lesser known difference is that *New* uses an internal creation mechanism when it instantiates a class in this part of the active application, while *CreateObject* always uses the COM+ activation method.[11]

---

11. *CreateObject* also offers the possibility for supplying an optional machine name parameter to instantiate remote components, in which case the *CoCreateInstanceEx* function is called.

The following code fragment uses the *New* keyword to access an object via *IDispatch*:

```
Dim myDispatch As Object
Dim myRef As New InsideCOM

' myRef->QueryInterface(IID_IDispatch, (void**)&myDispatch);
Set myDispatch = myRef

Print "Sum(4, 6) = " & myDispatch.Sum(4, 6)
```

If you are curious about how Visual Basic's *CreateObject* function is implemented, here is C++ pseudocode for the call.

```
IDispatch* CreateObject(LPCOLESTR szProgID)
{
    CLSID clsid;
    IDispatch* pDispatch = 0;
    CLSIDFromProgID(szProgID, &clsid);
    CoCreateInstance(clsid, 0, CLSCTX_SERVER, IID_IDispatch,
        (void**)&pDispatch);
    return pDispatch;
}
```

Scripting

Over the last 20 years, interpreted programming languages have gradually been replaced by compilers. Compilers are now available for all major programming languages. The rise of the Internet and the interpreted HTML document format has been accompanied by a renewed interest in interpreted languages for scripting. You can use scripting languages to automate user-driven administrative tasks or to create server-side Web applications. You can even write COM+ objects entirely in script. (We'll cover this topic shortly.)

In the past, when macro programming languages were embedded in major applications such as WordPerfect or CorelDraw, the user had to learn a new macro programming language for each application. This problem has been partially addressed through the adoption of Visual Basic for Applications by many major applications. Scripting presents similar difficulties in that each environment that uses script might adopt a proprietary scripting language. There is nothing wrong with having multiple scripting languages (Perl is obviously designed for different tasks than JScript), but the problem is that every environment generally locks you into one scripting language. Ideally, you should be able to choose the scripting language that is best suited for the job and simply plug that language into the environment at run time.

To address this issue, Microsoft created the ActiveX Scripting specification, which defines two types of components: scripting engines and scripting hosts. Scripting engines are COM+ components that implement the *IActiveScript* and *IActiveScriptParse* interfaces to provide support for a specific scripting language. Scripting hosts are applications that make use of scripting engines, including Internet Explorer, IIS, and the Windows Scripting Host.

The great thing about the scripting facility is that a scripting environment such as Internet Explorer can execute scripts written in any programming language for which a scripting engine is available. Today, Microsoft ships two scripting engines with Windows: VBScript and JScript. VBScript is a lightweight version of Visual Basic; JScript[12] is a more object-oriented scripting language that is distantly related to Java. Third-party scripting engines are available for many popular scripting languages, including PerlScript, PScript, and Python.

Building Automation Clients in Script

You can automate components that support the *IDispatch* interface using script code written in any compatible scripting language, such as VBScript or JScript. Internet Explorer, IIS, and the Windows Scripting Host support these scripting languages. Listing 5-1 shows an HTML document that you can view with Internet Explorer to test the component.

client.html

```
<HTML>
<HEAD><TITLE>HELLO THERE</TITLE></HEAD>
<BODY>
This is a VBScript sample that uses the Component.InsideCOM
object.<BR> VBScript will talk only to a component using
IDispatch.<BR>
Here we go: 4 + 5 =
<OBJECT ID="MyComponent"
    CLASSID="CLSID:10000002-0000-0000-0000-000000000001">
</OBJECT>
<SCRIPT LANGUAGE="VBScript">
    Document.Write MyComponent.Sum(4, 5)
</SCRIPT>
</BODY>
</HTML>
```

Listing 5-1.
An HTML document containing VBScript code that uses the InsideCOM *component.*

---

12. This is an implementation of the ECMA 262 language specification with some proprietary enhancements.

When Internet Explorer opens this HTML file, it might ask the user if the object is safe for scripting, depending on the current security settings. Internet Explorer is quite wary when executing scripts against components because of the potential for malicious script to turn even a usually benign component into a terror. To placate Internet Explorer, you should mark components in the registry as being safe for use by scripting languages, indicating that the component cannot do any damage to the user's data even if operated by a malevolent script. Because the *ISum* interface of our *InsideCOM* component cannot do any harm, it is safe to add this setting in the registry.

To mark an object as safe for scripting, you create an Implemented Categories subkey under the object's CLSID entry, as shown in Figure 5-9. This subkey should contain additional subkeys of the category identifiers (CATIDs) of any categories supported by this component. The available categories are listed in the registry under HKEY_CLASSES_ROOT\Component Categories. The CATID {7DD95801-9882-1CF-9FA9-00AA006C42C4} indicates that a component is safe for scripting. (For more on component categories, see Chapter 7.) Once these registry entries are added, Internet Explorer can work with our Automation component without prior warning to the user.

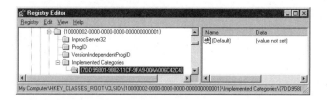

Figure 5-9.
An Implemented Categories subkey indicating that a component is safe for scripting.

The Windows Scripting Host

The Windows Scripting Host is a language-independent scripting host supplied with Windows. It was designed to replace MS-DOS batch files. Using a scripting language, you can write real programs to automate administrative and end user tasks. The neat thing about the Windows Scripting Host is that it is extensible through COM+. Client applications running in the Windows Scripting Host can access any Automation-compatible COM+ components via the *CreateObject* function; components installed on remote machines are also accessible via the second parameter of the *CreateObject* function, which specifies the target machine.

To test the Automation component from the Windows Scripting Host, open the file shown in Listing 5-2 from the Windows shell or run the script file from the command prompt using the cscript.exe or wscript.exe utility.

client.vbs

```
Dim myRef
Set MyRef = CreateObject("Component.InsideCOM")

MsgBox "Sum(5, 3) = " & myRef.Sum(5, 3)
```

Listing 5-2.
A Windows Scripting Host file containing VBScript code that uses the InsideCOM *component.*

Scriptlets

Continuing in the grand tradition of making COM+ objects accessible to any language, Microsoft enables scripts that are embedded in an HTML document or in a Windows Scripting Host file to access COM+ objects. What's even more amazing, however, is that you can actually create COM+ objects in script code stored in an Extensible Markup Language (XML) file. COM+ objects defined in this way are called *scriptlets*. Another type of scriptlet, called a Dynamic HTML scriptlet, is written using Dynamic HTML with user interface elements; these components are exposed as ActiveX controls. Thus, you have three ways to package a COM+ object:

- Native code (.dll and .exe files)
- Java classes (.class files)
- Scriptlets (.sct files)

Scriptlets are a powerful packaging technique because they let you create COM+ objects using XML and an interpreted scripting language. For example, the scriptlet shown in Listing 5-3 qualifies as a COM+ object. This scriptlet is written in VBScript, but you could use any scripting language for which a scripting engine is available.

Component.sct

```
<?XML version="1.0"?>
<scriptlet>

<registration
    description="Component"
    progid="Component.InsideCOM"
```

Listing 5-3.
A scriptlet written in VBScript.

(continued)

Listing 5-3. *continued*

```
      version="1.00"
      classid="{10001111-0000-0000-0000-000000000001}"
>
</registration>

<public>
    <method name="Sum">
        <PARAMETER name="X"/>
        <PARAMETER name="Y"/>
    </method>
</public>
<script language="VBScript">
<![CDATA[


function Sum(X, Y)
    Sum = X + Y
end function


]]>
</script>

</scriptlet>
```

At run time, scriptlets are executed by the scriptlet run-time component (scrobj.dll), which is a sort of virtual machine for scriptlet components. When a scriptlet is registered, its InprocServer32 subkey refers to the scrobj.dll file. The *<registration>* tag defines the information that must be added to the registry when the scriptlet is registered. This tag includes the attributes for the description, ProgID, CLSID, and version number for a scriptlet. You can register scriptlets by running RegSvr32, or more easily by right-clicking on the scriptlet file and choosing Register from the context menu. The *<registration>* tag shown in Listing 5-3 creates the following registry entries in the HKEY_ CLASSES_ ROOT\CLSID section of the registry.[13]

```
[HKCR\CLSID\{10001111-0000-0000-0000-000000000001}]
@="Component"

[HKCR\CLSID\{10001111-0000-0000-0000-000000000001}\
    VersionIndependentProgID]
@="Component.InsideCOM"
```

---

13. HKCR is used as an abbreviation of the HKEY_CLASSES_ROOT key in the registry.

```
[HKCR\CLSID\{10001111-0000-0000-0000-000000000001}\ProgID]
@="Component.InsideCOM.1.00"

[HKCR\CLSID\{10001111-0000-0000-0000-000000000001}\ScriptletURL]
@="file://C:\\WINDOWS\\Desktop\\Component.sct"

[HKCR\CLSID\{10001111-0000-0000-0000-000000000001}\
    InprocServer32]
@="C:\\WINDOWS\\SYSTEM\\SCROBJ.DLL"
"ThreadingModel"="Apartment"
```

The *<?XML version="1.0"?>* declaration at the top of the scriptlet file indicates that this file conforms to the XML protocol.[14] The *<scriptlet>* tag encloses an entire scriptlet definition. Each *<scriptlet>* tag in a .sct file defines one coclass. If multiple *<scriptlet>* tags are to be defined in a single .sct file, you use the *<package>* tag to contain all of the scriptlets in the component. The example shown in Listing 5-3 defines only a single scriptlet, so the *<package>* tag is not required. The *<public>* tag defines the properties, methods, and events of the dispinterface exposed by each scriptlet. Finally, the *<script>* tag is where the actual scripting code is implemented. You must define this in a *<![CDATA[]]>* tag for XML compatibility. Also, you can use a *<comment>* tag to provide comments in the scriptlets source code. The various XML elements that can go into a scriptlet are described in the table below:

Tag	Description
<comment>	Contains text that is ignored when the scriptlet is parsed and executed.
<implements>	Specifies the COM+ interface implemented by the scriptlet. Interfaces are implemented using an interface handler. (Scriptlets currently support three interface handlers: Automation (*IDispatchEx*), Active Server Pages (ASP), and DHTML behaviors. In the future, it might be possible to build custom interface handlers that plug into the scriptlet at run time.)
<object>	Contains information about an object that you use in your script, such as another COM+ component.
<package>	Multiple *<scriptlet>* elements can appear in the same .sct file and are contained within a master *<package>* element.

(continued)

14. This element is optional; if you leave it out, a looser syntax can be used when defining the scriptlet.

Tag	Description
<public>	Encloses definitions for properties, methods, and events that your scriptlet exposes via the Automation interface handler. These definitions point to variables or functions defined in a separate *<script>* block.
<reference>	References a type library containing constants you want to use in script.
<registration>	Includes information used to register your scriptlet.
<resource>	Contains values that should not be hard-coded into scriptlet code. Resource elements can include information that might change between versions, strings that might be translated, and other values.
<script>	Contains the script used to implement the logic of your scriptlet.
<scriptlet>	Encloses one entire scriptlet definition.

You can build client applications that use scriptlet components in any development environment that supports COM+. For example, a scriptlet can be called from an HTML page displayed by Internet Explorer or from a Java applet executed by the Microsoft Java VM. For demonstration purposes, let's build a client program in Visual Basic that calls the scriptlet shown in Listing 5-3. Here are the steps to follow:

1. In Visual Basic, open a Standard EXE project.

2. Place a command button on the form.

3. In the Code window, enter the following code:

```
Private Sub Command1_Click()
    Dim ref As Object
    Set ref = CreateObject("Component.InsideCOM")
    MsgBox ref.Sum(4, 6)
End Sub
```

4. Run the program and test it by clicking the button.

CHAPTER SIX

Exceptions

Error handling is a contentious issue among developers. For a long time, most C programmers subscribed to the every-function-call-returns-an-error-code style of coding. While effective, this error-handling mechanism has its drawbacks. To start with, error-handling code is sprinkled throughout an application, which makes the code hard to read and costly to maintain. This approach can also be inefficient because it requires a great deal of usually unnecessary code that simply checks for error return codes.

More recently, languages such as C++ and Java have introduced an error-handling mechanism known as *exceptions*. Exceptions are run-time errors by another name. Programming languages that support exceptions have special language directives that allow exceptions to be caught and raised. Raising an exception is a way to report an error; catching an exception means intercepting and responding to the error condition. C++ and Java support the *try* and *catch* keywords for trapping exceptions, while the *throw* keyword is used to raise exceptions. Even Microsoft Visual Basic supports trapping exceptions with the *On Error* statement; you use the *Err.Raise* method to raise exceptions.

To the designers of COM+, error handling represented a unique challenge because each programming language has its own ideas about error handling. As a language-neutral component architecture, COM+ must deal with errors in a way that is compatible with all major programming languages, some of which might not support exceptions. To meet that goal, COM+ supports both the errors-as-return-codes technique and the more modern idea of exceptions.

For method return codes, COM+ defines the *HRESULT*, a 32-bit value that identifies an error. In the exception-handling arena, COM+ defines several interfaces that support those semantics. Some high-level languages such as Visual Basic automatically map COM+ exceptions to the language's native exception-handling mechanism. In lower-level languages such as C++, COM+ exceptions are not automatically mapped to the C++ exception-handing mechanism. Instead, C++ developers must work directly with the COM+ exception interfaces or roll their own mapping layer that converts COM+ exceptions to C++ exceptions and vice versa. The Microsoft Java Virtual Machine (VM) also provides nearly automatic COM+ to Java exception translation. The error-handling technique you employ will depend on the programming language you use and your preferences about how to deal with errors.

Error Codes

Practically all COM+ interface methods return an *HRESULT* value. An *HRESULT* is defined simply as a *long* type, which means that it is a signed 32-bit value. The term *HRESULT* is a holdover from the days when 16-bit operating systems ruled the world and an *HRESULT* was a handle to a result. Today, an *HRESULT* is the result value itself. All *HRESULT* values are composed of three parts: the severity, the facility, and the status code. For many *HRESULT* names, these parts are separated by underscores. For example, the code for *MK_E_MUSTBOTHERUSER* is a combination of the moniker facility (*MK*), an error severity (*E*), and a status code indicating that user input is required for the operation to succeed (*MUSTBOTHERUSER*).

Figure 6-1 shows how an *HRESULT* is laid out in memory. The R, C, N, and r bits are reserved.

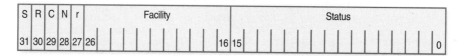

Figure 6-1.
The memory layout of an HRESULT.

The top bit (31) defines the severity code of the *HRESULT* value. The severity code contains *0* for success or *1* for an error. The facility codes are shown in the following table.

Facility	Value	Meaning
FACILITY_NULL	0	Used for general error codes such as S_OK
FACILITY_RPC	1	Errors from Remote Procedure Calls (RPCs)
FACILITY_DISPATCH	2	Errors from the IDispatch interface

Facility	Value	Meaning
FACILITY_STORAGE	3	Errors from the IStorage or IStream interface
FACILITY_ITF	4	Error codes defined by custom interfaces
FACILITY_WIN32	7	Errors from the Win32 API
FACILITY_WINDOWS	8	Errors from standard interfaces
FACILITY_SSPI	9	Errors from the Security Support Provider Interface (SSPI)
FACILITY_MSMQ	14	Errors from the Microsoft Message Queue Server (MSMQ)
FACILITY_COMPLUS	17	Errors from COM+ component services

FACILITY_ITF Error Codes

To ensure that facility codes don't conflict, developers outside Microsoft are not permitted to define new facility codes. In addition, you can define new status codes using only the *FACILITY_ITF* facility code, and then only in the range *0x0200* through *0xFFFF* to avoid conflicting with Microsoft-defined status codes in the range *0x0000* through *0x01FF*. It is legal for different interfaces to reuse identical status codes of the *FACILITY_ITF* facility for completely different errors. This reuse is possible because the *HRESULT* values returned by interface methods are considered part of the interface contract and therefore must be interpreted in the context of that interface.

Helper Macros

Microsoft provides several helpful macros that can help you work directly with *HRESULT* values. The *HRESULT_SEVERITY*, *HRESULT_FACILITY*, and *HRESULT_CODE* macros extract the severity, facility, and status codes from an *HRESULT*, respectively. The *SUCCEEDED* and *FAILED* macros test the severity portion of an *HRESULT*. If the top bit of the *HRESULT* is *0*, the *SUCCEEDED* macro returns *true*. For an error severity code of *1*, the *SUCCEEDED* macro returns *false*. The *FAILED* macro works in the exact opposite manner of the *SUCCEEDED* macro, returning *true* when the top bit of the *HRESULT* is *1*. The *MAKE_HRESULT* macro composes an *HRESULT* value from severity, facility, and status codes.

All COM+ and Windows errors as well as the aforementioned macros are defined in the winerror.h system include file. To obtain a meaningful string that explains a system error code at run time, you can call the Win32 function *FormatMessage*. The *ErrorMessage* routine shown in the following code is a simple wrapper for *FormatMessage* that you can use; you call it with a user-provided string and the *HRESULT*. The companion CD contains a simple utility named Error that interactively decodes *HRESULT* values.

```
void ErrorMessage(char* szMessage, HRESULT hr)
{
    if(HRESULT_FACILITY(hr) == FACILITY_WINDOWS)
        hr = HRESULT_CODE(hr);

    char* szError;
    if(FormatMessage(FORMAT_MESSAGE_ALLOCATE_BUFFER|
        FORMAT_MESSAGE_FROM_SYSTEM, NULL, hr,
        MAKELANGID(LANG_NEUTRAL, SUBLANG_DEFAULT),
        (LPTSTR)&szError, 0, NULL) != 0)
    {
        printf("%s: (%0x) %s", szMessage, hr, szError);
        LocalFree(szError);
    }
    else
        printf("Error number not found\n");
}
```

Rich Error Information

*HRESULT*s do not work well for applications written in Java or Visual Basic because these high-level languages hide *HRESULT* values from the programmer. In Java and Visual Basic, the parameter marked with the *[out, retval]* IDL attributes replaces the *HRESULT* as the method's return value. In these languages, errors are dealt with as exceptions, not return codes. Therefore, Visual Basic raises an exception if the *HRESULT* returned by a method indicates an error. You can trap this error in Visual Basic using an *On Error* statement. Unfortunately, Visual Basic programmers do not have much information to work with when they try to respond to an error message represented by an *HRESULT*. To overcome these limitations and to provide richer error information for components of all languages, COM+ offers the *IErrorInfo*, *ICreateErrorInfo*, and *ISupportErrorInfo* interfaces.

When a run-time error occurs inside a component, a COM+ exception can be propagated back to the client application. In order for the COM+ exception-handling mechanism to work, both the client and the component must support COM+ exceptions. The component implements the *ISupportErrorInfo* interface and, when an error occurs, makes use of the system implementation of the *ICreateErrorInfo* interface. The component then returns a standard error code to the client, whereupon the client can retrieve the additional information configured in the system error object.

The *ISupportErrorInfo* Interface

A component that wants to provide rich error information to its client must first implement the *ISupportErrorInfo* interface to indicate this capability. The *ISupportErrorInfo* defines only one method, as shown in the following IDL definition:

```
interface ISupportErrorInfo : IUnknown
{
    HRESULT InterfaceSupportsErrorInfo([in] REFIID riid);
}
```

Both the Visual Basic and Java VMs query for *ISupportErrorInfo* and then call the *ISupportErrorInfo::InterfaceSupportsErrorInfo* method for every custom interface exposed by the component and accessed by the client program. Some C++ client programs, such as those written using MFC, also do this. It is easy to implement this interface to return *S_OK* or *S_FALSE* when a client attempts to determine whether your component offers rich error information for the methods of a specific interface. The following code fragment shows a sample implementation:

```
HRESULT CInsideCOM::InterfaceSupportsErrorInfo(REFIID riid)
{
    if(riid == IID_ISum)
        return S_OK;
    else
        return S_FALSE;
}
```

The *ICreateErrorInfo* Interface

During method execution, a component that supports the COM+ exception mechanism calls the *CreateErrorInfo* function to instantiate a generic error object. The *CreateErrorInfo* function returns an *ICreateErrorInfo* interface pointer. The methods of the *ICreateErrorInfo* interface set the rich error information describing the *HRESULT* value that will be returned by the component. The following code shows the IDL definition of the *ICreateErrorInfo* interface:

```
interface ICreateErrorInfo : IUnknown
{
    HRESULT SetGUID([in] REFGUID rguid);
    HRESULT SetSource([in] LPOLESTR szSource);
    HRESULT SetDescription([in] LPOLESTR szDescription);
    HRESULT SetHelpFile([in] LPOLESTR szHelpFile);
    HRESULT SetHelpContext([in] DWORD dwHelpContext);
}
```

After setting the desired method error information using the *ICreateErrorInfo* interface, the component calls the *SetErrorInfo* function. *SetErrorInfo* assigns the error object to the current thread of execution, enabling the client program to retrieve the error information using the *GetErrorInfo* function. The only problem is that *SetErrorInfo* requires an *IErrorInfo* interface pointer and the component currently has an *ICreateErrorInfo* interface pointer. The component can obtain the correct interface pointer for *SetErrorInfo* simply by calling the *QueryInterface* method on the *ICreateErrorInfo* interface pointer to request *IErrorInfo*; the standard error object implements both interfaces. The following code shows a special implementation of the *ISum::Sum* method that returns rich error information if either parameter is negative:

```
HRESULT CInsideCOM::Sum(int x, int y, int* retval)
{
    // If either x or y is negative, return error info.
    if(x < 0 || y < 0)
    {
        // Create generic error object.
        ICreateErrorInfo* pCreateErrorInfo;
        CreateErrorInfo(&pCreateErrorInfo);

        // Set rich error information.
        pCreateErrorInfo->SetDescription(
            L"Negative numbers not allowed.");
        pCreateErrorInfo->SetGUID(IID_ISum);
        pCreateErrorInfo->SetSource(L"Component.InsideCOM");

        // Exchange ICreateErrorInfo for IErrorInfo.
        IErrorInfo* pErrorInfo;
        pCreateErrorInfo->QueryInterface(IID_IErrorInfo,
            (void**)&pErrorInfo);

        // Make the error information available to the client.
        SetErrorInfo(0, pErrorInfo);

        // Release the interface pointers.
        pErrorInfo->Release();
        pCreateErrorInfo->Release();

        // Return the actual error code.
        return E_INVALIDARG;
    }

    // Business as usual...
    *retval = x + y;
    return S_OK;
}
```

Visual Basic and Java automatically map the error information interfaces offered by COM+ to their language-based exception-handling mechanisms. This mapping enables a client program running in Visual Basic to trap a COM+ error as if it were a regular Visual Basic exception, as shown here:

```
Private Sub Command1_Click()
    On Error GoTo MyHandler
    Dim Test As New Component.InsideCOM
    Print Test.Sum(4, 3) ' Everything is OK.
    Print Test.Sum(-1, 5) 'Raises exception.
    Exit Sub

MyHandler: 'Exception transfers execution control here.
    MsgBox Err.Description 'Displays: Negative numbers
                         '            not allowed.

End Sub
```

Obtaining Error Information

A component written in Java can return rich error information by throwing an instance of *ComFailException*, a class provided by the com.ms.com package. The *ComFailException* class is derived from the *com.ms.com.ComException* abstract class, which in turn inherits from the *java.lang.RuntimeException* class. This class hierarchy means it is legal to use an instance of the *ComFailException* class anywhere an instance of the *RuntimeException* class is required, such as with the *throw* statement. The *com.ms.com.ComSuccessException* class (also derived from *ComException*) is used to return an *HRESULT* of *S_FALSE*. The Java component shown in Listing 6-1, with the code that throws the exception in boldface, behaves identically to the C++ component on page 254.

insidecom.java

```
/**
 * This class is designed to be packaged with a COM DLL output
 * format. The class has no standard entry points other than the
 * constructor. Public methods are exposed as methods on the
 * default COM interface.
 * @com.register ( clsid=DB379AA0-D639-11D2-BB51-006097B5EAFC,
       typelib=DB379AA1-D639-11D2-BB51-006097B5EAFC )
 */
import com.ms.com.*;
```

Listing 6-1. *(continued)*

The insidecom.java source file showing how a Java component can raise COM+ exceptions.

insidecom.java *continued*

```
/**
 * @com.register ( clsid=2652CA66-D6CF-11D2-BB51-006097B5EAFC,
       typelib=2652CA65-D6CF-11D2-BB51-006097B5EAFC )
 */
public class InsideCOM implements component.ISum
{
    // TODO: Add additional methods and code here
    public int Sum(int x, int y)
    {

        if(x < 0 || y < 0)
            throw new ComFailException(0x80070057,
                "Negative numbers not allowed");

        return x + y;
    }


    /**
     * NOTE: To add auto-registration code, refer to the
     * documentation on the following method:
     *   public static void onCOMRegister(boolean unRegister) {}
     */
}
```

The *IErrorInfo* Interface

Client applications that want to obtain rich error information use the methods of the *IErrorInfo* interface. The IDL definition of the *IErrorInfo* interface is shown here:

```
interface IErrorInfo : IUnknown
{
    HRESULT GetGUID([out] GUID * pGUID);
    HRESULT GetSource([out] BSTR * pBstrSource);
    HRESULT GetDescription([out] BSTR * pBstrDescription);
    HRESULT GetHelpFile([out] BSTR * pBstrHelpFile);
    HRESULT GetHelpContext([out] DWORD * pdwHelpContext);
}
```

Before it calls the methods of the *IErrorInfo* interface, the client must determine whether the component reporting the error provides rich error information. To do this, the client calls the *QueryInterface* method to request the *ISupportErrorInfo* interface. If this call is successful, the client calls *ISupportErrorInfo::InterfaceSupportsErrorInfo* to verify that rich error information is available for the methods of the interface in question. If this call is successful, the client can call the *GetErrorInfo* function to obtain an *IErrorInfo* pointer to the object containing the rich error information. The methods of the *IErrorInfo* interface shown in the preceding code can now be called to obtain the error information. Later, the *IErrorInfo* and *ISupportErrorInfo* interface pointers must be released. The following code fragment shows how a C++ client program can obtain the error information thrown by our sample Java component:

```
hr = pSum->Sum(-2, 3, &sum);
if(SUCCEEDED(hr))
    cout <<"Sum = " << sum << endl;
else
{
    ISupportErrorInfo* pSupportErrorInfo;
    if(SUCCEEDED(pSum->QueryInterface(IID_ISupportErrorInfo,
        (void**)&pSupportErrorInfo)))
    {
        if(pSupportErrorInfo->InterfaceSupportsErrorInfo(
            IID_IInsideCOM) == S_OK)
        {
            IErrorInfo* pErrorInfo;
            GetErrorInfo(0, &pErrorInfo);

            BSTR description;
            pErrorInfo->GetDescription(&description);
            wprintf(L"HRESULT = %x, Description: %s\n", hr,
                description);
            SysFreeString(description);

            pErrorInfo->Release();
        }
        pSupportErrorInfo->Release();
    }
}
```

CHAPTER SEVEN

Component Categories

A COM+ object exposes its functionality through interfaces; a client learns about these interfaces through the *IUnknown::QueryInterface* method. The *QueryInterface* method has two purposes: to enable clients to determine what interfaces are supported by an object, and to retrieve pointers to those interfaces. The first purpose does not scale well as objects become increasingly complex and begin to support not several but dozens of interfaces. Of course, regardless of the number of interfaces an object supports, *QueryInterface* is still the method to call when you need an interface pointer.[1]

As objects and their clients become increasingly complex, they require more functionality from one another. Generally speaking, most COM+ interfaces have between three and seven methods, but legally an interface can have any number of methods. Pragmatically, an interface seems to work best if a programmer can grasp it quickly. As coclasses evolve, they add functionality by implementing new interfaces.

These days, most components need to support a gamut of interfaces that work together to accomplish a single task. Microsoft Visual Basic, for example, requires that an ActiveX control support a dozen or more interfaces. When the user chooses Components from the Project menu in Visual Basic, a list of available ActiveX controls is displayed, as shown in Figure 7-1. Here's the problem: How can client programs such as Visual Basic determine which objects installed on the user's computer support all the interfaces necessary to qualify as ActiveX controls?

---

1. Actually, if you need to retrieve many interfaces implemented by an object, you should use the *QueryMultipleInterfaces* method of the *IMultiQI* interface; for details, see Chapter 13.

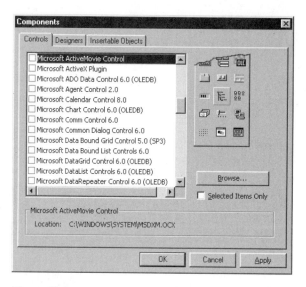

Figure 7-1.

The Components dialog box in Visual Basic, showing a list of available ActiveX controls.

With only the *QueryInterface* mechanism at its disposal, Visual Basic would have to traverse the HKEY_CLASSES_ROOT\CLSID section of the registry, instantiate each object, and then call *QueryInterface* a dozen or more times per object simply to determine whether the necessary interfaces are available. This technique would take an unreasonable amount of time. Ideally, Visual Basic should be able to determine whether a component meets the requirements of its client prior to instantiation.

Component categories make this possible. One solution might be to identify a coclass's functionality by simply listing the interfaces it implements. This might sound like a good approach, but in practice most components belong to a certain type, or category. For example, controls, documents, scripting engines, and Automation objects are different types of components. A component declares its support for one or more categories via registry keys. A client program can then identify and locate the components that support a particular category by a quick scan of the registry. The desired component is then instantiated, and interface pointers are obtained by calling *QueryInterface* in the usual way.

Standard Component Categories

A component identifies its type using a category identifier (CATID), which is identical to a 128-bit globally unique identifier. For example, any component that implements the CATID {40FC6ED4-2438-11CF-A3DB-080036F12502} is a control, and any component that implements the CATID {F0B7A1A1-9847-11CF-8F20-00805F2CD064} is an active scripting engine. By design, component categories are extensible, which means that you can define additional CATIDs for custom component types. Of course, it is strongly recommended that you use an existing component category if it meets your needs. Like the signature of an interface, the semantics of a CATID are immutable. You must define a new component category instead of expanding the required interfaces for an existing component type.

The defined CATIDs on an individual machine are stored in the HKEY_CLASSES_ROOT\Component Categories section of the registry. Stored with each CATID value is a human-readable name that describes the category. Figure 7-2 shows the standard CATIDs that can be easily located in the registry.

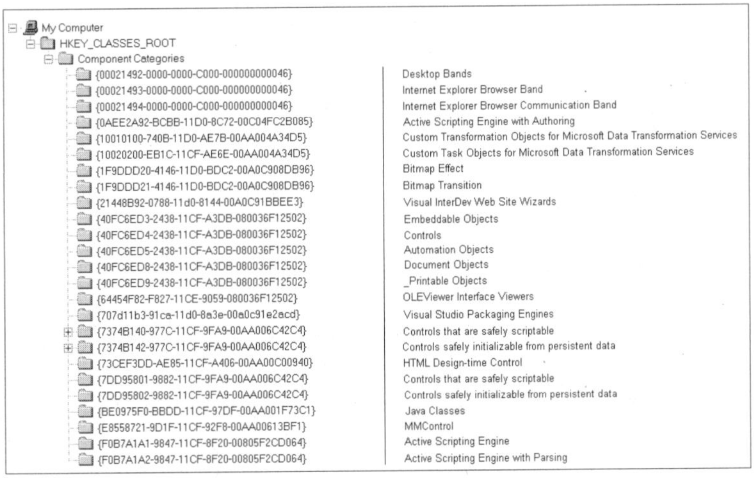

Figure 7-2.
Some standard CATIDs.

An object declares its support for a particular component category using the Implemented Categories registry key. An object can support multiple component categories by listing all its supported CATIDs in the registry. Component categories can also be a two-way street. Not only can a client search for components that are members of a certain category, but a component can also declare that it requires certain functionality of the client. If a component does not indicate the type of client it is willing to work with, the user might select a component only to discover that it won't work with the application. An object declares categories of acceptable clients using the Required Categories registry key. You should use this registry key with restraint because it severely limits the clients that can access an object.

Figure 7-3 shows a hypothetical registry entry for a coclass. Based on this information, we can deduce that the object is a control that requires a container to support Visual Basic–style data binding.

Figure 7-3.
The registry entries for a coclass that uses the Required Categories subkey to specify required client functionality.

Default Components

In some cases, it might be useful to associate a CATID with a default object. This technique allows clients to instantiate an object of a particular type without even knowing the object's CLSID! For example, imagine an e-mail application that checks the spelling of a message before it is sent. If the application does not care what spell checker component it uses, it can simply call *CoCreateInstance* with the CLSID parameter set to the CATID for spell checker components, as shown here:

```
// Instantiate the default object, implementing the
// Spell Checker component category.
CoCreateInstance(CATID_SpellChecker, NULL, CLSCTX_INPROC_SERVER,
    IID_IUnknown, (void**)&pUnknown);
```

```
// Now we know that the object must support the
// ISpellChecker interface.
pUnknown->QueryInterface(IID_ISpellChecker, (void**)&pSpell);
```

CoCreateInstance locates the default spell checker by looking in the HKEY_CLASSES_ROOT\CLSID section of the registry for the particular CATID. The CATID is defined there using the TreatAs subkey, which references the CLSID of the spell checker component, as shown in Figure 7-4.

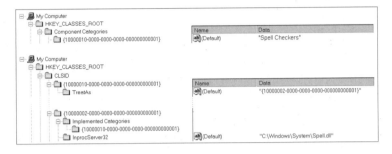

Figure 7-4.
The default component of a certain category, referenced in the HKEY_CLASSES_ROOT\CLSID\\{ComponentCategoryID\}\TreatAs registry key.

This mechanism can be helpful when you don't want to tie a client program to a particular CLSID and you also don't want to force the user to select from a list of available components. You can design an application so that the setup program asks the user to make a selection during the installation process and then configures that component as the default.

You can also define a default icon for every component category. This might allow an application to present the user with different icons for components that belong to different categories. Default icons come in two standard sizes, the standard 32-by-32-pixel icon and the smaller 16-by-16-pixel icon that is typically displayed on toolbox buttons. To associate a standard-sized icon with a specific component category, you create a subkey of HKEY_CLASSES_ROOT\CLSID with the component category's CATID and populate that key with a DefaultIcon subkey. For a toolbox-sized icon, you use the ToolBoxBitmap32 subkey.

The registry entry for the *OLEViewer Interface Viewers* component category used by the OLE/COM Object Viewer utility is shown in Figure 7-5. The icon is identified by a number, which references a resource stored in the component. Incidentally, the OLE/COM Object Viewer displays the toolbox-sized icon for all component categories that have one configured.

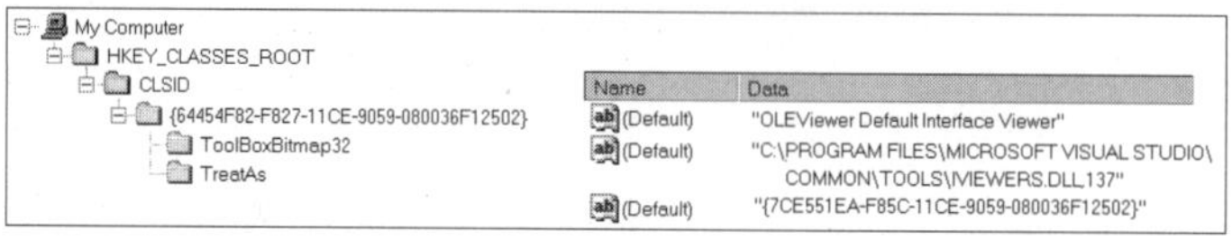

Figure 7-5.
The icon configured for the OLEViewer Interface Viewers *component category.*

Class Emulation

As a coclass evolves, it can add support for new interfaces or drop support for older ones. In most cases, a new version of an existing coclass should be assigned a new CLSID so that a client application can specify the class it wants. Client applications that predate the new version of a component use the older coclass. If the new version of a coclass is fully backward-compatible with the older version, it might make sense for older clients to be routed to the new class.

The *CoTreatAsClass* and *CoGetTreatAsClass* functions allow a coclass represented by a CLSID to evolve over time while still supporting older clients. You can call the *CoTreatAsClass* function to insert the TreatAs subkey into the registry entry of a particular CLSID. Any client requests for that CLSID will be automatically routed to the CLSID specified by the TreatAs key. You can use the *CoGetTreatAsClass* function to learn the current emulation setting of a specific CLSID.

Let's say that the *CLSID_InsideCOM* coclass is extended and that the class identifier *CLSID_InsideCOM2* identifies the new version. If the new version of the class is backward-compatible, you can call the *CoTreatAsClass* function to configure class emulation, as shown in the following code fragment:

```
hr = CoTreatAsClass(CLSID_InsideCOM, CLSID_InsideCOM2);
```

This code configures the registry so that the *CLSID_InsideCOM2* class is used even when clients request the *CLSID_InsideCOM* class—for example, via a call to *CoCreateInstance*. The actual registry entries in place after the execution of the *CoTreatAsClass* function are shown in Figure 7-6.

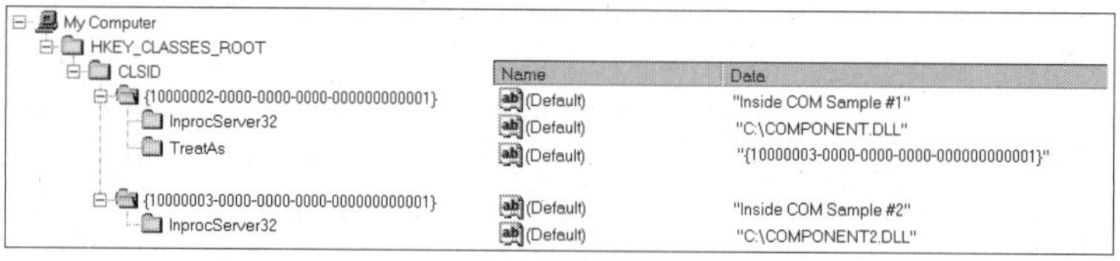

Figure 7-6.
The effect of the CoTreatAsClass *function on the registry.*

Registering a Component Category

In contrast to component registration, where COM+ leaves it up to you to write the code that manually registers objects, component categories have a lot of built-in registration support. COM+ provides a coclass called the Component Categories Manager that implements the *ICatRegister* interface. Through this interface, a client application can create and manipulate component categories.

The *ICatRegister* Interface

You can use the six methods of the *ICatRegister* interface to define component categories and register coclasses that implement or require them. Remember that there is no reason to implement the *ICatRegister* interface; the Component Categories Manager already provides a satisfactory implementation. The following code shows the *ICatRegister* interface in IDL notation:

```
interface ICatRegister : IUnknown
{
// Register a new component category.
HRESULT RegisterCategories(
    [in] ULONG cCategories,
    [in, size_is(cCategories)] CATEGORYINFO rgCategoryInfo[]);

// Remove an existing component category.
HRESULT UnRegisterCategories(
    [in] ULONG cCategories,
    [in, size_is(cCategories)] CATID rgcatid[]);

// Register a CLSID as implementing a component category.
HRESULT RegisterClassImplCategories(
    [in] REFCLSID rclsid,
    [in] ULONG cCategories,
    [in, size_is(cCategories)] CATID rgcatid[]);

// Remove an implemented component category from the CLSID.
HRESULT UnRegisterClassImplCategories(
    [in] REFCLSID rclsid,
    [in] ULONG cCategories,
    [in, size_is(cCategories)] CATID rgcatid[]);

// Register a CLSID as requiring a component category.
HRESULT RegisterClassReqCategories(
    [in] REFCLSID rclsid,
    [in] ULONG cCategories,
    [in, size_is(cCategories)] CATID rgcatid[]);
```

(continued)

```
// Remove a required component category from the CLSID.
HRESULT UnRegisterClassReqCategories(
    [in] REFCLSID rclsid,
    [in] ULONG cCategories,
    [in, size_is(cCategories)] CATID rgcatid[]);
}
```

To use the component category interfaces, you must include the comcat.h file in the source. The following code defines a new CATID, *CATID_Math*, which is implemented by the *InsideCOM* coclass:

```
#include <comcat.h> // For component category stuff

// CATID for the Arithmetic Objects category
CATID CATID_Math =
    {0x10000010,0x0000,0x0000,
    {0x00,0x00,0x00,0x00,0x00,0x00,0x00,0x01}};
```

After making a call to *CoInitializeEx*, a client program can instantiate the Component Categories Manager object, which is identified as *CLSID_StdComponentCategoriesMgr* or with the GUID {0002E 005-0000-0000-C000-000000000046}. A quick scan of the registry reveals that this class is implemented by the in-process server ole32.dll, which is in the Windows\System folder. (In Microsoft Windows 2000, this file is in the WINNT\System32 folder.) COM+'s implementation of the component category interfaces is no different from an in-process component you might create. The following code retrieves a pointer to the *ICatRegister* interface:

```
// Instantiate COM+'s implementation of component categories.
ICatRegister* pCatRegister;
CoCreateInstance(CLSID_StdComponentCategoriesMgr, NULL,
    CLSCTX_INPROC_SERVER, IID_ICatRegister,
    (void**)&pCatRegister);
```

To register the new component category, you build a CATEGORYINFO structure and then call the *ICatRegister::RegisterCategories* method. The CATEGORYINFO structure contains the CATID, a locale identifier (lcid) for localizing the descriptive string, and a string description of the new component category. This structure is shown below:

```
typedef struct tagCATEGORYINFO {
    CATID      catid;
    LCID       lcid;
    OLECHAR szDescription[CATDESC_MAX];
    } CATEGORYINFO, *LPCATEGORYINFO;
```

The Component Categories Manager in addition implements the *IEnumCATEGORYINFO* interface, which enumerates the CATIDs and description strings for the component categories registered on the current system.

After the new component category is registered, you can call the *Release* method to free the *ICatRegister* interface pointer. The following code is normally executed with other self-registration code in the component:

```
// Set up the CATEGORYINFO structure.
CATEGORYINFO catinfo;
catinfo.catid = CATID_Math;
catinfo.lcid = 0x0409; // English
wcsncpy(catinfo.szDescription, L"Arithmetic Objects", 128);

// Install the component category.
pCatRegister->RegisterCategories(1, &catinfo);

// Release COM+'s implementation of component categories.
pCatRegister->Release();
```

If it becomes necessary to unregister a component category, you can call the *ICatRegister::UnRegisterCategories* method, as shown here:

```
pCatRegister->UnRegisterCategories(1, &CATID_Math);
```

Under most circumstances, however, it is unnecessary to remove a component category from the registry; there are likely to be many components of any particular category.

Perhaps more common than registering or unregistering component categories is the task of declaring that a particular coclass implements or requires one or more component categories. The following code calls the *ICatRegister::RegisterClassImplCategories* method to declare that the InsideCOM coclass implements the *Arithmetic Objects* component category. This method adds the Implemented Categories key below the HKEY_CLASSES_ROOT\ CLSID\{*CLSID_InsideCOM*} entry in the registry. The actual CATIDs supported are inserted below the Implemented Categories key. The following code would probably be executed as part of a component self-registration procedure:

```
CATID rgcatid[1];
rgcatid[0] = CATID_Math;
pCatRegister->RegisterClassImplCategories(CLSID_InsideCOM,
    1, rgcatid);
```

Removing a particular CATID from the registration of a coclass, as shown in the following code, is less commonly performed. During the unregister

267

procedure, most components simply delete all their registry settings, so removing implemented categories specifically is unnecessary. It does no harm, however.

```
CATID rgcatid[1];
rgcatid[0] = CATID_Math;
pCatRegister->UnRegisterClassImplCategories(CLSID_InsideCOM, 1,
    rgcatid);
```

Obtaining Component Category Information

When you need to obtain information about available components from the registry, the Component Categories Manager can again be invaluable. In addition to the *ICatRegister* interface, the Component Categories Manager also implements the *ICatInformation* interface, through which you can get information about the categories of already registered components.

The *ICatInformation* Interface

Clients that want to locate one or more components that implement or require certain categories should use the *ICatInformation* interface. Visual Basic, for example, uses the *ICatInformation::EnumClassesOfCategories* method to populate the Components dialog box, which lists the available ActiveX controls. Here is the *ICatInformation* interface in IDL notation:

```
interface ICatInformation : IUnknown
{
// Get an enumerator for the registered categories.
HRESULT EnumCategories(
    [in] LCID lcid,
    [out] IEnumCATEGORYINFO** ppenumCategoryInfo);

// Get the description of a registered component category.
HRESULT GetCategoryDesc(
    [in] REFCATID rcatid,
    [in] LCID lcid,
    [out] LPWSTR* pszDesc);

// Get an enumerator for the classes that support a
// component category.
HRESULT EnumClassesOfCategories(
    [in] ULONG cImplemented,
    [in,size_is(cImplemented)] CATID rgcatidImpl[],
    [in] ULONG cRequired,
    [in,size_is(cRequired)] CATID rgcatidReq[],
    [out] IEnumCLSID** ppenumClsid);
```

```
// Determine whether a class supports a component category.
HRESULT IsClassOfCategories(
    [in] REFCLSID rclsid,
    [in] ULONG cImplemented,
    [in,size_is(cImplemented)] CATID rgcatidImpl[],
    [in] ULONG cRequired,
    [in,size_is(cRequired)] CATID rgcatidReq[]);

// Get an enumerator for component categories implemented by
// a class.
HRESULT EnumImplCategoriesOfClass(
    [in] REFCLSID rclsid,
    [out] IEnumCATID** ppenumCatid);

// Get an enumerator for component categories required by
// a class.
HRESULT EnumReqCategoriesOfClass(
    [in] REFCLSID rclsid,
    [out] IEnumCATID** ppenumCatid);
}
```

The methods of this interface do not affect the information stored in the registry. You use the *ICatInformation* interface to retrieve component category information from the registry in a meaningful format. The following code instantiates the Component Categories Manager and retrieves a pointer to the *ICatInformation* interface:

```
// Instantiate COM+'s implementation of component categories.
// Notice that now we request the ICatInformation interface.
ICatInformation* pCatInformation;
CoCreateInstance(CLSID_StdComponentCategoriesMgr, NULL,
    CLSCTX_INPROC_SERVER, IID_ICatInformation,
    (void**)&pCatInformation);
```

The following code shows the *ICatInformation::EnumClassesOfCategories* method retrieving a pointer to an enumerator that contains the CLSIDs of the coclasses that implement the *Arithmetic Objects* component category:

```
// Get an enumerator for the CLSIDs of Arithmetic Objects.
IEnumCLSID* pEnumCLSID;
pCatInformation->EnumClassesOfCategories(1, &CATID_Math, 0,
    NULL, &pEnumCLSID);
pCatInformation->Release();
```

Next, the code loops through the elements in the enumerator and displays the CLSIDs of all the *Arithmetic Objects* coclasses, as shown in the following code. At the very least, this display should include the CLSID of the *InsideCOM*

269

coclass because it was previously registered as implementing the *Arithmetic Objects* component category.

```
// Loop through the CLSIDs in the enumeration.
CLSID clsid = CLSID_NULL;
DWORD fetched = 0;
while(true)
  {
    // Get the next CLSID.
    pEnumCLSID->Next(1, &clsid, &fetched);
    if(fetched == 0)
        break;

    // Convert the CLSID to a string.
    char buffer[39];
    OLECHAR ppsz[39];
    StringFromGUID2(clsid, ppsz, 39);
    WideCharToMultiByte(CP_ACP, 0, ppsz, 39, buffer, 39,
        NULL, NULL);

    // Print the string form of CLSID.
    cout <<
        "CLSID that supports the Arithmetic Objects component "
        << "category is " << buffer << endl;
}
pEnumCLSID->Release();
```

This code is similar to that executed by Visual Basic when it presents the user with a list of controls. Visual Basic, of course, enumerates classes that implement the ActiveX control CATID {40FC6ED4-2438-11CF-A3DB-080036F12502}. All COM+ components built with Microsoft Visual J++ are automatically labeled as supporting the Java Classes component category.

CHAPTER EIGHT

Connection Points

A client uses the *IUnknown::QueryInterface* method to discover the functionality supported by an object. The more interfaces that are common to the client and the object, the more intertwined their relationship is. But regardless of the number of interfaces the object supports, the basic model remains the same: the client calls the methods implemented by the object, the object performs the desired service, and then the object returns the results to the client. This type of relationship is rather one-sided—the client always makes requests of the object. COM+ supports connection points, a technology that enables an object to "talk back" to its client. Objects that support connection points are often called *connectable objects*.

An object generally uses connection points to notify the client when something interesting happens in the object's sphere; this is known as firing an event. ActiveX controls are the best-known type of the objects that use this technology to raise events in their container. Sometimes objects use connection points to get further information from the client about the service it has requested. At other times, objects use connection points to request that the client perform a service—in effect turning the tables on their relationship. Regardless of the reason for using connection points, this generic COM+ facility supports bidirectional communication between a client and an object.

Connection points involve some rather peculiar terminology, which deserves a moment of attention. A *source interface,* also called an outgoing interface, is an interface defined in the object but implemented by the client. A *sink object,* which resides within the client, is the object that implements the object's source interface. Knowing these definitions will help you understand connection points. Figure 8-1 shows the layout of these elements.

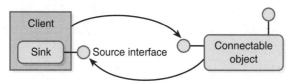

Figure 8-1.
A connectable object using a source interface to "talk back" to the client.

A Simple Connectable Object

To support connection points, Microsoft offers these four interfaces: *IConnectionPointContainer, IEnumConnectionPoints, IConnectionPoint,* and *IEnumConnections.* Due to their generic design, these interfaces can initially seem overwhelmingly complex. To make this technology more comprehensible, let's build a simple, pared-down connectable object. Keep in mind that this example is not a full implementation of all the connection point interfaces—we'll develop a full-fledged example later in this chapter.

The example implements the *IConnectionPoint* and *IConnectionPoint-Container* interfaces. The two other interfaces, *IEnumConnectionPoints* and *IEnumConnections,* enumerate the available connection points and the current connections, respectively. While these latter two interfaces are not difficult to implement, enumerators are not simple to understand and they detract from the discussion of connection points, so we'll add the enumerators in the full version of the connection point example.

The Source Interface

As with most other programming tasks in COM+, working with connection points starts in Interface Definition Language (IDL). First, we must define the source interface that will be implemented by the sink and called by the connectable object. For demonstration purposes, we'll define a source interface named *IOutGoing,* shown below in IDL notation. The *GotMessage* method of the *IOutGoing* interface notifies the sink that something has happened in the connectable object.

```
[ object, uuid(10000005-0000-0000-0000-000000000001),
  oleautomation ]
interface IOutGoing : IUnknown
{
    HRESULT GotMessage(int Message);
}
```

Next, we need to add this interface to the *coclass* statement, as shown in the following IDL code. Notice that we declare the *IOutGoing* interface using the *source* attribute, as shown in boldface. In the type library created by the Microsoft IDL (MIDL) compiler, this attribute indicates that *IOutGoing* is a source of events and that the interface is called rather than implemented by the *InsideCOM* coclass. Every *coclass* statement in the IDL file can have a default incoming interface (the standard kind) as well as a default source interface. If the default is not indicated using the *default* attribute, the first outgoing and incoming interfaces are treated as the defaults.[1] This assignment of defaults is important because high-level languages such as Microsoft Visual Basic automatically call *IUnknown::QueryInterface* for the interface marked with the *default* attribute.

```
[ uuid(10000003-0000-0000-0000-000000000001),
  helpstring("Inside COM+ Component Type Library"),
  version(1.0) ]
library Component
{
    importlib("stdole32.tlb");

    interface ISum;
    interface IOutGoing;
    [ uuid(10000002-0000-0000-0000-000000000001) ]
    coclass InsideCOM
    {
        interface ISum;
        [source] interface IOutGoing;
    }
};
```

The *IConnectionPoint* Interface

A connection point is an object managed by the connectable object that implements the *IConnectionPoint* interface. The main purpose of this interface is to let a client provide a connectable object with a pointer to the client's sink, as shown in Figure 8-2. Each connection point supports exactly one source interface.

---

1. Actually, the first outgoing and incoming interfaces not marked with the *restricted* IDL attribute are assumed to be the defaults. The *restricted* attribute hides the specified interface from use in languages that rely on type libraries, such as Visual Basic and Java.

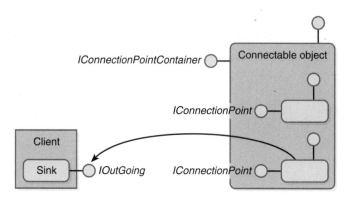

Figure 8-2.
A pointer to the client's sink obtained via the IConnectionPoint *interface.*

Here is the *IConnectionPoint* interface in IDL notation:

```
interface IConnectionPoint : IUnknown
{
    // Get the IID of the outgoing interface.
    HRESULT GetConnectionInterface
    (
        [out]   IID * piid
    );

    // Get the IConnectionPointContainer that we belong to.
    HRESULT GetConnectionPointContainer
    (
        [out]   IConnectionPointContainer ** ppCPC
    );

    // Here's a pointer to my sink.
    HRESULT Advise
    (
        [in]    IUnknown * pUnkSink,
        [out]   DWORD *    pdwCookie
    );

    // Don't call us--we'll call you.
    HRESULT Unadvise
    (
        [in]    DWORD dwCookie
    );
```

```
// Who else do you talk to?
HRESULT EnumConnections
(
    [out]   IEnumConnections ** ppEnum
);
}
```

Of the five methods of *IConnectionPoint*, we'll initially implement only the two most important ones: *Advise* and *Unadvise*. All the other methods simply return *E_NOTIMPL* for now. The client calls the *IConnectionPoint::Advise* method to provide the connectable object with a pointer to the client's sink object. In a way, you can consider this call a *QueryInterface* call in reverse. A client uses the *IUnknown::QueryInterface* method to discover the interfaces exposed by an object. It calls *IConnectionPoint::Advise* to provide an object with a pointer to its sink. So instead of the question asked by *QueryInterface*, "What interfaces do you support?" the *Advise* method tells the object, "Here is a pointer to my sink."

Although the *IConnectionPoint::Advise* method provides the connectable object with a pointer to the client sink's *IUnknown* interface, this pointer alone is not sufficient. To call the methods of the client's sink object, we must obtain a pointer to one of the more interesting interfaces implemented by the sink. Thus, the *IUnknown::QueryInterface* method is the first call made from the connectable object to the client's sink! Then the *IConnectionPoint::Advise* method returns a unique number to the client that identifies the advisory relationship that has been established. The client retains this number, called a *cookie*, for later use in terminating the connection.

A simple implementation of the *Advise* method looks like this:

```
HRESULT CInsideCOM::Advise(IUnknown* pUnknown, DWORD* pdwCookie)
{
    // Hard-code the cookie value.
    *pdwCookie = 1;

    // Get a pointer to the sink's source interface.
    return pUnknown->QueryInterface(IID_IOutGoing,
        (void**)&g_pOutGoing);
}
```

Since this code is prepared to handle only a single connection, the cookie returned to the client is a dummy placeholder. The connectable object then calls the sink object's *IUnknown::QueryInterface* method to obtain a pointer to its *IOutGoing* interface. This pointer is stored in a global variable for later use. Conveniently, the *IUnknown::AddRef* operation required to increment the reference counter is encapsulated within the *QueryInterface* call.

The *QueryInterface* call might seem redundant. After all, since each connection point supports one source interface, why doesn't the client simply provide that interface pointer in the *Advise* call in place of the *IUnknown* pointer? The answer is that connection points are designed to be a general-purpose mechanism for configuring bidirectional communication in COM+. Because the designers of the connection point interfaces had no way of knowing what custom interfaces a sink object might implement, *IUnknown* was the only option.

The *IConnectionPoint::Unadvise* method terminates an advisory relationship that was previously established using the *Advise* method. The cookie argument passed to *Unadvise* identifies which connection should be terminated. In the following implementation, the *Unadvise* method simply releases the interface pointer obtained previously:

```
HRESULT CInsideCOM::Unadvise(DWORD dwCookie)
{
    // Ignoring dwCookie; only one connection is
    // supported anyway.
    g_pOutGoing->Release();
    return NOERROR;
}
```

At this stage, the component has a pointer to the sink object and can call the *GotMessage* method of the *IOutGoing* interface. An interesting question remains, however: how does the client get a pointer to the *IConnectionPoint* interface in the first place? This is the job of the *IConnectionPointContainer* interface.

The *IConnectionPointContainer* Interface

The methods of the *IConnectionPoint* interface establish and release connections between a client and a connectable object; the methods of the *IConnectionPointContainer* interface discover the connection points of a connectable object. When implemented by an object, the *IConnectionPointContainer* interface embodies the qualities that make an object "connectable." The two methods of the *IConnectionPointContainer* interface are shown here:

```
interface IConnectionPointContainer : IUnknown
{
    // Tell me about your connection points.
    HRESULT EnumConnectionPoints
    (
        [out] IEnumConnectionPoints ** ppEnum
    );
```

```
// Do you support a specific connection point?
HRESULT FindConnectionPoint
(
    [in] REFIID riid,
    [out] IConnectionPoint ** ppCP
);
}
```

Clients that want to enumerate all the source interfaces supported by a connectable object should call *IConnectionPointContainer::EnumConnection-Points*, which retrieves a pointer to an object that supports the *IEnumConnection-Points* enumeration interface. At this stage, we do not support enumerator objects, so this method returns *E_NOTIMPL*. Note that returning *E_NOTIMPL* from *IConnectionPointContainer::EnumConnectionPoints* is not recommended because with the exception of type information, a client cannot determine the interface identifiers (IIDs) of the source interfaces that a connectable object supports.

The *IConnectionPointContainer::FindConnectionPoint* method is the *QueryInterface* of connection points. It asks the connectable object, "Do you support a particular source interface?" If the connectable object supports the requested interface, the method returns a pointer to that source interface's connection point (an object that implements the *IConnectionPoint* interface). *QueryInterface* actually obtains the *IConnectionPoint* interface pointer, as shown in the following implementation of the *IConnectionPointContainer:: FindConnectionPoint* method:

```
HRESULT CInsideCOM::FindConnectionPoint(REFIID riid,
    IConnectionPoint** ppCP)
{
    // If we support the source interface, then QI for
    // the connection point.
    if(riid == IID_IOutGoing)
        return QueryInterface(IID_IConnectionPoint,
            (void**)ppCP);
    return E_NOINTERFACE;
}
```

This implementation of *FindConnectionPoint* supports only one source interface, *IOutGoing*. *E_NOINTERFACE* is returned if the client is looking for the connection point of some other source interface. Assuming that the client wants *IOutGoing*, *QueryInterface* is called to obtain a pointer to the connection point, and that pointer is returned to the client. This answers the question of how the client obtains the pointer to the *IConnectionPoint* interface. If you're wondering how the *IConnectionPointContainer* interface is obtained, just remember your good friend *QueryInterface*. The *InsideCOM* coclass implements *QueryInterface* in the standard fashion, simply handing out pointers to the *IConnectionPointContainer* interface as requested, as shown below in boldface:

```
HRESULT CInsideCOM::QueryInterface(REFIID riid, void** ppv)
{
    if(riid == IID_IUnknown)
        *ppv = (ISum*)this;
    else if(riid == IID_ISum)
        *ppv = (ISum*)this;
    else if(riid == IID_IConnectionPointContainer)
        *ppv = (IConnectionPointContainer*)this;
    else if(riid == IID_IConnectionPoint)
        *ppv = (IConnectionPoint*)this;
    else
    {
        *ppv = NULL;
        return E_NOINTERFACE;
    }
    AddRef();
    return S_OK;
}
```

The final bit of code required in the component is the call to the *IOutGoing::GotMessage* method. To make things interesting, we'll call this method whenever the user presses a key on the keyboard. The ASCII key code is sent to the client in the *Message* parameter of *GotMessage*. To make things even more interesting, you can configure the client and component on different computers and then watch the events fire across the network. The following code reads keyboard input from the console by using the Win32 function *ReadConsoleInput* (shown in boldface) and then calls the *GotMessage* method of the sink object:

```
// Press any key to fire an event at the client.
HANDLE handles[2] =
    { g_hEvent, GetStdHandle(STD_INPUT_HANDLE) };

// READY...
while(WaitForMultipleObjects(2, handles, FALSE, INFINITE) -
    WAIT_OBJECT_0 == 1)
{
    INPUT_RECORD ir;
    DWORD read;
```

```
// AIM...
    ReadConsoleInput(handles[1], &ir, 1, &read);
    if(ir.EventType == KEY_EVENT &&
        ir.Event.KeyEvent.bKeyDown == TRUE)

// FIRE!!!
        g_pOutGoing->
            GotMessage(ir.Event.KeyEvent.uChar.AsciiChar);
}
```

Implementing a Sink in C++

To test the connectable object, we must expand the client program built in the previous chapters to include a sink object that receives and responds to the fired events. The client code is where the *IOutGoing* interface is actually implemented by the *CSink* class, as shown here:

```
class CSink : public IOutGoing
{
public:
    // IUnknown
    ULONG __stdcall AddRef();
    ULONG __stdcall Release();
    HRESULT __stdcall QueryInterface(REFIID riid, void** ppv);

    // IOutGoing
    HRESULT __stdcall GotMessage(int Message);

    CSink() : m_cRef(0) { }
    ~CSink() { }

private:
    long m_cRef;
};
```

As you can see, the *CSink* class implements the *IUnknown* and *IOutGoing* interfaces. We won't bore you with the all-too-standard implementations of *IUnknown::AddRef, Release*, and *QueryInterface*. The *IOutGoing::GotMessage* method, shown here, is more interesting because the connectable object calls it whenever the user presses a key:[2]

---

2. A quacking sound can be heard whenever the B key is pressed. Readers of Kraig Brockschmidt's *Inside OLE* (Microsoft Press, 1995) will understand.

```
HRESULT CSink::GotMessage(int Message)
{
    if(Message == (int)'b' || Message == (int)'B')
        PlaySound("BrockschmidtQuack", NULL,
            SND_RESOURCE|SND_ASYNC);
    cout << "CSink::GotMessage is " << (char)Message << endl;
    return S_OK;
}
```

Setting Up a Connection Point

The client code starts out in the standard fashion, calling *CoCreateInstance* to instantiate the *InsideCOM* coclass, as shown here:

```
// Instantiate the object.
IUnknown* pUnknown;
CoCreateInstance(CLSID_InsideCOM, NULL, CLSCTX_LOCAL_SERVER,
    IID_IUnknown, (void**)&pUnknown);
```

Next, the client calls *IUnknown::QueryInterface* to determine whether *InsideCOM* is a connectable object, as shown in the following code. If the object supports the *IConnectionPointContainer* interface, it qualifies as "connectable."

```
// Query for IConnectionPointContainer.
IConnectionPointContainer* pConnectionPointContainer;
hr = pUnknown->QueryInterface(IID_IConnectionPointContainer,
    (void**)&pConnectionPointContainer);
```

The *IConnectionPointContainer::FindConnectionPoint* method is then called to retrieve the connection point for the *IOutGoing* interface, as shown below. Notice that we are not yet using the *IConnectionPointContainer::Enum-ConnectionPoints* method because this method currently returns *E_NOTIMPL*.

```
// Find the connection point for IOutGoing.
IConnectionPoint* pConnectionPoint;
hr = pConnectionPointContainer->FindConnectionPoint(
    IID_IOutGoing, &pConnectionPoint);
```

Using the pointer obtained from *FindConnectionPoint*, the client calls *IConnectionPoint::Advise* to provide the connectable object with a pointer to the sink object. Of course, the sink object must be instantiated in the client before its pointer can be sent to the component! This task is accomplished using the C++ keyword *new*, as shown here:

```
// Instantiate the sink object.
CSink* mySink = new CSink;

// Give the connectable object a pointer to the sink.
DWORD dwCookie;
pConnectionPoint->Advise((IUnknown*)mySink, &dwCookie);
```

At this stage, there is an advisory relationship between the client's sink and the connectable object. Whenever the user presses a key from within the component, the sink's *IOutGoing::GotMessage* method is called. When the user tires of this fantastic program and decides to exit, the *IConnectionPoint::Unadvise* method is called to terminate this connection, as shown here:

```
// Terminate the connection.
pConnectionPoint->Unadvise(dwCookie);
```

This call is followed by several calls to *IUnknown::Release* to free all the pointers used in the course of this exercise, as shown in the following code snippet:

```
// Release everything in sight.
pConnectionPoint->Release();
pConnectionPointContainer->Release();
pUnknown->Release();
```

Figure 8-3 shows the calls made by the client and the connectable object to establish their relationship; the numbers indicate the order of the calls.

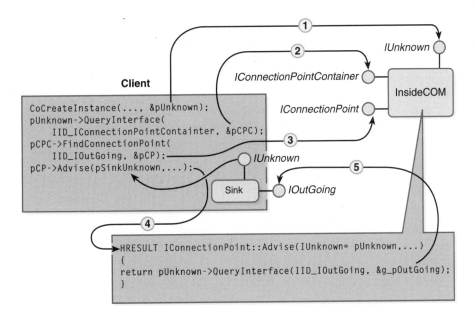

Figure 8-3.
The steps that the client and the connectable object take so the InsideCOM connectable object can obtain a pointer to its client's sink and fire back events.

Multicasting with Connection Points

A one-to-one relationship is typical but not required between a client and a connectable object. The connection point architecture is generic enough to support a connectable object that fires events at multiple sinks, or a sink that gets hooked up to several connectable objects. Figure 8-4 shows several clients connecting their sinks to a single connectable object.

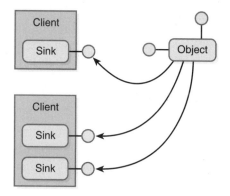

Figure 8-4.
A connectable object firing events at multiple sinks.

Although the connection point architecture supports multicasting, this doesn't happen automatically. The connectable object itself must keep track of its client sinks and then fire the events individually. It can sequentially fire the same event at all the client sinks that called *IConnectionPoint::Advise* by iterating through its current connections using the following code:

```
IOutGoing* pOutGoing;
for(int count = 0; count < CCONNMAX; count++)
    if(m_rgpUnknown[count] != NULL)
    {
        pOutGoing = (IOutGoing*)m_rgpUnknown[count];
        pOutGoing->SomethingHappened(WhatHappened);
    }
```

Figure 8-5 shows the inverse of this topology: a single client application has advised several connectable objects of its sink. Now the same client sink receives events fired by any of the connectable objects. This setup is most useful when a client wants to listen to several connectable objects at the same time in one sink.

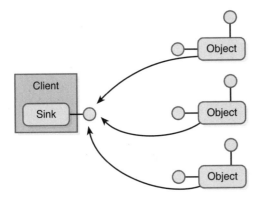

Figure 8-5.
A single sink receiving events fired from multiple connectable objects.

A Visual Basic Sink

To liven things up a bit, let's use Visual Basic to test our simple connectable object. After slogging through the preceding *CSink* code, you'll find that intercepting events in Visual Basic is almost dishearteningly easy. You simply use the *WithEvents* keyword when you declare an object variable, and Visual Basic dynamically creates a sink object that implements the source interface supported by the connectable object. Then you instantiate the object using the Visual Basic *New* keyword. Now, whenever the connectable object calls methods of the source interface, Visual Basic's sink object checks to see whether you have written any code to handle the call. For example, in the following code, the standard-looking *myRef_GotMessage* event procedure handles the *InsideCOM* coclass's *GotMessage* event:

```
' Declare the object variable.
Dim WithEvents myRef As InsideCOM

Private Sub Form_Load()
    ' Instantiate the connectable object.
    Set myRef = New InsideCOM
End Sub

' Catch events here...
Private Sub myRef_GotMessage(ByVal Message As Long)
    Print Chr(Message)
End Sub
```

The rules of COM+ state that the *InsideCOM* coclass is not an entirely legitimate connectable object because it does not implement all the connection point interfaces. But since Visual Basic is willing to work with it, it has a great deal of credibility.[3] If you have only a relatively basic need for a connectable object, this code might be sufficient. Connectable objects were designed for ActiveX controls and thus can seem unnecessarily complicated if the full power of this paradigm is not required.

Creating a Sink Dynamically

This simple Visual Basic code raises an interesting question: How does Visual Basic's sink implement the *IOutGoing* interface? In Figure 8-3, on page 281, the sink object exposes the *IOutGoing* interface, which is easy enough to accomplish because the code we wrote in the *CSink* class inherited the interface definition and implemented its methods. Visual Basic, however, has no knowledge of the *IOutGoing* interface, but it can still respond correctly to the *IOutGoing::GotMessage* event.

This fact is as amazing as it seems. For Visual Basic to correctly respond to events fired from connectable objects, it must dynamically synthesize a sink object that implements the designated source interface. This means that at run time, Visual Basic must create a v-table containing entry points for each member function, and later it must call the Visual Basic procedure that handles the event (if one exists), properly constructing a stack frame on the way.

Figure 8-6 shows the steps that Visual Basic takes to perform this miraculous feat. First, it obtains the component's type information[4] to learn about the source interface supported by the connectable object. Using this information about the interface, its methods, and their arguments, Visual Basic dynamically constructs a v-table for the source interface. Now, when the connectable object fires an event at Visual Basic, everything works properly. The connectable object is not aware of the extraordinary lengths to which Visual Basic has gone to make this work.

The problem with creating a generic sink, such as that provided by Visual Basic, is that at compile time the methods of the source interfaces supported by the connectable object are unknown. C++ does not help solve this problem because a C++ compiler adds only virtual functions that are known at compile time to a v-table. To dynamically create a v-table, as Visual Basic does, you must

---

3. Or perhaps it simply proves that Visual Basic is a most forgiving client.
4. The type information is obtained via the *IProvideClassInfo* interface; see Chapter 9.

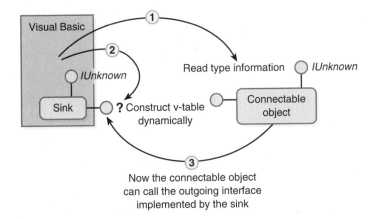

Now the connectable object
can call the outgoing interface
implemented by the sink

Figure 8-6.
*The steps that Visual Basic takes to handle events fired from a
connectable object.*

drop below the level of functionality offered by virtual functions in C++ and
handcraft the v-table structure normally generated automatically by the C++
compiler. You can define the sink object using a structure, which in C++ is equivalent to a class with public members anyway.

In the following declaration, you can see the binary standard that defines
all COM+ objects. The first entry in the memory structure of a COM+ object
must always be a pointer to the v-table. Normally, this entry is created automatically and hidden from view by C++ for any class containing virtual functions.

```
// This sink can implement any interface at run time.
// In C++, struct == public class.
struct CStink // Class for the generic sink object
{
    // The first item must be a pointer to the v-table
    // of the sink, declared as a pointer to one or more
    // function pointers.
    // Here we can see the binary standard that defines COM+.
    void (__stdcall **pVtbl)();

    // Next comes the object's data.
    long m_cRef; // Reference-counting variable
};
```

Since *IUnknown* is the only interface that a COM+ object is required to
implement, it is the only interface that can be predefined for a truly generic sink

object. Because all three *IUnknown* methods are no longer members of a C++ class, they take a first parameter that points to the current object. This parameter replaces the implicit C++ *this* pointer that is normally available in all nonstatic member functions. Because all C++ compilers provide this argument automatically, it is a de facto part of the binary COM+ standard. In the following code, the first argument is named *me* to avoid collision with the *this* keyword. Also notice that any access to the member variable *m_cRef* is done through the *me* pointer. A little bit of this type of code can quickly make you appreciate the work normally done automatically by C++.

```
// Nonstatic methods in a class always have an implicit this
// argument that points to the current object. Since
// these methods are not part of a class, we make believe....
// Every method in the interface must pretend to have a this
// argument because all callers will provide it.
ULONG __stdcall CStink_AddRef(CStink* me)
{
    // me is a stand-in for this, a reserved keyword in C++.
    // Everything must be explicitly accessed through the
    // pointer to the object.
    // Now we can appreciate what C++ does automatically.
    return ++me->m_cRef;
}


ULONG __stdcall CStink_Release(CStink* me)
{
    if(--me->m_cRef != 0)
        return me->m_cRef;
    delete me; // We can even use delete.
    return 0;
}


HRESULT __stdcall CStink_QueryInterface(CStink* me, REFIID riid,
    void** ppv)
{
    if(riid == IID_IUnknown || riid == IID_IOutGoing)
        *ppv = &me->pVtbl; // Here's a pointer to our interface.
    else
    {
        *ppv = NULL;
        return E_NOINTERFACE;
    }
    CStink_AddRef(me);
    return S_OK;
}
```

When the time comes to instantiate the sink object, you can use the standard C++ *new* operator, as shown in the following code fragment. The result does not qualify as a COM+ object, however, because it does not yet support the *IUnknown* methods.

```
// Instantiate the object, sort of...
CStink* mySink = new CStink;
```

Now you allocate memory for a v-table and initialize the individual function pointers. The following code uses the COM+ memory allocation function *CoTaskMemAlloc*. This function automatically gets a pointer to the system's implementation of the memory allocation interface *IMalloc* and then allocates memory by calling *IMalloc::Alloc*. The size of the v-table allocated depends on the number of methods in the source interface being implemented. The minimum size is always 12 bytes: 4 bytes for each of the three methods of *IUnknown*. Since the *IOutGoing* interface defines the one additional *GotMessage* method, four v-table entries are required, consuming a grand total of 16 bytes.

```
// 3 methods in IUnknown + number of methods in the
// source interface
int num_methods = 4;

// Allocate memory for the v-table, and cast the returned
// void* to a pointer to an array of function pointers.
void (__stdcall **IStink)() =
    (void (__stdcall **)())CoTaskMemAlloc(
        num_methods * sizeof(void*));
    // sizeof(void*) = 4 bytes per pointer.
```

Now you must initialize each entry in the v-table so that it points to the correct function, as shown in the following code. Note that the order of these functions is not arbitrary. The order in which an interface's methods appear in the v-table is a defined part of every interface. For *IUnknown*, the order is *QueryInterface*, *AddRef*, and then *Release*.

```
// Initialize the v-table to point to our implementations.
// These three methods always come first (and in this order)!
*(IStink + 0) = (void (__stdcall *)())CStink_QueryInterface;
*(IStink + 1) = (void (__stdcall *)())CStink_AddRef;
*(IStink + 2) = (void (__stdcall *)())CStink_Release;
```

At this stage, the *IUnknown* functionality is in place. Now a truly generic implementation of a sink object, such as that provided by Visual Basic, gets the type information for the connectable object's source interface. Additional functions can be synthesized once the sink has learned about all the methods (and their associated arguments) of the source interface. How to accomplish this task is a bit beyond the scope of this section, so we'll stick with simply wiring the last v-table entry to point to an implementation of the *IOutGoing::GotMessage* method discussed earlier.

```
// Now add any additional methods to the v-table based on the
// available type information for the source interface.

// IOutGoing has only one additional method.
*(IStink + 3) = (void (__stdcall *)())GotMessage;
```

Finally, the v-table structure must be plugged into the sink object itself, and its reference counter must be initialized, as shown here:

```
// Give the sink a brain.
mySink->pVtbl = IStink;

// Initialize the sink's reference counter.
mySink->m_cRef = 0;
```

Now a pointer to the sink object can be passed to the connectable object using the standard *IConnectionPoint::Advise* method, as shown in the following code. To the connectable object, our handcrafted sink should be indistinguishable from one mass-produced by C++. You can test this by running the client with the connectable object we built earlier in this chapter in the section titled "A Simple Connectable Object."

```
DWORD dwCookie;
hr = pConnectionPoint->Advise((IUnknown*)mySink, &dwCookie);
```

After *IConnectionPoint::Unadvise* is called to terminate the connection, the v-table we worked so hard to create must be destroyed. Here the *CoTaskMemFree* function, the analogue of *CoTaskMemAlloc*, does the job:

```
// Now free the v-table; the object has probably already
// deleted itself.
CoTaskMemFree(IStink);
```

You can implement unfamiliar source interfaces in a sink only if type information describing the outgoing interface is available. Through type information, Visual Basic learns about all the attributes, methods, and method arguments of an interface—enough information to correctly generate a sink object that implements the interface and to connect that sink with the connectable object. Without this information, a client that encounters an unfamiliar outgoing interface is completely out of luck. In fact, the idea of type information was originally developed in conjunction with connectable objects for the ActiveX Controls specification (then called OLE Controls). Fortunately, most clients need not be as generic as Visual Basic and thus know at compile time what source interfaces must be implemented by their sink.

Visual Basic and high-level scripting languages such as VBScript do have one limitation relating to connection points: they do not support nondefault source interfaces. For example, the following IDL code defines a coclass containing two source interfaces, *IOutGoing* and *INonDefaultOutGoing*, shown in boldface. Currently Visual Basic and scripting languages ignore the *INonDefaultOutGoing* interface, restricting you to events of the default source interface. Of course, client applications written in C++ or Java can access any source interface defined by a connectable object.

```
[ uuid(10000003-0000-0000-0000-000000000001) ]
library Component
{
    importlib("stdole32.tlb");

    interface IOutGoing;
    interface INonDefaultOutGoing;

    [ uuid(10000002-0000-0000-0000-000000000001) ]
    coclass InsideCOM
    {
        [default, source] interface IOutGoing;
        [source] interface INonDefaultOutGoing;
    }
};
```

A Java Sink

A program written in Java can also intercept events fired by a connectable object. Implementing a sink in Java is nearly as simple as in Visual Basic. First, you use the Project/Add COM Wrapper command in Microsoft Visual J++ and select the Inside COM+ Component Type Library. Visual J++ creates a subdirectory named *component* and then generates Java wrappers for the coclasses and interfaces described in the type library of the component: InsideCOM.java, ISum.java, and IOutGoing.java.

The *JavaSink* class shown in Listing 8-1 implements the *GotMessage* method of the *IOutGoing* interface. Hooking up the sink to the connectable object is quite easy using the *com.ms.com.ConnectionPointCookie* class provided with Microsoft's Java Virtual Machine (VM). The constructor of the *ConnectionPointCookie* class creates a connection between the connectable object and the sink using the IID of the source interface. Notice the use of the *import* statement to access the classes and interfaces of the *component* package. This reference lets you access the classes and interfaces of the component package by prefixing each reference with *component*.

JavaSink.java

```java
import component.*;
import com.ms.com.ConnectionPointCookie;

public class JavaSink implements IOutGoing
{
    public void GotMessage(int Message)
    {
        System.out.println((char)Message);
    }
}

class Driver
{
    public static void main(String[] args)
    {
        ISum ref = (ISum)new component.InsideCOM();
        System.out.println("8 + 9 = " + ref.Sum(8, 9));

        try
        {
            JavaSink j = new JavaSink();
            ConnectionPointCookie EventCookie = new
                ConnectionPointCookie(ref, j,
                    Class.forName("component.IOutGoing"));
            System.out.println("Press Enter to exit.");
            System.in.read();
        }
        catch(Exception e)
        {
        }
    }
}
```

Listing 8-1.
A Java client that implements a sink that can handle GotMessage *events fired from the* InsideCOM *connectable object.*

A Complete Connectable Object

Now that we've explored the basic architecture of connection points, it's time to examine a complete implementation of a connectable object, replete with enumerators and full implementations of the *IConnectionPointContainer* and the *IConnectionPoint* interfaces. Let's begin with the main interface exposed by an object that expresses the existence of outgoing interfaces: *IConnection-PointContainer*. A client that wants to hook up with a connectable object initially queries for the *IConnectionPointContainer* interface. From there, the client can locate individual connection points by calling *IConnectionPointContainer::FindConnectionPoint* or *IConnectionPointContainer::EnumConnectionPoints*. *FindConnectionPoint* takes the IID of the desired source interface and, if successful, returns a pointer to the relevant *IConnectionPoint* interface. *EnumConnectionPoints* is more complicated because it returns a pointer to an object that implements the *IEnumConnectionPoints* interface. (Enumerators are discussed next in this chapter.)

An implementation of *IConnectionPointContainer::EnumConnectionPoints* might look like this:

```
HRESULT CInsideCOM::EnumConnectionPoints(
    IEnumConnectionPoints** ppEnum)
{
    CEnumConnectionPoints* pEnum = new CEnumConnectionPoints(
        reinterpret_cast<IUnknown*>(this), (void**)m_rgpConnPt);
    return pEnum->QueryInterface(IID_IEnumConnectionPoints,
        (void**)ppEnum);
}
```

This code instantiates the *CEnumConnectionPoints* class using the *new* operator and then returns a pointer to the *IEnumConnectionPoints* interface exposed by the object. To the constructor of the *CEnumConnectionPoints* class, we pass a pointer to the current object (*this*) for reference counting and an array of connection points that can be enumerated (*m_rgpConnPt*).

The array of connection points is set up during the construction phase of the *InsideCOM* object, as shown here:

```
const NUM_CONNECTION_POINTS = 1;

CInsideCOM::InsideCOM() : m_cRef(0)
{
    g_cComponents++;
    m_cRef = 0;
```

(continued)

```
    // Initialize all the connection points to NULL.
    for(int count = 0; count < NUM_CONNECTION_POINTS; count++)
        m_rgpConnPt[count] = NULL;

    // Create our connection point.
    m_rgpConnPt[0] = new CConnectionPoint(this, IID_IOutGoing);
    m_rgpConnPt[0]->AddRef();

    // Additional connection points can be instantiated here.
}
```

In this example, *NUM_CONNECTION_POINTS* equals *1*, indicating that this connectable object supports only one source interface. The code, however, is defined in such a way that you can easily extend it to support connectable objects with multiple source interfaces. You simply set the *NUM_CONNECTION_POINTS* constant to the number of source interfaces supported by an object and instantiate the individual connection point objects with the IID of each supported source interface. More sophisticated implementations of the *IConnectionPointContainer::EnumConnectionPoints* method might use a linked list instead of an array to more flexibly support an arbitrary number of connection points.

Enumerators

An *enumerator object* iterates through a sequence of items. You can use an enumerator object in COM+ when a set of items lends itself to enumeration. Each enumerator object implements a different interface depending on the type of object it enumerates. A number of enumerator interfaces are defined, including *IEnumUnknown*, *IEnumString*, and *IEnumMoniker*, each of which is implemented by an enumerator object that enumerates objects of the specified type. However, all of the enumerator interfaces have the same four methods: *Next*, *Skip*, *Reset*, and *Clone*. This is not to say that all enumerators are alike; the methods of each enumerator interface generally take parameters of different types since each enumerator enumerates different kinds of things. Behind the facade of the four methods, you can implement the enumerator object in whatever way you see fit (using a linked list, an array, and so on).

The concept of an enumerator interface can perhaps best be expressed using C++ templates, as shown here:

```
template <class T> class IEnum : public IUnknown
{
public:
    virtual HRESULT Next(ULONG cElement, T* pElement,
        ULONG* pcFetched)=0;
```

```
virtual HRESULT Skip(ULONG cElement)=0;
virtual HRESULT Reset(void)=0;
virtual HRESULT Clone(IEnum<T>** ppEnum)=0;
};
```

If you ever need to design a set of custom interfaces in COM+, you might need to enumerate objects of a certain type that you have defined. In this case, it is a good idea to design a custom enumerator interface using the same four methods and following the pattern set by standard enumerator interfaces.

The *IEnumConnectionPoints* Enumerator

Here is the IDL definition of the enumerator interface *IEnumConnectionPoints*, which enumerates objects that implement the *IConnectionPoint* interface:

```
interface IEnumConnectionPoints : IUnknown
{
    // Get me the next connection point(s).
    HRESULT Next(
        [in] ULONG cConnections,
        [out, size_is(cConnections), length_is(*pcFetched)]
            IConnectionPoint* ppCP,
        [out] ULONG* pcFetched);

    // Skip the next connection point(s).
    HRESULT Skip([in] ULONG cConnections);

    // Start at the beginning.
    HRESULT Reset(void);

    // Give me a new enumerator object.
    HRESULT Clone([out] IEnumConnectionPoints** ppEnum);
}
```

The *CEnumConnectionPoints* class we created for the full connection points sample (which is on the companion CD in the Samples\Connection Points\Full folder) is publicly derived from *IEnumConnectionPoints* and thus implements the three methods of *IUnknown* plus the four methods of *IEnumConnectionPoints*. The *Next* method, shown in the following code, is the heart of every enumerator. You call it to retrieve one or more consecutive items from the enumeration. The first parameter of the *Next* method is always the number of items to be retrieved. The number of items actually retrieved from the enumerator is returned in the third parameter, a pointer to a long value allocated by the caller. This pointer must point to a valid address unless the client is retrieving only one item, in which case the third parameter can be *NULL*. The second parameter of the enumerator retrieves the desired items from enumeration. In the case of the

IEnumConnectionPoints interface, the *Next* method retrieves pointers to connection point objects:

```
HRESULT CEnumConnectionPoints::Next(ULONG cConnections,
    IConnectionPoint** rgpcn, ULONG* pcFetched)
{
    if(rgpcn == NULL)
        return E_POINTER;
    if(pcFetched == NULL && cConnections != 1)
        return E_INVALIDARG;
    if(pcFetched != NULL)
        *pcFetched = 0;

    while(m_iCur < NUM_CONNECTION_POINTS && cConnections > 0)
    {
        *rgpcn = m_rgpCP[m_iCur++];
        if(*rgpcn != NULL)
            (*rgpcn)->AddRef();
        if(pcFetched != NULL)
            (*pcFetched)++;
        cConnections--;
        rgpcn++;
    }
    return S_OK;
}
```

Recall from Chapter 2 that you must call *IUnknown::AddRef* when a method returns an interface pointer. Since the *IEnumConnectionPoints::Next* method hands out pointers to the *IConnectionPoint* interface, it must first call *AddRef*. The caller is responsible for calling *Release* through each pointer enumerated by this method.

The *IEnumXXXX::Skip* method instructs the enumerator to skip a specified number of elements; if successful, subsequent calls to *IEnumXXXX::Next* return elements after those that were skipped. In the following implementation of *IEnumConnectionPoints::Skip*, the *m_iCur* private member variable is incremented so that it correctly identifies the element immediately following those that were skipped:

```
HRESULT CEnumConnectionPoints::Skip(ULONG cConnections)
{
    if(m_iCur + cConnections >= NUM_CONNECTION_POINTS)
        return S_FALSE;
    m_iCur += cConnections;
    return S_OK;
}
```

The *IEnumXXXX::Reset* method orders the enumerator to position itself at the first element in the enumeration. Note that enumerators are not required to return the same set of elements on each pass through the list, even if *Reset* is not called. For example, an enumerator for a list of files in a directory might continually change in response to changes in the underlying file system. In this sample, the implementation of *IEnumConnectionPoints::Reset* simply sets *m_iCur* to *0*, causing it to refer to the first element in the array:

```
HRESULT CEnumConnectionPoints::Reset()
{
    m_iCur = 0;
    return S_OK;
}
```

The *IEnumXXXX::Clone* method creates and returns a pointer to an exact copy of the enumerator object, making it possible to record a point in an enumeration sequence, create a clone and work with that enumerator, and later return to the previous element in the first enumerator. In the implementation of the *IEnumConnectionPoints::Clone* method shown in the following code, the *new* operator creates a new instance of the *CEnumConnectionPoints* class. In the *CEnumConnectionPoints* constructor, a copy of the array of connection points referenced by *m_rgpCP* is created and *AddRef* is called on each. The *m_iCur* member variable that references the current element in the enumerator is also copied, ensuring that the new enumerator has the same state as the current enumerator.

```
HRESULT CEnumConnectionPoints::Clone(IEnumConnectionPoints** ppEnum)
{
    if(ppEnum == NULL)
        return E_POINTER;
    *ppEnum = NULL;

    // Create the clone.
    CEnumConnectionPoints* pNew = new CEnumConnectionPoints(
        m_pUnkRef, (void**)m_rgpCP);
    if(pNew == NULL)
        return E_OUTOFMEMORY;

    pNew->AddRef();
    pNew->m_iCur = m_iCur;
    *ppEnum = pNew;
    return S_OK;
}
```

The Complete Implementation of *IConnectionPoint*

Earlier in this chapter, we coded a hobbled version of the *IConnectionPoint* interface that implemented only the *Advise* and *Unadvise* methods. The time has come to implement the remaining three *IConnectionPoint* methods: *GetConnectionInterface*, *GetConnectionPointContainer*, and *EnumConnections*. *GetConnectionInterface* returns the IID of the source interface managed by the connection point. A client might call this method to learn the IID of a connection point retrieved from the *IEnumConnectionPoints* enumerator. A standard implementation of *GetConnectionInterface* is shown here:

```
HRESULT CConnectionPoint::GetConnectionInterface(IID *pIID)
{
    if(pIID == NULL)
        return E_POINTER;
    *pIID = m_iid;
    return S_OK;
}
```

The *GetConnectionPointContainer* method is even simpler. It returns a pointer to the *IConnectionPointContainer* interface associated with the connection point. It exists to enable a client that happens to have a pointer to a connection point to work backward to the connection point's container. The following implementation of *GetConnectionPointContainer* simply calls *QueryInterface* to obtain the pointer. Conveniently, *QueryInterface* automatically calls *AddRef*.

```
HRESULT CConnectionPoint::GetConnectionPointContainer(
    IConnectionPointContainer** ppCPC)
{
    return m_pObj->QueryInterface(IID_IConnectionPointContainer,
        (void**)ppCPC);
}
```

The *EnumConnections* method returns a pointer to the *IEnumConnections* interface, enabling a client to enumerate all the connections that exist on a connection point. The following code implements the *EnumConnections* method by instantiating the *CEnumConnections* class that implements the *IEnumConnections* enumeration interface:

```
HRESULT CConnectionPoint::EnumConnections(
    IEnumConnections** ppEnum)
{
    *ppEnum = NULL;
    CONNECTDATA* pCD = new CONNECTDATA[m_cConn];
```

```
    for(int count1 = 0, count2 = 0; count1 < CCONNMAX; count1++)
        if(m_rgpUnknown[count1] != NULL)
        {
            pCD[count2].pUnk = (IUnknown*)m_rgpUnknown[count1];
            pCD[count2].dwCookie = m_rgnCookies[count1];
            count2++;
        }
    CEnumConnections* pEnum = new CEnumConnections(this,
        m_cConn, pCD);
    delete [] pCD;
    return pEnum->QueryInterface(IID_IEnumConnections,
        (void**)ppEnum);
}
```

Another Enumerator: *IEnumConnections*

The *IEnumConnections* interface enables a client to enumerate the known connections of a connection point. This information about each connection is encapsulated in the CONNECTDATA structure defined in the ocidl.idl system IDL file and is shown here:

```
typedef struct tagCONNECTDATA
{
    IUnknown *  pUnk;
    DWORD       dwCookie;
} CONNECTDATA;
```

The CONNECTDATA structure contains the *IUnknown* pointer to the connected sink as well as the cookie value that identifies the connection as returned by the *IConnectionPoint::Advise* method. The *IEnumConnections* interface defines the four methods common to every COM+ enumerator: *Next*, *Skip*, *Reset*, and *Clone*. To avoid dragging you through another enumerator, we'll omit the code for *IEnumConnections* here; you can find it on the companion CD in the Samples\Connection Points\Full\component.cpp source file.

When to Use Connection Points

Connection points offer a flexible and extensible way to enable bidirectional communication between an object and its clients. The fundamental architecture was derived from that developed for use by Visual Basic controls. As we've seen, Visual Basic has to deal with numerous requirements and issues when it works with events fired by objects. The connection points architecture makes this feasible for Visual Basic. Most applications do not have such stringent requirements, however. Not only is the connection points model complex, it can also be inefficient when it is used in a distributed environment by components spread across a network. Setting up a single connection point requires a minimum of four round-trips, as shown in the following list.[5]

1. The client calls the connectable object's *IUnknown::QueryInterface* method to request a pointer to the *IConnectionPointContainer* interface.

2. The client calls the *IConnectionPointContainer::FindConnectionPoint* method to request a pointer to the *IOutGoing* connection point.

3. The client calls the *IConnectionPoint::Advise* method to provide the connectable object with a pointer to the *IUnknown* interface of its sink object.

4. The connectable object calls the client sink object's *IUnknown:: QueryInterface* method to request a pointer to the *IOutGoing* interface.

Now the connectable object can call the methods of the *IOutGoing* interface implemented by the client's sink.

The four calls needed for a client to establish a relationship with a connectable object are not a significant performance problem when you use in-process components. The connection points architecture was designed primarily for working with in-process components. ActiveX controls that work with Visual Basic are always implemented as in-process components. When local or remote calls are involved, however, this overhead makes connection points less efficient. Of course, these four calls are required only once to establish the connection prior to the first outgoing method call. Subsequent outgoing calls require no special setup.

Thus, in the process of developing a component, you must consider whether connection points are the best means of enabling bidirectional communication with clients. If the object needs to work with Visual Basic clients, whether as an ActiveX control or simply as a nonvisual COM+ object using Visual Basic's *WithEvents* keyword, connection points are required. If the object needs to work with Java clients via the *ConnectionPointCookie* class, connection points are also required. If support for scripting languages such as VBScript and JScript is desirable, connection points are again the only way to go.

---

5. It might help to refer back to Figure 8-3 on page 281 as you examine these steps. Note that step 1 in the list correlates to call number 2 in Figure 8-3 because here we are assuming that a client has already instantiated the object.

However, if Visual Basic, Java, and scripting language compatibility is not a concern, it might be more efficient to develop a simple custom interface through which the client passes an interface pointer implemented by its sink to the component. Such a protocol might require only one round-trip to set up the connection. Simply passing an interface pointer to a custom interface implemented by a sink object is sufficient. As a model for such a design, you can examine the architecture of the standard *IDataObject* and *IAdviseSink* interfaces. Although the *IDataObject* and *IAdviseSink* interfaces were designed before the generic connection points architecture became available, they are a good model on which to base a simpler, custom callback mechanism.

CHAPTER NINE

Type Information

The architectures of connection points and type information were developed together. In fact, connection points as implemented by high-level languages such as Microsoft Visual Basic and Java could not exist without the presence of type information. As you saw in Chapter 3, a type library is the binary form of an interface definition. The Microsoft Interface Definition Language (MIDL) compiler was initially designed to generate C language bindings for programmers using Remote Procedure Calls[1] (RPCs) but has since been extended to create type library files. MIDL does not contain all the code necessary to create a type library, however. Microsoft has defined and implemented interfaces that do this job; MIDL is only a consumer of these interfaces.

The two primary interfaces that MIDL uses to create type libraries are *ICreateTypeLib(2)* and *ICreateTypeInfo(2)*. Together, these interfaces enable MIDL to generate a type library that describes practically any interface you might write in IDL.[2] The *ITypeLib(2)* and *ITypeInfo(2)* interfaces implemented by COM+ enable applications to read type information stored in type libraries.

Other programs besides the MIDL compiler use the *ICreateTypeLib(2)* and *ICreateTypeInfo(2)* interfaces. Visual Basic, for example, automatically generates a type library for all components. So does Microsoft Visual J++.[3] To understand the structure and contents of a type library, you must take at least a cursory look at these interfaces. In the following section, we'll use these interfaces and their associated methods to create a type library that exactly matches the type library produced by the MIDL compiler when it is fed the IDL file shown in Listing 9-1. The numbers in parentheses in the comments correspond to the numbers in the code that creates those elements of type information later in this section.

---

1. See Appendix A for more information about RPCs.

2. Type libraries do not accurately represent the IDL interface definition in certain cases; see Chapter 16 for details.

3. A Visual Basic or Java program can read the information stored in an existing type library by setting a reference to the TypeLib Information (tlbinf32.dll) component, as described later in this chapter.

mylib.idl

```
import "unknwn.idl";

[ object, uuid(10000001-0000-0000-0000-000000000001),   // (6)
  oleautomation ]                                        // (7)
interface ISum                                           // (5)
    : IUnknown                                           // (12)
{
    HRESULT Sum(int x, int y, [out, retval] int* retval);// (13)
}
[ uuid(10000003-0000-0000-0000-000000000001),            // (1)
  helpstring("Inside COM+ Component Type Library"),       // (4)
  version(1.0) ]                                          // (3)
library Component                                         // (2)
{
    importlib("stdole32.tlb");                            // (12)

    interface ISum;

    [ uuid(10000002-0000-0000-0000-000000000001) ]        // (9)
    coclass InsideCOM                                     // (8)
    {
        [default]                                         // (11)
            interface ISum;                               // (10)
    }
};
```

Listing 9-1.
*An IDL file containing library information that the MIDL compiler
uses to produce a type library file.*

Creating a Type Library

You can enter the exclusive world of type information if you know the magic
words. Too many developers treat type information as a kind of black box that
only the MIDL compiler knows how to create. It is both enlightening and interesting to investigate how MIDL goes about creating this information. A type
library file created by MIDL is simply a collection of type information about the
interfaces and coclasses supported by a component. You call the *CreateTypeLib2*[4]

---

4. The obsolete *CreateTypeLib* function creates a type library in the older format and returns a
pointer to the *ICreateTypeLib* interface.

function to create a type library in the modern format[5] and obtain a pointer to the system implementation of the *ICreateTypeLib2* interface. The following code fragment creates a type library file named mylib.tlb:

```
// Create the type library file.
ICreateTypeLib2* pCreateTypeLib2;
CreateTypeLib2(SYS_WIN32, L"C:\\mylib.tlb", &pCreateTypeLib2);
```

With the interface pointer obtained from *CreateTypeLib2*, you can call all the methods of the *ICreateTypeLib2* interface. The *ICreateTypeLib2* interface is shown below in IDL notation:

```
interface ICreateTypeLib2 : ICreateTypeLib
{
    // Deletes the specified type information from the
    // type library
    HRESULT DeleteTypeInfo([in] LPOLESTR szName);

    // Sets a value to custom data
    HRESULT SetCustData([in] REFGUID guid,
        [in] VARIANT* pVarVal);

    // Sets the Help string context number
    HRESULT SetHelpStringContext(
        [in] ULONG dwHelpStringContext);

    // Sets the DLL name to be used for Help string lookup
    // (for localization purposes)
    HRESULT SetHelpStringDll([in] LPOLESTR szFileName);
}
```

You can also use the interface pointer returned by *CreateTypeLib2* to call the methods of the *ICreateTypeLib* interface, as shown below in IDL notation:

```
interface ICreateTypeLib : IUnknown
{
    // Creates a new type information object within the
    // type library
    HRESULT CreateTypeInfo([in] LPOLESTR szName,
        [in] TYPEKIND tkind,
        [out] ICreateTypeInfo ** ppCTInfo);

    // Sets the name of the type library
    HRESULT SetName([in] LPOLESTR szName);
```

(continued)

---

5. The *CreateTypeLib2* function creates type libraries using the memory-mapped file capabilities of Win32.

```
// Sets the major and minor version numbers of the
// type library
HRESULT SetVersion([in] WORD wMajorVerNum,
    [in] WORD wMinorVerNum);

// Sets the GUID associated with the type library
HRESULT SetGuid([in] REFGUID guid);

// Sets the documentation string associated with the
// type library
HRESULT SetDocString([in] LPOLESTR szDoc);

// Sets the name of the help file
HRESULT SetHelpFileName([in] LPOLESTR szHelpFileName);

// Sets the help context ID for retrieving general help for
// the type library
HRESULT SetHelpContext([in] DWORD dwHelpContext);

// Sets the locale identifier associated with the
// type library
HRESULT SetLcid([in] LCID lcid);

// Sets general type library flags
HRESULT SetLibFlags([in] UINT uLibFlags);

// Save all the type information to the type library
HRESULT SaveAllChanges(void);
}
```

The *ICreateTypeLib::SetGuid* method sets the globally unique identifier (GUID) of a type library, as shown here:

```
// (1) Set the library LIBID to
// {10000003-0000-0000-0000-000000000001}.
GUID LIBID_Component =
    {0x10000003,0x0000,0x0000,
    {0x00,0x00,0x00,0x00,0x00,0x00,0x00,0x01}};
pCreateTypeLib2->SetGuid(LIBID_Component);
```

The *ICreateTypeLib::SetName* method sets the name of our type library to *Component*, as shown in the following code. Note that this is not the name of the type library (.tlb) file but rather the name of the type library stored in the type library file.

```
// (2) Set the library name to Component.
pCreateTypeLib2->SetName(L"Component");
```

ICreateTypeLib2::SetVersion sets the version number for the type description. The following code sets this value to *1.0*:

```
// (3) Set the library version number to 1.0.
pCreateTypeLib2->SetVersion(1, 0);
```

The *helpstring* attribute in IDL corresponds to the *ICreateTypeLib2::SetDocString* method. The following code sets the *helpstring* attribute to *"Inside COM+ Component Type Library"*:

```
// (4) Set helpstring to "Inside COM+ Component Type Library".
pCreateTypeLib2->SetDocString(
    L"Inside COM+ Component Type Library");
```

ICreateTypeLib2::SetLcid sets the locale identifier of the type library, which is used to designate the national language for which this type library is created. By default, MIDL generates a language-neutral type library; the following code has the same effect:

```
pCreateTypeLib2->SetLcid(LANG_NEUTRAL);
```

Adding Type Information

After you configure the basic attributes of the type library, you can use the *ICreateTypeLib::CreateTypeInfo* method to insert additional kinds of fundamental type information into the type library. The supported kinds of type information are defined by the *TYPEKIND* enumeration; these types, along with their IDL equivalents, are described in the table below.

TYPEKIND Value	IDL Keyword	Description
TKIND_ALIAS	typedef	A type that is an alias for another type.
TKIND_COCLASS	coclass	A set of implemented component object interfaces.
TKIND_DISPATCH	dispinterface	A set of methods and properties that are accessible through *IDispatch::Invoke*. By default, dual interfaces return *TKIND_DISPATCH*.
TKIND_ENUM	enum	A set of enumerators.
TKIND_INTERFACE	interface	A type that has virtual functions, all of which are pure.
TKIND_MODULE	module	A module that can have only exported functions and data (for example, a DLL).
TKIND_RECORD	struct	A structure with no methods.
TKIND_UNION	union	A union, all of whose members have an offset of *0*.
TKIND_MAX	enum	End of an enum marker.

These values are the eight fundamental elements you can describe using type information. The following code calls the *ICreateTypeLib::CreateTypeInfo* method to create type information for an interface (*TKIND_INTERFACE*) named *ISum*. If successful, *CreateTypeInfo* returns a pointer to the system implementation of the *ICreateTypeInfo* interface.

```
// (5) Create the ISum interface.
ICreateTypeInfo* pCreateTypeInfoInterface;
pCreateTypeLib2->CreateTypeInfo(L"ISum", TKIND_INTERFACE,
    &pCreateTypeInfoInterface);
```

Using the methods of *ICreateTypeInfo*, you can set the attributes of the type information in much the same way that the *ICreateTypeLib2* interface operates on the type library as a whole. The *ICreateTypeInfo* interface is shown below in IDL notation:

```
interface ICreateTypeInfo: IUnknown
{
    // Sets the GUID associated with the type information
    HRESULT SetGuid([in] REFGUID guid);

    // Sets type flags of the type information being created
    HRESULT SetTypeFlags([in] UINT uTypeFlags);

    // Sets the documentation string displayed by type browsers
    HRESULT SetDocString([in] LPOLESTR pStrDoc);

    // Sets the Help context ID of the type information
    HRESULT SetHelpContext([in] DWORD dwHelpContext);

    // Sets the major and minor version number of the
    // type information
    HRESULT SetVersion([in] WORD wMajorVerNum,
        [in] WORD wMinorVerNum);

    // Adds a reference to other type information
    HRESULT AddRefTypeInfo([in] ITypeInfo* pTInfo,
        [in] HREFTYPE* phRefType);

    // Adds a method to the type information
    HRESULT AddFuncDesc([in] UINT index,
        [in] FUNCDESC* pFuncDesc);

    // Specifies an interface implemented by a coclass
    HRESULT AddImplType([in] UINT index,
        [in] HREFTYPE hRefType);
```

```
// Sets the attributes for an implemented interface
// of a type
HRESULT SetImplTypeFlags([in] UINT index,
    [in] INT implTypeFlags);

// Specifies the data alignment for a structure
HRESULT SetAlignment([in] WORD cbAlignment);

// Reserved
HRESULT SetSchema([in] LPOLESTR pStrSchema);

// Adds a variable or data member description to the
// type information
HRESULT AddVarDesc([in] UINT index,
    [in] VARDESC * pVarDesc);

// Sets the name of a function and the names of
// its parameters to the names in the array of
// pointers rgszNames
HRESULT SetFuncAndParamNames([in] UINT index,
    [in, size_is((UINT) cNames)] LPOLESTR * rgszNames,
    [in] UINT cNames);

// Sets the name of a variable
HRESULT SetVarName([in] UINT index, [in] LPOLESTR szName);

// Sets the type description for which this type description
// is an alias
HRESULT SetTypeDescAlias([in] TYPEDESC * pTDescAlias);

// Associates a DLL entry point with the function that has
// the specified index number
HRESULT DefineFuncAsDllEntry([in] UINT index,
    [in] LPOLESTR szDllName,
    [in] LPOLESTR szProcName);

// Sets the documentation string for a method
HRESULT SetFuncDocString([in] UINT index,
    [in] LPOLESTR szDocString);

// Sets the documentation string for the variable with the
// specified index
HRESULT SetVarDocString([in] UINT index,
    [in] LPOLESTR szDocString);
```

(continued)

```
    // Sets the Help context ID for the function with the
    // specified index
    HRESULT SetFuncHelpContext([in] UINT index,
        [in] DWORD dwHelpContext);

    // Sets the Help context ID for the variable with the
    // specified index
    HRESULT SetVarHelpContext([in] UINT index,
        [in] DWORD dwHelpContext);

    // Sets the marshaling opcode string associated with the
    // type description or the function
    HRESULT SetMops([in] UINT index, [in] BSTR bstrMops);

    // Sets IDL attributes (not supported)
    HRESULT SetTypeIdlDesc([in] IDLDESC * pIdlDesc);

    // Assigns virtual function table (VTBL) offsets for
    // virtual functions and instance offsets for per-instance
    // data members
    HRESULT LayOut(void);
}
```

ICreateTypeInfo2, an extension of the *ICreateTypeInfo* interface, offers methods for deleting items that were added using the methods of *ICreateTypeInfo*. To upgrade to the *ICreateTypeInfo2* interface, you simply call *QueryInterface* using the *ICreateTypeInfo* interface pointer returned by the *ICreateTypeLib::CreateTypeInfo* method. The *ICreateTypeInfo2* interface is shown below in IDL notation:

```
interface ICreateTypeInfo2: ICreateTypeInfo
{
    // Deletes a method from the type information by
    // index number
    HRESULT DeleteFuncDesc([in] UINT index);

    // Deletes a method from the type information by member ID
    HRESULT DeleteFuncDescByMemId([in] MEMBERID memid,
        [in] INVOKEKIND invKind);

    // Deletes a variable from the type information by
    // index number
    HRESULT DeleteVarDesc([in] UINT index);

    // Deletes a variable from the type information by member ID
    HRESULT DeleteVarDescByMemId([in] MEMBERID memid);
```

```
// Deletes the IMPLTYPE flags for an interface
HRESULT DeleteImplType([in] UINT index);

// Sets a value for custom data
HRESULT SetCustData([in] REFGUID guid,
    [in] VARIANT* pVarVal);

// Sets a value for custom data for the specified method
HRESULT SetFuncCustData([in] UINT index, [in] REFGUID guid,
    [in] VARIANT* pVarVal);

// Sets a value for the custom data for the
// specified parameter
HRESULT SetParamCustData([in] UINT indexFunc,
    [in] UINT indexParam, [in] REFGUID guid,
    [in] VARIANT* pVarVal);

// Sets a value for custom data for the specified variable
HRESULT SetVarCustData([in] UINT index, [in] REFGUID guid,
    [in] VARIANT* pVarVal);

// Sets a value for custom data for the specified
// implementation type
HRESULT SetImplTypeCustData([in] UINT index,
    [in] REFGUID guid, [in] VARIANT* pVarVal);

// Sets the context number for the specified Help string
HRESULT SetHelpStringContext(
    [in] ULONG dwHelpStringContext);

// Sets a Help context value for a specified function
HRESULT SetFuncHelpStringContext([in] UINT index,
    [in] ULONG dwHelpStringContext);

// Sets a Help context value for a specified variable
HRESULT SetVarHelpStringContext([in] UINT index,
    [in] ULONG dwHelpStringContext);

// Reserved
HRESULT Invalidate(void);

// Sets the name of the type information
HRESULT SetName([in] LPOLESTR szName);
}
```

The following code obtains the *ICreateTypeInfo2* interface pointer using *QueryInterface*, followed by a call to the *ICreateTypeInfo::SetGuid* method to set the GUID of the *ISum* interface:

```
ICreateTypeInfo2* pCreateTypeInfo2 = 0;
pCreateTypeInfoInterface->QueryInterface(IID_ICreateTypeInfo2,
    (void**)&pCreateTypeInfo2);

IID IID_ISum = { 0x10000001, 0x0000, 0x0000,
    { 0x00, 0x00, 0x00, 0x00, 0x00, 0x00, 0x00, 0x01 } };

// (6) Set the ISum IID to
// {10000001-0000-0000-0000-000000000001}.
pCreateTypeInfo2->SetGuid(IID_ISum);
```

You can use the *ICreateTypeInfo::SetTypeFlags* method to configure numerous attributes of the type information you are creating. The following table lists the *TYPEFLAGS* values:

TYPEFLAGS Value	IDL Keyword	Description
TYPEFLAG_FAPPOBJECT	appobject	A type description that describes an application object.
TYPEFLAG_FCANCREATE	The default*	Instances of this type can be created by *ITypeInfo:: CreateInstance.*
TYPEFLAG_FLICENSED	licensed	This type is licensed.
TYPEFLAG_FHIDDEN	hidden	This type should not be displayed to browsers.
TYPEFLAG_FCONTROL	control	This type is a control from which other types are derived and should not be displayed to users.
TYPEFLAG_FDUAL	dual	The types in this interface derive from *IDispatch* and are fully compatible with Automation.
TYPEFLAG_FNONEXTENSIBLE	nonextensible	This interface cannot add members at run time.

* The MIDL compiler automatically sets the *TYPEFLAG_FCANCREATE* flag; no IDL keyword is necessary. If you don't want this behavior, use the IDL keyword *noncreatable.*

TYPEFLAGS Value	IDL Keyword	Description
TYPEFLAG_FOLEAUTOMATION	*oleautomation*	The types used in this interface are fully compatible with Automation and can be displayed in an object browser. Specifying *dual* on an interface sets this flag automatically.
TYPEFLAG_FRESTRICTED	*restricted*	The item on which this flag is specified is not accessible from high-level languages such as Visual Basic.
TYPEFLAG_FAGGREGATABLE	*aggregatable*	The class supports aggregation.
TYPEFLAG_FREPLACEABLE	*replaceable*	The interface has default behaviors.
TYPEFLAG_FDISPATCHABLE	(none)	The interface derives from *IDispatch*.

Because the *ISum* interface is fully Automation-compatible, you set the *TYPEFLAG_FOLEAUTOMATION* flag using the *SetTypeFlags* method, as shown in the code below. This flag offers the additional benefit of causing the *LoadTypeLibEx* function to automatically set up type library marshaling for the *ISum* interface when the component is registered. (See Chapter 12 for more information.) Notice that the *TYPEFLAG_FOLEAUTOMATION* flag is different from the *TYPEFLAG_FDISPATCHABLE* flag, which indicates that the interface is derived from *IDispatch*. *TYPEFLAG_FOLEAUTOMATION* simply indicates that the interface restricts itself to Automation-compatible types.

```
// (7) Set the oleautomation flag.
pCreateTypeInfoInterface->SetTypeFlags(TYPEFLAG_FOLEAUTOMATION);
```

At this stage, the basic structure of the *ISum* interface is specified. Still missing from the type information for *ISum*, however, is the *Sum* method. Before we add this method, let's turn our attention to the *InsideCOM* coclass. Using the pointer to the *ICreateTypeLib2* interface originally obtained from the call to *CreateTypeLib2*, you can create a new bit of type information, this time describing the coclass (*TKIND_COCLASS*) *InsideCOM*:

```
// (8) Create type information for the coclass InsideCOM.
ICreateTypeInfo* pCreateTypeInfoCoClass;
pCreateTypeLib2->CreateTypeInfo(L"InsideCOM", TKIND_COCLASS,
    &pCreateTypeInfoCoClass);
```

Following the familiar pattern, you call the *ICreateTypeInfo::SetGuid* method to set the GUID of the *InsideCOM* coclass, as shown here:

```
// (9) Set the InsideCOM CLSID to
// {10000002-0000-0000-0000-000000000001}.
CLSID CLSID_InsideCOM =
    {0x10000002,0x0000,0x0000,
    {0x00,0x00,0x00,0x00,0x00,0x00,0x00,0x01}};
pCreateTypeInfoCoClass->SetGuid(CLSID_InsideCOM);
```

Now the class must be marked so that it can be created by clients using the *ITypeInfo::CreateInstance* method. Type libraries generated by MIDL automatically have this flag set, but when you create a type description manually as described here, you must call the *SetTypeFlags* method using the *TYPEFLAG_FCANCREATE* argument, as shown here:

```
// Specify that this coclass can be instantiated.
pCreateTypeInfoCoClass->SetTypeFlags(TYPEFLAG_FCANCREATE);
```

Now the *InsideCOM* coclass and the *ISum* interface have been defined. However, no relationship exists between the two. To express the fact that the *InsideCOM* coclass implements the *ISum* interface, you must insert the type description for *ISum* into that of *InsideCOM*. You use the *ICreateTypeInfo:: AddImplType* method to do this. The second parameter of *AddImplType* requires a handle that identifies the type information, which is declared as an *HREFTYPE*. To obtain the *HREFTYPE* for the *ISum* interface, you must first call the *ICreateTypeInfo::AddRefTypeInfo* method. This method in turn requires an *ITypeInfo* interface pointer. You obtain it in a two-step process by calling *QueryInterface* to request a pointer to the system implementation of the *ITypeLib* interface, and then using the resultant *ITypeLib* interface pointer to call the *ITypeLib::GetTypeInfoOfGuid* method to obtain an *ITypeInfo* pointer to the type information describing the *ISum* interface. This process is shown in the code fragment below:

```
// Get a pointer to the ITypeLib interface.
ITypeLib* pTypeLib;
pCreateTypeLib2->QueryInterface(IID_ITypeLib,
    (void**)&pTypeLib);

// Get a pointer to the ITypeInfo interface for ISum.
ITypeInfo* pTypeInfo;
pTypeLib->GetTypeInfoOfGuid(IID_ISum, &pTypeInfo);
```

With the *ITypeInfo* interface pointer at your disposal, you call the *ICreateTypeInfo::AddRefTypeInfo* method to obtain the *HREFTYPE*. The *HREFTYPE* handle returned by *AddRefTypeInfo* enables you to finally call the *ICreateTypeInfo::AddImplType* method to declare that the *InsideCOM* coclass implements the *ISum* interface, as shown here:

```
// Trade in the ITypeInfo pointer for an HREFTYPE.
HREFTYPE hRefTypeISum;
pCreateTypeInfoCoClass->AddRefTypeInfo(pTypeInfo,
    &hRefTypeISum);

// (10) Insert the ISum interface into the InsideCOM coclass.
pCreateTypeInfoCoClass->AddImplType(0, hRefTypeISum);
```

The *ICreateTypeInfo::SetImplTypeFlags* method sets attributes for an implemented interface of a type. You can use this method to set one or more of the flags listed in the following table.

IMPLTYPEFLAG Value	IDL Keyword	Description
IMPLTYPEFLAG_FDEFAULT	*default*	The interface or *dispinterface* represents the default for the source or sink.
IMPLTYPEFLAG_FSOURCE	*source*	This member of a coclass is called rather than implemented.
IMPLTYPEFLAG_FRESTRICTED	*restricted*	This member should not be displayed or be programmable by users.
IMPLTYPEFLAG_FDEFAULTVTABLE	*defaultvtbl*	Sinks receive events through the v-table.

The following code calls the *SetImplTypeFlags* method to set the default (*IMPLTYPEFLAG_FDEFAULT*) flag for the *ISum* interface in the *InsideCOM* coclass. This call is important to languages such as Visual Basic that automatically connect the client with the default interface of an object. Note that MIDL automatically sets the default flag for the first unrestricted interface.

```
// (11) Specify ISum as the default interface.
pCreateTypeInfoCoClass->SetImplTypeFlags(0,
    IMPLTYPEFLAG_FDEFAULT);
```

The next step in the creation of the type library is to express the fact that the *ISum* interface is derived from *IUnknown*. To do this, you have two choices: define *IUnknown* using the methods of the *ICreateTypeInfo* interface as we did for *ISum*, or load the existing type description of *IUnknown* from the Automation type library (stdole32.tlb) supplied by Microsoft. To make things easier and more standard, let's opt for the latter approach. You obtain access to the type information contained in the Automation type library using the *LoadRegTypeLib* function. You use the *ITypeLib* pointer returned by *LoadRegTypeLib* to call the *ITypeLib::GetTypeInfoOfGuid* method to retrieve an *ITypeInfo* pointer to type information for the *IUnknown* interface, as shown here:

```
// Get a pointer to the ITypeLib interface for Automation.
ITypeLib* pTypeLibStdOle;
GUID GUID_STDOLE = { 0x00020430, 0x00, 0x00, 0xC0, 0x00, 0x00,
    0x00, 0x00, 0x00, 0x00, 0x46 };
LoadRegTypeLib(GUID_STDOLE, STDOLE_MAJORVERNUM,
    STDOLE_MINORVERNUM, STDOLE_LCID, &pTypeLibStdOle);

// Get a pointer to the ITypeInfo interface for IUnknown.
ITypeInfo* pTypeInfoUnknown;
pTypeLibStdOle->GetTypeInfoOfGuid(IID_IUnknown,
    &pTypeInfoUnknown);
```

After you call the *ICreateTypeInfo::AddRefTypeInfo* method to retrieve an *HREFTYPE* handle to the type information, you call the *ICreateTypeInfo:: AddImplType* method to declare that *ISum* derives from *IUnknown*, as shown here:

```
// Get the HREFTYPE handle for IUnknown's type information.
HREFTYPE hRefType;
pCreateTypeInfoInterface->AddRefTypeInfo(pTypeInfoUnknown,
    &hRefType);

// (12) Declare that ISum is derived from IUnknown.
pCreateTypeInfoInterface->AddImplType(0, hRefType);
```

You need a final bit of type information to describe the *ISum::Sum* method, which you create by calling the *ICreateTypeInfo::AddFuncDesc* method. Unfortunately, using the *AddFuncDesc* interface to manually describe methods is not tremendously enjoyable—you must examine and describe every aspect of the method in the most exacting and detailed manner. You use the FUNCDESC structure to describe all the attributes of a method. Figure 9-1 shows the FUNCDESC structure in IDL notation, along with its associated structures.

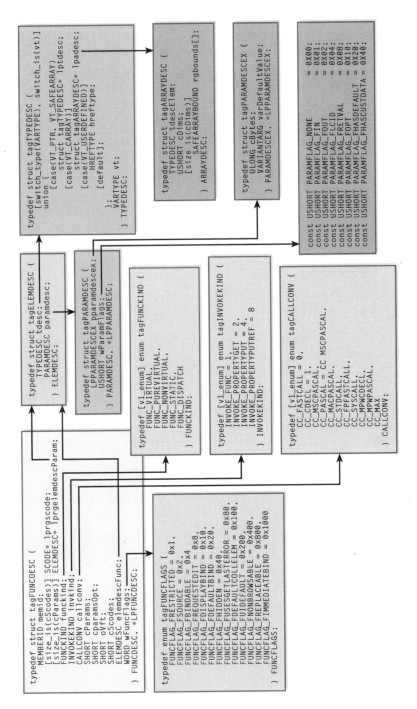

Figure 9-1.
The FUNCDESC structure and friends.

One of the more important fields in the FUNCDESC structure is the *lprgelemdescParam* pointer to an array of ELEMDESC structures, each of which describes a single parameter of the method. As you can see in Figure 9-1, the ELEMDESC structure is basically a container for the TYPEDESC and PARAMDESC structures. The TYPEDESC structure describes the parameter type, while the PARAMDESC structure contains flags that indicate whether the parameter is passed to and/or from the object.

The following code defines an array of three ELEMDESC structures and initializes it for the three parameters (*x*, *y*, and *retval*) of the *ISum::Sum* method. The first two structures are declared as integers (*VT_INT*), and the third is declared as a pointer (*VT_PTR*) to an integer, with special flags (*PARAMFLAG_FRETVAL* and *PARAMFLAG_FOUT*) indicating that this is an *[out, retval]* parameter.

```
// Structures for the x, y, and retval parameters of the
// Sum method
TYPEDESC tdescParams = { 0 };
tdescParams.vt = VT_INT;

ELEMDESC myParams[3] = { 0 };
myParams[0].tdesc.vt = VT_INT;                    // x
myParams[0].tdesc.lptdesc = &tdescParams;
myParams[1].tdesc.vt = VT_INT;                    // y
myParams[1].tdesc.lptdesc = &tdescParams;
myParams[2].tdesc.vt = VT_PTR;                    // retval
myParams[2].tdesc.lptdesc = &tdescParams;
myParams[2].paramdesc.wParamFlags =
    PARAMFLAG_FRETVAL|PARAMFLAG_FOUT;
```

Next you allocate and initialize the FUNCDESC structure using a number of settings. You declare the *Sum* method (*INVOKE_FUNC*) as a pure virtual function (*FUNC_PUREVIRTUAL*) using the standard calling convention (*CC_STDCALL*), which accepts three parameters (*cParams*) and returns an *HRESULT* (*VT_HRESULT*). Then you call the *ICreateTypeInfo::AddFuncDesc* method to add the *Sum* method as described by the FUNDESC structure to the *ISum* interface, as shown here:

```
// Additional data describing the Sum method and its
// return value
TYPEDESC tdescUser = { 0 };
FUNCDESC FuncDesc = { 0 };
FuncDesc.funckind = FUNC_PUREVIRTUAL;
FuncDesc.invkind = INVOKE_FUNC;
FuncDesc.callconv = CC_STDCALL;
```

```
FuncDesc.elemdescFunc.tdesc.vt = VT_HRESULT;
FuncDesc.elemdescFunc.tdesc.lptdesc = &tdescUser;
FuncDesc.cParams = 3;
FuncDesc.lprgelemdescParam = myParams;

// (13) Add the Sum method to the ISum interface.
pCreateTypeInfoInterface->AddFuncDesc(0, &FuncDesc);
```

Notice that we have not yet provided names for the parameters of the *Sum* method. To attach names to the *Sum* method and its parameters, you call *ICreateTypeInfo::SetFuncAndParamNames* with an array of the names to be attached, as shown here:

```
// Set names for the Sum function and its parameters.
OLECHAR* Names[4] = { L"Sum", L"x", L"y", L"retval" };
pCreateTypeInfoInterface->SetFuncAndParamNames(0, Names, 4);
```

You call the *ICreateTypeInfo::LayOut* method to assign v-table offsets for the virtual functions, as shown here:

```
// Assign the v-table layout.
pCreateTypeInfoInterface->LayOut();
```

Unless you call the *ICreateTypeLib2::SaveAllChanges* method, all of your efforts will have been for naught, since nothing will have been saved to disk! This call is followed by calls to the *Release* method for all the objects accumulated during this exercise, as shown here:

```
// Save changes.
pCreateTypeLib2->SaveAllChanges();

// Release all references.
pTypeInfoUnknown->Release();
pTypeLibStdOle->Release();
pTypeInfo->Release();
pTypeLib->Release();
pCreateTypeLib2->Release();
pCreateTypeInfoInterface->Release();
pCreateTypeInfoCoClass->Release();
```

Once you have a basic understanding of how to create type libraries using the *ICreateTypeLib* and *ICreateTypeInfo* interfaces, you'll have a much better understanding of the information contained in a type library.[6]

---

6. Of course, we recommend that you consider using MIDL if your future component development plans call for a type library.

Obtaining Type Information

So far, we've examined how type information can be synthesized at run time. In comparison, obtaining access to predefined type information is relatively easy. Normally, a client can find the type library of a coclass simply by looking in the registry. The type library identifier (LIBID) of the class is stored in the TypeLib subkey beneath the CLSID key. With this LIBID, you can obtain type information about the class by calling the *LoadRegTypeLib* function. However, not all objects have a CLSID and the complementary registry entries—for example, subobjects such as connection points do not have a CLSID. You cannot obtain type information about such objects unless the object supports the *IProvideClassInfo* interface. Objects that do not have a CLSID but still want to expose type information to their clients must implement this interface. Adding support for the *IProvideClassInfo* interface is not particularly difficult. The lone method of this interface, *GetClassInfo*, retrieves the type information of the class. Here is the *IProvideClassInfo* interface in IDL notation:

```
interface IProvideClassInfo : IUnknown
{
    // Get a pointer to the type information for this CLSID.
    HRESULT GetClassInfo([out] ITypeInfo** ppTI);
}
```

How the *GetClassInfo* method is implemented depends entirely on where the type information for the object is stored. If the type information is created dynamically and stored only in memory, the method should simply return a pointer to the *ITypeInfo* interface. If the type information is available in a type library file, call *LoadRegTypeLib* and then call *ITypeLib::GetTypeInfoOfGuid*, as shown here:

```
HRESULT CInsideCOM::GetClassInfo(ITypeInfo** pTypeInfo)
{
    ITypeLib* pTypeLib;
    LoadRegTypeLib(LIBID_Component, 1, 0, LANG_NEUTRAL,
        &pTypeLib);
    HRESULT hr = pTypeLib->GetTypeInfoOfGuid(CLSID_InsideCOM,
        &pTypeInfo);
    pTypeLib->Release();
    return hr;
}
```

Now the client can simply call *QueryInterface* for the *IProvideClassInfo* interface and follow that with a call to *IProvideClassInfo::GetClassInfo*. This is an equal opportunity interface: every coclass can expose *IProvideClassInfo* regardless of whether it has a CLSID. For objects with a CLSID, the *IProvideClassInfo* interface allows clients to use the standard *QueryInterface* mechanism instead of having to perform a registry lookup to locate the LIBID.

The *IProvideClassInfo2* interface offers a further improvement; its definition is shown here:

```
interface IProvideClassInfo2 : IProvideClassInfo
{
    // Get the IID of this object's default source interface.
    HRESULT GetGUID(
        [in]  DWORD dwGuidKind,
        [out] GUID * pGUID);
}
```

As you can see, this interface derives from *IProvideClassInfo*; the only addition is the *GetGUID* method, which makes it quick and easy for a client to retrieve the interface identifier (IID) of an object's default source interface. The *dwGuidKind* parameter can be one of the values in the *GUIDKIND* enumeration. Currently, *GUIDKIND_DEFAULT_SOURCE_DISP_IID* is the only value defined. Using this value, the client requests the IID of the object's default source *dispinterface*. Because the sample source interfaces shown in Chapter 8 are not based on *IDispatch*, officially we should return an error. But never mind that. This is how an implementation of *IProvideClassInfo2::GetGUID* might look:

```
HRESULT CInsideCOM::GetGUID(DWORD dwGuidKind, GUID* pGUID)
{
    if(pGUID == NULL)
        return E_INVALIDARG;
    *pGUID = IID_IOutGoing;
    return S_OK;
}
```

The *ITypeLib* Interface

Regardless of the technique you use to obtain type information, the end result is an *ITypeLib* or *ITypeInfo* interface pointer. The *ITypeLib* interface provides a container for the type information stored in a type library, as well as general information and flags that apply to the type library as a whole. The *ITypeLib* interface is shown below in IDL notation:

```
interface ITypeLib : IUnknown
{
    // Returns the number of type descriptions in the
    // type library
    UINT GetTypeInfoCount(void);
```

(continued)

319

```
    // Retrieves the specified type description in the library
    HRESULT GetTypeInfo([in] UINT index,
        [out] ITypeInfo** ppTInfo);

    // Retrieves the type of a type description
    HRESULT GetTypeInfoType([in] UINT index,
        [out] TYPEKIND* pTKind);

    // Retrieves the type description that corresponds to the
    // specified GUID
    HRESULT GetTypeInfoOfGuid([in] REFGUID guid,
        [out] ITypeInfo** ppTinfo);

    // Retrieves the structure that contains the
    // library's attributes
    HRESULT GetLibAttr([out] TLIBATTR** ppTLibAttr);

    // Enables a client compiler to bind to a library's types,
    // variables, constants, and global functions
    HRESULT GetTypeComp([out] ITypeComp ** ppTComp);

    // Retrieves the library's documentation string, the
    // complete Help file name and path, and the context
    // identifier for the library Help topic in the Help file
    HRESULT GetDocumentation([in] INT index,
        [out] BSTR* pBstrName, [out] BSTR* pBstrDocString,
        [out] DWORD* pdwHelpContext, [out] BSTR* pBstrHelpFile);

    // Indicates whether a passed-in string contains the name
    // of a type or member described in the library
    HRESULT IsName([in, out] LPOLESTR szNameBuf,
        [in] ULONG lHashVal, [out] BOOL* pfName);

    // Finds occurrences of a type description in a type
    // library. This can be used to quickly verify that a name
    // exists in a type library.
    HRESULT FindName([in, out] LPOLESTR szNameBuf,
        [in] ULONG lHashVal,
        [out, size_is(*pcFound),
            length_is(*pcFound)] ITypeInfo** ppTInfo,
        [out, size_is(*pcFound),
            length_is(*pcFound)] MEMBERID* rgMemId,
        [in, out] USHORT* pcFound);

    // Releases the TLIBATTR originally obtained from
    // ITypeLib::GetLibAttr
    void ReleaseTLibAttr([in] TLIBATTR* pTLibAttr);
}
```

The *ITypeLib* interface was extended to produce the *ITypeLib2* interface; the enhancements allow you to retrieve custom data values and localized help file information. To obtain a pointer to the *ITypeLib2* interface, you simply call *QueryInterface* on the *ITypeLib* interface pointer. The *ITypeLib2* interface is shown below in IDL notation:

```
interface ITypeLib2 : ITypeLib
{
    // Gets custom data
    HRESULT GetCustData([in] REFGUID guid,
        [out] VARIANT* pVarVal);

    // Returns statistics about a type library that are required
    // for efficient sizing of hash tables
    HRESULT GetLibStatistics([out] ULONG* pcUniqueNames,
        [out] ULONG* pcchUniqueNames);

    // Gets localized documentation information about the
    // type library
    HRESULT GetDocumentation2([in] INT index, [in] LCID lcid,
        [out] BSTR* pbstrHelpString,
        [out] DWORD* pdwHelpStringContext,
        [out] BSTR* pbstrHelpStringDll);

    // Gets all custom data items for the library
    HRESULT GetAllCustData([out] CUSTDATA* pCustData);
}
```

The *ITypeInfo* Interface

You use the *ITypeInfo* interface to obtain type information about an object. Generally speaking, an application obtains access to type information by calling the *ITypeLib::GetTypeInfo* or *ITypeLib::GetTypeInfoOfGuid* methods, both of which return an *ITypeInfo* interface pointer. The *ITypeInfo* interface is shown below in IDL notation:

```
interface ITypeInfo : IUnknown
{
    // Retrieves a TYPEATTR structure that contains the
    // attributes of the type description
    HRESULT GetTypeAttr([out] TYPEATTR** ppTypeAttr);

    // Retrieves the ITypeComp interface for the type
    // description, which enables a client compiler to bind
    // to the type description's members
    HRESULT GetTypeComp([out] ITypeComp** ppTComp);
```

(continued)

```
// Retrieves the FUNCDESC structure for a specified function
HRESULT GetFuncDesc([in] UINT index,
    [out] FUNCDESC** ppFuncDesc);

// Retrieves a VARDESC structure that describes the
// specified variable
HRESULT GetVarDesc([in] UINT index,
    [out] VARDESC** ppVarDesc);

// Retrieves the variable with the specified member ID (or
// the name of the property or method and its parameters)
// that corresponds to the specified function ID
HRESULT GetNames([in] MEMBERID memid,
    [out, size_is(cMaxNames), length_is(*pcNames)]
        BSTR* rgBstrNames,
    [in] UINT cMaxNames, [out] UINT* pcNames);

// Retrieves the type description of the implemented
// interface types for a coclass. For an interface, it
// returns the type information for inherited interfaces,
// if any.
HRESULT GetRefTypeOfImplType([in] UINT index,
    [out] HREFTYPE* pRefType);

// Retrieves the IMPLTYPEFLAGS an interface in a
// type description
HRESULT GetImplTypeFlags([in] UINT index,
    [out] INT* pImplTypeFlags);

// Maps between member names and member IDs and between
// parameter names and parameter IDs
HRESULT GetIDsOfNames(
    [in, size_is(cNames)] LPOLESTR* rgszNames,
    [in] UINT cNames,
    [out, size_is(cNames)] MEMBERID* pMemId);

// Invokes a method defined by the type description
HRESULT Invoke([in] PVOID pvInstance, [in] MEMBERID memid,
    [in] WORD wFlags, [in, out] DISPPARAMS* pDispParams,
    [out] VARIANT* pVarResult, [out] EXCEPINFO* pExcepInfo,
    [out] UINT* puArgErr);

// Retrieves the documentation information for a
// type description
HRESULT GetDocumentation([in] MEMBERID memid,
    [out] BSTR* pBstrName, [out] BSTR* pBstrDocString,
    [out] DWORD* pdwHelpContext, [out] BSTR* pBstrHelpFile);
```

```
// Retrieves a description or specification of an entry
// point for a function in a DLL
HRESULT GetDllEntry([in] MEMBERID memid,
    [in] INVOKEKIND invKind, [out] BSTR* pBstrDllName,
    [out] BSTR* pBstrName, [out] WORD* pwOrdinal);

// Retrieves the referenced type descriptions
HRESULT GetRefTypeInfo([in] HREFTYPE hRefType,
    [out] ITypeInfo** ppTInfo);

// Gets the addresses of static functions or variables,
// such as those defined in a DLL
HRESULT AddressOfMember([in] MEMBERID memid,
    [in] INVOKEKIND invKind, [out] PVOID* ppv);

// Creates a new instance of a type that describes a coclass
HRESULT CreateInstance([in] IUnknown* pUnkOuter,
    [in] REFIID riid, [out, iid_is(riid)] PVOID* ppvObj);

// Retrieves marshaling information
HRESULT GetMops([in] MEMBERID memid, [out] BSTR* pBstrMops);

// Retrieves the containing type library and the index of
// the type description within that type library
HRESULT GetContainingTypeLib([out] ITypeLib** ppTLib,
    [out] UINT* pIndex);

// Releases a TYPEATTR previously returned by GetTypeAttr
void ReleaseTypeAttr([in] TYPEATTR* pTypeAttr);

// Releases a FUNCDESC previously returned by GetFuncDesc
void ReleaseFuncDesc([in] FUNCDESC* pFuncDesc);

// Releases a VARDESC previously returned by GetVarDesc
void ReleaseVarDesc([in] VARDESC* pVarDesc);
}
```

The enhanced version of *ITypeInfo*, *ITypeInfo2*, permits clients to obtain localized help file information as well as custom data items stored in the type library. To obtain a pointer to the *ITypeInfo2* interface, you simply call *QueryInterface* from any *ITypeInfo* interface pointer. The *ITypeInfo2* interface is shown below in IDL notation:

```
interface ITypeInfo2 : ITypeInfo
{
    // Returns the TYPEKIND enumeration quickly, without doing
    // any allocations
```

(continued)

```
HRESULT GetTypeKind([out] TYPEKIND* pTypeKind);

// Returns the type flags without any allocations
HRESULT GetTypeFlags([out] ULONG* pTypeFlags);

// Binds to a specific member based on a known DISPID,
// where the member name is not known
HRESULT GetFuncIndexOfMemId([in] MEMBERID memid,
    [in] INVOKEKIND invKind, [out] UINT* pFuncIndex);

// Binds to a specific member based on a known DISPID,
// where the member name is not known
HRESULT GetVarIndexOfMemId([in] MEMBERID memid,
    [out] UINT* pVarIndex);

// Gets the custom data
HRESULT GetCustData([in] REFGUID guid,
    [out] VARIANT* pVarVal);

// Gets the custom data from the specified function
HRESULT GetFuncCustData([in] UINT index, [in] REFGUID guid,
    [out] VARIANT *pVarVal);

// Gets the specified custom data parameter
HRESULT GetParamCustData([in] UINT indexFunc,
    [in] UINT indexParam, [in] REFGUID guid,
    [out] VARIANT* pVarVal);

// Gets the variable for the custom data
HRESULT GetVarCustData([in] UINT index, [in] REFGUID guid,
    [out] VARIANT* pVarVal);

// Gets the implementation type of the custom data
HRESULT GetImplTypeCustData([in] UINT index,
    [in] REFGUID guid, [out] VARIANT* pVarVal);

// Gets localized documentation information for the
// type description
HRESULT GetDocumentation2([in] MEMBERID memid,
    [in] LCID lcid, [out] BSTR* pbstrHelpString,
    [out] DWORD* pdwHelpStringContext,
    [out] BSTR* pbstrHelpStringDll);

// Gets all custom data items for the library
HRESULT GetAllCustData([out] CUSTDATA* pCustData);
```

```
// Gets all custom data from the specified function
HRESULT GetAllFuncCustData([in] UINT index,
    [out] CUSTDATA* pCustData);

// Gets all of the custom data for the specified
// function parameter
HRESULT GetAllParamCustData([in] UINT indexFunc,
    [in] UINT indexParam, [out] CUSTDATA* pCustData);

// Gets the variable for the custom data
HRESULT GetAllVarCustData([in] UINT index,
    [out] CUSTDATA* pCustData);

// Gets all custom data for the specified
// implementation type
HRESULT GetAllImplTypeCustData([in] UINT index,
    [out] CUSTDATA* pCustData);
}
```

The *ITypeComp* Interface

The *ITypeComp* interface, an optimization for use by compilers, is implemented in oleaut32.dll. This interface enables clients to quickly locate a certain piece of type information in a type library without having to navigate through many of the methods of *ITypeLib* and *ITypeInfo*. The *ITypeComp* interface is shown below in IDL notation:

```
interface ITypeComp : IUnknown
{

    HRESULT Bind(
            [in] LPOLESTR szName,
            [in] ULONG lHashVal,
            [in] WORD wFlags,
            [out] ITypeInfo ** ppTInfo,
            [out] DESCKIND * pDescKind,
            [out] BINDPTR * pBindPtr
        );

    HRESULT BindType(
            [in] LPOLESTR szName,
            [in] ULONG lHashVal,
            [out] ITypeInfo ** ppTInfo,
            [out] ITypeComp ** ppTComp
        );
}
```

Reading Type Information Using High-Level Languages

While type information is usually created and read automatically by the run-time support provided for high-level languages, type information can also be obtained programmatically in languages such as Visual Basic, Java, or even script via the TypeLib Information (tlbinf32.dll) component. This component encapsulates the type information interfaces offered by COM+—*ITypeLib(2)* and *ITypeInfo(2)*—in high-level dual interfaces. The Visual Basic code below reads and displays the type information from the type library we created earlier in this chapter.

```
Private Sub Command1_Click()
    Dim refTypeLibInfo As TLI.TypeLibInfo

    ' Load the type library from the registry based on
    ' the LIBID.
    Set refTypeLibInfo = _
        TLI.TLIApplication.TypeLibInfoFromRegistry( _
        "{10000003-0000-0000-0000-000000000001}", 1, 0, 0)

    Dim refCoClassInfo As TLI.CoClassInfo
    For Each refCoClassInfo In refTypeLibInfo.CoClasses
        ' Print the coclass name.
        Print "Coclass: " & refCoClassInfo.Name

        ' Display info about all interfaces implemented by
        ' the coclass.
        PrintInterfaces refCoClassInfo.Interfaces
    Next
End Sub


Sub PrintInterfaces(refInterfaces As TLI.Interfaces)
    Dim refInterfaceInfo As TLI.InterfaceInfo
    For Each refInterfaceInfo In refInterfaces
        ' Print interface name.
        Print "Interface: " & refInterfaceInfo.Name;

        ' Print interface IID.
        Print " " & refInterfaceInfo.Guid

        Dim refMemberInfo As TLI.MemberInfo
        For Each refMemberInfo In refInterfaceInfo.Members
            ' Print the return type.
```

```
        Select Case refMemberInfo.ReturnType
        Case TliVarType.VT_HRESULT
            Print vbTab & "HRESULT ";
        Case TliVarType.VT_INT
            Print vbTab & "int ";
        Case TliVarType.VT_UI4
            Print vbTab & "ULONG ";
        End Select

        ' Print method name.
        Print refMemberInfo.Name & "(";

        Dim refParameterInfo As TLI.ParameterInfo
        For Each refParameterInfo In _
            refMemberInfo.Parameters
            ' Print parameter direction.
            Select Case refParameterInfo.Flags
            Case ParamFlags.PARAMFLAG_FIN
                Print "[in] ";
            Case ParamFlags.PARAMFLAG_FOUT
                Print "[out] ";
            Case ParamFlags.PARAMFLAG_FRETVAL
                Print "[retval] ";
            End Select

            ' Print parameter type.
            Select Case refParameterInfo.VarTypeInfo.VarType
            Case TliVarType.VT_INT
                Print "int ";
            Case TliVarType.VT_VOID
                Print "void ";
            End Select

            ' Print parameter name.
            Print refParameterInfo.Name & ", ";
        Next
        Print ")"
    Next

    ' Recursive calls to print all base interfaces,
    ' including IUnknown
    PrintInterfaces refInterfaceInfo.ImpliedInterfaces
  Next
End Sub
```

CHAPTER TEN

Persistence

Once an interface is published, its survival depends on how useful an abstraction it offers. If developers perceive that the functionality defined by an interface is useful for exposing or accessing a certain service, they'll write components that implement that interface and client applications that use it. The more components that implement or work with a certain interface, the more important that interface becomes. By this measure, *IUnknown* is the most important interface because all COM+ components must implement it. Other interfaces, such as *IMoniker* and *IConnectionPoint*, are also important, but less so.

Most of the original persistence interfaces that are part of COM+ were originally designed to solve project-specific problems in OLE. Over time, however, many developers found these interfaces useful, so they now rank among the more important standard interfaces in COM+. As these interfaces have become more widely used, the persistence facility of COM+ itself has become more important because it makes integration possible between a wide variety of software components. Today, even the Microsoft Visual Basic and Microsoft Java virtual machines provide nearly automatic support for persistence, which means that a tremendous variety of persistable objects are available. This leads to an interesting truth about COM+: as more components are built that reuse standard interfaces for basic facilities such as persistence, naming, and events, the stronger and more important the overall COM+ architecture becomes.

The *IPersist* Interface Family

At run time, most objects maintain certain information about their current state. The exact nature of the data and its format are defined by the author of each coclass, not by COM+. However, several standard persistence interfaces allow a client application to obtain and save the state of an object. An object declares its ability to serialize its state by implementing one or more of these interfaces. The persistence interfaces also enable a client to clone an object by loading its serialized state back into an object. Visual Basic, for example, invokes the persistence interfaces implemented by Microsoft ActiveX controls to obtain their current property values when a project is saved. When the project is reopened, the controls are instantiated and their property values are initialized from the persisted data. Microsoft Message Queue (MSMQ) uses the persistence interfaces to save an object's state for transmission in a message.

At the root of all the persistence interfaces is the *IPersist* interface itself, shown below in Interface Definition Language (IDL) notation:

```
interface IPersist : IUnknown
{
    HRESULT GetClassID([out] CLSID* pClassID);
}
```

This interface simply allows a client to obtain the class identifier (CLSID) of the object. Typically, a client application stores the CLSID of an object together with its state. In this way, the client application knows which object to activate when it reinstantiates the class. For stateless objects, the *IPersist* interface is sufficient because the client application needs to know only which class to activate. Most objects, however, need to store data in addition to their CLSID. Those objects can choose among several types of persistence interfaces that derive from the base *IPersist* interface. These are described in the table below.

Persistence Interface	Description
IPersistStream	Implemented by objects that save and load their state using a simple serial stream
IPersistStreamInit	Like *IPersistStream* but with the addition of the *InitNew* method for initialization
IPersistMemory	Like *IPersistStreamInit* except that the caller can provide a fixed-sized memory block instead of an arbitrarily expandable stream
IPersistStorage	Implemented by objects that save and load their state using a storage object
IPersistFile	Implemented by objects that save and load their state using a file
IPersistPropertyBag(2)	Implemented by controls that save and load their state using a property bag
IPersistMoniker	Implemented by objects that save and load their state using a moniker
IPersistHistory	Implemented by objects running in Microsoft Internet Explorer that want to save and load their state when the user navigates among Web pages

IPersistStream is one of the fundamental interfaces in the *IPersist* family. Any object that implements the *IPersistStream* interface tells the world that it is happy to load and save its state to any stream object provided by the client. The four methods of *IPersistStream* are shown below in IDL notation:

```
interface IPersistStream : IPersist
{
    // Check the object for changes since it was last saved.
    HRESULT IsDirty(void);

    // Load the object's state from the stream.
    HRESULT Load([in, unique] IStream *pStm);

    // Save the object's state to the stream.
    HRESULT Save([in, unique] IStream *pStm,
        [in] BOOL fClearDirty);

    // How many bytes are required to the save the
    // object's state?
    HRESULT GetSizeMax([out] ULARGE_INTEGER *pcbSize);
}
```

Objects that implement *IPersistStream* expect to be initialized by the client via the *IPersistStream::Load* method before the client calls other methods of the *IPersistStream* interface. One variation of *IPersistStream* is the *IPersistStreamInit* interface, which is identical to *IPersistStream* except for the addition of the *InitNew* method. Clients can use this method to initialize the object to a default state instead of restoring a saved state via the *IPersistStreamInit::Load* method. The *IPersistStreamInit* interface is shown below in IDL notation; the *InitNew* method is shown in boldface.

```
interface IPersistStreamInit : IPersist
{
    HRESULT IsDirty(void);
    HRESULT Load([in] LPSTREAM pStm);
    HRESULT Save([in] LPSTREAM pStm, [in] BOOL fClearDirty);
    HRESULT GetSizeMax([out] ULARGE_INTEGER * pCbSize);

    // Initialize the object to its default state.
    HRESULT InitNew(void);
}
```

The *IStream* Interface

Notice that the first argument of both the *Load* and *Save* methods of the *IPersistStream(Init)* interface accepts an *IStream* pointer. *IStream* is a basic interface that encompasses the functionality of reading and writing to a sequential byte stream. Interestingly, *IStream* derives from the *ISequentialStream*[1] interface, which defines the *Read* and *Write* methods, as shown here in IDL notation:

```
interface ISequentialStream : IUnknown
{
    // Reads a specified number of bytes from the stream object
    // into memory, starting at the current seek pointer
    HRESULT Read(
        [out, size_is(cb), length_is(*pcbRead)] void *pv,
        [in] ULONG cb,
        [out] ULONG *pcbRead);

    // Writes a specified number of bytes into the stream
    // object, starting at the current seek pointer
    HRESULT Write(
        [in, size_is(cb)] void const *pv,
        [in] ULONG cb,
        [out] ULONG *pcbWritten);
}
```

The *IStream* interface contains methods similar to those that can be executed on a file handle in that each stream has its own access rights and seek pointer. The *IStream* interface also provides support for a transacted mode and for restricting access to a range of bytes in the stream. The members of the *IStream* interface are described in the following table.

IStream Method	Description
Seek	Moves the seek pointer to a new location relative to the beginning of the stream, the end of the stream, or the current seek pointer
SetSize	Changes the size of the stream object
CopyTo	Copies a specified number of bytes from the current seek pointer in one stream to the current seek pointer in another stream

1. Stream objects that require only simple sequential access implement the *ISequentialStream* interface. Typically, the *ISequentialStream* interface is not implemented by itself. Instead, a more sophisticated stream object implements the *ISequentialStream::Read* and *ISequentialStream::Write* methods as part of an *IStream* interface implementation. For example, the stream object implemented as part of the structured storage service fails when *QueryInterface* is called for the *ISequentialStream* interface; calling *QueryInterface* for *IStream* succeeds.

IStream Method	Description
Commit	Ensures that any changes made to a stream object open in transacted mode are reflected in the parent storage object
Revert	Discards all changes that have been made to a transacted stream since the last *IStream::Commit* call
LockRegion	Restricts access to a specified range of bytes in the stream
UnlockRegion	Removes the access restriction on a range of bytes previously restricted using *IStream::LockRegion*
Stat	Retrieves the STATSTG structure for this stream.*
Clone	Creates a new stream object that references the same bytes as the original stream but provides a separate seek pointer to those bytes

* The STATSTG structure contains statistical information about an open storage, stream, or byte array object.

COM+ provides several standard implementations of the *IStream* interface, so you generally don't need to implement this interface yourself unless you require special functionality. The most popular implementation of this interface is provided by the structured storage service (described later in this chapter), which you can use to save a stream to a disk-based file. You can obtain an even more general implementation of the *IStream* interface by calling the *CreateStreamOnHGlobal*[2] API function, which creates a stream object based on a block of global memory.

Persisting an Object

You persist an object by obtaining a pointer to its persistence interface using the *QueryInterface* method and then calling the appropriate *Save* method for that persistence interface. The *Save* method always requires a pointer to an object implemented by the client where the persistable object can store its data. These steps are illustrated in Figure 10-1, which shows a client directing the object to persist itself to a stream object.

---

2. The *GetHGlobalFromStream* function returns a pointer to the memory block allocated by the *CreateStreamOnHGlobal* function.

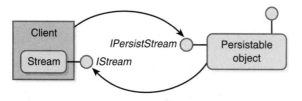

Figure 10-1.
A client asks an object to store its state in a stream using the
IPersistStream *interface.*

The code fragment below illustrates how a client application obtains a pointer to the *IPersistStream* interface implemented by a persistable object and then saves the object's state to a memory-based stream:

```
// Create the object.
IUnknown* pUnknown;
HRESULT hr = CoCreateInstance(CLSID_SomePersistentObject, NULL,
    CLSCTX_INPROC_SERVER, IID_IUnknown, (void**)&pUnknown);
if(FAILED(hr))
    cout << "CoCreateInstance failed." << endl;

// Ask the object for IPersistStreamInit.
IPersistStreamInit* pPersistStreamInit;
hr = pUnknown->QueryInterface(IID_IPersistStreamInit,
    (void**)&pPersistStreamInit);
if(FAILED(hr))
    cout << "IPersistStreamInit not supported." << endl;

// Create a memory-based stream.
IStream* pStream = 0;
hr = CreateStreamOnHGlobal(NULL, TRUE, &pStream);
if(FAILED(hr))
    cout << "CreateStreamOnHGlobal failed." << endl;

// Initialize the object to its default state.
hr = pPersistStreamInit->InitNew();
if(FAILED(hr))
    cout << "IPersistStreamInit::InitNew failed." << endl;

// Save the object to the stream.
hr = pPersistStreamInit->Save(pStream, TRUE);
if(FAILED(hr))
    cout << "IPersistStreamInit::Save failed." << endl;
```

```
// Release the object.
pPersistStreamInit->Release();
pUnknown->Release();
```

Once you have a stream containing the state of an object, you can create a clone of the object simply by instantiating a new object of the same coclass and passing the stream to the *IPersistStream(Init)::Load* method. Assuming that the object has properly implemented its persistence code, the newly created object should be indistinguishable from the original; the code fragment below shows how it's done:

```
// Rewind the stream to the beginning.
LARGE_INTEGER zero = { 0, 0 };
hr = pStream->Seek(zero, STREAM_SEEK_SET, NULL);
if(FAILED(hr))
    cout << "IStream::Seek failed." << endl;

// Create a new object.
hr = CoCreateInstance(CLSID_SomePersistentObject, NULL,
    CLSCTX_INPROC_SERVER, IID_IUnknown, (void**)&pUnknown);
if(FAILED(hr))
    cout << "CoCreateInstance failed." << endl;

// Ask the object for IPersistStreamInit.
hr = pUnknown->QueryInterface(IID_IPersistStreamInit,
    (void**)&pPersistStreamInit);
if(FAILED(hr))
    cout << "IID_IPersistStreamInit not supported." << endl;

// Initialize the object from the stream.
hr = pPersistStreamInit->Load(pStream);
if(FAILED(hr))
    cout << "IPersistStreamInit::Load failed." << endl;

// Release the stream.
pStream->Release();
```

Implementing a Persistable Object

As you can see from the code above, using the *IPersist* interfaces is not difficult. Implementing the *IPersistStream(Init)* interface in an object is also not difficult; it simply entails implementing the five methods of *IPersistStream* or the six methods of *IPersistStreamInit*. Let's begin with the *IPersist::GetClassID* method required by all implementations of the *IPersist* family of interfaces. The *GetClassID* method should simply return the CLSID of the object, as shown below:

```
HRESULT CInsideCOM::GetClassID(CLSID* pClassID)
{
    *pClassID = CLSID_InsideCOM;
    return S_OK;
}
```

The purpose of the *IPersist::GetClassID* method might not be clear initially, since this method has nothing to do with the persistence of a specific object. But its importance becomes obvious when you realize that once an object is persisted to a stream, nothing in that stream identifies the object itself. In other words, if you were to obtain a stream containing the persisted state of an unknown object, you wouldn't be able to re-create the original object from the stream. To address this problem, most client applications obtain the object's CLSID using the *IPersist::GetClassID* method and store that in the stream before the object's data.

The only problem with this approach is that client applications might choose to store an object's CLSID in a stream differently. For example, one client might convert the CLSID to a string before storing it in the stream, and another might store it as a hexadecimal byte array. This would lead to a situation in which a stream containing the persisted state of an object created by one client application could not be read by another client application. The *WriteClassStm* function automates the chore of saving an object's CLSID to a stream in a standard way; it ensures uniformity among all client applications that use it, as shown in the client-side code below:

```
// Get the CLSID of the persistable object.
CLSID clsid;
hr = pPersistStream->GetClassID(&clsid);

// Store the object's CLSID in the stream.
hr = WriteClassStm(pStream, clsid);

// Save the object's data to the stream.
hr = pPersistStream->Save(pStream, TRUE);
```

To re-create an object from a stream, you call the *ReadClassStm* function to obtain the CLSID stored by *WriteClassStm*. This allows the client application to instantiate the correct object via a call to *CoCreateInstance(Ex)* and then call *IPersistStream(Init)::Load* to initialize the object with the remaining data in the stream, as shown in the following code.

```
// Get the CLSID of the persistable object.
CLSID clsid;
hr = ReadClassStm(pStream, &clsid);

// Instantiate the appropriate object.
IPersistStream* pPersistStream;
hr = CoCreateInstance(clsid, NULL, CLSCTX_INPROC_SERVER,
    IID_IPersistStream, (void**)&pPersistStream);

// Load the object's data from the stream.
hr = pPersistStream->Load(pStream);
```

The sequence of operations illustrated by the two preceding code fragments are so standard that two helper functions have been defined to automate the entire procedure: *OleSaveToStream* and *OleLoadFromStream*. *OleSaveToStream* calls *IPersist::GetClassID* to obtain the object's CLSID, calls *WriteClassStm* to save the object's CLSID to the stream, and then calls *IPersistStream::Save* to save the object's persistent data to the stream. *OleLoadFromStream* calls *ReadClassStm* to obtain the object's CLSID from the stream, calls *CoCreateInstance* to instantiate the object, and then calls *IPersistStream::Load* to initialize the object from the data in the stream. Thus all the code in the two fragments can be reduced to two function calls:

```
// Save the object to stream (with its CLSID).
hr = OleSaveToStream(pPersistStream, pStream);

// Sometime later, create a new object based on the
// persisted stream.
IUnknown* pObject;
hr = OleLoadFromStream(pStream, IID_IUnknown, (void**)&pObject);
```

The *IPersistStream(Init)::IsDirty* method lets the client know whether the object has changed since it was last saved. A return value of *S_OK* indicates that the object is dirty; *S_FALSE* indicates that it is clean. A client application can use this information to decide whether the object needs to be persisted again using *IPersistStream(Init)::Save*. The code below is a simple implementation of the *IPersistStream(Init)::IsDirty* method:

```
HRESULT CInsideCOM::IsDirty(void)
{
    if(m_dirty)
        return S_OK;    // The object is dirty.
    else
        return S_FALSE; // The object is clean.
}
```

The *Save* and *Load* methods are the heart of the *IPersistStream(Init)* interface. When the *Save* method is called, the object should use the *ISequentialStream::Write* method to store its current state in the *IStream* pointer provided as the first parameter to the *Save* method. The second parameter of the *IPersistStream(Init)::Save* method tells the object whether it should reset its dirty flag. If *fClearDirty* is TRUE, the dirty flag should be cleared, assuming that the object can successfully save its state to the stream; otherwise, the dirty flag should be left unchanged. The implementation of the *IPersistStream::Save* method for the *InsideCOM* coclass is shown below. Note that the *ISequentialStream::Write* method is used to save the values of the *m_x* and *m_y* variables obtained from the client during a prior call to the *ISum::Sum* method.

```
HRESULT CInsideCOM::Save(IStream *pStm, BOOL fClearDirty)
{
    // Save the data in the client's stream.
    ULONG written = 0;
    int data[2] = { m_x, m_y };
    HRESULT hr = pStm->Write(data, sizeof(data), &written);

    // Clear the dirty flag?
    if(fClearDirty)
        m_dirty = FALSE;

    return S_OK;
}
```

The *IPersistStream(Init)::Load* method is responsible for reading data from the stream object provided in the first parameter and restoring the object's internal state to that specified by the stream data. The sample implementation of the *Load* method shown below uses the *ISequentialStream::Read* method to read data from the stream and restore the values of the *m_x* and *m_y* member variables:

```
HRESULT CInsideCOM::Load(IStream *pStm)
{
    // Read the data from the client's stream.
    ULONG read = 0;
    int data[2] = { 0, 0 };
    pStm->Read(data, sizeof(data), &read);

    // Restore the data back to our private variables.
    m_x = data[0];
    m_y = data[1];

    // Clear the dirty flag.
    m_dirty = FALSE;
```

```
    return S_OK;
}
```

GetSizeMax, the last method of the *IPersistStream* interface, tells the client how many bytes are needed in the stream to store the object's data. Since the *InsideCOM* coclass saves only two 32-bit integer values during the *IPersistStream::Save* operation, *GetSizeMax* returns 8.

```
HRESULT CInsideCOM::GetSizeMax(ULARGE_INTEGER *pcbSize)
{
    (*pcbSize).QuadPart = 8;
    return S_OK;
}
```

If you are implementing the *IPersistStreamInit* interface, you must implement the *IPersistStreamInit::InitNew* method in addition to the methods of *IPersistStream*. The *InitNew* method initializes the object to a default state; the client can call it instead of *IPersistStreamInit::Load*. If the client has already called *Load*, the *InitNew* method must return *E_UNEXPECTED*. In the case of the *InsideCOM* coclass, the *InitNew* method is used only to initialize the dirty flag:

```
HRESULT CInsideCOM::InitNew(void)
{
    // Initialize the dirty flag.
    m_dirty = FALSE;
    return S_OK;
}
```

Building Persistable Objects in Visual Basic

Persistence is supported by higher-level languages such as Visual Basic and Java. Visual Basic supports building persistable classes using the *Persistable* property of public class modules. If the *Persistable* property is set to *1 – Persistable*, Visual Basic automatically provides an implementation of the *IPersist*, *IPersistStream*, *IPersistStreamInit*, and *IPersistPropertyBag* interfaces for the coclass. The *IPersistPropertyBag* interface is shown below in IDL notation:

```
interface IPersistPropertyBag : IPersist
{
    HRESULT InitNew(void);
    HRESULT Load([in] IPropertyBag* pPropBag,
        [in] IErrorLog* pErrorLog);
    HRESULT Save([in] IPropertyBag* pPropBag,
        [in] BOOL fClearDirty,
        [in] BOOL fSaveAllProperties);
}
```

The *IPersistPropertyBag* interface is similar to the *IPersistStreamInit* interface in that it has the *InitNew*, *Load*, and *Save* methods.[3] Notice, however, that the *Load* and *Save* methods of the *IPersistPropertyBag* interface do not access data using the *IStream* interface; instead, they expect to be provided with a property bag object that implements the *IPropertyBag*[4] interface, which is shown below in IDL notation:

```
interface IPropertyBag : IUnknown
{
    // Called by the object to read a property from the storage
    // provided by the client
    HRESULT Read([in] LPCOLESTR pszPropName,
        [in, out] VARIANT* pVar,
        [in] IErrorLog* pErrorLog);

    // Called by the object to write each property in turn to
    // the storage provided by the client
    HRESULT Write([in] LPCOLESTR pszPropName,
        [in] VARIANT* pVar);
}
```

Because it has *Read* and *Write* methods, the *IPropertyBag* interface is superficially similar to the *ISequentialStream* interface. However, instead of storing data as a sequential stream of bytes as the *ISequentialStream* interface does, the *IPropertyBag* interface was designed as an optimization for objects, such as ActiveX controls, that store primarily text-based property values. Most ActiveX controls implement the *IPersistPropertyBag* interface, and the Visual Basic development environment itself implements the *IPropertyBag* interface to collect and store the property values saved by controls into Visual Basic project files.

The *IErrorLog* interface is an abstraction of an "error log" for communicating detailed error information between a client and an object. It is used as part of the *IPropertyBag* and *IPersistPropertyBag* protocol to report any errors that occur using the *IErrorLog::AddError* method. The first parameter of the *AddError* method is the name of the property involved in the error, and the second parameter is an *EXCEPINFO* structure containing the error information. The *IErrorLog* interface is shown on the following page in IDL notation:

---

3. The *GetSizeMax* method is not applicable to property bag objects; the *IsDirty* method was added to the *IPersistPropertyBag2* interface—although Visual Basic does not currently implement this interface.

4. The enhanced version of this interface, *IPropertyBag2*, has several new methods.

```
    // Here's what happened...
    HRESULT AddError(
interface IErrorLog : IUnknown
{

        [in] LPCOLESTR pszPropName,
        [in] EXCEPINFO * pExcepInfo);
}
```

While this is all fascinating information, you're probably wondering why Visual Basic automatically implements the *IPersistPropertyBag* interface in every persistable class. The reason will become clear as we examine the three event procedures that are implemented in Visual Basic by every persistable class module—*InitProperties*, *ReadProperties*, and *WriteProperties*:

```
' Similar to IPersistPropertyBag::InitNew
Private Sub Class_InitProperties()
End Sub

' Similar to IPersistPropertyBag::Load
Private Sub Class_ReadProperties(PropBag As PropertyBag)
End Sub

' Similar to IPersistPropertyBag::Save
Private Sub Class_WriteProperties(PropBag As PropertyBag)
End Sub
```

Notice the one-to-one mapping between the three event procedures exposed in Visual Basic and the methods of the *IPersistPropertyBag* interface. The *InitProperties* event corresponds to the *IPersistPropertyBag::InitNew* or *IPersistStreamInit::InitNew* methods and is fired at the class module when the client calls one of those methods. The *ReadProperties* and *WriteProperties* events correspond to the *IPersistPropertyBag::Load* and *IPersistPropertyBag::Save* or *IPersistStream(Init)::Load* and *IPersistStream(Init)::Save* methods, respectively, and are fired when the client calls those methods. In fact, although Visual Basic also implements the *IPersistStream(Init)* interface for all persistable coclasses, the two additional methods of *IPersistStream(Init)* not addressed by *IPersistPropertyBag*, *IPersistStream(Init)::IsDirty* and *IPersistStream(Init)::GetSizeMax*, are not exposed in Visual Basic. Instead, in current versions of Visual Basic, the *IsDirty* method always returns *S_OK*[5] and *GetSizeMax* returns *E_NOTIMPL*.

---

5. This indicates that the object always thinks it's dirty.

Notice that the *ReadProperties* and *WriteProperties* procedures both have a *PropertyBag* parameter, which you use when you actually save and load the state of an object in Visual Basic. The methods and properties of Visual Basic's *PropertyBag* class are shown below; notice the close correlation of these methods with the *IPropertyBag* interface described previously.

```
' A byte array representing the contents of the PropertyBag
Property Contents As Variant

' Returns a persisted value from a PropertyBag
' Similar to IPropertyBag::Read
Function ReadProperty(Name As String, [DefaultValue]) As Variant

' Writes a value to be persisted to a PropertyBag
' Similar to IPropertyBag::Write
Sub WriteProperty(Name As String, Value, [DefaultValue])
```

The code below is a fragment from a persistable class module written in Visual Basic that stores its state in a Visual Basic–provided *PropertyBag* object:

```
Private Sub Class_ReadProperties(PropBag As PropertyBag)
    m_x = PropBag.ReadProperty("x", 0)
    m_y = PropBag.ReadProperty("y", 0)
End Sub

Private Sub Class_WriteProperties(PropBag As PropertyBag)
    PropBag.WriteProperty "x", m_x
    PropBag.WriteProperty "y", m_y
End Sub
```

A client application written in C++ can obtain this data by calling *IPersistStreamInit::Save* or *IPersistPropertyBag::Save*. Since we've already seen how the *IPersistStreamInit* interface works, let's examine how the *IPersistPropertyBag* interface is used in C++. The code below invites a Visual Basic object to save its state in a property bag using the *IPersistPropertyBag* interface:

```
// Get the IPersistPropertyBag interface.
IPersistPropertyBag* pPersistPropertyBag;
HRESULT hr = pUnknown->QueryInterface(IID_IPersistPropertyBag,
    (void**)&pPersistPropertyBag);
if(FAILED(hr))
    cout << "IID_IPersistPropertyBag not supported." << endl;

// Initialize the object to its default state.
// This fires the InitProperties event in Visual Basic.
```

```
hr = pPersistPropertyBag->InitNew();
if(FAILED(hr))
    cout << "IPersistPropertyBag::InitNew failed" << endl;

// Instantiate the property bag object.
IPropertyBag* pPropertyBag = new CPropertyBag();

// Tell the object to save its state to the property bag.
// This fires the WriteProperties event in Visual Basic.
hr = pPersistPropertyBag->Save(pPropertyBag, TRUE, TRUE);
if(FAILED(hr))
    cout << "IPersistPropertyBag::Save failed" << endl;
```

The main difference between *IPersistPropertyBag* and *IPersistStreamInit* is that when you use *IPersistStreamInit* you create a stream object that implements the *IStream* interface simply by calling the *CreateStreamOnHGlobal* function, and when you use *IPersistPropertyBag* you must create a property bag object that implements the *IPropertyBag* interface. Unfortunately, there is no system-provided implementation of a property bag as there is with a stream; you're left to implement this interface yourself. Below is a simple implementation of the *IPropertyBag::Write* method that simply prints out the name of the property and the value saved by the persistent object:

```
// This method called by the persistable object during
// IPersistPropertyBag::Save.
HRESULT CPropertyBag::Write(LPCOLESTR pszPropName,
    VARIANT* pVar)
{
    // Just print the property name and value.
    wprintf(L"PropertyName = %s Value = %s\n", pszPropName,
        pVar->bstrVal);
    return S_OK;
}
```

Controlling Persistence from Visual Basic

In addition to implementing several members of the *IPersist* interface family in Visual Basic, a Visual Basic application can also act as a client of these same persistence interfaces implemented by another object. When Visual Basic instantiates a coclass, it automatically calls *QueryInterface* to obtain the object's *IPersistPropertyBag*, *IPersistStreamInit*, or *IPersistStream* interface, in that order. The object is not required to support any of the persistence interfaces, but if it does, Visual Basic allows you to persist the object into a *PropertyBag* and to initialize a new object from the data saved in a *PropertyBag*. The Visual Basic code below shows how it's done; for demonstration purposes, it uses the C++ implementation of *IPersistStreamInit* described earlier in this chapter.

```
' InsideCOM supports IPersistStreamInit.
Dim ref As New InsideCOM

' The first time we touch the object, Visual Basic creates it
' and calls IPersistStreamInit::InitNew.
Print ref.SumPersist

' Internally, the object saves the values 3 and 4.
Print ref.Sum(3, 4)

' Create a PropertyBag object for our use.
Dim pb As New PropertyBag

' Save a string property named String.
pb.WriteProperty "String", "Guy"

' Persist the InsideCOM object into a property named COM+.
' Visual Basic calls IPersistStreamInit::GetClassID and
' IPersistStreamInit::Save.
pb.WriteProperty "COM+", ref

' Display the contents of the PropertyBag (not a pretty sight).
Print pb.Contents

' Create another reference to the InsideCOM coclass.
Dim newref As InsideCOM

' Create a new InsideCOM object.
' Visual Basic calls IPersistStreamInit::Load with the data from the
' PropertyBag.
Set newref = pb.ReadProperty("COM+")

' The new object prints 3 + 4 = 7, proving that the persistence
' worked.
Print newref.SumPersist
```

Building Persistable Objects in Java

A class written in Java can support persistence by implementing the *java.io.Serializable* interface. This interface has no methods or properties—it serves only as a signal interface to indicate that the class supports persistence.

For classes that implement the *java.io.Serializable* interface, the Microsoft Java Virtual Machine (VM) automatically supports the *IPersist, IPersistStreamInit,* and *IPersistStorage* interfaces. When a client application asks a Java class to save its state using one of the supported *IPersist* interfaces, the object's nonstatic and nontransient fields are automatically serialized. When the state of the object is later restored using the same *IPersist* interface, Java automatically restores the member variables saved previously. In this way, a Java component can participate in persistence operations with other COM+ components.

Java classes that require special control during the serialization and deserialization process can implement two methods, *writeObject* and *readObject,* with the exact signatures shown below:

```
// Called during IPersistStreamInit::Save
private void writeObject(java.io.ObjectOutputStream out)
    throws java.io.IOException

// Called during IPersistStreamInit::Load
private void readObject(java.io.ObjectInputStream in)
    throws java.io.IOException, ClassNotFoundException
```

Within the *writeObject* and *readObject* methods, you can use the methods of the *java.io.ObjectOutputStream* and *java.io.ObjectInputStream* classes to write and read data from the stream, respectively. You can invoke the default mechanism for serialization by calling the *ObjectOutputStream.defaultWriteObject* method in the *writeObject* method and the *ObjectInputStream.defaultReadObject* method in the *readObject* method, as shown in the code fragment below:

```
private void writeObject(java.io.ObjectOutputStream out)
    throws java.io.IOException
{
    // Default write method
    out.defaultWriteObject();
}

private void readObject(java.io.ObjectInputStream in)
    throws java.io.IOException, ClassNotFoundException
{
    // Default read method
    in.defaultReadObject();
}
```

Structured Storage

As software has become increasingly sophisticated, it has also become more demanding of the services offered by the operating system. Operating systems, in turn, have become resource managers that have to ration the available resources among the various applications. In the area of persistent storage, most operating systems are willing to provide an application with controlled access to the hard disk. Normally, the application receives a file handle through which it can read from and write to certain areas of the disk. In a typical file system, each file is treated as a raw sequence of bytes, with no meaning other than that given to it by the application that created the file. Although the bytes that comprise a file might actually be fragmented into small blocks scattered throughout the drive, the file system is responsible for understanding the layout of the data and presenting the application with a sequential view of it.

Structured storage is a facility that takes a unique approach to saving data. It enables a component (or components) to save data in a single file in a standardized, structured format. In the past, most sophisticated applications developed complex proprietary formats for saving the user's data. While workable, this approach was limited in two significant respects. First, only the application itself had any idea what data was stored in a file. Other applications, such as the system shell or other file viewers, had no information about the file other than its name, size, and other file system trivia. Second, the proprietary format made it almost impossible for other applications to embed their data in the same file. For instance, if the user of a word processing application embedded a picture produced by a graphics utility in a document, and if the picture data was saved in a proprietary format, the application would have difficulty storing the embedded data. Structured storage addresses these limitations by offering a standard mechanism for applications to use when saving data.

Structured storage is sometimes called "a file system within a file" because it can treat a single file as if it is capable of storing directories and files. A file created using the structured storage service contains one or more *storages*, roughly equivalent to directories, and each storage can contain zero or more *streams*, roughly equivalent to files. A storage can also contain any number of *substorages*.

The advantages offered by structured storage are numerous. First, instead of developing a proprietary protocol for saving data, an application can use structured storage to develop a more standardized solution. For example, a word processing application might save a document by creating distinct storages and streams for summary information, embedded objects, macros, and the user's data. The storage for embedded objects might contain substorages, one for each application whose data has been embedded in the document. Each of those substorages might have one or more streams, each containing the data of a single embedded object. This hypothetical example is illustrated in Figure 10-2.

The structured storage service is accessible through two interfaces: *IStorage* and *IStream*. *IStorage* offers methods that can be executed on a storage object, and *IStream* offers methods that can be executed on a stream object. Microsoft provides implementations of these interfaces as part of the structured storage service. As you'll see, the structured storage service is so easy to use that there's almost no excuse for not using it to read and write data.

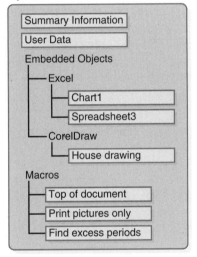

Figure 10-2.
A single file containing different types of data saved in a structured format.

The *IStorage* and *IStream* Interfaces

Like a directory in the file system, a storage object has a certain number of standard operations that it can perform. To get a general idea of the functionality provided by a storage object, consider the standard command-line utilities that are often executed on a directory. These utilities include md (make directory), cd (change directory), deltree (delete a directory tree), xcopy (copy a file or directory), and move (move a file or directory). All of these operations can be executed as methods of the *IStorage* interface and are described in the following table.

IStorage Method	Description
CreateStream	Creates and opens a stream object with the specified name contained in this storage object
OpenStream	Opens an existing stream object within this storage object by using the specified access permissions
CreateStorage	Creates and opens a new storage object within this storage object
OpenStorage	Opens an existing storage object with the specified name according to the specified access mode
CopyTo	Copies the entire contents of this open storage object into another storage object
MoveElementTo	Copies or moves a substorage or stream from this storage object to another storage object
Commit	Reflects changes for a transacted storage object to the parent level
Revert	Discards all changes made to the storage object since the last commit operation
EnumElements	Returns an enumerator object that can be used to enumerate the storage and stream objects contained in this storage object
DestroyElement	Removes the specified storage or stream from this storage object
RenameElement	Renames the specified storage or stream in this storage object
SetElementTimes	Sets the modification, access, and creation times of the indicated storage element, if supported by the underlying file system
SetClass	Assigns the specified CLSID to this storage object
SetStateBits	Stores up to 32 bits of state information in this storage object
Stat	Returns the STATSTG structure for this open storage object

To create or open a structured storage file, call the *StgCreateStorageEx* or *StgOpenStorageEx* function. Using the *IStorage* interface pointer returned by the *StgCreateStorageEx* function, you can create streams or additional substorages using the methods in the table above. The following code fragment creates a structured storage file named TestFile.stg and obtains a pointer to the root storage object's *IStorage* interface:

```
hr = StgCreateStorageEx(L"C:\\TestFile.stg",
    STGM_DIRECT|STGM_CREATE|STGM_READWRITE|STGM_SHARE_EXCLUSIVE,
    STGFMT_STORAGE, 0, 0, 0, IID_IStorage, (void**)&pStorage);
```

This seemingly simple request to create a new file actually creates on the disk a file that already contains 1.5 KB of data. This overhead is required by the implementation of the structured storage service.

Using the *IStorage* interface pointer to create a stream is straightforward. The following code fragment creates a stream named *MyDataStream* and retrieves a pointer to the stream object's *IStream* interface:

```
IStream* pStream;
hr = pStorage->CreateStream(L"MyDataStream",
    STGM_DIRECT|STGM_CREATE|STGM_WRITE|STGM_SHARE_EXCLUSIVE,
    0, 0, &pStream);
```

When working with standard files, developers typically use a file handle to execute read and write operations on a file. For structured storage files, you use the *IStream* interface to execute read and write operations on a stream within the file. You use the *ISequentialStream::Write* method to write data into a stream, as shown here:

```
ULONG bytes_written;
char data[] = "HELLO THERE!";
pStream->Write(data, strlen(data), &bytes_written);
```

The *IPropertySetStorage* and *IPropertyStorage* Interfaces

The actual data stored by an individual stream might be in a proprietary format, but it's important that the structure of a file saved using the structured storage interfaces be accessible to all applications through a standard protocol. Not only is the data saved in an organized fashion, but utilities and other applications might be able to obtain information about the data stored in the file if certain streams in the file are stored in a standardized format. For example, a file might have a summary information stream in the root storage that contains information about the file's contents. Other applications, such as the system shell, might allow the user to execute sophisticated queries based on this information—such as a request for a list of all documents written by a certain person or containing information about a certain subject.

As part of the structured storage service, Microsoft offers a property set format that you can use to store summary information in a standard way. This information can then be accessed by anyone who wants it. Microsoft Windows, for example, displays this information when the user right-clicks the icon for a file and then chooses Properties from the context menu to display a Properties dialog box, as shown in Figure 10-3. When viewing a folder as a Web page, Internet Explorer automatically displays this information for any selected file.

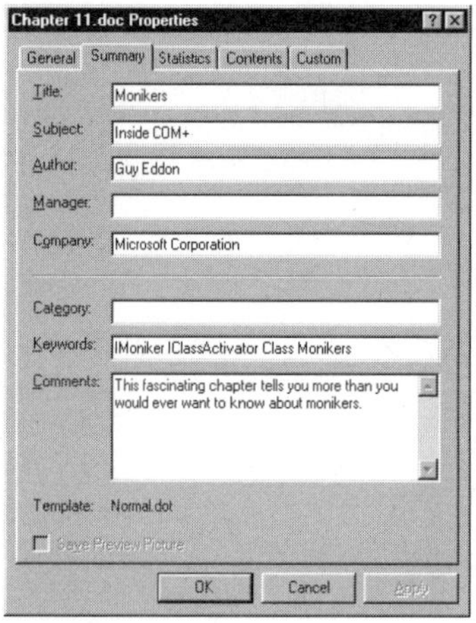

Figure 10-3.
The Properties dialog box displaying the summary information stream for a file.

The *IPropertySetStorage* and *IPropertyStorage* interfaces encapsulate the functionality needed to create property sets, such as the summary information stream described above. The confusing thing about the property storage interfaces is that from the point of view of a structured storage file, a property set is written into a single stream. Therefore, *IPropertySetStream* and *IPropertyStream* might seem to be more appropriate names for these interfaces. However, the *IPropertySetStorage* and *IPropertyStorage* interfaces were not designed to be used only by structured storage. Since other services might benefit from these interfaces, conceptually these interfaces abstract the storage of properties.

When you work with the property set implementation provided by the structured storage service, you obtain a pointer to the *IPropertySetStorage* interface by calling *QueryInterface* on an *IStorage* pointer, as shown here:

```
IPropertySetStorage* pPropertySetStorage;
pStorage->QueryInterface(IID_IPropertySetStorage,
    (void**)&pPropertySetStorage);
```

Every property set is identified by a globally unique identifier (GUID) called a format identifier (FMTID). This identifier allows any application that might come across this property set to quickly determine whether it under-stands the contents of the property set. The two most widely used FMTIDs are *FMTID_SummaryInformation* and *FMTID_DocSummaryInformation*. The latter stores extended summary information for documents created by Microsoft Office applications. When you create a new property set, you must define its FMTID. The following code uses the *IPropertySetStorage* interface to create a new property set with the format identifier *FMTID_SummaryInformation*:

```
IPropertyStorage* pPropertyStorage;
pPropertySetStorage->Create(FMTID_SummaryInformation,
    NULL, PROPSETFLAG_ANSI,
    STGM_CREATE|STGM_READWRITE|STGM_SHARE_EXCLUSIVE,
    &pPropertyStorage);
```

The methods of the *IPropertySetStorage* interface are described in the fol-lowing table.

IPropertySetStorage Methods	Description
Create	Creates a new property set
Open	Opens a previously created property set
Delete	Deletes an existing property set
Enum	Creates and retrieves a pointer to an object that can be used to enumerate property sets

The *IPropertySetStorage::Create* method returns an *IPropertyStorage* inter-face, which you can use to work with an individual property set. The methods of the *IPropertyStorage* interface are described in the following table.

IPropertyStorage Methods	Description
ReadMultiple	Reads property values in a property set
WriteMultiple	Writes property values in a property set
DeleteMultiple	Deletes properties in a property set
ReadPropertyNames	Gets corresponding string names for given property identifiers (PROPIDs)

(continued)

IPropertyStorage Methods	Description
WritePropertyNames	Creates or changes string names corresponding to given PROPIDs
DeletePropertyNames	Deletes string names for given PROPIDs
SetClass	Assigns a CLSID to the property set
Commit	As in *IStorage::Commit*, flushes or commits changes to the property storage object
Revert	When the property storage is opened in transacted mode, discards all changes since the last commit operation
Enum	Creates and gets a pointer to an enumerator for properties within this property set
Stat	Receives statistics about this property set
SetTimes	Sets modification, creation, and access times for the property set

Two structures are used in defining a property set: PROPSPEC and PROPVARIANT. The PROPSPEC structure defines the property based on a property identifier (PROPID) or a string name; properties are typically defined by a PROPID. More than a dozen PROPIDs are defined for the summary information property set; they define everything from the document's author to a thumbnail sketch of the document. Of course, an application will work only with the properties it requires.

The value of the property itself is defined in the PROPVARIANT structure. This is a variation on a structure used to store variants. For example, to store string data, you simply declare the *VT_LPSTR* variant type. The code fragment below stores a single property in a property storage. Notice that the string *"Anna"* is not saved in Unicode. Although in general all strings used by COM+ must be in Unicode, string data stored in a property set need not be. In fact, for the data stored in a summary information property set to display properly on non-Unicode systems such as Windows 98, the string data must not be stored in Unicode.

```
PROPSPEC ps;
ps.ulKind = PRSPEC_PROPID;
ps.propid = PIDSI_AUTHOR;
```

```
PROPVARIANT pv;
pv.vt = VT_LPSTR;
pv.pszVal = "Anna";

hr = pPropertyStorage->WriteMultiple(1, &ps, &pv, 0);
```

In Windows 2000, the New Technology File System version 5.0 (NTFS5) has been updated so that it supports native property sets on any file or directory using the *IPropertyStorage* and *IPropertySetStorage* interfaces. You can use these interfaces to attach a property set to flat files (such as bitmaps) in addition to structured storage files. NTFS stores this data on the disk in a special part of the file structure; this enables applications such as Microsoft Index Server to index and search the contents of native NTFS property sets.

CHAPTER ELEVEN

Monikers

Naming is a crucial aspect of any system. Files are the most obvious kind of object for which naming matters, but many other types of objects are affected by naming. Because different developers typically work on different aspects of a system, the naming rules for certain categories of objects can differ radically. Monikers (sometimes known as *intelligent names*) are a standard and extensible way of naming and connecting to objects throughout the system. Simply put, a moniker is an object that identifies another object.

Like other areas of COM+, the namespace is rich and complex. Unlike other parts of COM+, monikers have been slow to gain acceptance by developers both inside and outside Microsoft. This situation is changing, however, because monikers are used throughout Microsoft Windows 2000, including technologies such as Active Directory as well as COM+ component services such as queued components. In this chapter, we'll explain why monikers are so important and how you can take advantage of this technology in your designs.

Initializing Objects

In earlier chapters, we identified coclasses by their class identifier (CLSID) and instantiated objects using the rather primitive *CoCreateInstance* function. *CoCreateInstance* is typically one of the first functions that new COM+ programmers learn, so many of those programmers overuse it until they gain some experience and insight into the richness of the COM+ namespace. Part of the problem is that some programmers see *CoCreateInstance* as the COM+ analogue of the *new* operator in C++. This parallel is further reinforced by the fact that *CoCreateInstance* is actually called by Microsoft Visual Basic and Java programs when the *New* keyword is applied to a coclass. Unfortunately, *CoCreateInstance* is a poor substitute for the functionality provided by the *new* operator in C++. For example, say that you have defined a C++ class that computes prime numbers, as shown on the following page.

```
class prime
{
public:
    prime(int starting_prime) : m_first(starting_number) { }
    int get_next_prime(void);

private:
    int m_first;
};
```

The constructor for this class accepts one argument, whose value becomes the starting prime number. Each call to the *get_next_prime* method returns a subsequent prime number, which implies the following usage:

```
prime* my_prime = new prime(7);      // Calls constructor
cout << my_prime->get_next_prime() << endl; // Displays 11
```

Now imagine that you want to turn the C++ *prime* class into a coclass that implements the *IPrime* interface. First you need to define the *IPrime* interface containing the *GetNextPrime* method, as shown below:

```
interface IPrime : IUnknown
{
    HRESULT GetNextPrime([out, retval] int* next_prime);
};
```

Noticeably absent from this interface definition is the constructor. Typically, the client program calls *CoCreateInstance* to instantiate the object, automatically invoking the constructor. Unfortunately, *CoCreateInstance* doesn't accept an extra argument for our constructor. As you know, *CoCreateInstance* is a high-level object creation function that is implemented using the *CoGetClassObject* function. The following pseudo-code shows the implementation of *CoCreateInstance*:[1]

```
HRESULT CoCreateInstance(REFCLSID rclsid, IUnknown* pUnkOuter,
    DWORD dwClsContext, REFIID riid, void** ppv)
{
    IClassFactory* pClassFactory;
    CoGetClassObject(rclsid, dwClsContext, NULL,
        IID_IClassFactory, (void**)&pClassFactory);
    pClassFactory->CreateInstance(pUnkOuter, riid, ppv);
    pClassFactory->Release();
}
```

1. When instantiating an object on a remote machine, the system provides an optimization of *CoCreateInstance*. Instead of making two round-trips (one for *CoGetClassObject* and another for *IClassFactory::CreateInstance*), the Service Control Manager (SCM) on the remote machine executes these steps and returns the desired pointer to the caller.

Class Objects

In most contexts, you can substitute the phrase *class factory* with *class object*, but this is not always the case. A class factory is an object that implements the two methods of the *IClassFactory* interface, *CreateInstance* and *LockServer*. This implementation enables *CoCreateInstance* to easily instantiate a coclass. However, notice that the function used by *CoCreateInstance* in the preceding code to obtain a pointer to the *IClassFactory* interface is named *CoGetClassObject*—not *CoGetClassFactory*. In fact, *CoCreateInstance* passes the *IID_IClassFactory* interface identifier to *CoGetClassObject* to ensure that the interface pointer received can be used to call the *IClassFactory::CreateInstance* method.

A class object is a powerful abstraction that you can use to implement a custom activation interface instead of or in addition to *IClassFactory*. Therefore, while a class factory (an object that implements *IClassFactory*) can be called a class object, a class object is not necessarily a class factory. Since the *IClassFactory::CreateInstance* method is what really instantiates most coclasses, it, not *CoCreateInstance*, is the true analogue of the *new* operator. The declaration of the *CreateInstance* method shown below clearly illustrates that no parameter is provided to pass an argument to a class's constructor. By creating a class object with a custom activation interface (not *IClassFactory*), you can effectively redefine (or overload, in C++-speak) the *new* operation for a particular coclass:

```
HRESULT IClassFactory::CreateInstance(IUnknown* pUnkOuter,
    REFIID riid, void** ppvObject);
```

Custom Activation Interfaces

By defining a custom activation interface and implementing that interface in a class object, you can pass extra arguments for the constructor, as expressed by the *IPrimeFactory*[2] interface shown here:

```
interface IPrimeFactory : IUnknown
{
    HRESULT CreatePrime(
        [in] int starting_prime,
        [out, retval] IPrime** ppPrime);
};
```

A class object implementing the *IPrimeFactory* interface works as well with the *CoGetClassObject* function called by the client as it does with the *DllGetClassObject* function exported by in-process components or the

---

2. It is customary, but not required, to name custom activation interfaces in the form of I*Thing*Factory, where *Thing* is the name of the coclass being instantiated by the class object.

CoRegisterClassObject function called by executable components.[3] The only requirement of both functions is that the class object implement *IUnknown*, not *IClassFactory*. However, because the *CoCreateInstance* helper function depends on the existence of the *IClassFactory* interface, it does not work with class objects that don't implement this interface. Thus, a client program will most likely have to access an object that implements a custom activation interface using the *CoGetClassObject* function, as shown here:

```
// Calling CoGetClassObject but requesting IPrimeFactory,
// not IClassFactory
IPrimeFactory* pPrimeFactory;
CoGetClassObject(CLSID_Prime, CLSCTX_SERVER, NULL,
    IID_IPrimeFactory, (void**)&pPrimeFactory);

// Calling the IPrimeFactory::CreatePrime method and
// passing 7 to the constructor
IPrime* pPrime;
pPrimeFactory->CreatePrime(7, &pPrime);
pPrimeFactory->Release();

// Now we have a Prime object.
int next_prime;
pPrime->GetNextPrime(&next_prime);
cout << next_prime << endl; // Displays 11
```

While this mechanism works well for C++ programs, a Visual Basic application will have a hard time instantiating the *Prime* object because its *New* keyword results in a call to *CoCreateInstance*. Since *CoCreateInstance* depends on finding an implementation of *IClassFactory*, it does not work with the *Prime* object. Calling *CoGetClassObject* directly from Visual Basic is theoretically possible, but this is not something most Visual Basic programmers would entertain.

More on Monikers

After following our analysis to this point, you probably have two questions on your mind:

- Why bother creating a class object that implements a custom activation interface if Visual Basic refuses to work with it?

- How on earth is this related to monikers?

---

3. Executable components that implement custom activation interfaces in place of *IClassFactory* have special lifetime issues that you must address. For more information, see the section titled "Managing the Lifetime of an Executable Component" in Chapter 13.

Monikers are the answer to the first question, and consequently they provide the answer to the second question. As mentioned earlier, a moniker is an object that names another object. Names are used throughout Windows to identify everything from files to event objects. The difficulty is that every type of object has its own naming rules. Monikers allow all objects to deal with naming through a single, standard interface: *IMoniker*. COM+ provides several system implementations of the *IMoniker* interface, described in the following table. Notice that monikers are not instantiated by calling *CoCreateInstance* but instead offer their own custom creation function because most monikers require extra information about the object they name.

Moniker Type	Creation Function	Purpose
File moniker	*CreateFileMoniker*	A file moniker acts as a wrapper for the pathname of a file.
Item moniker	*CreateItemMoniker*	An item moniker identifies an object contained in another object.
Pointer moniker	*CreatePointerMoniker*	A pointer moniker identifies an object that can exist only in the active or running state.
Anti-moniker	*CreateAntiMoniker*	An anti-moniker is the inverse of another moniker; when the two are combined, they obliterate each other.
Composite moniker	*CreateGenericComposite*	A composite moniker is composed of other monikers.
Class moniker	*CreateClassMoniker*	A class moniker acts as a wrapper for the CLSID of a COM class.
URL moniker	*CreateURLMoniker*	A URL moniker represents and manages a Uniform Resource Locator (URL).
OBJREF moniker*	*CreateObjrefMoniker*	An OBJREF moniker encapsulates a marshaled *IUnknown* interface pointer to an object.

* For information about the OBJREF moniker, see Chapter 15.

The *IMoniker* Interface

In many cases, one of the system monikers implemented by COM+—or some combination of these monikers—will suffice for the purpose of naming objects. At other times, only a custom moniker will do. A custom moniker is an object you create that implements the *IMoniker* interface. Contrary to popular belief, implementing the *IMoniker* interface is not that difficult.

The myth that the *IMoniker* interface is difficult to implement probably arose because the interface has 15 methods. To ensure that all moniker objects support persistence, *IMoniker* is derived from the *IPersistStream* interface (4 methods), which is derived from the *IPersist* interface (1 method), which is in turn derived from the *IUnknown* interface (3 methods). That makes a grand total of 23 methods required to implement a custom moniker. This interface hierarchy is shown in Figure 11-1.

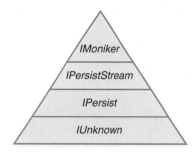

Figure 11-1.
The IMoniker *interface hierarchy.*

In practice, not all monikers need to implement all of the methods. Many of the *IMoniker* methods were designed primarily for file monikers and thus are not applicable to certain custom monikers. In addition, not all monikers need to support persistence, which means that the methods of the *IPersist* and *IPersistStream* interfaces might simply return *E_NOTIMPL*. The system-supplied pointer moniker operates in this fashion.

A warning flag should be raised in your mind whenever several methods of an interface implementation return *E_NOTIMPL*. Either the implementation is incomplete or certain methods of that interface are not applicable. If, as is the case with pointer monikers, certain methods of an interface simply are not relevant to a specific implementation, this might indicate that the interface was designed improperly. Monikers do not take advantage of the richness offered by the *IUnknown::QueryInterface* method to determine the capabilities offered by a particular moniker coclass. Every implementation of the *IMoniker* interface is forced to provide an implementation of the *IPersistStream* and *IPersist* interfaces, even if those methods do nothing more than return *E_NOTIMPL*. This design flaw is more annoyance than limitation, but it does illustrate the importance of careful interface design.

The following table describes the methods of the *IMoniker* interface.

IMoniker Method	Description
BindToObject	Binds to the object named by the moniker
BindToStorage	Binds to the object's storage
Reduce	Reduces the moniker to its simplest form
ComposeWith	Combines the moniker with another moniker to create a composite moniker (a collection of monikers stored in left-to-right sequence)
Enum	Enumerates component monikers
IsEqual	Compares the moniker with another moniker
Hash	Returns a hash value
IsRunning	Checks whether the object is running
GetTimeOfLastChange	Returns time the object was last changed
Inverse	Returns the inverse of the moniker
CommonPrefixWith	Finds the prefix that the moniker has in common with another moniker
RelativePathTo	Constructs a relative moniker between this moniker and another
GetDisplayName	Returns the display name
ParseDisplayName	Converts a display name to a moniker
IsSystemMoniker	Checks whether the moniker is one of the system-supplied types

Bind Contexts

Roughly half of *IMoniker*'s methods take a pointer to a *bind context* as an argument. A bind context is an object that implements the *IBindCtx* interface and contains information about a moniker binding operation. The *IBindCtx* interface is shown below in IDL notation:

```
interface IBindCtx : IUnknown
{
    // Registers an object with the bind context
    HRESULT RegisterObjectBound([in, unique] IUnknown* punk);

    // Revokes an object's registration
    HRESULT RevokeObjectBound([in, unique] IUnknown* punk);
```

(continued)

```
        // Releases all objects registered via RegisterObjectBound
        HRESULT ReleaseBoundObjects(void);

        // Sets the binding options
        HRESULT SetBindOptions([in] BIND_OPTS* pbindopts);

        // Returns the binding options stored in this bind context
        HRESULT GetBindOptions([in, out] BIND_OPTS* pbindopts);

        // Returns a pointer to the IRunningObjectTable interface
        HRESULT GetRunningObjectTable(
            [out] IRunningObjectTable** pprot);

        // Associates an object with a string key
        HRESULT RegisterObjectParam([in] LPOLESTR pszKey,
            [in, unique] IUnknown* punk);

        // Returns the object associated with a given string key
        HRESULT GetObjectParam([in] LPOLESTR pszKey,
            [out] IUnknown** ppunk);

        // Enumerates all the string keys in the table
        HRESULT EnumObjectParam([out] IEnumString** ppenum);

        // Revokes association between an object and a string key
        HRESULT RevokeObjectParam([in] LPOLESTR pszKey);
}
```

A binding operation connects a moniker with the object that it names. In some situations, a bind context enables certain optimizations to occur during the binding of composite monikers. There is no need to implement the *IBindCtx* interface because the system provides a fully functional implementation of this interface. To create a bind context for use with a moniker, you simply call the *CreateBindCtx* function, as shown here:

```
IBindCtx* pBindCtx;
CreateBindCtx(0, &pBindCtx);
```

The heart of the *IMoniker* interface is the *BindToObject* method. This method enables a moniker to bind to the object it names. A client application might call this method as shown in the code below. Notice the use of the *pBindCtx* parameter passed to the *IMoniker::BindToObject* method.

```
IMyInterface* pMyInterface;
pMoniker->BindToObject(pBindCtx, NULL, IID_IMyInterface,
    (void**)&pMyInterface);
```

Once a moniker is bound to the underlying object that it names, a pointer to the requested interface of that object is returned to the client application. The client can proceed to use the object in the typical fashion by calling any methods of the requested interface. When the client has finished working with the object, the object must be released, along with the bind context and the moniker itself.

To reify monikers without an explicit binding context, use the helper function *BindMoniker*. The *BindMoniker* function takes an *IMoniker* interface pointer and binds that moniker to the object it names. The bind context required to perform the binding operation is automatically acquired by the *BindMoniker* function. In the following code fragment, *pMoniker* is a pointer to a moniker that is being bound to the underlying object it names. Notice the explicit use of a bind context:

```
IBindCtx* pClassBindCtx;
CreateBindCtx(0, &pClassBindCtx);
pMoniker->BindToObject(pClassBindCtx, NULL, IID_IUnknown,
    (void**)&pUnknown);
pClassBindCtx->Release();
```

The functionally equivalent code shown here uses the *BindMoniker* helper function, resulting in code that is significantly easier to read:

```
BindMoniker(pMoniker, 0, IID_IUnknown, (void**)&pUnknown);
```

The primary reason you might bother to explicitly create a bind context and then call the *IMoniker::BindToObject* method instead of using the *BindMoniker* function is if you need to set custom options in the bind context. Bind context options are set using the *IBindCtx::SetBindOptions* method, which takes a pointer to a BIND_OPTS or BIND_OPTS2 structure. For example, using the BIND_OPTS2 structure, you can set the *pServerInfo* member to point to a COSERVERINFO structure containing the name of the machine on which the binding operation should occur.[4] The BIND_OPTS2 structure is shown below:

```
typedef struct tagBIND_OPTS2 {
    DWORD           cbStruct;              // sizeof(BIND_OPTS2)
    DWORD           grfFlags;              // BIND_FLAGS
    DWORD           grfMode;               // STGM flags
    DWORD           dwTickCountDeadline;   // How long should
                                           //    binding take
    DWORD           dwTrackFlags;          // SLR flags
    DWORD           dwClassContext;        // CLSCTX flags
```

(continued)

---

4. Currently the class moniker does not honor the *BIND_OPTS2.pServerInfo* member.

```
    LCID           locale;               // Passed to
                                         //   IClassActivator
    COSERVERINFO* pServerInfo;           // Server name and
                                         //   security
    } BIND_OPTS2;
```

The *MkParseDisplayName* Function

A coclass is identified by a CLSID; a running COM+ object is identified by a marshaled interface pointer. Instead of using a CLSID or marshaled interface pointer, monikers employ a somewhat user-friendly string called a display name to identify COM+ objects. Monikers require that string names be used to represent objects in much the same way that a file system identifies files—at least to the user—by string name. For example, a file moniker's display name takes the form of a path, such as C:\My Documents\Story.doc, whereas a class moniker supports strings in the form *clsid:10000013-0000-0000-0000-0000000000001*.

The *IMoniker::GetDisplayName* method returns the display name of any moniker; and the *IMoniker::ParseDisplayName* method converts a display name into a moniker object. Of course, before you can call either the *GetDisplayName* or *ParseDisplayName* methods, you must already have a moniker object of the desired type. This is where the *MkParseDisplayName* function comes in, as defined here:

```
HRESULT MkParseDisplayName(IBindCtx* pbc, LPCWSTR szDisplayName,
    ULONG* pchEaten, IMoniker** ppmk);
```

Technically speaking, *MkParseDisplayName* converts a string to a moniker that identifies the object named by that string. This process is similar to calling the *IMoniker::ParseDisplayName* method, except that you don't have to have a moniker to begin with—a string is sufficient. You can use a string because the *MkParseDisplayName* function is the entry point into the COM+ namespace; a custom moniker can hook into this namespace and provide any user-defined naming functionality you require.

MkParseDisplayName accepts two primary string formats. The first format is a pathname, such as C:\My Documents\Letter.doc. *MkParseDisplayName* has hard-coded support for file monikers and thus knows that any pathname should be converted to a file moniker. The second string format is the more general and thus more important of the two formats. In this format, *MkParseDisplayName* accepts any string in the form *ProgID:ObjectName*, where *ProgID* is a registered program identifier. This architecture allows anyone to write a custom moniker that hooks into the COM+ namespace simply by creating a program identifier (ProgID) entry in the registry.

The following steps are executed when *MkParseDisplayName* encounters a string that has the *ProgID:ObjectName* format:

1. The ProgID is converted to a CLSID using the *CLSIDFromProgID* function. The result is the CLSID of the moniker.

2. *CoGetClassObject* is called to instantiate the moniker.

3. *IUnknown::QueryInterface* is called to request the *IParseDisplayName* interface.

4. The *IParseDisplayName::ParseDisplayName* method is called to parse the string passed to *MkParseDisplayName*.

5. In the moniker's *IParseDisplayName::ParseDisplayName* method, a moniker that names the object identified by the string is created.

6. The resulting *IMoniker* pointer is returned to the client.

For example, if the string "*Hello:Maya*" is passed to *MkParseDisplayName*, the HKEY_CLASSES_ROOT section of the registry is searched for the ProgID *Hello*. If *Hello* is found, the CLSID subkey below the ProgID is used to locate and load the moniker. The moniker's *IParseDisplayName::ParseDisplayName* method is then called to create a moniker object that names the *Maya* object. Figure 11-2 shows the registry entries involved in this hypothetical example; the numbered labels indicate the order in which the information is obtained from the registry.

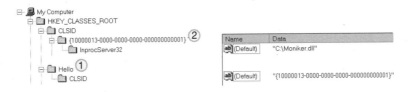

Figure 11-2.
The steps to locate a moniker's coclass from a ProgID.

The *CoGetObject* Helper Function

Once you obtain an *IMoniker* interface pointer using *MkParseDisplayName*, the next step is typically to bind to the object named by the moniker. You can do this by creating an explicit bind context and then calling the *IMoniker::BindToObject* method; or you can use the *BindMoniker* helper function discussed previously.

Yet another helper function, *CoGetObject*,[5] simplifies the process of converting a display name into a moniker and then binding to the named object. Like the *BindMoniker* function, *CoGetObject* obviates the need for an explicit binding context. Unlike *BindMoniker*, however, *CoGetObject* also lets you set binding options using the BIND_OPTS(2) structures. Below is pseudo-code for the internal implementation of the *CoGetObject* function:

```
HRESULT __stdcall CoGetObject(LPCWSTR pszDisplayName,
    BIND_OPTS* pBindOptions, REFIID riid, void** ppv)
{
    HRESULT hr = 0;

    // Create the bind context.
    IBindCtx* pBindCtx = 0;
    hr = CreateBindCtx(0, &pBindCtx);

    // Call MkParseDisplayName with the user's string.
    ULONG chEaten;
    IMoniker* pMoniker = 0;
    hr = MkParseDisplayName(pBindCtx, pszDisplayName,
        &chEaten, &pMoniker);

    // Set the bind options requested by the caller.
    hr = pBindCtx->SetBindOptions(pBindOptions);

    // Call IMoniker::BindToObject to get the user's object.
    hr = pMoniker->BindToObject(pBindCtx, NULL, riid, ppv);

    // Release stuff.
    pMoniker->Release();
    pBindCtx->Release();

    return hr;
}
```

The Visual Basic and Java Perspective

One of the neat things about the *CoGetObject* wrapper for *MkParseDisplayName* is that Visual Basic programmers already know and love this function. Well, actually, most Visual Basic programmers know the *MkParseDisplayName* function by a different moniker—they call it *GetObject*. Like the *CoGetObject* helper function designed for C++ developers, Visual Basic's *GetObject* function takes a string

---

5. Although it was undocumented until recently, the *CoGetObject* function is now a legitimate member of the COM+ run-time library.

and internally calls *MkParseDisplayName* to obtain a moniker. Then it calls the *IMoniker::BindToObject* method of the moniker to obtain a pointer to the object requested by the Visual Basic programmer in the string passed to *GetObject*. C++ pseudo-code for Visual Basic's *GetObject* function is shown below:[6]

```
IUnknown* GetObject(LPCOLESTR szDisplayName)
{
    IUnknown* pUnknown = 0;
    // Convert a display name to a moniker,
    // and then bind to the object.
    CoGetObject(szDisplayName, 0, IID_IUnknown,
        (void**)&pUnknown);

    // Return a pointer to the object's IUnknown.
    return pUnknown;
}
```

Java has no native analogue to the *CoGetObject* function. Instead, the J/Direct feature of the Microsoft Java Virtual Machine (VM) enables Java programs to call native Win32 API functions; you can use it to directly invoke the standard *CoGetObject* function. To avoid forcing Java developers to provide J/Direct declarations for the functions of the Win32 API, Microsoft provides these in the com.ms.win32 package. The COM+ library of API primitives is defined in the com.ms.win.Ole32 class, of which *CoGetObject* is a method.

The Class Moniker

Although monikers were originally developed to enable OLE to deal with objects that were linked to a compound document in a standard way, monikers are now important for different reasons altogether. To understand how you can use monikers as part of a component-based design, it is instructive to examine some of the newer system monikers implemented as part of COM+. The class moniker is an excellent example of modern implementations of the *IMoniker* interface, so we'll use it as a starting point for understanding how monikers can be integrated with current software projects. The genius of the class moniker is its utter simplicity: it wraps the CLSID of a coclass. Thus, the class moniker enables a client application, using the standard *IMoniker* interface, to reference a coclass identified by a CLSID. Actually, the class moniker always returns a pointer to the class object of the named coclass, so the caller can instantiate the object itself.

---

6. The *GetObject* function has an additional code path executed for file monikers and objects registered in the Running Object Table, which is not discussed here.

In fact, the class moniker is so simple that in most cases its implementation of the *IMoniker::BindToObject* function simply calls *CoGetClassObject*, as shown here:

```
HRESULT CClassMoniker::BindToObject(IBindCtx *pbc,
    IMoniker *pmkToLeft, REFIID riidResult, void **ppvResult)
{
    BIND_OPTS2 bopts;
    bopts.cbStruct = sizeof(bopts);
    pbc->GetBindOptions(&bopts);
    if(pmkToLeft == NULL)
        return CoGetClassObject(m_clsid, bopts.dwClassContext,
            0, riidResult, ppvResult);

    // Code to deal with moniker to the left omitted...

    // Since a composite moniker is a collection of other
    // monikers stored in left-to-right sequence, there
    // might be a moniker to the left of this class moniker.
}
```

Using the class moniker via the *MkParseDisplayName* function, you can name any object based on its CLSID and then activate it by calling the *IMoniker:: BindToObject* method. You can use this method instead of the more standard activation sequence of *CoGetClassObject* followed by *IClassFactory:: CreateInstance*, as executed by *CoCreateInstance*. Binding to a coclass named by a class moniker, however, does not in itself instantiate the object. Only a pointer to the class object is returned by the binding operation, which means that in order to instantiate the object you still have to call *IClassFactory:: CreateInstance* or a method of some custom activation interface.

The class moniker works for the same reasons that the imaginary *Hello* moniker described earlier does; no special support for class monikers is built into the *MkParseDisplayName* function. When a string that has the form *clsid:10000013-0000-0000-0000-000000000001* is passed to the function *MkParseDisplayName*, the *clsid* program identifier is searched for in the registry. Of course, we all know about the HKEY_CLASSES_ROOT\CLSID section of the registry—after all, it's one of the most important areas of the registry in which coclasses are registered. To the *MkParseDisplayName* function, however, HKEY_CLASSES_ROOT\CLSID is just another ProgID in the registry. Once it locates this ProgID, the function opens the HKEY_CLASSES_ROOT\ CLSID\clsid subkey, which contains the actual CLSID of the class moniker.

When you use a tool such as the registry editor (regedit.exe), this clsid subkey is visible as the final entry in the HKEY_CLASSES_ROOT\CLSID section of the registry, after all of the true class identifiers. The CLSID of the class moniker can be searched for in HKEY_CLASSES_ROOT\CLSID\ {0000031A-0000-0000-C000-000000000046}, where the InprocServer32 key has the value ole32.dll, which tells you that the class moniker is implemented as part of ole32.dll. This neat setup is what makes the class moniker work.

Once a moniker has been returned to the client, it can immediately bind to the underlying object using the *IMoniker::BindToObject* method. The following code uses *MkParseDisplayName* to obtain the moniker and then, by binding the moniker to the named object, obtains a pointer to the *Prime* class object. Using the custom activation interface implemented by the class object, you can create the *Prime* object and then call its *GetNextPrime* method. Then all the interface pointers must be released.

```
// We always need a bind context.
IBindCtx* pBindCtx;
CreateBindCtx(0, &pBindCtx);

// Convert the string to a moniker.
ULONG eaten;
IMoniker* pMoniker;
OLECHAR string[] =
    L"clsid:10000013-0000-0000-0000-000000000001";
MkParseDisplayName(pBindCtx, string, &eaten, &pMoniker);

 // Bind the moniker to the named object.
IPrimeFactory* pPrimeFactory;
pMoniker->BindToObject(pBindCtx, NULL, IID_IPrimeFactory,
    (void**)&pPrimeFactory);

// Use the custom class object to create a Prime object.
IPrime* pPrime;
pPrimeFactory->CreatePrime(7, &pPrime);

// Now we have a Prime object.
int next_prime;
pPrime->GetNextPrime(&next_prime);
cout << next_prime << endl; // Displays 11

// Release all.
pPrimeFactory->Release();
pPrime->Release();
pBindCtx->Release();
pMoniker->Release();
```

By this time, you are almost certainly wondering what the advantages are of using *MkParseDisplayName* and *IMoniker::BindToObject* compared to simply calling *CoGetClassObject*. The fact that you can deal with any coclass using the standard *IMoniker* interface is a powerful concept. In this instance, you can combine what you know about the class moniker with Visual Basic's *GetObject* function to make it possible for an application written in Visual Basic to access the *IPrimeFactory* custom activation interface implemented by the class object of the *Prime* coclass.[7] The code below shows how it's done:

```
Dim myPrimeFactory As IPrimeFactory
Dim myPrime As IPrime

' Call MkParseDisplayName and IMoniker::BindToObject.
Set myPrimeFactory = _
    GetObject("clsid:10000013-0000-0000-0000-000000000001")

' Call IPrimeFactory::CreatePrime.
Set myPrime = myPrimeFactory.CreatePrime(7)

' Call IPrime::GetNextPrime.
Print myPrime.GetNextPrime          ' Displays 11
```

The Marvelous Moniker: Improving the Class Moniker

The class moniker is powerful in its own right. It even offers Visual Basic programmers access to custom activation interfaces implemented by class objects. But it is missing one important piece of functionality: the ability to name coclasses on remote machines. As you've seen, the class moniker takes a string in the form *clsid:10000013-0000-0000-0000-000000000001* and converts it to a moniker after performing a lookup in the local registry. The class moniker would be much more powerful if it could be supplied with a string in the form *host:myserver!clsid:10000013-0000-0000-0000-000000000001*. (An exclamation point is typically used to delineate the sections of a composite moniker.) This form would enable you to create a moniker that names a coclass on another computer. Imagine the power of a Visual Basic program that could pass a magic string to the *GetObject* function that would provide access to any coclass on any machine!

Although COM+ does not currently provide this functionality in the system-supplied class moniker, Microsoft did consider that other developers

---

7. Visual Basic can access any custom activation interface as long as it uses Automation-compatible types. Interestingly, this restriction means that *IClassFactory* is not directly accessible to Visual Basic programmers.

might want to extend the class moniker by adding the ability to name classes on other machines. To this end, the class moniker is aware that it might have another moniker to its left. If it is told that such a moniker exists, the class moniker attempts to determine whether the moniker to its left implements the *IClassActivator* interface. The *IClassActivator* interface is a hook that lets you modify the default behavior of the class moniker. The *IClassActivator* interface is shown here in IDL notation:

```
interface IClassActivator : IUnknown
{
    HRESULT GetClassObject(
        [in] REFCLSID rclsid,
        [in] DWORD dwClassContext,
        [in] LCID locale,
        [in] REFIID riid,
        [out, iid_is(riid)] void **ppv);
}
```

Because this functionality is not currently available in the system, let's implement a custom moniker that provides the functionality needed to redirect the class moniker to another machine.[8] We'll build this functionality into a custom moniker called the marvelous moniker. To create a custom moniker, you generally begin with a standard in-process component. The object will be a moniker, so it must implement the *IMoniker* interface, which includes the methods of *IPersistStream* and *IPersist* as well as *IUnknown*. If the moniker is to be accessible via the *MkParseDisplayName* function, it must also have a registered ProgID. Since the desired display name of the moniker is *host:myserver!clsid:????????-????-????-????-????????????*, the registered ProgID must be *host*.[9] The registration procedure for this moniker, shown in the following code, creates the correct registry entries:

```
HRESULT __stdcall DllRegisterServer()
{
    // The ProgID host must be registered
    // in order for the moniker to work.
    return RegisterServer("moniker.dll",
        CLSID_MarvelousMoniker, "Marvelous Moniker",
        "Host", "Host", NULL);
}
```

---

8. Although no implementation of the *IClassActivator* interface currently exists in a system-supplied moniker, Microsoft might provide one in the future.

9. ProgIDs are not case sensitive.

With the registration in place, all calls to the *MkParseDisplayName* function beginning with the string *Host* are directed to the CLSID of the moniker (*CLSID_MarvelousMoniker*). The class object of the moniker is then obtained using *CoGetClassObject*, and *QueryInterface* is called to determine whether the moniker's class object implements the *IParseDisplayName* interface. Thus, the class object of a moniker typically implements only the *IParseDisplayName* activation interface; there is no need to implement *IClassFactory*. The *IParseDisplayName* interface is defined to enable *MkParseDisplayName* to load a moniker and request that it parse its own display name, since obviously *MkParseDisplayName* is a general function and doesn't have any information about the string format of a specific custom moniker. The *IParseDisplayName* interface is shown here in IDL notation:

```
interface IParseDisplayName : IUnknown
{
    HRESULT ParseDisplayName
    (
        [in, unique] IBindCtx *pbc,
        [in] LPOLESTR pszDisplayName,
        [out] ULONG *pchEaten,
        [out] IMoniker **ppmkOut
    );
}
```

The *IParseDisplayName* interface has only one method: *ParseDisplayName*. The first moniker to be instantiated by *MkParseDisplayName* is handed the entire string provided by the caller. Its job is to digest as much of the string as possible and return a moniker that names the object specified in the string. The following code shows the marvelous moniker's implementation of the *IParseDisplayName::ParseDisplayName* method. This method simply parses the display name into its two components: the host name and the CLSID. These values are stored in the moniker's member variables for later use during the binding operation.

```
HRESULT CClassObject::ParseDisplayName(IBindCtx *pbc,
    LPOLESTR pszDisplayName, ULONG *pchEaten,
    IMoniker **ppmkOut)
{
    // Instantiate the moniker.
    CMarvyMoniker* pCMarvyMoniker = new CMarvyMoniker();

    // Parse and check the display name.
    // It must have the following format:
    // host:hostname!clsid:????????-????-????-????-????????????
    if(_wcsicmp(wcstok(pszDisplayName, L":"), L"host") == 0)
```

```
        {
            pCMarvyMoniker->m_CoServerInfo.pwszName =
                wcscpy(pCMarvyMoniker->m_hostname,
                wcstok(NULL, L"!"));
            if(_wcsicmp(wcstok(NULL, L":"), L"clsid") == 0)
            {
                wchar_t clsid_with_braces[39] = L"{";
                wcscat(wcscat(clsid_with_braces,
                    wcstok(NULL, L"!")), L"}");
                CLSIDFromString(clsid_with_braces,
                    &pCMarvyMoniker->m_clsid);
            }
        }

        // Get IMoniker* to return to caller.
        pCMarvyMoniker->QueryInterface(IID_IMoniker, (void**)ppmkOut);
        pCMarvyMoniker->Release();

        // Indicate that we have digested the entire display name.
        *pchEaten = (ULONG)wcslen(pszDisplayName);
        return S_OK;
}
```

Once the *MkParseDisplayName* function returns, the client holds a valid
moniker that names a unique coclass on a particular machine. To use the object
named by the moniker, the client typically binds to the object by calling the
IMoniker::BindToObject method, as shown here:

```
IPrimeFactory* pPrimeFactory;
pMoniker->BindToObject(pBindCtx, NULL, IID_IPrimeFactory,
    (void**)&pPrimeFactory);
```

Now comes the hard part: the moniker must actually instantiate the coclass
on the machine identified in the moniker's display name. Since the marvelous
moniker is really an extension of the system-supplied class moniker, as part of
its implementation of the *IMoniker::BindToObject* method it creates a standard
class moniker for the specified CLSID using the *CreateClassMoniker* function.
Next, the moniker binds to the object by calling the class moniker's implementation of the *IMoniker::BindToObject* method. The steps are shown in the
following code:

```
// An AddRef a day keeps the doctor away...
AddRef();

// Create a normal class moniker for this CLSID.
IMoniker* pClassMoniker;
HRESULT hr = CreateClassMoniker(m_clsid, &pClassMoniker);
```

(continued)

373

```
// Bind to the COM class named by the class moniker;
// tell the class moniker that we are to its left.
hr = pClassMoniker->BindToObject(pbc, (IMoniker*)this,
    riidResult, ppvResult);
pClassMoniker->Release();
```

Typically, the class moniker's implementation of the *IMoniker::BindToObject* method simply calls *CoGetClassObject*. However, if the class moniker is aware that there is a moniker to its left, it takes special action. Notice that in the *BindToObject* call in the preceding code, the second parameter of the *BindToObject* call is a *this* pointer that informs the class moniker that the marvelous moniker is to its left. The following pseudo-code shows the steps executed by the class moniker in its *BindToObject* method; the section dealing with the moniker to its left is shown in boldface:

```
HRESULT CClassMoniker::BindToObject(IBindCtx *pbc,
    IMoniker *pmkToLeft, REFIID riidResult, void **ppvResult)
{
    BIND_OPTS2 bopts;
    bopts.cbStruct = sizeof(bopts);
    pbc->GetBindOptions(&bopts);
    if(pmkToLeft == NULL)
        return CoGetClassObject(m_clsid, bopts.dwClassContext,
            0, riidResult, ppvResult);

    // Code to deal with moniker to the left...
    // Make a recursive call to the BindToObject method
    // of the moniker on the left to obtain a
    // pointer to the IClassActivator interface.
    IClassActivator* pActivate;
    pmkToLeft->BindToObject(pbc, IID_IClassActivator,
        (void**)&pActivate);

    // Call IClassActivator::GetClassObject.
    HRESULT hr = pActivate->GetClassObject(m_clsid,
        bopts.dwClassContext, bopts.locale, riidResult,
        ppvResult);
    pActivate->Release();
    return hr;
}
```

Note that if the class moniker discovers another moniker to its left, it makes a recursive call to that moniker's *BindToObject* method. This recursive call has an effect similar to that of the *QueryInterface* method because the class moniker is attempting to obtain a pointer to our moniker's implementation of the *IClassActivator* interface. To trap this recursive call from the class moniker and to avoid an endless loop of recursion, the marvelous moniker's implementation of the *BindToObject* method first checks whether someone is attempting to obtain a pointer to the *IClassActivator* interface. If so, it simply casts the *this* reference to an *IClassActivator* interface pointer and returns *S_OK*. The marvelous moniker's implementation of the *IMoniker::BindToObject* method is shown below; the section relevant to the *IClassActivator* interface is in boldface:

```
HRESULT CMarvyMoniker::BindToObject(IBindCtx *pbc, IMoniker
    *pmkToLeft, REFIID riidResult, void **ppvResult)
{
    // This catches the recursive call by the class moniker.
    if(riidResult == IID_IClassActivator)
    {
        *ppvResult = (IClassActivator*)this;
        return S_OK;
    }

    // An AddRef a day keeps the doctor away...
    AddRef();

    // Create a normal class moniker for this CLSID.
    IMoniker* pClassMoniker;
    HRESULT hr = CreateClassMoniker(m_clsid, &pClassMoniker);
    if(FAILED(hr))
        return hr;

    // Bind to the COM class named by the class moniker;
    // tell the moniker that the new moniker is to its left.
    hr = pClassMoniker->BindToObject(pbc, (IMoniker*)this,
        riidResult, ppvResult);
    pClassMoniker->Release();
    return hr;
}
```

Because the marvelous moniker itself implements the *IClassActivator* interface in addition to the *IMoniker* interface, a simple cast in the *BindToObject* method is sufficient. As you saw in the pseudo-code for the class moniker's implementation of the *IMoniker::BindToObject* method, the class moniker calls the sole method of the *IClassActivator* interface: *GetClassObject*. The *GetClassObject* method retrieves the class object of the coclass named by the moniker. This hook method lets you override the default local machine behavior of the class moniker and redirect it to bind with a class object on a specific host. The marvelous moniker's implementation of the *IClassActivator::GetClassObject* method simply calls *CoGetClassObject*. However, it uses the COSERVERINFO structure to specify the host name from which the class object is to be retrieved.[10] The implementation of the *GetClassObject* method is shown here:

```
HRESULT CMarvyMoniker::GetClassObject(REFCLSID pClassID,
    DWORD dwClsContext, LCID locale, REFIID riid, void** ppv)
{
    // Call CoGetClassObject using the COSERVERINFO structure
    // that contains the host name from the moniker's
    // display name.
    return CoGetClassObject(pClassID, CLSCTX_SERVER,
        &m_CoServerInfo, riid, ppv);
}
```

The *CoGetClassObject* function in the preceding code obtains and returns the class object from the specified host. The pointer to the remote class object is returned to the class moniker, back to the marvelous moniker, and finally to the client. The client can then use the class object without regard to the fact that the object was instantiated on a remote machine. Once installed and registered, the marvelous moniker can be used from any language. From C++, you simply call *MkParseDisplayName* or the *CoGetObject* helper function; in Visual Basic, you call the *GetObject* function. Here is a snippet of Visual Basic code that uses the marvelous moniker to access the *Prime* coclass on any machine:

```
Dim myPrimeFactory As IPrimeFactory
Dim myPrime As IPrime

' Call MkParseDisplayName.
Set myPrimeFactory = GetObject( _
    "host:HostNameHere!clsid:10000013-0000-0000-0000-000000000001")

' Call IPrimeFactory::CreatePrime.
Set myPrime = myPrimeFactory.CreatePrime(7)

Dim Count As Integer
For Count = 0 To 10
    ' Call IPrime::GetNextPrime.
    Print myPrime.GetNextPrime
Next
```

The marvelous moniker also exports a moniker creation function named *CreateMarvelousMoniker*. This function enables a marvelous moniker to be

---

10. The class moniker could simply have used the COSERVERINFO information defined in the BIND_OPTS2 structure to achieve the same result. However, the class moniker does not currently use this information when binding to a class object.

created directly rather than from a display name. The declaration for the *CreateMarvelousMoniker* function is shown here:

```
HRESULT CreateMarvelousMoniker(REFCLSID clsid,
    COSERVERINFO* pCoServerInfo, IMoniker** ppMoniker)
```

The New Moniker

The class moniker is powerful because it affords the programmer a way of dealing with coclasses using monikers. As we saw, one limitation of the class moniker is that it does not obey the parameters specified by the BIND_OPTS(2) structures. So to instantiate a coclass on a remote machine using the class moniker, we had to create a custom moniker (the marvelous moniker) that implemented the *IClassActivator* interface and called *CoGetClassObject* itself. Another peculiarity of the class moniker is that it always binds to the class object of the specified coclass, leaving the client to instantiate the object using *IClassFactory::CreateInstance* or whatever custom activation interface that class object happens to implement. Since the *CreateInstance* method cannot be called directly from Visual Basic, this means that Visual Basic developers cannot use the class moniker to instantiate a coclass whose class object implements the *IClassFactory* interface.

The new moniker was introduced to address many these issues. Rather than binding to the class object of the specified coclass, the new moniker operates more like the *CoCreateInstance(Ex)* function. After obtaining the class object, the new moniker automatically calls *IClassFactory::CreateInstance* to instantiate the desired coclass. This means that like the *CoCreateInstance(Ex)* function, the new moniker requires that the class object implement the *IClassFactory* interface; it cannot be used with custom activation interfaces such as *IPrimeFactory*. Unlike the class moniker, however, the new moniker obeys the parameters specified in the BIND_OPTS(2) structures. Therefore, you can use the new moniker to instantiate an object on a remote machine, as shown in the code fragment below:

```
COSERVERINFO csi = { 0, 0, 0, 0 };
csi.pwszName = L"RemoteMachineName";

BIND_OPTS2 bopts;
bopts.dwClassContext = CLSCTX_LOCAL_SERVER;
bopts.cbStruct = sizeof(BIND_OPTS2);
bopts.pServerInfo = &csi;

ISum* pSum = 0;
hr = CoGetObject(L"new:10000002-0000-0000-0000-000000000001",
    &bopts, IID_ISum, (void**)&pSum);
```

(continued)

```
// Now we can use the object--the new moniker has already
// instantiated it.
int sum = 0;
hr = pSum->Sum(4, 9, &sum);
cout << "Client: Calling Sum() return value is " << sum << endl;

pSum->Release();
```

As a convenience, the new moniker also accepts ProgIDs in place of CLSIDs. For example, instead of specifying the CLSID of the *InsideCOM* coclass, you can simply use the ProgID *Component.InsideCOM*, as shown below:

```
hr = CoGetObject(L"new:Component.InsideCOM", &bopts, IID_ISum,
    (void**)&pSum);
```

Because the new moniker automatically instantiates the coclass using the *IClassFactory::CreateInstance* method, you can easily use this moniker from Visual Basic with any standard class object that implements the *IClassFactory* interface, as shown below. Unfortunately, a Visual Basic client does not have the opportunity to set the BIND_OPTS(2) structure, so the new moniker can be used only for default activation based on registry information.

```
Private Sub Command1_Click()
    Dim ref As Component.InsideCOM
    Set ref = GetObject("new:Component.InsideCOM")

    ' Or use the CLSID.
    ' Set ref = _
    '     GetObject("new:10000002-0000-0000-0000-000000000001")

    Print ref.Sum(5, 3)
End Sub
```

The Java Moniker

The Microsoft Java VM offers its own special moniker called the Java moniker. Java monikers are identified by a string name in the form *java:myclass.class*, where *java* is a registered ProgID that refers to the CLSID of Microsoft's Java VM. The Java moniker enables an application written in any language to access Java code via *MkParseDisplayName*. In Visual Basic, you can access Java code using the syntax *GetObject("java:myclass.class")*. The following Visual Basic code fragment uses the *Date* class implemented as part of the java.util package:

```
Private Sub Command1_Click()
    Dim x As Object
    Set x = GetObject("java:java.util.Date")
    MsgBox x.toString() ' Displays current date and time
End Sub
```

Using the same syntax, you can access methods of a custom-built Java class. The following code shows a Java class:

```
//
//
// SumClass
//
//
public class SumClass
{
    public int Sum(int x, int y)
    {
        return x + y;
    }
}
```

In Chapter 3, we exposed the *SumClass* class as a coclass by generating coclass wrappers for the Java class and using Visual J++ to build a type library. To avoid this drudgery, we could have simply used the Java moniker to access *SumClass*, as shown here:

```
Private Sub Command1_Click()
    Dim x As Object
    Set x = GetObject("java:SumClass")
    MsgBox x.Sum(5, 3)
End Sub
```

The Running Object Table

The Running Object Table (ROT) is a machine-wide table in which objects can register themselves. The ROT enables a moniker to check whether an object is already running when the client application calls the *IMoniker::BindToObject* method to bind to the object. Thus, the ROT acts mainly as a binding optimization to help you avoid unnecessarily instantiating a new object when binding. You access the ROT through the *IRunningObjectTable* interface. The *GetRunningObjectTable* function provides access to the system implementation of this interface. The *IRunningObjectTable* interface is defined here in IDL notation:

```
interface IRunningObjectTable : IUnknown
{
    // Add an object to the ROT.
    HRESULT Register(
        [in] DWORD grfFlags,
        [in, unique] IUnknown *punkObject,
```

(continued)

```
    [in, unique] IMoniker *pmkObjectName,
    [out] DWORD *pdwRegister);

// Remove an object from the ROT.
HRESULT Revoke(
    [in] DWORD dwRegister);

// Check whether the object named by a moniker is
// in the ROT.
HRESULT IsRunning(
    [in, unique] IMoniker *pmkObjectName);
// Get a pointer to the object named by a moniker from
// the ROT.
HRESULT GetObject(
    [in, unique] IMoniker *pmkObjectName,
    [out] IUnknown **ppunkObject);

// Specify the time an object in the ROT was last modified.
HRESULT NoteChangeTime(
    [in] DWORD dwRegister,
    [in] FILETIME *pfiletime);

// Get the time an object in the ROT was last modified.
HRESULT GetTimeOfLastChange(
    [in, unique] IMoniker *pmkObjectName,
    [out] FILETIME *pfiletime);

// Get an enumerator for all objects in the ROT.
HRESULT EnumRunning(
    [out] IEnumMoniker **ppenumMoniker);
}
```

You can get a feel for the information stored in the ROT by examining its contents. You can do this using the *IRunningObjectTable::EnumRunning* method, which simply enumerates all the objects currently registered in the ROT. The *IEnumMoniker* interface returned by the *EnumRunning* method enumerates the registered objects by their monikers. To turn this data into easily browsable information, you can call the *IMoniker::GetDisplayName* method on each moniker in the ROT. The following code snippet is from the Running Object Table.cpp sample on the companion CD:

```
// Open the ROT.
IRunningObjectTable* pRunningObjectTable;
GetRunningObjectTable(NULL, &pRunningObjectTable);
```

```
// Get an enumerator.
IEnumMoniker* pEnumMoniker;
pRunningObjectTable->EnumRunning(&pEnumMoniker);

IMoniker* pMoniker;
IBindCtx* pBindCtx;
OLECHAR* moniker_name;

// Loop until there are no more monikers.
while(pEnumMoniker->Next(1, &pMoniker, NULL) == S_OK)
{
    // Create a silly bind context.
    CreateBindCtx(0, &pBindCtx);

    // Get the display name, print it, and free the buffer.
    pMoniker->GetDisplayName(pBindCtx, NULL, &moniker_name);
    wprintf(L"DisplayName is %s\n", moniker_name);
    CoTaskMemFree(moniker_name);

    // Code omitted here that determines the moniker type...

    // Release the moniker and the silly bind context.
    pMoniker->Release();
    pBindCtx->Release();
}

// Free the enumerator and close the ROT.
pEnumMoniker->Release();
pRunningObjectTable->Release();
```

When you register an object in the ROT, the *IRunningObjectTable::Register* method requires a flag specifying the type of registration that should occur. This value should be *0*, indicating a weak registration, or *ROTFLAGS_REGISTRATIONKEEPSALIVE*, which holds the object in memory even if no other references to the object exist. When an object is registered, the ROT calls *IUnknown::AddRef* on the object. For a weak registration, the ROT releases the object when the last reference to the object is released. For a strong registration (*ROTFLAGS_REGISTRATIONKEEPSALIVE*), the ROT prevents the object from being destroyed until the object's registration is explicitly revoked via the *IRunningObjectTable::Revoke* method. You can also use the *ROTFLAGS_ALLOWANYCLIENT* flag when an object registered in the ROT needs to be accessed by clients running from different security contexts. Without this flag, the moniker is registered with a security descriptor that allows only clients from the same security context to access it.

REMOTING
ARCHITECTURE

CHAPTER TWELVE

Surrogates

Location transparency—the idea that it doesn't matter whether code runs locally or remotely, in-process or out-of-process—has been part of COM from the very beginning. But the full power of location transparency has been realized only in COM+. Due to the foresight of the COM designers, the transition from a single machine to a distributed model has been smooth.

In previous chapters, we built and tested in-process components and examined a wide range of COM+ services, including connection points, monikers, and persistence. In this chapter, we'll move beyond the in-process model and begin to examine the remoting architecture.

Remoting is the mechanism used to communicate with two types of components, local and remote. A local component is an executable file that runs on the same machine as its client but in a separate address space. A remote component executes on a machine separate from that of its client and is a more elusive entity. As you know, in-process components are dynamic-link libraries (DLLs) and local components are executable files (EXEs). Microsoft Windows does not provide a third type of code module, so how do you set about remoting a DLL or an EXE? Well, executable components don't need much help in this regard because they can simply be launched on a remote computer. As you'll see, however, an executable file is not always the best housing for COM+ objects.

Most COM+ objects feel much more at home with an in-process component. Why? Since a DLL runs in the process address space of its caller, DLLs usually run faster than equivalent executable components. Also, the COM+ runtime environment works only with in-process components. But does the much-vaunted location transparency apply to in-process components as well as executable components? In other words, can you launch and call a DLL remotely? Contrary to what logic might lead you to believe, in-process components can be remoted. Permit us to explain.

DLL Surrogates

DLLs are like children; they need constant attention. A DLL can never run without a parent process nearby to protect it. However, DLL components can be remoted if a surrogate is available to provide round-the-clock supervision and security. COM+ provides a default DLL surrogate (dllhost.exe[1]) that loves and protects your in-process components when they are away from home. The file dllhost.exe is an executable component that can be remoted and then instructed to load any in-process component, providing the component with a surrogate parent process and security context. Since an in-process component can be remoted using a DLL surrogate, this is where we'll begin our discussion of the COM+ remote infrastructure.

Running In-Process Components Locally

To activate an in-process component in the context of a DLL surrogate, you must configure two settings in the registry. You can add these settings in the component's self-registration code, but for this discussion we'll add the entries by using the following surrogate.reg file:

```
REGEDIT4

[HKEY_CLASSES_ROOT\CLSID\{10000002-0000-0000-0000-000000000001}]
"AppID"="{10000002-0000-0000-0000-000000000001}"

[HKEY_CLASSES_ROOT\AppID\{10000002-0000-0000-0000-000000000001}]
@="Inside COM+ Sample"
"DllSurrogate"=""
```

The *AppID* value in the class identifier (CLSID) section links clients with the component's entry in the application identifier (AppID) section of the registry. In the AppID section, we define the *DllSurrogate* value, which requests that the in-process component be run inside a surrogate and specifies the name of that surrogate. Since no surrogate name is provided in this case, the system-supplied surrogate, dllhost.exe, is used by default.

The AppID Registry Key

An AppID is a 128-bit globally unique identifier (GUID) that groups the configuration and security options for all the coclasses exposed by a COM+ application in one centralized location in the registry: HKEY_CLASSES_ROOT\AppID. To associate a coclass with an AppID, you place the named-value of *AppID*, which contains the string corresponding to the AppID listed under

---

1. COM+ also provides an alternative version of the standard surrogate, dllhst3g.exe, that supports a 3-GB user-mode address space.

the AppID subkey, in its CLSID entry in the registry. This mapping sequence is shown in Figure 12-1.

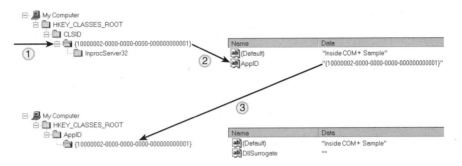

Figure 12-1.
The registry mapping of a CLSID to an AppID.

To simplify management of common security and configuration settings, COM+ objects hosted by the same component are grouped together under one AppID. Executables can also be registered under the AppID key in a subkey indicating the module name (for example, component.exe). These subkeys contain an AppID value that indicates the AppID associated with the executable and are used to obtain the default access permissions. The following table shows the valid named-values that can be present in an AppID subkey. Note that you can set most of these values using the Distributed COM Configuration utility (discussed later in this chapter).

AppID Named-Values	Description
AccessPermission	Sets the access control list (ACL) that determines default access permissions
ActivateAtStorage	Configures the client to activate on the same system as persistent storage
AuthenticationLevel	Sets the default authentication level
DllSurrogate	Names the surrogate process used to load DLLs remotely
LaunchPermission	Sets the ACL that determines who can launch the application
LocalService	Configures the component to run as a Microsoft Windows NT Service
RemoteServerName	Names a remote server
RunAs	Sets an application to run only as a given user
ServiceParameters	Sets parameters to be passed to *LocalService* on invocation

Instantiating an In-Process Object in a Surrogate

We're almost there, but we still need to change the call to create the object. In the client, you first adjust the *CoCreateInstance* call to specify a local component. That's right—a local component. Even though our component is still implemented as an in-process component, we call *CoCreateInstance* to instantiate a local component as shown in the following code. With the addition of the AppID and *DllSurrogate* information, this code is now legal.

```
CoCreateInstance(CLSID_InsideCOM, NULL, CLSCTX_LOCAL_SERVER,
    IID_IUnknown, (void**)&pUnknown);
```

Now it's time to rebuild and run the client. Notice that only messages displayed by the client are visible. Messages from the component are nowhere to be seen because the component is running in the address space of the dllhost surrogate. The dllhost surrogate doesn't display a user interface, so no output messages from the component appear. You can verify that the surrogate is running by displaying the task list and observing that the dllhost.exe process is running.

> **NOTE:** If the HKEY_CLASSES_ROOT\CLSID\{10000002-0000-0000-0000-000000000001}\LocalServer32 registry key is present, you must delete it to run the in-process version of the *InsideCOM* object within the DLL surrogate.

You might wonder why you'd ever want to run an in-process component in a DLL surrogate. Doing so offers these benefits:

- Provides fault isolation and allows you to service multiple clients simultaneously

- Enables an in-process component to service remote clients in a distributed environment

- Permits clients to protect themselves from untrusted components while still allowing access to the services provided by the in-process component

- Provides the in-process component with the surrogate's security context

Running Components Remotely

In most cases, to enable remote execution, you run an in-process component under the guidance of a surrogate. To configure existing COM+ components to run remotely, you need not change one iota of code. Because you can specify all the necessary information in the registry, even legacy components written prior to the advent of surrogates can still use these features.

If a client calls *CoCreateInstance* using the flag *CLSCTX_LOCAL_SERVER*, the client is not necessarily restricted to local servers—it might in fact end up using a remote server. Here's how the process works: when the Service Control Manager (SCM) tries to activate an executable component, it first checks for the *AppID* named-value in HKEY_CLASSES_ROOT\CLSID\{*YourCLSID*} key of the registry. If it finds the *AppID* named-value, it looks for the same GUID in the HKEY_CLASSES_ROOT\AppID section of the registry, where it might find some of the named-values that specify where and how the component should be activated.

For example, to launch a component on another machine, the *RemoteServerName* value should indicate the name of the desired computer. When you request an object on a remote machine, the SCM on the local machine contacts the SCM on the remote machine designated by the *RemoteServerName* value to request that the remote SCM locate and load the component on its machine. In this way, remote capabilities can be configured for legacy clients and components.

To configure a surrogate process to run remotely, you must make sure that all the standard registry entries configured via the component's self-registration routine are present on the client machine, along with the following entries:

```
REGEDIT4

[HKEY_CLASSES_ROOT\CLSID\{10000002-0000-0000-0000-000000000001}]
"AppID"="{10000002-0000-0000-0000-000000000001}"

[HKEY_CLASSES_ROOT\AppID\{10000002-0000-0000-0000-000000000001}]
@="Inside COM+ Sample"
"RemoteServerName"="Remote_Computer_Name"
```

These entries specify that when a client looks for the component, the component should actually be run on another machine specified by the *RemoteServerName* named-value. You need not modify that client's call to *CoCreateInstance* to specify *CLSCTX_REMOTE_SERVER* instead of *CLSCTX_LOCAL_SERVER*. The *RemoteServerName* entry in the registry provides all the information the SCM needs. The remote computer on which the component actually runs must have the registry configured as before, with the *DllSurrogate* named-value but not the *RemoteServerName* named-value. Note that if you have both the *DllSurrogate* and *RemoteServerName* entries in the registry, the client's call to *CoCreateInstance* must specify *CLSCTX_REMOTE_SERVER* in order to connect with the component remotely. Otherwise, the client will launch the DLL surrogate locally.

The Distributed COM Configuration Utility

The Distributed COM Configuration utility (dcomcnfg.exe) was designed solely to help configure the registry so that legacy clients and components can participate in a distributed environment.[2] This utility has four pages: Applications, Default Properties, Default Security, and Default Protocols. The Applications tab shows a list of executable components and allows the user to configure them for remote execution by selecting a component and clicking the Properties button, as shown in Figure 12-2. The other three tabs are used to control default settings for components.

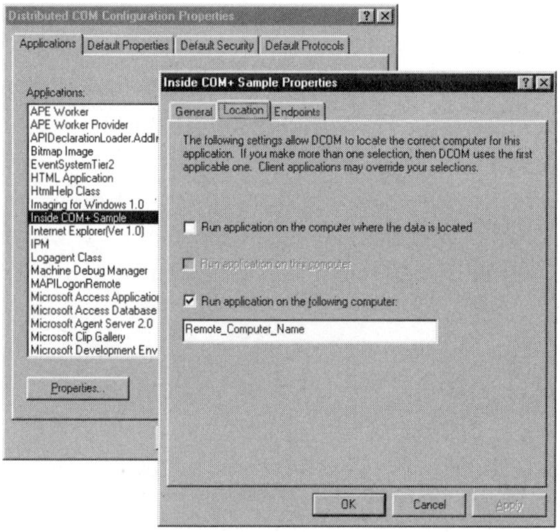

Figure 12-2.
Setting the Inside COM+ Sample properties using dcomcnfg.exe.

To entirely disable DCOM on the current machine, you deselect the Enable Distributed COM On This Computer option on the Default Properties tab or set the *EnableDCOM* value in the HKEY_LOCAL_MACHINE\SOFTWARE \Microsoft\OLE key of the registry to *N*.

NOTE: Every time the Distributed COM Configuration utility runs, it generates AppIDs in the registry for any coclasses that have a CLSID\LocalServer32 key but not an AppID key.

---

2. Modern components, which were designed for use in a distributed environment, normally offer their own configuration options and thus have no use for the Distributed COM Configuration utility.

Custom Surrogates

The default DLL surrogate provided by the system is quite flexible; it even allows multiple in-process components to be loaded into a single surrogate process. Generally speaking, the default surrogate is more than adequate for well-behaved in-process components. However, misbehaving components might not run properly in the default surrogate. Any code executed by the component under the assumption that it is running in the process space of its client will fail. Such assumptions include access to global variables and callback functions implemented using function pointers. Running this type of component in a surrogate requires a special surrogate that is trained to deal with the unique needs of that component. In other words, you must write a custom surrogate process. Here are some reasons you might decide to do so:

- A custom surrogate can provide special optimizations for a particular component.

- You can tailor a custom surrogate to deal with in-process components that depend on being in the same process as their client.

- A custom surrogate can more flexibly manage the security context for a component.

If the features provided by the default DLL surrogate don't meet your needs, you can build your own custom surrogate by implementing the *ISurrogate* interface in a local component. The definition of the *ISurrogate* interface is shown below in Interface Definition Language (IDL) notation:

```
interface ISurrogate : IUnknown
{
    // Load the specified in-process component.
    HRESULT LoadDllServer([in] REFCLSID clsid);

    // Exiting...
    HRESULT FreeSurrogate();
}
```

A Custom DLL Surrogate: *DllNanny*

To further illustrate the concept of surrogates, let's look at some code fragments from a simple DLL surrogate named *DllNanny*. Surrogate processes are launched automatically by the SCM when a client instantiates an in-process object registered for execution within the surrogate. The SCM provides the surrogate with the CLSID of the in-process object as a command-line argument. On start-up, a surrogate process registers its threading model by calling *CoInitializeEx*. Next, it calls *CoRegisterSurrogate* to provide the system with a pointer to its *ISurrogate* interface.

In the following code fragment from dllnanny.cpp, the surrogate follows this start-up procedure with a call to the *ISurrogate::LoadDllServer* method to indicate the presence of a client activation request. The first (and only) command-line argument provided to the surrogate process on start-up specifies the CLSID for the desired in-process object. This CLSID is converted from a string to a binary CLSID using the *CLSIDFromString* function, and then it is passed as a parameter to the *LoadDllServer* method.

```
void main(int argc, char** argv)
{
    // Initialize COM and create the multithreaded
    // apartment (MTA).
    CoInitializeEx(NULL, COINIT_MULTITHREADED);

    // Instantiate and register the surrogate.
    CSurrogate surrogate;
    CoRegisterSurrogate(&surrogate);

    // Convert the ASCII string-form CLSID in
    // argv[1] to Unicode.
    OLECHAR wszCLSID[39];
    mbstowcs(wszCLSID, argv[1], 39);

    // Convert the Unicode CLSID to a binary CLSID.
    CLSID clsid;
    CLSIDFromString(wszCLSID, &clsid);

    surrogate.LoadDllServer(clsid);

    // Code omitted...
```

Upon receiving the client request via the *ISurrogate::LoadDllServer* method, the surrogate instantiates and registers a class object. This class object is not the actual class object implemented by the in-process component. It is a generic class object implemented by the surrogate process that must support the *IUnknown* and *IClassFactory* interfaces.

Next, the implementation of the *ISurrogate::LoadDllServer* method should call the *CoRegisterClassObject* function to register the surrogate class object for the specified CLSID. All surrogate class objects should be registered using the *REGCLS_SURROGATE* flag when the *CoRegisterClassObject* function is called; surrogate processes should not use *REGCLS_SINGLEUSE* and *REGCLS_MULTIPLEUSE*. Here is *DllNanny*'s implementation of the *ISurrogate:: LoadDllServer* method:

```
HRESULT CSurrogate::LoadDllServer(REFCLSID rclsid)
{
    // Instantiate the surrogate class factory object.
    m_pcf = new CGenericFactory(rclsid);

    // Register the surrogate class factory object;
    // note the use of the REGCLS_SURROGATE flag.
    return CoRegisterClassObject(rclsid, (IClassFactory*)m_pcf,
        CLSCTX_LOCAL_SERVER, REGCLS_SURROGATE,
        &m_pcf->m_dwRegister);
}
```

When the client calls *CoCreateInstance* to instantiate the desired in-process object as a local server, the surrogate's *IClassFactory::CreateInstance* method is called. The surrogate class factory must use the real class factory to create an instance of the object. Calling *CoCreateInstance* on the in-process object itself does the trick. Thus, *DllNanny*'s implementation of the *IClassFactory:: CreateInstance* method looks like this:

```
HRESULT CGenericFactory::CreateInstance(IUnknown* pUnknownOuter,
    REFIID riid, void** ppv)
{
    return CoCreateInstance(m_clsid, pUnknownOuter,
        CLSCTX_INPROC_SERVER, riid, ppv);
}
```

During the lifetime of the surrogate process, it is important that *CoFreeUnusedLibraries* be called periodically. This function, normally called repeatedly by a low-priority thread, unloads any DLLs that are no longer in use. Later, after all clients have exited and all the in-process components running in the surrogate process have terminated, the system calls the *ISurrogate:: FreeSurrogate* method. At that point, the surrogate should revoke all registered class factories using the *CoRevokeClassObject* function and then cause the surrogate process to exit, as shown here:

```
HRESULT CSurrogate::FreeSurrogate()
{
    // Revoke the surrogate class factory.
    HRESULT hr = CoRevokeClassObject(m_pcf->m_dwRegister);

    // Set an event that causes the surrogate to exit.
    SetEvent(g_hEvent);
    return hr;
}
```

The *SetEvent* function signals a global event object created in the surrogate's *main* function, where the *WaitForSingleObject* function has been called, as shown in the following code fragment. This call causes the surrogate to wait until it is time to exit. Once the event is signaled, *WaitForSingleObject* returns and the surrogate terminates cleanly.

```
// The main function...

// Create the event.
g_hEvent = CreateEvent(NULL, FALSE, FALSE, NULL);

// Wait for the event to be signaled
// by ISurrogate::FreeSurrogate.
WaitForSingleObject(g_hEvent, INFINITE);
CloseHandle(g_hEvent);

CoUninitialize();
}
```

An Introduction to Marshaling

When the *InsideCOM* coclass is run in the surrogate as described previously, the object implements the *ISum* interface, which has the methods *QueryInterface*, *AddRef*, *Release*, and *Sum*. Did you pause to marvel at how the parameters to and from these methods happen to pass successfully between the client and the component? In earlier chapters, we built in-process components, which ran in the address space of the client, obviating the issue of parameter passing. However, in the surrogate process example, our in-process component ran first in the address space of the surrogate process and then on another computer altogether. How did the parameter passing work, then? This whole issue of how parameters are passed between processes, called *marshaling*, is an area of great importance.

In-process components don't have to worry about marshaling because all the action takes place in a single address space. The function parameters are simply pushed onto the stack for a function call and then popped off the stack when the function executes. Executable components, whether they're running on the same machine as the client or on a remote computer, must concern themselves with marshaling. While marshaling is a concern for executable components, cross-computer marshaling has added network bandwidth issues, making marshaling an even more important concern. Figure 12-3 illustrates how marshaling is used to send data to and from a component.

Process Boundary

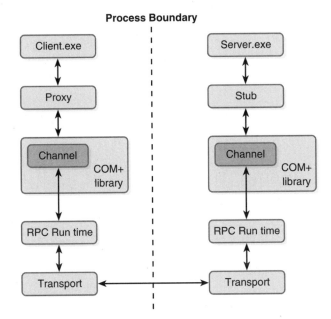

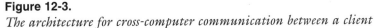

Figure 12-3.
The architecture for cross-computer communication between a client and a component.

To put it more precisely, marshaling is the process of packaging method calls and their parameters into a transmittable packet and then sending that packet to a component. This process can be quite simple or complex. For example, marshaling an integer parameter involves simply copying its value into a transmission buffer and sending it off. Marshaling an array of characters, however, is more complicated. How does the marshaler know the size of the array? Even if the size of the entire array can be determined, perhaps only the first several bytes are in use; transmitting the entire array would be a waste of bandwidth. Finally, what if you have a pointer to an element in a doubly linked list? How can the marshaler possibly know how to package this complex data structure for transmission?

In the case of most standard interfaces, marshaling is handled by objects instantiated from the system ole32.dll component. The main issue for most developers is what to do about custom interfaces. Marshaling custom interfaces is too often explained away as black magic that requires various incantations to work smoothly. Here we'll expose it for what it really is.

COM+ offers three basic marshaling options, which we'll discuss in detail in the sections that follow:

- Standard marshaling
- Type library marshaling
- Custom marshaling

Standard Marshaling

Don't confuse the term *standard marshaling* with standard interfaces. Remember that standard interfaces are interfaces defined by Microsoft as part of COM+. For most of these interfaces, Microsoft has already built marshaling code. Standard marshaling is used for custom interfaces such as *ISum*. The easiest way to take advantage of standard marshaling is to use the Microsoft IDL (MIDL) compiler. You simply create an IDL file describing your custom interfaces and then compile the IDL file using the MIDL compiler to generate the standard marshaling code. The following table lists the files created by the MIDL compiler when it is used to compile interface definitions.

Filename	Description
idlname.h	Header file for the interface definitions
*idlname*_i.c	Definitions of the IID and CLSID constants
*idlname*_p.c	Marshaling code
idlname.tlb	Type library (only if the IDL contains a *library* statement)
dlldata.c	DLL entry points for the marshaling code

By compiling and linking these files, you can produce a proxy/stub DLL that correctly marshals your interfaces. A proxy/stub DLL is a library that can be loaded by both the client and the component to properly marshal data back and forth. In order for the system to automatically load this DLL when needed, the proxy/stub DLL must be registered as the *ISum* interface marshaler. Luckily, the DLL built from the code generated by the MIDL compiler exports the *DllRegisterServer* function, which knows how to correctly register the proxy/stub DLL. You simply compile the proxy/stub DLL with the *REGISTER_PROXY_DLL* symbol defined, and the necessary code is included in the component. When the *DllRegisterServer* function is called, it creates all the necessary registry entries. Recall that this self-registration feature allows the proxy/stub component to be registered using the RegSvr32 utility. In sum, the advantage of standard marshaling is that you have to write only the IDL—the rest is automatic.

Building a Proxy/Stub DLL for Standard Marshaling

To build a proxy/stub DLL when you use standard marshaling, follow these steps:

1. Compile your IDL file (component.idl) using MIDL.

2. Open Visual C++ and choose the File/New command.

3. Select the Projects tab, and then select Win32 Dynamic-Link Library.

4. In the Project Name text box, type *ProxyStub*, and then click OK.

5. When asked by the wizard, create an empty DLL project and click Finish. Then click OK.

6. Choose the Project/Add To Project/Files command.

7. Select the dlldata.c, component_i.c, and component_p.c files generated by MIDL, and then click OK.

8. Choose the File/New command, select the Files tab, and then select Text File.

9. In the File Name text box, type *ProxyStub.def*, and then click OK.

10. Enter the following module definition file:

```
; ProxyStub.def
LIBRARY              ProxyStub.dll
DESCRIPTION          'Proxy/Stub DLL'
EXPORTS
    DllGetClassObject    @1 PRIVATE
    DllCanUnloadNow      @2 PRIVATE
    DllRegisterServer    @3 PRIVATE
    DllUnregisterServer  @4 PRIVATE
```

11. Choose the File/Save command, and then choose Project/Settings.

12. In the Settings For list box, select All Configurations.

13. Select the C/C++ tab, and in the Category list box, select General.

14. In the Preprocessor Definitions box, add *REGISTER_PROXY_DLL* and *_WIN32_DCOM*, separated by commas.

15. Select the Link tab, and in the Category list box, select General.

16. In the Object/Library Modules box, add *rpcndr.lib*, *rpcns4.lib*, and *rpcrt4.lib*, separated by spaces, and then click OK.

17. Choose the Build/Build ProxyStub.dll command.

18. Assuming that all has gone well, choose the Tools/Register Control command.

Self-registering proxy/stub DLLs should generally include a version information resource containing the *OLESelfRegister* value. (See Chapter 2 for details.)

Type Library Marshaling

Type library marshaling uses the Automation (*IDispatch*) marshaler. Normally, components implement the *IDispatch* interface to work with scripting languages such as VBScript or JScript since these languages require that a component support the *IDispatch* interface. A component implementing the *IDispatch* interface need not worry about marshaling since this is a standard interface and the system has a built-in marshaler for *IDispatch* in oleaut32.dll, which is included with every 32-bit Windows system.

While the *IDispatch* interface has its uses, it also has its problems (as described in Chapter 5). Thus, many components opt for custom interfaces rather than *IDispatch*. You can, however, use the marshaling infrastructure developed for the *IDispatch* interface without implementing this interface in your component. This option is intriguing, and you can use it only if your custom interfaces restrict themselves to Automation-compatible data types.[3] In order for the Automation marshaler to obtain the information it needs to correctly marshal your custom interfaces, you must also register a type library for the component. You must declare these interfaces as Automation-compatible in the IDL file used to build the type library. You do this by including the *oleautomation* flag, as shown here:

```
[ object, uuid(10000001-0000-0000-0000-000000000001),
  oleautomation ]
interface ISum : IUnknown
{
    HRESULT Sum(int x, int y, [out, retval] int* retval);
}
```

Setting the *oleautomation* flag does not mean that you're using the *IDispatch* interface—only that your interface is compatible with *IDispatch*. Because the Automation marshaler is generic, it is not as efficient as the marshaling code generated by MIDL. Moreover, it imposes a slight performance penalty due to the time consumed by the type library lookup. However, because the Automation marshaler is flexible and easy to use, it is often an excellent choice. As an added benefit, you don't need to build a proxy/stub DLL and register it on each machine—the Automation marshaler is automatically available in Windows. To enable type library marshaling for your components, you simply register

---

3. These data types are listed in the section titled "Automation Types" in Chapter 5.

each custom interface by setting the *ProxyStubClsid32* value to *{00020424-0000-0000-C000-000000000046}*, as shown here:

```
REGEDIT4

[HKEY_CLASSES_ROOT\Interface\
{10000001-0000-0000-0000-000000000001}\ProxyStubClsid32]
@="{00020424-0000-0000-C000-000000000046}"
```

At run time, the SCM locates this CLSID and performs a lookup in the HKEY_CLASSES_ROOT\CLSID section of the registry. The Automation marshaler CLSID has the following entries in the registry:

```
HKEY_CLASSES_ROOT\
    CLSID\
        {00020424-0000-0000-C000-000000000046}\
            (Default)="PSOAInterface"
            InprocServer32
                (Default)="oleaut32.dll"
                ThreadingModel="Both"
```

Notice that oleaut32.dll is listed as the proxy/stub Automation (*PSOAInterface*) coclass housed by oleaut32.dll. If you use type library marshaling, calling the *LoadTypeLibEx* or *RegTypeLib* function during the self-registration process automatically adds the necessary registry entries, as shown in the code fragment below. In the previous discussion of DLL surrogates, marshaling worked correctly because of the *oleautomation* attribute in the IDL file. Just imagine: you used type library marshaling without even realizing it!

```
ITypeLib* pTypeLib;
HRESULT hr = LoadTypeLibEx(L"mytypelib.tlb", REGKIND_DEFAULT,
    &pTypeLib);
pTypeLib->Release();
```

Custom Marshaling

Custom marshaling, the fundamental marshaling architecture of COM+, gives you complete control over the marshaling process. Not surprisingly, it is also the most difficult marshaling technique to implement. Custom marshaling is the generic mechanism by which one object can specify exactly how it communicates with a proxy in another process. Custom marshaling involves taking an interface pointer in one process and making it accessible to another process, either on the same machine or remotely. Standard marshaling is simply one way to achieve this goal. The standard marshaling architecture is built on top of custom marshaling, and type library marshaling is built on top of standard marshaling. These relationships are shown in Figure 12-4.

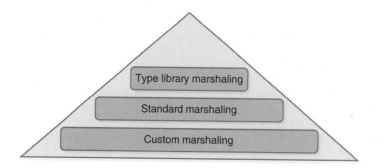

Figure 12-4.
The relationship between the three marshaling options.

Marshaling an interface pointer is far more complex than marshaling simple Remote Procedure Calls (RPCs). With RPCs, marshaling is only a matter of packaging the parameters of a fixed set of functions in a data packet and then unpacking the data structure on the other side. In COM+, each interface specifies a different set of functions that must be marshaled uniquely. The client might not know in advance what interfaces it will use. Visual Basic and the Microsoft Java Virtual Machine (VM), for example, can connect to any custom interface you might dream up. How can these run-time interpreters possibly know how to marshal the parameters to methods in your custom interface? The custom marshaling architecture must somehow deal with the dynamic nature of COM+.

While you ponder possible solutions to this dilemma, we'll discuss executable components in Chapter 13 and custom marshaling in Chapter 14. These will lead up to the detailed discussion of standard marshaling in Chapter 15.

CHAPTER THIRTEEN

Executable Components

Executable components, also known as out-of-process or local components, are EXE files that house COM+ objects. Both executable and in-process components (with the help of a surrogate) can run on remote machines in a distributed environment. The promise of location transparency in COM+ means that you don't have to modify the client process, regardless of whether it's accessing an in-process or an executable component running on a local or remote machine. In previous chapters, we implemented in-process components; in this chapter, we'll discuss how you can convert an in-process component to an executable component and then call it remotely.

Figure 13-1 compares a client calling an in-process component to a client calling a component running in a separate address space.

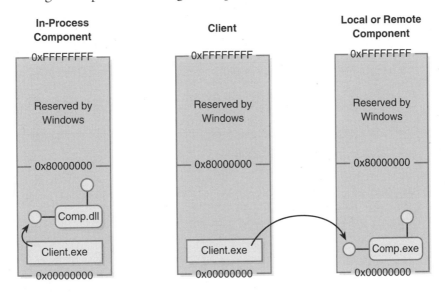

Figure 13-1.
The memory layout of in-process components, executable components, and their clients.

Before you build an executable component, you should carefully weigh the advantages and disadvantages of using executable components instead of their in-process siblings. As you know, you need not create an executable component to call a component remotely; DLL surrogates enable in-process components to run both locally and remotely.

The two primary advantages of executable components are that they can run as services, as described in Chapter 18, and that the user can run them as double-clickable applications. In both cases, you can still build the desired functionality into an in-process component and then create an executable front to call the component. Another reason that some developers favor executable components is that since they run in a separate address space from the client, they pose less of a security risk to the client. But you can also address this security risk by using a DLL surrogate. In fact, in the future there might not be any need for executable components that are not surrogates for in-process components.[1]

In some situations, the outgoing parameters of a method call made on an in-process component work slightly differently from a method call made on an executable component. For example, when a method running in an in-process component writes data using pointers provided by the method's *out* parameters, the caller's address space is updated immediately; if the method is running in an out-of-process component, the caller's address space is updated only when the method returns. Normally, this rather subtle difference is of no consequence. However, if a method running in an out-of-process component makes a call back to the caller, the caller might reasonably expect that its variables have been updated by the method. This will not be the case because the method has not yet returned. You can resolve this by specifying that methods should not write data through *out* parameters until just before they return, as is the case automatically with out-of-process components. In this way, this minor variation between the operation of in-process and out-of-process components is better masked.

What about the disadvantages of executable components? The main disadvantage is that they run much more slowly than in-process components because cross-process calls must be made. Of course, an in-process component running in a surrogate or any kind of component running on a remote machine suffers the same performance hit. The following table lists some questions you should ask yourself when you consider whether to implement an in-process component, an in-process component running in the default surrogate, or an executable component:

---

1. The COM+ run-time environment supports only in-process components.

Question	In-Process Component	In-Process Component Running in the Default DLL Surrogate	Executable Component
Do you want instances of the object to be shared by more than one client?	No	Yes	Yes
Do you plan to enter the object in the Running Object Table (ROT)?	No	No	Yes
Does the object need to expose nonremotable interfaces (such as *IViewObject*)?	Yes	No	No
Do you want the object to be insulated from client crashes?	No	Yes	Yes
Do you want to run the component in the COM+ run-time environment?	Yes	Yes	No
Do you want the object to have its own security context?	No	Yes	Yes
Does the object require superior performance?	Yes	No	No
Do you want the object to be run as a stand-alone application under the user's direct control?	No	No	Yes
Does the object need to expose internal data structures directly to the client?	Yes	No	No

Building an Executable Component

Fortunately, changing an in-process component into an executable component, or vice-versa, is not all that difficult because it primarily involves changing
the housing for your coclasses. Nevertheless, if after careful consideration of
the alternatives you decide to proceed with an executable component, keep in
mind that executable components differ from in-process components in several
ways. One of the major differences is that EXEs cannot export functions as DLLs
can, which means that the well-known entry points *DllGetClassObject*,

DllCanUnloadNow, *DllRegisterServer*, and *DllUnregisterServer* are specific to in-process components only. An executable component must have a *main* or *WinMain* start-up function where execution begins and must include special code to deal with termination. The remaining concerns with executable components relate to race conditions that can arise in multithreaded EXEs; these are explained later in this chapter.

Originally, DLLs worked simply by exporting functions. Other programs could load a DLL and ask for a pointer to a particular function either by name or by number. In-process components use the *IUnknown::QueryInterface* method to return interface pointers through which calls can be made, while COM+ relies on standard exported functions such as *DllGetClassObject* to retrieve the initial interface pointer.

Executable files, unlike DLLs, do not export functions. An executable file can hand out function pointers only while it is running. COM+ addresses this difference between DLLs and EXEs by using command-line parameters that are communicated to the EXE on start-up. Thus, the four functions exported by in-process components are replaced by three command-line arguments that can be supplied to executable components. The following table lists the exported functions and their equivalent command-line arguments:

Function Exported from an In-Process Component	Equivalent Command-Line Argument Passed to an Executable Component
DllGetClassObject	*−Embedding*
DllCanUnloadNow	No equivalent; see the section titled "Managing the Lifetime of an Executable Component" later in this chapter
DllRegisterServer	*−RegServer*
DllUnregisterServer	*−UnregServer*

Note that when an executable is launched in the normal way (in response to the user clicking an icon), no special command-line arguments are passed to the application, so the application can easily determine whether it has been launched in response to a client request or by the user. Typical executable components, such as Microsoft Internet Explorer or Microsoft Word, do not show any user interface when they are launched via COM+, so a client process can request services from these applications without the desktop becoming unnecessarily cluttered. Of course, most executable components also provide methods that enable the client to request that they show themselves to the user.

When you develop components that will run remotely, displaying a user interface is usually not a good idea. Due to the COM+ security architecture, most components executing remotely run on a desktop separate from that displayed on the server.[2] Therefore, ignoring the fact that the user might be a great distance from the server, the user interface might not even be visible on the server. The following start-up code is typical of that normally executed by executable components in their *main* function:

```
int main(int argc, char** argv)
{
    if(argc > 1)
    {
        char* szToken = strtok(argv[1], "-/");
        if(_stricmp(szToken, "RegServer") == 0)
            return RegisterComponent(...);
        if(_stricmp(szToken, "UnregServer") == 0)
            return UnregisterComponent(...);
        if(_stricmp(szToken, "Embedding") == 0)
        {
            // Launched by COM+!
            // Don't show a user interface.
            // Then register a class factory.
        }
    }
    // No COM+ arguments; run in the normal fashion.
    // Show user interface here.
    return 0;
}
```

This code determines whether more than one command-line argument is present, since the first command-line argument (*argv[0]*) is always the name of the application itself. The *strtok* function finds the first dash (–) or slash (/) character in the first command-line argument; either character is a legal prefix to the command-line arguments provided by the system. Next, the *_stricmp* function compares lowercase versions of the command-line argument with the three standard strings that can be provided by COM+. If *–RegServer* or *–UnregServer* is found, the appropriate registration steps are performed and execution is terminated. That's right—if an executable component is executed using either of the registration commands, the program exits immediately after performing the requested action. This design allows setup programs to launch an executable component and instruct the component to register itself without any danger that it will display a user interface or take some other action.

---

2. Actually, they run in a separate window station. See Chapter 18 for details.

Note that you must call *CoInitializeEx* prior to the registration or de-registration routine if type libraries are to be registered using *LoadTypeLibEx* or *RegisterTypeLib* or unregistered using *UnRegisterTypeLib*. Although the samples on the companion CD always refresh their registry settings when they are launched, this is for convenience only and is not generally recommended for production code. Depending on the security environment, a component might not have write access to critical areas of the registry.

The actual registration of an executable component is similar to that of an in-process object. The main difference is that instead of using the InprocServer32 subkey, executable components are registered in a LocalServer32 subkey. The same coclass can be registered in both the InprocServer32 and the LocalServer32 subkeys. In such cases, COM+ provides the client with whatever form of the object was requested via the class context values (*CLSCTX_LOCAL_SERVER* or *CLSCTX_INPROC_SERVER*). If the client passes the value *CLSCTX_SERVER* or *CLSCTX_ALL*, COM+ defaults to the most efficient implementation of the coclass: an in-process component. If an in-process implementation is not available—in other words, if the InprocServer32 key is not found—COM+ looks for local and then remote components.

The *RegisterServer*[3] function automatically checks its first parameter to determine whether an EXE or a DLL component is being registered. For example, if the *RegisterServer* function is called using the name of an executable file, the component is registered in a LocalServer32 subkey. In-process (DLL) components are registered in the InprocServer32 subkey. The following code fragment is from the *RegisterServer* function:

```
// Add the component's filename subkey under the CLSID key.
// Is it an EXE?
if(strstr(szModuleName, ".exe") == NULL)
{
    // No; use InprocServer32.
    setKeyAndValue(szKey, "InprocServer32", szModule);
    // More code here...
}
else
    // Yes; use LocalServer32.
    setKeyAndValue(szKey, "LocalServer32", szModule);
```

---

3. Alternatively, you can use the *RegisterServerEx* function (also provided in registry.cpp on the companion CD) to configure the registry information based on a tabular data structure. See Chapter 2 for details.

Registering the Class Objects

If the *–Embedding* flag is located in the command-line arguments, the component knows that it is being launched in response to a client's activation request. The name of this flag originates from the linking and embedding days of OLE. The component should respond to the *–Embedding* flag by registering its class object using the *CoRegisterClassObject* function and taking other steps similar to those performed by a DLL when the *DllGetClassObject* function is called. If no COM+ command-line argument is detected, the executable component should assume that it has been launched at the request of the user and thus behave like a normal application. For executable components designed to be activated only via COM+, the absence of the *–Embedding* flag should also be interpreted as the user's attempt to launch the application and an appropriate message should be displayed, after which the application should terminate.

Once the processing of command-line parameters is out of the way, executable components must call *CoInitializeEx*. Recall that in-process components do not normally call *CoInitializeEx* because they run in the process of their caller, which has already called *CoInitializeEx*. Besides initializing COM+, *CoInitializeEx* gives the component an opportunity to specify its supported threading model. In-process components are forced to do this via the *ThreadingModel* value in the registry. An executable component can use the *COINIT_MULTITHREADED* flag of *CoInitializeEx* to declare itself as multithreaded, as shown in the following code:

```
CoInitializeEx(NULL, COINIT_MULTITHREADED);
```

The *CoRegisterClassObject* Function

In place of the *DllGetClassObject* function, an executable component uses the *CoRegisterClassObject* function to inform COM+ about the objects it supports. Each call to *CoRegisterClassObject* registers one class identifier (CLSID) and its associated class object. If a component supports multiple coclasses, it must call *CoRegisterClassObject* once for each object. *CoRegisterClassObject* takes the CLSID of the coclass being registered as its first parameter and a pointer to the coclass's class object as its second parameter. Thus, you must first create an instance of the class object using the C++ *new* operator, as shown here:

```
IClassFactory *pClassFactory = new CFactory();

DWORD dwRegister;
CoRegisterClassObject(CLSID_InsideCOM, pClassFactory,
    CLSCTX_LOCAL_SERVER, REGCLS_MULTIPLEUSE, &dwRegister);
```

Each class object can specify certain settings via the third and fourth parameters of the *CoRegisterClassObject* function. The third parameter determines whether the class object is visible only to client code running in the process space of the component (*CLSCTX_INPROC_SERVER*) or to clients running in a separate address space on the local machine or a remote machine (*CLSCTX_LOCAL_SERVER*). The fourth parameter accepts flags from the *REGCLS* enumeration, as shown here:

```
typedef enum tagREGCLS
{
    REGCLS_SINGLEUSE = 0,
    REGCLS_MULTIPLEUSE = 1,
    REGCLS_MULTI_SEPARATE = 2,
    REGCLS_SUSPENDED = 4,
    REGCLS_SURROGATE = 8
} REGCLS;
```

The *REGCLS_SINGLEUSE* flag is a legacy setting that enables only one client to access the class object. Subsequent client requests cause COM+ to load a new instance of the entire component. The *REGCLS_MULTIPLEUSE* flag is more commonly used because it enables multiple client applications to connect to a single instance of a class object. In addition, class objects registered with the *REGCLS_MULTIPLEUSE* flag are automatically accessible to code running in the process space of the component itself, regardless of whether the *CLSCTX_INPROC_SERVER* flag was specified in the third parameter of *CoRegisterClassObject*.

The *REGCLS_MULTI_SEPARATE* flag is a variation on the flag *REGCLS_MULTIPLEUSE*, which restricts client code running in the process of the component from accessing the class object. This flag enables a component to register different class objects for in-process clients (*CLSCTX_INPROC_SERVER*) and out-of-process clients (*CLSCTX_LOCAL_SERVER*). COM+ specifically allows multiple registrations of the same class object; each registration is independent and returns a unique key via the fifth parameter of the *CoRegisterClassObject* function. A class object registered with the *CLSCTX_LOCAL_SERVER* class context and *REGCLS_MULTI_SEPARATE* registration flag would exhibit rather odd behavior. Out-of-process clients would share one instance of the component, but client code running in the process of the component would cause COM+ to launch another instance of the component!

The following table describes the behavior exhibited by various combinations of the class context and registration flags. For information about the *REGCLS_SURROGATE* flag, see Chapter 12. We'll discuss the flag *REGCLS_SUSPENDED* later in this chapter.

Class Context Flags	Registration Flags		
	REGCLS_ SINGLEUSE	*REGCLS_ MULTIPLEUSE*	*REGCLS_ MULTI_ SEPARATE*
CLSCTX_INPROC_SERVER	Illegal	In-process	In-process
CLSCTX_LOCAL_SERVER	Local	In-process or local	Local
CLSCTX_INPROC_SERVER| CLSCTX_LOCAL_SERVER	Illegal	In-process or local	In-process or local

Remote Instantiation

While you can control many basic COM+ settings directly using the registry editor or indirectly by using the Distributed COM Configuration utility, components written today generally do not rely on these methods. Modern applications want precise run-time control over which server they're connected to and over what security settings are involved. The *CoCreateInstanceEx* function creates a single object on a specified machine, whether local or remote. The ability to create an object on a remote machine is an extension of the functionality available in the *CoCreateInstance* function, which creates an object on the local machine only.

In addition, rather than requesting a single interface and obtaining a single pointer to that interface, you can use *CoCreateInstanceEx* to request multiple interface pointers in a single call. Although *QueryInterface* calls to in-process components are fast, calling *QueryInterface* multiple times to request many different interface pointers from a component that is located on another machine is much less efficient. The *CoCreateInstanceEx* function offers an optimization that enables a developer to obtain multiple interface pointers from an object with a single remote call.

CoCreateInstanceEx lets you specify an array of MULTI_QI structures, each containing a pointer to an interface identifier (IID). The MULTI_QI structure optimizes *QueryInterface* so that fewer round-trips are made between machines. When *CoCreateInstanceEx* returns, each MULTI_QI structure contains (if available) a pointer to the requested interface and the return value of the *QueryInterface* call for that interface. A return value of *E_NOINTERFACE* means that no interface pointers were available; the distinguished error *CO_S_NOTALLINTERFACES* means that the object did not implement all of the requested interfaces. The MULTI_QI structure used by *CoCreateInstanceEx* is shown in the code on the following page.

```
typedef struct tagMULTI_QI
{
    const IID* pIID;
    IUnknown* pItf;
    HRESULT hr;
} MULTI_QI;
```

CoCreateInstanceEx supports this functionality because of the *IMultiQI* interface, shown in Interface Definition Language (IDL) notation in the following code. Like the *CoCreateInstanceEx* function, the *IMultiQI:: QueryMultipleInterfaces* method accepts an array of MULTI_QI structures and in a single remote call can obtain multiple interface pointers from an object. In fact, the internal implementation of *CoCreateInstanceEx* actually calls the *QueryMultipleInterfaces* method to provide its functionality.

```
interface IMultiQI : IUnknown
{
    HRESULT QueryMultipleInterfaces(
        [in]      ULONG     cMQIs,
        [in, out] MULTI_QI* pMQIs);
}
```

You do not have to implement the *IMultiQI* interface; together, the proxy and the stub conspire to implement this interface for all objects that use standard marshaling or type library marshaling. You can simply call the *IUnknown:: QueryInterface* method to request the *IMultiQI* interface and then use the resultant interface pointer to call the *IMultiQI::QueryMultipleInterfaces* method, as shown in the following code fragment. Note that calling *QueryInterface* to request the *IMultiQI* interface pointer does not execute a round-trip to the server because the in-process proxy implements this interface.

```
MULTI_QI qi[2];
qi[0].pIID = &IID_IHello;
qi[0].pItf = 0;
qi[0].hr = S_OK;
qi[1].pIID = &IID_IGoodbye;
qi[1].pItf = 0;
qi[1].hr = S_OK;

IMultiQI* pMultiQI = 0;
pUnknown->QueryInterface(IID_IMultiQI, (void**)&pMultiQI);
pMultiQI->QueryMultipleInterfaces(2, &qi);
```

The *CoCreateInstanceEx* function also accepts an argument of the type COSERVERINFO, as shown in the following code. COSERVERINFO identifies the remote machine on which the object should be instantiated as well as the security provider to be used. The most important field of this structure is the *pwszName* variable, which refers to the name of the remote machine. The name used to identify a machine depends on the naming scheme of the underlying network transport. By default, all Universal Naming Convention (UNC) paths, such as \\server or server, and Domain Name Service (DNS) names, such as *server.com*, *www.server.com*, and *144.19.56.38*, are allowed.

```
typedef struct _COSERVERINFO
{
    DWORD dwReserved1;
    LPWSTR pwszName;
    COAUTHINFO* pAuthInfo;
    DWORD dwReserved2;
} COSERVERINFO;
```

Note that *CoCreateInstanceEx* does not search the client's registry for the desired CLSID but instead contacts the Service Control Manager (SCM) residing on the specified remote machine and requests that it search the registry on the server. This technique is advantageous because it means that the CLSID of the remote component does not need to be registered on the client's machine. It also obviates the need for the *RemoteServerName* entry in the AppID section of the registry. Of course, using *CoCreateInstanceEx* doesn't relieve you from having to provide marshaling code for any custom interfaces consumed by the client.

The following code shows the use of the *CoCreateInstanceEx* function; you can use it to replace calls to *CoCreateInstance* in a client-side application. Notice the use of the *CLSCTX_REMOTE_SERVER* flag.

```
COSERVERINFO ServerInfo = { 0, L"Remote_Computer_Name", 0, 0 };
MULTI_QI qi = { &IID_IUnknown, NULL, 0 };

CoCreateInstanceEx(CLSID_InsideCOM, NULL, CLSCTX_REMOTE_SERVER,
    &ServerInfo, 1, &qi);

pUnknown = qi.pItf;
```

Integrating the Marshaling Code

Since we're building an executable component, marshaling is a concern. Of the three basic marshaling options—standard, type library, and custom—we strongly recommend standard marshaling or type library marshaling for most components. The easiest way to use standard marshaling is simply to build and register a proxy/stub DLL from the files generated by the MIDL compiler following the steps described in Chapter 12. To use type library marshaling, you simply make sure that the interface is marked with the *oleautomation* attribute in the IDL file and that the type library is properly registered. No further work is required if you're using type library marshaling because the type library marshaler is available as part of the system. If, however, you use standard marshaling with a proxy/stub DLL, the DLL must be copied to every machine and properly registered using the RegSvr32 utility.

It is sometimes desirable to avoid distributing and registering a proxy/stub marshaling DLL on every computer that runs either the client application or the component itself. The main reason for wanting to avoid this drudgery is simply to minimize the amount of baggage that must be distributed and installed with an application. Of course, the simplest way to obviate the need for a proxy/stub DLL is to use the type library marshaling facility built into the system. If this technique proves unacceptable due to performance or other reasons, it is possible to integrate the proxy/stub code generated by MIDL directly into the client and component executables instead of building a marshaling DLL. You do this by statically linking the proxy/stub code generated by MIDL into the client and component executables.

Be forewarned that integrating proxy/stub code directly with an application is normally frowned upon. For one thing, it means that other client programs cannot access the services of the component because they won't have access to the marshaling code. Also, it becomes crucial that the proxy/stub code statically linked into the client and component executables be synchronized. If the component's stub code is updated, the client's proxy code must be updated as well.

If after careful consideration of the alternatives you decide to integrate the proxy/stub code directly with the application's executable file, follow the steps below. After following these steps, you can run and test the application. Everything should work as it did before the changes except that the proxy/stub DLL will no longer be needed.

1. Add the *idlname*_p.c, *idlname*_i.c, and dlldata.c files generated by the MIDL compiler to both the client and component projects.

2. In the main source files of both the client and component, add the following code in boldface immediately after the call to *CoInitializeEx* but replace *IID_ICustom* with the name of the custom interface that the proxy/stub code knows how to marshal. If the proxy/stub code generated by MIDL is used to marshal multiple interfaces, repeat this code once for each custom interface.

```
int main(int argc, char** argv)
{
    CoInitializeEx(NULL, COINIT_MULTITHREADED);

    IUnknown* pUnknown;
    DWORD dwUnused;
    DllGetClassObject(IID_ICustom, IID_IUnknown,
        (void**)&pUnknown);
    CoRegisterClassObject(IID_ICustom, pUnknown,
        CLSCTX_INPROC_SERVER, REGCLS_MULTIPLEUSE, &dwUnused);
    CoRegisterPSClsid(IID_ICustom, IID_ICustom);
```

3. Rebuild the client and the component.

The *CoGetPSClsid* and *CoRegisterPSClsid* Functions

Normally, COM+ locates the proxy/stub marshaling code for a custom interface by searching the HKEY_CLASSES_ROOT\Interfaces section of the registry. As a subkey of the desired interface, the ProxyStubClsid32 key includes the CLSID of the in-process component containing the marshaling code. COM+ uses the *CoGetPSClsid* function to help retrieve this information from the registry. In some cases, however, an application might not want to store this information in the registry. A component might have been downloaded across a network and due to security settings might not have permission to access the local registry. Or, as in the situation discussed here, the application might already contain the necessary proxy/stub code.

In such cases, you can call the *CoRegisterPSClsid* function used in the preceding code fragment to register the proxy/stub marshaling code for custom interfaces within the context of a running process. The *CoGetPSClsid* function used by COM+ to locate the marshaling code returns the CLSID of the proxy/stub code registered using the *CoRegisterPSClsid* function. Thus, you can use *CoRegisterPSClsid* to perform temporary run-time registration that remains in effect only as long as the process is running, in place of a more permanent registration that would actually be written to the system registry.

Note that in the preceding code, the IID *IID_ICustom* is passed as a CLSID parameter to the *DllGetClassObject*, *CoRegisterClassObject*, and *CoRegisterPSClsid* functions. By convention, the IID of a custom interface is used as the CLSID of that interface's proxy/stub marshaling code. Since both IIDs and CLSIDs are 128-bit GUIDs, this seemingly odd conversion presents no difficulty to the compiler.

Managing the Lifetime of an Executable Component

At this stage, the executable component is fully operational, but it has a serious problem. Because the program will continue executing, it will soon reach the end of its *main* function and terminate. Clients of our component will be justifiably upset if the component simply exits without warning, so we must find a way to keep our component alive. In-process components do not have to worry about this problem because they are loaded into the address space of their client and politely wait to be called. When a client finishes using an in-process component, COM+ calls the exported function *DllCanUnloadNow* before unloading the DLL.

Executable components, however, are responsible for managing their own lifetimes. How this issue is addressed depends on whether the executable component runs in a single-threaded apartment (STA) or the multithreaded apartment (MTA). Multithreaded components typically address this problem by creating an event object using the Win32 *CreateEvent* function, as shown in the following code. This function call is followed by a call to the Win32 function *WaitForSingleObject*, which waits for the event to be signaled.

```
g_hEvent = CreateEvent(NULL, FALSE, FALSE, NULL);
WaitForSingleObject(g_hEvent, INFINITE);
```

Because the *INFINITE* flag is used in the call to *WaitForSingleObject*, the code will wait forever until the event is signaled, solving the problem of the component exiting prematurely. A client can request all the services it wants from the executable component, and only when all clients have finished using the component do we want it to exit. Exiting can be accomplished by adding code in the object's destructor to detect whether this is the last outstanding reference to the component, as shown here:

```
CInsideCOM::~CInsideCOM()
{
    if(CoReleaseServerProcess() == 0)
        SetEvent(g_hEvent);
}
```

When the *SetEvent* function is called, the *WaitForSingleObject* call that was on hold in the *main* function returns. After performing a few cleanup steps, the component is permitted to exit. First, the component must inform COM+ that it is no longer offering any objects for use. This notification is sent using the *CoRevokeClassObject* function, the ancillary of *CoRegisterClassObject*. Once there is no danger of more clients calling to request objects, you release what should be the final class factory pointer. The *IUnknown::Release* method is followed immediately by a call to *CoUninitialize*. The entire *main* function for an executable component is shown on the following page:

```
void main(int argc, char** argv)
{
    CommandLineParameters(argc, argv);

    CoInitializeEx(NULL, COINIT_MULTITHREADED);
    g_hEvent = CreateEvent(NULL, FALSE, FALSE, NULL);

    DWORD dwRegister;
    IClassFactory *pClassFactory = new CFactory();

    CoRegisterClassObject(CLSID_InsideCOM,
        pClassFactory, CLSCTX_LOCAL_SERVER,
        REGCLS_SUSPENDED|REGCLS_MULTIPLEUSE, &dwRegister);
    CoResumeClassObjects();

    WaitForSingleObject(g_hEvent, INFINITE);
    CloseHandle(g_hEvent);

    CoRevokeClassObject(dwRegister);
    pClassFactory->Release();
    CoUninitialize();
}
```

Race Conditions

In the preceding code fragments, you might have noticed some unfamiliar functions, including *CoReleaseServerProcess*, *CoResumeClassObjects*, and *CoRevokeClassObject*. These belong to a set of four helper functions, described in the table below, that simplify the job of writing robust server-side code in multithreaded executable components. Collectively, these functions address the unique race conditions afflicting multithreaded executable components. While they are designed for use by multithreaded executable components, you can use them just as easily with single-threaded components. In-process components have no use for these functions.

Function	Description
CoResumeClassObjects	Called by a server to inform the SCM about all registered classes; permits activation requests for those class objects
CoSuspendClassObjects	Prevents any new activation requests from the SCM on all class objects registered within the process
CoAddRefServerProcess	Increments a global per-process reference count
CoReleaseServerProcess	Decrements a global per-process reference count

During the start-up and initialization phase of a local component, the *CoRegisterClassObject* function is called once for each CLSID supported by the component. This function tells COM+ about the component's classes and gives it a pointer to each class's class object. After it registers all of its class objects, the component is ready for use. For multithreaded components, however, calls might arrive after the first object is registered. This is a problem because, at least theoretically, a client might instantiate an object and perform the final *IUnknown::Release* call before the rest of the component has had a chance to finish initializing. This final *IUnknown::Release* call would decrement the usage reference counter to 0 and initiate a shutdown of the component process.

To avoid this type of activation race condition and simplify the developer's job, a multithreaded component with more than one class object should use the *REGCLS_SUSPENDED* flag when calling the *CoRegisterClassObject* function, as shown in boldface in the following code. This flag tells COM+, "I'm registering a class, but please don't tell anyone else just yet." The component can peacefully register the remainder of its class objects, passing the *REGCLS_SUSPENDED* flag with every call to *CoRegisterClassObject*. Once all the classes have been registered with COM+ and the component is ready to accept client requests, the component calls the *CoResumeClassObjects* function to tell COM+ that the classes are available for use.

```
DWORD dwRegister;
IClassFactory *pIFactory = new CFactory();
CoRegisterClassObject(CLSID_InsideCOM,
    pIFactory, CLSCTX_LOCAL_SERVER,
    REGCLS_SUSPENDED|REGCLS_MULTIPLEUSE, &dwRegister);
// Register more class objects here.
// Use the REGCLS_SUSPENDED flag with each call.

// Now tell the SCM about all the call objects in one blow.
CoResumeClassObjects();
```

The *CoResumeClassObjects* function tells COM+ to inform the SCM about all the registered classes. This technique offers several advantages, the most important of which is that no activation or shutdown requests are received before the component is ready. Aside from solving the aforementioned race condition, this call is also more efficient because COM+ needs to make only one call to the SCM to tell it about all the class objects instead of working in the piecemeal fashion used when *CoRegisterClassObject* is called without the *REGCLS_SUSPENDED* flag. This technique also reduces the overall start-up and registration time required by the component.

One additional function, *CoSuspendClassObjects*, prevents any new activation requests from the SCM on all class objects registered within the process. This function is not usually called directly by local components, but it is nonetheless the complement of *CoResumeClassObjects*. Note also that *CoSuspendClassObjects* does not relieve the component of the need to call *CoRevokeClassObject* for each registered class object.

A similar race condition might occur when a client calls the *CoGetClassObject* function to obtain a pointer to an object's class factory. This call is often followed by a call to the *IClassFactory::LockServer(TRUE)* method to prevent the component from exiting. However, a window of opportunity exists between the time the class object is obtained and the time the client calls the *LockServer* method during which another client can connect to the same component. This second client can instantiate an object and then immediately call *IUnknown::Release*, causing the component to shut down and thus leave the first client with a disconnected *IClassFactory* pointer.

To prevent this race condition, COM+ implicitly calls the *IClassFactory:: LockServer(TRUE)* method as part of *CoGetClassObject* and implicitly calls *IClassFactory::LockServer(FALSE)* when the client releases the *IClassFactory* interface pointer. This obviates the need for the client process to call the *LockServer* method because COM+ handles this step automatically. In fact, the standard proxy for the *IClassFactory::LockServer* method implemented by ole32.dll simply returns *S_OK* without actually making a remote call.

Executable Component Shutdown

To shut down properly, a local component must keep track of how many objects it has instantiated and the number of times its *IClassFactory::LockServer* method has been called. Only when both of these counts, often represented in code as the variables *g_cComponents* and *g_cServerLocks*, reach 0 can the component legally exit. In a thread-oblivious component, the decision to shut down is automatically coordinated with incoming activation requests by virtue of the fact that all incoming requests are serialized by the message queue. Upon receiving a call to the *IUnknown::Release* method for its last object and deciding to shut down, a component revokes its class objects using the *CoRevokeClassObject* function. This function tells COM+ not to accept any more activation requests. If an activation request comes in after this point, COM+ recognizes that the class objects are revoked and returns an error to the SCM. The SCM then automatically attempts to launch a new instance of the component process, beginning the entire process anew.

If multiple objects are running in the MTA or in multiple STAs, another thread in the component will hand out a new object while the last object in a component is shutting down. If the component proceeds with the shutdown at this critical stage, somewhere a client thinks it has a valid interface pointer.

You can imagine what happens if the client tries to use that pointer. Thus, the decision to shut down must be coordinated across multiple threads, possibly in different apartments, so that a thread of the component does not shut down while another thread is busy handing out objects. To help you coordinate a component's shutdown across multiple threads, COM+ provides two reference-counting functions: *CoAddRefServerProcess* and *CoReleaseServerProcess*.

CoAddRefServerProcess increments a processwide reference count. *CoReleaseServerProcess* decrements that reference count; also, when the reference counter reaches 0, it automatically calls the *CoSuspendClassObjects* function. After this call, any incoming activation requests are refused. This technique permits the component to peacefully deregister its class objects from its various threads without the risk that a simultaneous activation request will be accepted. Activation requests received during or after the shutdown procedure are handled by directing the SCM to launch a new instance of the component process.

You can use *CoAddRefServerProcess* and *CoReleaseServerProcess* to replace the global object count (*g_cComponents*) and the global *IClassFactory:: LockServer* count (*g_cServerLocks*) as well as solve the race condition discussed earlier. The simplest way for a local component to use these functions is to call *CoAddRefServerProcess* in the constructor of each of its instance objects and call *CoReleaseServerProcess* in the destructor of each of its instance objects,[4] as shown in the following code:

```
CInsideCOM::CInsideCOM() : m_cRef(1)
{
    CoAddRefServerProcess();
}

CInsideCOM::~CInsideCOM()
{
    if(CoReleaseServerProcess() == 0)
        InitiateComponentShutdown();
}
```

Also, *CoAddRefServerProcess* should be called in the *IClassFactory:: LockServer* method when the *bLock* flag is *TRUE*, as shown in the following code. If the *bLock* flag is *FALSE*, the *CoReleaseServerProcess* function should be called.

```
HRESULT CFactory::LockServer(BOOL bLock)
{
    if(bLock)
        CoAddRefServerProcess();
```

---

4. By *instance objects,* we mean regular COM+ objects that are not class objects.

```
    else
        if(CoReleaseServerProcess() == 0)
            InitiateComponentShutdown();
    return S_OK;
}
```

As you can see in the preceding code, the application should check the value returned by the *CoReleaseServerProcess* function. A value of 0 indicates that *CoReleaseServerProcess* has automatically called *CoSuspendClassObjects* and that the component can initiate shutdown. In the STA case this means that the component should signal all of its STAs to exit their message loops, and then it should call *CoRevokeClassObject* and *CoUninitialize*. It signals an STA to exit its message loop by posting a *WM_QUIT* message to the queue using the Win32 *PostQuitMessage(0)* function, as shown here:

```
void InitiateComponentShutdown()
{
    PostQuitMessage(0);
}
```

If the component supports the MTA model, it need only revoke its class objects and then call *CoUninitialize*, since MTA-based code does not use a message loop. (Unless you use the functions *CoAddRefServerProcess* and *CoReleaseServerProcess* diligently in both the constructors and destructors of instance objects as well as in the *IClassFactory::LockServer* method, the component process can shut down prematurely.) The following code sets an event object to prod the MTA-based component to exit:

```
void InitiateComponentShutdown()
{
    SetEvent(g_hEvent);
}
```

The following code shows the complete *main* function of a typical MTA-based component. The *WaitForSingleObject* function, shown in boldface, is waiting for the event to be set. When the *SetEvent* function is called by the shutdown code, it wakes up and executes the remaining steps needed to exit cleanly.

```
void main(int argc, char** argv)
{
    CommandLineParameters(argc, argv);

    CoInitializeEx(NULL, COINIT_MULTITHREADED);
    g_hEvent = CreateEvent(NULL, FALSE, FALSE, NULL);
```

(continued)

```
    DWORD dwRegister;
    IClassFactory *pIFactory = new CFactory();
    CoRegisterClassObject(CLSID_InsideCOM, pIFactory,
        CLSCTX_LOCAL_SERVER,
        REGCLS_SUSPENDED|REGCLS_MULTIPLEUSE,
        &dwRegister);
    CoResumeClassObjects();

    WaitForSingleObject(g_hEvent, INFINITE);
    CloseHandle(g_hEvent);

    CoRevokeClassObject(dwRegister);
    pIFactory->Release();
    CoUninitialize();
}
```

Custom Activation Interfaces

In Chapter 11, we discussed building class objects that implement a custom activation interface instead of, or in addition to, *IClassFactory*. As we saw, actually implementing a custom activation interface in a class object is not difficult. Those objects, however, were housed by in-process components. Managing the lifetime of an executable component whose class objects do not support the *IClassFactory* interface is more difficult.

As described in Chapter 3, poorly written executable components are often structured in such a way that a client holding a reference only to a class object is not sufficient to keep the component process running. The following code in boldface shows how the *IUnknown::Release* call destroys the object, thereby invoking the destructor, which sets a global event and finally causes the component to exit:

```
ULONG CPrime::Release()
{
    unsigned cRef = InterlockedDecrement(&m_cRef);
    if(cRef != 0)
        return cRef;
    delete this;
    return 0;
}

CPrime::~CPrime()
{
    if(CoReleaseServerProcess() == 0)
        SetEvent(g_hEvent);
}

void main(int argc, char** argv)
```

```
{
    // Initialization and CoRegisterClassObject omitted

    // Create the event to wait for.
    g_hEvent = CreateEvent(NULL, FALSE, FALSE, NULL);

    // Now wait for SetEvent...
    WaitForSingleObject(g_hEvent, INFINITE);

    // Event set. Exit now.
    CloseHandle(g_hEvent);
    CoRevokeClassObject(dwRegister);
    pPrimeFactory->Release();
    CoUninitialize();
}
```

The difficulty arises when the client releases a pointer to an object but
doesn't release a pointer to that object's class object. The client thinks that
retaining an open pointer to the class object means that the server will remain
running. Later, the client might want to use that class object pointer to create new
instances of the actual object. This problem is illustrated in the following code
using the example of the *IPrimeFactory* custom activation interface described in
Chapter 11; the release of the *Prime* object is shown in boldface:

```
// Get the PrimeFactory class object.
IPrimeFactory* pPrimeFactory;
CoGetClassObject(CLSID_Prime, CLSCTX_LOCAL_SERVER, NULL,
    IID_IPrimeFactory, (void**)&pPrimeFactory);

// Use the custom class object to create a Prime object.
IPrime* pPrime;
pPrimeFactory->CreatePrime(7, &pPrime);

// Use the Prime object here...
int next_prime;
pPrime->GetNextPrime(&next_prime);

// Release the Prime object.
pPrime->Release();

// Give the component a chance to exit.
Sleep(1000);

// Use pPrimeFactory to create another Prime object.
// Unfortunately, the component has already exited!
// Prepare for system meltdown.
pPrimeFactory->CreatePrime(7, &pPrime);
pPrime->GetNextPrime(&next_prime);
```

421

Typically, the system sidesteps this problem by automatically calling the *IClassFactory::LockServer(TRUE)* method when the first pointer is marshaled to a client. This call forces the component to keep running until the corresponding *IClassFactory::LockServer(FALSE)* call is made, which COM+ does automatically after the final client disconnects. Notice that this solution relies on the implementation of the *IClassFactory* interface in the class object. Class objects that implement a custom activation interface instead of *IClassFactory* cannot take advantage of this built-in functionality. Thus, a class object that does not implement the *IClassFactory* interface must correctly manage its own lifetime.

The *IExternalConnection* Interface

When an executable component calls *CoRegisterClassObject*, COM+ does not immediately marshal the interface pointer. Instead, it calls the *IUnknown::AddRef* method on the class object and then stores the pointer in an internal class object lookup table. Only when a client calls *CoGetClassObject* does the system find the interface pointer in the lookup table and then marshal the interface pointer back to the client, where it is subsequently unmarshaled. Since each marshaling operation represents a new client, you need hooks into this marshaling mechanism only to correctly control the lifetime of an executable component. This is where the *IExternalConnection* interface comes in—it offers complete lifetime control in COM+. The interface has only two methods, as shown here in IDL notation:

```
interface IExternalConnection : IUnknown
{
    DWORD AddConnection
    (
        [in] DWORD extconn,
        [in] DWORD reserved
    );

    DWORD ReleaseConnection
    (
        [in] DWORD extconn,
        [in] DWORD reserved,
        [in] BOOL  fLastReleaseCloses
    );
}
```

By implementing the *IExternalConnection* interface in a custom class object, you can prevent the component from exiting prematurely. When an interface pointer is first marshaled from the component to the client, the stub manager[5] calls *IUnknown::QueryInterface* to request the *IExternalConnection* interface from the class object. Objects that implement *IExternalConnection* must explicitly destroy the stub manager before exiting via the *CoDisconnectObject*[6] function. Most class objects do not implement this interface, and thus the stub manager first queries for the *IClassFactory* interface and, if found, proceeds to call the *IClassFactory::LockServer* method as discussed previously.

Responding affirmatively to the *QueryInterface* call with a valid pointer to an implementation of the *IExternalConnection* interface causes the stub manager to make calls to your methods *IExternalConnection::AddConnection* and *IExternalConnection::ReleaseConnection*. The *AddConnection* method is called whenever an interface pointer is marshaled to a client; the *ReleaseConnection* method is called when the pointer is released. The *extconn* parameter passed to the *AddConnection* and *ReleaseConnection* methods specifies the type of connection being added or released. The following table lists the valid values for this parameter. Currently, only the *EXTCONN_STRONG* value is used, indicating that the external connection must keep the object alive until all strong external connections are cleared using the *IExternalConnection:: ReleaseConnection* method.

Connection Type	Description
EXTCONN_STRONG	Strong connection
EXTCONN_WEAK	Weak connection (table, container)
EXTCONN_CALLABLE	Table vs. callable connection

By implementing *IExternalConnection*, an object can obtain a true count of external connections. In this way, you can ensure that a client retaining only a reference to a class object is sufficient to keep the component alive. Here is a relatively standard implementation of *IExternalConnection*'s two methods:

```
DWORD CPrimeFactory::AddConnection(DWORD extconn,
    DWORD dwreserved)
{
    if(extconn & EXTCONN_STRONG)
        return CoAddRefServerProcess();
    return 0;
}
```

(continued)

---

5. For more information about the stub manager, see Chapter 15.

6. The *CoDisconnectObject* function terminates all client connections. See Chapter 14.

```
DWORD CPrimeFactory::ReleaseConnection(DWORD extconn,
    DWORD dwreserved, BOOL fLastReleaseCloses)
{
    if(extconn & EXTCONN_STRONG)
    {
        if(CoReleaseServerProcess() == 0 && fLastReleaseCloses)
        {
            // No client references exist at all!
            // Destroy the stub manager.
            CoDisconnectObject(this, 0);
            return 0;
        }
    }
    return 1;
}
```

You can use the *CoLockObjectExternal* function to increment or decrement an object's external references as identified by the first parameter. To increment the object's lock count, you simply call *CoLockObjectExternal* with the second parameter set to *TRUE*. As a result, the stub manager calls the *IExternalConnection::AddConnection* method to notify the object of the new external lock. To decrement the lock count, you pass *FALSE* as the second parameter of the *CoLockObjectExternal* function; the stub manager will call *IExternalConnection::ReleaseConnection*. The third parameter of *CoLockObjectExternal* determines whether the stub manager should be destroyed when the final external lock is released. If so, the *CoDisconnectObject* function is called in the *IExternalConnection::ReleaseConnection* method, as shown above. The declaration of the *CoLockObjectExternal* function is shown below:

```
HRESULT __stdcall CoLockObjectExternal(IUnknown* pUnk,
    BOOL fLock, BOOL fLastUnlockReleases);
```

Singletons

The typical COM+ component creates a new class object for each client, and the client uses the *IClassFactory::CreateInstance* method to instantiate new objects. This is a good design for most objects, but some objects—such as objects that do not store any information about their clients—fit better in the singleton model. A singleton creates only one instance of a coclass and offers that object to all clients.[7] For example, a singleton object might plausibly implement the following interface:

---

7. Note that singletons are not supported by the COM+ run-time environment.

```
interface IPrime : IUnknown
{
    HRESULT IsPrime(long testnumber,
        [out, retval] boolean* retval);
}
```

The *IPrime* interface does not store a client state between method calls. Implementing the *IPrime* interface in a typical multi-instance component is not difficult, but instantiating a new *Prime* object for each client that connects when all clients could be sharing a single instance of the object does consume unnecessary resources. In theory, the singleton design would enable a prime number component to scale better when accessed by a large number of clients concurrently. While COM+ does not offer any special APIs or interfaces designed specifically for implementing singletons, building a singleton object does not present any special challenges either. Arguably the simplest way to implement a singleton object is to return the same instance from every call to the *IClassFactory::CreateInstance* method, as shown here:

```
HRESULT CFactory::CreateInstance(IUnknown* pUnknownOuter,
    REFIID riid, void** ppv)
{
    if(pUnknownOuter != NULL)
        return CLASS_E_NOAGGREGATION;

    static CPrime SingletonPrime;
    return SingletonPrime.QueryInterface(riid, ppv);
}
```

This practical technique works acceptably well, but aesthetically it leaves much to be desired. Returning a pointer to the same object each time the *CreateInstance* method is called seems almost unethical. Whereas the *CreateInstance* method is obviously designed to create a new instance of a class, the *CoGetClassObject* function is designed only to obtain a pointer to a class object, not necessarily to create one. Thus, a second way to design singleton objects in COM+ is to implement a custom interface directly in the class object.[8]

While this technique is semantically better than altering the behavior of the *CreateInstance* method as just described, it is not without its shortcomings. As we discussed previously, building a custom class object in an executable component requires that you implement the *IExternalConnection* interface. It also means that *CoCreateInstance* will no longer work, which in turn means that client applications written in Microsoft Visual Basic or Java cannot access the singleton object using the *new* operator or Visual Basic's *CreateObject* function.

---

8. Custom class objects are discussed in detail in Chapter 11.

The solution to this problem, at least for Visual Basic clients, is to use the class moniker via the *GetObject* function.

Whatever mechanism you choose to expose a singleton COM+ object, be aware that reference counting is normally disabled for such objects—because the final *Release* method should not execute a *delete this* statement! Typically, singleton objects stay in memory for the lifetime of the process they live in, so reference counting is not terribly important. A common way to implement this type of object is to code the *AddRef* and *Release* methods so that they simply return dummy values, as shown here:

```
ULONG CPrime::AddRef()
{
    return 2;
}

ULONG CPrime::Release()
{
    return 1;
}
```

CHAPTER FOURTEEN

Custom Marshaling

As you know, in-process components always run within the address space of their caller, except when run in a surrogate. This means that transferring function parameters, whether values or pointers to data, between the client and the component is a relatively trivial matter. When you make cross-process calls to a component running on the local machine or on a remote machine, things get more complicated. In such cases, all the data that needs to be shared by the client and the component must be neatly packaged and transmitted by any means available. This process is called *marshaling*, which according to the closest available dictionary means to arrange in proper order. We touched on marshaling in earlier chapters, and in this chapter we'll delve into the details of this interesting and rather complex subject.

Any component designed to run outside the context, apartment, process, or local machine of the client process must address the issue of marshaling. When a method call is executed on an object in another address space, COM+ needs to organize the data to be transferred. All of the method's parameters must be packed and transmitted from the caller's address space to the receiver's address space. For primitive data types such as characters and integers, marshaling does not sound all that difficult. But for more complex types such as structures, strings, arrays, linked lists, and interface pointers, marshaling can become exceedingly complex.

The subject of marshaling function parameters, whether integers or linked lists, was thoroughly researched during the development of Remote Procedure Call (RPC) systems.[1] Most RPC systems, including Microsoft Windows, transmit method parameters using the Network Data Representation (NDR)[2] standard adopted by the Open Software Foundation (OSF). Because COM+ is built on top of Microsoft RPC, it can leverage most of the RPC functionality—except in the area of interface pointers. RPC systems have no concept of interface pointers. In fact, the COM+ marshaling architecture deals almost exclusively with

---

1. See the appendix for details.

2. For more on NDR, see the sidebar titled "Network Data Representation" on page 431.

how to pass an interface pointer from the component to the client. In this chapter, we'll show you how to use custom marshaling, the basic marshaling architecture of COM+, to handle the marshaling requirements of the *ISum* interface.[3]

Marshaling Interface Pointers: An Overview

What does it mean to marshal an interface pointer? To answer this question, we first need to address a more basic question: What is an interface pointer? As you know, an interface pointer is a pointer to a pointer to a memory-based table, the v-table, which contains pointers to the virtual functions contained in that interface. For example, the *ISum* interface has four methods—the three methods of *IUnknown* plus the *ISum::Sum* method. The v-table structure at the location specified by an *ISum* interface pointer is shown in Figure 14-1. Although this figure shows a new interface pointer being obtained via the well-known *IUnknown::QueryInterface* method, this is certainly not the only method that can return an interface pointer; any method of a custom interface can return interface pointers.

```
hr = pUnknown->QueryInterface(IID_ISum, (void**)&pSum);
```

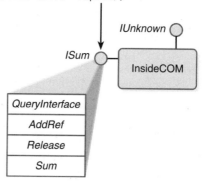

Figure 14-1.
The layout of a v-table structure.

Now let's return to the broader issue of marshaling. The question remains: How is it possible to take an *ISum* interface pointer and return it to a client in another process, which might or might not be on the same machine? The short answer is that it isn't possible. What constitutes a valid interface pointer in one apartment is complete gibberish in another.

---

3. The system also provides a built-in implementation of custom marshaling called standard marshaling, which is described in Chapter 15.

Re-Creating an Interface's V-Table

When a component returns an interface pointer to the client—via *QueryInterface* or any other method—that interface pointer must be marshaled. But given that passing an interface pointer from one process to another is a fruitless pursuit, the next best option is to have the client think that it is talking directly to the component. For each interface pointer returned to the client, you must re-create that interface's v-table structure in the client's address space. In other words, marshaling an interface pointer means re-creating that interface's v-table in the client's address space.

This v-table is fabricated by loading into the client's address space a proxy object that exposes the same interfaces as those implemented by the real object. When the client makes a method call on the object, it actually calls the in-process proxy. The proxy then communicates the method request to the object running in the component process. This architecture, however, requires that the component contain code to communicate directly with the proxy. To simplify the job of developing a component, this code is sometimes encased in another object, called the *stub,* which is loaded into the component's address space.

The Proxy/Stub DLL

Recall that marshaling an interface pointer simply means re-creating that interface's v-table within the client's address space. You use a proxy object to do this. Proxy objects are typically built as DLLs so they can be loaded into the client's address space when necessary. There is an important reason for building the proxy code as an in-process component rather than just statically linking it into the client code. Let's say that you've written a coclass that implements a custom interface and have packaged it into an executable component. A developer using Microsoft Visual Basic might want to access this component. In order for Visual Basic to call the object, a proxy must be loaded into Visual Basic's address space. If the proxy code is statically linked into one client program, other clients (such as Visual Basic) will not be able to access it. Unless you don't care about this restriction,[4] the proxy code for each custom interface that might be remoted should be implemented in a DLL.

There is no such requirement for stub code. The stub code that communicates with the proxy in the client's address space can be statically linked with the component. This is generally not as desirable as implementing the stub in a separate DLL, but we'll use this technique for the sake of simplicity. When you use standard marshaling (as described in Chapter 15), the proxy/stub code is always implemented as a separate in-process component.

---

4. For information on how to embed proxy and stub code in an application, see Chapter 13.

Interprocess Communication

Marshaling requires a proxy object in the client's address space and, at least conceptually, a stub object in the component's address space. When the client calls the proxy, the proxy communicates with the stub and the stub makes the actual calls into the object. The proxy packs any method parameters for transmission to the stub; the stub unpacks the parameters and calls the object. Everything goes in the reverse order on the way back: the object returns to the stub, the stub to the proxy, and the proxy to the client. Of course, the stub is responsible for packing any outgoing parameters and the method's return value for transmission back to the proxy; the proxy unpacks the arguments and returns them to the client. This process is illustrated in Figure 14-2.

Figure 14-2.
Communication between a client and a component via the proxy/stub mechanism.

The form and format of the interprocess communication between the proxy and the stub is private to these objects. If the client and the component run in different processes on one machine, shared memory can be used. If they run on different machines, a networking interface such as named pipes is required. COM+ does not define the format of the interprocess communication between a proxy and a stub, so you must determine the most efficient and appropriate way to implement this communication. If interfaces are remoted to other machines over a network, the transmitted data should conform to a published standard. The proxy/stub marshaling code generated by the Microsoft IDL (MIDL) compiler, for example, adheres to the Network Data Representation (NDR) standard.

In previous chapters, we dealt with the marshaling needs of custom interfaces using either type library or MIDL-generated marshaling code. Recall that type library marshaling relies on the Automation proxy/stub DLL to perform the necessary magic. Using MIDL-generated code is nearly as simple; you simply build and register a proxy/stub DLL. Again, the marshaling problem is solved. In most cases one of these two prepackaged solutions will suffice, but some situations call for a higher degree of control over the marshaling process.

Will That Be Custom or Standard Marshaling?

Custom marshaling, the fundamental marshaling mechanism of COM+, is generally the most difficult way to provide marshaling code for an interface. The raw power of this model is unparalleled, but most objects do not require the fine degree of control it offers. One typical situation in which you might use custom marshaling is when an object has one or more clients running on the same machine that want to access the object's state in memory. Suppose you're developing an image-processing component to which clients send bitmaps for a specific type of processing. If a client process is running on the same machine but in a different process from the component, it makes little sense to copy the bitmap from the client's address space to the component's address space. It is much more efficient to simply allocate shared memory between the two processes. Custom marshaling gives you full control over the marshaling process, and implementing marshaling using shared memory is one possibility. Obviously, this type of custom marshaling is limited to processes running on a single machine.

Network Data Representation

The NDR standard was originally developed by Apollo Corporation and was later adopted by the OSF as part of its Distributed Computing Environment (DCE). Windows uses NDR in its DCE-compatible RPC implementation and, therefore, in COM+. NDR provides a mapping of Interface Definition Language (IDL) data types to the streams sent over the wire. NDR supports a multi-canonical format, which means that certain aspects of NDR support alternative representations. Data properties such as byte order, character sets, and floating-point representation can assume one of several predefined forms. For example, NDR supports ASCII and EBCDIC character sets. This flexibility is accommodated by following a "reader makes right" policy. The proxy is allowed to write the data in the best way it sees fit from the available choices, and the stub (the reader) is expected to be able to read data in any of the NDR flavors. The proxy, however, must inform the stub of the particular variation of NDR transfer syntax being used. Note that the "reader makes right" strategy was chosen over the alternative approach, "writer makes right," whereby the proxy must determine the transfer syntax supported by the stub before writing the data.

Another common use of custom marshaling is for obtaining marshal-by-value semantics. Some objects, such as monikers, have an immutable state: their internal data never changes. For an object whose state never changes, it doesn't make sense to require the client to make remote method calls to retrieve data. For example, imagine an object that represents a rectangle. If the dimensions and coordinates of the rectangle never change after the object is created, the object is a good candidate for the marshal-by-value optimization. In such cases, the data that defines the object can be transmitted to the proxy using custom marshaling, and the data can be used to create an exact replica of the object. This technique allows the client to make in-process calls to obtain the same information that a remote call would; the client is none the wiser.[5]

When you use shared memory to implement custom marshaling, you must still consider what happens when the clients and components do not run on the same machine. In such cases, you can either build the support necessary to remote the interface across a network or delegate to the standard marshaler for this task. In fact, it is recommended that implementations of custom marshaling delegate to the standard marshaler for destination contexts they do not understand or for which they do not provide special functionality.

Before you marshal interface pointers, the system must know what type of marshaling is called for. To see how COM+ makes this determination, take a look at the following code, which shows the tentative first steps taken by a typical client:

```
// client.cpp

// Start your engines.
CoInitializeEx(NULL, COINIT_MULTITHREADED);

// Get a pointer to the object's class factory.
IClassFactory* pClassFactory;
CoGetClassObject(CLSID_InsideCOM, CLSCTX_LOCAL_SERVER, NULL,
    IID_IClassFactory, (void**)&pClassFactory);
```

CoGetClassObject instructs the Service Control Manager (SCM) to locate the executable component containing the *InsideCOM* coclass and launch it. Recall that *CoGetClassObject* is also used internally by *CoCreateInstance(Ex)*, the standard object creation function in COM+; we'll use the *CoGetClassObject* function for clarity.

---

5. We'll describe how to use custom marshaling to implement marshal-by-value semantics later in this chapter.

On start-up, a typical executable component performs the following standard steps:

```
// component.cpp

// Start your engines.
CoInitializeEx(NULL, COINIT_MULTITHREADED);

// Instantiate the class factory object.
IClassFactory* pClassFactory = new CFactory();

// Register the object in the global object table.
DWORD dwRegister;
CoRegisterClassObject(CLSID_InsideCOM, pClassFactory,
    CLSCTX_LOCAL_SERVER, REGCLS_MULTIPLEUSE, &dwRegister);
```

The *CFactory* class is instantiated using the C++ *new* operator, and the resulting *IClassFactory* interface pointer is passed to the *CoRegisterClassObject* function. *CoRegisterClassObject* must somehow take this *IClassFactory* pointer and marshal it to any client process (on any machine) that calls *CoCreateInstance(Ex)* or *CoGetClassObject*. *CoRegisterClassObject* in turn calls *CoMarshalInterface* to do the dirty work of marshaling the *IClassFactory* interface pointer.

CoMarshalInterface is the fundamental COM+ interface pointer marshaling function. It starts by asking the object, "Hey, will that be custom or standard marshaling?" by calling *IUnknown::QueryInterface* for the *IMarshal* interface. *IMarshal* is the fundamental custom marshaling interface. If an object implements *IMarshal*, *CoMarshalInterface* knows that the object wants to use custom marshaling. If an object does not support *IMarshal*, as shown in the following code, *CoMarshalInterface* assumes that the object wants to use standard marshaling:

```
// component.cpp

HRESULT CFactory::QueryInterface(REFIID riid, void** ppv)
{
    if((riid == IID_IUnknown) || (riid == IID_IClassFactory))
        *ppv = (IClassFactory*)this;
    else
    {
        // IID_IMarshal?! No way!
        *ppv = NULL;                // No implementation of IMarshal,
        return E_NOINTERFACE; // so standard marshaling is used.
    }
    AddRef();
    return S_OK;
}
```

Since *IClassFactory* is a standard interface, Microsoft provides marshaling code as part of ole32.dll, the system-wide COM+ run time. You are able to override the built-in marshaling to provide custom marshaling code for *IClassFactory*, but the benefits of doing so are dubious. Thus, in the class object's *IUnknown::QueryInterface* implementation shown in the preceding code, any request for the *IMarshal* interface returns *E_NOINTERFACE*. Once *CoMarshalInterface* determines that standard marshaling is in order, it marshals the *IClassFactory* interface using the proxy/stub code provided by ole32.dll.

Returning to our examination of the client application, the next step normally executed is shown here in boldface:

```
// client.cpp

// Start your engines.
CoInitializeEx(NULL, COINIT_MULTITHREADED);

// Get a pointer to the object's class factory.
IClassFactory* pClassFactory;
CoGetClassObject(CLSID_InsideCOM, CLSCTX_LOCAL_SERVER, NULL,
    IID_IClassFactory, (void**)&pClassFactory);

// Instantiate the InsideCOM object
// and get a pointer to its IUnknown interface.
IUnknown* pUnknown;
pClassFactory->CreateInstance(NULL, IID_IUnknown,
    (void**)&pUnknown);
```

The client calls *IClassFactory::CreateInstance* to request that the *InsideCOM* coclass be instantiated and a pointer to *IUnknown* be returned. The *IUnknown* interface pointer about to be returned by the *IClassFactory::CreateInstance* method must be marshaled to the client, so the system-provided marshaling code for the *IClassFactory* interface calls *CoMarshalInterface* to marshal the *IUnknown* interface pointer. *CoMarshalInterface*[6] calls the *InsideCOM* object's *IUnknown::QueryInterface* method, requesting the *IMarshal* interface to determine whether the object wants to use standard or custom marshaling.

At this point, thoroughly exhausted by the narrative sequence above, you think, "What the heck, I'll take standard marshaling and call it a day." After all, *IUnknown* is a very standard interface, so surely you don't need to provide custom marshaling code for *IUnknown*. Custom marshaling, however, is done on a per-object basis, not on a per-interface basis like standard marshaling, so

---

6. *CoMarshalInterface* first calls *QueryInterface* for your *IUnknown* interface pointer several times as part of its standard stub creation and identity testing.

it really is an all-or-nothing proposition. While the system will be more than happy to provide you with standard marshaling for *IUnknown*, the *InsideCOM* object also implements the *ISum* custom interface, which the system knows nothing about. So although the standard marshaler would properly handle the *IUnknown* interface, any attempt to get the *ISum* interface would fail. Thus, we are now at a crucial juncture. You must either respond affirmatively to the *CoMarshalInterface* query for *IMarshal*, opening your mind to the path of custom marshaling, or again respond with *E_NOINTERFACE*, indicating a desire to proceed with standard marshaling.

Can You Say "Custom Marshaling"?

The *InsideCOM* object's implementation of the *IUnknown::QueryInterface* method is shown in the following code; support for the *IMarshal* interface is indicated in boldface:

```
HRESULT CInsideCOM::QueryInterface(REFIID riid, void** ppv)
{
    if(riid == IID_IUnknown)
        *ppv = (ISum*)this;

    // IMarshal? Absolutely!
    else if(riid == IID_IMarshal)
        *ppv = (IMarshal*)this;

    else if(riid == IID_ISum)
        *ppv = (ISum*)this;
    else
    {
        *ppv = NULL;
        return E_NOINTERFACE;
    }
    AddRef();
    return S_OK;
}
```

Once a pointer to *IMarshal* is returned by the *QueryInterface* method, the *CoMarshalInterface* function, called by the standard marshaling code for *IClassFactory::CreateInstance*, is entitled to call any of the six methods in the *IMarshal* interface. These methods are shown here in IDL notation:

```
interface IMarshal : IUnknown
{
    // Object implements this method.
    // Get the CLSID of the proxy object.
```

(continued)

```
HRESULT GetUnmarshalClass(
    [in] REFIID riid,
    [in, unique] void* pv,
    [in] DWORD dwDestContext,
    [in, unique] void* pvDestContext,
    [in] DWORD dwFlags,
    [out] CLSID *pClsid);

// Object implements this method.
// Get the maximum space needed to marshal the interface.
HRESULT GetMarshalSizeMax(
    [in] REFIID riid,
    [in, unique] void* pv,
    [in] DWORD dwDestContext,
    [in, unique] void* pvDestContext,
    [in] DWORD dwFlags,
    [out] DWORD* pSize);

// Object implements this method.
// Marshal that interface and write it to the stream.
HRESULT MarshalInterface(
    [in, unique] IStream* pStream,
    [in] REFIID riid,
    [in, unique] void* pv,
    [in] DWORD dwDestContext,
    [in, unique] void* pvDestContext,
    [in] DWORD dwFlags);

// Object implements this method.
// Tell the proxy that we're going to shut down.
HRESULT DisconnectObject([in] DWORD dwReserved);

// Object implements this method.
// Release the marshaled data in the stream.
HRESULT ReleaseMarshalData([in, unique] IStream* pStream);

// Proxy implements this method.
// Unmarshal that interface from the stream.
HRESULT UnmarshalInterface(
    [in, unique] IStream *pStream,
    [in] REFIID riid,
    [out] void** ppv);
}
```

IMarshal is a peculiar interface because the first five of its six methods are called in the object and the remaining method, *UnmarshalInterface*, is called in the proxy. Although COM+ requires that any object returning an interface pointer from *QueryInterface* fully support that interface, in the case of *IMarshal* some of these methods are never called in the object or in the proxy. Nevertheless, you must provide dummy implementations of all six *IMarshal* methods in both the object and the proxy. For example, the object provides the following dummy implementation of the *IMarshal::UnmarshalInterface* method:

```
HRESULT CInsideCOM::UnmarshalInterface(IStream* pStream,
    REFIID riid, void** ppv)
{
    // This method should be called only in the proxy, not here.
    return E_UNEXPECTED;
}
```

After the object says, "Yes, I perform custom marshaling," the following steps are executed in the component:

1. *IMarshal::GetUnmarshalClass* is called to obtain the CLSID of the proxy object.

2. *IMarshal::GetMarshalSizeMax* is called to determine the size of the marshaling packet that the interface needs.

3. The system allocates the memory and then creates a stream object that wraps the memory buffer.

4. *IMarshal::MarshalInterface* is called to tell the object to marshal the interface pointer into the stream.

At this point, the buffer allocated in step 3 contains all the information necessary to create and initialize the proxy object within the client's address space. This buffer is communicated back to the client process, where the proxy object is created. Then *IMarshal::UnmarshalInterface* is called in the proxy to initialize the interface proxy. That's it—the whole purpose of the *IMarshal* interface is to give the object a chance to send one measly message back to the proxy!

Now that you have a high-level overview of the process, let's look at custom marshaling in detail.

Pardon Me, What Is the CLSID of Your Proxy Object?

CoMarshalInterface first calls the *IMarshal::GetUnmarshalClass* method to request that the object provide the CLSID of the proxy object. In effect, *GetUnmarshalClass* asks the object, "What is the CLSID of your proxy object?" This value is returned via the CLSID pointer in the last parameter of

GetUnmarshalClass. An implementation of *IMarshal::GetUnmarshalClass* might look like this:

```
CLSID CLSID_InsideCOMProxy =
    {0x10000004,0x0000,0x0000,0x00,0x00,0x00,0x00,
    0x00,0x00,0x00,0x01};

HRESULT CInsideCOM::GetUnmarshalClass(REFIID riid, void* pv,
    DWORD dwDestContext, void* pvDestContext, DWORD dwFlags,
    CLSID* pClsid)
{
    // We handle only the local marshaling case.
    if(dwDestContext == MSHCTX_DIFFERENTMACHINE)
    {
        IMarshal* pMarshal;
        // Create a standard marshaler (proxy manager).
        CoGetStandardMarshal(riid, (ISum*)pv, dwDestContext,
            pvDestContext, dwFlags, &pMarshal);

        // Load the interface proxy.
        HRESULT hr = pMarshal->GetUnmarshalClass(riid, pv,
            dwDestContext, pvDestContext, dwFlags, pClsid);
        pMarshal->Release();
        return hr;
    }
    *pClsid = CLSID_InsideCOMProxy;
    return S_OK;
}
```

COM+ holds onto this CLSID, which it sends to the client as part of the marshaling packet for use in launching the proxy object in the client's address space. Notice that much of the code in *GetUnmarshalClass* deals with the situation in which the client runs on a different machine. Since this custom marshaling example uses shared memory, we must delegate marshaling to the standard marshaler when the client is not running on the local machine. *CoGetStandardMarshal* returns a pointer to the standard marshaler's implementation of the *IMarshal* interface, on which we call the *IMarshal::GetUnmarshalClass* method to get the CLSID of the standard marshaler's proxy.

How Big Did You Say Your Interface Is?

Next, *CoMarshalInterface* calls *IMarshal::GetMarshalSizeMax*, as shown in the following code. *GetMarshalSizeMax* asks the object, "What is the maximum space you need for marshaling your interface?" In this implementation, the object declares that it currently needs a maximum of 255 bytes. Notice that once again the code checks to see whether the client is running on the same machine. If it is not, we delegate the call to the standard marshaler.

```
HRESULT CInsideCOM::GetMarshalSizeMax(REFIID riid, void* pv,
    DWORD dwDestContext, void* pvDestContext, DWORD dwFlags,
    DWORD* pSize)
{
    // We handle only the local marshaling case.
    if(dwDestContext == MSHCTX_DIFFERENTMACHINE)
    {
        IMarshal* pMarshal;
        CoGetStandardMarshal(riid, (ISum*)pv, dwDestContext,
            pvDestContext, dwFlags, &pMarshal);
        HRESULT hr = pMarshal->GetMarshalSizeMax(riid, pv,
            dwDestContext, pvDestContext, dwFlags, pSize);
        pMarshal->Release();
        return hr;
    }

    // We need 255 bytes of storage to marshal the ISum
    // interface pointer.
    *pSize = 255;
    return S_OK;
}
```

To the value returned by the *GetMarshalSizeMax* method, *CoMarshalInterface* adds the space needed for the marshaling data header and for the proxy CLSID obtained in the call to *IMarshal::GetUnmarshalClass*. This technique yields the true maximum size in bytes required to marshal the interface, which is used to allocate a buffer large enough to hold the marshaled interface pointer. This buffer is then turned into a stream[7] by calling the *CreateStreamOnHGlobal* function. *CoMarshalInterface*, before it does anything else, writes the CLSID of the proxy object into the stream object by calling the *WriteClassStm* function.

Finally, *CoMarshalInterface* is ready to marshal the interface, so it calls *IMarshal::MarshalInterface* to say to the component, "Pack up that interface and let's get moving!" *MarshalInterface* marshals the requested interface pointer into the stream object provided as the first parameter. It normally does this by calling the *IStream::Write* method to write the marshaled interface pointer into the stream object.

---

7. An object that implements the *IStream* interface

What Is a Marshaled Interface Pointer?

Perhaps you're wondering exactly what a marshaled interface pointer consists of. A marshaled interface pointer can be whatever you want it to be. Once the *IMarshal* dance is over, you want the proxy to be able to communicate with the component to make method calls. That's right, *IMarshal* is designed to marshal interface pointers only. Once the interface pointer is available on the client side, all the work of packing function parameters, sending them to the component, and unpacking them is left to you! You can perform these tasks however you like. For cross-machine calls, you might use sockets or named pipes; for cross-process calls, you might use a file-mapping object for shared memory.

Your implementation of *IMarshal::MarshalInterface* must write to the stream whatever data is needed to initialize the proxy on the client side. Such data might include the information needed to connect to the object, such as a handle to a window, the name of a named pipe, or an Internet Protocol (IP) address and port number. When you implement custom marshaling to obtain marshal-by-value semantics, the marshaled interface pointer should contain the entire state of the object.

In the following code, *MarshalInterface* creates a file-mapping object to share memory between the proxy and the component in order to pass function parameters. Then it creates two event objects that are later used for synchronizing method calls. The names of these Win32 kernel objects are written into the marshaling stream. In other words, a marshaled interface pointer for *ISum* consists of the string "*FileMap,StubEvent,ProxyEvent*".

```
HRESULT CInsideCOM::MarshalInterface(IStream* pStream,
    REFIID riid, void* pv, DWORD dwDestContext,
    void* pvDestContext, DWORD dwFlags)
{
    // We handle only the local marshaling case.
    if(dwDestContext == MSHCTX_DIFFERENTMACHINE)
    {
        IMarshal* pMarshal;
        CoGetStandardMarshal(riid, (ISum*)pv, dwDestContext,
            pvDestContext, dwFlags, &pMarshal);
        HRESULT hr = pMarshal->MarshalInterface(pStream,
            riid, pv, dwDestContext, pvDestContext, dwFlags);
        pMarshal->Release();
        return hr;
    }
```

```
ULONG num_written;
char* szFileMapName = "FileMap";
char* szStubEventName = "StubEvent";
char* szProxyEventName = "ProxyEvent";
char buffer_to_write[255];

// Don't let your object fly away.
AddRef();

hFileMap = CreateFileMapping((HANDLE)0xFFFFFFFF, NULL,
    PAGE_READWRITE, 0, 255, szFileMapName);
hStubEvent = CreateEvent(NULL, FALSE, FALSE,
    szStubEventName);
hProxyEvent = CreateEvent(NULL, FALSE, FALSE,
    szProxyEventName);

strcpy(buffer_to_write, szFileMapName);
strcat(buffer_to_write, ",");
strcat(buffer_to_write, szStubEventName);
strcat(buffer_to_write, ",");
strcat(buffer_to_write, szProxyEventName);

return pStream->Write(buffer_to_write,
    strlen(buffer_to_write)+1, &num_written);
}
```

As with the *IMarshal::GetUnmarshalClass* and *IMarshal:: GetMarshal-SizeMax* methods shown earlier, the *MarshalInterface* method delegates to the standard marshaler if the destination context does not indicate that the client is running on the local machine. The extra *AddRef* thrown into the preceding *MarshalInterface* code is necessary. When you use custom marshaling, no stub is available to hold a reference count on the object itself. Without this *AddRef*, the *InsideCOM* object would simply exit before the client has had a chance to call it. In the next section, you'll see that the proxy eventually calls *Release*, which is forwarded to the component to undo this *AddRef*.

Remember that *CoMarshalInterface* carefully orchestrates all of these steps. To review what we've covered so far, look at the following pseudo-code for *CoMarshalInterface*, which shows how interface pointers are marshaled:

```
// AddRef the incoming pointer to verify that it is safe.
pUnknown->AddRef();

// Do you support custom marshaling?
IMarshal* pMarshal;
HRESULT hr = pUnknown->QueryInterface(IID_IMarshal,
    (void**)&pMarshal);
```

(continued)

```
// I guess not, so we'll use standard marshaling.
if(hr == E_NOINTERFACE)
    CoGetStandardMarshal(riid, pUnknown, dwDestContext,
        pvDestContext, dwFlags, &pMarshal);

// OK, what's the CLSID of your proxy?
CLSID clsid;
pMarshal->GetUnmarshalClass(riid, pUnknown, dwDestContext,
    pvDestContext, dwFlags, &clsid);

// How much space do you need?
ULONG packetSize;
pMarshal->GetMarshalSizeMax(riid, pUnknown, dwDestContext,
    pvDestContext, dwFlags, &packetSize);

// Allocate that memory.
HGLOBAL pMem = GlobalAlloc(GHND, packetSize + sizeof(CLSID));

// Turn it into a stream object.
IStream* pStream;
CreateStreamOnHGlobal(pMem, FALSE, &pStream);

// Write the CLSID of the proxy into the stream.
WriteClassStm(pStream, clsid);

// Marshal that interface into the stream.
pMarshal->MarshalInterface(pStream, riid, pUnknown,
    dwDestContext, pvDestContext, dwFlags);

// Release everything in sight.
pStream->Release();
pMarshal->Release();
pUnknown->Release();
```

At this point, the SCM is ready to send the stream object back to the client process. Since the SCM was responsible for launching the component to begin with, it knows exactly what sort of a barrier lies between the client and the component. This barrier is described by one of the marshaling contexts in the *MSHCTX* enumeration, shown in the table below. The mechanism you use to transmit data between the client and the component depends on the marshaling context. For example, if the client is communicating with the component process on the same machine (*MSHCTX_LOCAL*), you can use a file-mapping object to share memory. If the two processes run on different computers (*MSHCTX_DIFFERENTMACHINE*), you can use a network protocol such as named pipes, sockets, RPC, NetBIOS, or mailslots.

MSHCTX Enumeration	Value	Description
MSHCTX_LOCAL	0	The object is running in another process of the current machine.
MSHCTX_NOSHAREDMEM	1	The object does not have shared memory access; unused.
MSHCTX_DIFFERENTMACHINE	2	The object is running on a different machine.
MSHCTX_INPROC	3	The object is running in another apartment of the current process.
MSHCTX_CROSSCTX	4	The object is running in another context of the current apartment.

At the end of the marshaling sequence, we're left with a marshaled interface pointer that can be sent directly to the client or be stored in a table waiting for a client to request it. The flag passed as the last parameter to *CoMarshalInterface* indicates whether the marshaled data is to be transmitted back to the client process—the normal case—or written to the class table, from which multiple clients can retrieve it. This flag can be one of the values from the *MSHLFLAGS* enumeration constants listed in the following table.

MSHLFLAGS Enumeration	Description
MSHLFLAGS_NORMAL	Indicates that unmarshaling is occurring immediately.
MSHLFLAGS_TABLESTRONG	Unmarshaling is not occurring immediately. Keeps object alive; must be explicitly released.
MSHLFLAGS_TABLEWEAK	Unmarshaling is not occurring immediately. Doesn't keep object alive; still must be released.
MSHLFLAGS_NOPING	Turns off garbage collection by not pinging objects to determine whether they are still alive.* Can be combined with any of the other *MSHLFLAGS* enumeration constants.

* For more about garbage collection, see Chapter 19.

The *MSHLFLAGS_NORMAL* flag indicates that the unmarshaling is occurring immediately, such as when the component returns an interface pointer in response to a client's call to *IUnknown::QueryInterface*. *MSHLFLAGS_TABLESTRONG* and *MSHLFLAGS_TABLEWEAK*, however, indicate that the unmarshaling isn't happening at the present time. These flags indicate that the marshaled interface pointer is to be stored in a global table that is accessible to all processes via COM+. When a client process wants to connect, the marshaled interface pointer is already there, ready and waiting. For example, table marshaling is used by the *CoRegisterClassObject* function, which is called by executable components. Internally, *CoRegisterClassObject* calls *CoMarshalInterface* with the *MSHLFLAGS_TABLESTRONG* flag. This stores a marshaled interface pointer to the class object in the class table, which clients can request using *CoGetClassObject*. Only when a client calls *CoGetClassObject* is the marshaled interface pointer sent to the client for unmarshaling.

If *MSHLFLAGS_TABLESTRONG* is specified, the *IUnknown::AddRef* method is automatically called to ensure that the object remains in memory. In other words, the presence of the marshaled interface pointer in the class table counts as a strong reference to the interface being marshaled, meaning that it is sufficient to keep the object alive. This is the case with *CoRegisterClassObject*. When the *CoRevokeClassObject* function is later called to remove the marshaled interface pointer from the class table, *CoRevokeClassObject* calls the *CoRelease-MarshalData* function to free the stream object containing the marshaled interface pointer. *CoReleaseMarshalData* is a relatively simple helper function that instantiates the proxy and invokes the *IMarshal::ReleaseMarshalData* method.

MSHLFLAGS_TABLEWEAK indicates that the presence of the marshaled interface pointer in the class table acts as a weak reference to the interface being marshaled, which means that it is not sufficient to keep the object alive because *AddRef* is not called. You typically use *MSHLFLAGS_TABLEWEAK* when you register an object in the Running Object Table (ROT). The presence of this flag prevents the object's entry in the ROT from keeping the object alive in the absence of any other connections.[8]

Unmarshaling the Interface Pointer

The *IMarshal* interface provides a mechanism by which the component can marshal its interface pointer into a stream object that the client can unmarshal. Just as *CoMarshalInterface* directs the marshaling of an interface pointer, *CoUnmarshalInterface* directs the unmarshaling of an interface pointer. Look at the following function declaration for *CoUnmarshalInterface*; you should be able to tell that *QueryInterface* will be involved somewhere along the way:

```
STDAPI CoUnmarshalInterface(IStream* pStream, REFIID riid,
    void** ppv);
```

---

8. See Chapter 11 for more information on the ROT.

CoUnmarshalInterface examines the stream object containing the marshaled interface pointer to find the CLSID of the proxy object, which is required to unmarshal the remainder of the stream object. The CLSID is read out of the stream by the *ReadClassStm* function. The SCM then instantiates the proxy object specified by the CLSID by calling *CoCreateInstance* and requesting the *IMarshal* interface. A proxy used for custom marshaling an object must implement the *IMarshal* interface.[9]

Figure 14-3 shows how the SCM loads the proxy in the client's address space and that the proxy and the object communicate directly via a private protocol of their own choosing.

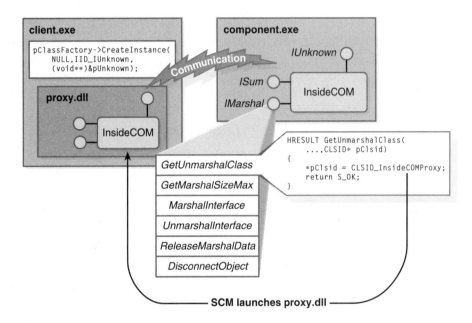

Figure 14-3.
An example of custom marshaling showing the proxy and the object communicating.

Here's a quick recap. The client calls *CoCreateInstance* to instantiate the *InsideCOM* component. Then *CoMarshalInterface* calls *IUnknown::QueryInterface* to determine whether the object supports the *IMarshal* interface and hence custom marshaling. Since this is the case, the *ISum* interface pointer is marshaled into a stream object and returned to the proxy manager.

---

9. If standard marshaling is used, the CLSID in the stream is *CLSID_StdMarshal*, or *{00000017-0000-0000-C000-000000000046}*.

The *CoUnmarshalInterface* function instantiates the proxy and manages the unmarshaling of the stream object. Once a pointer to the *IMarshal* interface of the proxy object has been retrieved, *CoUnmarshalInterface* calls *IMarshal::UnmarshalInterface*. This method, implemented by the proxy, reads data from the marshaling stream using *IStream::Read*, and uses that information to establish a connection with the object. Again, you can use any communication mechanism (named pipes, sockets, and so on). From this communication, the *UnmarshalInterface* method returns the unmarshaled pointer to the requested interface. In reality, the unmarshaled pointer is simply a pointer to the proxy's implementation of the requested interface that is now loaded in the client's address space. *CoUnmarshalInterface* also calls *IMarshal::ReleaseMarshalData* to free whatever data might be stored in the marshaling packet; this means that you need not call the *CoReleaseMarshalData* function when unmarshaling an interface pointer.

Here is the proxy's implementation of *IMarshal::UnmarshalInterface*, which reads the data from the stream previously marshaled by the object in *IMarshal::MarshalInterface*:

```
HRESULT CInsideCOM::UnmarshalInterface(IStream* pStream,
    REFIID riid, void** ppv)
{
    unsigned long num_read;
    char buffer_to_read[255];
    char* pszFileMapName;
    char* pszStubEventName;
    char* pszProxyEventName;

    pStream->Read((void*)buffer_to_read, 255, &num_read);

    pszFileMapName = strtok(buffer_to_read, ",");
    pszStubEventName = strtok(NULL, ",");
    pszProxyEventName = strtok(NULL, ",");

    hFileMap = OpenFileMapping(FILE_MAP_WRITE, FALSE,
        pszFileMapName);
    pMem = MapViewOfFile(hFileMap, FILE_MAP_WRITE, 0, 0, 0);

    hStubEvent = OpenEvent(EVENT_MODIFY_STATE, FALSE,
        pszStubEventName);
    hProxyEvent = OpenEvent(EVENT_MODIFY_STATE|SYNCHRONIZE,
        FALSE, pszProxyEventName);

    return QueryInterface(riid, ppv);
}
```

Eventually, when the component exits, *CoDisconnectObject* is called, which in turn calls the *IMarshal::DisconnectObject* method in the object. Note that clients do not call *CoDisconnectObject*; they should use *IUnknown::Release* for that purpose. *CoDisconnectObject* is a helper function that disconnects all remote client connections that maintain interface pointers to the specified object. First, *CoDisconnectObject* queries the object for its *IMarshal* interface pointer; if the object does not support custom marshaling, *CoGetStandardMarshal* is called to obtain a pointer to the standard marshaler. *CoDisconnectObject* then uses the *IMarshal* pointer to call the *IMarshal::DisconnectObject* method. It is the job of *DisconnectObject* to notify the proxy that the object itself is exiting and that it should return the error *CO_E_OBJECTNOTCONNECTED* to client requests.

The following pseudo-code summarizes the steps taken in the client process by *CoUnmarshalInterface* to ensure that unmarshaling is done correctly:

```
// Turn the marshaled interface pointer into a stream object.
IStream* pStream;
CreateStreamOnHGlobal(hMem, FALSE, &pStream);

 // Get the CLSID of the proxy object out of the stream.
CLSID clsid;
ReadClassStm(pStream, &clsid);

// Instantiate that proxy object.
IMarshal* pMarshal;
CoCreateInstance(clsid, 0, CLSCTX_INPROC_SERVER, IID_IMarshal,
    (void**)&pMarshal);

// Clone the stream.
IStream* pStreamClone;
pStream->Clone(&pStreamClone);

// Unmarshal your interface.
pMarshal->UnmarshalInterface(pStream, riid, ppv);

// Release any data in the stream.
pMarshal->ReleaseMarshalData(pStreamClone);

// Release anything left.
pStream->Release();
pStreamClone->Release();
pMarshal->Release();

// Free the marshaled memory packet.
GlobalFree(hMem);
```

When the client calls the *ISum::Sum* method, it is actually talking to the in-process proxy object. One of the major reasons for performing custom marshaling is to be able to intelligently reduce the number of cross-process or cross-machine calls. For example, rather than making a call to the component every time the client calls *AddRef* or *Release*, the proxy simply keeps a reference count locally. Only when the last *Release* call is made and the reference count returns to 0 does the proxy actually forward the *Release* call to the object. Interestingly, the remoting infrastructure of COM+ performs this type of *IUnknown* optimization automatically for objects that use standard marshaling.[10]

Here is the proxy's implementation of the *Release* method:

```
ULONG CInsideCOM::Release()
{
    // Regular Release; don't bother calling the object.
    if(--m_cRef != 0)
        return m_cRef;

    // Notify the object that this is the last Release.
    short method_id = 1; // ISum::Release
    memcpy(pMem, &method_id, sizeof(short));
    SetEvent(hStubEvent);
    delete this;
    return 0;
}
```

When the reference count returns to 0, this function copies the value of the *method_id* variable into the file-mapping memory shared by the proxy and the component. It then calls *SetEvent* to notify the object that it is requesting service. The object is waiting for this event in the following code:

```
void TalkToProxy()
{
    while(hStubEvent == 0)
        Sleep(0);

    void* pMem = MapViewOfFile(hFileMap, FILE_MAP_WRITE,
        0, 0, 0);
    short method_id = 0;

    while(true)
    {
        WaitForSingleObject(hStubEvent, INFINITE);
        memcpy(&method_id, pMem, sizeof(short));
        switch(method_id) // What method did the proxy call?
```

---

10. This optimization is discussed further in Chapter 19.

```
    {
    case 1:     // IUnknown::Release
        CoDisconnectObject(reinterpret_cast<IUnknown*>(
            g_pInsideCOM), 0);
        g_pInsideCOM->Release();
        return;
    case 2:     // ISum::Sum
        SumTransmit s;
        memcpy(&s, (short*)pMem+1, sizeof(SumTransmit));
        g_pInsideCOM->Sum(s.x, s.y, &s.sum);
        memcpy(pMem, &s, sizeof(s));
        SetEvent(hProxyEvent);
    }
  }
}
```

After the proxy sets the stub event, the object retrieves the first byte, which indicates what method is being called. In this simple implementation, the object expects to receive only one of two calls from the proxy: *Release* or *Sum*. The object then deciphers the call and forwards it to the actual implementation. The *Sum* method, for example, requires that the object unpack the parameters from the SumTransmit structure and then repack the return value. The SumTransmit structure, defined below, stores the parameters and the return value of the *Sum* method:

```
struct SumTransmit
{
    int x;
    int y;
    int sum;
};
```

As shown in the following proxy code, we wait until the object has finished adding the values before we retrieve the result for the client. We use a second event object (*hProxyEvent*) to determine when the component has finished processing.

```
HRESULT CInsideCOM::Sum(int x, int y, int* sum)
{
    SumTransmit s;
    s.x = x;
    s.y = y;
    short method_id = 2; // ISum::Sum

    memcpy(pMem, &method_id, sizeof(short));
    memcpy((short*)pMem+1, &s, sizeof(SumTransmit));
```

(continued)

449

```
    SetEvent(hStubEvent);
    WaitForSingleObject(hProxyEvent, INFINITE);

    memcpy(&s, pMem, sizeof(s));

    *sum = s.sum;
    return S_OK;
}
```

The custom marshaling mechanism in this example depends on shared memory being available between the proxy and the object; this is possible only if both the client and the object are running on the same machine. To create a custom marshaling sample that works across machines, we would have to use a network-capable mechanism.

Marshal-by-Value

One specialized use of custom marshaling is known as marshal-by-value. When interface pointers are unmarshaled in COM+, the client always receives a pointer, usually through a proxy, to the original object; this is known as marshal-by-reference because the client receives a reference to the object. With marshal-by-value, on the other hand, the client receives its very own copy of the object rather than a reference to the original object. This is most useful for objects whose state is immutable—such as an object that is initialized with some data during creation and whose state never changes after that. Monikers are a great example: after you create a moniker, you can never change the object that it names. If you want to name a different object, you must create a new moniker.

For objects with immutable state, marshal-by-reference makes little sense because it requires that every call to the object be made across whatever marshaling context separates the client and the object. Obviously, the overhead is greatest if calls are made across machines. Marshal-by-value support can offer a significant optimization because a clone of the object is created in the client's apartment. Monikers, for example, have built-in marshal-by-value support.

Adding marshal-by-value support in COM+ is not easy because the standard marshaler provides marshal-by-reference semantics. You must use custom marshaling to accomplish this. Basically, the technique used to support marshal-by-value is simply to serialize the entire state of the object into the marshaling stream during the *IMarshal::MarshalInterface* method call. Since COM+ automatically returns the marshaling stream to the proxy, the proxy can read the object's state in the *IMarshal::UnmarshalInterface* method and create what is effectively a clone of the original object in the client's address space. Objects that support marshal-by-value must be designed as in-process components so they can be instantiated in the client and server processes.

As you've seen, implementing the *IMarshal* interface is not easy. However, if you examine the methods of *IMarshal* and *IPersistStream*,[11] you'll find that they share several methods that have similar purposes, as shown in the table below.

IMarshal Methods	*IPersistStream* Methods
GetMarshalSizeMax	*GetSizeMax*
GetUnmarshalClass	*GetClassID*
MarshalInterface	*Save*
UnmarshalInterface	*Load*

This realization means that you can implement several of the methods of the *IMarshal* interface by delegating to the methods of *IPersistStream*. Since many more objects support *IPersistStream* than *IMarshal*, this is an important discovery. Part of the challenge of supporting marshal-by-value semantics is obtaining the object's state; for objects that implement the *IPersistStream* interface, this is almost trivial because the object automatically saves its state to a stream in the *IPersistStream::Save* method. You can actually provide an aggregatable implementation of *IMarshal* that performs custom marshaling simply by delegating to the outer object's implementation of *IPersistStream*; Figure 14-4 illustrates this architecture.

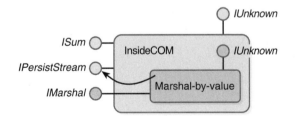

Figure 14-4.
An object that implements IPersistStream *obtains support for* IMarshal *by aggregating a marshal-by-value object.*

11. For information about object persistence, see Chapter 10.

451

On the companion CD, in the Samples\Custom Marshaling\Marshal By Value folder, you'll find an implementation of an aggregatable object that provides an implementation of *IMarshal* with marshal-by-value semantics for any object that aggregates it and implements *IPersistStream*. The following code fragment shows the relevant methods of the *IMarshal* implementation that delegate to the outer object's *IPersistStream* methods:

```
HRESULT CMarshalByValue::GetUnmarshalClass(REFIID riid,
    void* pv, DWORD dwDestContext, void* pvDestContext,
    DWORD dwFlags, CLSID* pClsid)
{
    IPersistStream* pPersistStream = 0;
    HRESULT hr = m_pUnknownOuter->QueryInterface(
        IID_IPersistStream, (void**)&pPersistStream);

    // Call the outer object's GetClassID method.
    pPersistStream->GetClassID(pClsid);

    pPersistStream->Release();
    return S_OK;
}


HRESULT CMarshalByValue::GetMarshalSizeMax(REFIID riid,
    void* pv, DWORD dwDestContext, void* pvDestContext,
    DWORD dwFlags, DWORD* pSize)
{
    IPersistStream* pPersistStream = 0;
    m_pUnknownOuter->QueryInterface(IID_IPersistStream,
        (void**)&pPersistStream);

    // Call the outer object's GetSizeMax method.
    ULARGE_INTEGER size;
    pPersistStream->GetSizeMax(&size);
    *pSize = size.LowPart;

    pPersistStream->Release();
        return S_OK;
}

HRESULT CMarshalByValue::MarshalInterface(IStream* pStream,
    REFIID riid, void* pv, DWORD dwDestContext,
    void* pvDestContext, DWORD dwFlags)
{
    AddRef();
```

```
    IPersistStream* pPersistStream = 0;
    m_pUnknownOuter->QueryInterface(IID_IPersistStream,
        (void**)&pPersistStream);

    // Call the outer object's Save method.
    HRESULT hr = pPersistStream->Save(pStream, TRUE);

    pPersistStream->Release();
    return hr;
}

HRESULT CMarshalByValue::UnmarshalInterface(IStream* pStream,
    REFIID riid, void** ppv)
{

    IPersistStream* pPersistStream = 0;
    m_pUnknownOuter->QueryInterface(IID_IPersistStream,
        (void**)&pPersistStream);

    // Call the outer object's Load method.
    pPersistStream->Load(pStream);

    pPersistStream->Release();
    return m_pUnknownOuter->QueryInterface(riid, ppv);
}
```

CHAPTER FIFTEEN

Standard Marshaling

In earlier chapters, we used the term *standard marshaling* to refer to marshaling code generated by the MIDL compiler since this generated code actually uses the standard marshaling technique. In this chapter, we'll discuss standard marshaling without the support of the MIDL compiler, and we'll introduce *handler marshaling*—a variation of marshaling that lies somewhere between standard marshaling and custom marshaling.

From the programmer's perspective, the main difference between standard marshaling and custom marshaling is that the standard marshaler provides built-in support for transmitting data between the proxy and the stub in all marshaling contexts. When you use custom marshaling, it is your responsibility to determine what form of communication is best for the job.

Standard marshaling is a specific implementation of the generic custom marshaling architecture, just as type library marshaling is a specific implementation of standard marshaling. Remember that both standard and custom marshaling are appropriate marshaling solutions for custom interfaces such as *ISum*. Most standard interfaces, such as *IDispatch*, already have marshaling code provided by Microsoft. You could replace this code with your own marshaling code, but this would be a fruitless effort.

Standard marshaling is the marshaling mechanism used by MIDL-generated proxy/stub code. However, you can write a proxy/stub DLL without using the MIDL compiler to generate the code. In many situations, handcrafted code is desirable. Recall the image-processing example from Chapter 14, in which clients sent bitmaps to an object for processing. These bitmaps might be very large and could bog down the network if the client and the object are run on different machines. To reduce the amount of network traffic when transferring large bitmaps, you can write proxy code that compresses the bitmap before sending it and stub code that decompresses the bitmap before forwarding it to the object. Granted, you can build such compression code directly into the client and the object, but doing so would place the burden of compression on the clients. Isolating the compression-related code in the proxy and the stub code insulates the client and the object from this bandwidth optimization.

When you use standard marshaling, you don't have to modify the client code or the object code. Instead, you build and register a single DLL containing both the proxy and stub code. Generally speaking, every custom interface needs a proxy/stub DLL for marshaling purposes. When an interface pointer is marshaled back to a client, the system automatically loads the proxy/stub DLL into the client's and the component's address spaces. The proxy object is instantiated in the client's address space; the stub object is instantiated in the component's address space.

The Standard Marshaling Architecture

In standard marshaling, COM+ provides a generic proxy object, called the *proxy manager*, and a generic stub object, sometimes called the *stub manager*. These communicate through an RPC-based channel. When you marshal a custom interface pointer, the standard marshaling architecture lets you plug in an interface marshaler that knows how to marshal that specific interface; proxies and stubs for most of the standard interfaces are loaded from ole32.dll. When loaded, interface proxies are always aggregated with the proxy manager, giving clients the illusion that all of the interfaces are exposed from a single object and thus preserving the identity of the object even when it is remoted to another address space. Without this feature, there would be no way to distinguish between calls to the same interfaces implemented on entirely different objects.

A client holding a pointer to the proxy manager's *IUnknown* interface believes that it holds a pointer to the actual object in the component's address space because the proxy manager represents the object in the client process. The proxy manager appears to implement the interfaces of the actual object, but this bit of subterfuge is supported by interface proxies that are aggregated into the proxy manager. The proxy manager also implements *IMarshal*, the fundamental marshaling interface of COM+. While complex, this general purpose mechanism is required because the standard marshaler cannot know in advance what custom interfaces a particular object might implement.

To see how standard marshaling fits into the custom marshaling model and to provide some context for the upcoming discussion of standard marshaling for the *ISum* interface, let's review the code executed by the prototypical client application:

```
// client.cpp

// Start your engines.
CoInitializeEx(NULL, COINIT_MULTITHREADED);

// Get a pointer to the object's class factory.
IClassFactory* pClassFactory;
CoGetClassObject(CLSID_InsideCOM, CLSCTX_LOCAL_SERVER,
    NULL, IID_IClassFactory, (void**)&pClassFactory);
```

```
// Instantiate the InsideCOM object
// and get a pointer to its ISum interface.
ISum* pSum = 0;
pClassFactory->CreateInstance(NULL, IID_ISum, (void**)&pSum);

// Client uses pSum...
```

The client calls *IClassFactory::CreateInstance* to request that the *InsideCOM* object be instantiated and a pointer to *ISum* be returned. In the component's address space, the stub code for *IClassFactory::CreateInstance* realizes that the *ISum* interface pointer about to be returned to the client must be marshaled. The stub then calls the *CoMarshalInterface* function to marshal the *ISum* interface pointer. *CoMarshalInterface* queries the *InsideCOM* object for the *IMarshal* interface to determine whether the object wants standard or custom marshaling. By the simple act of returning *E_NOINTERFACE* in the *QueryInterface* call for the *IMarshal* interface, we tell the system of our desire to use standard marshaling.

Having determined that our object wants standard marshaling, *CoMarshalInterface* calls the *CoGetStandardMarshal* function to obtain a pointer to the system-provided implementation of the *IMarshal* interface; this is the standard marshaler. *CoMarshalInterface* uses the default implementation of *IMarshal* to call the *IMarshal::GetUnmarshalClass* method in order to determine the CLSID of the proxy coclass that should be loaded into the client's address space. In the case of the standard marshaler, the CLSID provided is that of the proxy manager.

The CLSID returned by *GetUnmarshalClass* is written into the marshaling stream, along with any other data the standard marshaler provides in its implementation of the *IMarshal::MarshalInterface* method. The marshaling stream is returned to the client's address space, where the proxy code for the *IClassFactory::CreateInstance* method calls the *CoUnmarshalInterface* function. *CoUnmarshalInterface* reads the CLSID from the marshaling stream and instantiates the object by calling *CoCreateInstance*. This loads the specified proxy in the client's address space; in the case of standard marshaling, this has the effect of creating the proxy manager. *CoUnmarshalInterface* then calls the *IMarshal::UnmarshalInterface* method in the proxy manager. The proxy manager uses the interface identifier (IID) of the interface being marshaled, which is provided by *UnmarshalInterface*, to load the interface proxy registered for that interface. You are responsible for implementing the interface proxy and the interface stub in the standard marshaling model.

When the proxy manager instantiates a new interface proxy, it provides the interface proxy with a pointer to the proxy manager's implementation of *IUnknown*, to which the interface proxy delegates all *QueryInterface*, *AddRef*, and *Release* calls as dictated by the aggregation model. Each interface proxy

457

implements two interfaces: the custom interface it represents and *IRpcProxyBuffer*. The custom interface is exposed directly to clients, which obtain access to the interface through the *QueryInterface* mechanism; the proxy manager uses the *IRpcProxyBuffer* interface to communicate with the interface proxy. The standard marshaling architecture is depicted in Figure 15-1.

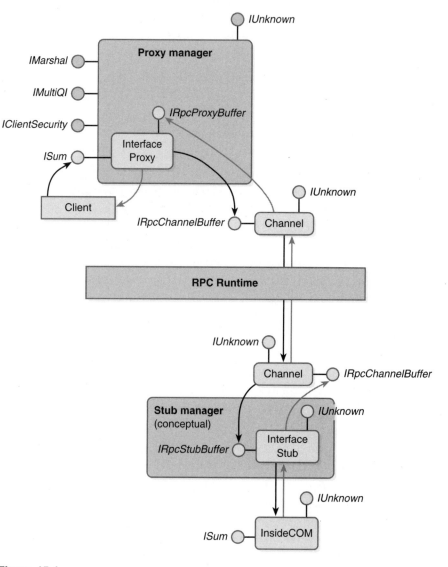

Figure 15-1.
The standard marshaling architecture.

The client calls *QueryInterface* to obtain an *ISum* interface exposed by the interface proxy object. The interface proxy is part of the greater proxy manager; it communicates with the *InsideCOM* object through the *IRpcChannelBuffer* interface implemented by the standard marshaling channel. On the server side, the channel communicates with the interface stub through the *IRpcStubBuffer* interface, which in turn calls the actual *InsideCOM* object. The stub manager represents the client in the object's address space; because the stub manager does not need to present a unified identity to any clients, interface stubs are not aggregated with the stub manager.[1]

The Service Control Manager (SCM) knows which proxy/stub DLL to load based on the IID of the interface pointer returned to the client. In the HKEY_CLASSES_ROOT\Interface section of the registry, the IID must be declared along with the subkey ProxyStubClsid32. This subkey must contain the CLSID of the proxy/stub component for this interface. The SCM then proceeds to the HKEY_CLASSES_ROOT\CLSID section of the registry to locate the CLSID and the InprocServer32 value specifying the name of the proxy/stub DLL to load. Notice that with respect to the HKEY_CLASSES_ROOT\CLSID section of the registry, proxy/stub DLLs are not treated any differently than regular components.

Figure 15-2 illustrates the registry scenario for a proxy/stub DLL configured to marshal an interface. In this case, the interface uses the type library marshaler. (The numbers indicate the order in which the SCM traverses the registry.) Remember that type library marshaling is built on top of standard marshaling, and thus the registry settings follow the same rules.

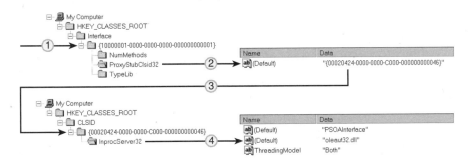

Figure 15-2.
The order in which the SCM scours the registry to find a proxy/stub DLL for standard marshaling.

---

1. Figure 15-1 shows the stub manager for conceptual purposes; the stub manager does not actually exist as a separate entity.

The Standard Marshaling Interfaces

Standard marshaling involves four interfaces: *IPSFactoryBuffer*, *IRpcProxyBuffer*, *IRpcStubBuffer*, and *IRpcChannelBuffer*. The proxy/stub DLL is itself an in-process component that implements the *IPSFactoryBuffer*, *IRpcProxyBuffer*, and *IRpcStubBuffer* interfaces. The *IRpcChannelBuffer* interface is implemented by a built-in object called the channel, which is provided by the standard marshaler and is called by the proxy/stub DLL for interprocess communication. But before we launch into a detailed explanation of these interfaces and the ways in which they are used, take a moment to peruse Figure 15-3.

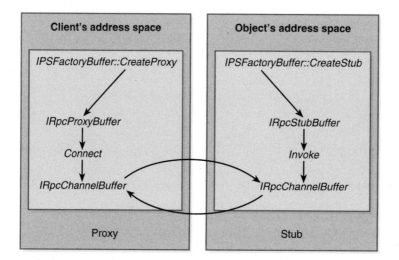

Figure 15-3.
How a proxy/stub DLL turns into a proxy in the client's address space and into a stub in an object's address space.

Figure 15-3 shows how proxy and stub objects start from the same code base and then diverge. In both the client and server address spaces, the proxy/stub coclass's class object implements the *IPSFactoryBuffer* interface in place of the standard *IClassFactory* interface typically implemented by class objects. Then something dramatic happens. In the client's address space, the *IPSFactoryBuffer::CreateProxy* method is called to create an interface proxy object that implements the *IRpcProxyBuffer* interface; in the server's address space, the *IPSFactoryBuffer::CreateStub* method is called to instantiate an interface stub object that implements the *IRpcStubBuffer* interface. From there, the proxy calls *IRpcProxyBuffer::Connect* and then communicates with the stub using the

IRpcChannelBuffer interface. In response to a request by the proxy, the stub is awakened using the *IRpcStubBuffer::Invoke* method.

The *IPSFactoryBuffer* Interface

Proxy/stub DLLs that support standard marshaling are themselves COM+ objects, but their class objects do not need to implement the *IClassFactory* interface. Recall that clients typically call the *IClassFactory::CreateInstance* method to instantiate objects in a component. Unlike the method *IClassFactory::CreateInstance*, a proxy/stub DLL does not instantiate a single coclass; it can instantiate a proxy or a stub object for a particular interface. Thus, instead of supporting *IClassFactory*, the class objects of proxy/stub coclasses implement the *IPSFactoryBuffer* interface.

IPSFactoryBuffer is the interface through which proxies and stubs are created. Every proxy/stub DLL must implement the *IPSFactoryBuffer* interface on a class object accessible through its *DllGetClassObject* entry point. As shown in the following code, the implementation of the *DllGetClassObject* function in a proxy/stub DLL is not substantially different from that of a normal component:

```
HRESULT __stdcall DllGetClassObject(REFCLSID clsid,
    REFIID riid, void** ppv)
{
    // This is a proxy/stub object.
    if(clsid != CLSID_InsideCOMStdProxy)
        return CLASS_E_CLASSNOTAVAILABLE;

    // Create the PSFactoryBuffer object.
    CPSFactoryBuffer* pPSFactoryBuffer = new CPSFactoryBuffer;
    if(pPSFactoryBuffer == NULL)
        return E_OUTOFMEMORY;

    // Calling QueryInterface for IPSFactoryBuffer
    return pPSFactoryBuffer->QueryInterface(riid, ppv);
}
```

As described earlier in this chapter, the SCM consults the registry for the ProxyStubClsid32 subkey of the HKEY_CLASSES_ROOT\Interface entry to get the CLSID of the coclass that provides for the interface's marshaling needs. *DllGetClassObject* is then called to request the *IPSFactoryBuffer* interface. Here is the *IPSFactoryBuffer* interface declared in IDL notation:

```
interface IPSFactoryBuffer : IUnknown
{
    HRESULT CreateProxy
```

(continued)

461

```
(
    [in] IUnknown* pUnkOuter,
    [in] REFIID riid,
    [out] IRpcProxyBuffer** ppProxy,
    [out] void** ppv
);

HRESULT CreateStub
(
    [in] REFIID riid,
    [in, unique] IUnknown* pUnkServer,
    [out] IRpcStubBuffer** ppStub
);
}
```

From this single interface, the gender of a proxy/stub DLL is decided. In the client's address space, *IPSFactoryBuffer::CreateProxy* is called to instantiate the proxy object, and in the component's address space, the same DLL is loaded but *IPSFactoryBuffer::CreateStub* is called. The client-side pseudo-code for the steps executed by the proxy manager after locating the ProxyStubClsid32 in the registry is shown here:

```
clsid = LookUpInRegistry(riid);
CoGetClassObject(clsid,
    CLSCTX_INPROC_HANDLER|CLSCTX_INPROC_SERVER,
    NULL, IID_IPSFactoryBuffer, (void**)&pPSFactoryBuffer);
pPSFactoryBuffer->CreateProxy(pUnkOuter, riid, &pRpcProxyBuffer,
    (void**)&ppv);
```

In the object's address space, the stub manager executes the following pseudo-code:

```
clsid = LookUpInRegistry(riid);
CoGetClassObject(clsid,
    CLSCTX_INPROC_HANDLER|CLSCTX_INPROC_SERVER,
    NULL, IID_IPSFactoryBuffer, (void**)&pPSFactoryBuffer);
pPSFactoryBuffer->CreateStub(riid, pUnkServer, &pRpcStubBuffer);
```

In our proxy/stub DLL, the *IPSFactoryBuffer::CreateProxy* method is written to instantiate a new *CRpcProxyBuffer* object, as shown in the code on the next page. *CRpcProxyBuffer* is the class that actually implements the *IRpcProxyBuffer* interface as well as the *ISum* custom interface that we are marshaling in this DLL. Notice that when a new interface proxy is instantiated using the *CreateProxy* method, it receives as its first parameter a pointer to the *IUnknown* interface of the proxy manager, to which the interface proxy must delegate all *QueryInterface*, *AddRef*, and *Release* calls. This is how the proxy manager aggregates interface proxies into its identity. In the following code, we simply pass this interface pointer to the constructor of the *CRpcProxyBuffer* class, where it is stored for use in the methods of the *IUnknown* interface.

```
HRESULT CPSFactoryBuffer::CreateProxy(IUnknown* pUnknownOuter,
    REFIID riid, IRpcProxyBuffer** ppProxy, void** ppv)
{
    // Create the proxy object; pUnknownOuter is the
    // proxy manager.
    CRpcProxyBuffer* pRpcProxyBuffer =
        new CRpcProxyBuffer(pUnknownOuter);

    // Code omitted...

}
```

As with standard aggregation,[2] the goal is to have the proxy present a single identity to the client. To achieve this, the object must delegate any *IUnknown* method calls to the outer object; this is why the *IPSFactoryBuffer::CreateProxy* method provides the *pUnknownOuter* parameter. The delegating implementation of *IUnknown* is the one seen by all external clients. In addition to the delegating implementation of *IUnknown*, the interface proxy must also implement a second, nondelegating version of *IUnknown* for use only by the outer object. Standard aggregation requires the outer object to first request the inner object's *IUnknown* interface via the *IClassFactory::CreateInstance* method so that the inner object can return a pointer to its nondelegating version of the *IUnknown* interface.

Unfortunately for us, proxy/stub DLLs don't implement the *IClassFactory* activation interface—they implement *IPSFactoryBuffer* instead. To add insult to injury, the *IPSFactoryBuffer::CreateProxy* method does not request the interface proxy's *IUnknown* interface first; it requests the *IRpcProxyBuffer* interface. So in place of a nondelegating version of *IUnknown*, we must implement a nondelegating version of the *IRpcProxyBuffer* interface. The code below shows the declaration of the *INoAggregationRpcProxyBuffer* custom interface that mimics the v-table layout of the real *IRpcProxyBuffer* interface but uses a custom implementation of *IUnknown* whose methods do not delegate to the proxy manager:

```
interface INoAggregationRpcProxyBuffer
{
    virtual HRESULT __stdcall QueryInterface_NoAggregation(
        REFIID riid, void** ppv)=0;
    virtual ULONG __stdcall AddRef_NoAggregation()=0;
```

(continued)

---

2. Standard aggregation is done via the *IClassFactory* interface; proxy/stub components use the *IPSFactoryBuffer* interface. Both types of aggregation follow the same principles as described in Chapter 2.

```
virtual ULONG __stdcall Release_NoAggregation()=0;
virtual HRESULT __stdcall Connect(
    IRpcChannelBuffer* pRpcChannel)=0;
virtual void __stdcall Disconnect(void)=0;
};
```

Next the code in the *IPSFactoryBuffer::CreateProxy* method calls the nondelegating version of the *QueryInterface* method for a pointer to the *ISum* interface. This is the *ISum* interface pointer that is returned to the client. Now you can see how a v-table is fabricated in the client's address space—a fake object implementing the custom interface is created so the client has an in-process object on which to call methods. Finally, the code calls the nondelegating version of *QueryInterface* so that a pointer to the nondelegating version of the *IRpcProxyBuffer* interface implemented by the interface proxy can be returned to the proxy manager:

```
HRESULT CPSFactoryBuffer::CreateProxy(IUnknown* pUnknownOuter,
    REFIID riid, IRpcProxyBuffer** ppProxy, void** ppv)
{
    // Create the proxy object; pUnknownOuter is the
    // proxy manager.
    CRpcProxyBuffer* pRpcProxyBuffer =
        new CRpcProxyBuffer(pUnknownOuter);

    // Call QueryInterface for IID_ISum.
    HRESULT hr = pRpcProxyBuffer->QueryInterface_NoAggregation(
        riid, ppv);

    // Return a pointer to the IRpcProxyBuffer interface.
    return pRpcProxyBuffer->QueryInterface_NoAggregation(
        IID_IRpcProxyBuffer, (void**)ppProxy);
}
```

Meanwhile, on the server-side, the *IPSFactoryBuffer::CreateStub* method is called to instantiate the *CRpcStubBuffer* class, which then implements the *IRpcStubBuffer* interface. The code below shows how the *CreateStub* method receives a pointer to the *InsideCOM* object for later use by the interface stub when it needs to call the object. *CreateStub* also provides the IID of the interface we are marshaling—in this case, *IID_ISum*. This IID is passed to the *CRpcStubBuffer* class's constructor for safekeeping by the stub. The *IRpcStubBuffer::Connect* method is then called to provide the interface stub with a pointer to this object. Finally, the code calls *QueryInterface* for *IRpcStubBuffer* so that a pointer to the interface stub can be returned to the stub manager.

```
HRESULT CPSFactoryBuffer::CreateStub(REFIID riid,
    IUnknown* pUnkServer, IRpcStubBuffer** ppStub)
```

```
{
    // Create the stub object.
    CRpcStubBuffer* pRpcStubBuffer = new CRpcStubBuffer(riid);

    // Give the stub the pointer to the object.
    pRpcStubBuffer->Connect(pUnkServer);

    // Return a pointer to the IRpcStubBuffer interface.
    return pRpcStubBuffer->QueryInterface(IID_IRpcStubBuffer,
        (void**)ppStub);
}
```

The *IRpcProxyBuffer* Interface

The *IRpcProxyBuffer* interface is the primary interface implemented by an interface proxy. It is the interface through which the proxy manager talks to an interface proxy that it has aggregated. The *IRpcProxyBuffer* interface is shown here in IDL notation:

```
interface IRpcProxyBuffer : IUnknown
{
    // Here is a pointer to the channel so you can talk
    // to the stub.
    HRESULT Connect
    (
        [in, unique] IRpcChannelBuffer *pRpcChannelBuffer
    );

    // Disconnect from the stub.
    void Disconnect
    (
        void
    );
}
```

Connect is obviously the more interesting of *IRpcProxyBuffer*'s two methods. It is called by the proxy manager shortly after the interface proxy is created in the *IPSFactoryBuffer::CreateProxy* method. The first (and only) argument for *Connect* is a pointer to a channel object implementing the *IRpcChannelBuffer* interface through which the proxy communicates with the stub. The implementation of *Connect* can be as simple as this:

```
HRESULT CRpcProxyBuffer::Connect(IRpcChannelBuffer* pRpcChannel)
{
    // Store the pointer to the channel.
    m_pRpcChannel = pRpcChannel;
```

(continued)

465

```
    // AddRef the pointer.
    m_pRpcChannel->AddRef();
    return S_OK;
}
```

This code simply stores the *IRpcChannelBuffer* pointer in a member variable and then calls *AddRef* as dictated by the COM+ reference counting rules. This pointer will be used whenever the client calls a method of the object. As we've seen, the client thinks it has a pointer to the object, but it in fact has only a pointer to the proxy. Therefore, all client calls actually end up in the proxy; from there, the request is forwarded to the stub using the *IRpcChannelBuffer* pointer.

The *IRpcProxyBuffer::Disconnect* method notifies the proxy that it is no longer connected to the stub. At this stage, the RPC channel must be released to counteract the *AddRef* method called in *IRpcProxyBuffer::Connect*. A sample implementation of the *Disconnect* method is shown here:

```
void CRpcProxyBuffer::Disconnect()
{
    // Release the channel pointer and set it to NULL.
    m_pRpcChannel->Release();
    m_pRpcChannel = NULL;
}
```

The *IRpcStubBuffer* Interface

Like *IRpcProxyBuffer*, *IRpcStubBuffer* is the main interface of an interface stub. The stub manager dynamically loads the interface stub into the component's address space and uses the *IRpcStubBuffer* interface to communicate with it. The following code shows the *IRpcStubBuffer* interface in IDL notation:

```
interface IRpcStubBuffer : IUnknown
{
    // Connect to the object.
    HRESULT Connect([in] IUnknown* pUnkServer);

    // Disconnect from the object.
    void Disconnect();

    // Call a method of the object.
    HRESULT Invoke
    (
        [in] RPCOLEMESSAGE* _prpcmsg,
        [in] IRpcChannelBuffer* _pRpcChannelBuffer
    );
```

```
    // Do you support other interfaces?
    IRpcStubBuffer* IsIIDSupported([in] REFIID riid);

    // How many references are you holding?
    ULONG CountRefs(void);

    HRESULT DebugServerQueryInterface(void** ppv);

    void DebugServerRelease(void* pv);
}
```

The *IRpcStubBuffer::Connect* method provides the interface stub with a pointer to the actual object in the component's address space to which the stub is connected. The stub forwards all client requests from the proxy to this object. To obtain the correct interface pointer for this object, the implementation of *IRpcStubBuffer::Connect* should call *QueryInterface* for the interface we are marshaling—in this case, *ISum*. As shown in the following code, *QueryInterface* takes care of the need to call *AddRef*. The resulting pointer is stored for later use in the *m_pObj* member variable.

```
HRESULT CRpcStubBuffer::Connect(IUnknown* pUnknown)
{
    // Need to keep track of component references for later.
    m_cConnection++;

    // Get a pointer to the interface we are marshaling.
    return pUnknown->QueryInterface(m_iid, (void**)&m_pObj);
}
```

The *IRpcStubBuffer::IsIIDSupported* method is called to determine if a stub is designed to handle the unmarshaling of a particular interface, as shown in the code on the following page. When a new interface pointer is remoted on a given object, the existing interface stubs are first queried using the *IsIIDSupported* method in an attempt to locate a stub that can handle marshaling for the interface before the system goes to the trouble of creating a new interface stub. An interface stub is usually designed to support only one interface. In such cases, the *IsIIDSupported* method should simply check whether the requested interface is the one the stub was designed to handle. If it is, the method should return *true*; otherwise, it should return *false*. If the interface stub supports multiple interfaces, the *IsIIDSupported* method should check whether the IID provided is one of the supported ones. If so, *IsIIDSupported* should return an appropriate *IRpcStubBuffer* pointer for that interface.

```
IRpcStubBuffer* CRpcStubBuffer::IsIIDSupported(REFIID riid)
{
    // Do we support this IID?
    if(riid == m_iid)
        return (IRpcStubBuffer*)true;
    return (IRpcStubBuffer*)false;
}
```

The *IRpcStubBuffer::CountRefs* method returns the total number of references the stub is holding on the component's object, as shown in the following code. The counter value returned should be incremented in every call to *IRpcStubBuffer::Connect* and decremented in *IRpcStubBuffer::Disconnect*.

```
ULONG CRpcStubBuffer::CountRefs()
{
    // Return component connection reference count.
    return m_cConnection;
}
```

IRpcStubBuffer::Disconnect informs the stub that it should disconnect from the component's object. The following implementation of *Disconnect* releases the object reference stored in *m_pObj* and then decrements the connection counter *m_cConnection*:

```
void CRpcStubBuffer::Disconnect()
{
    // Release our reference on the object.
    m_pObj->Release();
    m_cConnection--;
}
```

The *DebugServerQueryInterface* and *DebugServerRelease* methods of the *IRpcStubBuffer* interface are designed to support debuggers that provide the ability to step into remote invocations on objects. For our purposes, the implementation shown in the following code is sufficient.[3]

```
HRESULT CRpcStubBuffer::DebugServerQueryInterface(void**)
{
    return E_NOTIMPL;
}

void CRpcStubBuffer::DebugServerRelease(void*)
{
}
```

3. See the original COM specification for more information about the recommended implementation of these functions.

At this stage, the proxy and stub are fully set up, and the client can make calls into the component through the marshaling code. When a call is made by the interface proxy through the channel, it is received by the stub in the *IRpcStubBuffer::Invoke* method. To better understand how it works, we'll defer our discussion of the *Invoke* method until after we discuss the *IRpcChannelBuffer* interface.

The *IRpcChannelBuffer* Interface

At the core of the functionality offered by standard marshaling is the built-in channel, through which a proxy communicates with its corresponding stub. Conceptually, the channel provides a magic box into which the proxy puts data in the client's address space. When the proxy tells the channel to send the data, the channel transmits the data to the component's address space and wakes up the stub, regardless of the nature of the boundaries separating those two processes. The great thing about the channel is that it completely handles the transmission of marshaled data between processes, regardless of whether the processes are on the same machine or on different machines connected over a network.

The channel implements the *IRpcChannelBuffer* interface; the proxy and stub obtain this interface through the *IRpcProxyBuffer::Connect* and *IRpcStubBuffer::Invoke* methods, respectively. The *IRpcChannelBuffer* interface is internal to and implemented by the COM+ remoting infrastructure and is not available outside of the standard marshaling interfaces. Here is the *IRpcChannelBuffer* interface in IDL notation:

```
interface IRpcChannelBuffer : IUnknown
{
    // Allocate a transmission buffer.
    HRESULT GetBuffer
    (
        [in] RPCOLEMESSAGE* pMessage,
        [in] REFIID riid
    );

    // Invoke a method and wait for it to return.
    HRESULT SendReceive
    (
        [in, out] RPCOLEMESSAGE* pMessage,
        [out] ULONG* pStatus
    );

    // Free the transmission buffer.
    HRESULT FreeBuffer([in] RPCOLEMESSAGE* pMessage);
```

(continued)

469

```
// What is the nature of the boundary between the
// proxy and stub?
HRESULT GetDestCtx
(
    [out] DWORD* pdwDestContext,
    [out] void** ppvDestContext
);

// Am I connected to the stub?
HRESULT IsConnected(void);
}
```

The RPCOLEMESSAGE Data Structure

Of the five *IRpcChannelBuffer* methods, we'll focus initially on the *GetBuffer*, *SendReceive*, and *FreeBuffer* methods. Common to these three methods is the RPCOLEMESSAGE data structure—the structure actually transmitted from the proxy to the stub and back. This data structure is declared as shown here:

```
typedef struct tagRPCOLEMESSAGE
    {
        void                *reserved1;
        RPCOLEDATAREP       dataRepresentation;
        void                *Buffer;
        ULONG               cbBuffer;
        ULONG               iMethod;
        void                *reserved2[5];
        ULONG               rpcFlags;
    } RPCOLEMESSAGE;
```

The most significant field in this structure is the *Buffer* pointer. The proxy packs the parameters of a method into this buffer and then transmits it to the stub. The *cbBuffer* member of the RPCOLEMESSAGE data structure specifies the current size in bytes of the marshaling buffer. Memory is allocated for the *Buffer* pointer by a call to the *IRpcChannelBuffer::GetBuffer* method, not by the proxy. The *GetBuffer* method uses the value of the *cbBuffer* field to determine how much memory to allocate for the channel's transmission buffer.

The *dataRepresentation* field of the RPCOLEMESSAGE structure is an unsigned long (4-byte) value defined as the RPCOLEDATAREP type. This field contains the Network Data Representation (NDR) format label that identifies the data formats used to represent primitive values. The stub can use this value to identify the particular variation of NDR transfer syntax being used. Figure 15-4 shows the layout of this 4-byte structure.

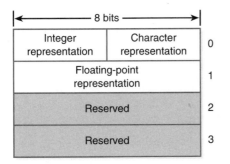

Figure 15-4.
The layout of the RPCOLEMESSAGE dataRepresentation field.

The bit flags that you can set in the format label are shown in the following table.

Data Type	Value	Format
Character representation	0	ASCII
	1	EBCDIC
Integer and floating-point byte order	0	Big endian
	1	Little endian
Floating-point representation	0	IEEE
	1	VAX
	2	Cray
	3	IBM

Let's pause and retrace our steps back to the client to see how all these pieces fit together. To retrieve an interface pointer from the component, the client executes the following code:

```
ISum* pSum;
HRESULT hr = pUnknown->QueryInterface(IID_ISum, (void**)&pSum);
int retval;
hr = pSum->Sum(2, 7, &retval);
```

The *QueryInterface* call actually returns the pointer to the proxy's implementation of *ISum*. When the client calls the *ISum::Sum* method, the proxy's implementation of this method is invoked in the client's address space. At this stage, the proxy must pack the necessary method parameters into a buffer for transmission to the stub. Here is the proxy's implementation of the *Sum* method, which is invoked when the client calls *ISum::Sum*:

```
HRESULT CRpcProxyBuffer::Sum(int x, int y, int* retval)
{
    RPCOLEMESSAGE Message = { 0, 0, 0, 0, 0, 0, 0, 0, 0, 0, 0 };
    ULONG status;

    // Specify how much memory to allocate for Message.Buffer.
    Message.cbBuffer = sizeof(int)*2;

    // Allocate the memory for Message.Buffer.
    m_pRpcChannel->GetBuffer(&Message, IID_ISum);

    // Marshal the Sum method's x and y arguments.
    ((int*)Message.Buffer)[0] = x;
    ((int*)Message.Buffer)[1] = y;

    // Set the v-table entry for ISum::Sum.
    Message.iMethod = 3;

    // Send the packet to the stub.
    m_pRpcChannel->SendReceive(&Message, &status);

    // Now the result is available.
    *retval = ((int*)Message.Buffer)[0];

    // Free the memory used for Message.Buffer.
    m_pRpcChannel->FreeBuffer(&Message);
    return S_OK;
}
```

The marshaling of method arguments takes place in the *CRpcProxyBuffer:: Sum* method shown above. This surrogate implementation of the *Sum* method declares a variable named *Message* of type RPCOLEMESSAGE. *Message.cbBuffer* is then set to the size of two integers—the total space needed to store the two *in* arguments accepted by the *Sum* method. *IRpcChannelBuffer::GetBuffer* is called to allocate the memory required for the transmission buffer. The following simple code marshals both the *x* and *y* arguments of the *Sum* method into the allocated buffer:

```
// Marshal the Sum method's x and y arguments.
((int*)Message.Buffer)[0] = x;
((int*)Message.Buffer)[1] = y;
```

Note that if any interfaces were transmitted as method arguments, they would also have to be packed into the RPCOLEMESSAGE structure. Of course, actual interface pointers would be useless to the recipient, so you should call *CoMarshalInterface* to marshal the interface into a stream and then transmit the contents of the stream in the RPCOLEMESSAGE structure. The stub will need to pass the stream to the *CoUnmarshalInterface* function to load a proxy and obtain a usable interface pointer.

Before the marshaled data packet can be sent to the proxy, you must indicate which method of the *ISum* interface is being called. Recall that *ISum* has four methods—the three methods of *IUnknown* plus *ISum::Sum*. The *iMethod* field of the RPCOLEMESSAGE structure specifies the desired method. This value is a zero-based number for the desired method's v-table entry in the interface. In the case of *ISum*, the order of the entries in the v-table is *QueryInterface*, *AddRef*, *Release*, and finally *Sum*. Thus, *Sum* exists as the third method in a zero-based enumeration of the v-table entries, as shown here:

```
// Set the v-table entry for ISum::Sum.
Message.iMethod = 3;
```

Now we're ready to send the marshaled data packet from the proxy to the stub. The *SendReceive* method is the heart of the *IRpcChannelBuffer* interface. Using the RPC infrastructure, this two-way method transmits the entire RPCOLEMESSAGE structure to the stub. The proxy then goes to sleep while it waits for the actual method to execute and for the return values to be sent back through the RPC channel to the proxy. In the interface stub, the *IRpcStubBuffer::Invoke* method is called automatically when data is received in the channel from the proxy as the result of a call to *SendReceive*.

In the *IRpcStubBuffer::Invoke* method, the stub first determines which method in the interface is being called. The *iMethod* field of the RPCOLEMESSAGE structure provides this crucial information. If it doesn't know which method is being called, the stub has no idea how to interpret the data in the channel. In the following code, a *switch* statement is used to execute the correct code for the specified method being invoked. In this case, we check only for the third method—the *Sum* method.

```
HRESULT CRpcStubBuffer::Invoke(RPCOLEMESSAGE* pMessage,
    IRpcCha~nnelBuffer* pRpcChannel)
{
    // What method of ISum is the proxy calling?
    switch(pMessage->iMethod)
    {
    case 3: // The proxy is calling ISum::Sum.
        int result;
```

(continued)

```
    // Calling the Sum method!!!
    m_pObj->Sum(((int*)pMessage->Buffer)[0],
        ((int*)pMessage->Buffer)[1], &result);

    // How much memory is needed for the return value?
    pMessage->cbBuffer = sizeof(int);

    // Free the proxy buffer and allocate a new one.
    pRpcChannel->GetBuffer(pMessage, m_iid);

    // Pack the return value into the buffer.
    ((int*)pMessage->Buffer)[0] = result;

    // Take it away...
    return NOERROR;

// case n: Other methods here...
}
return E_UNEXPECTED;
}
```

By using the *m_pObj* member variable that points to the actual *Sum* interface in the component, we can call the real *Sum* method. The two parameters, *x* and *y*, are retrieved from the buffer packed by the proxy. For efficiency's sake, the *Sum* method is passed direct pointers into the message buffer; no copy of the data is made. Now the real *Sum* method executes, adds the two values, and returns the result to the stub. The stub then transmits the method's *out* parameters back to the proxy. First, the *cbBuffer* field is set to the size (in bytes) of the memory required for the *out* parameters. Then the *IRpcChannelBuffer::GetBuffer* method is called to allocate the memory needed to pack the *out* parameters for transmission. Before allocating a reply buffer, the *GetBuffer* method automatically frees the memory buffer allocated for the proxy's buffer. Then the result of the *Sum* method is stored in the transmission buffer. Returning from *IRpcStubBuffer::Invoke* sends the RPCOLEMESSAGE structure to the proxy.

In the proxy, the *IRpcChannelBuffer::SendReceive* function returns and the RPCOLEMESSAGE structure contains the data returned by the stub. The proxy unpacks the *out* parameters from the buffer and copies them into variables returned to the client, as shown in the following code. Finally, the *IRpcChannelBuffer::FreeBuffer* method is called to free the buffer containing the marshaled data packet from the stub.

```
// Send the packet to the stub.
m_pRpcChannel->SendReceive(&Message, &status);
// Now the result is available.
*retval = ((int*)Message.Buffer)[0];

// Free the memory used for Message.Buffer.
m_pRpcChannel->FreeBuffer(&Message);
```

You can use the *IRpcChannelBuffer::GetDestCtx* method to obtain the destination context information for this interface. The destination context is identified by one of the *MSHCTX* enumeration constants, which describe the barrier between the object and its client. You can use *IsConnected*, the last method of the *IRpcChannelBuffer* interface, to determine whether the channel is still connected to the other side. Interface proxies can use this method as an optimization for quickly returning an error to the client if the proxy is not connected to the stub. This technique saves the time wasted by attempting a call to *IRpcChannelBuffer::SendReceive* simply to receive the *E_RPCFAULT* error.

Registering the Proxy/Stub DLL

Although proxy/stub DLLs are full-fledged COM+ components, they are registered a little differently from more standard components. First, a proxy/stub DLL has no need for a program identifier (ProgID) entry in the registry because it is unlikely that any code aside from the marshaling infrastructure will want to instantiate a proxy or a stub object. Second, proxy/stub DLLs must have the special subkey ProxyStubClsid32 for the specified interface in the HKEY_CLASSES_ROOT\Interface section of the registry. The table below shows the legal subkeys of the HKEY_CLASSES_ROOT\Interface section of the registry.

Interface Subkey	Description
BaseInterface	The IID of the interface that this interface derives from.
NumMethods	The number of methods in the interface, including the three methods of *IUnknown*.
ProxyStubClsid	CLSID of the 16-bit proxy/stub coclass.
ProxyStubClsid32	CLSID of the 32-bit proxy/stub coclass.

The following code sets up the REG_DATA structure so that the correct registry entries are added for the *ISum* interface marshaler. You simply pass this structure to the *RegisterServerEx* and *UnregisterServerEx* functions as usual. Notice that proxy/stub DLLs should be registered with the *ThreadingModel = Both* setting to ensure that they are always instantiated in the apartment of their creator. This also means that they must be thread-safe.

```
const REG_DATA g_regData[] = {
    { "CLSID\\{10000006-0000-0000-0000-000000000001}", 0, "PSSum" },
    { "CLSID\\{10000006-0000-0000-0000-000000000001}\\InprocServer32", 0,
```

(continued)

```
            (const char*)-1 },
  { "CLSID\\{10000006-0000-0000-0000-000000000001}\\InprocServer32",
      "ThreadingModel", "Both" },
  { "Interface\\{10000001-0000-0000-0000-000000000001}", 0, "ISum" },
  { "Interface\\{10000001-0000-0000-0000-000000000001}\\ProxyStubClsid32",
      0, "{10000006-0000-0000-0000-000000000001}" },
  { "Interface\\{10000001-0000-0000-0000-000000000001}\\NumMethods", 0,
      "4"},
  { 0, 0, 0 }
};
```

Converting Marshaled Interface Pointers to Strings

In Chapter 14, we saw that a marshaled interface pointer can be as simple as the string *"FileMap,StubEvent,ProxyEvent"*. When you use custom marshaling, it is up to you to decide what constitutes a marshaled interface pointer. Since the standard marshaling architecture is built on top of custom marshaling, the standard marshaler must decide what constitutes a marshaled interface pointer. It should come as no surprise that interface pointers marshaled by the standard marshaler are stored in a very different format from that in the custom marshaling example in Chapter 14. To obtain the marshaled form of an arbitrary interface pointer, regardless of whether it uses custom or standard marshaling, you need only create a stream object and then call the *CoMarshalInterface* function, as shown in the following code fragment:

```
IStream* pStream = 0;
hr = CreateStreamOnHGlobal(0, TRUE, &pStream);
hr = CoMarshalInterface(pStream, riid, pObject,
    MSHCTX_DIFFERENTMACHINE, 0, MSHLFLAGS_NORMAL);
```

Now you can examine the marshaled interface pointer stored in the stream. Of course, the data is stored in a binary format that does not lend itself to casual inspection. One common technique for viewing binary data is to convert it to a string that can be displayed. You can use many algorithms to convert binary data to a string format; one of the simplest is to convert each byte of data into two hexadecimal characters. This means, for example, that a decimal value of 0 is converted to the characters 00, the decimal value 78 is converted to the characters 4E, and 255 becomes FF. To automate this conversion, we wrote a function that converts an arbitrary interface pointer to a hexadecimal string using this technique; the code for the function, named *IPToHexString*, is shown here:

```
HRESULT IPToHexString(REFIID riid, IUnknown* pObject,
    char** output)
{
```

```
HRESULT hr;
IStream* pStream = 0;
hr = CreateStreamOnHGlobal(0, TRUE, &pStream);

hr = CoMarshalInterface(pStream, riid, pObject,
    MSHCTX_DIFFERENTMACHINE, 0, MSHLFLAGS_NORMAL);

ULONG size;
hr = CoGetMarshalSizeMax(&size, riid, pObject,
    MSHCTX_DIFFERENTMACHINE, 0, MSHLFLAGS_NORMAL);

HGLOBAL hg;
hr = GetHGlobalFromStream(pStream, &hg);
unsigned char* buffer = (unsigned char*)GlobalLock(hg);

*output = (char*)CoTaskMemAlloc((size * 2) + 1);

char hex[] = { '0', '1', '2', '3', '4', '5', '6', '7',
    '8', '9', 'a', 'b', 'c', 'd', 'e', 'f' };

for(ULONG count = 0; count < size; count++)
{
    (*output)[count*2] = hex[buffer[count] / 16];
    (*output)[(count*2)+1] = hex[buffer[count] -
        (buffer[count] / 16) * 16];
}
(*output)[((count-1)*2)+2] = 0;

GlobalUnlock(hg);
pStream->Release();

return hr;
}
```

This function reveals the fascinating world of standard marshaled interface pointers. After converting an interface pointer to a string, you can easily display it using a *printf*-style function. The other day we found a really good one, shown below. If you are wondering what this data means, don't despair—the exact contents of a standard marshaled interface pointer are covered in Chapter 19.

4d454f5701000000010000100000000000000000000000000100000000000000004
00500004d3b9e044a0500004d3b9e0401000000e5b5f6ff31baf6ff0100000023
00140007003100390039002e00330034002e00350038002e00330030005b00310
0330035005d00000000000a00000044004f004d00410049004e005c0047004100
4c004900000000000000004c0100a034643435334663537303130303030303031

You might be thinking, "Hey, that's pretty neat. But what can I do with a marshaled interface pointer in string form?" The great thing about having a string form of a marshaled interface pointer is that you can easily transfer it. For example, you can e-mail the interface pointer shown above to a friend. And what can your friend do with a marshaled interface pointer in string form? She can convert the string back to a binary marshaled interface pointer and then unmarshal it, yielding a valid interface pointer to your object. The code you need to convert a hexadecimal stream back to a binary block of memory is on the companion CD. Here is the code that unmarshals the interface pointer and provides an actual interface pointer, which is named *pObject*:

```
IStream* pStream = 0;
hr = CreateStreamOnHGlobal(pointer, TRUE, &pStream);
hr = CoUnmarshalInterface(pStream, riid, pObject);
pStream->Release();
```

This technique for transmitting interface pointers works whether you transmit the interface pointer across the hall or across the continent. Of course, the unmarshaled interface pointer is valid only as long as the original object is running; once the object terminates, the interface pointer is useless. And of course the client machine must have a registered proxy installed that knows how to unmarshal the interface pointer.

The OBJREF Moniker

In the first edition of this book, we suggested that an interesting project would be to build a custom moniker that uses the string form of a marshaled interface pointer as its display name, and we left this as an exercise for the reader. Since then, Microsoft has taken us up on the challenge and built the OBJREF moniker. As its display name, the OBJREF moniker uses the marshaled form of an interface pointer that has been converted to a string. But instead of converting the marshaled interface pointer to a hexadecimal string, Microsoft chose to do the conversion using a 64-bit encoding scheme. The result, although even less readable, is similar to the hexadecimal string shown earlier:

```
objref:TUVPVwEAAAAAAAAAAAAAMAAAAAAAABGAQAAAAAAAAPDgAAmijNCBkOAACaKM0
IAQAAACPj9v8D4PbAQAAACIAFAAHADEAOQA5AC4AMwA0AC4ANQA4AC4AMwA5AFsAMQAzAD
UAXQAAAAAACgAAAEQATwBNAEEASQBOAFwARwBVAFkkAAAAAA==:
```

Notice that the ProgID of the OBJREF moniker is *objref*. You are able to create an OBJREF moniker by calling the *CreateObjrefMoniker* function. *CreateObjrefMoniker* requires only the *IUnknown* interface pointer of the object you want the moniker to represent. The OBJREF moniker representing that interface pointer is returned as the second parameter of the *CreateObjrefMoniker* function. Using the OBJREF moniker, you can call the

IMoniker::GetDisplayName method to obtain the string representation of the object reference, as shown previously.

The string representation of an OBJREF moniker can then be passed to a client by any available means. One popular way to transmit this type of data over the Internet is to use an Active Server Pages (ASP) file that instantiates a COM+ object using the *CreateObject* function. The server-side script calls a method of the object that returns its display name using the OBJREF moniker and embeds that display name in the HTML returned to the client's browser. VBScript code running in the browser can then gain access to the object on the server by calling the *GetObject* function with the OBJREF moniker's display name. As you know from Chapter 11, internally the VBScript *GetObject* function calls the *MkParseDisplayName* function to re-create the OBJREF moniker from the display name, followed by the *IMoniker::BindToObject* method to connect with the original object on the server. A client application written in C++ might call the *CoGetObject* convenience function in place of *MkParseDisplayName* and *IMoniker::BindToObject*.

Handler Marshaling

Handler marshaling is closely related to standard marshaling. You can think of it as a middle ground between regular standard marshaling and full custom marshaling. Handler marshaling is useful for objects that want to perform some of the work in the client's address space, making remote calls only when absolutely necessary. An object might decide to use handler marshaling for a variety of reasons. Sometimes the overhead of a remote call simply overshadows the amount of work the object will perform. For example, making a remote call simply to add two values, as was shown with the *ISum* interface, is terribly inefficient. It would be much more efficient to implement that call within an in-process handler.

Objects that want to support handler marshaling implement the interface *IStdMarshalInfo* instead of *IMarshal*. The *IStdMarshalInfo* interface is shown here in IDL notation:

```
interface IStdMarshalInfo : IUnknown
{
    HRESULT GetClassForHandler
    (
        [in] DWORD dwDestContext,
        [in, unique] void *pvDestContext,
        [out] CLSID *pClsid
    );
}
```

When marshaling an interface pointer, *CoMarshalInterface* automatically calls *QueryInterface* for the *IStdMarshalInfo* interface. If the object implements *IStdMarshalInfo*, *CoMarshalInterface* calls the *IStdMarshalInfo::GetClass-ForHandler* method to retrieve the CLSID of the handler object to be loaded into the client's address space. The *IStdMarshalInfo::GetClassForHandler* method is similar to the *IMarshal::GetUnmarshalClass* method, which obtains the CLSID of a proxy that is to be loaded in the client's address space for custom marshaling (as described in Chapter 14). The InprocHandler32 subkey in the HKEY_CLASSES_ROOT\CLSID section of the registry references the handler coclass. When the interface pointer is unmarshaled, *CoUnmarshalInterface* activates the handler object in the client's address space using the *CoCreateInstance* function. The following code illustrates a standard implementation of the *IStdMarshalInfo::GetClassForHandler* method:

```
const CLSID CLSID_InsideCOMHandler =
    {0x11000006,0x0000,0x0000,0x00,0x00,0x00,0x00,
    0x00,0x00,0x00,0x01};

HRESULT CInsideCOM::GetClassForHandler(DWORD dwDestContext,
    void* pvDestContext, CLSID* pClsid)
{
    // Load this handler into the client's address space.
    *pClsid = CLSID_InsideCOMHandler;
    return S_OK;
}
```

In the client's address space, *CoCreateInstance* is called with the *CLSCTX_INPROC_HANDLER* flag to instantiate the handler. The *CLSCTX_INPROC_HANDLER* flag indicates that the handler coclass must be registered using the InprocHandler32 subkey. Handlers, like regular proxies and stubs, should be registered with the *ThreadingModel = Both* setting so that they are always loaded into the apartment of their creator. The REG_DATA structure for registering the handler is shown below:

```
const REG_DATA g_regData[] = {
    { "CLSID\\{11000006-0000-0000-0000-000000000001}", 0,
      "InsideCOM Handler" },
    { "CLSID\\{11000006-0000-0000-0000-000000000001}\\InprocHandler32", 0,
      (const char*)-1 },
    { "CLSID\\{11000006-0000-0000-0000-000000000001}\\InprocHandler32",
      "ThreadingModel", "Both" },
    { 0, 0, 0 }
};
```

As you'd expect, *CoCreateInstance* calls the handler's *DllGetClassObject* function, followed by its *IClassFactory::CreateInstance* method. Using this

CreateInstance method, *CoUnmarshalInterface* informs the handler that it is being aggregated and passes it a pointer to the controlling *IUnknown* interface implemented by the system identity object, to which the handler should delegate its own implementation of *IUnknown*. While the *IClassFactory:: CreateInstance* method executes, the handler should create an aggregated standard marshaler (proxy manager) using the *CoGetStdMarshalEx* function.

When the *CoGetStdMarshalEx* function is called by the handler, it takes a pointer to the controlling *IUnknown* interface provided by the *CreateInstance* method and the *SMEXF_HANDLER* flag, which indicates that the function is being called from the client's address space, as shown in the following code fragment. The third parameter of the *CoGetStdMarshalEx* function returns a pointer, named *m_pUnknownInner* here, to the *IUnknown* interface implemented by the proxy manager. Through this pointer, the handler can communicate with the interface proxy and therefore with the actual object in the component's address space.

```
IUnknown* m_pUnknownInner = 0;
CoGetStdMarshalEx(pUnknownOuter, SMEXF_HANDLER,
    &m_pUnknownInner);
```

Figure 15-5 shows how the identity object aggregates the handler and how the handler, in turn, aggregates the proxy manager. Of course, the proxy manager aggregates the interface proxy as dictated by standard marshaling. The identity object, also called the *controlling unknown*, is a built-in system object that gives the system control over the lifetime and the identity of the standard marshaler.

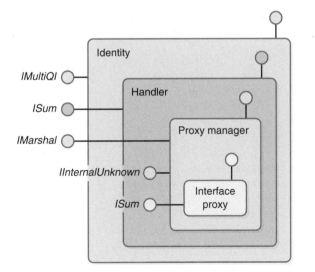

Figure 15-5.
Lightweight client-side handlers are sandwiched between the proxy manager and the identity object.

Recall that the real goal of most handlers is to enable some work to be done in the client's address space while delegating other work to the actual object in the component's address space. With this in mind, a handler's implementation of the *ISum::Sum* method might perform some calculations in-process while delegating others to the *InsideCOM* object via the *m_pUnknownInner* pointer. Because the proxy manager aggregates the interface proxy, the handler can obtain a pointer to the *ISum* interface implemented by the interface proxy simply by calling *QueryInterface* on the *m_pUnknownInner* pointer, which is actually a pointer to the proxy manager. This concept is illustrated in the following code, in which the handler's implementation of the *Sum* method adds only numbers smaller than 50. For summations involving values of 50 or higher, the method executes a cross-process or possibly even a cross-machine call to the *InsideCOM* object running in the component's address space.

```
HRESULT CInsideCOM::Sum(int x, int y, int* retval)
{
    if(x > 50 || y > 50)
    {
        // Numbers bigger than 50 had better call the
        // real object.
        ISum* pSum = 0;

        // Ask the proxy manager for a pointer to the ISum
        // interface proxy.
        m_pUnknownInner->QueryInterface(IID_ISum,
            (void**)&pSum);

        // Now call the interface proxy's ISum::Sum method.
        // This results in a call the object's Sum method.
        HRESULT hr = pSum->Sum(x, y, retval);

        pSum->Release();
        return hr;
    }

    // Numbers smaller than 50 need not call the object.
    // We'll do the work right here in the handler.
    *retval = x + y;
    return S_OK;
}
```

If you compare Figure 15-5 and Figure 15-1, you'll notice that the *IMultiQI* and *IClientSecurity* interfaces implemented by the proxy manager in Figure 15-1 are missing in Figure 15-5, where the *IInternalUnknown* is implemented instead. The proxy manager is a very sensitive object, and it does not like handlers to blindly expose its internal interfaces. To prevent this, when the proxy manager is aggregated by a handler via the *CoGetStdMarshalEx* function, it does not expose some of its internal interfaces via the standard *IUnknown::QueryInterface* method. Instead, handlers that require access to internal interfaces implemented by the proxy manager go through the *IInternalUnknown* interface, which is shown below in IDL notation. The *IInternalUnknown::QueryInternalInterface* method, which has the same semantics as the regular *IUnknown::QueryInterface* method, allows the handler to obtain access to these hidden interfaces.

```
interface IInternalUnknown : IUnknown
{
    HRESULT QueryInternalInterface(
        [in]  REFIID riid,
        [out] void** ppv);
}
```

Another variation on handler marshaling allows the object to return extra data to the handler via the marshaling packet. The object can use this technique to initialize the handler with extra data. In this case, the object must implement both the *IStdMarshalInfo* and *IMarshal* interfaces. The object aggregates the standard marshaler by calling *CoGetStdMarshalEx* with the flag *SMEXF_SERVER*, indicating that you want to aggregate the stub manager. The first part of the marshaling operation is delegated to the standard marshaler, but the object must add the size of the data it wants to send to the client to the value returned from the *IMarshal::GetMarshalSizeMax* method. After delegating to the standard marshaler's *IMarshal::MarshalInterface* method, the object writes its own extra data into the marshaling stream. This architecture is shown in Figure 15-6.

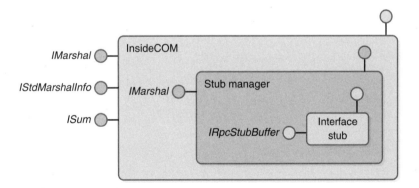

Figure 15-6.
The InsideCOM *object aggregates the standard marshaler.*

In the client's process, the handler must read the extra data stored by the object in the marshaling stream. The handler implements the *IMarshal* interface by delegating to the proxy manager's implementation of the *IMarshal::UnmarshalInterface* method and then reading the extra data that remains.

Of course, you could build this type of example using the standard marshaling technique described earlier in this chapter. Notice, however, how much easier it is to use handler marshaling to override certain aspects of standard marshaling. We don't have to implement or call any of the standard marshaling interfaces, such as *IPSFactoryBuffer*, *IRpcProxyBuffer*, *IRpcStubBuffer*, or *IRpcChannelBuffer*. Of course, a standard proxy/stub DLL is still needed, but you can fulfill this requirement using the type library marshaler or MIDL-generated marshaling code.

Interface Definition Language

It is widely acknowledged that the language used to express an idea both limits and shapes what can be expressed. Likewise, while the COM+ infrastructure is entirely divorced from the source-level languages used to access or create components, the available tools and languages have heavily influenced its design. The design of COM, and by consequence COM+, was strongly affected by C++, the most widely used object-oriented programming language; by Microsoft Windows, the platform that gave birth to COM+; and by Remote Procedure Calls (RPC).

RPC has contributed to the design of COM+ in several key areas. The RPC infrastructure enables COM+ to work across a network, and Interface Definition Language (IDL), the language developed to define RPC client/server interfaces, was adopted and extended for the definition of COM+ interfaces and classes. You can create components without IDL, and tools far better than Microsoft IDL (MIDL) might be developed in the future. Nevertheless, the importance and centrality of IDL to the design of COM+ cannot be underestimated. In this chapter, we'll explore IDL and its effect on the COM+ programming model.

As anyone who has worked on large-scale projects involving network communications knows, defining the interface between a client and a server and ensuring that both sides correctly adhere to that interface is one of the biggest challenges faced by the developer. The original goal of IDL was to encourage the client and server projects to agree upon and specify the communication interfaces and then follow those contracts. To achieve this end, the designers of IDL had to surmount several problems, which we'll describe below.

Types

IDL has to make up for the shortcomings of the rather weakly typed C programming language on which it is loosely based. C and C++ have a number of implementation-dependent features, including the size of the *short*, *int*, and *long* types. When you use a single compiler on a single computer, you needn't be overly concerned with internal data formats because data is handled in a consistent manner. However, a distributed environment involving multiple machines with different architectures can become a minefield of inconsistencies. For example, some compilers define the internal representation of an integer as 16 bits, while others use 32 bits. In order for IDL to define interfaces between programs that run on different machine architectures, implementation-dependent data types are unacceptable. For this reason, IDL's designers developed a strongly typed language that concretely defines the size of all base types in IDL. These base types are listed in the following table.

Base Type	Description
boolean	A data item that can have the value *TRUE* or *FALSE*
byte	An 8-bit data item guaranteed to be transmitted without any change
char	An 8-bit unsigned character data item
double	A 64-bit floating-point number
float	A 32-bit floating-point number
handle_t	A primitive handle that can be used for RPC binding or data serializing
hyper	A 64-bit integer that can be declared as either signed or unsigned
int	A 32-bit integer that can be declared as either signed or unsigned
long	A 32-bit integer that can be declared as either signed or unsigned
short	A 16-bit integer that can be declared as either signed or unsigned
small	An 8-bit integer that can be declared as either signed or unsigned
wchar_t	A 16-bit wide-character type

In addition, different machines might be designed around the little endian or big endian architecture that determines the order in which bytes are stored in memory. The little endian architecture used by the Intel platform assigns the least significant byte of data to the lowest memory address and the most significant byte to the highest address. Processors that use the big endian architecture do the opposite. For example, the base-10 value *654* (*0x028E* in base 16) is represented in memory as *0x8E02* by an Intel CPU but as *0x028E* on a Motorola CPU of the big endian variety. IDL uses the Network Data Representation (NDR) transfer format to ensure that network transmissions are independent of the data-type format on any particular computing architecture.[1]

Enumerated Types

You can define enumerated types in IDL using the *enum* keyword, as shown in the next code fragment. Note the use of the *[v1_enum]* attribute, which directs the marshaling code generated by MIDL to transmit the enumerated type as a 32-bit entity; by default, enumerated types are transmitted as 16-bit values. Enumerated types defined in IDL are also added to the type library file generated by MIDL. This means that high-level languages such as Microsoft Visual Basic and Java can use this information to provide syntax-completion information for enumerated types used as method parameters.

```
interface IWeek : IUnknown
{
    typedef [v1_enum] enum DaysOfTheWeek
    {
        Monday,
        Tuesday,
        Wednesday,
        Thursday,
        Friday,
        Saturday,
        Sunday
    } DaysOfTheWeek;

    HRESULT Test(DaysOfTheWeek day);
}
```

Directional Attributes

The C++ programming languages were designed as general-purpose languages for systems running within a single address space on one computer. Although you can use these languages to develop distributed systems by adding networking libraries such as Windows Sockets, the languages themselves have no special features in this regard. As a result, passing parameters to a function is as simple as pushing them onto the stack, jumping to the function address, and then popping the parameters off the stack. With the exception of the function's return value, parameters need not be passed back to the caller when the function returns because C++ specifies that parameters are passed by value. This means

---

1. See Chapter 14 for information on the NDR transfer syntax.

that a copy of the values is passed to a function, and any changes made to those values within the function are not reflected back to the caller when the function returns. The following code fragment illustrates this situation:

```
void sum(int x, int y, int sum)
{
    sum = x + y
}

void main()
{
    int result = 0;
    sum(5, 3, result);
    printf("5 + 3 = %d\n", result);    // Prints 0
}
```

Pass-by-value semantics in C++ can be contrasted with languages such as Visual Basic and Fortran, which, by default, pass parameters by reference, as shown in the following Visual Basic code:[2]

```
Sub Sum(X As Integer, Y As Integer, Sum As Integer)
    Sum = X + Y
End Sub

Sub Form_Load()
    Dim Result As Integer
    Sum 5, 3, Result
    Print "5 + 3 = " & Result              ' Prints 8
End Sub
```

Of course, in C++ you can achieve pass-by-reference functionality using pointers or references. When you use pointers, the address of the variable is passed to the function, causing any changes to the memory pointed to by the pointer to be immediately visible to the caller, as shown in the following code:

```
void sum(int x, int y, int* sum)
{
    *sum = x + y
}
```

---

2. Java hedges by passing primitive types by value but user-defined types by reference.

```
void main()
{
    int result = 0;
    sum(5, 3, &result);
    printf("5 + 3 = %d\n", result);    // Prints 8
}
```

When you pass parameters by value to a remote function, the system sends the value of the variable across the network to the server. However, several problems arise when you use pointers to pass data to code in another address space. The most obvious problem is that passing the address of a variable in one address space to a function in another address space does not work. To overcome this situation, the system must send the data that is stored at the location specified by the pointer across the network to the server. Memory is allocated to store the value in the address space of the server process, and then the address of the newly allocated memory is passed to the function. All this must be done as transparently as possible.

One of the problems with passing pointers is that C++ syntax does not indicate whether the function actually modifies the data that a specific function argument points to. For example, a pointer to some data might be passed to a function that uses that data in a read-only manner. In other cases, such as the *sum* function in the preceding code, a pointer is passed to a function for the sole purpose of retrieving data when the function returns. In a third variation on the same theme, a function might both read and write data that is passed via a pointer. The C++ syntax does not express these variations because it assumes that the caller and the function are both running in the same address space. Note that you can use the *const* keyword to indicate that a function does not modify data through a pointer.

For calls between machines, however, this situation is not merely syntactical hairsplitting. The system must pass the data located at the address specified by any pointer parameters to the server when the call is made and then back to the client when the function returns. Since IDL was designed to facilitate the development of distributed systems, one of its goals is to reduce the amount of network traffic generated by remote calls. For this reason, IDL offers three directional attributes to standard C++-style syntax: *[in]*, *[out]*, and *[in, out]*. If no attribute is specified, by default parameters are passed to the server as part of the request message used to invoke a method, as shown in the following illustration.

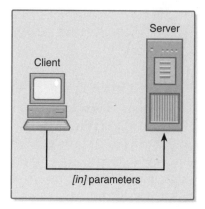

The *[out]* attribute indicates that data must be sent back to the client in the response message when the function call completes. This attribute is meaningful only when applied to a pointer argument because, by default, function parameters in C++ are passed by value. When the call returns, the system allocates memory in the client's address space to store the data returned; the caller is responsible for freeing this memory. The *[out]* attribute is a good choice when a pointer is passed to a function solely to retrieve data, as in the *sum* function shown previously. The process of passing a parameter with the *[out]* attribute is illustrated below.

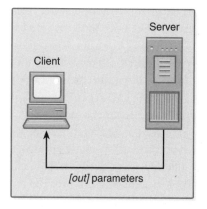

The *[in, out]* attribute indicates that the data at the location specified by a pointer parameter must be passed to the server as part of the request message and then back to the client in the response message. On the server side, the function frees and then reallocates a new buffer, if necessary. On the client side, the system copies the new data returned by the function over the original data, and the client ultimately frees this memory. This technique is used when a function expects to receive meaningful data and the caller expects it to return meaningful data to the same memory address. Since the *[in, out]* attribute transparently models the way normal C++ code works at the expense of extra network traffic, you should use it only when necessary. The action of a parameter with the *[in, out]* attribute is illustrated below.

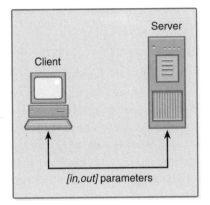

Arrays

C++ affords great flexibility when you deal with pointers and arrays. In fact, there is almost no difference between pointers and arrays in C++. This flexibility can translate into great ambiguity in some cases. Consider the following code:

```
int* x;        // A pointer, but to how many integers?

int z;         // One integer
int y[50];     // 50 integers (0 through 49)

x = &z;        // x is a pointer to one integer.
x = (int*)&y;  // x is a pointer to an array of 50 integers.
```

You can see that the intended use of pointer types defined by C++ is not always clear; from the first line of code, you can't tell whether *x* will point to one integer or to many integers. The truth is, it doesn't matter to C++. If you use a pointer to write data past the end of the allocated space, that's your problem. The flexibility of pointers and arrays is the main reason that pointers are considered a dangerous language feature and are not directly available in higher-level languages such as Java and Visual Basic.

Fixed Arrays

When you make remote calls, it is crucial that you know whether an argument points to a single item or to multiple items because all the data at the memory location pointed to by the argument must be transferred to the server. Unless otherwise indicated by the interface definition, a pointer parameter in IDL is assumed to point to a single element of the specified type. By this rule, the *[out]* attribute in the following function declaration is assigned to a parameter that is a pointer to a single integer:

```
HRESULT SquareInteger([in] int myInteger, [out] int* square);
```

When you need an actual array, the number of elements in that array must be clearly defined so that the system knows how much data to transmit over the network. When you design a distributed system, remember that every unnecessary byte sent across the network slows the entire system. The simplest technique for passing an array of elements to a function is known as a *fixed array*. From the following code fragment, you can see how fixed arrays got their name—the array holds a fixed number of elements that is known at compile time:

```
HRESULT SumOfIntegers1([in] int myIntegers[5], [out] int* sum);
```

At run time, the marshaler for this method copies the 20 bytes (5 integers multiplied by 4 bytes each) of memory pointed to by *myIntegers* into a transmission buffer. This buffer is then sent to the server, where the *myIntegers* pointer passed to the *SumOfIntegers1* method is adjusted to point directly to the buffer received by the server. In theory, fixed arrays are the most efficient means of passing data. In practice, however, it can be difficult to predict exactly how much data will need to be transferred. Choosing too small a size is an obvious problem, and choosing a larger size can mean that a mostly empty buffer is sent across the network.

As you might recall from Chapter 15, for efficiency reasons the stub often passes—as a method's parameters—direct pointers into the message buffer obtained from the client. With fixed arrays, this is possible because the data transmitted in the buffer is an exact copy of the data in the client's address space, as shown in Figure 16-1.

Conformant Arrays

IDL defines several attributes that help define and control the size of arrays and the data transmitted. These attributes are listed in the following table.

Attribute	Description
first_is	Index of the first array element transmitted
last_is	Index of the last array element transmitted
length_is	Total number of array elements transmitted
max_is	Highest valid array index value
min_is	Lowest valid array index value (not supported—always 0)
size_is	Total number of array elements allocated for the array

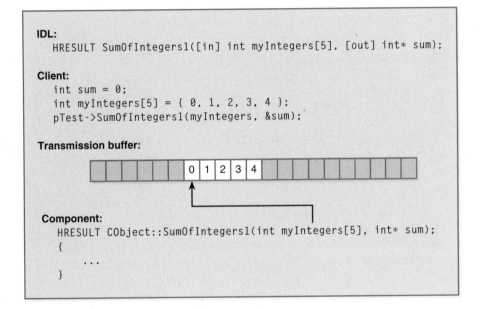

Figure 16-1.
The marshaled form of a fixed array.

To allow the number of elements transmitted to the server to be determined at run time, IDL supports *conformant arrays*. The *size_is* attribute indicates a conformant array. As shown in the following declaration, the caller specifies the actual number of elements in the array at run time. This technique allows the marshaling code to dynamically determine how many elements are in the array, and it has the added advantage of helping the implementation of this method determine how many numbers to add.

```
HRESULT SumOfIntegers2([in] int cMax, [in, size_is(cMax)] int*
    myIntegers, [out] int* sum);
```

Methods that use conformant arrays can be declared using the preceding pointer notation or with the array notation below; they are functionally identical:

```
HRESULT SumOfIntegers2([in] int cMax, [in, size_is(cMax)] int
    myIntegers[], [out] int* sum);
```

Either of these two declarations implies that the client will call the *SumOfIntegers2* method, as shown in the following code fragment:

```
int sum = 0;
int myIntegers[] = { 4, 65, 23, -12, 89, -23, 8 };
pTest->SumOfIntegers2(7, myIntegers, &sum);
cout << "Sum = " << sum;
```

Conformant arrays might also be embedded in structures, as shown in the following example. Note that no more than one conformant array can be nested in a structure and that it must be the last element of the structure.

```
typedef struct tagSUM_STRUCT
{
    int cMax;
    [size_is(cMax)] int* myIntegers;
} SUM_STRUCT;

HRESULT SumOfIntegers3([in] SUM_STRUCT* myIntegers,
    [out] int* sum);
```

The client-side call is shown in the following code:

```
int sum = 0;
int myIntegers[] = { 4, 65, 23, -12, 89, -23, 8 };

SUM_STRUCT x;
x.cMax = 7;
x.myIntegers = myIntegers;
pTest->SumOfIntegers3(&x, &sum);
```

The *max_is* attribute is nearly identical to the *size_is* attribute. The only difference is that the *size_is* attribute specifies the total number of elements in an array and the *max_is* attribute specifies the highest (zero-based) index value into the array. Thus, a *size_is* value of 7 is equivalent to a *max_is* value of 6.

Conformant arrays using the *size_is* or *max_is* attribute work well for parameters with *[in]* attributes but not as well for parameters with *[out]* or even *[in, out]* attributes. The problem is that the server gets stuck with the number of array elements specified by the caller. Imagine the case of a parameter with an *[out]* attribute. The following method returns a specified number of integers:

```
HRESULT ProduceIntegers1([in] int cMax, [out, size_is(cMax)]
    int* myIntegers);
```

The client must allocate a buffer large enough to hold all the data that the method might return, as shown in the following code fragment:

```
int myIntegers[7];
pTest->ProduceIntegers1(7, myIntegers);
```

This is all well and good as long as the server returns exactly seven integers every time. Since the client states the maximum buffer size, the server cannot return more than seven integers; if the server returns less than a full load of integers, network bandwidth is wasted. As with fixed arrays, conformant arrays are passed directly to the method implementation from the message buffer received in the stub because the complete array is always in the request message sent by the client, as shown in Figure 16-2.

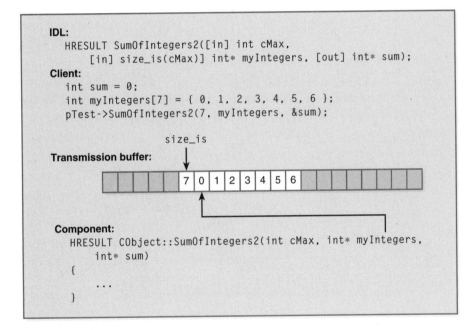

Figure 16-2.
The marshaled form of a conformant array.

Varying Arrays

To deal with the problem of the server returning less than the full number of elements, IDL introduces the concept of *varying arrays*. As with fixed arrays, the bounds of a varying array are decided at compile time, but the range of elements actually transmitted is determined at run time. The *length_is* attribute specifies the number of elements to be transmitted at run time, as shown in the following function declaration:

```
HRESULT ProduceIntegers2([out] int* pcActual,
    [out, length_is(*pcActual)] int myIntegers[4096]);
```

The client-side call is shown here:

```
int how_many_did_we_get = 0;
int myIntegers[4096];
pTest->ProduceIntegers2(&how_many_did_we_get, myIntegers);
cout << how_many_did_we_get << " integers returned.";
```

This mechanism lets the method determine how many integers, up to a preset maximum, should be transmitted back to the client in the response message. The first *[out]* parameter, *pcActual*, is also used to tell the client how many elements were returned. This technique ensures that the client code does not walk into part of the uninitialized buffer accidentally. Varying arrays are also useful for methods with *[in, out]* parameters, as shown in the following declaration:

```
HRESULT SendReceiveIntegers([in, out] int* pcActual,
    [in, out, length_is(*pcActual)] int myIntegers[4096]);
```

This method allows the client to send a variable number of elements and then receive a different number of elements back, as shown here:

```
int num_integers = 5;
int myIntegers[4096] = { 0, 1, 2, 3, 4 };
pTest->SendReceiveIntegers(&num_integers, myIntegers);
cout << num_integers << " integers returned";
```

You can use the *first_is* and *last_is* attributes to mark a certain range of elements in the transmission array. Unless you otherwise specify with the *first_is* attribute, the zero-index element is always the first element of the array transmitted. Using the *first_is* attribute, you can specify a certain element in the array as the starting point for transmission. The *last_is* attribute specifies the index of the last element in the array that is marked for transmission. Like the *max_is* variation on *size_is*, the *last_is* attribute defines an index into the array rather than the count defined by *length_is*. In practice, the *first_is* and *last_is* attributes are rarely used.

When used judiciously, varying arrays reduce network traffic, but they can also hurt performance because the data packet received by the marshaling code is not in the correct format to be handed over to the client or server code. Instead, another block of memory must be allocated on the receiving end and the data reconstructed, as shown in Figure 16-3.

Open Arrays

In practice, varying arrays can be somewhat restrictive because there is always a fixed maximum amount of data that can be transmitted. To combat this problem, IDL lets you create arrays with attributes of both conformant and varying arrays, known as *open arrays* (sometimes called *conformant varying arrays*). An open array is distinguished by the use of both the *size_is* attribute of a conformant array and the *length_is* attribute of a varying array. The caller can control the size of the buffer, but the method itself controls the number of elements transmitted over the wire, as shown in the following code:

```
HRESULT ProduceIntegers3([in] int cMax, [out] int* pcActual,
    [out, size_is(cMax), length_is(*pcActual)] int*
    myIntegers);
```

The client calls the *ProduceIntegers3* method like this:

```
int how_many_did_we_get = 0;
int myIntegers[5];
pTest->ProduceIntegers3(5, &how_many_did_we_get, myIntegers);
cout << how_many_did_we_get << " integers returned.";
```

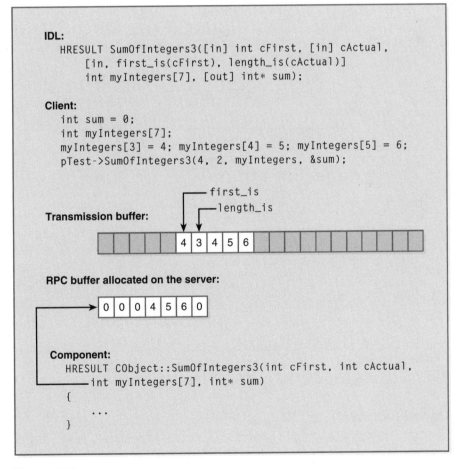

Figure 16-3.
The marshaled form of a varying array.

Generally, conformant arrays are most useful for *[in]* parameters, and open arrays work best for *[out]* and *[in, out]* parameters. Like varying arrays, open arrays must be reconstructed in the second block of memory allocated on the receiving side. The flexibility of varying and open arrays comes with a memory and performance penalty commensurate with the size of the buffer, as shown in Figure 16-4.

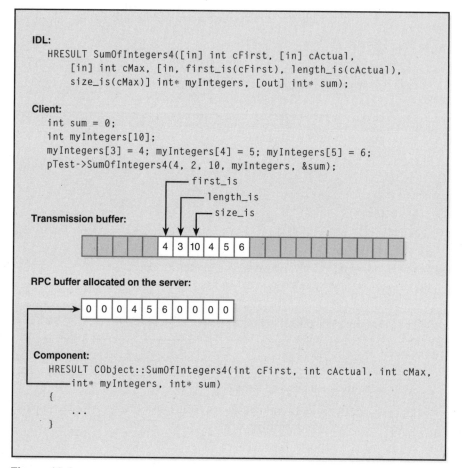

Figure 16-4.
The marshaled form of an open array.

Character Arrays

In C++, a string is fundamentally expressed as an array of characters with a 0 byte indicating the end of the string. Therefore, you can simply pass a string parameter in the same way as other arrays, as shown here:

```
HRESULT SendString1([in] int cLength, [in, size_is(cLength)]
    wchar_t* myString);
```

The client calls this function as follows:

```
wchar_t wszHello[] = L"Inside COM+";
pTest->SendString1(wcslen(wszHello), wszHello);
```

Because passing string parameters is such a common programming practice, IDL offers the *[string]* attribute to make this job easier. IDL can automate the process of calling the appropriate string length function based on the knowledge that all strings end with a null character. With the *[string]* attribute, the *SendString2* method declaration looks like this:

```
HRESULT SendString2([in, string] wchar_t* myString);
```

The client calls this function as shown here:

```
wchar_t wszHello[] = L"Inside COM+";
pTest->SendString2(wszHello);
```

A potential problem arises when the *[string]* attribute is combined with the *[in, out]* attributes, as shown in the following code:

```
HRESULT SendReceiveString1([in, out, string] wchar_t*
    myString);
```

See whether you can find the error in the following code:

```
// Client-side usage
wchar_t wszHello[256] = L"Inside COM+";
pTest->SendReceiveString1(wszHello);
wprintf(L"Received string: %s\n", wszHello);    // ???

// Server-side implementation of the function
HRESULT CObject::SendReceiveString1(wchar_t* myString)
{
    wprintf(L"Received string: %s\n", myString); // Inside COM+
    wcscpy(myString, L"Nice weather today");    // Uh-oh
    return S_OK;
}
```

This code works fine as long as the length of the string returned by the *SendReceiveString1* method is smaller than or equal to the length of the string sent. In this sample, however, the method returns a string several characters longer than that sent by the client. This might not seem like a problem because the client has allocated a buffer of 256 characters, which is more than enough to hold a few extra characters. Nevertheless, the *[string]* attribute used by the *SendReceiveString1* method tells the system to compute the length of the client's string and then allocate only the minimum amount of memory needed on the server side. The result is that the implementation on the server side writes past the end of the character array and onto random bits of memory.

We can correct this problem using the following IDL declaration:

```
HRESULT SendReceiveString2([in] int cMax, [in, out, string,
    size_is(cMax)] wchar_t* myString);
```

The client calls the function as shown here:

```
wchar_t wszHello[256] = L"Inside COM+";
pTest->SendReceiveString2(256, wszHello);
wprintf(L"Received string: %s\n", wszHello);
```

Even this solution is incomplete because the client still must specify the maximum size of the buffer. Yet the exact amount of memory necessary for the result can be determined only inside the method itself. If the client guesses too small a value, the server is out of luck. To avoid these dire straits, robust interfaces usually force the method's implementation to allocate space for the *[out]* buffer. This dynamically allocated buffer is then returned to the client, where it must later be freed. Thus, the IDL declaration of the method is simplified, as shown here:

```
HRESULT SendReceiveString3([in, out, string] wchar_t**
    myString);
```

But the implementation of the *SendReceiveString3* method is made more complex by the addition of the memory allocation call, as shown in the following example:

```
// Server-side implementation of the function
HRESULT CObject::SendReceiveString3(wchar_t** myString)
{
    wprintf(L"Received string: %s\n", *myString);
    CoTaskMemFree(*myString);

    wchar_t returnString[] = L"Nice weather today";
    *myString = (wchar_t*)CoTaskMemAlloc(
        (wcslen(returnString)+1)*sizeof(wchar_t));
    wcscpy(*myString, returnString);
    return S_OK;
}
```

The client-side code is responsible for freeing this memory, as shown here:

```
wchar_t* wszHello = L"Inside COM+";
wchar_t* myString = (wchar_t*)CoTaskMemAlloc(
    (wcslen(wszHello)+1)*sizeof(wchar_t));
```

```
wcscpy(myString, wszHello);
pSum->SendReceiveString3(&myString);

wprintf(L"Received string: %s\n", myString);
CoTaskMemFree(myString);
```

Multidimensional Arrays

IDL can also deal with multidimensional arrays. The biggest problem with marshaling multidimensional arrays is their ambiguous nature in C++. Take a look at the following declaration:

```
int** test;
```

In C++, this declaration can have a number of possible meanings. Is *test* a pointer to a pointer to an integer? A pointer to a pointer to an array of integers? A pointer to an array of pointers to integers? A pointer to an array of pointers to integer arrays? The intended use of *test* is unclear because as far as C++ is concerned, it doesn't make any difference. When you marshal calls between different address spaces, however, these distinctions become crucial. IDL manages these subtle differences by using a special syntax. The *size_is* and *length_is* attributes can work with a variable number of arguments, each indicating the conformance and variance of one level of indirection.

The simplest case is a pointer to a pointer to a single integer, because if no additional attributes are specified, IDL assumes a pointer to a single element. This situation is illustrated by the following IDL declaration:

```
HRESULT SendInteger([in] int** test);
```

The second possibility is that of a pointer to a pointer to an array of integers. In this case, you can use the following IDL declaration, in which the first level of indirection is omitted and the default value of 1 is used. Note that the *size_is* values are read right to left; the rightmost value affects the rightmost pointer of the parameter.

```
HRESULT SendIntegers([in, size_is(, 2)] int** test);
```

A pointer to an array of pointers to integers is declared using the IDL syntax on the following page.

501

```
HRESULT SendIntegers([in, size_is(3, )] int** test);
```

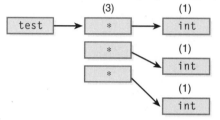

Last, a pointer to an array of pointers to integer arrays defines both positions of the *size_is* attribute, as shown here:

```
HRESULT SendIntegers([in, size_is(3, 2)] int** test);
```

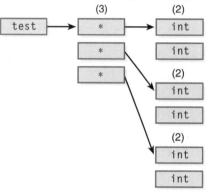

Passing Arrays of User-Defined Types from Visual Basic

From Visual Basic, you can call a method of an interface that accepts an array of structures without using the safe array type described in Chapter 5. For example, the following interface definition contains a method that accepts an array of MYTYPE structures. The MYTYPE structure is also defined in the interface definition.

```
interface ISum : IUnknown
{
    typedef struct MYTYPE
    {
        short a;
        long b;
    } MYTYPE;

    HRESULT Sum([in] long cMax, [in, size_is(cMax)] MYTYPE*
        myarray);
}
```

If you assume that an arbitrary coclass has implemented the *ISum* interface, calling the *ISum::Sum* method from Visual Basic is not difficult. The trick is to pass the array as if you were passing only the first element of that array. For example, if the array is named *myarray*, instead of passing the parameter by using the standard Visual Basic notation *myarray()*, you would use *myarray(0)*, as shown here:

```
Private Sub Command1_Click()
    Dim myRef As New InsideCOM
    Dim myarray(3) As MYTYPE
    myarray(0).a = 1
    myarray(0).b = 5
    myarray(1).a = 2
    myarray(1).b = 4
    myarray(2).a = 3
    myarray(2).b = 3
    myRef.Sum 3, myarray(0)      ' myarray(0) makes arrays work!
End Sub
```

Pointers

As you've seen, the flexibility afforded by pointers in C++ can inflict pain on the unwary when it comes to making remote calls. In C++, pointers can do the following:

- Point to any memory location

- Have the value 0 (*null*)

- Be set to point to a different memory location at any time

- Be aliased

Because IDL must actually transmit the data pointed to by a pointer, it must have a lot of information about what that pointer is pointing to and in what format the data is stored. The designers of IDL were faced with the choice between modeling the language to work as transparently as possible with C++-style pointers, even if the result was greater overhead, or exposing the complexity to the developer in the hope of gaining efficiency. In the end, they decided to offer several options.

To better accommodate a wide range of programs, IDL offers three pointer types: *full, unique,* and *reference.* These are specified in IDL with the *ptr, unique,* and *ref* attributes, respectively, and cannot be combined. If you don't specify a pointer type, the pointer type is determined by the *pointer_default* attribute in the interface header. If you don't specify the *pointer_default* attribute, all non-attributed pointers are assumed to be unique pointers. In this section, we'll look at how and when to use the IDL pointer attributes, as well as how to pass interface pointers as parameters.

Full Pointers

Full pointers most closely model the attributes of C++-style pointers. Although they are rather inefficient, full pointers are useful when you distribute code that was formerly executed within a single process. Full pointers are expensive because they permit pointer aliasing, which means that they allow more than one pointer to point to the same memory location. For example, imagine a complex memory structure such as a doubly linked list. If you have a pointer to an arbitrary element in the list, several pointers reference the same memory location, as shown in Figure 16-5.

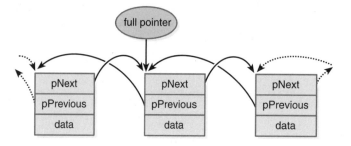

Figure 16-5.
Aliasing with a full pointer.

This situation complicates matters for the marshaling code because the marshaling code must manage several pointers to the data. This is done by maintaining a dictionary of all marshaled pointers. The underlying stub code does this by resolving the various pointers to the addresses and then determining whose copy of the data is the most recent version. In general, you can avoid the need for full pointers by developing a careful interface design.

Unique Pointers

A unique pointer is identical to a full pointer in every respect but one. The difference is that unique pointers cannot cause aliasing of data, which means that storage referred to by a unique pointer cannot be accessed through any other pointer in the function. If you are certain that a pointer will not be aliased, you can mark it as a unique pointer in the IDL code. The MIDL compiler can generate efficient marshaling code for unique pointers because it can make certain assumptions about how that pointer will be used. Unique pointers have the following characteristics:

- They can point to any memory location.
- They can have the value 0 (*null*).
- They can change from non-*null* to *null* or vice-versa during a call.
- IDL ignores changes from one non-*null* value to another non-*null* value during a call.
- They cannot be aliased.

When you pass an uninitialized pointer to a method to retrieve an outbound parameter, you must set the pointer to *null*. Uninitialized pointers might work when you make in-process calls, but proxies and stubs assume that all pointers are either initialized with a valid address or are set to *null* when the call is made. This requirement is a common source of programming errors and can be difficult to track down.

Reference Pointers

From the perspective of IDL, reference pointers are the simplest type of pointer and thus require the least amount of processing by the marshaling code. Like unique pointers, reference pointers do not permit pointer aliasing. Unlike unique pointers, they cannot have the value *null*. A reference pointer must always refer to a valid memory address. Reference pointers are mainly used to implement C++-style reference semantics and allow for outgoing parameters. Function return types, however, cannot be reference pointers.

To summarize, reference pointers have the following characteristics:

- They can point to any memory location.
- They cannot have the value 0 (*null*).
- They cannot be aliased.
- They cannot be set to point to a different memory location during a call.

Interface Pointers

Although IDL can support most types of pointers to data, pointers to C++ classes or functions are off-limits to remote method calls. The only way to access code running in another address space is through an interface pointer. For this reason, a method of an interface will occasionally need to return a pointer to another interface. You might ask, "Wait a minute, isn't that what *QueryInterface* is for?" Well, *QueryInterface* is useful for retrieving an interface pointer on an object, but sometimes a method needs more information in order to return an interface pointer. In such cases, it makes sense to design a method in a custom interface to do the job.

Many standard interfaces have methods that return pointers to other interfaces. To see some examples of such interfaces, you can look up the definitions of the *IServiceProvider::QueryService*, *IMoniker::BindToObject*, *IClassFactory:: CreateInstance*, *IClassActivator::GetClassObject*, *IStorage::CreateStream*, *IOleItem-Container::GetObject*, and *ITypeInfo::CreateInstance* methods, to name but a few.

The simplest way to design a method that accepts an interface pointer as a parameter is to prototype the interface pointer argument as *void***, as shown in the following declaration:

```
HRESULT GetInterfacePointer1([out] void** ppvObject); // Error
```

The problem with this approach is that the MIDL compiler cannot generate proxy/stub code for this method because it doesn't know how to marshal a *void*** argument. For this reason, the preceding declaration will result in a compile error reported by the MIDL compiler. For interfaces designed to be implemented by in-process components only, you can prefix the method declaration with the *[local]* attribute, indicating that no marshaling code needs to be generated by the MIDL compiler, as shown here:

```
[local] HRESULT GetInterfacePointer1([out] void** ppvObject);
```

For interfaces that might be implemented in executable or remote components, you must provide more information about the parameter in the IDL file so that the correct proxy/stub code can be generated. Perhaps the simplest way to do this is to specify the *IUnknown* interface, as shown in the following code. This approach is flexible because all interfaces derive from *IUnknown*. However, the client of this object probably doesn't want an *IUnknown* pointer, which means that the client will most likely follow with an immediate *QueryInterface* call for the desired interface. This approach puts an extra burden on the client code and is less efficient because two round-trips must be made to the component in order to retrieve the desired interface pointer.

```
HRESULT GetInterfacePointer2([out] IUnknown** ppvObject);
```

Recall from Chapter 8 that connection points suffer from this problem. The *IConnectionPoint::Advise* method is declared below in IDL notation. Although clients always pass the *IUnknown* pointer of their sink to the *Advise* method, it is a rare object that is interested in the sink for its *IUnknown* interface. The typical connectable object simply calls *QueryInterface* to request the desired interface.

```
HRESULT Advise
    (
        [in]    IUnknown * pUnkSink,
        [out]   DWORD *    pdwCookie
    );
```

Another approach to this problem is to name the interface being passed, as shown in the following code. Although this tight coupling technique works well initially, it can return to haunt the project at a later date. Problems begin when an improved version of the interface—for example, *IMyCustomInterface2*—is released; the client will need to obtain a pointer to the *IMyCustomInterface* interface before calling *QueryInterface* to request the *IMyCustomInterface2* interface.

```
HRESULT GetInterfacePointer3([out] IMyCustomInterface**
    ppvObject);
```

By now, you might be wondering how the *IUnknown::QueryInterface* method is defined. After all, *QueryInterface* seems to be able to correctly handle interface pointers for any interface, standard or custom. The definition of the *QueryInterface* method taken from the unknwn.idl file is shown here:

```
HRESULT QueryInterface(
    [in] REFIID riid,
    [out, iid_is(riid)] void **ppvObject);
```

The IDL attribute *iid_is* is designed specifically for methods that have an interface pointer as a parameter. You use it to specify the interface identifier (IID) of the interface pointer being transmitted. The *QueryInterface* method obtains this IID from its first parameter. You can use this design when you create methods that return interface pointers, as shown in the following code. This approach effectively solves the issue of versioning custom interfaces because you always specify the interface pointer being marshaled. Specifying the interface pointer also obviates the need for the client to make an extra *QueryInterface* call to obtain the desired interface.

```
HRESULT GetInterfacePointer4([in] REFIID riid,
    [out, iid_is(riid)] void** ppvObject);
```

The *GetInterfacePointer4* method definition implies the following client-side code:

```
IMyCustomInterface* pCustomInterface;
pObject->GetInterfacePointer4(IID_IMyCustomInterface,
    (void**)pCustomInterface);
```

You can also use the IDL attribute *call_as* to help map a nonremotable method, such as one that uses *void* ** as an argument, to a method that can be remoted. For example, without the *call_as* attribute, the method declared here cannot be remoted because it uses a *void* ** argument, and thus the method must be defined using the *local* attribute:

```
[local] HRESULT GetInterfacePointer([in] REFIID riid,
    [out] void** ppvObject);
```

Using the *call_as* attribute, you can map the *GetInterfacePointer* method to a remotable version of the function, appropriately named *RemoteGetInterface-Pointer*, as shown here:

```
[call_as(GetInterfacePointer)] HRESULT
    RemoteGetInterfacePointer([in] REFIID riid,
    [out, iid_is(riid)] IUnknown** ppvObject);
```

Using the *call_as* attribute to map local-only methods to those that can be remoted requires you to write binding routines that map the local types to the remotable ones. These binding routines must be compiled and then linked with the proxy/stub code generated by the MIDL compiler. Listing 16-1 shows the binding routines required for the *GetInterfacePointer* method declared above using the *call_as* attribute:

call_as.cpp

```cpp
// Compile and then link this file with the proxy/stub code
// generated by MIDL.
#include "component.h"

HRESULT __stdcall ITest_GetInterfacePointer_Proxy(ITest* Me,
    REFIID riid, void** ppv)
{
    return ITest_RemoteGetInterfacePointer_Proxy(Me, riid,
        (IUnknown**)ppv);
}

HRESULT __stdcall ITest_GetInterfacePointer_Stub(ITest* Me,
    REFIID riid, IUnknown** ppv)
{
    return Me->GetInterfacePointer(riid, (void**)ppv);
}
```

Listing 16-1.
Binding routines used with the GetInterfacePointer *method.*

Interface Design Recommendations

To help you define custom interfaces, this section provides several guidelines for improved designs. Although no design guidelines can be considered recipes for creating a useful interface specification, we hope that these suggestions will provide you with ideas. If you have found techniques of your own that have proved successful, let us know; perhaps we will be able to include them in a future edition of this book.

First, you should study the standard interfaces that are defined by Microsoft as part of COM+ and its fundamental services, such as structured storage, monikers, connection points, type libraries, automation, and apartments. While not always perfect, Microsoft's designs reflect the goals and objectives of COM+ itself. This knowledge will be invaluable when you define a set of custom interfaces. In addition to this general recommendation, we offer the following more specific guidelines:

- **Make interfaces as simple as possible, but no simpler**   A successful interface can be grasped as a whole entity in a single sitting. As a general rule, most interfaces have between five and seven methods. Again, this is only a general rule—and very good reasons exist to break it. For example, the *IClassActivator* interface has only 1 method, but the *IMoniker* interface has 15. An interface with too many methods is probably trying to cover too much ground and will result in implementations of the interface that return *E_NOTIMPL* for many methods.

- **Be exact when you specify semantics**   Although an interface is a contract, we all know that some contracts are more restrictive than others. When you define a custom interface, you must specify the exact semantics of the interface. If you explicitly permit some methods to return *E_NOTIMPL*, the resulting interface definition is relatively fluid. We've learned from experience that strict interface definitions that do not permit methods to return *E_NOTIMPL* tend to work better in the long run. This fact raises the issue of interface factoring. It is probably better to factor an interface into two or more interfaces instead of designing one interface that permits certain methods to go unimplemented. Factoring allows a more rigid interface definition but doesn't require you to implement undesired functionality.

- **Avoid the one-interface-per-object design**   Sometimes you might design an object for use in a single project. "Since I will be the only one to use this object," you might reason, "it's OK if I design it so that the object has only one interface with 100 methods." (Developers who work for large corporations whose main business is not software development are often guilty of this shortsightedness.) This type of one-interface-per-object design is particularly poor because it overlooks a major design goal of COM+: the ability of an object to implement multiple interfaces and for the client to use the *QueryInterface* method to navigate among them. Your reasoning might be correct now, but you never know when someone else might want to implement your interface in a different project. Of course, the one-interface-per-object design is a self-fulfilling prophecy; no one in his or her right mind would ever voluntarily implement an interface with 100 methods.

■ **Evaluate different methods of passing information**   The number of parameters passed with each method of a given interface is another design concern. In most cases, it is obvious what information the method requires to do its job, but there are different ways to provide this information. For example, if a method might be called repeatedly, it makes sense for that method to pass the minimum amount of data possible, thus reducing the network bandwidth used when making remote calls. In such cases, it might make sense to define an "initialization" method that is called once with the required information, in advance of the worker method calls. Also, because all the standard interfaces that deal with strings use Unicode characters, we strongly recommend that you do likewise when you design your own interfaces.

■ **Obey the versioning rules**   When new versions of COM+ interfaces are created, it is customary to place a revision number at the end of the interface name. For example, the *IHello* interface becomes *IHello2*. This numbering technique has made COM+ the subject of some derision, especially since COM+ is supposed to resolve many of the versioning issues facing applications. The truth is that COM+ does help solve these versioning problems by introducing the notion of a *binary contract* (otherwise known as an interface) to which both clients and implementers must adhere. Once it is published, an interface can never be changed because doing so would break the binary compatibility promised by COM+.

CHAPTER SEVENTEEN

Asynchronous Calls

The standard COM+ model is completely synchronous. When a client application calls a method of an interface implemented by an object, the client thread blocks until the method executes and returns. This synchronous model, which originated in Remote Procedure Calls (RPCs) to emulate standard procedure calls, is not necessarily the best for all scenarios, however. Clients usually want to make synchronous calls, but sometimes a client application will want to do other work while the object is processing a method call. This is true especially in distributed scenarios with high network latency or in cases where the object will do a lot of processing during a single method call, such as a database query.

Even in the synchronous model, it is possible for the client application to spawn multiple threads, some of which might call methods of COM+ objects and some of which might do processing on the client side. While this is a reasonable way of making asynchronous calls when there is no alternative, it is advantageous to have a service of this type built into the system infrastructure. If you make many concurrent calls, spawning hundreds of threads can cause the system to spend more time switching between threads than doing productive work. Where asynchronous calls are a feature of the infrastructure, the system can optimize the calls to lessen the overall load.

Making Asynchronous Calls

In Microsoft Windows 2000, COM+ includes support for asynchronous calls. A client thread can execute a method asynchronously. COM+ starts the call and then immediately returns control back to the client. The client thread is then free to do other work and can later obtain the results of the method call. If the client thread reaches a point where it can no longer do any useful work without the results of the asynchronous method call, it can block until the object has finished processing the call. COM+ also enables the client thread to cancel the method call. For example, the client might decide that it no longer needs the results of the method call or that the object is simply taking too long.

Defining Asynchronous Interfaces

As with all other programming tasks in COM+, Interface Definition Language (IDL) is the starting place for defining asynchronous interfaces. For each interface defined in IDL that you want to call asynchronously, you must add the *async_uuid* IDL attribute. When the Microsoft IDL (MIDL) compiler sees this attribute in a COM+ interface definition, it automatically generates two versions of that interface: one for traditional synchronous use and the other for asynchronous calls. The asynchronous version of the interface will have the same name as the synchronous interface except with an *Async* prefix. For example, the asynchronous version of the *IUnknown* interface defined in the unknown.idl system IDL file is named *AsyncIUnknown*.

For the asynchronous version of an interface, MIDL splits every method in the interface into two methods named *Begin_*methodname and *Finish_*methodname. Each *Begin_* method accepts all of the *[in]* and *[in, out]* parameters of the synchronous version of that method; each *Finish_* method includes all of the *[out]* and *[in, out]* parameters. The interface definition shown below includes the *async_uuid* attribute; notice that the asynchronous version of the interface has its own globally unique identifier (GUID):

```
[ object, uuid(10000001-AAAA-0000-0000-A00000000001),  // IID_IPrime
    async_uuid(10000001-AAAA-0000-0000-B00000000001) ] // IID_AsyncIPrime
interface IPrime : IUnknown
{
    HRESULT IsPrime(int testnumber, [out, retval] int* retval);
}
```

The corresponding asynchronous version of this interface generated by MIDL in the component.h file is shown below. Notice that the single *IsPrime* method of the synchronous *IPrime* interface has been converted to the *Begin_IsPrime* and *Finish_IsPrime* methods of the asynchronous *AsyncIPrime* interface. The *[in]* parameter (*testnumber*) of the *IPrime::IsPrime* method becomes an argument of the *AsyncIPrime::Begin_IsPrime* method. The *[out]* parameter (*retval*) of the *IPrime::IsPrime* method becomes an argument of the *AsyncIPrime::Finish_IsPrime* method.

```
MIDL_INTERFACE("10000001-AAAA-0000-0000-B00000000001")
AsyncIPrime : public IUnknown
{
public:
    virtual HRESULT STDMETHODCALLTYPE Begin_IsPrime(
        int testnumber) = 0;

    virtual HRESULT STDMETHODCALLTYPE Finish_IsPrime(
        /* [out][retval] */ int __RPC_FAR *retval) = 0;
};
```

512

Interesting entries are created in the HKEY_CLASSES_ROOT\Interface section of the registry when you build and register the proxy/stub code generated by the MIDL compiler for an asynchronous interface. The entry for the interface identifier (IID) of the synchronous version of the interface contains a subkey named AsynchronousInterface that references the IID of the asynchronous version of the interface. The entry for the IID of the asynchronous version of the interface contains a subkey named SynchronousInterface that points back to the synchronous version. Figure 17-1 shows all of the registry entries created by the proxy/stub dynamic-link library (DLL).

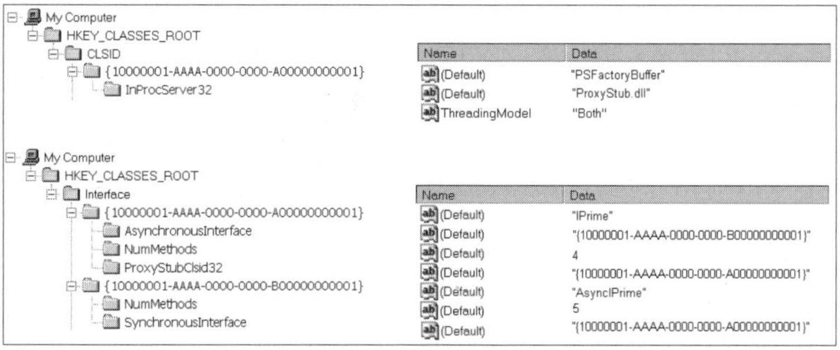

Figure 17-1.
The registry entries created by a proxy/stub DLL for an asynchronous interface.

Calling Asynchronous Interfaces

Typically, a single coclass does not implement both the synchronous and asynchronous versions of an interface. Instead, the coclass that implements the synchronous version of the interface acts as a class object for the coclass that implements the asynchronous version. A separate object, known as a call object, implements the asynchronous version of the interface. The coclass that implements the synchronous version of the interface also implements the standard *ICallFactory* interface. The *ICallFactory* interface has only one method, *CreateCall*, which is shown below in IDL notation:

```
interface ICallFactory : IUnknown
{
    HRESULT CreateCall(
        [in]  REFIID                riid,
        [in]  IUnknown              *pCtrlUnk,
        [in]  REFIID                riid2,
        [out, iid_is(riid2)] IUnknown **ppv );
}
```

The client calls *QueryInterface* to obtain the *ICallFactory* interface pointer. Using this pointer, the client calls the *ICallFactory::CreateCall* method to instantiate the call object that implements the asynchronous version of the desired interface. The client can then call the *Begin_* method to start the asynchronous call, followed sometime later with a call to the *Finish_* method to obtain the results of the asynchronous call. The following code fragment illustrates these steps:

```
IPrime* pPrime = 0;
hr = CoCreateInstance(CLSID_InsideCOM, 0, CLSCTX_LOCAL_SERVER,
    IID_IPrime, (void**)&pPrime);

ICallFactory* pCallFactory = 0;
hr = pPrime->QueryInterface(IID_ICallFactory,
    (void**)&pCallFactory);

AsyncIPrime* pAsyncPrime = 0;
hr = pCallFactory->CreateCall(IID_AsyncIPrime, 0,
    IID_AsyncIPrime, (IUnknown**)&pAsyncPrime);

int result = 0;
hr = pAsyncPrime->Begin_IsPrime(testnumber);

// Do other work here.

// Sometime later...
hr = pAsyncPrime->Finish_IsPrime(&result);
if(result)
    cout << endl << testnumber << " is prime." << endl;

pAsyncPrime->Release();
pCallFactory->Release();
pPrime->Release();
```

Each call object can process only one asynchronous call at a time. If a second asynchronous call is invoked on the same call object while the first call is still executing, the *Begin_* method returns RPC_S_CALLPENDING. The client calls the *Finish_* method when it is ready to retrieve the results of the asynchronous call. If the asynchronous call is still executing when the *Finish_* method is called, the *Finish_* method automatically blocks the client thread until the object has completed executing the call. The *Finish_* method must be called before a new asynchronous call can be issued on the call object. If you're not interested in the values returned by the *Finish_* method and don't intend to issue another asynchronous call on the call object, you can simply release the call object; COM+ detects this condition and automatically cleans up the call.

If you simply want to find out whether the object has finished processing the asynchronous call, you should query the call object for the *ISynchronize*

interface and call the *ISynchronize::Wait* method. The *ISynchronize* interface is
shown below in IDL notation:

```
interface ISynchronize : IUnknown
{
    // Waits for the synchronization object to be signaled or
    // for a specified timeout period to elapse, whichever
    // comes first
    HRESULT Wait([in] DWORD dwFlags, [in] DWORD dwMilliseconds);

    // Sets the synchronization object's state to signaled
    HRESULT Signal();

    // Resets the synchronization object to the
    // not signaled state
    HRESULT Reset();
}
```

The *ISynchronize::Wait* method accepts two parameters: an options flag from
the *COWAIT_FLAGS* enumeration shown below, and the number of milliseconds
to block before timing out. COM+ provides two built-in implementations of the
ISynchronize interface: *CLSID_StdEvent* and *CLSID_ManualResetEvent*. Because
the system provides these two coclasses that implement *ISynchronize*, there is
typically no need to implement this interface; if your object wants to expose
ISynchronize, you can simply aggregate one of the two built-in implementations.

```
typedef enum tagCOWAIT_FLAGS
{
    COWAIT_WAITALL = 1,
    COWAIT_ALERTABLE = 2
} COWAIT_FLAGS;
```

Internally, the system-provided implementation of the *ISynchronize::Wait*
method calls the *CoWaitForMultipleHandles* function. This synchronization
primitive waits for handles to be signaled or for the specified timeout period to
elapse. In the STA model, *CoWaitForMultipleHandles* enters a modal message
loop so it won't freeze the application's user interface; in the MTA model, this
function simply puts the calling thread to sleep until the handles become signaled or the timeout period expires. So to find out whether an asynchronous
call has completed, you simply call the *ISynchronize::Wait* method with a timeout
of 0, as shown below:

```
hr = pSynchronize->Wait(0, 0);
if(hr == RPC_S_CALLPENDING)
    cout << "Call is still pending." << endl;
```

Implementing Asynchronous Interfaces

Objects that want to support asynchronous calls need to implement the *ICallFactory* interface. The *ICallFactory::CreateCall* method is called by a client that is preparing to make an asynchronous call. The implementer of this method should instantiate a call object that implements the asynchronous version of the interface. The first parameter of the *CreateCall* method comes from the client; it specifies the IID of the asynchronous interface for which the client wants a call object. In the code fragment shown below, the object supports only the *AsyncIPrime* interface; if the client has requested any other interface, an error is returned.

The second parameter of *CreateCall* is a pointer to the controlling *IUnknown*. Call objects are typically aggregated by the system so that COM+ can provide automatic implementation of interfaces such as *ISynchronize*. Even though the client typically passes *null* for this parameter, COM+ automatically aggregates the object on the server side and provides the call object with a pointer to the controlling unknown of the outer object. The third and fourth parameters of *CreateCall* are standard *QueryInterface*-style arguments. The client specifies which interface implemented by the call object it would like in the third parameter, and that interface pointer is returned in the fourth parameter.

A sample implementation of the *ICallFactory::CreateCall* method is shown below. Note that because the call object is aggregated by COM+, it must provide a delegating version of *QueryInterface* in addition to the standard implementation. The call object's nondelegating implementation of *QueryInterface* need only check for the *IUnknown* and *AsyncIPrime* interfaces.

```
HRESULT CInsideCOM::CreateCall(REFIID riid, IUnknown* pCtrlUnk,
    REFIID riid2, IUnknown** ppv)
{
    HRESTUL hr = 0;

    if(riid != IID_AsyncIPrime)
        return E_INVALIDARG;

    CPrimeCall* pPrimeCall = new CPrimeCall(pCtrlUnk);
    hr = pPrimeCall->Init();
    hr = pPrimeCall->QueryInterface_NoAggregation(riid2,
        (void**)ppv);
    pPrimeCall->Release_NoAggregation();
    return hr;
}
```

The *CPrimeCall* constructor simply stores the *IUnknown* pointer of the outer object (named *pCtrlUnk* in the code on the previous page) for use in its delegating implementation of *IUnknown*. The call object is then initialized in the *CPrimeCall::Init* method, as shown below. Assuming that the call object is being aggregated by COM+, we query the outer object for the *ISynchronize* interface and store that interface pointer for later use when signaling the client that an asynchronous call is complete. The *ISynchronize* interface pointer is eventually released in the *CPrimeCall* destructor.

```
HRESULT CPrimeCall::Init()
{
    if(m_pCtrlUnk)
        return m_pCtrlUnk->QueryInterface(IID_ISynchronize,
            (void**)&m_pSynchronize);
    return E_UNEXPECTED;
}
```

When the client invokes the *Begin_IsPrime* message to start an asynchronous call, COM+ calls the *Begin_IsPrime* method in the call object. The *Begin_IsPrime* method does its work in the usual fashion, but instead of returning the result back to the client, it stores the return value in a member variable (*m_retval*) of the call object. Then it signals the outer object's synchronization object to let the client know that the asynchronous call is complete. The changed portions of the *IsPrime* method are shown in boldface below:

```
HRESULT CPrimeCall::Begin_IsPrime(int testnumber)
{
    unsigned long count;
    unsigned long halfnumber = testnumber / 2 + 1;
    HRESULT hr = 0;

    for(count = 2; count < halfnumber; count++)
        if(testnumber % count == 0)
        {
            m_retval = false;
            m_pSynchronize->Signal();
            return S_OK;
        }

    m_retval = true;
    m_pSynchronize->Signal();
    return S_OK;
}
```

The implementation of the *AsyncIPrime::Finish_IsPrime* method simply returns the *m_retval* value saved in the call object by the *Begin_IsPrime* method, as shown below. Note that only the *Begin_* method of an asynchronous interface is actually called asynchronously; the client thread is always blocked during calls to *Finish_* methods. For this reason, it is desirable to do as little processing as a possible in a *Finish_* method.

```
HRESULT CPrimeCall::Finish_IsPrime(int* retval)
{
    *retval = m_retval;
    return S_OK;
}
```

Interoperability

Although every asynchronous interface has a unique IID, asynchronous and synchronous interfaces are considered two parts of one interface. This idea leads to some interesting scenarios in which a client might attempt to invoke methods of an asynchronous interface on an object that implements only the synchronous version of that interface. In such cases, the client can trap the failed *QueryInterface* call for the *ICallFactory* interface and default to the synchronous version of the interface.

This solution, however, places the onus on the client to detect and compensate for a feature not provided by the object. To better support interoperability between clients and objects, the standard marshaling infrastructure of COM+ automatically supports the *ICallFactory* interface in the proxy even if the object does not implement this interface. When the client calls the *Begin_* method, the proxy converts this into a standard call on the synchronous version of the interface. The proxy then holds the values returned by the method until the client calls the *Finish_* method to obtain the results.

Only standard marshaling provides this built-in support for mapping asynchronous client calls to synchronous calls on the object. If the object uses custom marshaling, COM+ cannot provide an automatic implementation of *ICallFactory* on the proxy. In addition, if the client and the object are running in the same process and are not separated by apartments or contexts, no proxy/stub code is loaded and consequently COM+ cannot provide the automatic asynchronous to synchronous translation. In such cases, the client's only recourse is to obtain a pointer to the synchronous version of the interface and make synchronous calls.

Another interesting case occurs when a client makes calls to the synchronous version of an interface on an object that implements the synchronous and asynchronous versions of that interface. In this case, the object must provide two implementations of what is fundamentally a single interface. To avoid the unnecessary duplication of functionality in the synchronous and asynchronous versions of an interface, the standard marshaling infrastructure automatically marshals synchronous client calls to the asynchronous version of the interface if they are supported by the object. Thus, the object does not have to actually implement the synchronous version of the interface so long as it provides a call object that implements the asynchronous version.

When the client makes a synchronous call on the synchronous version of the interface, the proxy in the client's address space calls the *Begin_* method and blocks until the method returns. Then the proxy automatically calls the *Finish_* method to obtain the results of the call before returning control to the client. This programming model greatly simplifies life for both the client and the object. The client can make asynchronous calls even if the object does not support this functionality. The object can implement only the asynchronous version of an interface that will be used to service both synchronous and asynchronous client calls.

Call Cancellation

Client applications can make asynchronous calls to ensure that their threads are not blocked during the execution of a method. Sometimes the user might request that a long operation be canceled, so it can be useful for the client application to notify the server that it is no longer interested in the results of a call. COM+ supports call cancellation for such cases. Call cancellation in COM+ is handled through the *ICancelMethodCalls* interface, which is shown below in IDL notation:

```
interface ICancelMethodCalls : IUnknown
{
    // Called by the client
    // Requests that a method be canceled
    HRESULT Cancel         ([in] ULONG ulSeconds);

    // Called by the object
    // Determines if a call has been canceled
    HRESULT TestCancel     (void);
}
```

To request the cancellation of an outstanding call, the client obtains a pointer to the *ICancelMethodCalls* interface and then calls the *ICancelMethodCalls::Cancel* method. As long as the object uses standard marshaling, the object need not actually implement the *ICancelMethodCalls* interface; the proxy manager creates a cancel object that implements this interface when the call is marshaled. After the object requests the cancellation of a method, it will be unable to retrieve any return values and the method will return the *RPC_E_CALL_CANCELED* code. Objects that use custom marshaling must provide their own implementation of *ICancelMethodCalls* if they want to support call cancellation. The *CoSwitchCallContext* function enables custom-marshaled objects to install their own call context object. Proxies use the *CoSetCancelObject* function to register or unregister a cancel object for use during subsequent cancel operations on the calling thread.

Requesting Method Call Cancellation

When the client makes an asynchronous call, the cancellation request should follow at some point after the *Begin_* method but before the *Finish_* method. In the code fragment shown below, the client simply calls *QueryInterface* on the call object to obtain the *ICancelMethodCalls* interface implemented by the proxy manager and then calls *ICancelMethodCalls::Cancel*. The *Cancel* method accepts one argument that specifies the number of seconds the *Cancel* method should wait for the object to cancel the call. If the value is 0, the *Cancel* method returns immediately. A value of *RPC_C_CANCEL_INFINITE_TIMEOUT* indicates the client's willingness to wait however long it might take for the object to cancel the method. Note that for all values except 0, the specified timeout passed to the *Cancel* method is only a suggestion. The cancel object can consider factors such as the context of the call (in-process, out-of-process, or remote) and the threading model when determining how long to block. The return value of the *Cancel* method indicates whether the method finished executing (*RPC_E_CALL_COMPLETE*) or if the cancellation request was submitted (*S_OK*). Then the *ICancelMethodCalls* interface pointer is released.

```
ICancelMethodCalls* pCancelMethodCalls = 0;

hr = pSynchronize->QueryInterface(IID_ICancelMethodCalls,
    (void**)&pCancelMethodCalls);
if(SUCCEEDED(hr))
{
    hr = pCancelMethodCalls->Cancel(0);

    if(hr == RPC_E_CALL_COMPLETE)
        cout << "The call finished executing before it was cancelled."
            << endl;
    if(hr == S_OK)
        cout << "The cancel request was submitted." << endl;

    pCancelMethodCalls->Release();
}
```

When the client makes a synchronous method call, only another thread in the client process can issue the cancellation request because the thread that made the synchronous call is blocked for the duration of the method. In this scenario, COM+ provides the *CoEnableCallCancellation* and *CoGetCancelObject* functions. Unlike with asynchronous method calls, call cancellation is disabled by default for synchronous method calls. Before invoking any synchronous methods that might be canceled, the client thread must call the *CoEnableCallCancellation* function[1]—otherwise, the *CO_E_CANCEL_DISABLED* error will be returned by the *ICancelMethodCalls::Cancel* method. The client thread can then obtain its thread identifier by calling the *GetCurrentThreadID* Win32 API function before making a synchronous method call.

The code fragment below shows a client thread that gets its thread identifier and stores it in a global variable, enables call cancellation, spawns a new thread, and then makes a synchronous method call:

```
IPrime* pPrime = 0;
hr = CoCreateInstance(CLSID_InsideCOM, 0, CLSCTX_LOCAL_SERVER,
    IID_IPrime, (void**)&pPrime);

// Get the current thread identifier and store it in a
// global variable.
g_threadid = GetCurrentThreadId();

// Turn on call cancellation for this thread.
CoEnableCallCancellation(0);

// Start a new thread to cancel the synchronous method
// call below.
DWORD newthread = 0;
HANDLE thread_handle = CreateThread(0, 0,
    (LPTHREAD_START_ROUTINE)MyThread, 0,
    0, &newthread);

int result = 0;
hr = pPrime->IsPrime(testnumber, &result);
if(hr == RPC_E_CALL_CANCELED)
    cout << "The call was canceled." << endl;
else if(SUCCEEDED(hr))
    if(result)
        cout << testnumber << " is prime." << endl;

pPrime->Release();
```

---

1. The *CoDisableCallCancellation* function disables cancellation of synchronous method calls made on the calling thread.

The newly created thread uses the thread identifier of the first thread when it calls *CoGetCancelObject* to obtain the *ICancelMethodCalls* interface implemented by the cancel object of the first thread. The *ICancelMethodCalls:: Cancel* method is then called in the standard way, as shown in the code below. COM+ also provides the *CoCancelCall* helper function, which you can use in place of the *CoGetCancelObject, ICancelMethodCalls::Cancel*, and *Release* calls.

```
void __stdcall MyThread(DWORD nothing)
{
    HRESULT hr = CoInitializeEx(NULL, COINIT_MULTITHREADED);

    // Get the cancel object of the first thread.
    ICancelMethodCalls* pCancelMethodCalls = 0;
    hr = CoGetCancelObject(g_threadid, IID_ICancelMethodCalls,
        (void**)&pCancelMethodCalls);

    // Request that the first thread's synchronous call
    // be canceled.
    hr = pCancelMethodCalls->Cancel(0);

    // Release the cancel object.
    pCancelMethodCalls->Release();

    CoUninitialize();
}
```

Terminating the Method

Even when the client requests cancellation of a method call, there is no guarantee that the method executing in the object will actually abort. The object must be coded explicitly to detect a client's cancellation request via the *ICancelMethodCalls::TestCancel* method and then abort execution. The object obtains a pointer to the cancel object by calling the *CoGetCallContext* function and requesting an *ICancelMethodCalls* interface pointer. A modified version of the *AsyncIPrime::Begin_IsPrime* method that supports call cancellation is shown below; the relevant sections are in boldface:

```
HRESULT CPrimeCall::Begin_IsPrime(int testnumber)
{
    unsigned long count;
    unsigned long halfnumber = testnumber / 2 + 1;
    HRESULT hr = 0;

    for(count = 2; count < halfnumber; count++)
```

```
{
    ICancelMethodCalls* pCancelMethodCalls = 0;

    CoGetCallContext(IID_ICancelMethodCalls,
        (void**)&pCancelMethodCalls);

    hr = pCancelMethodCalls->TestCancel();

    pCancelMethodCalls->Release();

    if(hr == RPC_E_CALL_CANCELED)
        return RPC_E_CALL_CANCELED;

    if(testnumber % count == 0)
    {
        m_retval = false;
        m_pSynchronize->Signal();
        return S_OK;
    }

    m_retval = true;
    m_pSynchronize->Signal();
    return S_OK;
}
```

Alternatively, objects can call the *CoTestCancel* helper function to determine whether the client has requested the cancellation of a method call. *CoTestCancel* calls *CoGetCallContext* to obtain the *ICancelMethodCalls* interface pointer on the current cancel object, and then it calls the *ICancelMethodsCalls::Cancel* method. After the cancellation request is submitted, *CoTestCancel* automatically releases the cancel object.

Pipes

The standard mechanism for communication in COM+ is the method call. When a client calls a method, the *[in]* arguments are sent to the server and the *[out]* arguments are returned at the end of the call. This marshaling technique was originally designed to make RPCs as transparent as possible. While the *[in]* and *[out]* attributes are useful for passing regular function parameters, they were not designed for transferring large amounts of data over the network. Developers who build distributed applications often require an optimized mechanism for high-speed data transfer. Pipes were introduced in COM+ to meet this need.

Fundamentally, a pipe is an ordered sequence of elements of the same type. The number of elements in a pipe grows and shrinks dynamically as data is pushed into or pulled from the pipe; there are no hard limits on the size of a pipe. COM+ pipes are also bidirectional: an application can intersperse push and pull operations on pipes. Thus, pipes provide a useful mechanism for transferring large amounts of data in an efficient and location-transparent manner.

COM+ defines three pipe interfaces—*IPipeByte*, *IPipeLong*, and *IPipeDouble*—from a template-like interface definition, which is shown below in IDL notation. Each pipe interface has two methods, *Pull* and *Push*, but the methods of each interface pull and push parameters of a different type. *IPipeByte* transfers 8-bit *byte* values, *IPipeLong* transfers 32-bit *long* values, and *IPipeDouble* transfers 64-bit *double* values.

```
interface IPipe##name : IUnknown
{
    HRESULT Pull(
        [out, size_is(cRequest), length_is(*pcReturned)]
            type* buf,
        [in]  ULONG  cRequest,
        [out] ULONG* pcReturned);

    HRESULT Push(
        [in, size_is(cSent)] type* buf,
        [in] ULONG cSent);
}
```

One neat aspect of COM+ pipes is that this functionality is provided by regular interfaces that can be implemented by coclasses and called by clients. This means that a pointer to one of the pipe interfaces can be passed as regular *[in]* or *[out]* method parameters of some other interface. For each pipe interface, COM+ also provides a corresponding asynchronous version. The proxy/stub code for the pipe interfaces performs read-ahead and write-behind optimizations using the asynchronous versions of the pipe interfaces. This improves the performance of large data transfer transparently to the application. Although an application can make direct use of the asynchronous pipe interfaces, this technique overrides the built-in buffering in the proxy/stub code.

The code fragment below shows an implementation of the *IPipeLong::Pull* method that generates sequential numbers when called by the client:

```
HRESULT CInsideCOM::Pull(long* buf, ULONG cRequest,
    ULONG* pcReturned)
{
    long data = 1;

    for(ULONG count = 0; count < cRequest; count++)
        buf[count] = data++;
```

```
        *pcReturned = count;
        return S_OK;
}
```

The corresponding client side that calls the *IPipeLong::Pull* method is shown below. First, the client calls *QueryInterface* to obtain a pointer to the *IPipeLong* interface implemented by the object. Then it calls the *Pull* method and prints out the data. Finally, the pipe is released.

```
IPipeLong* pPipeLong = 0;
hr = pPrime->QueryInterface(IID_IPipeLong, (void**)&pPipeLong);

ULONG pulled = 0;
long bugger[100000];
hr = pPipeLong->Pull(bugger, 100000, &pulled);
if(FAILED(hr))
    cout << "Pull 10000 FAILED" << endl;

cout << "Pulled " << pulled << endl;
_getch();

for(ULONG count = 0; count < pulled; count++)
    cout << bugger[count] << " ";

pPipeLong->Release();
```

CHAPTER EIGHTEEN

Security

In these paranoid times of globally interconnected computer networks, the issue of security preoccupies individual users as well as large organizations. Computer security encompasses a diverse body of knowledge. Cryptography, virus detection, authentication, auditing, certificates, permissions, access control, digital signatures, and firewalls are but a few of the topics that fall under the rubric of security. Although the security of computer networks is an important subject, we believe that for most projects, security is more of an administration and deployment issue than a development issue. Security sometimes receives too much attention too early in a project—attention that might be better devoted to other areas of the system. Like a broken clock that tells the correct time twice a day, the most secure systems are those that don't work.

It is certainly important for component developers to understand the COM+ security model, since this is one area of COM+ that can bite you where you least expect it. A few words of caution before we begin: Before you read this chapter, be sure that you are intimately familiar with COM+. And after you read this chapter, be sure to learn about the role-based security services that are available to configured components. Role-based security simplifies security and administration issues for middle-tier components; it is covered in volume 2 of *Inside COM+*. In this chapter, we'll examine the declarative and programmatic security options that COM+ offers to system administrators and component developers. You'll learn how to protect a component from launch and access by unauthorized clients and how to protect the confidentiality of data transmitted across a network.

The Windows Distributed Security Model

The basic Microsoft Windows security model focuses on two areas: authentication and access control. Authentication is usually encountered when a user attempts to log on to a network or call a process on another machine. In such cases, the system wants to be sure that the user is who she claims to be. Access control in Windows enables applications to selectively grant or deny certain users access to specific services. While any executable code presents a potential security risk, Windows mitigates this risk by limiting the access permissions of a given process, depending on the user account it is running under. To this end, Windows maintains an access token for each user logged on to the system; the access token contains information identifying the user and the user groups to which the user belongs and information about other privileges that might be available. A copy of this access token is later associated with each process launched by that user. The operating system selectively grants or denies access to system services by comparing the access token of the running process with the security information attached to the system object that the user wants to access.

Each user and user group is identified in the access token by a unique value called a *security identifier* (SID). Every system object—such as a thread, a mutex, a semaphore, an event, or a file—can contain a *security descriptor* that includes the SID of the object's owner and of the primary user group to which the owner belongs. Also stored in this security descriptor is the *discretionary access control list* (DACL), which controls access permissions, and the *system access control list* (SACL), which specifies operations on the object that should generate audit messages. Both types of *access control lists* (ACLs) are really linked lists of *access control entries* (ACEs). Each ACE in a DACL either grants or denies a certain permission to a specific user or user group. The system checks each ACE in the DACL to determine whether permission has been granted or denied. Once it makes the determination, it does not examine the remaining ACEs, as shown in Figure 18-1.

The COM+ Security Model

When you're learning about the COM+ security model, it is helpful to understand what resources must be secured. Here are the primary goals of the COM+ security model:

- Activation control
- Access control
- Authentication control
- Identity control

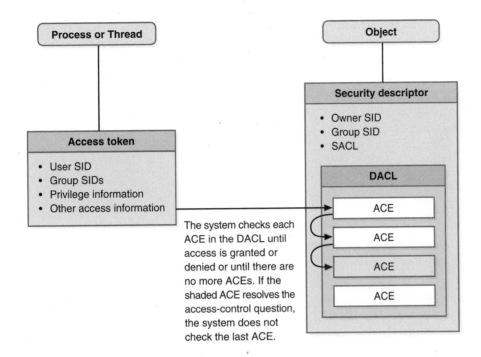

Figure 18-1.
Checking an object's DACL to determine whether the client has the requisite permissions.

Activation control enforces who is permitted to launch components. Once a component has been launched, access control limits access to the component's objects. In some cases, it might be acceptable for certain users to have access to certain areas of functionality while other services of a component are restricted. For example, perhaps all users connecting over the World Wide Web are permitted to access certain areas of the component's functionality, but other services are reserved for authorized users only. Authentication control ensures that a network transmission is authentic and protects the data from unauthorized viewers. Different authentication levels can be set so that all the data is encrypted before being transmitted. Identity control determines the security credentials under which the component will execute. These credentials can be a specific user account configured for this purpose or the security credentials of the client application.

529

Security information for COM+ components is configured in two ways: using declarative security and using programmatic security. Declarative security settings are configured in the registry external to the component. A system administrator typically configures declarative security. Programmatic security is incorporated into a component by the developer. Activation, access, authentication, and identity security settings for a component can be configured in the declarative manner via the registry, using a utility such as the Distributed COM Configuration utility (dcomcnfg.exe). Access and authentication security can also be controlled programmatically by using several interfaces and helper functions provided by COM+. Activation and identity security cannot be controlled programmatically because these settings must be specified before a component is launched.

Running the Distributed COM Configuration Utility on Windows 95 and Windows 98

By default, Windows 95 and Windows 98 are set for share-level access control—access control that allows a password to be assigned to each shared resource. Although the Distributed COM Configuration utility refuses to run in this mode, remote calls can still be executed, albeit without any security. Because this utility refuses to run with share-level access control, you must use the registry editor to adjust the registry settings for remote execution of a component. Basically, this amounts to disabling authentication and enabling remote connections. Only in a network with a domain controller that can be used to provide pass-through security can COM+ security be enabled for Windows 95 and Windows 98 machines. When pass-through security is used, the domain controller provides security information to a system. In a networked environment with a domain controller, follow these steps to configure Windows 95 and Windows 98 for user-level access control:

1. Choose Start/Settings/Control Panel.

2. Open the Network applet in the Control Panel, and click the Access Control tab.

3. Select User-Level Access Control, and click OK.

After rebooting, you can run dcomcnfg.exe.

COM+ Security Packages

Perhaps you're wondering why COM+ needs a special security model. Windows is a secure operating system platform, so why can't COM+ components simply leverage that security model? The answer is that they can—but they shouldn't. As you know, the design of COM+ is not tied to the design of Windows in any way. In addition to the various flavors of Windows, COM+ components can run on many other operating systems. Most of these operating systems have their own notion of security, and certainly none support the security functions of the Win32 API. In fact, neither Windows 95 nor Windows 98 supports many of these security functions. COM+ requires a security model that can be supported on all platforms on which COM+ services are available.

COM+ defines a higher-level security model by abstracting the underlying security mechanisms of both Windows and Remote Procedure Calls (RPCs)—which explains why many of the security flags used by COM+ have been borrowed from the RPC security infrastructure. Aside from platform-independence, the COM+ security model insulates component developers from the Windows and RPC security mechanisms so that as these technologies evolve, components will be able to derive benefits from the new security services automatically. This flexible security model is built around the Security Support Provider Interface (SSPI), a standard API designed to support the security needs of applications running in a distributed environment.

The design of the SSPI can be compared with the architecture of Open Database Connectivity (ODBC). ODBC was designed to insulate database application developers from a specific back-end database server by offering numerous drivers that implement the standard ODBC API for use by client-side developers but that communicate with a specific back-end database server using the proprietary interface that the server understands. To support the varying security requirements of different applications, vendors can implement the SSPI API in a dynamic-link library (DLL) called a Security Support Provider (SSP). An application written to work with one SSP would require few or perhaps no modifications to work with another SSP. All SSPs must implement the SSPI, but internally they are free to use different mechanisms to enforce security.

The following sections provide an overview of the primary SSPs available to COM+ applications: NTLMSSP, Kerberos, and Snego. Understanding the general features of each authentication package can help you make a choice that is right for the security needs of your application. Once you choose a security package, however, COM+ insulates you from the internals of the various authentication protocols, so this chapter will focus primarily on the higher-level security model defined by COM+.

NTLMSSP

Prior to Windows 2000, only one SSPI-compliant SSP was available—the Microsoft Windows NT LAN Manager Security Support Provider (NTLMSSP). This security package is based on the NTLM authentication protocol, a challenge-response protocol that authenticates clients. In the challenge-response model, the server issues a challenge to the client that consists of some data. The client uses an encoded version of the user's password to encrypt the data provided by the server. This encrypted challenge is then sent back to the server, where it is decrypted and compared with the original data sent to the client. If the data are the same, the user is authenticated. Note that the user's password is never sent across the network by the NTLM challenge-response protocol. For this reason, the server cannot use the client's password during impersonation to access network resources for which the client might have permissions.

Kerberos

Windows 2000 offers both NTLMSSP and a new SSP that implements the Kerberos network authentication service version 5. Kerberos is a more sophisticated authentication protocol than NTLMSSP that supports features such as mutual authentication and the delegation of security information from one machine to another. This can allow a server process to cloak itself with the client's identity when making remote calls to another service. In Windows 2000, Kerberos is the fundamental security protocol of the operating system.

Snego

While NTLMSSP and Kerberos are real authentication packages that support the SSPI, the Snego (Simple Negotiation Mechanism) package is used to negotiate between real SSPs. This pseudo-SSP does not provide any actual authentication features of its own—its only use is to help applications select a real SSP. Currently, applications can use Snego to negotiate between the NTLMSSP and Kerberos protocols. For Snego to work properly, both the client and server must use it. Snego selects an actual authentication protocol by comparing the authentication packages available on the client machine with those available on the server machine.

Declarative Security: The Registry

As it does for many other aspects of COM+, the registry contains a great deal of information relating to the COM+ security model. You can control many, although not all, of the COM+ security settings by setting various options in the registry. You can also configure security settings programmatically, but there are decided advantages to using the registry. By manipulating the registry, a knowledgeable system administrator can flexibly configure and customize the security environment. But the best thing about configuring security settings in the registry is that COM+ enforces all of these settings automatically. This technique reduces the amount of security-related code you need to write—a definite plus, in our opinion. For example, you can specify that a user named "Mary" or users belonging to the "Accountants" group are not permitted to launch or access a particular component. You need never worry that Mary or Accountants will be able to use the component.

The easiest place to begin exploring the COM+ security model is the Distributed COM Configuration utility. You use this powerful tool to set component and security settings in the registry. In the first half of this chapter, we'll explore the options that this utility makes available and where in the registry these settings are stored. Note that there is no security risk associated with storing security information in the registry. Like other parts of the Windows system, the registry is fully securable and permits only privileged users to access and modify sensitive areas. In fact, only administrators are permitted to run the utility on Windows NT and Windows 2000. Of course, there are also certain disadvantages to using the registry to configure security information, but we'll save these for later in the chapter.

The declarative security information stored in the registry can be neatly divided into two arenas: default security and component security. Default security settings are for all components running on the local machine that do not in some way override these default settings. Component security settings can provide special security for a specific component, thereby overriding the default security settings.[1] Let's begin by examining the default security settings.

Default Security

Launching the Distributed COM Configuration utility and clicking the Default Properties tab displays the options shown in Figure 18-2. The administrator can use these options to set the default authentication and impersonation options on a machinewide basis. The Enable Distributed COM On This Computer check box is the master switch of COM+. If this check box is deselected, all remote calls to and from the machine are rejected. When the system is first installed, this

---

1. You can use programmatic security—discussed later in this chapter in the section titled "Programmatic Security"—to override both default and component security settings in the registry.

check box is selected. The Enable COM Internet Services On This Computer check box determines whether COM+ Internet Services (CIS) is available; by default, it's disabled. Select this check box if you're planning to use COM+ over the Internet, and then see the section titled "Internet Services" in Chapter 19.

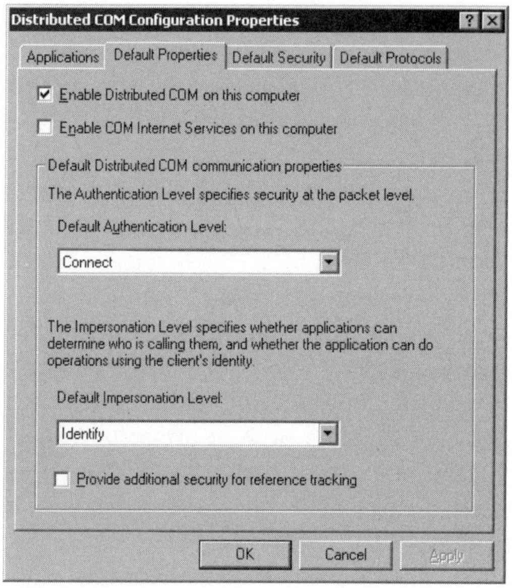

Figure 18-2.
The Default Properties tab of the Distributed COM Configuration utility.

The Default Authentication Level setting specifies the base authentication level for the system, assuming that a component does not override the value programmatically or through other registry settings. When the system is first installed, this setting is configured for connect-level authentication. The possible authentication levels and their attributes are shown in the following table. Although Windows 95 and Windows 98 machines can make calls at any authentication level, they can only receive calls made at the *RPC_C_AUTHN_LEVEL_NONE* or *RPC_C_AUTHN_LEVEL_CONNECT* levels. Note that datagram transports, such as User Datagram Protocol (UDP), default to packet-level authentication if a lower authentication level is requested, which is logical because datagram transports do not maintain a virtual connection between the client and the server. Therefore, each transmitted packet should be authenticated individually.

Value	Authentication Level	Flag	Description
0	Default	RPC_C_AUTHN_ LEVEL_DEFAULT	The authentication level is chosen automatically using the normal COM+ security blanket negotiation algorithm.
1	None	RPC_C_AUTHN_ LEVEL_NONE	No authentication.
2	Connect	RPC_C_AUTHN_ LEVEL_CONNECT	Authenticates the client only when the client first connects to the server.
3	Call	RPC_C_AUTHN_ LEVEL_CALL	Authenticates the client at the beginning of each remote call.
4	Packet	RPC_C_AUTHN_ LEVEL_PKT	Authenticates that all of the data received is from the expected client.
5	Packet Integrity	RPC_C_AUTHN_ LEVEL_PKT_ INTEGRITY	Authenticates data integrity and verifies that it has not been modified when transferred between the client and the server.
6	Packet Privacy	RPC_C_AUTHN_ LEVEL_PKT_- PRIVACY	Authenticates, verifies, and encrypts the arguments passed to every remote call.

The Default Impersonation Level setting specifies the base impersonation level that clients running on this system grant to their servers, again assuming that a component does not override this value. Impersonation levels protect the client from rogue components. From the client's point of view, anonymous-level impersonation is the most secure because the component cannot obtain any information about the client. With each successive impersonation level, a component is granted further liberties with the client's security credentials. When the system is first installed, this setting is configured for identify-level impersonation. The possible impersonation levels and their attributes are shown in the table below. Note that Windows NT supports only the RPC_ C_IMP_LEVEL_IDENTIFY and RPC_C_IMP_LEVEL_IMPERSONATE impersonation levels; Windows 2000 also supports the RPC_C_IMP_LEVEL_ DELEGATE impersonation level when the Kerberos security protocol is used.

The Provide Additional Security For Reference Tracking check box indicates whether calls to the *IUnknown::AddRef* and *IUnknown::Release* methods are secured. When the system is first installed, this option is turned off. Selecting this check box causes COM+ to perform additional callbacks to authenticate

Value	Impersonation Level	Flag	Description
0	Default	*RPC_C_IMP_LEVEL_ DEFAULT*	The impersonation level is chosen automatically using the normal security blanket negotiation algorithm of COM+.
1	Anonymous	*RPC_C_IMP_LEVEL_ ANONYMOUS*	The client is anonymous to the server. The server cannot obtain the client's identification information, and it cannot impersonate the client.*
2	Identify	*RPC_C_IMP_LEVEL_ IDENTIFY*	The server can obtain the client's identification information. The server can impersonate the client for ACL checking, but it cannot access system objects as the client.
3	Impersonate	*RPC_C_IMP_LEVEL_ IMPERSONATE*	The server can impersonate the client's security context while acting on behalf of the client. This level of impersonation can be used only to access resources on the server's machine.
4	Delegate	*RPC_C_IMP_LEVEL_ DELEGATE*	The server can impersonate the client's security context when making outgoing calls to other servers (on other machines) on behalf of the client.

* *RPC_C_IMP_LEVEL_ANONYMOUS* is currently not supported.

distributed reference count calls, ensuring that objects are not released maliciously. This option improves the security of the system but slows execution.[2]

Configuring Default Access and Launch Permissions

The Distributed COM Configuration utility's Default Security tab, shown in Figure 18-3, enables the administrator to configure default access and launch permissions on a machinewide basis. These settings are for components that do not provide their own settings. Clicking the Edit Default button presents a list of users and user groups that can be explicitly granted or denied permissions. When the system is first installed, only administrators, the system account, and the interactive user have access and launch permissions. If the default security information is deleted from the registry, only the system account and the interactive user retain permissions. In general, you should avoid changing these values; instead of changing the machinewide default settings that affect all components, it is preferable to adjust the security settings on a component-by-component basis, as described in the next section.

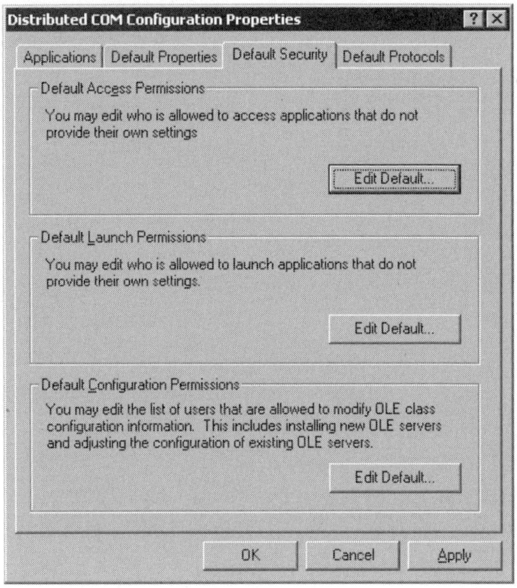

Figure 18-3.
The Distributed COM Configuration utility's Default Security tab.

---

2. Chapter 19 includes more information about secure reference counting.

The system account is a highly privileged local account used by system processes. It must always have launch and access permissions because the Service Control Manager (SCM; rpcss.dll) runs in this account. If a component does not grant the system account launch permission, the component can never be launched.

The requirement that the system account have launch permission explains a common source of confusion regarding the CLSID\LocalServer32 registry key. Component launch always fails if the LocalServer32 registry key contains a Universal Naming Convention (UNC) path in the form *server**share**directory**component.exe*, because although the system account has the right to do most anything on the local machine, it has no network privileges.[3] This means that the SCM cannot launch an executable component that resides on a remote machine. Keep in mind that UNC paths fail even if they refer to an executable component that resides on the local machine.

In the Default Configuration Permissions area of the Default Security tab, the administrator can control the security of the entire HKEY_CLASSES_ROOT section of the registry. These settings can be used to restrict ordinary users from being able to view or modify the contents of this crucial area in the registry. To view or change the security settings of individual registry keys, you use the old registry editor (regedt32.exe) instead of the new one (regedit.exe). Note that some legacy components are designed to refresh their registry settings every time they run.[4] Refreshing the registry settings can cause components to fail if you restrict write access to the registry. Therefore, it is recommended that modern components do not refresh their entries in the HKEY_CLASSES_ROOT section of the registry every time they are executed.

In Windows 95 and Windows 98, only the default access permissions are configurable; all the other settings are not applicable because of the limited security available on these platforms. However, an additional option, Enable Remote Connection, is available. This option determines whether remote clients are permitted to connect to objects running on the local computer. Although Windows 95 and Windows 98 do not support remote launching of components, they do permit connections to running objects. When the system is first installed, however, this option is disabled; you enable it using the Distributed COM Configuration utility or another registry editor.

---

3. An administrator can give the system account network privileges by setting the HKEY_LOCAL_MACHINE\SYSTEM\CurrentControlSet\Services\LanmanServer\ Parameters\RestrictNullSessionAccess registry value to *0*, but this technique is not generally recommended because it significantly compromises system security.

4. All components written in Microsoft Visual Basic do this.

All of the options presented on the Default Properties and Default Security tabs of the Distributed COM Configuration utility are controlled by registry values stored in the HKEY_LOCAL_MACHINE\Software\Microsoft\OLE key. The following table describes the named-values that can be stored in this registry key.

HKEY_LOCAL_MACHINE\ Software\Microsoft\OLE Values	Description
DefaultLaunchPermission	Specifies the default ACL that determines who can launch components
DefaultAccessPermission	Specifies the default ACL that determines who can access components
EnableDCOM	Specifies whether Distributed COM is enabled on this machine
EnableRemoteConnect	Specifies whether objects running on the machine accept remote connections; by default, it is set to no *(N)**
LegacyAuthenticationLevel	Sets the default authentication level
LegacyImpersonationLevel	Sets the default impersonation level
LegacySecureReferences	Specifies whether *AddRef* and *Release* method calls are secured
LegacyMutualAuthentication	Specifies whether mutual authentication is enabled**

* Windows 95 and Windows 98 only.
** Windows 2000 only.

Configuring Component Security: The AppID Key

So far, we've explored how you can use the Distributed COM Configuration utility to set the registry entries that control the default COM+ security settings. In this section, we'll examine the registry settings that control security on a per-component basis. For components with more specialized security requirements, you can use these settings to override the machinewide default settings.

The AppID registry key was designed to group the configuration options for one or more objects housed by a component into one centralized location in the registry. A unique class identifier (CLSID) is assigned to each coclass, but all coclasses housed by one component must map to the same application identifier (AppID).[5] The following table describes the four security-related values

5. Chapter 12 covers the AppID registry key in more detail.

that can be stored in an AppID registry entry. These four named values correspond precisely to the four areas of the COM+ security model: launch, access, authentication, and identity control.

Security-Related AppID Values	Description
LaunchPermission	Specifies the ACL that determines who can launch the component
AccessPermission	Specifies the ACL that determines who can access the component
AuthenticationLevel	Sets the authentication level to be used for the component
RunAs	Sets the user account in which the component will execute

When you run the Distributed COM Configuration utility, it presents a list of components registered on the local machine. To configure the security settings for a particular component, you select it from the list and click the Properties button. Then you click the Security tab and specify the launch and access permissions for a specific component. These options affect the *AccessPermission* and *LaunchPermission* values in the component's AppID registry key. You select the Use Default Access Permissions and Use Default Launch Permissions options to instruct COM+ to use the machinewide default security settings for this component. Otherwise, select Use Custom Access Permissions or Use Custom Launch Permissions and click the corresponding Edit button to control the security for this specific component, as shown in Figure 18-4.

Recall that when the system is first installed, the machinewide default launch and access permissions enable only administrators, the system account, and the interactive user to launch and access components. We recommend that you not change these machinewide settings. However, because remote clients are not likely to be logged on as administrators, you'll typically modify the component's launch and access security to grant or deny permissions to everyone, various user groups, or even specific users. This technique is preferable to adjusting the machinewide default security settings that affect all components. Granting launch and access permissions to all users (*Everyone*) and setting the authentication level to none (*RPC_C_AUTHN_LEVEL_NONE*) enables anonymous activation and access.[6]

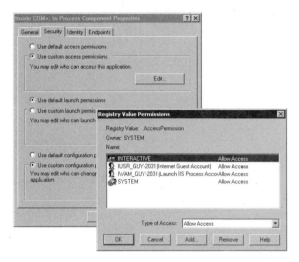

Figure 18-4.
Using the Distributed COM Configuration utility to set the access permissions for a component.

The *IAccessControl* Interface

Although large parts of the COM+ security model, such as authentication and impersonation, are platform-independent through the use of the SSPI, until recently access control was performed exclusively using Windows DACLs. The Win32 API includes functions that can create and manipulate ACLs. These ACLs can then be serialized into the registry keys that control COM+ security, allowing you to configure launch and access permissions. However, because ACLs created in Windows NT or Windows 2000 are obviously not portable (they aren't even supported in Windows 95 and Windows 98), Microsoft needed a platform-independent solution for the COM+ security model. That solution is the *IAccessControl* interface, shown on the following page in IDL notation.

---

6. Note that you cannot use the launching user identity setting when security is turned off in this way.

```
interface IAccessControl : IUnknown
{
    // Merge the new rights with the existing access rights.
    HRESULT GrantAccessRights([in] PACTRL_ACCESSW pAccessList);

    // Replace the existing access rights with the new rights.
    HRESULT SetAccessRights([in] PACTRL_ACCESSW pAccessList);

    // Set an item's owner or group.
    HRESULT SetOwner(
        [in] PTRUSTEEW pOwner,
        [in] PTRUSTEEW pGroup);

    // Remove explicit entries for the list of trustees.
    HRESULT RevokeAccessRights(
        [in] LPWSTR lpProperty,
        [in] ULONG cTrustees,
        [in, size_is(cTrustees)] TRUSTEEW prgTrustees[]);

    // Get the entire list of access rights.
    HRESULT GetAllAccessRights(
        [in] LPWSTR lpProperty,
        [out] PACTRL_ACCESSW_ALLOCATE_ALL_NODES* ppAccessList,
        [out] PTRUSTEEW* ppOwner,
        [out] PTRUSTEEW* ppGroup);

    // Determine whether a trustee has access rights.
    HRESULT IsAccessAllowed(
        [in] PTRUSTEEW pTrustee,
        [in] LPWSTR lpProperty,
        [in] ACCESS_RIGHTS AccessRights,
        [out] BOOL* pfAccessAllowed);
}
```

Although it is possible to write security code that uses the Win32 API security functions, doing so unnecessarily ties a component to the Windows platform. Component developers who want to write portable code that works on Windows as well as on other platforms that support COM+ should use the *IAccessControl* interface instead. The true goal of the *IAccessControl* interface is to provide programmatic security, but we'll first explore its use in creating platform-independent access control information stored in the registry.

Although it is considered wiser to let the administrator configure the security settings using the Distributed COM Configuration utility, it might occasionally be advantageous to control the registry settings from within a component. Relying on an administrator to configure critical security settings can sometimes be a mistake. In such cases, configuring the registry-based security settings for a component might be a necessary part of the installation program. Of course, the administrator could later adjust these settings using the Distributed COM Configuration utility.

The System Implementation of *IAccessControl*

Windows provides an implementation of the *IAccessControl* interface in the *CLSID_DCOMAccessControl* coclass. In addition to implementing the *IAccessControl* interface, this system object also implements the *IPersist* and *IPersistStream* interfaces, which you can use to configure an ACL using the methods of the *IAccessControl* interface. You can then store these settings in a registry key that COM+ will use to determine access and launch permissions. The Distributed COM Configuration utility itself uses the *DCOMAccessControl* object to create these registry entries in Windows 95 and Windows 98, where the Win32 API security functions are not available, while the Windows NT and Windows 2000 versions of this utility use the Win32 API security functions to put this information in the registry.[7]

The ACTRL_ACCESS structure, which is used as a parameter by several methods of the *IAccessControl* interface, is somewhat complicated. It has several levels of structures nested within one another, as shown in Figure 18-5. Aficionados of the Win32 API security functions will recognize the TRUSTEE structure buried deep within the ACTRL_ACCESS structure. The *IAccessControl* interface has borrowed the TRUSTEE structure from the security functions of the Win32 API. A trustee identifies a security principal, which can be a user account, a group account, or a logon session. The TRUSTEE structure enables you to use a name (*ptstrName*) or an SID (*pSid*) to identify a trustee. When you work within the COM+ security model, it is certainly preferable to identify trustees by name instead of a Windows-specific SID. The Windows NT and Windows 2000 implementations of the *DCOMAccessControl* object automatically look up the SID that corresponds to the trustee name.

---

7. The format of the security information produced by the *DCOMAccessControl* object is not the same as that produced by the Win32 API security functions. While COM+ itself supports both formats, the Distributed COM Configuration utility on Windows NT and Windows 2000 is unable to read security information created by the *DCOMAccessControl* object.

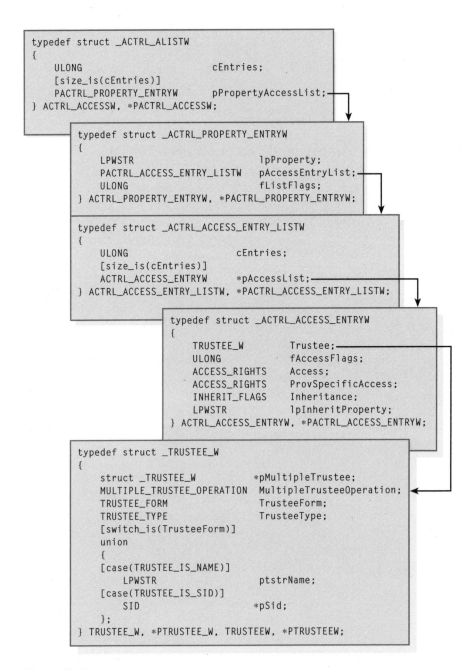

Figure 18-5.
The structures nested in the ACTRL_ACCESS structure.

The following sample program shows how to use the *DCOMAccessControl* object to read and display COM+ security information stored in registry entries in a platform-independent manner. The numbers shown in parentheses here correspond to the numbered elements shown in boldface in the code. The program calls *CoCreateInstance* to instantiate the *CLSID_DCOMAccessControl* coclass and obtain a pointer to its *IPersistStream* interface (1). Then the *IPersistStream::Load* method is called to initialize the object with the security information stored in the AppID\AccessPermission registry value of a component (2). Next, the program calls the *IUnknown::QueryInterface* method to request a pointer to the *IAccessControl* interface (3) for use in calling the *IAccessControl::GetAllAccessRights* method (4). Not shown in this code is a loop that displays all of the trustees enumerated in the ACL obtained from the *GetAllAccessRights* method. The companion CD also includes a program, based on a sample from the Microsoft Platform SDK, that illustrates how to write security settings to the registry using the *CLSID_DCOMAccessControl* implementation of the *IAccessControl* interface.

```
#include <windows.h>
#include <stdio.h>
#include <iaccess.h> // For IAccessControl

// Need to define this ourselves!
const IID IID_IAccessControl =
    {0xEEDD23E0,0x8410,0x11CE,
    {0xA1,0xC3,0x08,0x00,0x2B,0x2B,0x8D,0x8F}};

// This is the header stored in the registry.
typedef struct
{
    WORD version;
    WORD pad;
    GUID classid;
} SPermissionHeader;

void main()
{
    HRESULT hr = CoInitialize(NULL);

    // Open the AppID key.
    // Replace the AppID below with an AppID for which you
    // have configured custom access permission.
```

(continued)

```
HKEY key = 0;
hr = RegOpenKeyEx(HKEY_CLASSES_ROOT,
    "AppID\\{10000002-0000-0000-0000-000000000001}", 0,
    KEY_READ, &key);

 // Read the value from the registry.
DWORD dwSize = 0;
hr = RegQueryValueEx(key, "AccessPermission", NULL, NULL,
    NULL, &dwSize);

void* pMemory = (void*)CoTaskMemAlloc(dwSize);
hr = RegQueryValueEx(key, "AccessPermission", NULL, NULL,
    (unsigned char*)pMemory, &dwSize);

IStream* pStream;
hr = CreateStreamOnHGlobal(pMemory, TRUE, &pStream);

// (1) Create an instance of the
// CLSID_DCOMAccessControl object.
IPersistStream* pPersistStream = NULL;
hr = CoCreateInstance(CLSID_DCOMAccessControl, NULL,
    CLSCTX_INPROC_SERVER, IID_IPersistStream,
    (void**)&pPersistStream);

LARGE_INTEGER size;
size.QuadPart = sizeof(SPermissionHeader);
hr = pStream->Seek(size, STREAM_SEEK_SET, NULL);

// (2) Initialize the CLSID_DCOMAccessControl object with
// the data from the registry.
hr = pPersistStream->Load(pStream);

// (3) Request a pointer to the IAccessControl interface.
IAccessControl* pAccessControl = NULL;
hr = pPersistStream->QueryInterface(IID_IAccessControl,
    (void**)&pAccessControl);

ACTRL_ACCESSW* pAccess = NULL;
TRUSTEEW* pOwner = NULL;
TRUSTEEW* pGroup = NULL;
// (4) Call the IAccessControl::GetAllAccessRights method.
hr = pAccessControl->GetAllAccessRights(NULL, &pAccess,
    &pOwner, &pGroup);

// Program proceeds to enumerate all security principals
// returned by IAccessControl::GetAllAccessRights.
```

```
        // Release everything and bail out.
        CoTaskMemFree(pAccess);
        CoTaskMemFree(pOwner);
        CoTaskMemFree(pGroup);

        pPersistStream->Release();
        pStream->Release();
        pAccessControl->Release();

        RegCloseKey(key);
        CoUninitialize();
}
```

Configuring Component Identity

The Identity tab of the Distributed COM Configuration utility for a selected component, shown in Figure 18-6, enables the administrator to determine which user account the component will execute in. The Identity tab provides three options for defining the user account: The Interactive User, The Launching User, and This User. Changes made on the Identity tab affect the *RunAs* value in the component's AppID registry key.

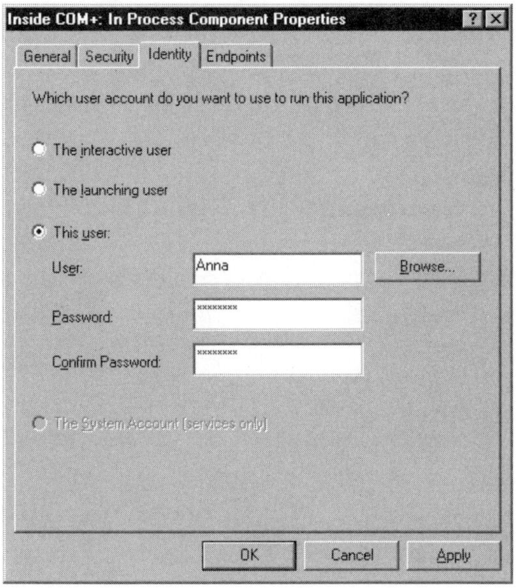

Figure 18-6.
The Identity tab of the Distributed COM Configuration utility for a selected component.

The Launching User

The default identity setting for components is that of the launching user. With this setting, the *RunAs* value is not present in the component's AppID registry key. Running as the launching user means that the component executes under the security credentials of the client process, which is somewhat analogous to using impersonation for the lifetime of the component. Each distinct client gets a new instance of the server, and each server runs in its own window station. This happens regardless of whether the coclass used the *REGCLS_MULTIPLEUSE* flag when calling the *CoRegisterClassObject* function. Because each client has its own instance of the server, this is the most secure setting but also the most resource-intensive one. Imagine a thousand users connecting to a component and each one causing a new window station and process to be created! Also note that components launched under the identity of the launching user do not have access to the interactive desktop visible to the end user.

In Windows NT, components that are run as the launching user receive somewhat crippled security credentials because the system does not support delegation-level impersonation. For example, remote calls to other machines cannot be made when the component runs under the identity of the launching user; nor can the component access files be shared across the network. If this access were allowed, impersonation could form an endless chain from one computer to another, allowing a rogue component to assume the client's security credentials and do all sorts of bad things with them.

In Windows 2000, delegation-level impersonation is supported via the Kerberos security provider. The Kerberos security protocol has built-in safeguards that limit what can be done with delegation-level impersonation. However, the launching user setting is a special case when you use Kerberos authentication. Because the server's secret key is not available to decrypt the service ticket presented by the client, "user-to-user" authentication must be employed. This means that the client must use Kerberos to activate the server at delegate level impersonation in the *CoCreateInstanceEx* call.[8]

The Interactive User

When a component is configured to run as the interactive user, it runs under the identity of the currently logged-on end user, which means that it has access to the interactive desktop visible to the user. This configuration has three problems.

---

8. For information on how to set this up, see the section titled "Activation Credentials: The COAUTHINFO Structure" later in this chapter.

First, a user must be logged on in order for the component to execute. Second, you never know who will log on, so the component might have many rights (if the administrator is logged on) or few rights (if a guest is logged on). Third, if the user logs off while the component is running, the component dies. This configuration is most useful for a system such as a distributed whiteboard-style drawing application that needs to interact with the user, as well as for debugging purposes. It is not recommended for other types of server or middle-tier components. The *RunAs* registry value is set to *Interactive User* for components configured to run under the identity of the end user.

A Specific User

The third identity option is to configure the component for execution under a specific user account. When an attempt is made to launch the component, COM+ automatically initiates a system logon using the specified user account by calling the Win32 API function *LogonUser*, followed by a call to the *CreateProcessAsUser* function. As part of the logon procedure, a new, noninteractive window station is created for use by the component. This setting is often the best option for components that will serve many client programs simultaneously because all instances of the component will be loaded into one window station. In addition, if the class was registered with the *REGCLS_MULTIPLEUSE* flag, multiple clients will be able to share access to a single instance of the component.

Window Stations

Windows supports a security environment known as a *window station*. The Windows desktop visible on the screen is part of the interactive window station. All programs executing in the interactive window station receive the security credentials of the logged-on user. It is possible to create additional, noninteractive window stations for use when you launch processes under the security credentials of different user accounts. However, processes running in noninteractive window stations are not visible to the user and cannot receive input from the user. This technique is sometimes advantageous because it insulates a process from the actions of an end user, who might be working on the server machine.

The *RunAs* value in the component's AppID registry key is set to a string in the form *domain\user*, and the password is stored in a secure part of the registry managed by the Local Security Authority (LSA) subsystem of Windows. The LSA is a protected subsystem used to maintain information about all aspects of local security on a system; only an administrator can use the LSA API functions to read and write the secured password information stored in the registry.

Note that components registered to run under a specific account will always fail if you attempt to run them manually under the guise of a different user account. Suffering from an identity crisis, the *CoRegisterClassObject* function will return the error *CO_E_WRONG_SERVER_IDENTITY*. This error occurs because the code calling *CoRegisterClassObject* can't be trusted. Only the securable registry settings that specify which component to run and under what identity can be trusted. This restriction prevents a malicious component from spoofing client programs by masquerading as an upstanding class object with a registered CLSID.

User accounts that COM+ uses for logon purposes must be assigned the special right Log On As A Batch Job. Otherwise, COM+ cannot successfully log on using the account. The Distributed COM Configuration utility automatically grants this right to any user account specified on the Identity tab. It can do this because the user of this utility must be an administrator and therefore has the right to confer special privileges on other users. Note that the identity of components implemented as services is not configured using the Distributed COM Configuration utility or the *RunAs* registry value. Instead, the *LocalService* value of the AppID registry key names the service, and the identity is configured in the Services section of the Component Services management console.

Programmatic Security

Configuring security settings in the registry has its advantages: it doesn't require any special work on the part of the component developer, and it allows the administrator great flexibility in configuring the security settings. As you know, component activation security and identity control is always configured using the registry. However, declarative security isn't always the best answer for all security concerns. Certain features of the COM+ security model can be accessed only via a programming interface. For example, it might sometimes be necessary to temporarily increase the security of sensitive data transmitted across the network. In these cases, taking programmatic control of security settings offers a solution. The best answer for most components is a combined approach—using declarative security for most security jobs and programmatic security for more specialized tasks that require a finer degree of control than that available using the registry settings.

The *CoInitializeSecurity* Function

The COM+ security infrastructure is initialized on a per-process basis at start-up. The *CoInitializeSecurity* function sets the default security values for the process. If an application does not call *CoInitializeSecurity*, COM+ calls the function automatically the first time an interface pointer is marshaled into or out of an apartment (or context) in the process. Attempting to call *CoInitializeSecurity* after marshaling takes place yields the infamous *RPC_E_TOO_LATE* error. Thus, programs that want to call *CoInitializeSecurity* explicitly are advised to do so immediately after calling *CoInitializeEx*. This rule makes it difficult to call *CoInitializeSecurity* from languages such as Microsoft Visual Basic and Java, where the virtual machine might call *CoInitializeSecurity* before running any application code. Note that *CoInitializeSecurity* is called only once per process, not in each thread that calls *CoInitializeEx*.

For applications that do not call *CoInitializeSecurity*, COM+ calls this function with parameters obtained from the security settings in the registry. In this way, legacy components written prior to the advent of the COM+ security model are not left unsecured.[9] Although most of the security settings can be configured using the registry, it is often desirable to have programmatic control over the security environment so that a component can override both the machinewide default and the component-specific security settings configured in the registry by an administrator. The declaration of the *CoInitializeSecurity* function is shown here:

```
HRESULT __stdcall CoInitializeSecurity(
    PSECURITY_DESCRIPTOR        pSecDesc,       // Server
    LONG                        cAuthSvc,       // Server
    SOLE_AUTHENTICATION_SERVICE *asAuthSvc,     // Server
    void                        *pReserved1,    // NULL
    DWORD                       dwAuthnLevel,   // Client/Server
    DWORD                       dwImpLevel,     // Client
    SOLE_AUTHENTICATION_LIST    *pAuthList,     // Client
    DWORD                       dwCapabilities, // Client/Server
    void                        *pReserved3);   // NULL
```

---

9. For more information about how to configure these settings, see the section titled "Declarative Security: The Registry" earlier in this chapter.

The following discussion examines these parameters in detail, with the exception of parameters 4 and 9, which are reserved and must be set to *NULL*.

The first parameter of *CoInitializeSecurity*, *pSecDesc*, is declared as a *PSECURITY_DESCRIPTOR*, which is simply a pointer to void (*void**). This polymorphic argument defines the component's access permissions in one of three ways. Typically, *pSecDesc* points to a Win32 security descriptor that COM+ uses to check access permissions on new connections. The *pSecDesc* parameter can also point to a globally unique identifier (GUID) that references an AppID in the registry where declarative security information is stored, or it can point to an implementation of the *IAccessControl* interface. Figure 18-7 shows the three ways that the polymorphic *pSecDesc* parameter can be used to perform access control.

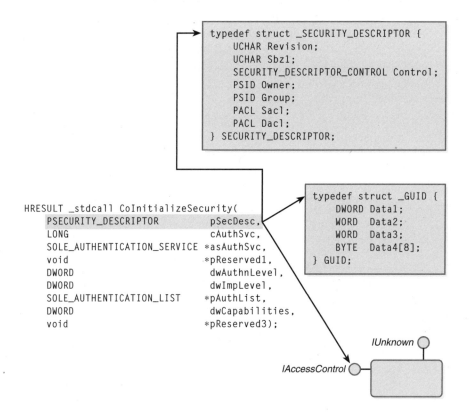

Figure 18-7.
Three ways to perform access control using the pSecDesc *parameter.*

CoInitializeSecurity interprets the *pSecDesc* parameter based on the value of the *dwCapabilities* parameter. If *dwCapabilities* contains the *EOAC_APPID* flag, *pSecDesc* must point to a GUID of an AppID in the registry. In this case, COM+ obtains all the security settings from the registry and all other parameters of the *CoInitializeSecurity* function are ignored. If the *EOAC_APPID* flag is set in the *dwCapabilities* parameter but the *pSecDesc* parameter is *NULL*, *CoInitializeSecurity* looks for the .exe name of the process in the HKEY_CLASSES_ROOT\AppID section of the registry and uses the AppID stored there. This behavior is identical to the default behavior obtained when you allow COM+ to call *CoInitializeSecurity* automatically.

If the *EOAC_ACCESS_CONTROL* flag is set in the *dwCapabilities* parameter, *CoInitializeSecurity* interprets *pSecDesc* as a pointer to a COM+ object that implements the *IAccessControl* interface. COM+ calls this implementation of *IAccessControl* to determine access permissions at run time. If neither the *EOAC_APPID* nor *EOAC_ACCESS_CONTROL* flag is set in the *dwCapabilities* parameter, *CoInitializeSecurity* interprets *pSecDesc* as a pointer to a Win32 security descriptor structure that is used for access checking. If *pSecDesc* is *NULL*, no ACL checking is performed.

The SOLE_AUTHENTICATION_SERVICE Structure

The second parameter of *CoInitializeSecurity*, *cAuthSvc*, specifies the number of authentication services that are being registered. A value of 0 means that no authentication services are being registered and the process cannot receive secure calls; a value of −1 instructs COM+ to choose which authentication services to register. The third parameter, *asAuthSvc*, is a pointer to an array of SOLE_AUTHENTICATION_SERVICE structures, each of which identifies one authentication service to be registered. If −1 was passed as the *cAuthSvc* parameter to instruct COM+ to choose the authentication services, the parameter must be *NULL*. The definition of the SOLE_AUTHENTICATION_SERVICE structure is shown here:

```
typedef struct tagSOLE_AUTHENTICATION_SERVICE
{
    DWORD dwAuthnSvc;          // RPC_C_AUTHN_xxx
    DWORD dwAuthzSvc;          // RPC_C_AUTHZ_xxx
    OLECHAR *pPrincipalName;   // Should be NULL
    HRESULT hr;
} SOLE_AUTHENTICATION_SERVICE;
```

The first field of the SOLE_AUTHENTICATION_SERVICE structure, *dwAuthnSvc*, specifies which authentication service should be used to authenticate client calls; this field can be set to one of the constants shown in the following table. The authentication service specified by *CoInitializeSecurity* determines which security providers are used for incoming calls; outgoing calls can use any security provider installed on the machine.

*RPC_C_AUTHN_*xxx Flag	Description
RPC_C_AUTHN_NONE	No authentication.
RPC_C_AUTHN_DCE_PRIVATE	Distributed Computing Environment (DCE) private key authentication.
RPC_C_AUTHN_DCE_PUBLIC	DCE public key authentication.
RPC_C_AUTHN_GSS_NEGOTIATE	Snego security support provider.
RPC_C_AUTHN_WINNT	NTLMSSP.
RPC_C_AUTHN_GSS_KERBEROS	Kerberos authentication.
RPC_C_AUTHN_DEFAULT	COM+ uses its normal security blanket negotiation algorithm to pick an authentication service.

The second field of the SOLE_AUTHENTICATION_SERVICE structure, *dwAuthzSvc*, indicates the authorization service to be used by the server. This field can be set to one of the constants shown in the following table. Note that the *RPC_C_AUTHN_WINNT* and *RPC_C_AUTHN_GSS_KERBEROS* authentication packages do not use an authorization service, so this field must be set to *RPC_C_AUTHZ_NONE* when you use NTLMSSP or Kerberos authentication.

*RPC_C_AUTHZ_*xxx Flag	Description
RPC_C_AUTHZ_NONE	Server performs no authorization.
RPC_C_AUTHZ_NAME	Server performs authorization based on the client's principal name.
RPC_C_AUTHZ_DCE	Server performs authorization checking using the client's DCE privilege attribute certificate information, which is sent to the server with each RPC made using the binding handle.
RPC_C_AUTHZ_DEFAULT	COM+ uses its normal security blanket negotiation algorithm to pick an authorization service.

The third field, *pPrincipalName*, defines the principal name to be used with the authentication service. The NTLMSSP and Kerberos authentication packages ignore this parameter, assuming the current user identifier, so most applications set this value to the constant *COLE_DEFAULT_PRINCIPAL*. The last field, *hr*, contains the *HRESULT* value indicating the status of the call to register this authentication service. If the *asAuthSvc* parameter is not *NULL* and *CoInitializeSecurity* cannot successfully register any of the authentication services specified in the list, the *RPC_E_NO_GOOD_SECURITY_PACKAGES* error is returned. You should check the *SOLE_AUTHENTICATION_SERVICE.hr* attribute for error codes specific to each authentication service.

Authentication and Impersonation Levels

The fifth parameter of *CoInitializeSecurity*, *dwAuthnLevel*, specifies the default authentication level. This parameter can be set to one of the *RPC_C_AUTHN_LEVEL_xxx* flags shown in the table on page 535. Client applications set the *dwAuthnLevel* parameter to determine the default authentication level for outgoing calls. The *dwAuthnLevel* setting specified in the component's call to *CoInitializeSecurity* becomes the minimum level at which client calls will be accepted. Any calls arriving at an authentication level below the minimum watermark specified by the component will fail. When making a connection between a particular client and a particular component, COM+ automatically negotiates the actual authentication level to be the higher of the two settings. In this way, the server does not need to reject client calls because they arrive at an authentication level below the minimum level required by the component. Also note that, by default, *IUnknown* calls are made at the authentication level specified in the call to *CoInitializeSecurity*.

If the first parameter passed to *CoInitializeSecurity*, *pSecDesc*, is a valid pointer to a Win32 security descriptor, a GUID, or an implementation of the *IAccessControl* interface, the *dwAuthnLevel* parameter cannot be set to *RPC_C_AUTHN_LEVEL_NONE*. On the other hand, if *pSecDesc* is *NULL*, no ACL checking is performed and therefore the *dwAuthnLevel* parameter can be set to *RPC_C_AUTHN_LEVEL_NONE*, indicating that anonymous access is permitted.

The sixth parameter of *CoInitializeSecurity*, *dwImpLevel*, specifies the default impersonation level for proxies. This parameter can be set to one of the *RPC_C_IMP_LEVEL_xxx* flags shown in the table on page 536. The *dwImpLevel* setting specified in the client's call to *CoInitializeSecurity* specifies the default impersonation level that the client grants to the component. Applications should set this value carefully since, by default, all *IUnknown* calls are made at the impersonation level set by the client's call to *CoInitializeSecurity*. The *dwImpLevel* parameter is not used on the server side.

The seventh parameter, *pAuthList*, must be set to *NULL* on Windows NT systems. In Windows 2000, the *pAuthList* parameter points to a SOLE_AUTHENTICATION_LIST structure, which contains a pointer to an array of SOLE_AUTHENTICATION_INFO structures, as shown in Figure 18-8. This list contains the default authentication information to use with each authentication service. Each SOLE_AUTHENTICATION_INFO structure identifies an authentication service (*dwAuthnSvc*—one of the *RPC_C_AUTHN_LEVEL_xxx* flags on page 535), authorization service (*dwAuthzSvc* —one of the *RPC_C_IMP_LEVEL_xxx* flags on page 536), and a pointer to authentication information (*pAuthInfo*) whose type is determined by the type of authentication service.

For the NTLMSSP and Kerberos security packages, this value points to the SEC_WINNT_AUTH_IDENTITY_W structure containing the user name and password. For Snego, the *pAuthInfo* parameter should be *NULL* or point to a SEC_WINNT_AUTH_IDENTITY_EXW structure, in which case the structure's *PackageList* member must point to a string containing a comma-delimited list of authentication packages; the *PackageListLength* member should contain the number of bytes in the *PackageList* string. If *pAuthInfo* is *NULL*, Snego automatically picks a number of authentication services to try from those available on the client machine.

The client specifies these values in the call to *CoInitializeSecurity* so that when COM+ negotiates the default authentication service for a proxy, it uses the default information specified in the *pAuthInfo* parameter for that authentication service. If the *pAuthInfo* parameter for the desired authentication service is *NULL*, COM+ uses the process identity to represent the client. Applications that don't fill in the SEC_WINNT_AUTH_IDENTITY_W structure can simply set the *pAuthInfo* pointer to *COLE_DEFAULT_AUTHINFO* (*-1*).

The eighth parameter, *dwCapabilities*, can be used to set additional client-side and server-side capabilities. This value can be composed of a combination of the values from the *EOLE_AUTHENTICATION_CAPABILITIES* enumeration shown in the table on page 558. *CoInitializeSecurity* interprets the data pointed to by the *pSecDesc* parameter based on the flags set in the *dwCapabilities* parameter. If *pSecDesc* points to a GUID, the *EOAC_APPID* flag must be set; if *pSecDesc* points to an implementation of the *IAccessControl* interface, the *EOAC_ACCESS_CONTROL* flag must be set. By default, if neither the *EOAC_APPID* nor the *EOAC_ACCESS_CONTROL* flag is set in the *dwCapabilities* parameter, *pSecDesc* is assumed to point to a Win32 security descriptor structure. Note that the *EOAC_APPID* and *EOAC_ACCESS_CONTROL* flags are mutually exclusive, as are *EOAC_STATIC_CLOAKING* and *EOAC_DYNAMIC_CLOAKING.*

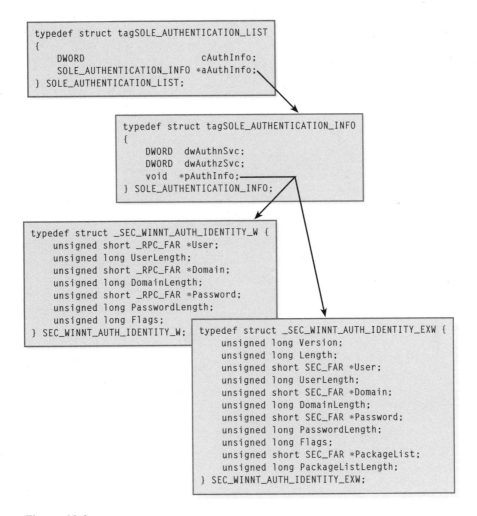

Figure 18-8.
The pAuthList *parameter of* CoInitializeSecurity *points to the SOLE_AUTHENTICATION_LIST structure that contains an array of SOLE_AUTHENTICATION_INFO structures.*

EOLE_AUTHENTICATION_ CAPABILITIES Enumeration	Description
EOAC_NONE	No capability flags.
EOAC_DEFAULT	Tells COM+ to pick the capabilities using its normal security blanket negotiation algorithm.
EOAC_MUTUAL_AUTH	Not used. Mutual authentication is supported automatically by some authorization services.
EOAC_STATIC_CLOAKING	Tells COM+ that calls should be made under the identity of the client thread token. The client's identity is determined during the first call on a proxy and whenever the *IClientSecurity::SetBlanket* method is called.
EOAC_DYNAMIC_CLOAKING	Tells COM+ that calls should be made under the identity of the client thread token. The client's identity is determined during every call on a proxy.
EOAC_SECURE_REFS	Causes COM+ to perform additional callbacks to authenticate distributed reference count calls, to ensure that objects are not released maliciously.
EOAC_ACCESS_CONTROL	*CoInitializeSecurity* expects *pSecDesc* to point to an implementation of the *IAccessControl* interface. COM+ uses this pointer to call the *IAccessControl::IsAccessAllowed* method when performing security checks.
EOAC_APPID	*CoInitializeSecurity* expects *pSecDesc* to point to a GUID that is installed in the HKEY_CLASSES_ROOT\AppID section of the registry. *CoInitialize- Security* uses the security information read from the registry.

EOLE_AUTHENTICATION_ CAPABILITIES Enumeration	Description
EOAC_DISABLE_AAA	Causes any activation in which a server process would be launched under the caller's identity (activate-as-activator, also known as launching user in the Distributed COM Configuration utility) to fail with *E_ACCESSDENIED*. This value allows an application that runs under a privileged account (such as LocalSystem) to prevent its identity from being used to launch untrusted components.

Security Blanket Negotiation

COM+ uses security blanket negotiation to select the appropriate security settings when it first instantiates a proxy. The client and server security blankets are defined by their calls to *CoInitializeSecurity* on start-up. When instantiating a proxy, COM+ compares the settings of the server's security blanket with those of the client in order to select appropriate values for the proxy's default security blanket. COM+ picks an authentication service that is available to both the client and the server. Then it chooses an authorization service and principal name that work with the selected authentication service. For the authentication level, COM+ uses the formula *max(client, server)*. The impersonation level and other flags used are those given by the client, and the authentication identity used is that given by the client for the selected authentication service. These negotiated values are assigned to the newly created proxy and affect all calls made on the proxy unless they are overridden by a client call to *IClientSecurity::SetBlanket*.[10]

The *CoQueryAuthenticationServices* Function

The *CoQueryAuthenticationServices* function retrieves the list of authentication services that were registered when the process called *CoInitializeSecurity*. This information is primarily of interest to custom marshaling code that needs to

---

10. The *IClientSecurity* interface is described later in this chapter.

determine what principal names an application can use. The declaration of the *CoQueryAuthenticationServices* function is shown here:

```
HRESULT __stdcall CoQueryAuthenticationServices(
    DWORD *pcAuthSvc,
    SOLE_AUTHENTICATION_SERVICE** asAuthSvc);
```

Using the *IAccessControl* Interface with *CoInitializeSecurity*

Earlier in this chapter, we explained how to use the *DCOMAccessControl* object and its implementation of the *IAccessControl* and *IPersistStream* interfaces to read and write access permissions from the registry. Although the *IAccessControl* interface can be useful in some cases, it is not designed for this type of administration and configuration code. It is primarily intended for use by code that needs to perform programmatic access checking.

As you know, the first parameter of the *CoInitializeSecurity* function can point to a Win32 security descriptor, an AppID, or an implementation of the *IAccessControl* interface. For *CoInitializeSecurity* to accept an *IAccessControl* interface pointer as the first parameter, the *dwCapabilities* parameter must have the *EOAC_ACCESS_CONTROL* flag set. When a pointer to an access control object is passed to *CoInitializeSecurity*, COM+ calls the object's *IAccessControl::IsAccessAllowed* method to perform access checking at run time. This method determines whether the trustee (user account, group account, or logon session) has access to the object and then simply returns a value of *true* or *false*, indicating that permission is granted or denied.

You can use the system implementation of the *IAccessControl* interface provided by the *DCOMAccessControl* object for this purpose. First, you instantiate the object by calling *CoCreateInstance*, and then you request a pointer to the *IAccessControl* interface. Then you call any of the first five methods of the *IAccessControl* interface (*GrantAccessRights*, *SetAccessRights*, *SetOwner*,[11] *RevokeAccessRights*, and *GetAllAccessRights*) to configure the process-wide access permissions. Finally, you call the *CoInitializeSecurity* function, passing the *IAccessControl* pointer in the first parameter and the *EOAC_ACCESS_ CONTROL* flag in the last parameter. After you call the *CoInitializeSecurity* security function, the access control object can be released using the *IUnknown:: Release* method; following the reference counting rules of COM+, *CoInitialize- Security* calls the *AddRef* method internally. COM+ performs all access checking by calling the *IAccessControl::IsAccessAllowed* method. The implementation of this method provided by *CLSID_DCOMAccessControl* uses the access

---

11. The *IAccessControl::SetOwner* method is currently not implemented by the *DCOMAccessControl* object.

permissions configured in the object to determine whether to grant or deny access to individual trustees.

The following code illustrates these steps by configuring an access control object that grants access to the system account and the Everyone group but denies access to a specific user account. Explicit calls to methods of the *IAccessControl* interface are shown in boldface.

```
// Create a DCOMAccessControl object, and get its IAccessControl
// interface pointer.
IAccessControl* pAccessControl = NULL;
hr = CoCreateInstance(CLSID_DCOMAccessControl, NULL,
    CLSCTX_INPROC_SERVER, IID_IAccessControl,
    (void**)&pAccessControl);

// Set up the property list. We use the NULL property because we
// are trying to adjust the security of the object itself.
ACTRL_ACCESSW access;
ACTRL_PROPERTY_ENTRYW propEntry;
access.cEntries = 1;
access.pPropertyAccessList = &propEntry;

ACTRL_ACCESS_ENTRY_LISTW entryList;
propEntry.lpProperty = NULL;
propEntry.pAccessEntryList = &entryList;
propEntry.fListFlags = 0;

// Set up the ACL for the default property.
ACTRL_ACCESS_ENTRYW entry;
entryList.cEntries = 1;
entryList.pAccessList = &entry;

// Set up the ACE.
entry.fAccessFlags = ACTRL_ACCESS_ALLOWED;
entry.Access = COM_RIGHTS_EXECUTE;
entry.ProvSpecificAccess = 0;
entry.Inheritance = NO_INHERITANCE;
entry.lpInheritProperty = NULL;

// Windows NT requires the system account to have access.
entry.Trustee.pMultipleTrustee = NULL;
entry.Trustee.MultipleTrusteeOperation = NO_MULTIPLE_TRUSTEE;
entry.Trustee.TrusteeForm = TRUSTEE_IS_NAME;
entry.Trustee.TrusteeType = TRUSTEE_IS_USER;
entry.Trustee.ptstrName = L"NT Authority\\System";
```

(continued)

```
// Setting access rights: allow access to
// NT Authority\System.
hr = pAccessControl->SetAccessRights(&access);

// Deny access to an individual user.
entry.fAccessFlags = ACTRL_ACCESS_DENIED;
entry.Trustee.TrusteeType = TRUSTEE_IS_USER;
entry.Trustee.ptstrName = L"Domain\\User";
hr = pAccessControl->GrantAccessRights(&access);

// Grant access to everyone.
entry.fAccessFlags = ACTRL_ACCESS_ALLOWED;
entry.Trustee.TrusteeType = TRUSTEE_IS_GROUP;
entry.Trustee.ptstrName = L"*";
hr = pAccessControl->GrantAccessRights(&access);

// Call CoInitializeSecurity and pass a pointer to the access
// control object.
hr = CoInitializeSecurity(pAccessControl, -1, NULL, NULL,
    RPC_C_AUTHN_LEVEL_CONNECT, RPC_C_IMP_LEVEL_IDENTIFY,
    NULL, EOAC_ACCESS_CONTROL, NULL);

// Release the access control object. CoInitializeSecurity holds
// a reference.
pAccessControl->Release();
```

Implementing the *IAccessControl* Interface

Besides using the system-provided *DCOMAccessControl* object, you can provide *CoInitializeSecurity* with a custom implementation of the *IAccessControl* interface. The first five methods of *IAccessControl* must be implemented so that the caller can configure access permissions. How this access control information is stored internally in the object is entirely implementation-dependent. The last method, *IAccessControl::IsAccessAllowed*, is called by COM+ when an access check is required to determine whether a client has sufficient rights. Note that implementations of *IAccessControl* must be completely thread-safe because COM+ can call the access control object on any thread, at any time.

Although time and space do not permit us to provide a more complete implementation of the *IAccessControl* interface, allow us to humbly present *CMyAccessControl*. *CMyAccessControl* is a C++ class that returns *E_NOTIMPL* for all the methods of the *IAccessControl* interface except one: *IsAccessAllowed*. The implementation of the *IAccessControl::IsAccessAllowed* method is shown in the following code. As you can probably guess by looking at the code, each client access causes the method to display a message box asking the user whether permission should be granted or denied. If the user clicks Yes, *IsAccessAllowed* returns *TRUE* in the *pfAccessAllowed* parameter; otherwise, it returns *FALSE*. This security system is ironclad.

```
HRESULT CMyAccessControl::IsAccessAllowed(PTRUSTEEW pTrustee,
    LPWSTR lpProperty, ACCESS_RIGHTS AccessRights,
    BOOL* pfAccessAllowed)
{
    if(MessageBoxW(NULL, pTrustee->ptstrName,
        L"Grant permission?",
        MB_SERVICE_NOTIFICATION|MB_SETFOREGROUND|MB_YESNO) ==
        IDYES)
        *pfAccessAllowed = TRUE;
    else
        *pfAccessAllowed = FALSE;
    return S_OK;
}
```

Before *CoInitializeSecurity* is called, a static instance of the *CMyAccessControl* object is created. The address of this simple access control object is then passed as the first parameter of *CoInitializeSecurity*, as shown in the following code. COM+ later calls the *CMyAccessControl::IsAccessAllowed* method to determine whether prospective clients should be granted or denied access.

```
CMyAccessControl ac;
hr = CoInitializeSecurity(&ac, -1, NULL, NULL,
    RPC_C_AUTHN_LEVEL_CONNECT, RPC_C_IMP_LEVEL_IDENTIFY,
    NULL, EOAC_ACCESS_CONTROL, NULL);
```

Activation Credentials: The COAUTHINFO Structure

Our discussion of security settings to this point has centered on access permissions, which can be configured in the registry or by calling *CoInitializeSecurity*. Recall that launch permissions can be configured only in the registry because the server's SCM needs this information before a component is launched. The client, of course, is running when it issues an activation request using one of the COM+ object instantiation functions, which gives the client the opportunity to specify authentication settings that will be used by the client machine's SCM when making the remote activation request to the server machine's SCM.

Imagine that a component's security settings have been configured in such a way that user Joe is granted launch permission and both user Joe and user Julie are granted access permission. A client process running under the security credentials of user Julie wants to launch and access the component. Unfortunately, Julie has not been granted launch permission, so the client's call to the *CoCreateInstanceEx* function fails with the error *E_ACCESSDENIED*. However, if the client process (running under the security credentials of Julie) happens to know the password for user account Joe, the client can use the security credentials of Joe when making the launch request. This launch request will be successful because the administrator has granted launch permission to Joe.

All of the standard instantiation functions, such as *CoCreateInstanceEx* and its friends *CoGetClassObject*, *CoGetInstanceFromFile*, and *CoGetInstanceFrom-IStorage*, accept an argument of the type *COSERVERINFO*. *CoGetObject* and many other moniker functions use the BIND_OPTS2 structure, which contains a pointer to the COSERVERINFO structure. COSERVERINFO contains two interesting fields: the name of the server machine on which the object should be instantiated[12] and a pointer to authentication information provided in the form of a COAUTHINFO structure. The COAUTHINFO structure in turn contains a pointer to a COAUTHIDENTITY structure. The definitions of the COSERVERINFO, COAUTHINFO, and COAUTHIDENTITY structures are shown in IDL notation in Figure 18-9.

The first two parameters of the COAUTHINFO structure, *dwAuthnSvc* and *dwAuthzSvc*, specify which authentication and authorization services should be used to authenticate the client. Each field can be set to one of the *RPC_C_AUTHN*_xxx and *RPC_C_AUTHZ*_xxx flags shown in the tables on page 554. The third parameter of the COAUTHINFO structure, *pwszServer-PrincName*, points to a string indicating the server principal name to use with the authentication service. If you're using the NTLMSSP authentication service, the principal name is ignored. If you're using the Kerberos authentication service, the principal name specified should be the name of the machine account on which you're launching the component.

The fourth and fifth parameters of the COAUTHINFO structure, *dwAuthn-Level* and *dwImpersonationLevel*, specify the authentication and impersonation levels. These fields can be set to one of the progressively higher levels of authentication and impersonation shown in the tables on pages 535 and 536. Typically, the impersonation level must be set to at least *RPC_C_IMP_LEVEL_IMPERSONATE* because the system needs an impersonation token to create a process on behalf of the client. If you're using Kerberos and specify the impersonation level *RPC_C_IMP_LEVEL_DELEGATE*, the machine account named by the *pwszServerPrincName* property must have the Computer Is Trusted For Delegation setting configured in Active Directory. The last parameter of the COAUTHINFO structure, *dwCapabilities*, defines flags that indicate further capabilities of the proxy. Currently, no capability flags are defined, so this flag must be set to *EOAC_NONE*.

---

12. This field is covered in the section titled "Remote Instantiation" in Chapter 13.

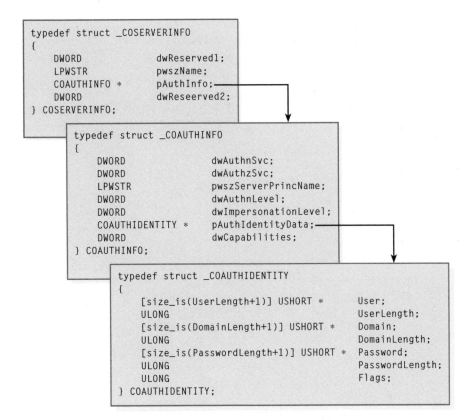

Figure 18-9.
The relationship between the COSERVERINFO, COAUTHINFO, and COAUTHIDENTITY structures.

The sixth parameter of the COAUTHINFO structure, *pAuthIdentityData*, points to a COAUTHIDENTITY structure that establishes the identity of the client. You can use the COAUTHIDENTITY structure to pass a particular user name and password to COM+ for the purpose of authentication. The *User* field specifies the user name, the *Domain* field specifies the domain or workgroup to which the user belongs, and the *Password* field contains the user's password. The *Flags* field specifies whether the strings are stored in Unicode (*SEC_WINNT_AUTH_IDENTITY_UNICODE*) or ASCII (*SEC_WINNT_AUTH_IDENTITY_ANSI*). Since all COM+ functions work with Unicode strings, the *Flags* field must be set to *SEC_WINNT_AUTH_IDENTITY_UNICODE*. The corresponding string length fields indicate the string length minus the terminating null character.

When, as is typically the case, the *COAUTHINFO* pointer in the CO-SERVERINFO structure passed to *CoCreateInstanceEx* and company is set to *NULL*, COM+ uses the default values for the COAUTHINFO structure based on the default machine security configured in the registry. The following code fragment shows how a client process can use the COAUTHINFO and COAUTHIDENTITY structures to specify its activation credentials when using the *CoCreateInstanceEx* function to instantiate an object on a remote machine:

```
COAUTHIDENTITY AuthIdentity;
AuthIdentity.User = L"User";
AuthIdentity.UserLength = wcslen(L"User");
AuthIdentity.Domain = L"Domain";
AuthIdentity.DomainLength = wcslen(L"Domain");
AuthIdentity.Password = L"Password";
 AuthIdentity.PasswordLength = wcslen(L"Password");
AuthIdentity.Flags = SEC_WINNT_AUTH_IDENTITY_UNICODE;

COAUTHINFO AuthInfo;
AuthInfo.dwAuthnSvc = RPC_C_AUTHN_GSS_KERBEROS;
AuthInfo.dwAuthzSvc = RPC_C_AUTHZ_NONE;
AuthInfo.pwszServerPrincName = L"Domain\\MachineName";
AuthInfo.dwAuthnLevel = RPC_C_AUTHN_LEVEL_CONNECT;
AuthInfo.dwImpersonationLevel = RPC_C_IMP_LEVEL_IMPERSONATE;
AuthInfo.pAuthIdentityData = &AuthIdentity;
AuthInfo.dwCapabilities = EOAC_NONE;

COSERVERINFO ServerInfo;
ServerInfo.dwReserved1 = 0;
ServerInfo.pwszName = L"RemoteServerName";
ServerInfo.pAuthInfo = &AuthInfo;
ServerInfo.dwReserved2 = 0;

MULTI_QI qi;
qi.pIID = &IID_IUnknown;
qi.pItf = NULL;
qi.hr = 0;

HRESULT hr = CoCreateInstanceEx(CLSID_InsideCOM, NULL,
    CLSCTX_REMOTE_SERVER, &ServerInfo, 1, &qi);
```

The *IServerSecurity* Interface

A server can enforce higher levels of security on a per-method basis using the *IServerSecurity* interface. A component uses this interface to identify the client and impersonate the client's security credentials. The stub implements the

IServerSecurity interface, so there is typically no reason to implement this interface unless you're using custom marshaling. The IDL definition of the *IServerSecurity* interface is shown below in IDL notation.

```
interface IServerSecurity : IUnknown
{
    // Called by the server to find out about the client that
    // has invoked one of its methods
    HRESULT QueryBlanket(
        [out] DWORD     *pAuthnSvc,
        [out] DWORD     *pAuthzSvc,
        [out] OLECHAR **pServerPrincName,
        [out] DWORD     *pAuthnLevel,
        [out] DWORD     *pImpLevel,
        [out] void    **pPrivs,
        [out] DWORD     *pCapabilities);

    // Allows a server to impersonate a client for the duration
    // of a call
    HRESULT ImpersonateClient();

    // Restores the authentication information on a thread to
    // the process's identity
    HRESULT RevertToSelf();

    // Indicates whether the server is currently impersonating
    // the client
    BOOL IsImpersonating();
}
```

To obtain a pointer to the stub's implementation of the *IServerSecurity* interface, the server process calls the function *CoGetCallContext*, as shown in the following code. Note that *CoGetCallContext* can be called only from within a method invoked by a client.

```
HRESULT MyObject::MyMethod()
{
    IServerSecurity* pServerSecurity;
    HRESULT hr = CoGetCallContext(IID_IServerSecurity,
        (void**)&pServerSecurity);

    // Use IServerSecurity interface pointer.

    pServerSecurity->Release();
    return S_OK;
}
```

Using the *IServerSecurity* interface pointer, the server can call any of the four methods of the interface. To make this easier, COM+ provides several helper functions that call *CoGetCallContext* to obtain the *IServerSecurity* interface pointer, call one of its methods, and then release the interface pointer. The helper functions are listed in the following table, along with their interface method counterparts.

IServerSecurity Method	Equivalent API Function
QueryBlanket	*CoQueryClientBlanket*
ImpersonateClient	*CoImpersonateClient*
RevertToSelf	*CoRevertToSelf*
IsImpersonating	(none)

The server uses the *IServerSecurity::QueryBlanket* method to find out about the client that invoked the current method. This technique can be useful for determining the security credentials of the client and then taking special action that depends on the user identity of the client process. The following code fragment uses the *QueryBlanket* method to obtain and display information about the client's security blanket:

```
HRESULT CInsideCOM::Sum(int x, int y, int* retval)
{
    DWORD AuthnSvc;
    DWORD AuthzSvc;
    OLECHAR* ServerPrincName;
    DWORD AuthnLevel;
    RPC_AUTHZ_HANDLE Privs;
    DWORD Capabilities;

    hr = CoQueryClientBlanket(&AuthnSvc, &AuthzSvc,
        &ServerPrincName, &AuthnLevel, NULL, &Privs,
        &Capabilities);

    // Code omitted here that displays the authentication and
    // authorization packages...

    // Display the current principal name.
    wprintf(L"ServerPrincName %s\n", ServerPrincName);

    // Free the memory allocated by QueryBlanket.
    CoTaskMemFree(ServerPrincNam);
```

```
// Code omitted here that displays the
// authentication level...

// Display the domain\user information.
wprintf(L"Privs %s\n", Privs);

*retval = x + y;
return S_OK;
}
```

Note that implementations of the *IUnknown::QueryInterface* method must never perform access control checking. COM+ requires an object that supports a particular interface identifier (IID) to always return success when queried for that IID. Besides, checking access permissions in *QueryInterface* does not provide any real security. If client A has a legal *ISum* interface pointer to a component, it can hand that interface pointer to client B without any calls back to the component. Also, COM+ caches interface pointers and does not necessarily call the component's *QueryInterface* method for each client call.

Impersonating the Client

Using the *IServerSecurity* interface pointer, the server can call the *IServerSecurity:: ImpersonateClient* method to temporarily assume the security credentials of the client.[13] While impersonating the client's security credentials, the server is limited by the impersonation level granted by the client. For example, if the client has limited the impersonation level to *RPC_C_IMP_LEVEL_IDENTIFY*, the server can impersonate the client only for the purpose of checking permissions using a Win32 API function such as *AccessCheck*. If the client has granted the server *RPC_C_IMP_LEVEL_IMPERSONATE* rights, the server can access system objects such as local files using the credentials of the client, but not any network resources. If the server is running on the same machine as the client, the server can access network resources as the client. In either case, only one machine hop is permitted, after which the server can access only local resources using the client's credentials.

---

13. Note that during an asynchronous call, the server cannot impersonate the client after the server's call to *ISynchronize::Signal* completes, even if the *Begin_* method has not yet completed. For example, if a client calls the *Begin_* method and the server calls *ISynchronize::Signal* to indicate that it is finished processing, even if work remains to be done in the *Begin_* method, the server cannot impersonate the client after the call to *ISynchronize::Signal*. If the server impersonates the client before it calls *ISynchronize::Signal*, the impersonation token is not removed from the thread until the server calls *IServerSecurity::RevertToSelf* or until the *Begin_* method returns, whichever comes first. See Chapter 17 for more information on asynchronous calls.

In Windows 2000, which supports the impersonation level *RPC_C_IMP_LEVEL_DELEGATE*, a server with this right can impersonate the client's security credentials when making cross-machine calls. Any number of machine hops is supported by delegate-level impersonation. In order for delegate-level impersonation to work, however, several requirements must be met. The client account that will be delegated must not be marked Account Is Sensitive And Can Not Be Delegated in Active Directory, and the account under which the server executes must be marked Account Is Trusted For Delegation. Also, because Kerberos support is required, the client, server, and all downstream servers must be running Windows 2000 in a Windows 2000 domain.

The primary reason to use impersonation is so that access checks are performed against the client's identity. Imagine that a client calls an object and asks it to read some data from a file. If the client has access rights to the file but the server does not, the server's attempt to read from the file will fail unless impersonation is activated. One can also imagine the reverse situation, in which the client is forbidden to access the file but the server has the necessary permissions; in this case, the server's attempt to read from the file will succeed and the client will receive unauthorized data unless impersonation is activated. As you can see, the access rights of the server process might be diminished or expanded depending on the rights of the client that is being impersonated.

Cloaking

Normally, when a method executes, the primary access token of the server's process is used to determine what access rights are available when the thread interacts with a securable object. However, when the thread on which the method is executing is impersonating the client, it is granted a special impersonation token representing the client's security context in addition to the primary access token of the process. While the server impersonates the client, the thread's impersonation token is used for all access checking. When the server finishes impersonating the client, it calls the *IServerSecurity::RevertToSelf* method to revert to the primary access token of the process, thereby restoring its own security credentials. Regardless of the impersonation level permitted by the client, the impersonation information lasts only until the end of the method. If, after impersonating the client, the server neglects to call the *RevertToSelf* method prior to the completion of the method, COM+ restores the server's security credentials automatically.

Imagine a scenario in which client A calls server B, which in turn calls server C. When client A calls server B, the access token for server B is used for access checking. If client A sets impersonate-level or delegate-level impersonation and server B impersonates client A, client A's ACL is used for access checking. But what happens if server B calls server C while impersonating client A? Assuming that client A has set delegate-level impersonation, this will work, but the access token for process B will be used when making the call to server C. This means that server C will see the identity of its caller as server B—not client A.

This might seem odd since the idea of delegate-level impersonation is to enable an object at the end of a call chain to impersonate its caller (the client) at the very start of the call chain. When the server impersonates the client, the client's ACL is used for access checking. But if a server makes calls to a downstream server while impersonating the client, its process token represents the identity of the caller to the downstream server. This is done for reasons of compatibility with the behavior of COM prior to Windows 2000. In Windows NT 4.0 Kerberos and later, delegate-level impersonation was not available, so this was really not an issue. In order to not break existing COM applications in Windows 2000, COM+ does not change the existing semantics of impersonation.

To achieve true delegation of security principals, COM+ has introduced the idea of cloaking. Fundamentally, cloaking does what delegate-level impersonation is supposed to do: it controls which identity is set on the proxy when you make a call, and it controls which identity the server sees when it impersonates. When a server process impersonates a client and then makes calls to downstream servers, the impersonating server's thread token is used. Let's return to the scenario in which client A calls server B, which in turn calls server C. If client A sets delegate-level impersonation before calling server B, and server B sets the cloaking flag and impersonates client A before calling server C, server C will think that its caller is client A and will be able to perform any actions permitted to client A. Thus, we achieve the true delegation of security principals. If server B neglects to set the cloaking flag before calling server C, server C will see server B as its client, even if client A has set delegate-level impersonation.

Cloaking can be set in two ways: the process can set a cloaking flag in the call to *CoInitializeSecurity*, or the cloaking attribute can be set on an individual proxy by calling *CoSetProxyBlanket*. The two cloaking flags supported in Windows 2000 are *EOAC_STATIC_CLOAKING* and *EOAC_DYNAMIC_CLOAKING*. Dynamic cloaking is the option that is typically used, and this is the way most people expect delegate-level impersonation to work. When server B sets the dynamic cloaking flag, impersonates client A, and then calls server C, server C sees client A as the identity of its caller. In other words, the current impersonation token, if available, is always used in the case of dynamic cloaking. While dynamic cloaking can have performance overhead, it provides the flexibility that is usually required by circumstances that necessitate the use of impersonation in the first place.

Static cloaking determines the identity of the caller during the first call on a proxy or whenever *CoSetProxyBlanket* is called, and that identity is used on all subsequent method calls. Imagine that server B sets static cloaking and makes a call to server C, thereby setting server C's proxy in server B's address space to the identity of server B. Later, client A calls server B, which impersonates client A and makes a call to server C. Server C sees as its caller the identity of server B, since that identity was fixed during the previous call. Now, if server C sets the cloaking attribute and calls server D, server D sees server B as its caller.

The *IClientSecurity* Interface

IClientSecurity, the twin of *IServerSecurity*, is an interface that client processes use to adjust security settings on the proxy of a remote object. As with the *IServerSecurity* interface, there is typically no need to implement the *IClientSecurity* interface, since all proxies generated by the MIDL compiler automatically support it, as does the Automation marshaler employed by components using type library marshaling. The *IClientSecurity* interface is shown here in IDL notation:

```
interface IClientSecurity : IUnknown
{
    // Retrieves the current authentication information
    HRESULT QueryBlanket(
        [in]  IUnknown *pProxy,
        [out] DWORD    *pAuthnSvc,
        [out] DWORD    *pAuthzSvc,
        [out] OLECHAR **pServerPrincName,
        [out] DWORD    *pAuthnLevel,
        [out] DWORD    *pImpLevel,
        [out] void    **pAuthInfo,
        [out] DWORD    *pCapabilites);

    // Sets the authentication information that will be used
    // to make calls on the specified proxy
    HRESULT SetBlanket(
        [in] IUnknown *pProxy,
        [in] DWORD    AuthnSvc,
        [in] DWORD    AuthzSvc,
        [in] OLECHAR *pServerPrincName,
        [in] DWORD    AuthnLevel,
        [in] DWORD    ImpLevel,
        [in] void    *pAuthInfo,
        [in] DWORD    Capabilities);
```

```
// Makes a copy of the specified proxy
HRESULT CopyProxy(
    [in]  IUnknown  *pProxy,
    [out] IUnknown  **ppCopy);
}
```

You can use the methods of the *IClientSecurity* interface to examine (*IClientSecurity::QueryBlanket*) or modify (*IClientSecurity::SetBlanket*) the current security settings for a particular connection to an out-of-process object. One typical use of the *IClientSecurity* interface is for the client process to escalate the authentication level used by a particular interface. Most interfaces of an object are rather pedestrian, but one interface could require the client to submit sensitive data such as the user's credit card information. In this case, it might make sense to establish a default authentication level of *RPC_C_AUTHN_LEVEL_CONNECT* but use the *IClientSecurity::SetBlanket* method to raise that setting to *RPC_C_AUTHN_LEVEL_PKT_PRIVACY* on the interface dealing with the credit card information. The *IClientSecurity:: SetBlanket* method can never set the authentication level lower than was specified by the component in its call to *CoInitializeSecurity.*

The *IClientSecurity::SetBlanket* method can also be used to set the static or dynamic cloaking flags discussed previously. The code fragment below shows a proxy being set with the dynamic cloaking attribute. Note that for all attributes of the proxy that are not being adjusted in this call, we simply pass the default flags. Although security settings assigned to the proxy by the *SetBlanket* method are not subject to the COM+ security blanket negotiation algorithm described previously, this algorithm is used to decide the value for all default parameters such as *RPC_C_AUTHN_LEVEL_DEFAULT.*

```
hr = pClientSecurity->SetBlanket(pInterface,
    RPC_C_AUTHN_GSS_KERBEROS, RPC_C_AUTHZ_DEFAULT,
    COLE_DEFAULT_PRINCIPAL, RPC_C_AUTHN_LEVEL_DEFAULT,
    RPC_C_IMP_LEVEL_DELEGATE, COLE_DEFAULT_AUTHINFO,
    EOAC_DYNAMIC_CLOAKING);
```

The *IClientSecurity::CopyProxy* method makes a private copy of the proxy. If you call *IClientSecurity::SetBlanket* on an interface pointer, the security settings will also affect all other code in the client process using that interface pointer. To limit the scope of the security settings, the client can make a copy of the proxy before adjusting the security blanket. In this way, the client receives a pointer to another proxy through which the object can be invoked. Adjusting the security settings for this proxy does not affect any other code running in the client process.

Obtaining a pointer to the proxy-supplied implementation of the *IClient-Security* interface is as simple as calling the *IUnknown::QueryInterface* method, as shown in the following code. This interface is always available for out-of-process objects that employ standard or type library marshaling. If the *IUnknown::QueryInterface* call for *IClientSecurity* fails, the object is either in-process or custom marshaled. Custom marshalers can implement the *IClientSecurity* interface for consistency if necessary.

```
IClientSecurity* pClientSecurity;
HRESULT hr = pUnknown->QueryInterface(IID_IClientSecurity,
    (void**)&pClientSecurity);
if(FAILED(hr))
    cout << "QueryInterface for IClientSecurity failed." << endl;

// Use the IClientSecurity interface pointer.

pClientSecurity->Release();
```

Note that the *IClientSecurity::SetBlanket* method returns an error if you set the *EOAC_SECURE_REFS*, *EOAC_ACCESS_CONTROL*, or *EOAC_APPID* flags in the *dwCapabilities* parameter. These settings are valid for use only when you call *CoInitializeSecurity*. As with the *IServerSecurity* interface, COM+ provides several helper functions that assist in calling the methods of the *IClientSecurity* interface. These functions are shown in the following table, along with their equivalent methods.

IClientSecurity Method	Equivalent API Function
QueryBlanket	*CoQueryProxyBlanket*
SetBlanket	*CoSetProxyBlanket*
CopyProxy	*CoCopyProxy*

CHAPTER NINETEEN

The Network Protocol

While COM+ is usually thought of as a specification for building interoperable components, when you use it for distributed communications it is simply a high-level network protocol that enables objects to work together across a network. From this perspective, COM+ is a high-level network protocol because it is built on top of several layers of existing protocols.

For example, say that a computer has an Ethernet network interface card and is using User Datagram Protocol (UDP). The layering of protocols ranges from the Ethernet frame at the lowest level to COM+ at the highest. Sandwiched in the middle are Internet Protocol (IP), UDP, and Remote Procedure Calls (RPCs), as shown in Figure 19-1. This is just one of many possible configurations—any available protocols can be used below the RPC layer. COM+ automatically chooses the best underlying network protocol based on the protocols available on the client and server machines.

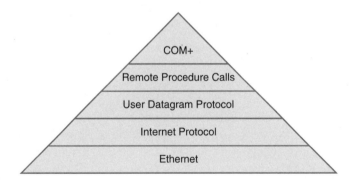

Figure 19-1.
An example of the layering of protocols from the Ethernet frame to COM+.

It can also be useful to think of a COM+ protocol stack in terms of the Open Systems Interconnection (OSI) seven-layer model. Figure 19-2 shows this model juxtaposed with our sample protocol stack. The figure shows how the COM+ protocol stack fits into the OSI seven-layer model on the Microsoft Windows platform. Different operating systems might implement the protocols at different layers.

OSI Seven-Layer Model

Application	RPC/COM+
Presentation	
Session	(WinSock driver)
Transport	User Datagram Protocol
Network	Internet Protocol
Data Link	Ethernet driver
Physical	Ethernet card

Figure 19-2.
*The OSI seven-layer model and the corresponding sample COM+
protocol stack.*

The packet sent across the network for each protocol in the protocol stack consists of a header followed by the actual data. Each protocol considers the protocol directly above it in the protocol stack as part of its data. For example, IP consists of a header followed by data; this IP data actually consists of the header for UDP followed by UDP's data. Thus, a packet that is transmitted across the network contains the header and data sections of each protocol in the protocol stack. This transmission packet is depicted in Figure 19-3.

Although it is convenient to think of COM+ as an independent network protocol layered on top of the RPC protocol, this is not really the case. COM+ is actually akin to a parasite on its RPC host. It infects the RPC header and data, using the fields of the RPC structures for its own devices. Thus, to better indicate the close relationship between the RPC and the COM+ protocol at the network level, the COM+ network protocol is often called Object RPC, or ORPC. ORPC leverages the functionality of the Open Software Foundation (OSF) Distributed Computing Environment (DCE) RPC network protocol.

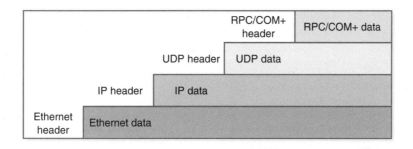

Figure 19-3.
A network transmission packet.

For example, the authentication, authorization, and message integrity features of the RPC protocol are present in ORPC. ORPC extends the standard RPC protocol in two areas:

■ How calls are made on remote objects

■ How object references are represented, transmitted, and maintained

Most discourse on COM+ focuses on the fundamental programming architecture. In other words, you are told what COM+ function to call in order to perform a specific task. This chapter examines COM+ from the bottom up. By analyzing the data packets transmitted across a network during the execution of COM+ applications, you can learn a lot about how the COM+ remoting architecture works. This knowledge will increase your overall understanding of the COM+ programming model and can help you design and develop better components.

Spying on the Network Protocol

Because nearly every aspect of the network protocol is hidden from the COM+ programmer, the most interesting and concrete way to examine the network protocol is to spy on the transmissions between computers during the execution of a COM+ client and component. To do this, you need a special type of software (and/or hardware) popularly known as a *lanalyzer*. A variety of third-party tools are available, for every need and budget, that let you capture and view network traffic. Network Monitor, a Microsoft utility included with Windows 2000 and Microsoft Systems Management Server, is perhaps the simplest and cheapest way to capture meaningful network traffic. Figure 19-4 shows Network Monitor in action.

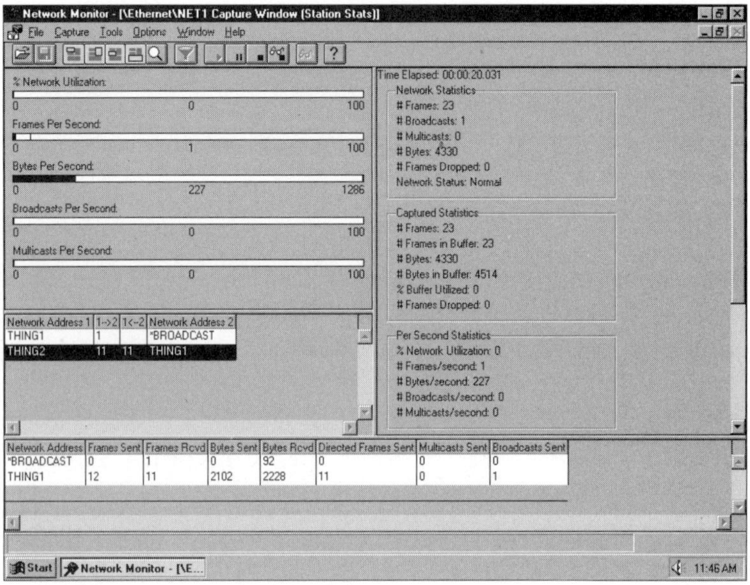

Figure 19-4.
Using Network Monitor to capture network traffic.

Unfortunately, Network Monitor does not currently support ORPC, so we're forced to look at ORPC through the eyes of RPC. This affliction does not have to be a permanent one: Network Monitor does have a publicly documented interface for building parser dynamic-link libraries (DLLs) that understand a specific network protocol and interpret the captured data in an intelligent manner.[1]

---

1. We'll leave it as an exercise for you to develop a Network Monitor parser DLL that understands the ORPC protocol.

Interpreting Marshaled GUIDs

Globally unique identifiers (GUIDs) that are transmitted over the network must be interpreted in accordance with the Interface Definition Language (IDL) definition of a GUID, shown here:

```
typedef struct _GUID
{
    DWORD Data1;
    WORD  Data2;
    WORD  Data3;
    BYTE  Data4[8];
} GUID;
```

Because the GUIDs are marshaled in little endian format, the original GUID can be reconstructed using a two-step process. First, the GUID found in a captured network packet must be formatted to look like a standard GUID. For example, imagine that you have located the GUID *78 56 34 12 34 12 34 12 12 34 12 34 56 78 9A BC* in a network packet. The following figure shows this GUID in standard formation:

Better already, isn't it? Now the little endian format must be taken into account to obtain the actual GUID. The first three elements of the GUID structure (labeled *Data1*, *Data2*, and *Data3* in the structure shown above) must be reversed byte by byte. The last element of the GUID structure (*Data4*) does not need to be modified because it is already stored as a simple byte array. Thus, after the first three elements of the GUID structure are reversed, the completed second step of the process provides the true GUID, 12345678-1234-1234-1234-123456789ABC.

Running Network Monitor

To turn on Network Monitor's capture facility, simply choose Start from the Capture menu. Then run a COM+ test program to generate the desired network traffic. After the program has completed execution, return to Network Monitor and choose Stop And View from the Capture menu to disable the network capture facility and display the captured packets. Network Monitor is quite clever—rather than simply displaying the raw captured packets, it actually understands many standard network protocols and thus presents the captured data in an intelligent and descriptive format. As far as ORPC-related protocols are concerned, Network Monitor can recognize and comprehend Ethernet, IP, UDP, and RPC. To view only the packets captured for certain network protocols, choose Filter from the Display menu.

To analyze the ORPC protocol, we ran Network Monitor to capture packets as the executable version of the *InsideCOM* object (which we built in Chapter 13) executed. The client ran on one computer, named Thing1, and was configured to activate the *InsideCOM* object on a server named Thing2. After calling *CoInitializeEx*, the client called *CoCreateInstanceEx* to instantiate the remote object, as shown here:

```
CoInitializeEx(NULL, COINIT_MULTITHREADED);

COSERVERINFO ServerInfo = { 0, L"Thing2", 0, 0 };
MULTI_QI qi = { &IID_IUnknown, NULL, 0 };
CoCreateInstanceEx(CLSID_InsideCOM, NULL, CLSCTX_REMOTE_SERVER,
    &ServerInfo, 1, &qi);
```

The call to *CoCreateInstanceEx* shown above results in the Service Control Manager (SCM) on Thing1 (the client) calling the *IRemoteActivation:: RemoteActivation* method on the SCM on Thing2 (the server) to activate the *CLSID_InsideCOM* object and return the interface pointer identifier (IPID) for *IID_IUnknown*. Thing1 was configured with an IP address of *199.34.58.3*, and Thing2 was configured with an IP address of *199.34.58.4*. Figure 19-5 shows how this remote activation translates to the transmission of a network packet as viewed using Network Monitor.

You can see the layering of protocols in the network packet depicted in the figure. In the RPC header, you can see that the interface identifier (IID; labeled *A*) is *B8 4A 9F 4D 1C 7D CF 11 86 1E 00 20 AF 6E 7C 57*. Following the rules described in the sidebar on the preceding page, the actual IID is *4D9F4AB8-7D1C-11CF-861E-0020AF6E7C57*—the *IRemoteActivation* interface.

SCM on Thing1 (client) calls the *IRemoteActivation::RemoteActivation* method on the SCM on Thing2 (server) to activate *CLSID_InsideCOM* and return IPID for *IID_IUnknown*

Ethernet
1 Destination address
2 Source address
3 Type (Internet Protocol)

Internet Protocol
4 Protocol (UDP)
5 Source address
(199.34.58.3)
6 Destination address
(199.34.58.4)

User Datagram Protocol
7 Destination port: 135
(Service Control Manager)

RPC header
8 PDU Type (Request)
9 Object identifier
A *IID_IRemoteActivation*
B Interface version (0.0)

ORPCTHIS
C Client ORPC version
D Causality identifier

Other parameters
E *CLSID_InsideCOM*
F RPC_C_IMP_LEVEL_IDENTIFY
G *IID_IUnknown*

Ethernet	00000: 00 60 97 8E EB 19 00 60 97 92 D2 6C 08 00 45 00
Internet Protocol	00010: 00 E8 A6 01 00 00 80 11 91 B7 C7 22 3A 03 C7 22
	00020: 3A 04 04 04 00 87 00 D4 74 D7 04 00 08 00 10 00
User Datagram Protocol	00030: 00 00 00 00 00 00 00 00 00 00 00 00 00 00 00 00
	00040: 00 00 B8 4A 9F 4D 1C 7D CF 11 86 1E D1 11 20 AF 6E
RPC header	00050: 7C 57 86 C2 37 67 F7 1E D1 11 BC D9 00 60 97 92
	00060: D2 6C 79 BE 01 34 00 00 00 00 00 00 00 00 00 00
	00070: FF FF FF FF 68 00 00 00 0A 00 05 00 01 00 00 00
ORPCTHIS	00080: 00 00 00 00 00 00 F1 59 EB 61 FB 1E D1 11 BC D9
	00090: 00 60 97 92 D2 6C 00 00 00 00 02 00 00 00 10 00 00
Other parameters	000A0: 00 00 00 00 00 00 00 00 00 00 01 00 00 00 00 00 00
	000B0: 00 00 02 00 00 00 00 00 00 00 01 00 00 00 80 3F
	000C0: 15 00 01 00 00 00 00 00 00 00 00 00 00 00 C0 00
	000D0: 00 00 00 00 00 46 01 00 00 00 01 00 00 00 08 00
	000E0: 64 00 04 00 69 00 01 00 00 00 87 03 B2 D6 99 EE
	000F0: AC 65 C7 53 81 A4

Figure 19-5.
The network packet resulting from an activation request, IRemoteActivation::RemoteActivation, *as captured by Network Monitor.*

Remote Activation

IRemoteActivation is an RPC interface (not a COM+ interface) that is exposed by the SCM on each machine. The SCM on Windows 2000 machines is named rpcss.dll and runs in the svchost.exe surrogate.[2] The *IRemoteActivation* interface has only one method, *RemoteActivation*, which activates a COM+ object on a remote machine. This powerful feature is missing in pure RPC, in which the server must always be running before the client can connect.[3] The IDL definition of the *IRemoteActivation* interface is shown on the following page.

2. In other versions of Windows, the SCM is named rpcss.exe.

3. Remote activation works only in Windows NT and Windows 2000. Windows 95 and Windows 98 lack the necessary security infrastructure.

```
[ // No object keyword here. Not a COM+ interface!
    uuid(4d9f4ab8-7d1c-11cf-861e-0020af6e7c57),
    pointer_default(unique)
]
interface IRemoteActivation
{
    const unsigned long MODE_GET_CLASS_OBJECT = 0xffffffff;

    HRESULT RemoteActivation(
        [in] handle_t                          hRpc,
        [in] ORPCTHIS                          *ORPCthis,
        [out] ORPCTHAT                         *ORPCthat,
        [in] GUID                              *Clsid,
        [in, string, unique] WCHAR             *pwszObjectName,
        [in, unique] MInterfacePointer         *pObjectStorage,
        [in] DWORD                             ClientImpLevel,
        [in] DWORD                             Mode,
        [in] DWORD                             Interfaces,
        [in, unique, size_is(Interfaces)] IID  *pIIDs,
        [in] unsigned short                    cRequestedProtseqs,
        [in, size_is(cRequestedProtseqs)]
            unsigned short                     RequestedProtseqs[],
        [out] OXID                             *pOxid,
        [out] DUALSTRINGARRAY                  **ppdsaOxidBindings,
        [out] IPID                             *pipidRemUnknown,
        [out] DWORD                            *pAuthnHint,
        [out] COMVERSION                       *pServerVersion,
        [out] HRESULT                          *phr,
        [out, size_is(Interfaces)]
            MInterfacePointer                  **ppInterfaceData,
        [out, size_is(Interfaces)] HRESULT     *pResults
    );
}
```

Through the *IRemoteActivation* interface, the SCM on one machine contacts the SCM on another machine to request that it activate an object. The client machine's SCM calls the *IRemoteActivation::RemoteActivation* method of the server's SCM to request activation of the class object identified by the class identifier (CLSID) in the fourth parameter. The *RemoteActivation* method returns a marshaled interface pointer for the requested object and two special values: the interface pointer identifier (IPID) and the object exporter identifier

(OXID). The IPID identifies an interface of an object running in a component. The OXID identifies the RPC string binding[4] information needed to connect to the interface specified by an IPID.

The SCM resides at well-known endpoints, one for each supported network protocol. An endpoint identifies the virtual channel through which you are communicating; it is based on the network protocol in use. For example, when you use Transmission Control Protocol (TCP) or UDP, the endpoint is a port number such as 1066; if you use named pipes, the endpoint is a pipe name such as *pipe**mypipe*. The following table shows the endpoints for the SCM when some of the more popular protocols are used.

Protocol String	Description	Endpoint
ncadg_ip_udp	Connectionless over UDP/IP	135
ncacn_ip_tcp	Connection-oriented over TCP/IP	135
ncacn_http	Connection-oriented over Hypertext Transfer Protocol (HTTP)	593

Internet Services

While the SCM always uses port 135 to initiate a remote request, the actual conversation between a client and a server occurs over a port number selected dynamically by COM+ in the range 1024 to 65535. While this technique is perfectly suitable for an intranet environment, in Internet scenarios, in which there is often a proxy server that filters outbound traffic from the client machine as well as some kind of firewall that limits incoming network traffic at the server, communication is more complex. Typically, the security software restricts COM+ to a narrow set of protocol and endpoint combinations. To allow administrators to control the range of ports from which COM+ chooses, you can use the Default Protocols tab of the Distributed COM Configuration utility to restrict the available ports, as shown in Figure 19-6.

---

4. RPC string bindings are discussed in greater detail in the Appendix.

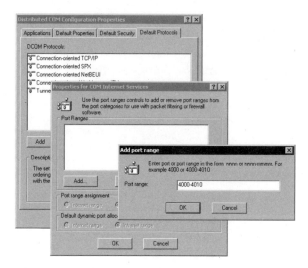

Figure 19-6.
Restricting COM+ to a limited range of ports.

Furthermore, port 135, which is used by the SCM, is often blocked by the firewall. To enable COM+ to work better in scenarios where the Internet is the vehicle for communication, COM+ supports the tunneling TCP/IP protocol. Tunneling TCP/IP uses a special handshake protocol at the beginning of each connection that is sent as HTTP traffic over port 80. After this initial handshake, all further COM+-generated traffic is sent via standard TCP/IP. Since part of the tunneling TCP/IP protocol is implemented as an Internet Server Application Programming Interface (ISAPI) extension and filter, this functionality works only in Internet scenarios where the Web server is Internet Information Server (IIS).[5]

To enable the use of tunneling TCP/IP on the client, you use the Distributed COM Configuration[6] utility to execute these steps, as shown in Figure 19-7.

1. Click the Default Protocols tab and use the Add button to select the Tunneling TCP/IP protocol. Then click OK.

---

5. In Windows 95 and Windows 98, this functionality is available in a separate utility named ciscnfg.exe.

6. Also, tunneling TCP/IP works only if the proxy servers and firewalls permit TCP/IP traffic over a port opened to HTTP.

2. You might want to move the Tunneling TCP/IP protocol up or down in the list. COM+ attempts to use the protocols in the order listed.

3. Reboot the system.

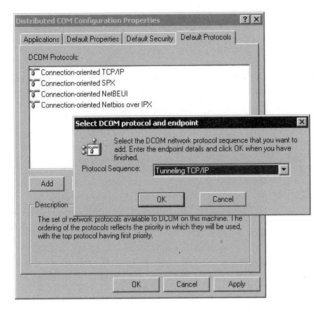

Figure 19-7.
Adding the Tunneling TCP/IP protocol.

On the server, you must follow the same steps but also select the Enable COM Internet Services On This Computer check box on the Default Properties tab of the Distributed COM Configuration utility.[7] On the server, you must also install the COM Internet Services Proxy. The client and server might also require additional configuration depending on whether a proxy server is used to connect to the Internet or whether an overly aggressive firewall is protecting the server. However, no coding changes are required to take advantage of the tunneling TCP/IP protocol.

---

7. You can disable this option to block any potential Internet access to COM+ components.

Calling All Remote Objects

Method calls made on remote COM+ objects are considered true DCE RPC invocations in that a standard request Protocol Data Unit (PDU) is transmitted across the network, requesting that a specific method be executed. A PDU is the basic unit of communication between two machines. The request PDU contains all of the *[in]* parameters that the method expects to receive. When method execution is complete, a response PDU containing the method's *[out]* parameters is transmitted back to the client.

This process sounds rather obvious, but it is quite amazing when you consider how it actually works. A remote method call requires two packets to be transmitted across the network, one from the client to the server containing the *[in]* parameters and the other from the server to the client containing the *[out]* parameters. The 19 defined PDU types and their values are listed in the table below. The table also shows whether a particular PDU type is specific to a connection-oriented (abbreviated as CO here) protocol, a connectionless (CL) protocol, or both.

PDU Type	Protocol(s)	Type Value
request	CO/CL	0
ping	CL	1
response	CO/CL	2
fault	CO/CL	3
working	CL	4
nocall	CL	5
reject	CL	6
ack	CL	7
cl_cancel	CL	8
fack	CL	9
cancel_ack	CL	10
bind	CO	11
bind_ack	CO	12
bind_nak	CO	13
alter_context	CO	14
alter_context_resp	CO	15
shutdown	CO	17
co_cancel	CO	18
orphaned	CO	19

A connection-oriented protocol, such as TCP, maintains a virtual connection for the client and server between transmissions and guarantees that messages are delivered in the order in which they were sent. A connectionless protocol, such as UDP, does not maintain a connection between the client and server and does not guarantee that a message from the client will actually be delivered to the server. And even if the messages are delivered, they might arrive in a different order from that in which they were sent. By default, COM+ uses the connectionless UDP. A connectionless protocol does not make COM+ unreliable, however, because RPC ensures robustness by using a customized mechanism for message ordering and acknowledgment.

An RPC PDU contains up to three parts, only the first of which is required:

- A PDU header containing protocol control information.

- A PDU body containing data. For example, the body of a request or response PDU contains data representing the input or output parameters for an operation. This information is stored in Network Data Representation (NDR) format.

- An authentication verifier containing data specific to an authentication protocol. For example, an authentication protocol can ensure the integrity of a packet by including an encrypted checksum in the authentication verifier.

The PDU header used for connectionless protocols is shown here in IDL notation:

```
typedef struct
{
    unsigned small rpc_vers = 4;  // RPC protocol major version
    unsigned small ptype;         // Packet type
    unsigned small flags1;        // Packet flags
    unsigned small flags2;        // Packet flags
    byte drep[3];                 // Data representation format label
    unsigned small serial_hi;     // High byte of serial number
    GUID object;                  // Object identifier (contains IPID)
    GUID if_id;                   // IID
    GUID act_id;                  // Activity identifier
    unsigned long server_boot;    // Server boot time
    unsigned long if_vers;        // Interface version
    unsigned long seqnum;         // Sequence number
    unsigned short opnum;         // Operation number
    unsigned short ihint;         // Interface hint
    unsigned short ahint;         // Activity hint
```

(continued)

587

```
      unsigned short len;          // Length of packet body
      unsigned short fragnum;      // Fragment number
      unsigned small auth_proto;   // Authentication protocol ID
      unsigned small serial_lo;    // Low byte of serial number
} dc_rpc_cl_pkt_hdr_t;
```

The packet type field (named *ptype* in this structure) of a PDU identifies the PDU type. This value is one of the 19 PDU types listed in the earlier table. ORPC uses the object identifier (OID) field (*object*) of a PDU to store an IPID. An IPID is a GUID that represents an interface of an object hosted by a component. The IID field (*if_id*) must contain the IID of the COM+ interface. This field is somewhat redundant given that the OID field contains the IPID, which already identifies the interface. However, placing the IID in the *if_id* field allows COM+ to work correctly when it is run on a standard implementation of OSF DCE RPC. On systems such as Windows, the RPC implementation has been optimized to enable method calls to be dispatched based solely on the information contained in the IPID, ignoring the IID. Finally, the interface version number (*if_vers*) must always be *0.0* because a COM+ interface can never be modified after it is published. COM+ interfaces are not versioned; a new interface is defined instead. All of these fields can be found in the RPC header section of the captured network packet (shown earlier in Figure 19-5).

The ORPCTHIS and ORPCTHAT Structures

All method invocations are transmitted across the network in a request PDU containing a special first parameter of type ORPCTHIS, which is inserted before all the other inbound parameters of the method. Thus, a COM+ method defined as *HRESULT Sum (int x, int y, [out, retval] int * result)* is transmitted in a request PDU as *Sum (ORPCTHIS orpcthis, int x, int y)*. The definition of the ORPCTHIS structure is shown here:

```
// Implicit "this" pointer is the first [in] parameter of
// every ORPC call.
typedef struct tagORPCTHIS
{
    COMVERSION      version;    // ORPC version number
    unsigned long   flags;      // ORPCF flags for presence
                                //   of other data.
    unsigned long   reserved1;  // Set to 0
    CID             cid;        // Causality ID of caller
    [unique] ORPC_EXTENT_ARRAY *extensions; // Extensions
} ORPCTHIS;
```

The first field of the ORPCTHIS structure specifies the version of the ORPC protocol used to make the method call. Because each remote method call contains an ORPCTHIS structure, the version of ORPC on the client machine is always transmitted to the server. At the server, the client's version of ORPC is compared with the server's, and if the major version numbers don't match, the *RPC_E_VERSION_MISMATCH* error is returned to the client. The server is allowed to have a higher minor version number than the client, however. In such cases, the server must limit its use of the ORPC protocol to match the features available in the client's version.

A causality identifier (CID) is a GUID used to link together what might be a long chain of method calls. For example, if client A calls component B, and component B, before ever returning to client A, proceeds to call component C, these calls are said to be causally related. Every time a new method call is made (but not during the processing of an existing method), a new CID is generated by the ORPC protocol. The same CID is propagated in any subsequent calls made by component B on behalf of client A. This happens even if component B uses connection points or some other mechanism to call back into client A. The *extensions* field of the ORPCTHIS structure is designed to allow extra data to be sent with a COM+ method call. Currently only two extensions are defined, one for extended error information and the other for debugging control. You can also define custom extensions to the ORPCTHIS structure using channel hooks.[8]

In every response PDU for a method call, a special outbound parameter of type ORPCTHAT is inserted before all other *[out]* parameters of the method. Thus, a method defined as *HRESULT Sum (int x, int y, [out, retval] int ∗ result)* is transmitted in a response PDU as *HRESULT Sum (ORPCTHAT orpcthat, int result)*. The definition of the ORPCTHAT structure is shown here:

```
// Implicit "that" pointer is the first [out] parameter of
// every ORPC call.
typedef struct tagORPCTHAT
{
    unsigned long      flags;        // ORPCF flags for presence
                                     // of other data.
    [unique] ORPC_EXTENT_ARRAY *extensions; // Extensions
} ORPCTHAT;
```

---

8. You can use channel hooks to pass extra data in the COM+ channel; see the section titled "Channel Hooks" later in this chapter.

Marshaled Interface Pointers

The ORPC protocol transmits method parameters in the NDR format specified by OSF DCE RPC. NDR specifies exactly how all the primitive data types understood by IDL should be marshaled into data packets for network transmission. The only extension made to the NDR standard by ORPC is support for marshaled interface pointers. Use of the *iid_is* IDL keyword[9] in an interface definition constitutes what can be considered a new primitive data type that can be marshaled: an interface pointer.

The term *interface pointer* is problematic because it conjures up a mental picture of a pointer to a pointer to a v-table structure that contains pointers to functions. But once it is marshaled into a data packet, an interface pointer does not look like that at all. It is a symbolic representation of access to an object and is therefore called an object reference. The format of a marshaled interface pointer is governed by the MInterfacePointer structure defined below.

```
// Wire representation of a marshaled interface pointer

typedef struct tagMInterfacePointer
{
    ULONG ulCntData;                    // Size of data
    [size_is(ulCntData)] BYTE abData[]; // Data (OBJREF)
} MInterfacePointer;
```

After the *ulCntData* field, which defines the size of the structure, comes the *abData* byte array, which contains the actual object reference in a structure called an OBJREF. An OBJREF is the data type used to represent a reference to an object. The definition of the OBJREF structure is shown in the following code. Notice that OBJREF takes one of three forms, depending on the type of marshaling being employed: standard, handler, or custom.[10]

```
// OBJREF is the format of a marshaled interface pointer.
typedef struct tagOBJREF
{
    unsigned long  signature;       // Must be OBJREF_SIGNATURE
    unsigned long  flags;           // OBJREF flags
    GUID           iid;             // IID

    [switch_is(flags), switch_type(unsigned long)] union {
        [case(OBJREF_STANDARD)] struct {
```

---

9. See Chapter 16 for a description of IDL keywords.

10. Chapters 14 and 15 cover these three types of marshaling in detail.

```
        STDOBJREF        std;         // Standard OBJREF
        DUALSTRINGARRAY  saResAddr;   // Resolver address
    } u_standard;

    [case(OBJREF_HANDLER)] struct {
        STDOBJREF        std;         // Standard OBJREF
        CLSID            clsid;       // CLSID of handler code
        DUALSTRINGARRAY  saResAddr;   // Resolver address
    } u_handler;

    [case(OBJREF_CUSTOM)] struct {
        CLSID            clsid;       // CLSID of unmarshaling code
        unsigned long    cbExtension; // Size of extension data
        unsigned long    size;        // Size of data that follows
        [size_is(size), ref] byte *pData; // Extension plus class-
                                           //   specific data
    } u_custom;
  } u_objref;
} OBJREF;
```

The OBJREF structure begins with a *signature* field that is defined as the unsigned long hexadecimal value *0x574F454D*. Interestingly, if you arrange this value in little endian format (*4D 45 4F 57*) and then convert each byte to its ASCII equivalent, the resulting characters spell *MEOW*. The great thing about the MEOW structure (a popular nickname for the OBJREF structure) is that when you scan through the mountains of packets captured by the Network Monitor utility it is easy to tell when you've hit upon an object reference: just say MEOW. Note that regardless of the format of the remainder of the NDR data, the wire representation of a marshaled interface pointer is always stored in little endian format.

Following the MEOW *signature* field is the *flags* field of the OBJREF structure, which identifies the type of object reference. You can set the *flags* field to *OBJREF_STANDARD* (*1*), *OBJREF_HANDLER* (*2*), or *OBJREF_CUSTOM* (*4*) to indicate the type of interface marshaling. The *iid* field is the last omnipresent field of the OBJREF structure; it specifies the IID of the interface being marshaled. Figure 19-8 shows a network packet that was captured as a result of the request PDU shown previously. There the *CoCreateInstanceEx* function had been called to request the object's *IUnknown* interface pointer. In this figure, you can see that the response PDU has returned to the client. It contains the marshaled interface pointer (decorated by MEOW and labeled 5) of the object's *IUnknown* interface.

IRemoteActivation::RemoteActivation returns an OBJREF

1 PDU Type (Response)	6 *flags*(OBJREF_STANDARD)	B *ipid*
2 *IID_IRemoteActivation*	7 *iid* (IID_IUnknown)	C *wNumEntries*
3 Server ORPC version	8 *cPublicRefs* (5)	D *wSecurityOffset*
4 *ulCntData* (130)	9 *oxid*	E *wTowerId* (NCADG_IP_UDP)
5 MEOW	A *oid*	F *wTowerId* (NCACN_IP_TCP)

```
Headers           00000:  00 60 97 92 D2 6C 00 60 97 8E EB 19 08 00 45 00   .`...l.`......E.
                  00010:  02 30 10 01 00 00 80 11 26 70 C7 22 3A 04 C7 22   .0......&p.":.."
                  00020:  3A 03 00 87 04 04 02 1C B8 28 04 02 08 00 10 00   :........(......
                  00030:  00 00 00 00 00 00 00 00 00 00 00 00 00 00 00 00   ................
                  00040:  00 00 B8 4A 9F 4D 1C 7D CF 11 86 1E 00 20 AF 6E   ...J.M.}..... .n
                  00050:  7C 57 86 C2 37 67 F7 1E D1 11 BC D9 00 60 97 92   |W..7g.....`..
                  00060:  D2 6C 79 BE 01 34 00 00 00 00 00 00 00 00 00 00   .ly..4..........
                  00070:  FF FF 6E 00 B0 01 00 00 0A 00 01 00 00 00 00 00   ..n.............
ORPCTHAT          00080:  00 00 3B 01 00 00 38 C2 35 21 28 A0 15 00 69 00   ..;...8.5!(...i.
                  00090:  00 00 69 00 14 00 08 00 31 00 39 00 39 00 2E 00   ..i.....1.9.9...
DUALSTRINGARRAY   000A0:  33 00 34 00 2E 00 35 00 38 00 2E 00 34 00 5B 00   3.4...5.8...4.[.
STRINGBINDING     000B0:  31 00 30 00 36 00 31 00 5D 00 00 00 00 00 0A 00   1.0.6.1.].......
SECURITYBINDING   000C0:  FF FF 41 00 64 00 6D 00 69 00 6E 00 54 00 68 00   ..A.d.m.i.n.T.h.
                  000D0:  69 00 6E 00 67 00 32 00 00 00 0C 00 FF FF 41 00   i.n.g.2.......A.
                  000E0:  64 00 6D 00 69 00 6E 00 54 00 68 00 69 00 6E 00   d.m.i.n.T.h.i.n.
                  000F0:  67 00 32 00 00 00 0C 00 FF FF 41 00 64 00 6D 00   g.2.......A.d.m
                  00100:  69 00 6E 00 54 00 68 00 69 00 6E 00 67 00 32 00   i.n.T.h.i.n.g.2.
                  00110:  00 00 0C 00 FF FF 41 00 64 00 6D 00 69 00 6E 00   ......A.d.m.i.n.
                  00120:  54 00 68 00 69 00 6E 00 67 00 32 00 00 00 0C 00   T.h.i.n.g.2...
                  00130:  FF FF 41 00 64 00 6D 00 69 00 6E 00 54 00 68 00   ..A.d.m.i.n.T.h.
                  00140:  69 00 6E 00 67 00 32 00 00 00 0B 00 FF FF 41 00   i.n.g.2.......A.
                  00150:  64 00 6D 00 69 00 6E 00 54 00 68 00 69 00 6E 00   d.m.i.n.T.h.i.n.
                  00160:  67 00 32 00 00 00 00 00 54 00 00 00 00 00 2F 00   g.2...T..../.
                  00170:  00 00 C9 00 00 00 00 00 00 00 00 00 02 00 00 00   ................
                  00180:  02 00 00 00 00 00 00 00 01 00 00 00 50 98 15 00   ............P...
MInterfacePointer 00190:  00 00 82 00 00 00 00 00 4D 45 4F 57 01 00 00 00   ........MEOW....
OBJREF            001A0:  00 00 00 00 00 00 00 00 C0 00 00 00 00 00 00 46   ...............F.
STDOBJREF         001B0:  00 00 05 00 00 00 3B 01 00 00 38 C2 35 21 44 01   ......;...8.5!D.
                  001C0:  00 00 38 C2 35 21 02 00 00 00 2F 00 00 00 CB 00   ..8.5!..../.
                  001D0:  00 00 02 00 00 00 1F 00 1B 00 08 00 31 00 39 00   ............1.9.
DUALSTRINGARRAY   001E0:  39 00 2E 00 33 00 34 00 2E 00 35 00 38 00 2E 00   9...3.4...5.8...
STRINGBINDING     001F0:  34 00 00 00 07 00 31 00 39 00 39 00 2E 00 33 00   4.....1.9.9...3.
                  00200:  34 00 2E 00 35 00 38 00 2E 00 34 00 00 00 00 00   4...5.8...4...
SECURITYBINDING   00210:  0A 00 FF FF 00 00 00 00 00 00 01 00 00 00 00 00   ................
                  00220:  00 00 00 00 00 00 00 00 00 00 04 00 00 00 01 00   ................
                  00230:  00 00 D8 45 F3 82 C9 F0 70 5E C7 53 81 A4         ...E...p^.S..
```

Figure 19-8.
The response PDU captured when IRemoteActivation::RemoteActivation *returns an OBJREF.*

The Standard Object Reference

As you can see in Figure 19-8, the *flags* field of the OBJREF structure indicates that standard marshaling (*OBJREF_STANDARD*) is being used. Based on this field, the remainder of the structure contains a structure of the type STDOBJREF followed by a DUALSTRINGARRAY structure. Here is the definition of the STDOBJREF structure:

```
typedef struct tagSTDOBJREF
{
    unsigned long  flags;        // SORF_ flags
    unsigned long  cPublicRefs;  // Count of references passed
    OXID           oxid;         // OXID of server with this OID
```

```
    OID         oid;         // OID of object with this IPID
    IPID        ipid;        // IPID of interface
} STDOBJREF;
```

The first field of the STDOBJREF structure specifies flags relating to the object reference. Although most of the possible settings for the *flags* parameter are reserved for use by the system, you can use the *SORF_NOPING* flag (*0x1000*) to indicate that the object does not need to be pinged. The ORPC network protocol uses pinging to implement a sophisticated garbage collection mechanism.[11] The second field of the STDOBJREF structure, *cPublicRefs*, specifies the number of reference counts on the IPID that are being transferred in this object reference. You can allocate multiple reference counts on an interface as an optimization to avoid making remote method calls every time the client calls *IUnknown::AddRef*.[12]

The third field of the STDOBJREF structure specifies the OXID of the server that owns the object. Although an IPID is used to identify an interface of an object hosted by a component, an IPID alone does not contain enough information to actually carry out a method invocation because the RPC infrastructure uses strings to specify the binding information needed to carry out a remote call. These strings, called RPC string bindings, contain information such as the underlying network protocol and security subsystem that should be used to carry out the call as well as the network address of the server machine on which the component is running. An unsigned hyper (64-bit integer), also called an OXID, is used to represent this connection information. Before making a call, the client translates an OXID into a set of string bindings that the RPC system understands.[13]

The fourth field of the STDOBJREF structure specifies the OID of the object that implements the interface being marshaled. OIDs are 64-bit values used as part of the pinging mechanism. The final parameter of the STDOBJREF structure is the actual IPID of the interface being marshaled.

The DUALSTRINGARRAY Structure

As part of an object reference, the STDOBJREF structure is followed by the DUALSTRINGARRAY structure. The DUALSTRINGARRAY structure is a container for a large array that contains two parts, STRINGBINDING

---

11. See the section titled "Garbage Collection" later in this chapter.

12. This optimization technique is covered later in this chapter in the section titled "The *IRemUnknown* Interface."

13. The details of this translation are covered later in this chapter in the section titled "The OXID Resolver."

structures and SECURITYBINDING structures. The definition of the DUALSTRINGARRAY structure is shown here:

```
// DUALSTRINGARRAYs are the return type for arrays of network
// addresses, arrays of endpoints, and arrays of both used in
// many ORPC interfaces.
typedef struct tagDUALSTRINGARRAY
{
    unsigned short    wNumEntries;      // Number of entries
                                        //   in array
    unsigned short    wSecurityOffset;  // Offset of security
                                        //   info

    // The array contains two parts, a set of STRINGBINDINGs
    // and a set of SECURITYBINDINGs. Each set is terminated by
    // an extra 0. The shortest array contains four 0s.

    [size_is(wNumEntries)] unsigned short aStringArray[];
} DUALSTRINGARRAY;
```

The first two fields of the DUALSTRINGARRAY structure simply specify the total number of entries in the array (*wNumEntries*) and the offset at which the STRINGBINDING structures end and the SECURITYBINDING structures begin (*wSecurityOffset*). The array itself is pointed to by the *aStringArray* field.

A STRINGBINDING structure represents the connection information needed to bind to an object. The layout of the STRINGBINDING structure is shown here:

```
// This is the return type for arrays of string bindings or
// protocol sequences (protseqs) used by many ORPC interfaces.

typedef struct tagSTRINGBINDING
{
    unsigned short    wTowerId;      // Cannot be 0
    unsigned short    aNetworkAddr;  // Zero-terminated
} STRINGBINDING;
```

The first field of the STRINGBINDING structure, *wTowerId*, specifies the network protocol that can be used to reach the server using the second parameter, *aNetworkAddr*. The *aNetworkAddr* parameter is a Unicode string specifying the network address of the server. For example, if the *wTowerId* value is set to the tower identifier *NCADG_IP_UDP*,[14] a valid network address for

---

14. The *NCA* prefix for each tower identifier is short for Network Computing Architecture. *CN* stands for a connection-oriented protocol, and *DG* stands for a connectionless, datagram-based protocol.

aNetworkAddr would be *199.34.58.4.* The following table lists the valid tower identifiers for common protocols that can be used with the *wTowerId* parameter.

Tower Identifier	Value	Description
NCADG_IP_UDP	*0x08*	Connectionless UDP
NCACN_IP_TCP	*0x07*	Connection-oriented TCP
NCADG_IPX	*0x0E*	Connectionless Internetwork Packet Exchange (IPX) Protocol
NCACN_SPX	*0x0C*	Connection-oriented Sequenced Packet Exchange (SPX) Protocol
NCACN_NB_NB	*0x12*	Connection-oriented NetBEUI over NetBIOS
NCACN_NB_IPX	*0x0D*	Connection-oriented NetBIOS over IPX
NCACN_HTTP	*0x1F*	Connection-oriented HTTP

Each STRINGBINDING structure ends with a null character to indicate the end of the *aNetworkAddr* string. The last STRINGBINDING in a DUALSTRINGARRAY is indicated by the presence of two extra 0 bytes. After that come the SECURITYBINDING structures. The definition of the SECURITYBINDING structure is shown here:

```
// This value indicates that the default authorization
// should be used.
const unsigned short COM_C_AUTHZ_NONE = 0xffff;

typedef struct tagSECURITYBINDING
{
    unsigned short    wAuthnSvc;    // Must not be 0
    unsigned short    wAuthzSvc;    // Must not be 0
    unsigned short    aPrincName;   // NULL terminated
} SECURITYBINDING;
```

The SECURITYBINDING structure contains fields indicating the authentication service, *wAuthnSvc*, and the authorization service, *wAuthzSvc*, to be used. The *wAuthzSvc* field is typically set to *0xFFFF*, which indicates that default authorization should be used.

The *IRemUnknown* Interface

IRemUnknown is a COM+ interface that handles reference counting and interface querying for remote objects. As its name suggests, *IRemUnknown* is the remote version of the holy *IUnknown* interface. Clients use the *IRemUnknown* interface to manipulate reference counts and request new interfaces based on IPIDs held by the client. Following standard reference counting rules in COM+, references are kept per interface rather than per object. The definition of the *IRemUnknown* interface is shown in the following IDL notation:

```
// The remote version of IUnknown is used by clients to
// query for new interfaces, get additional references (for
// marshaling), and release outstanding references.
[
    object,
    uuid(00000131-0000-0000-C000-000000000046)
]
interface IRemUnknown : IUnknown
{
    HRESULT RemQueryInterface
    (
        [in] REFIPID        ripid, // Interface to QueryInterface on
        [in] unsigned long  cRefs, // Count of AddRefs requested
        [in] unsigned short cIids, // Count of IIDs that follow
        [in, size_is(cIids)] IID* iids, // IIDs to QueryInterface for
        [out, size_is(,cIids)]
        REMQIRESULT**        ppQIResults // Results returned
    );

    HRESULT RemAddRef
    (
        [in] unsigned short    cInterfaceRefs,
        [in, size_is(cInterfaceRefs)]
        REMINTERFACEREF        InterfaceRefs[],
        [out, size_is(cInterfaceRefs)]
        HRESULT*               pResults
    );

    HRESULT RemRelease
    (
        [in] unsigned short    cInterfaceRefs,
        [in, size_is(cInterfaceRefs)]
        REMINTERFACEREF        InterfaceRefs[]
    );
}
```

A component developer never implements the *IRemUnknown* interface because the OXID object associated with each apartment already provides an implementation of this interface. The standard *IUnknown* interface is never remoted in COM+. The *IRemUnknown* interface is remoted in its place and results in local calls to *QueryInterface*, *AddRef*, and *Release* on the server. Client applications can call the *IUnknown::AddRef* method as often as they want.

COM+ remotes calls to *IUnknown::AddRef* only when the first *AddRef* call is made; *IUnknown::Release* is called only for the final *Release*.

The *IRemUnknown::RemQueryInterface* method differs from the *IUnknown::QueryInterface* method in that it can request several interface pointers in one call. The standard *IUnknown::QueryInterface* method is actually used to carry out this request on the server side. This optimization is designed to reduce the number of round-trips executed. The array of REMQIRESULT structures returned by *RemQueryInterface* contains the *HRESULT* from the *QueryInterface* call executed for each requested interface, as well as the STDOBJREF structure containing the marshaled interface pointer itself. The definition of the REMQIRESULT structure is shown here:

```
typedef struct tagREMQIRESULT
{
    HRESULT      hResult;     // Result of call
    STDOBJREF    std;         // Data for returned interface
} REMQIRESULT;
```

The *IRemUnknown::RemAddRef* and *IRemUnknown::RemRelease* methods increase and decrease, respectively, the reference count of the object referred to by an IPID. Like *RemQueryInterface*, *RemAddRef* and *RemRelease* differ from their local counterparts; they can increase and decrease the reference count of multiple interfaces by an arbitrary amount in a single remote call. Imagine a scenario in which an object that receives a marshaled interface pointer wants to pass that pointer to some other object. According to the COM+ reference counting rules, *AddRef* must be called before this interface pointer can be passed to another object, resulting in two round-trips, one to get the interface pointer and another to increment the reference counter. The caller can optimize this process by requesting multiple references in one call. Thereafter, the interface pointer can be given out multiple times without additional remote calls to increment the reference counter.

The Windows implementation of COM+ typically requests five references when marshaling an interface pointer, which means that the client process receiving the interface pointer can marshal it to four different apartments in the current process or in other processes. Only when the client attempts to marshal the interface pointer for the fifth time does COM+ make a remote call to the object to request an additional reference. Also, in the interest of performance on the client side, COM+ typically does not immediately translate each call to *IUnknown::AddRef* or *IUnknown::Release* into a remote call to *IRemUnknown:: RemAddRef* or *IRemUnknown::RemRelease*. Instead, it defers a remote call to the *RemRelease* method until all interfaces on an object have been released locally. Only then is a single *RemRelease* call made, with instructions to decrement the reference counter for all interfaces by the necessary amount.

It is important to note that in this scenario, when one component returns the interface pointer of another component to a client process, COM+ never allows one proxy to communicate with another proxy. For example, if client process A calls object B, which then returns an interface pointer for object C, any subsequent calls made by client A to object C are direct. This happens because the marshaled interface pointer contains information about how to reach the machine on which the actual object instance exists. In order for object B to call object C, object B must keep track of object C's OXID, IP address, IPID, and so on. When object B hands client A a pointer to object C, object B scribbles all that information into a new object reference (OBJREF) for client A. Object B is no longer part of the relationship, which saves network bandwidth and improves overall performance.

After calling the *CoCreateInstanceEx* function to instantiate the remote component, our client process possesses an initial *IUnknown* interface pointer. Typically, this call is followed by a call to the *IUnknown::QueryInterface* method to request another interface, as shown in the following code fragment:

```
hr = pUnknown->QueryInterface(IID_ISum, (void**)&pSum);
```

When the client process calls the *IUnknown::QueryInterface* method to request an interface pointer for *ISum*, the proxy manager in the client's address space calls the *IRemUnknown::RemQueryInterface* method on the server. Figure 19-9 shows the network packet that is transmitted for the *RemQueryInterface* method call. In this packet, you can clearly see that ORPC is requesting a count of five references for the *ISum* interface pointer.

IRemUnknown::RemQueryInterface(IPID, 5, 1, IID_ISum)

```
Headers      00000:  00 60 97 8E EB 19 00 60 97 92 D2 6C 08 00 45 00
             00010:  00 E8 A8 01 00 00 80 11 8F B7 C7 22 3A 03 C7 22
             00020:  3A 04 04 12 04 25 00 D4 02 48 04 00 08 00 10 00    PDU Type (Request)
             00030:  00 00 00 00 00 00 2F 00 00 00 C9 00 00 00 00 00
             00040:  00 00 31 01 00 00 00 00 00 00 C0 00 00 00 00 00    IID_IRemUnknown
             00050:  00 46 F2 59 EB 61 FB 1E D1 11 BC D9 00 60 97 92
             00060:  D2 6C 00 00 00 00 00 00 00 00 00 00 00 00 03 00
             00070:  FF FF FF FF 68 00 00 00 0A 00 05 00 02 00 00 00
ORPCTHIS     00080:  00 00 00 00 00 00 F1 59 EB 61 FB 1E D1 11 BC D9
             00090:  00 60 97 92 D2 6C 00 00 00 00 00 00 D2 00 00 00 2F 00    IPID
Parameters   000A0:  00 00 CB 00 00 00 02 00 00 00 05 00 00 00 01 00          cRefs (5)
             000B0:  00 00 01 00 00 00 01 00 00 10 00 00 00 00 00 00          clids (1)
             000C0:  00 00 00 00 00 01 00 00 00 00 00 00 00 00 00 00          IID_ISum
             000D0:  00 00 00 00 00 00 00 00 00 00 00 00 00 00 00 00
             000E0:  00 00 04 00 00 00 01 00 00 00 B1 55 95 9C 0C 86
             000F0:  D6 4A 6E 9F 2B 71
```

Figure 19-9.
The request PDU transmitted for the IRemUnknown::RemQueryInterface(IPID, 5, 1, IID_ISum) *call.*

On the server side, the actual *IUnknown::QueryInterface* call is executed to request an *ISum* interface pointer from the component. This interface pointer is then returned to the client in the marshaled form of a standard object reference (STDOBJREF). Figure 19-10 shows the response PDU that is returned to the client.

```
00000:  00 60 97 92 D2 6C 00 60 97 8E EB 19 08 00 45 00
00010:  00 C8 12 01 00 00 80 11 25 D8 C7 22 3A 04 C7 22
00020:  3A 03 04 25 04 12 00 B4 00 0C 04 02 08 00 10 00   Response PDU
00030:  00 00 00 00 00 00 2F 00 00 00 C9 00 00 00 00 00
00040:  00 00 31 01 00 00 00 00 00 00 C0 00 00 00 00 00   IID_IRemUnknown
00050:  00 46 F2 59 EB 61 FB 1E D1 11 BC D9 00 60 97 92
00060:  D2 6C 38 C5 01 34 00 00 00 00 00 00 00 00 03 00
00070:  FF FF 4A 00 48 00 00 00 0A 00 00 00 00 00 00 00
00080:  00 00 10 4B 15 00 01 00 00 00 00 00 00 00 20 02
00090:  14 00 00 00 00 00 05 00 00 00 3B 01 00 00 38 C2   HRESULT / cPublicRefs
000A0:  35 21 44 01 00 00 38 C2 35 21 03 00 00 00 2F 00   oxid
000B0:  00 00 94 00 00 00 03 00 00 00 00 00 00 00 00 00   oid
000C0:  00 00 04 00 00 00 01 00 00 00 45 21 81 9C 02 EF   ipid
000D0:  58 B7 6E 9F 2B 71
```
ORPCTHAT

Figure 19-10.
The response PDU transmitted for the IRemUnknown::RemQueryInterface *call.*

To prevent a malicious application from making a call to *IRemUnknown::RemRelease* and purposefully trying to force an object to unload while other clients might still be using it, a client can request private references. Private references are stored with the client's identity so that one client cannot release the private references of another. However, when you pass an interface pointer, private references cannot be provided from one object to another. Each client must request and release its own private references by explicitly calling the *RemAddRef* and *RemRelease* methods. These methods accept an argument that is an array of REMINTERFACEREF structures. The REMINTERFACEREF structure specifies an IPID and the number of public and private references that are being requested or released by the client. The definition of the REMINTERFACEREF structure is shown here:

```
typedef struct tagREMINTERFACEREF
{
    IPID          ipid;        // IPID to AddRef/Release
    unsigned long cPublicRefs;
    unsigned long cPrivateRefs;
} REMINTERFACEREF;
```

The *IRemUnknown2* Interface

The *IRemUnknown2* interface was introduced in version 5.2 of the ORPC protocol. Derived from the *IRemUnknown* interface, *IRemUnknown2* adds the *RemoteQueryInterface2* method, which enables clients to retrieve interface pointers to objects that supply additional data beyond the STDOBJREF in their marshaled interface packets. Like *RemQueryInterface*, this method queries for zero or more interfaces using the interface behind the IPID. Instead of returning the STDOBJREF marshaled interface packet, this method can return any marshaled data packet in the form of a byte array (including a traditional STDOBJREF). The IDL definition of the *IRemUnknown2* interface is shown in the following code:

```
interface IRemUnknown2 : IRemUnknown
{
    HRESULT RemQueryInterface2
    (
        [in] REFIPID                              ripid,
        [in] unsigned short                       cIids,
        [in, size_is(cIids)] IID                  *iids,
        [out, size_is(cIids)] HRESULT             *phr,
        [out, size_is(cIids)] MInterfacePointer   **ppMIF
    );
}
```

The OXID Resolver

The OXID Resolver is a service that runs on every machine that supports COM+. It performs two important duties:

- It stores the RPC string bindings that are necessary to connect with remote objects and provides them to local clients.

- It sends ping messages to remote objects for which the local machine has clients and receives ping messages for objects running on the local machine. This aspect of the OXID Resolver supports the COM+ garbage collection mechanism.

Similar to the way *CoCreateInstanceEx* incorporates the functionality of *CoGetClassObject* and *IClassFactory::CreateInstance*, the *IRemoteActivation* interface incorporates the functionality of the *IRemUnknown* and *IOXIDResolver* interfaces so that only one round-trip is needed to activate an object. The OXID Resolver resides at the same endpoints as the SCM (as described earlier in the section titled "Remote Activation.") Like the *IRemoteActivation* interface, the

OXID Resolver implements an RPC interface (not a COM+ interface) named
IOXIDResolver, which is shown in IDL notation in the following code. Notice that the *object* keyword is conspicuously absent from the interface header,
indicating that this is not a COM+ interface.

```
[ // No object keyword here. Not a COM+ interface!
    uuid(99fcfec4-5260-101b-bbcb-00aa0021347a),
    pointer_default(unique)
]
interface IOXIDResolver
{
    // Method to get the protocol sequences, string bindings,
    // and machine ID for an object server given its OXID.
    [idempotent] error_status_t ResolveOxid
    (
    [in]        handle_t         hRpc,
    [in]        OXID             *pOxid,
    [in]        unsigned short   cRequestedProtseqs,
    [in,  ref, size_is(cRequestedProtseqs)]
                unsigned short   arRequestedProtseqs[],
    [out, ref] DUALSTRINGARRAY **ppdsaOxidBindings,
    [out, ref] IPID             *pipidRemUnknown,
    [out, ref] DWORD            *pAuthnHint
    );
    // Simple ping is used to ping a set. Client machines use
    // this technique to inform the object exporter that it is
    // still using the members of the set. Returns S_TRUE if the
    // SetId is known by the object exporter, S_FALSE if not.
    [idempotent] error_status_t SimplePing
    (
    [in] handle_t  hRpc,
    [in] SETID    *pSetId // Must not be 0
    );
    // Complex ping is used to create sets of OIDs to ping. The
    // whole set can subsequently be pinged using SimplePing,
    // thus reducing network traffic.
    [idempotent] error_status_t ComplexPing
    (
    [in]        handle_t         hRpc,
    [in, out]   SETID            *pSetId, // An in value of 0 on
                                          // first call for new set
    [in]        unsigned short   SequenceNum,
    [in]        unsigned short   cAddToSet,
    [in]        unsigned short   cDelFromSet,
    [in, unique, size_is(cAddToSet)]   OID AddToSet[],
                // Add these OIDs to the set.
```

(continued)

601

```
        [in, unique, size_is(cDelFromSet)] OID DelFromSet[],
                    // Remove these OIDs from the set.
        [out]       unsigned short *pPingBackoffFactor
                    // 2^factor = multiplier
    );
    // In some cases, the client might be unsure that a
    // particular binding will reach the server--for example,
    // when the OXID bindings have more than one TCP/IP binding.
    // This call can be used to validate the binding from
    // the client.
        [idempotent] error_status_t ServerAlive
    (
    [in]        handle_t        hRpc
    );
}
```

> **NOTE** The *idempotent* flag specifies that a method does not modify the state of an object and returns the same results each time it is called. The RPC run-time library can invoke *idempotent* methods multiple times without adverse effects.

When the OXID Resolver is presented with an OXID, it obtains the associated RPC string binding necessary to connect to the object. On each machine, the OXID Resolver maintains a cached local table of mappings of OXIDs and their associated RPC string bindings. When asked to resolve an OXID into its associated string binding, the OXID Resolver first checks its cached local table for the OXID. If it finds the OXID, it returns the string binding immediately. If it cannot find the OXID, it contacts the server's OXID Resolver to request resolution of the OXID into a string binding.

The client machine's OXID Resolver then caches the string binding information provided by the server. This optimization enables the OXID Resolver to quickly resolve that OXID for other clients on the same machine that might want to connect in the future. If the client were to pass the object reference to a process running on a third machine, that computer's OXID Resolver service would not have a cached copy of the OXID's string bindings and thus would be obliged to make a remote call to the server to resolve the OXID for itself.

The purpose of the first method, *IOXIDResolver::ResolveOxid*, shown in the preceding code, is to resolve an OXID into the string bindings that are necessary to access an OXID object. The OXID being resolved is passed as the second parameter, *pOxid*, to the *ResolveOxid* method. When calling the *ResolveOxid* method, the client specifies what protocol sequences it is prepared to use when accessing the object, starting with the most preferred. The client passes this information in the *arRequestedProtseqs* array argument. The server's

OXID Resolver attempts to resolve the OXID and then returns an array of DUALSTRINGARRAY structures, *ppdsaOxidBindings*, which contains the string binding information—again in decreasing order of preference—that can be used to connect to the specified OXID.

The OXID resolution process is described in the following steps:

1. A server process calls *CoRegisterClassObject* to register itself with COM+.

2. The OXID Resolver on the server machine caches a reference to the object.

3. A client process calls *CoCreateInstanceEx* and receives an object reference for the object running on the server.

4. The client asks its OXID Resolver to resolve the OXID for the server object.

5. The client's OXID Resolver calls *IOXIDResolver::ResolveOxid* to request that the server's OXID Resolver return the string bindings for the OXID.

6. The server's OXID Resolver performs a lookup in its local table and returns the desired string bindings to the client's OXID Resolver.

7. The client's OXID Resolver caches the best string binding in its local table for future use and then returns the string binding for the OXID to the client process.

8. The client binds to the object using the given string binding. The client can now invoke methods on the object.

Because machines can have many network protocols installed, allocating endpoints for each available protocol sequence can be a time-consuming and resource-intensive operation. However, the server typically registers all available protocol sequences at initialization time. As an optimization, the OXID Resolver can decide to defer protocol registration. To implement lazy protocol registration, the server waits until a client machine calls its *IOXIDResolver::ResolveOxid* method. Rather than registering all available protocols at initialization time, the implementation of the *ResolveOxid* method registers only the protocols requested by the client at the time of OXID resolution. The network protocols available to COM+ are in the HKEY_LOCAL_MACHINE\Software\Microsoft\Rpc registry key under the DCOM Protocols named-value. There you'll find the supported protocols listed in order of preference.

Version 5.2 of the ORPC protocol added the *ResolveOxid2* method to the *IOXIDResolver* interface. This method enables a client to determine the version of the ORPC protocol used by the server when the server requests OXID resolution. Notice the addition of the last parameter in the IDL definition of the *IOXIDResolver::ResolveOxid2* method, shown here in boldface:

```
[idempotent] error_status_t ResolveOxid2
(
    [in]        handle_t          hRpc,
    [in]        OXID              *pOxid,
    [in]        unsigned short    cRequestedProtseqs,
    [in,  ref, size_is(cRequestedProtseqs)]
                unsigned short    arRequestedProtseqs[],
    [out, ref] DUALSTRINGARRAY  **ppdsaOxidBindings,
    [out, ref] IPID              *pipidRemUnknown,
    [out, ref] DWORD             *pAuthnHint,
    [out, ref] COMVERSION        *pComVersion
);
```

Garbage Collection

Although a distributed system can offer excellent availability (that is, little downtime) and protection against catastrophic failure, the probability of a failure somewhere in the system is far greater due to the higher complexity. From a client's perspective, a failure of either the network or the server is identified by the failure of a remote method call. In such cases, an *HRESULT* value such as *RPC_S_SERVER_UNAVAILABLE* or *RPC_S_CALL_FAILED* is returned.

A more complex situation exists on the server side if a client fails. Depending on the type of server, the failure of a client might or might not wreak havoc on the server. For example, a stateless object that always remains running and simply gives out the current time to any client that asks is not affected by the loss of a client process. However, any object that maintains state for its clients is obviously very interested in the death of those clients. Such objects typically have a method, such as *ByeByeNow*, that clients call before exiting. However, if the client process or a portion of the network fails, the client might not have the opportunity to notify the object of its intentions. This failure leaves the server in an unstable state because it is maintaining information for clients that might no longer exist.

RPC deals with this situation by using a logical connection called a *context handle* between the client and the server processes. If the connection between the two processes is broken for any reason, a special function called a *rundown routine* can be invoked on the server side to notify the server that a client connection has been broken. For performance reasons, COM+ does not leverage the functionality of RPC context handles. Instead, the ORPC protocol defines a pinging mechanism that determines whether a client is still alive. RPC context handles are implemented using a pinging mechanism as well, but because of the special needs of COM+, they are not suitable. A pinging mechanism is quite simple. Every so often, the client sends a ping message to an object saying, "I'm alive, I'm alive!" If the server does not receive a ping message within a specified period of time, the client is assumed to have died and all its references are freed.

This simplistic type of pinging algorithm is not sufficient for COM+ because it leads to too much unnecessary network traffic. In a distributed environment that includes hundreds, thousands, or hundreds of thousands of clients and components, network capacity can be overwhelmed simply by the number of ping messages being transmitted. To reduce the network traffic devoted to ping messages, COM+ relies on the OXID Resolver on each client machine to detect whether its local clients are alive and then send single ping messages on a per-machine basis instead of a per-object basis. This means that the client machine's OXID Resolver sends only one ping message to each computer that is serving its clients.

Even with only one message being sent to each computer, ping message traffic can still grow quite hefty—the ping data for each OID is 16 bytes. For example, if a client computer holds 5000 object references to an object running on another machine, each ping message is approximately 78 KB! To further reduce the amount of network traffic, ORPC includes a special mechanism called *delta pinging*. The idea behind delta pinging is that a server often has a relatively stable set of objects that are used by clients. Instead of including data for each individual OID in the ping message, delta pinging stipulates that a set of OIDs can be pinged by a single identifier called a *ping set* that refers to all the OIDs in that set. When delta pinging is employed, the ping message for five OIDs is the same size as a message for 1 million OIDs.

To establish a ping set, the client calls the *IOXIDResolver::ComplexPing* method. The *AddToSet* parameter of the *ComplexPing* method accepts an array of OIDs that should define the ping set. Once defined, all the OIDs in the set can be pinged simply by calling *IOXIDResolver::SimplePing* and passing it the ping set identifier (SETID) value returned from the *ComplexPing* method. If necessary, the *ComplexPing* method can be called again at any time to add or remove OIDs from the ping set.

To clean up after broken connections between a client and a server, the pinging mechanism uses a reclaiming process called *garbage collection*. The pinging mechanism activates garbage collection based on two values—the time that should elapse between each ping message and the number of ping messages that must be missed before the server can consider the client missing in action. The product of these two values determines the maximum amount of time that can elapse without a ping message being received before the server assumes that the client is dead.

By default, the ping period is set to 120 seconds; three ping messages must be missed before the client can be presumed dead. Currently, the user cannot change these default values. Thus, 6 minutes (3 × 120 seconds) must elapse before a client's references are implicitly reclaimed. Whether the server immediately reclaims the object references held by a client once the timeout has occurred is considered an implementation-dependent detail of the ORPC specification. In fact, if the server does not reclaim those references and later begins receiving ping messages from the heretofore-assumed-dead client, it can infer that whatever problem prevented the ping messages from being received has been fixed.

Some stateless objects, such as the time server example discussed at the beginning of this section, have no need for the COM+ garbage collection mechanism. These objects usually run forever and don't really care about a client after a method call has finished executing. For such objects, you can switch off the pinging mechanism by passing the *MSHLFLAGS_NOPING* flag to the *CoGetStandardMarshal* function. The following code fragment (with the relevant code in boldface) shows how to use the *MSHLFLAGS_NOPING* flag in an implementation of the *IClassFactory::CreateInstance* method:

```
IMarshal* pMarshal = NULL;

HRESULT CFactory::CreateInstance(IUnknown *pUnknownOuter,
    REFIID riid, void** ppv)
{
    if(pUnknownOuter != NULL)
        return CLASS_E_NOAGGREGATION;

    CObject *pObject = new CObject;

    if(pObject == NULL)
        return E_OUTOFMEMORY;

    IUnknown* pUnknown;
    pObject->QueryInterface(IID_IUnknown, (void**)&pUnknown);
    CoGetStandardMarshal(riid, pUnknown, 0, NULL,
        MSHLFLAGS_NOPING|MSHLFLAGS_NORMAL, &pMarshal);
    pUnknown->Release();
```

```
    // Call QueryInterface, which typically is for
    // IID_IUnknown.
    HRESULT hr = pObject->QueryInterface(riid, ppv);
    pObject->Release();
    return hr;
}
```

Just before exiting, the object should execute the following code to free the standard marshaler:

```
pMarshal->DisconnectObject(0);
pMarshal->Release();
```

Note that objects for which the *MSHLFLAGS_NOPING* flag has been specified never receive calls to their *IUnknown::Release* methods. Clients can call *Release*, but such calls are not remoted to the object itself. Due to the highly efficient delta pinging mechanism used by COM+, turning off this mechanism for an object does not cause a corresponding reduction in network traffic. As long as other objects on the server require ping messages, ORPC must send a ping message to the server machine by calling the *IOXIDResolver::SimplePing* method. The only difference is that the object that specified the *MSHLFLAGS_NOPING* flag is not added to the SETID that is being pinged.

A Remote Method Call

With an understanding of the ORPC network protocol under our belts, let's examine the data transmitted across the network during an actual remote method invocation. Figure 19-11 shows the request PDU sent when the client process calls the *ISum::Sum* method. Immediately following the ORPCTHIS structure are the *x* and *y* inbound parameters of the *Sum* method. Here the *Sum* method has been called with the values *4* and *9*.

Client (Thing1) calls *ISum::Sum(4,9)* on *InsideCOM* object on server (Thing2)

```
00000:   00 60 97 8E EB 19 00 60 97 92 D2 6C 08 00 45 00
00010:   00 A8 AA 01 00 00 80 11 8D F7 C7 22 3A 03 C7 22
00020:   3A 04 04 12 04 25 00 94 9A DD 04 00 08 00 10 00    1  Request PDU
00030:   00 00 03 00 00 00 2F 00 00 00 94 00 00 00 03 00    2  IPID
00040:   00 00 01 00 00 10 00 00 00 00 00 00 00 00 00 00    3  IID_ISum
00050:   00 01 F2 59 EB 61 FB 1E D1 11 BC D9 00 60 97 92
00060:   D2 6C 38 C5 01 34 00 00 00 00 01 00 00 00 03 00
00070:   FF FF 4A 00 28 00 00 00 0A 00 05 00 02 00 00 00    ORPCTHIS
00080:   00 00 00 00 00 00 F1 59 EB 61 FB 1E D1 11 BC D9
00090:   00 60 97 92 D2 6C 00 00 00 00 04 00 00 00 09 00
000A0:   00 00 04 00 00 00 01 00 00 00 A6 69 F1 50 E2 6B    4 + 9 = ???
000B0:   E9 D6 6F 9F 2B 71
```

Figure 19-11.
The request PDU transmitted when the client calls ISum::Sum *with the parameters* 4 *and* 9.

After the *Sum* method executes on the server, the response PDU is generated and sent back to the client. Clearly visible following the ORPCTHAT structure in the response PDU is the outbound value of *13 (4 + 9)*, as shown in Figure 19-12.

```
00000:   00 60 97 92 D2 6C 00 60 97 8E EB 19 08 00 45 00
00010:   00 90 13 01 00 00 80 11 25 10 C7 22 3A 04 C7 22
00020:   3A 03 04 25 04 12 00 7C 76 5F 04 02 08 00 10 00    1  Response PDU
00030:   00 00 03 00 00 00 2F 00 00 00 94 00 00 00 03 00    2  IPID
00040:   00 00 31 01 00 00 00 00 00 00 C0 00 00 00 00 00    3  IID_IRemUnknown
00050:   00 46 F2 59 EB 61 FB 1E D1 11 BC D9 00 60 97 92
00060:   D2 6C 38 C5 01 34 00 00 00 01 00 00 00 03 00
00070:   FF FF 4A 00 10 00 00 00 0A 00 00 00 00 00 00 00    ORPCTHAT
00080:   00 00 0D 00 00 00 00 00 00 00 04 00 00 00 01 00
00090:   00 00 45 21 81 9C C6 30 FA A9 6F 9F 2B 71           4 + 9 = 13 (0x000D)
```

Figure 19-12.
The response PDU transmitted when the component returns the value 13 *after executing the* ISum::Sum *method.*

Channel Hooks

A *channel* is the logical connection between a client and a component; all communication between the two parties is said to travel through the channel. Channel hooks enable a developer to hook into this communication mechanism. If you're experienced with the Microsoft Win32 API, you can compare channel hooking to the capabilities offered by the *SetWindowLong* function, which lets you store custom data inside a window structure held by Windows and later retrieve the data using the *GetWindowLong* function. In a similar way, channel hooks allow you to store custom data in the communication channel and then retrieve that data on the other side.

Recall that the last field in the ORPCTHIS and ORPCTHAT structures is an ORPC_EXTENT_ARRAY structure named *extensions*. You can use the *extensions* field of the ORPCTHIS structure to pass additional data in the channel when a method is invoked; you can use the *extensions* field of the ORPCTHAT structure to return additional data in the channel when a method returns. The ORPC_EXTENT_ARRAY itself does not contain the actual extension data—it simply records the number of *extents* that follow, each stored in an ORPC_EXTENT structure. The memory layout of the ORPC_EXTENT_ARRAY structure is shown here in IDL notation:

```
// Array of extensions
typedef struct tagORPC_EXTENT_ARRAY
```

```
{
    unsigned long size;       // Num extents
    unsigned long reserved;   // Must be 0
    [size_is((size+1)&~1,), unique]
        ORPC_EXTENT **extent; // Extents
} ORPC_EXTENT_ARRAY;
```

The actual extent data passed in the channel is stored in an array of
ORPC_EXTENT structures. Each extent is identified by a unique GUID. The
first field of the ORPC_EXTENT structure is the GUID of the extent data
being transmitted. The second field of the ORPC_EXTENT structure declares
the size of that data, followed by the extent data itself in the final field. The
ORPC_EXTENT structure is shown here in IDL notation:

```
// Extension to implicit parameters
typedef struct tagORPC_EXTENT
{
    GUID          id;            // Extension identifier
    unsigned long size;          // Extension size
    [size_is((size+7)&~7)] byte data[]; // Extension data
} ORPC_EXTENT;
```

To use channel hooks from an application, you must create a coclass that
implements the *IChannelHook* interface. This interface consists of six methods,
three that are called in the client process and three that are called in the server
process. Two of the three client-side methods are called automatically before
a client method call is made, and the third is called immediately upon its return. This technique lets you put extent data in the channel to be sent in the
ORPCTHIS structure of the request PDU and then retrieve any extent data from
the response PDU. On the server side, one method of the *IChannelHook* interface is called just before a method executes and the other two are called
immediately before it returns. This technique enables the server process to obtain
extent data stored in the request PDU and then store additional extent data to
be transmitted in the ORPCTHAT structure of the response PDU. The IDL
definition of the *IChannelHook* interface is shown here:

```
interface IChannelHook : IUnknown
{
// How big is your data?
    void ClientGetSize(
        [in]  REFGUID uExtent,
        [in]  REFIID  riid,
        [out] ULONG   *pDataSize );
```

(continued)

```
// Put the data in the channel.
    void ClientFillBuffer(
        [in]       REFGUID uExtent,
        [in]       REFIID  riid,
        [in, out] ULONG   *pDataSize,
        [in]       void    *pDataBuffer );

// Data has arrived from the server.
    void ClientNotify(
        [in] REFGUID uExtent,
        [in] REFIID  riid,
        [in] ULONG   cbDataSize,
        [in] void    *pDataBuffer,
        [in] DWORD   lDataRep,
        [in] HRESULT hrFault );

// Data has arrived from the client.
    void ServerNotify(
        [in] REFGUID uExtent,
        [in] REFIID  riid,
        [in] ULONG   cbDataSize,
        [in] void    *pDataBuffer,
        [in] DWORD   lDataRep );

// How big is your data?
    void ServerGetSize(
        [in]  REFGUID uExtent,
        [in]  REFIID  riid,
        [in]  HRESULT hrFault,
        [out] ULONG   *pDataSize );

// Put the data in the channel.
    void ServerFillBuffer(
        [in]       REFGUID uExtent,
        [in]       REFIID  riid,
        [in, out] ULONG   *pDataSize,
        [in]       void    *pDataBuffer,
        [in]       HRESULT hrFault );
};
```

The *riid* parameter of every *IChannelHook* method is actually a structure of type SChannelHookCallInfo that is passed by value, not a reference to an IID, as the interface definition would have you believe. The SChannelHookCallInfo structure provides channel hooks with additional information about a method call. For example, the fields available in this structure include the causality identifier (*uCausality*), the server's process identifier (*dwServerPid*), and a pointer

to the object (*pObject*). The declaration of the SChannelHookCallInfo structure is shown here:

```
typedef struct SChannelHookCallInfo
{
    IID             iid;
    DWORD           cbSize;
    GUID            uCausality;
    DWORD           dwServerPid;
    DWORD           iMethod;
    void            *pObject;
} SChannelHookCallInfo;
```

After creating an object that implements the *IChannelHook* interface, you
need to inform COM+ that you intend to hook into its communication channel. The *CoRegisterChannelHook* function is designed for this purpose. It accepts the GUID of the extent and a pointer to the object that implements the
IChannelHook interface, as shown here:

```
WINOLEAPI CoRegisterChannelHook(REFGUID ExtensionUuid,
    IChannelHook* pChannelHook);
```

A Useful Channel Hook: Obtaining the Client's Name

At this stage, you might be wondering why anyone would want to use a channel hook. After all, any data that you might want to pass from client to server
and back can be transmitted as one or more parameters of a particular method.
This technique is definitely easier than hooking into the communications channel! The advantage of a channel hook, however, is that the data being transmitted
is not visible in the interface definition. By hooking into the communications
channel, you can send additional data with each method call—data that is
invisible to someone examining the interface definition.

One example of how channel hooks can prove useful occurs when you want
to determine the name of the computer on which a particular client is executing. This information can prove valuable for a server-based administration application, since COM+ provides no built-in way to obtain a client's computer name.
The simplest solution to this problem is to add one additional parameter to every
method of the interface implemented by the server process, enabling the client
to voluntarily provide its computer name. However, this solution requires that
changes be made to the interface definition, thereby requiring that a new IID
be defined. This in turn means that the old interface must still be supported for
those clients that have not yet been updated to use the new interface. The new
parameter also indicates that the interface is designed for remote use; it doesn't
make sense to have a computer name parameter if the client and the component are running on the same machine.

Because the data that we want to pass to the server is not related to the primary purpose of that interface, it is bad design to force the two together. A channel hook can solve these problems because it can pass data in the channel outside the scope of the interface definition. With this goal in mind, you can build a custom channel hook that sends the client's computer name to the server as part of the ORPCTHIS structure in every method invocation. On the server side, the computer name is read from the channel and made available to the component. This makes for a nifty solution to a thorny problem.

We built this custom channel hook as an in-process component that can be loaded into the address space of any client or server process simply by calling *CoCreateInstance*. The *DllMain* function that is called on startup registers the channel hook by calling *CoRegisterChannelHook* and then obtains the computer's name by calling the Win32 *GetComputerName* function, as shown in boldface in the following code:

```
GUID EXTENTID_MyHook = {0x12345678, 0xABCD, 0xABCD, {0x99, 0x99,
0x99, 0x99, 0x99, 0x99, 0x99, 0x99}};

BOOL WINAPI DllMain(HINSTANCE h, DWORD dwReason, void* pv)
{
    static CChannelHook ChannelHook;
    if(dwReason == DLL_PROCESS_ATTACH)
    {
        if(FAILED(CoRegisterChannelHook(EXTENTID_MyHook,
            &ChannelHook)))
        {
            cout << "CoRegisterChannelHook failed." << endl;
            return FALSE;
        }
        ULONG length = MAX_COMPUTERNAME_LENGTH + 1;
        GetComputerName(g_mhtClientComputerName.computer_name,
            &length);
    }
    return TRUE;
}
```

A structure named MYHOOK_THIS encapsulates the data transmitted, making this channel hook easily extensible. Currently, the MYHOOK_THIS structure simply contains the string name of the computer on which the client is running. That name is obtained in the *DllMain* function shown in the preceding code and stored in *g_mhtClientComputerName*, as shown here:

```
struct MYHOOK_THIS
{
    char computer_name[MAX_COMPUTERNAME_LENGTH + 1];
} g_MYHOOK_THIS, g_mhtClientComputerName;
```

Although hooking into the COM+ communication channel sounds complex, the code required to implement the *IChannelHook* interface is relatively simple. When COM+ assembles the request PDU for a method invocation, the *IChannelHook::ClientGetSize* method is called to determine the size of the data to be transmitted. In the following code, the *pDataSize* value is set to the size of the MYHOOK_THIS structure:

```
// How big is your data?
void CChannelHook::ClientGetSize(REFGUID uExtent, REFIID riid,
    ULONG* pDataSize)
{
    if(uExtent == EXTENTID_MyHook)
        *pDataSize = sizeof(MYHOOK_THIS);
}
```

The *ClientGetSize* method is followed by a call to the *IChannelHook:: ClientFillBuffer* method to request the actual data that you want to transmit in the communication channel. In the code below, the data pointer is set to the address of the global *g_mhtClientComputerName* variable containing the client's computer name:

```
// Put the data in the channel.
void CChannelHook::ClientFillBuffer(REFGUID uExtent,
    REFIID riid, ULONG* pDataSize, void* pDataBuffer)
{
    if(uExtent == EXTENTID_MyHook)
    {
        MYHOOK_THIS *data = (MYHOOK_THIS*)pDataBuffer;
        *data = g_mhtClientComputerName;
        *pDataSize = sizeof(MYHOOK_THIS);
    }
}
```

COM+ now has sufficient information to build and transmit the request PDU to the server. The data transmitted in the channel hook travels coach in the ORPCTHIS structure of the request PDU. Once the server receives the request PDU, the *IChannelHook::ServerNotify* method is called in the server process, which means that the channel hook must be running on both the client and server computers to work properly. The *ServerNotify* method indicates that data has arrived from the client. The following code obtains that data from the *pDataBuffer* pointer and temporarily stores it in the *g_MYHOOK_THIS* variable for retrieval by the component:

```
// Data has arrived from the client.
void CChannelHook::ServerNotify(REFGUID uExtent, REFIID riid,
    ULONG cbDataSize, void* pDataBuffer, DWORD lDataRep)
```

(continued)

```
{
    if(uExtent == EXTENTID_MyHook &&
        lDataRep == NDR_LOCAL_DATA_REPRESENTATION)
    {
        MYHOOK_THIS* data = (MYHOOK_THIS*)pDataBuffer;
        strcpy(g_MYHOOK_THIS.computer_name,
            data->computer_name);
    }
}
```

Our channel hook is designed to transmit data from the client to the server, not vice-versa, so the *ClientNotify*, *ServerGetSize*, and *ServerFillBuffer* methods of the *IChannelHook* interface are all NO-OPs. Channel hooks that want to return data in the ORPCTHAT structure of a response PDU must implement these three methods as well. To make the client's computer name available to a component, our channel hook implements a custom interface called *IClientInfo* that offers only one method: *GetClientComputerName*. This method can be called by a server-side component from within a method invoked by the client. The implementation of this method, shown in the following code, simply retrieves and returns the client's computer name from the *g_MYHOOK_THIS* variable, where it was stored in the *IChannelHook:: ServerNotify* method:

```
HRESULT CClientInfo::GetClientComputerName(BSTR* bstr)
{
    int length = strlen(g_MYHOOK_THIS.computer_name);
    *bstr = SysAllocStringLen(0, length+1);
    strcpy((char*)*bstr, g_MYHOOK_THIS.computer_name);
    return S_OK;
}
```

Using *ClientChannelHook*

To use *ClientChannelHook*, both the client and server processes must load the channel hook by calling *CoCreateInstance*, as shown here:

```
// Load the channel hook.
void* silly;
CoCreateInstance(CLSID_ClientChannelHook, NULL,
    CLSCTX_INPROC_SERVER, IID_IUnknown, &silly);
```

In the client process, the channel hook is instantiated and every remote method call is sent with the client's computer name in the ORPCTHIS structure of the request PDU. In the server process, the channel hook retrieves the client's computer name and makes it available to the component using the

IClientInfo::GetClientComputerName method. For example, a method in the component that wants to obtain the client's computer name instantiates the *ClientChannelHook* object, requesting an *IClientInfo* interface pointer. Then the *GetClientComputerName* method is called to obtain the name of the client's computer from the channel hook. This process is shown in boldface in the following implementation of the *Sum* method:

```
HRESULT CInsideCOM::Sum(int x, int y, int* retval)
{
    IClientInfo* pClientInfo;
    CoCreateInstance(CLSID_ClientChannelHook, NULL,
        CLSCTX_INPROC_SERVER, IID_IClientInfo,
        (void**)&pClientInfo);

    BSTR bstr = 0;
    pClientInfo->GetClientComputerName(&bstr);
    MessageBox(NULL, (char*)bstr, "GetClientComputerName",
        MB_OK);
    SysFreeString(bstr);

    *retval = x + y;
    return S_OK;
}
```

Some overhead is associated with the second call to *CoCreateInstance* in the server process because the *ClientChannelHook* object is implemented as a singleton object. As described in Chapter 13, instead of instantiating a new object at each client request, a coclass designed to operate as a singleton always returns a reference to the same object. An easy way to implement a singleton is to declare a static object in the *IClassFactory::CreateInstance* method and then always provide a pointer to that one object, as shown in the following code. Like other singletons, the *ClientChannelHook* object is designed to stay in memory for the lifetime of its container process, so it does not support reference counting.

```
HRESULT CFactory::CreateInstance(IUnknown* pUnknownOuter,
    REFIID riid, void** ppv)
{
    if(pUnknownOuter != NULL)
        return CLASS_E_NOAGGREGATION;

    static CClientInfo ClientInfo;
    return ClientInfo.QueryInterface(riid, ppv);
}
```

Remote Procedure Calls

Microsoft's Remote Procedure Call (RPC) service was the first complete implementation of distributed processing available on the Microsoft Windows platform. RPC allows an application to call a function that executes on another computer on a network. To provide you with a detailed look at client/server technology and to shed light on the transition from RPC to COM+, this appendix describes a sample application that uses RPC to compute prime numbers; the calculations required are distributed across a network of computers.

Applications that use RPC usually have two parts: a client and a server. The client makes requests of the server, and the server's only purpose is to provide the client with the requested information. Servers are usually classified by the type of resource they offer. For instance, we're all familiar with file servers, print servers, and communications servers. Using RPC, a server in Windows can share not only its peripherals—such as hard disk space, printers, and modems—but also its computational horsepower.

RPC enables work to be distributed throughout a network. Idle computers on the network become compute servers. These compute servers do not have to be locked in a room with the file server because any computer on the network that runs Windows can be considered a compute server. RPC is Microsoft's answer to the complexity and reliability problems in client/server architecture compared with centralized systems.

The Design and Purpose of RPC

RPC alleviates the difficulties commonly associated with building distributed applications. These difficulties include all the errors that can occur in applications that communicate over a network. When an application sends a message, such as a Dynamic Data Exchange (DDE) message, to another application, it can be reasonably sure that the other application will receive it. However, even with DDE, a lot of programming effort is focused on error handling. What if an application engaged in the conversation doesn't follow the DDE protocol properly? What if it crashes? What if it sends garbage? These types of problems tend to increase exponentially when you communicate over a network. As anyone who has ever done low-level network programming knows, the number of errors that can occur is mind-boggling. Someone can trip over the network cable, the server can crash, or an application can fail to acknowledge a message. When you deal with network communications, the following rule of thumb still applies: if it can go wrong, it will.

RPC addresses these problems by providing a high-level procedural interface to the network. Until recently, all distributed computing was centered on the problem of I/O. Centralized systems, however, were not built based on I/O but rather on a procedural foundation. RPC resolved this discrepancy by providing a facility to build distributed systems based on the procedural model of its centralized ancestors. RPC is meant to be as unobtrusive as possible. The RPC model attempts to adhere closely to the Local Procedure Call (LPC) model. When RPC is implemented correctly, a programmer doesn't know whether a function has executed remotely or locally. This transparency is made possible by a special language originally designed for RPC and later commandeered by COM, Interface Definition Language (IDL).

Interface Definition Language

In RPC, as in COM, IDL defines the interface between the client and the server; all communications between the client and the server pass through the IDL interface. When programmers work on a project in which different applications are written by different teams, one problem is how to define a common interface to which everyone will adhere. With IDL, this process is automated. When the interface has been defined with IDL, all teams must adhere to it or they will not be able to compile their programs.

Here's how IDL works. You specify the name, version, and universally unique identifier (UUID) of the interface in the definition file. The UUID is a special number that ensures that RPCs are made to the correct server. Also included in the interface definition are special prototypes for all the exported functions that the client might call. All this data is saved in a file with an .idl extension. An interface definition file is somewhat analogous to a module definition (.def) file for a dynamic-link library (DLL).

The Microsoft IDL (MIDL) compiler compiles the source IDL file. Technically speaking, MIDL is a translator and not a compiler. It does not produce machine code—it translates IDL code into C. The C code generated by MIDL forms the remote procedure stubs in both the client and the server. Thus, the master IDL file produces code that is compiled and linked by both sides of the distributed application. If one side doesn't follow the specified interface, the compile and the link will fail.

You might find it interesting to examine the code produced by the MIDL compiler to see what it actually does. The MIDL compiler also uses the optional Application Configuration File (ACF) when it translates the IDL file. In the ACF, you can declare the type of binding handles used as well as optional server parameters.

Binding

The client connects to the server using a binding mechanism—a logical connection between the client and the server. Binding is a type of linking used for RPCs. Of the two standard types of linking, static and dynamic, binding is most similar to the latter. When you use dynamic linking, the address of the function called is resolved at run time. The binding mechanism in RPC differs from dynamic linking in that the procedure being called is located on a different computer. Therefore, the client cannot determine the correct address for the function because the function is in the server's address space. Only the server knows the actual address of the function called by the client. Thus, the client never actually calls the remote procedure; it asks the server to do so on its behalf. If you keep in mind that all communication is inherently I/O, it becomes obvious that the client cannot actually execute a jump to an address located on the server.

Two types of binding are available to RPC applications: manual and automatic. The manual method is more complex, and it requires that you both create and maintain the binding programmatically. However, it offers more control over the binding and the destination of RPCs. And since RPC applications are inherently complex, the manual binding method is used for most RPC applications.

When you use automatic binding, the MIDL compiler generates all the code to create and maintain the binding. This makes your job much easier, but the cost is less control. Automatic binding is usually used only in general applications that do not care which server they bind to. For example, an application that wants to get the time from a remote server is a good candidate for automatic binding.

Location Transparency

When the client calls the remote procedure, the code usually looks exactly as if it were written for an LPC. What happens, however, is radically different. When the RPC is executed, the client jumps to the client stub[1] generated by the MIDL compiler. The stub packages all the function parameters into a complex data structure in Network Data Representation (NDR) format. This structure is transmitted over the network to the server, where it is unpacked by the server stub and delivered to the remote procedure as regular function parameters. Because the client stub has the same name as the remote procedure, this whole process is transparent to the programmer.

Handles

An RPC application manages two main types of handles: binding handles and context handles. Binding handles contain information about the binding between the client and server, and context handles maintain state information.

A client initiates the binding process by calling several RPC run-time functions. If everything goes smoothly (if a valid server is found), the client receives a binding handle. A binding handle is an opaque data structure that the client uses when it makes RPCs and is always the first parameter passed to a remote procedure.

There are two ways to pass binding handles in an RPC application: implicitly and explicitly. Implicit binding handles are easier to use because the code for passing them is generated by the MIDL compiler. When you use an implicit binding handle, you declare it as a global variable so that the C code generated by the MIDL compiler can package it for transmission to the remote procedure's stub. All binding handles are eventually converted to explicit binding handles, but with implicit binding handles you need not be concerned with the details.

You pass explicit binding handles as the first parameter to every RPC. You gain control at the cost of extra complexity. With explicit binding handles, you can manage simultaneous connections to multiple servers. The RPC application presented later in this appendix uses explicit binding handles. Microsoft RPC also lets you define your own structures for use as binding handles. These handles can associate data unique to each binding for the application's use, similar to the ability to store application-defined data in a window handle.

Context handles, which are created and returned by the server, store information about the state of a server. Our sample RPC application uses context handles to determine when a client goes off line. If a client terminates, a special callback function known as a context handle rundown routine is executed on the server to notify the server that the client has terminated. The server can determine which client terminated by using the value stored in the context handle passed to the rundown routine.

---

1. In RPC the term *stub* is used on both the client and server sides. A client stub in RPC is conceptually equivalent to a proxy in COM.

The Prime Application

The RPC Prime application uses most of the RPC features described so far in this appendix to compute prime numbers. Prime number computation might not seem to be the pinnacle of application functionality, but it's an excellent vehicle for demonstrating the power of RPC. In this sample application, the prime number computations are widgets for any computationally intensive operation you might need to perform.

The client side of the Prime application has been designed so that it can operate whether or not a Prime server is available. When executed, the application creates a thread for each designated Prime server. Each thread then attempts to bind to its designated Prime server. The client sends work to all available Prime servers with which it has bound successfully. Each thread that was unsuccessful in binding to the server waits a predetermined period of time before trying to rebind. In addition, the client creates one local thread that computes prime numbers on the client's computer. The source code for the Prime client is in the primec.c source file on the companion CD.

To ensure that work is not replicated between the threads, the client keeps one global variable, *NextNumber*, which contains the value of the next number to be tested for prime status. Each thread increments this number within the context of a critical section to ensure that no other thread accesses it simultaneously. When the increment is complete, the thread copies the number to a local variable, *temp*, and exits the critical section. The *temp* variable can then be used safely because it is local to the thread, so no other thread can modify it. The next thread that accesses *NextNumber* retrieves the already incremented value of *NextNumber*, ensuring that no two threads test the same number. This technique is known as the "divide-and-conquer method" and is shown in the following code:

```
EnterCriticalSection(&GlobalCriticalSection);
if((temp = ++NextNumber) >= ULONG_MAX)
    break;
LeaveCriticalSection(&GlobalCriticalSection);
```

The client has several options that you can set. Type *PRIMEC /?* at a command prompt for a list of these features. You execute the client by typing this command:

```
PRIMEC -N \\FIRST_SERVER_NAME;\\SECOND_SERVER_NAME;...
```

Client Initialization

After parsing the command-line arguments, the client calls the *RpcString-BindingCompose* function, shown in the following code, to create a string binding for each server it intends to bind with. A string binding is a string of characters that defines all the attributes for the binding between the client and the server.

```
status = RpcStringBindingCompose(pszUuid,
    pszProtocolSequence, pszNetworkAddress[i],
    pszEndpoint[i], pszOptions, &pszStringBinding[i]);
```

The *RpcStringBindingCompose* function is a convenience function that combines all the pieces of a string binding and returns the combined string in a character array allocated by the function. This memory is later freed by a call to the *RpcStringFree* function.

As you can see from the example above, a string binding consists of the UUID, protocol sequence, network address, endpoint, and options. Using command-line arguments, the user can modify all the parameters used to create the string binding. The UUID specifies an optional number for identification purposes. This UUID allows clients and servers to distinguish between different objects. In this example, the field is set to *NULL* by default. The protocol sequence specifies the low-level network protocol for the network communication. Several network protocols are currently supported. Our example uses the named pipes (*ncacn_np*) protocol that is native to Windows NT. The currently supported network protocols are shown in the following table.

Protocol Sequence	Description
ncacn_np	Named pipes
ncacn_ip_tcp	Internet address
ncacn_dnet_nsp	DECNet phase IV
ncacn_osi_dna	DECNet phase V
ncadg_ip_udp	Internet address
ncacn_nb_tcp	NetBIOS
ncacn_nb_nb	NetBIOS Enhanced User Interface (NetBEUI)
ncacn_spx	Sequenced Package Exchange (SPX)
ncadg_mq	Microsoft Message Queue Server
ncacn_http	Microsoft Internet Information Server (IIS) as Hypertext Transfer Protocol (HTTP) proxy

Protocol Sequence	Description
ncacn_at_dsp	AppleTalk Data Stream Protocol (DSP)
ncacn_vns_spp	Banyan Vines Sequenced Packet Protocol (SPP) transport
ncadg_ipx	Internetwork Packet Exchange (IPX)
ncalrpc	Local RPC

The network address is the address of the server that the client wants to bind with. When the named pipes protocol sequence is used, the network address is described in the form \\servername, where servername is the name of the server computer. The type of valid network address depends on the protocol sequence used. Different protocol sequences have different methods of defining network addresses.

The endpoint used to create the binding specifies the network endpoint at which the server application listens. The endpoint is like a street address of a particular server application, and the network address is rather like the name of the city in which the server lives. Like the network address, the type of endpoint reflects the protocol sequence being used. When the named pipes protocol sequence is used, the valid endpoint specifies the pipe that the server is listening to. A valid endpoint for the named pipes protocol sequence is \pipe\pipename, where pipename is an application-defined name for the pipe used for low-level network communication between the client and the server.

The goal of RPC is to provide a high-level interface to networks, allowing a remote call to travel transparently over any type of available transport. The *options* parameter is a miscellaneous string that you use for whatever special settings are appropriate for a particular protocol sequence. In the case of the named pipes protocol sequence, the only available option is *security = true*. This setting turns on the security mechanisms for the RPC. For other network protocols, the valid options vary.

The *RpcStringBindingCompose* function combines the parts of a string binding. You bind a string in order to specify all the parameters for the protocol sequence (network protocol) used. The client then transforms each string binding into the actual binary binding using the *RpcBindingFromStringBinding* function, as shown here:

```
status = RpcBindingFromStringBinding(pszStringBinding[i],
    &BindingHandle[i]);
```

The binding becomes a sort of magic cookie, or handle, that you can use to make RPCs. The client then creates a thread to manage each server using the *CreateThread* function, as shown here:

```
hthread_remote[count - 1] = CreateThread(NULL, 0,
    (LPTHREAD_START_ROUTINE)thread_remote, (LPVOID)count, 0,
    &lpIDThread[count - 1]);
```

Each thread is passed a number that designates a server that the thread is responsible for. In addition, the client initializes a critical section object for later use when you access global variables from the threads, as shown in the following example:

```
InitializeCriticalSection(&GlobalCriticalSection);
```

The client calls the *GetComputerName* function so that it can pass the returned string to the server. The server uses this string for display purposes so the user can see which client is making RPCs, as shown here:

```
GetComputerName(computer_name_buffer,
    &Max_ComputerName_Length);
```

After the client obtains a valid binding to each server, it attempts to initialize these servers on a logical level. To do so, it calls a special remote procedure available on each Prime server: *InitializePrimeServer*. This function notifies the server that a client plans to make requests. As you can see in the following example, the *InitializePrimeServer* function accepts a binding handle, a context handle, and the name of the computer retrieved by the *GetComputerName* function:

```
RpcTryExcept
    {
    PrimeServerHandle[iserver] = InitializePrimeServer(
        BindingHandle[iserver],
        &phContext[iserver], computer_name_buffer);
    IsActiveServer[iserver] = TRUE;
    }
RpcExcept(1)
    {
    value = TRUE;
    IsActiveServer[iserver] = FALSE;
    }
RpcEndExcept
```

Client Computation

After the client initializes, prime number computation begins. The *thread_local* function computes prime numbers locally on the client computer using the *IsPrime* function, as shown here:

```
if(IsPrime(temp - 1) != 0)
```

The *thread_remote* function makes an RPC to determine whether a number is prime by using the *RemoteIsPrime* function. In this case, because *RemoteIsPrime* is an RPC, it is embedded in an exception handler, as shown below:

```
RpcTryExcept
    {
    if(RemoteIsPrime(BindingHandle[count-1],
        PrimeServerHandle[count-1], temp - 1) != 0)
        {
        /* Code displays prime number. */
        }
    }
RpcExcept(1)
    {
    /* If exception occurred, respond gracefully. */
    }
RpcEndExcept
```

If an exception occurs, the client attempts to recognize the error and displays an error message on the console. If the exception indicates that the server is off line, the client thread waits a specified period of time before attempting to rebind to that server. When the client terminates normally, via the Esc key, a special RPC called *TerminatePrimeServer* is made to notify the server of the client's plans to exit, as shown in the following code. The server can then take action to free memory and update its display to reflect the new status.

```
TerminatePrimeServer(BindingHandle[iserver],
    PrimeServerHandle[iserver]);
```

The Prime Server

The Prime server has an important, if unrewarding, job. It registers its interface and listens for client requests. The source code for the Prime server module is in the primes.c and primep.c files on the companion CD. The *RpcServerUseProtseqEp* function tells the RPC run-time module to register a protocol sequence, an endpoint, and a security attribute on which to accept RPCs. This call designates the station the server listens to so that it can hear the client's cries for help, as shown in the following code:

```
status = RpcServerUseProtseqEp(pszProtocolSequence,
    cMaxCalls, pszEndpoint, pszSecurity);
```

The *RpcServerRegisterIf* function registers the server's interface. It accepts the handle to the interface being registered and two optional management parameters (which are not used in this example). This interface is defined in the Prime IDL file as shown here:

```
status = RpcServerRegisterIf(prime_v1_0_s_ifspec, NULL,
    NULL);
```

The last RPC run-time function that the Prime server calls begins listening for client requests. In this example, the *RpcServerListen* function never returns:

```
status = RpcServerListen(cMinCalls, cMaxCalls, fDontWait);
```

Until a client initiates an RPC, the server can do nothing. To avoid this waste of resources, we created a special thread for the server to perform maintenance tasks even when the server is not in use. We created this thread using the *CREATE_SUSPENDED* flag so that we can subsequently modify it using the *THREAD_PRIORITY_LOWEST* flag. This technique ensures that the maintenance thread consumes the minimal amount of CPU cycles when it is restarted using the *ResumeThread* function. In the following example, the maintenance thread provides some prime number statistics and checks to see whether the Esc key was pressed:

```
hthread_server = CreateThread(NULL, 0,
    (LPTHREAD_START_ROUTINE)thread_server, NULL,
    CREATE_SUSPENDED, &lpIDThread);
SetThreadPriority(hthread_server, THREAD_PRIORITY_LOWEST);
ResumeThread(hthread_server);
```

Context Rundown

The Prime server also includes a special context rundown routine, which you can see in the primep.c file on the companion CD. As you might recall, the client calls the *TerminatePrimeServer* function when the user presses the Esc key. But what happens if the client terminates abnormally—for example, if the client crashes, the power goes out, or the computer fails? In any case, the server must be fault-tolerant and not allow such an event to impair its performance for other clients that might still be on line. The server must do whatever the

TerminatePrimeServer function would have done. The designers of RPC took this situation into account and came up with the special rundown facility. It is a user-defined function that the RPC calls automatically at run time when the client terminates. If the client terminates normally by calling the *TerminatePrimeServer* function, the rundown routine is skipped. If the client terminates abnormally, the rundown routine is called to perform the necessary cleanup.

The Prime interface definition file specifies this interface between the client and the server. The Prime interface is defined in the prime.idl file. The UUID, version number, and pointer type used are defined in the following code for the interface header. Following that is the actual interface definition, which consists of the function prototypes with special IDL flags.

```
[ uuid (906B0CE0-C70B-1067-B317-00DD010662DA),
    version(1.0),
    pointer_default(unique) ]
interface prime
    {
    /* Function definitions */
    }
```

Debugging

Debugging distributed RPC applications is slightly different from debugging conventional applications because of the added factor of the network. For this reason, it is best to separate the server initialization code from the remote procedures themselves. We did this in the Prime RPC application using the primes.c and primep.c source files. These files are linked to produce the server application, but during the debugging stage, separating them can be invaluable. By dividing the server application into two parts, you give yourself the option of linking the remote procedures directly with the client application to produce one standard application. You can then test the application as a whole without worrying about the network. Once your program works properly, you can divide it into a client and a server to test the distribution factor.

Distributed Computation

After all the effort we've exerted to compute prime numbers, it's a shame that there isn't more of a market for them. By now, we could probably package and sell them by the metric ton. Is there any advantage to computing prime numbers in a distributed manner across a network rather than on one computer? The Prime application provides some simple timer routines that indicate how long the computations take. The following table should give you an idea of the practicality of RPCs. You can see that when the number of computations is relatively small (1 to 1000), distributing an application can hurt performance because of the overhead of RPCs. But if the number of calculations is very large (10,000,000 and up), the overhead of RPCs becomes insignificant. Based on our tests, the improvement with the distributed prime computations approached an order of 3.5 times faster with four computers compared to only one. A well-written application will make RPCs only when the possible gain outweighs the cost in overhead.

Calculations	One Computer	Four Computers	Ratio
1–1000	35 seconds	40 seconds	0.88
100,000–101,000	40 seconds	42 seconds	0.95
1,000,000–1,001,000	100 seconds	61 seconds	1.64
10,000,000–10,001,000	581 seconds	170 seconds	3.42

BIBLIOGRAPHY

Bernstein, Philip A., and Eric Newcomer. *Principles of Transaction Processing*. San Francisco: Morgan Kaufmann, 1997.

Booch, Grady, James Rumbaugh, and Ivar Jacobson. *The Unified Modeling Language User Guide*. Reading, Mass.: Addison-Wesley, 1999.

Box, Don, et al. *Effective COM*. Reading, Mass.: Addison-Wesley, 1999.

Box, Don. *Essential COM*. Reading, Mass.: Addison-Wesley, 1998.

Brockschmidt, Kraig. *Inside OLE*. 2d ed. Redmond, Wash.: Microsoft Press, 1995.

Chappell, David. *Understanding ActiveX and OLE*. Redmond, Wash.: Microsoft Press, 1996.

Component Object Model Specification, version 0.9, October 1995. Microsoft Corporation, http://www.microsoft.com/com/comdocs.asp.

Custer, Helen. *Inside Windows NT*. Redmond, Wash.: Microsoft Press, 1993.

———. *Inside the Windows NT File System*. Redmond, Wash.: Microsoft Press, 1994.

DCE 1.1: Remote Procedure Call Open Group CAE Specification, Document Number C706, August 1997. The Open Group, http://www.opengroup.org/pubs/catalog/c706.htm.

DCE 1.2.2: Introduction to OSF DCE, Open Group Product Documentation, F201, November 1997. The Open Group, http://www.opengroup.org/pubs/catalog/f201.htm.

Distributed Component Object Model Protocol, version 1.0, January 1998. Microsoft Corporation, http://www.microsoft.com/oledev/olecom/draft-brown-dcom-v1-spec-02.txt.

Eddon, Guy. *RPC for NT*. Lawrence, Kans.: R&D Publications, 1994.

Eddon, Guy, and Henry Eddon. *Active Visual Basic 5.0*. Redmond, Wash.: Microsoft Press, 1997.

———. *Inside Distributed COM*. Redmond, Wash.: Microsoft Press, 1998.

———. *Programming Components with Microsoft Visual Basic 6.0*. 2d ed. Redmond, Wash.: Microsoft Press, 1998.

Ellis, Margaret A., and Bjarne Stroustrup. *The Annotated C++ Reference Manual*. Reading, Mass.: Addison-Wesley, 1990.

Flanagan, David. *Java in a Nutshell.* 2d ed. Sebastopol, Calif.: O'Reilly, 1997.

Gamma, Erich, et al. *Design Patterns.* Reading, Mass.: Addison-Wesley, 1995.

Gosling, James, and Ken Arnold. *The Java Programming Language.* Reading, Mass.: Addison-Wesley, 1996.

Kerberos Network Authentication Service, version 5, Internet Engineering Task Force RFC 1510, http://www.ietf.org/rfc/rfc1510.txt, 1993.

Kernighan, Brian W., and Dennis M. Ritchie. *The C Programming Language.* 2d ed. Englewood Cliffs, N.J.: Prentice Hall, 1988.

Knuth, Donald. *The Art of Computer Programming.* Vol. 1, *Fundamental Algorithms.* 3d ed. Reading, Mass.: Addison-Wesley, 1997.

―――. *The Art of Computer Programming.* Vol. 2, *Seminumerical Algorithms.* 3d ed. Reading, Mass.: Addison-Wesley, 1998.

―――. *The Art of Computer Programming.* Vol. 3, *Sorting and Searching.* 2d ed. Reading, Mass.: Addison-Wesley, 1998.

Meyers, Scott. *Effective C++: 50 Specific Ways to Improve Your Programs and Designs.* 2d ed. Reading, Mass.: Addison-Wesley, 1998.

―――. *More Effective C++: 35 New Ways to Improve Your Programs and Designs.* Reading, Mass.: Addison-Wesley, 1996.

Microsoft Corporation. *Automation Programmer's Reference.* Redmond, Wash.: Microsoft Press, 1997.

Petzold, Charles. *Programming Windows.* 5th ed. Redmond, Wash.: Microsoft Press, 1999.

Richter, Jeffrey. *Advanced Windows.* 3d ed. Redmond, Wash.: Microsoft Press, 1997.

Rogerson, Dale. *Inside COM.* Redmond, Wash.: Microsoft Press, 1997.

Schneier, Bruce. *Applied Cryptography.* 2d ed. New York: John Wiley & Sons, 1996.

Stroustrup, Bjarne. *The C++ Programming Language.* 3d ed. Reading, Mass.: Addison-Wesley, 1997.

―――. *The Design and Evolution of C++.* Reading, Mass.: Addison-Wesley, 1994.

Tanenbaum, Andrew S. *Computer Networks.* 3d ed. Upper Saddle River, N.J.: Prentice Hall PTR, 1996.

―――. *Distributed Operating Systems.* Englewood Cliffs, N.J.: Prentice Hall, 1995.

―――. *Modern Operating Systems.* Englewood Cliffs, N.J.: Prentice Hall, 1992.

INDEX

Note: Page numbers in italics refer to figures or tables.

Symbols

& (address-of operator), 45

<> (angle brackets), 103

== (comparison operator), 50

A

abstract base classes
  defined, 30
  ISum as, 30, 48
  IUnknown as, 30
access control. *See also IAccessControl* interface
  and *CoInitializeSecurity* function, 552–53, *552,* 560–63
  in COM+ security model, 528, 529, 530
  declarative security, 528, 529, 530
  declarative vs. programmatic security, 530
  defined, 528, 529
  programmatic security, 530
  Windows distributed security model, 527, 528, 529, 530
access control entries (ACEs), 528
access control lists (ACLs), 528
access tokens, 570, 571
ACEs. *See* access control entries (ACEs)
ACLs. *See* access control lists (ACLs)
activation control, 528, 529, 530
Active Server components, *113*
Active Template Library (ATL)
  ATL COM+ AppWizard, 112, *112*
  ATL Object Wizard, 113–16, *113*

Active Template Library (ATL), *continued*
  building COM+ objects, 116–17
  vs. Microsoft Foundation Classes, 111–12
  object model, 116, *116*
  overview, 111–12
  testing COM+ objects, 117
ActiveX
  and COM+, 10–11
  and component categories, 259–60, *260*
  and impact of components, 10–11
  integrating controls with Java Beans, 141–42
  and Internet Explorer, 14
  and scriptlets, 245
ActiveX Data Objects (ADO), 231
ACTRL_ACCESS structure, 543, *544*
AddConnection method, *IExternalConnection* interface, 423–24
add-in objects, *113*
Add method, collection objects, 227
AddRef method, *IUnknown* interface, 40–42, 49, 60, 61, 87–88, 90
AddRefTypeInfo method, *ICreateTypeInfo* interface, 313, 314
address-of operator (&), 45
ADOs. *See* ActiveX Data Objects (ADO)
Advise method, *IConnectionPoint* interface, 275
aggregation, 81, 85–90, *86. See also* free-threaded marshaler
angle brackets (<>), 103
anti-monikers, *359*
apartments. *See also* multi-threaded apartment (MTA) model; single-threaded apartment (STA) model
  comparing models, 183–85
  defined, 148
  interactions among, 166–72
  multi-threaded model, 157–58

apartments, *continued*
  neutral model, 181–83
  security issues, 185–87
  single-threaded model, 149–53
API functions. *See* Win32 API
AppIDs. *See* application identifiers (AppIDs)
applets. *See* Java
application identifiers (AppIDs)
  and COM+ security model, 539–41
  and DCOM Configuration utility, 390, 539–41
  list of named-values, *387*
  list of security-related values, 540
  overview, 386–87
  and remote machines, 389
architecture
  standard marshaling, 456–76, *458*
  three-tier, 18–20
arrays. *See also* safe arrays
  character, 498–501
  in C language, 491–503
  conformant, 492–95
  fixed, 492
  multidimensional, 501–2
  open, 496–98
  overview, 491
  passing from Visual Basic, 502–3
  vs. pointers, 491
  varying, 495–96
artificial reference counts, 61
asynchronous calls
  calling interfaces, 513–15
  cancelling, 519–23
  defining interfaces, 512–13
  ICallFactory interface, 513–14
  implementing interfaces, 516–18

asynchronous calls, *continued*
  overview, 511
  and registry entries, 513
ATL. *See* Active Template Library (ATL)
ATL COM+ AppWizard, 112, *112*
ATL Object Wizard, 113–16, *113*
atomic transaction property, 26
authentication control
  in COM+ security model, 528, 529, 530
  and *CoQueryAuthenticationServices* function, 559–60
  defined, 527–28
  setting authentication level, 534–35, 555–59
  and SOLE_AUTHENTICATION_SERVICE structure, 553–55
  Windows distributed security model, 527–28, 529, 530
Automation, COM+. *See also IDispatch* interface
  building client in C++, 235–39
  building client in scripts, 243–45
  building client in Visual Basic, 240–42
  compatible data types, 201
  marshaler for *IDispatch* interface, 200–212, 398
  overview, 197–98
  and type library marshaling, 200–201, 398–99

B
BASIC strings, 204–6
*Begin_* methods, 512, 514, 517–18, 519
big endian architecture, 486
binary reuse, 9
bind contexts, 361–64
binding, and RPC, 619
binding, early vs. late, 235, 241
binding handles, 620

binding operations, 361, 362

BindMoniker helper function, 363, 366

BIND_OPTS2 structure, 363–64

BindToObject method, *IMoniker* interface, *361*, 362, 363, 365, 367, 368, 369, 370, 373–74, 379

BindToStorage method, *IMoniker* interface, *361*

blankets, security, 559

boolean data type, *96, 201, 486*

BSTR data type, *96, 201*

BSTRs. *See* BASIC strings

business logic tier, three-tier system architecture

    and just-in-time activation, 20–22

    overview, 18, *18,* 19

byte data type, *95, 486,* 524

C

C and C++ programming languages

    and abstract base classes, 30, 48

    Active Template Library, 111–17

    Automation-compatible data types, *201*

    building Automation client, 235–39

    building sample client application using *ISum* interface, 46–47

    calling conventions, 30

    class *CFactory,* 59

    CoGetObject function vs. COM+ *MkParseDisplayName* function, 366, 367, 376

    and COM+, 29–30, 31, 51

    and COM+ error handling, 249–50, 257

    component threading issues, 192

    and directional attributes, 487–91

    elements of sample client application using *ISum* interface, 36–46

C and C++ programming languages, *continued*

    and *IDispatch* interface, 235–39

    and IDL arrays, 491–503

    and IDL-defined data types, 95, *95–96*

    and IDL pointers, 503–4

    implementing sink object, 279–83

    and *Isum* interface, 29, 48–57

    and MIDL compiler, 34–35

    and namespaces, 110–11

    new operator, 36, 57, 355–56

    and object-oriented programming, 7

    passing parameters, 487–91

    pointers vs. arrays, 491

    relationship to COM+ objects and classes, 31, 51

    and smart pointers, 105–9

    template overview, 102–5

    testing Visual Basic components from, 125

    testing Visual J++ components from, 141

.cab files, *139,* 143

call_as.cpp file, 508, *508*

calling conventions, 30

calls, asynchronous. *See* asynchronous calls

Cancel method, *ICancelMethodCalls* interface, 519, 520, 521, 522

category identifiers (CATIDs), 261–64

CATEGORYINFO structure, 266–67

CATIDs. *See* category identifiers (CATIDs)

CComCoClass ATL class, 116

CComObjectRootEx ATL class, 116

channel hooks, 608–15

channels, defined, 152, 608

character arrays, 498–501

char data type, *95, 486*

CInsideCOM class, 48–49, 57, 58, 60

class1.java file, 137, *137*

class emulation, 264

classes

  abstract base, 30, 48

  C++ vs. COM+, 31, 51

  defined, 7

  vs. objects, 7–8

  and virtual functions, 29–30

class factories. *See also IClassFactory* interface

  vs. class objects, 58, 357

  defined, 58

.class files, 138, 139–40, 142–43

class identifiers (CLSIDs). *See also* category
    identifiers (CATIDs)

  and class emulation, 264

  and *CoCreateInstance* function, 37

  and monikers, 367–70

  overview, 37

  and proxy objects, 437–38

  registering, 37

class keyword, 103

class moniker

  implementing, 368–69

  vs. marvelous moniker, 370–77

  vs. new moniker, 377–78

  overview, *359,* 367–70

  and Visual Basic, 370, 377

class objects

  vs. class factories, 58, 357

  and custom activation interfaces, 357, 420–24

  defined, 58

  in EXE components, 407–9

  and *IExternalConnection* interface, 422–24

  in Java, 138

  registering, 407–9

class templates, 103, 104–5

ClientChannelHook object, 614–15

client.cpp file, *47,* 456–57. *See also*
    easyclient.cpp file

ClientFillBuffer method, *IChannelHook*
    interface, 613

ClientGetSize method, *IChannelHook*
    interface, 613

client.html file, 243, *243*

ClientNotify method, *IChannelHook interface,* 614

client/server model vs. three-tier architecture,
    18, 19

client.vbs file, *245*

clipboard, 12, 13

cloaking, 570–72

Clone method, *IStream* interface, *333*

CloseHandle Win32 API function, 146

CLSID_DCOMAccessControl object and
    IAccessControl interface, 545–47

CLSIDs. *See* class identifiers (CLSIDs)

CoAddRefServerProcess helper function, 415,
    415, 418

COAUTHIDENTITY structure, 564, 565,
    565, 566

COAUTHINFO structure, 563–66, *565*

CoCreateFreeThreadedMarshaler function,
    175, 176

CoCreateGuid function, 34

CoCreateInstanceEx function

  calling from Java, 134–35

  vs. *CoCreateInstance* function, 409, 411

  and smart pointers, 105, 108

  and Visual Basic, 118

CoCreateInstance function, 67–68, *69*

  and aggregation, 86

  vs. C++ *new* operator, 36, 57, 355–56

CoCreateInstance function, *continued*

  vs. *CoCreateInstanceEx* function, 409, 411

  and *CoGetClassObject* function, 67–68, *69,* 356, 357, 358, 368, 370

  and *IClassFactory* interface, 358

  overview, 36–39

code libraries, 8–9

code reuse

  vs. binary reuse, 9

  in COM+ (*see* aggregation; containment)

  and inheritance, 8, 81

  and object-oriented programming, 8–9

CoEnableCallCancellation function, 521

CoFreeLibrary function, 66

CoFreeUnusedLibraries function, 66, 187, 393

CoGetCallContext function, 522, 523

CoGetCancelObject function, 521, 522

CoGetClassObject function, 67, 69, 182, 356, 357, 358, 368, 370, 374, 375, 376, 432, 433

CoGetCurrentProcess Win32 function, 151

CoGetInterfaceAndReleaseStream function, 158, 159, 160, 161, 173, 174, 176, 178, 180, 181

CoGetObject helper function, 365–66, 367, 376, 479

CoGetPSClsid function, 413

CoGetStandardMarshal function, 175, 438, 457

CoGetStdMarshalEx function, 481, 483

CoGetTreatAsClass function, 264

CoInitializeEx function, 36, 42–43, 118, 150, 157, 158, 182, 407

CoInitialize function, 42–43

CoInitializeSecurity function

  and access control, 552–53, *552,* 560–63

  and *CoQueryAuthenticationServices* function, 559–60

CoInitializeSecurity function, *continued*

  declaration, 551

  overview, 551

  registering authentication services, 553–55

  setting authentication levels, 555–59

  setting impersonation levels, 555–56

  and SOLE_AUTHENTICATION_INFO structure, 556, *557*

  and SOLE_AUTHENTICATION_LIST structure, 556, *557*

  and SOLE_AUTHENTICATION_SERVICE structure, 553–55

collection objects

  Add method, 227

  Count property, 227

  Item method, 227

  members, 227–29

  _*NewEnum* property, 227–28

  Remove method, 227

collections, Visual Basic, 227–29

CoLockObjectExternal function, 424

COM+. *See also* Automation, COM+

  and ActiveX, 10–11

  added features, 20–28, *20*

  classes vs. objects, 7–8

  class objects vs. class factories, 58, 357

  vs. COM, *20*

  custom interface design recommendations, 509–10

  error handling, 249–57

  evolution of, 11–28

  and interactions among threading models, 166–69

  interface overview, 11, 31

  and location transparency, 57, 385

COM+, *continued*

as network protocol layer, 575–76, *575*

overview, 16–18

programming in Java, 126–43

relationship to C++ objects, 31

security model overview, 528–32

ten commandments of threading, 193–94

threading model overview, 148–49

ways to package objects, 139, 245

COM+ AppWizard. *See* ATL COM+ AppWizard

COM+ channels, defined, 152

COM+ objects

adding to components using ATL Object
Wizard, 113–14

and aggregation, 85–90

building in Java, 135–36

building using ATL, 116–17

vs. C++ objects, 31

calling from Java, 132–36

and component categories, 259–70

containment technique, 83–85

implementing in Java, 136–41

instantiating using *CoCreateInstance,* 36–39

instantiating using *CreateInstance,* 58, 60–61

remote instantiation, 409–11

CoMarshalInterface function, 161, 174, 433,
434, 435, 437, 438, 439, 441–42, 443, 457,
476, 480

CoMarshalInterThreadInterfaceInStream
function, 158, 159, 160, 161, 173, 174, 176,
178, 180, 181

@com comments, 128–29, *129*

ComFailException class, 255

<comment> tag, 247, *247*

Commit method, *IStorage* interface, *348*

Commit method, *IStream* interface, *333*

CommonPrefixWith method, *IMoniker*
interface, *361*

comparison operator (==), 50

ComplexPing method, *IOXIDResolver*
interface, *605*

component categories, 259–70

Component Categories Manager, 265–70

component.cpp file, 70, *70–74*

component.def file, 70, *70*

component.h file, 34–35, 216

component.idl file, *32, 93–94*

component.rc file, 80, *80, 96*

component.reg file, 74, *74*

components. *See also* in-process components;
local components; remote components

adding COM+ objects using ATL Object
Wizard, 113–14

and apartment interactions, 166–69

building in Java, 140–41

building in Visual Basic, 124–26

building sample client application using
ISum interface, 46–47

categories of, 259–70

configuring security, 532–50

deactivation, 22

elements of sample client application using
ISum interface, 36–46

embedding type libraries in, 96, 101

just-in-time activation, 20–22

overview, 9–11

queued, 23–24

role of COM+, 14

running remotely, 388–90

self-registering, 75–81

components, *continued*
  singleton model, 424–26
  threading model overview, 148–49
component.sct file, *245–46*
component with registration.def file, 78, *79*
ComposeWith method, *IMoniker* interface, *361*
composite controls, *114*
composite monikers, *359*
compound documents
  creating using clipboard, 13
  creating using OLE, 13–14
  defined, 13
  and just-in-time activation, 14
COM Wrappers dialog box, 127, *128*
conformant arrays, 492–95
connectable objects. *See also* connection points
  complete implementation example, 291–99
  defined, 271, *272*
  IConnectionPointContainer interface, 276–79
  IConnectionPoint interface, 273–76
  simple example, 272–90
connectionless protocols, 587–88
Connection object, 231
connection points. *See also* connectable objects
  defined, 271
  multicasting with, 282–83
  and Visual Basic, 297–99
  when to use, 271, 297–99
Connect method, *IRpcProxyBuffer* interface, 465–66
Connect method, *IRpcStubBuffer* interface, 467, 468
consistent transaction property, 26
containment
  and aggregation support, 85–90, *86*
  as COM+ reuse mechanism, 81, 83–85, *83*

context, 38, 183. *See also* bind contexts
context handles, 604–5, 620
context menus, 82
CopyProxy method, *IClientSecurity* interface, 573
CopyTo method, *IStorage* interface, *348*
CopyTo method, *IStream* interface, *332*
CoQueryAuthenticationServices function, 559–60
CoRegisterChannelHook function, 612
CoRegisterClassObject function, 358, 407–9, 416, 434, 444, 550
CoRegisterMessageFilter function, 153
CoRegisterPSClsid function, 413
CoReleaseMarshalData helper function, 444
CoReleaseServerProcess helper function, 415, *415*, 418–19
CoResumeClassObjects helper function, 415, *415*, 416, 417
CoRevokeClassObject function, 414, 416
COSERVERINFO structure, 363, 410–11, 564, *565*
CoSuspendClassObjects helper function, 415, *415*, 416–17, 419
CoSwitchCallContext function, 520
CoTreatAsClass function, 264
CoUninitialize function, 66, 108–9, 118
CoUnmarshalInterface function, 161, 444–46, 447, 457, 480, 481
Count property, collection objects, 227
CoWaitForMultipleHandles function, 515
CreateCall method, *ICallFactory* interface, 513–14, 516
CreateClassMoniker function, 373
CreateErrorInfo function, 253
CreateInstance method
  IClassFactory interface, 58, 60–61, 86, 87, 89, 356, 434
  and singleton implementation, 424, 425

CreateMarvelousMoniker function, 376–77

CreateObject function, 118–19, 240, 241, 242, 479

CreateObjrefMoniker function, 478–79

CreateProcess Win32 API function, 146

CreateProxy method, *IPSFactoryBuffer* interface, 462–64

CreateStdDispatch function, 217, 218–19, 223

CreateStorage method, *IStorage* interface, *348*

CreateStream method, *IStorage* interface, *348*

CreateStreamOnHGlobal Win32 API function, 333

CreateStub method, *IPSFactoryBuffer* interface, 462, 464–65

CreateThread Win32 API function, 146, 148, 157–58

CreateTypeInfo method, *ICreateTypeLib* interface, 305, 306, 308

CreateTypeLib2 function, 302–3

CreateWindowEx Win32 API function, 150

Currency data type, *96, 201*

custom activation interfaces, 357–58, 420, 422–24

custom DLL surrogates, 391–94

custom interfaces
  defining *ISum* example, 29–31
  design recommendations, 509–10
  and dual interface overview, 213–15
  and marshaling, 395
  pure vs. dual interface, 213–14
  vs. standard interfaces, 29

custom marshaling
  marshal-by-value, 450–53
  overview, 399–400
  and shared memory, 431, 432, 440

custom marshaling, *continued*
  vs. standard marshaling, 399–400, *400,* 431–35
  when to choose, 431–35

CY data type, *96, 201*

D

DACLs. *See* discretionary access control lists (DACLs)

database servers
  and COM+, 17
  and Windows DNA, 18, *18,* 19–20

data types. *See also* type libraries
  Automation-compatible, *201*
  enumerated, 487
  and Interface Definition Language (IDL), 95, *95–96,* 485–87, *486*

Date data type, *96, 201*

DCOM. *See* Distributed COM (DCOM) Configuration utility

deactivation, just-in-time, 22

DebugServerQueryInterface method, *IRpcStubBuffer* interface, 468

DebugServerRelease method, *IRpcStubBuffer* interface, 468

declarative security
  in COM+ security model, 530
  component security settings, 539–41
  default security settings, 533–39
  vs. programmatic security, 26–27, 550
  and registry, 532–50

default attribute, 273

default objects, 262–64

DestroyElement method, *IStorage* interface, *348*

directional attributes, C++, 487–91

Disconnect method
    IRpcProxyBuffer interface, 466
    IRpcStubBuffer interface, 468
DisconnectObject method, *IMarshal* interface, 447
discretionary access control lists (DACLs), 528, *529*
DISPARAMS structure, 236–39
dispatch identifiers (DISPIDs)
    defined, 200
    and *IDispatchEX* interface, 232–34
    in sample automation client, 235, 236
DispatchMessage Win32 API function, 150
DISPIDs. *See* dispatch identifiers (DISPIDs)
dispinterface statement, 212–13
display names, 364. *See also* monikers
Distributed COM (DCOM) Configuration utility
    Default Properties tab, 533–37, *534*
    Default Protocols tab, 583–85, *584, 585*
    Default Security tab, 537–39, *539*
    Identity tab, 547–50, *547*
    overview, 533
    running on Windows 95 and Windows 98, 530
    Security tab, 540–41, *541*
distributed computing, defined, 3–4
Distributed Computing Environment (DCE), 16, 32, 576
Distributed interNet Applications Architecture. *See* Windows DNA
DllCanUnloadNow function, 63, 66, 70, 185, 186–87, 404
DllGetClassObject function, 61, 63, 64–66, 68, 70, 185, 186–87, 356, 403–4, 461, 480
DllMain function, 612
DllNanny custom DLL surrogate, 391–94
DllRegisterServer function, 75, 76–77, 78, 79, *79*, 396, 404

DLL surrogates
    default vs. custom surrogates, 391
    DllNanny, 391–94
    and in-process components, 386–94
    overview, 386
DllUnregisterServer function, 75, 76–77, 78, *79*, 97, 404
DNA (Distributed interNet Applications Architecture). *See* Windows DNA
double data type, *96, 201, 486*, 524
dual interfaces
    creating, 215–16
    IDL notation, 215
    overview, 213–15
    vs. pure Automation-based interface, 213–14
DUALSTRINGARRAY structure, 593–95
durable transaction property, 26
Dynamic Data Exchange (DDE)
    vs. Automation, 197
    defined, 12
    vs. Remote Procedure Calls, 617–18
    shortcomings, 148
dynamic-link libraries (DLLs).
    See DLL surrogates; in-process components; proxy/stub DLLs

E

early binding, 235, 241
easyclient.cpp file, 101, *101*
encapsulation in object-oriented programming, 8, 11
EnumClassesOfCategories method, *ICatInformation* interface, 268, 269
EnumConnectionPoints method, *IConnectionPointContainer* interface, 277, 291

EnumConnections method, *IConnectionPoint* interface, 296–97

enum data type, *201*

EnumElements method, *IStorage* interface, *348*

enumeration
  IEnumConnectionPoints interface, 292, 293–95
  IEnumConnections interface, 292, 297
  overview, 292–93

enumerator objects, 227, 292–97

enum keyword, 487

Enum method, *IMoniker* interface, *361*

EnumRunning method, *IRunningObjectTable* interface, 380

error handling
  and exceptions, 249, 252–57
  and *HRESULT* values, 249, 250–52

Ethernet, 575

event models
  external, 27–28
  internal vs. external, 27

exceptions, 249, 252–57

EXE components. *See also* local components
  advantages and disadvantages, 402–3
  building, 403–13
  vs. DLL components, 63, 401–3
  and *IExternalConnection* interface, 422–24
  vs. in-process components, 63, 385, 401–3
  keeping alive, 414–17
  local components as, 385
  and marshaling, 394–95
  overview, 63, 401–3
  registering, 75, 406, 407–9
  shutting down, 417–20
  start-up function, 404, 405, 414–15
  threading issues, 415, 417, 418, 419

executable components. *See* EXE components

ExitThread Win32 API function, 146

exported functions, 403–4

export library, 70

extends keyword, 131

F

facility codes, 250–51

file monikers, *359*

FindConnectionPoints method, *IConnectionPointContainer* interface, 277, 291

*Finish_* methods, 512, 514, 517–18, 519

firewalls, 583

fixed arrays, 492

float data type, *96, 201, 486*

For Each...Next statement, 227

FormatMessage Win32 API function, 251–52

FreeBuffer method, *IRpcChannelBuffer* interface, 470, 474

FreeLibrary Win32 API function, 63

FreeSurrogate method, *ISurrogate* interface, 393

free-threaded marshaler, 172–81

full controls, *114*

full pointers, 504

FUNCDESC structure, 314, *315*, 316–17

function calls, synchronous vs. asynchronous, 146

functions, exported, 403–4

function templates, 103–4

G

garbage collection, 118, 135, 605–7

GetAllAccessRights method, *IAccessControl* interface, 545, 560

GetBuffer method, *IRpcChannelBuffer* interface, 470, 472, 474

GetClassForHandler method, *IStdMarshalInfo* interface, 480

GetClassInfo method, *IProvideClassInfo* interface, 318

GetClassObject method, *IClassActivator* interface, 375–76

GetClientComputerName method, *IClientInfo* interface, 614, 615

GetConnectionInterface method, *IConnectionPoint* interface, 296

GetConnectionPointContainer method, *IConnectionPoint* interface, 297

GetCurrentThreadID Win32 API function, 151, 521

GetDestCtx method, *IRpcChannelBuffer* interface, 475

GetDispID method, *IDispatchEx* interface, 229, 232–33

GetDisplayName method, *IMoniker* interface, *361*, 364, 380

GetErrorInfo function, 254, 256

GetExitCodeThread Win32 API function, 146

GetGUID method, *IProvideClassInfo2* interface, 319

GetIDsOfNames method, *IDispatch* interface, 217, 221, 236

GetInterfaceFromGlobal method, *IGlobalInterfaceTable* interface, 180, 181

GetMarshalSizeMax method, *IMarshal* interface, 438–39, 441

GetMessage Win32 API function, 150

GetModuleFileName Win32 API function, 78, 98

GetObject function, 366–67, 376, 479

GetPriorityClass function, 147

GetProcAddress Win32 API function, 63, 68

GetRecordInfoFromGuids function, 211

GetRecordInfoFromTypeInfo function, 211–12

GetThreadPriority function, 147

GetTimeOfLastChange method, *IMoniker* interface, *361*

GetTypeInfoCount method, *IDispatch* interface, 219–20

GetTypeInfo method, *IDispatch* interface, 220–21

GetTypeInfoOfGuid method, *ITypeInfo* interface, 312

GetTypeInfoOfGuid method, *ITypeLib* interface, 314

GetUnmarshalClass method, *IMarshal* interface, 437–38, 439, 441, 457

GetWindowLong Win32 API function, 608

GIT. *See* Global Interface Table (GIT)

Global Interface Table (GIT), 178–81

globally unique identifiers (GUIDs)

  creating, 34

  defined, 34

  formatting, 579

  transmitted over networks, 579

  vs. universally unique identifiers (UUIDs), 34

GUIDs. *See* globally unique identifiers (GUIDs)

H

HandleInComingCall method, *IMessageFilter* interface, 154–55

handler marshaling, 479–84

handles

  binding, 620

  context, 604–5, 620

Hash method, *IMoniker* interface, *361*

header files, 34–35, 101–2

helper functions

  for BSTRs, 205–6

helper functions, *continued*

   IDispatch interface, 217–19

   for safe arrays, 207–10

   for variants, 203–4

HKEY_CLASSES_ROOT\CLSID registry key, 37–39, 261–64, *261, 262, 263*

HKEY_CLASSES_ROOT\Interface registry key, 97, *98*

HKEY_CLASSES_ROOT\TypeLib registry key, 96–97

HRESULT value, 30, 33, 249, 250–52

HTML controls, *114*

HTML documents, 243, *243*

hyper data type, *95, 486*

I

IAccessControl interface

   and *CLSID_DCOMAccessControl* implementation, 545–47

   and *CoInitializeSecurity* function, 560–63

   and *DCOMAccessControl* object, 543, 545

   GetAllAccessRights method, 545, 560

   IDL notation, 542

   IsAccessAllowed method, 560, 562–63

   overview, 541–43

IAdviseSink interface, 299

IBindCtx interface, 361–62, 363

ICallFactory interface, 513–14, 516, 518

ICancelMethodCalls interface, 519–22

ICatInformation interface, 268–69

ICatRegister interface

   IDL notation, 265–66

   RegisterCategories method, 266

   RegisterClassImplCategories method, 267

   UnRegisterCategories method, 267

IChannelHook interface

   ClientFillBuffer method, 613

   ClientGetSize method, 613

   ClientNotify method, 614

   IDL notation, 609–10

   ServerFillBuffer method, 614

   ServerGetSize method, 614

   ServerNotify method, 613, 614

IClassActivator interface

   GetClassObject method, 375–76

   IDL notation, 371

   and marvelous moniker, 371, 374–76

IClassFactory2 interface, 65–66

IClassFactory interface

   and *CoCreateInstance* function, 358

   CreateInstance method, 58, 60–61, 86, 87, 89, 356, 434

   vs. custom activation interfaces, 357, 420, 422

   vs. *IClassFactory2*, 65–66

   IDL notation, 58

   LockServer method, 58, 61–63, 417, 422

   and marshaling, 433, 434

   overview, 57–59

IClientInfo interface, 614, 615

IClientSecurity interface

   CopyProxy method, 573

   defined, 572

   equivalent API functions, 574

   IDL notation, 572–73

   QueryBlanket method, 573

   SetBlanket method, 559, 573, 574

IConnectionPointContainer interface

   EnumConnectionPoints method, 277, 291

   FindConnectionPoint method, 277, 291

   IDL notation, 276–77

IConnectionPoint interface
  Advise method, 275
  EnumConnections method, 296–97
  GetConnectionInterface method, 296
  GetConnectionPointContainer method, 297
  IDL notation, 274
  overview, 273, *274*
  Unadvise method, 276
ICreateErrorInfo interface, 252, 253–55
ICreateTypeInfo2 interface, 92, 93, 301, 308–10
ICreateTypeInfo interface, 306–8, 310, 311, 312, 313, 314, 316, 317
ICreateTypeLib2 interface, 92, 93, 301, 303, 304, 305, 311, 317
ICreateTypeLib interface, 303–4, 305, 306
IDataObject interface, 299
identity, rules of, 52–57, 81–82
identity control
  in COM+ security model, 528, 529, 530
  defined, 528, 529
IDispatchEx interface, 229–34
IDispatch interface
  and Automation marshaler, 200–212, 398
  and C++, 235–39
  dual interface overview, 213–15
  and early vs. late binding, 235, 241
  GetIDsOfNames method, 217, 221, 236
  GetTypeInfoCount method, 219–20
  GetTypeInfo method, 220–21
  helper functions, 217–19
  vs. *IDispatchEx* interface, 229–32
  IDL notation, 199–200
  implementing, 212–34
  Invoke method, 200, 217, 222–25, 236, 238–39

IDispatch interface, *continued*
  overview, 199–200
  pure vs. dual interface, 213–14
  and Visual Basic, 241
IDL. *See* Interface Definition Language (IDL)
IEnumConnectionPoints interface, 292, 293–95
IEnumConnections interface, 292, 297
IErrorInfo interface, 116, 252, 253, 256–57
IExternalConnection interface
  AddConnection method, 423–24
  IDL notation, 422
  ReleaseConnection method, 423–24
IGlobalInterfaceTable interface
  GetInterfaceFromGlobal method, 180, 181
  IDL notation, 179
  RegisterInterfaceInGlobal method, 180
  RevokeInterfaceFromGlobal method, 181
IIDs. *See* interface identifiers (IIDs)
IMarshal interface
  defined, 456
  DisconnectObject method, 447
  and free-threaded marshaler, 174, 176
  GetMarshalSizeMax method, 438–39, 441, 483
  GetUnmarshalClass method, 437–38, 439, 441, 457, 480
  IDL notation, 435–36
  and interface pointers, 440
  vs. *IPersistStream* interface, 451–52
  MarshalInterface method, 439–40, 446, 450, 451, 457, 483
  ReleaseMarshalData method, 444
  and standard vs. custom marshaling, 433–34, 435
  UnmarshalInterface method, 436–37, 446, 450, 457, 484

IMDB. *See* In-Memory Database (IMDB)

IMessageFilter interface, 153–57

IMoniker interface

and bind contexts, 361–64

BindToObject method, *361, 362, 363, 365, 367, 368, 369, 370, 373–74, 379, 479*

and class moniker, 367–70

GetDisplayName method, *361,* 364, 380

hierarchy, 360, *360*

list of methods, *361*

and marvelous moniker, 371, 373–74, 375

and *MkParseDisplayName* function, 364–67

overview, 359–60

ParseDisplayName method, *361,* 364

ImpersonateClient method, *IServerSecurity* interface, 569–70

impersonation levels, 535–36, 555, 569–70

implements keyword, 119, 131

<implements> tag, *247*

IMPLTYPEFLAG values, *313*

#import directive, 101, 110, 111, 133

import library, 70

import statement, 133

IMultiply interface

and aggregation, 86, 88

and containment, 83–85

and *ISum* interface, 83–85

Multiply method, 83

IMultiQI interface, 410

incline functions, 104

#include directive, 102

inheritance, 8, 81, 84–85, *84*

InitNew method, *IPersistStreamInit* interface, 331, 339

In-Memory Database (IMDB), 23

in-place activation, 14

in-process components

and apartment interactions, 166–69

apartment model support, 169–72

and DLL surrogates, 386–94

vs. executable components, 63, 385, 401–3

and free-threaded marshaler, 172–81

overview, 63

running locally, 386–88

running remotely, 385, 388–90

self-registration, 75–81

and threading models, 165–87

In Process.dsw workspace file, 46, 81

insidecom.java file, 131, *131–32, 255–56*

Instancing property, 188–89

int data type, *95, 201, 486*

intelligent names. *See* monikers

Intel processors, 486

interactive users, DCOM Configuration utility, 548–49

Interface Definition Language (IDL)

and character arrays, 498–501

and conformant arrays, 492–95

creating type libraries, 93–96

and data types, 95, *95–96, 485–87, 486*

defining *ISum* interface, 32–35

defining *IUnknown* interface, 33

and enumerated types, 487

and fixed arrays, 492

full pointers, 504

and MIDL compiler, 34–35, 618–19

and multidimensional arrays, 501–2

and open arrays, 496–98

overview, 32–35, 485

reference pointers, 505

Interface Definition Language (IDL), *continued*
  and Remote Procedure Calls, 618–19
    unique pointers, 504–5
    and varying arrays, 495–96
interface identifiers (IIDs), 39, 413
INTERFACEINFO structure, 155
interface pointer identifiers (IPIDs), 582–83, 593
interface pointers. *See also* object references
  converting to strings, 476–79
  in data packets, 590–600
  and Global Interface Table, 178–81
  and *IMarshal* interface, 440
  marshaled, 440, 476–79, 590–600
  marshaling between apartments, 158–62
  marshaling overview, 428–30
  overview, 428, 505–8
  unmarshaling, 444–50
  and v-tables, 44, 429
interfaces, programmatic. *See also*
    IClassFactory interface; *IDispatch* interface;
    Interface Definition Language (IDL);
    IUnknown interface
  asynchronous, 512–18
  custom activation, 357–58, 420, 422–24
  design recommendations, 509–10
  dual interface overview, 213–15
  overview, 11, 31
  pure-Automation vs. dual interface, 213–14
  source, 271, 272–73, *272*
  standard vs. custom, 29, 396
  synchronous vs. asynchronous versions, 512, 518–19
  translating into source files using MIDL compiler, 34–35
  Win32 API as example, 11

InterfaceSupportsErrorInfo method, *ISupportErrorInfo* interface, 253, 256
Internet Explorer, 14
Internet Explorer objects, *113*
Internet Information Server (IIS), 584
Internet protocol (IP), 575
Internet Server Application Programming Interface (ISAPI), 584
interoperability, 10–11
INumbers interface, 228
Inverse method, *IMoniker* interface, *361*
InvokeEx method, *IDispatchEx* interface, 229, 233–34
Invoke method, *IDispatch* interface, 200, 217, 222–25, 236, 238–39
Invoke method, *IRpcStubBuffer* interface, 473
IOXIDResolver interface, 600–604, 605, 607
IP. *See* Internet protocol (IP)
IParseDisplayName interface
  IDL notation, 372
  ParseDisplayName method, 365, 372–73
IPersist interface
  derived interfaces, 330, *330*
  family of interfaces, 329–45
  GetClassID method, 335–36
  IDL notation, 330
  relationship to *IMoniker* interface, 360
IPersistPropertyBag interface, 339–44
IPersistStreamInit interface
  GetSizeMax method, 341
  IDL notation, 331
  InitNew method, 331, 339
  IsDirty method, 337, 341
  Load method, 331, 335, 336, 338, 339
  Save method, 331, 338

IPersistStream interface, *330*, 334–35, *334*
  GetSizeMax method, 339
  IDL notation, 331
  vs. *IMarshal* interface, 451–52
  Load method, 331
  relationship to *IMoniker* interface, 360
  Save method, 338
IPIDs. *See* interface pointer identifiers (IPIDs)
IPipeByte interface, 524
IPipeDouble interface, 524
IPipeLong interface, 524
IPrimeFactory interface, 357–58, 421
IPropertyBag interface, 339, 342, 343
IPropertySetStorage interface
  list of methods, *351*
  overview, 349–53
IPropertyStorage interface
  list of methods, *351*
  overview, 349–53
IProvideClassInfo2 interface, 319
IProvideClassInfo interface, 318–19
  GetClassInfo method, 318
  IDL notation, 318
IPSFactoryBuffer interface
  CreateProxy method, 462–64
  CreateStub method, 462, 464–65
  defined, 461
  IDL notation, 461–62
IRecordInfo interface, 211
IRemoteActivation interface
  defined, 581
  IDL notation, 582
  RemoteActivation method, 581, 582
IRemUnknown2 interface, 600

IRemUnknown interface
  IDL notation, 596
  overview, 595–96
  RemAddRef method, 597, 599
  RemQueryInterface method, 597, 598
  RemRelease method, 597, 599
IRpcChannelBuffer interface
  FreeBuffer method, 470, 474
  GetBuffer method, 470, 472, 474
  GetDestCtx method, 475
  IDL notation, 469–70
  IsConnected method, 475
  RPCOLEMESSAGE structure, 470–75
  SendReceive method, 470, 473, 474, 475
IRpcProxyBuffer interface
  Connect method, 465–66
  Disconnect method, 466
  IDL notation, 465
  and standard marshaling architecture, 458, *458*
IRpcStubBuffer interface
  Connect method, 467, 468
  DebugServerQueryInterface method, 468
  DebugServerRelease method, 468
  Disconnect method, 468
  IDL notation, 466–67
  Invoke method, 473
  ISIIDSupported method, 467–68
  and standard marshaling architecture, *458*, 459
IRunningObjectTable interface
  EnumRunning method, 380
  IDL notation, 379–80
  Register method, 381
  Revoke method, 381
IsAccessAllowed method, *IAccessControl* interface, 560, 562–63

IsConnected method, *IRpcChannelBuffer* interface, 475

IsDirty method, *IPersistStreamInit* interface, 337

IsEqual method, *IMoniker* interface, *361*

ISequentialStream interface
  IDL notation, 332
  Read method, 332, 338, 446
  Write method, 332, 338, 439

IServerSecurity interface
  defined, 566
  equivalent API functions, 568
  IDL notation, 567
  ImpersonateClient method, 569–70
  list of methods, 568
  QueryBlanket method, 568
  RevertToSelf method, 570

IsIIDSupported method, *IRpcStubBuffer* interface, 467–68

isolated transaction property, 26

IsRunning method, *IMoniker* interface, *361*

IsSystemMoniker method, *IMoniker* interface, *361*

IStdMarshalInfo interface
  GetClassForHandler method, 480
  IDL notation, 479

IStorage interface, 347–49

IStream interface. *See also ISequentialStream* interface
  Clone method, *333*
  Commit method, *333*
  CopyTo method, *332*
  list of methods, *332–33*
  LockRegion method, *333*
  Revert method, *333*
  Seek method, *332*
  SetSize method, *332*

IStream interface, *continued*
  Stat method, *333*
  UnlockRegion method, *333*

ISum interface
  as abstract base class, 30, 48
  building sample client application, 46–47
  in C++, 29, 48–57
  compiling using MIDL compiler, 34–35
  component.h file, 34–35
  elements of sample client application, 36–46
  IDL notation, *32*, 48, 225
  in Java, 31, 131, 136–41
  relationship to *IUnknown* interface, 31, 33
  Sum method, 29–30, 33, 57
  in Visual Basic, 31, 124–26
  v-table structure, 29–30

isum.java file, *130*

ISupportErrorInfoImpl ATL class, 116

ISupportErrorInfo interface, 116, 252, 253, 256

ISurrogate interface, 392–93

ISynchronize interface, 514–15, 517, 569

Item method, collection objects, 227

item monikers, *359*

ITransactionDispenser interface, 24

ITransaction interface, 24

ITransactionOptions interface, 24

ITransactionOutcomeEvents interface, 24

ITypeComp interface, 325

ITypeInfo2 interface, 92, 323–24

ITypeInfo interface, 312, 321–23

ITypeLib2 interface, 92, 321

ITypeLib interface, 314, 319–20

IUnknown interface
  as abstract base class, 30
  AddRef method, 40–42, 49, 60, 61, 87–88, 90

IUnknown interface, *continued*

and aggregation, 85–90

defined, 29, 31, 33

IDL notation, 33

QueryInterface method, 39–40, 50–57, 259, 271

relationship to *ISum* interface, 31, 33

Release method, 40–42, 49

as standard interface, 29

J

Java. *See also* Microsoft Java Virtual Machine; ·Visual J++

applet security issues, 142–43

building COM+ clients, 135–36

building COM+ components, 140–41

building persistable objects in, 344–46

calling COM+ objects from, 132–36

.class files, 138, 139–40, 142–43

and COM+, 126–29

and COM+ error handling, 252–56

COM+ programming in, 126–43

component threading issues, 192–93

and IDL-defined data types, 95, *95–96*

implementing COM+ objects, 136–41

and *ISum* interface, 31, 131, 136–41

new keyword, 133

packaging components, 138–40

running applets in sandboxes, 142–43

sink object example, 289–90

trusted vs. untrusted applets, 142–43

and type libraries, 128

wrappers for COM+ objects, 127–32

Java Beans, integrating with ActiveX Controls, 141–42

javaclient.java file, 132, *132–33*

Java moniker, 378–79

JavaSink.java file, 289–90, *290*

Java Virtual Machine, defined, 127.
See also Microsoft Java Virtual Machine

JScript, defined, 243

just-in-time activation, 14, 20–22

K

Kerberos security protocol, 532

kernel objects, threads as, 146–47

L

lanalyzers, 578

languages. *See* programming languages

LAN Manager Security Support Provider.
See Windows NT LAN Manager Security
Support Provider (NTLMSSP)

late binding, 235, 241

launching users, DCOM Configuration utility, 548

LayOut method, *ICreateTypeInfo* interface, 317

LIBIDs. *See* type library identifiers (LIBIDs)

library keyword, 94. *See also* type libraries

lite controls, *114*

little endian architecture, 486

load balancing, 23

LoadDllServer method, *ISurrogate* interface, 392–93

LoadLibrary Win32 API function, 63, 68

Load method, *IPersistStreamInit* interface, 331, 335, 336, 338, 339

Load method, *IPersistStream* interface, 331

LoadRegTypeLibEx function, 97, 98–99, 200

LoadRegTypeLib function, 314, 318

LoadTypeLibEx function, 399, 406

local components
  as executable files, 385
  shutting down, 417–20
Local Procedure Call (LPC) model, 618
location transparency, 57, 385, 619–20
LockRegion method, *IStream* interface, *333*
LockServer method, *IClassFactory* interface, 58, 61–63, 417, 422
long data type, *95, 201, 486,* 524
LPC (Local Procedure Call) model, 618

M

macros, for HRESULT values, 251–52
main start-up function, 404, 405, 414–15
marshal-by-value, 450–53
marshaler, free-threaded, 172–81
marshaling
  and apartment interactions, 167–68
  basic COM+ options, 396
  custom (*see* custom marshaling)
  and custom interfaces, 395
  handler marshaling, 479–84
  and *IClassFactory* interface, 433, 434
  and *IDispatch* interface, 200
  integrating code with executable components, 411–13
  interface pointers, 428–30, 590–600
  overview, 153, 394–96
  and proxy/stub DLL, 167
  and RPCs, 456–76
  standard (*see* standard marshaling)
  and standard interfaces, 396
  type library, 200–201, 398–99
  which to choose, 431–35

MarshalInterface method, *IMarshal* interface, 439–40, 446, 450, 451, 457
marvelous moniker, 370–77
max function template, 103, 104
MEOW structure, 591
MessagePending method, *IMessageFilter* interface, 156–57
message queues, in STA threading model, 148, 149, 150–53
Microsoft Distributed Transaction Coordinator (MS DTC), 24, 25–26
Microsoft Foundation Classes (MFC), 111–12
Microsoft IDL (MIDL) compiler
  and asynchronous calls, 512
  creating type information, 93–96, 301
  introduction, 34–35
  and RPC, 618–19
  and standard marshaling, 396
Microsoft Java Virtual Machine. *See also* Visual J++
  and COM+ objects, 133, 134, 137–38
  component threading issues, 192–93
  integrating ActiveX Controls and Java Beans, 141–42
  as Java implementation, 127, 129
  Java moniker, 378–79
  trusted vs. untrusted applets, 142–43
Microsoft Message Queue (MSMQ), 23–24, *24*
Microsoft Spy++, 150, *151*
Microsoft Systems Management Server, 578
Microsoft Transaction Server (MTS), 17
  and roles, 27
Microsoft Windows NT LAN Manager Security Support Provider (NTLMSSP), 532

MkParseDisplayName function
  and class moniker, 368–70
  and *IMoniker* interface, 364–67
  and marvelous moniker, 371–72, 373
  and OBJREF moniker, 479
MMC snap-ins, *114*
monikers
  class moniker, 367–70
  custom, 359–64
  and *IMoniker* interface, 359–64
  marvelous moniker, 370–77
  new moniker, 377–78
  overview, 355, 358–59
MoveElementTo method, *IStorage* interface, *348*
MS-DOS, 12
MS DTC. *See* Microsoft Distributed Transaction
    Coordinator (MS DTC)
MSMQ. *See* Microsoft Message Queue (MSMQ)
MS Transaction Server components, *114*
MTA. *See* multi-threaded apartment (MTA)
    model
MTS. *See* Microsoft Transaction Server (MTS)
multidimensional arrays, 501–2
multiple inheritance, 84–85, *84*
Multiply method, *IMultiply* interface, 83
multiprocessing. *See* parallel processing
multi-threaded apartment (MTA) model
  interactions involving in-process components,
    166–70
  vs. other apartment models, 148, 149, 183–85
  overview, 157–58
  when to use, 162–64
mylib.idl file, 301, *302*

N
NA. *See* neutral apartment (NA) model
named pipes, 622–23
names. *See* monikers
namespaces, 110–11
NDR. *See* Network Data Representation (NDR)
Network Data Representation (NDR)
  and marshaled interface pointers, 590
  overview, 431
  and Protocol Data Units, 590
Network Monitor utility, 578, 580–81
network protocols, 575
neutral apartment (NA) model
  vs. other apartment models, 148, 149, 183–85
  overview, 181–83
  when to use, 162–64
_NewEnum property collection objects, 227–28
new keyword, Java, 133
New keyword, Visual Basic, 118, 241–42
new moniker, 377–78
new operator, C++, 36, 57, 355–56
NTLMSSP. *See* Windows NT LAN Manager
    Security Support Provider (NTLMSSP)

O
object exporter identifiers (OXIDs), 582–83, 593.
    See also OXID Resolver
object keyword, 601
object linking and embedding (OLE), 13–14
object-oriented programming (OOP)
  and code sharing and reuse, 8–9
  encapsulation in, 8
  examples of objects and classes, 7–8
  overview, 7–8
  and polymorphism, 8

object pooling, 22

object references, 590–600

Object RPC

analyzing, 580–81

defined, 576–77

and marshaled interface pointers, 590–600

and Protocol Data Units, 588–89

objects. *See also* COM+ objects

vs. classes, 7–8

connectable (*see* connectable objects)

<object> tag, *247*

OBJREF monikers, *359,* 478–79

OBJREF structure, 590–92

ODBC (Open Database Connectivity), 19, 531

OIDs, 593

OLE/COM Object Viewer utility, 99, 263, *264*

OLE DB, 19, 20

OleLoadFromStream helper function, 337

OleMainThreadWndClass window class, 150

OleSaveToStream helper function, 337

OLESelfRegister flag, 79–81

OleUIBusy function, 156

On Error statement, 252

open arrays, 496–98

Open Database Connectivity (ODBC), 19, 531

Open Software Foundation (OSF), 16, 32, 576

OpenStorage method, *IStorage* interface, *348*

OpenStream method, *IStorage* interface, *348*

Open Systems Interconnection (OSI) seven-layer
model, 576, *576*

ORPC. *See* Object RPC

ORPC_EXTENT_ARRAY structure, 608–9

ORPC_EXTENT structure, 608, 609

ORPCTHAT structure, 588–89, 608

ORPCTHIS structure, 588–89, 607

OSI seven-layer model, 576, *576*

out-of-process components. *See* EXE components

OXID Resolver, 600–604

OXIDs. *See* object exporter identifiers (OXIDs)

P

<package> tag, *247*

parallel processing, 3

paramaterized types. *See* templates, C++

parameter passing. *See also* marshaling

C and C++ languages, 487–91

and COM interface design, 510

ParseDisplayName method

IMoniker interface, *361,* 364

IParseDisplayName interface, 365, 372–73

Pascal calling convention, 30

PDUs. *See* Protocol Data Units (PDUs)

persistable objects

building in Java, 344–46

building in Visual Basic, 339–44

implementing, 334–39

persistence, 329–53. *See also* structured storage

persistent subscriptions, 28

phantom reference counts, 61

pinging, 605–7

pipes, 523–25

pointer monikers, *359*

pointers. *See also* interface pointers

vs. arrays, 491

in C language, 503

full, 504

IDL support, 503–5

overview, 503–4

passing, 488–91

pointers, *continued*
  reference, 505
  unique, 504–5
polymorphism, defined, 8
pooling, object, 22
ports, 583–84
Prime application
  client computation, 625
  client initialization, 622–24
  context rundown, 626–27
  debugging, 627
  distributed computation, 627–28
  overview, 621
  Prime server, 625–26
PRIVATE keyword, 70
processors, big endian vs. little endian
    architecture, 486
Process Viewer utility, 158
ProgIDs. *See* program identifiers (ProgIDs)
program identifiers (ProgIDs), 240, 364–65, 378
programmatic security
  CoInitializeSecurity function, 551–60
  in COM+ security model, 530, 550–74
  vs. declarative security, 26–27, 550
programming languages. *See also* C and C++
    programming languages; Interface Definition
    Language (IDL); Java; Visual Basic
  and apartment models, 187–93
  and dual interface issue, 214
Project Properties dialog box, Visual Basic,
    189–91, *190, 191*
properties, Visual Basic
  defining, 225–26
  IDL notation, 225
  as type of method, 225–26

property page objects, *114*
property sets, 349–53
Protocol Data Units (PDUs), 586–89
proxy manager, 457, *458,* 482–83
proxy objects, 429, 430, 437–38, 448
proxy/stub DLLs
  building, 397–98
  defined, 396
  integrating with executable components,
      411–13
  and interprocess communications, 430
  overview, 429
  registering, 396, 475–76
  and standard marshaling, 396–98, 455,
      459, 460
  vs. type library marshaling, 200–201, 398–99
<public> tag, 247, *248*
publishers, 27–28
Pull methods, 524
Push methods, 524

Q
QueryBlanket method
  IClientSecurity interface, 573
  IServerSecurity interface, 568
QueryInterface method
  and aggregation, 86–90
  IUnknown interface, 39–40, 50–57, 259, 271
  overview, 39–40
  problems with, 44–46
  reflexive rule, 53–54, *57*
  requirements for implementation, 52–57
  symmetric rule, 54–55, *57*
  transitive rule, 55–57, *57*
  and Visual Basic, 119–21

QueryMultipleInterfaces method, *IMultiQI* interface, 410

QueryPathOfRegTypeLib function, 97

queued components, 23–24

R

ReadConsoleInput Win32 API function, 278

Read method, *ISequentialStream* interface, 332, 338, 446

RecordInfo object, 211

recycling objects. *See* object pooling

Reduce method, *IMoniker* interface, *361*

reference counts
  artificial, 61
  in Java, 135
  overview, 40–42, 49
  phantom, 61
  and singleton implementation, 426

reference pointers, 505

<reference> tag, *248*

RegCloseKey Win32 API function, 75

RegCreateKeyEx Win32 API function, 75

RegDeleteKey Win32 API function, 75

RegEnumKeyEx Win32 API function, 75

RegisterCategories method, 266

RegisterClassImplCategories method, 267

RegisterClass Win32 API function, 150

RegisterInterfaceInGlobal method, *IGlobalInterfaceTable* interface, 180

Register method, *IRunningObjectTable* interface, 381

RegisterServerEx function, 76, 77, 165–66, 406, 475

RegisterServer function, 76, 77, 78, 165, 406

RegisterTypeLib function, 97, 200

<registration> tag, 246, *248*

registry
  and AppIDs, 386–87, 389
  and asynchronous interfaces, 513
  and class monikers, 368–69
  and class objects, 407–9
  and *CoCreateInstance* function, 37–39
  and COM+ security model, 532–50
  and component categories, 265–68
  context menu script, 82
  and declarative security, 532–50
  and DLL surrogates, 386–87, 388, 389, 390
  and executable components, 406, 407–9
  and proxy/stub DLLs, 396, 475–76
  and Running Object Table, 381
  and threading models, 165–66
  and type libraries, 96–100

registry.cpp file, 75

registry.h file, 76, *76*

RegOpenKeyEx Win32 API function, 75

RegSetValueEx Win32 API function, 75

RegSvr32 utility, 81, *81*

RegTlb utility, 99–100

RegTypeLib function, 399, 406

RelativePathTo method, *IMoniker* interface, *361*

ReleaseConnection method, *IExternalConnection* interface, 424

ReleaseMarshalData method, *IMarshal* interface, 444

Release method, *IUnknown* interface, 40–42, 49

reliability, and distributed computing, 4–5

RemAddRef method, *IRemUnknown* interface, 597, 599

RemoteActivation method, 581, 582

remote COM+ objects, 586–89

remote components

  DLL surrogates, 388–90

  overview, 385

  threading models, 152–53

remote instantiation, 409–11

Remote Procedure Calls (RPCs).
    See also Object RPC

  and binding, 619

  binding handles, 620

  and COM+, 15–16, 576–77

  and COM+ security model, 531–32

  debugging applications, 627

  design and purpose, 617–20

  and IDL, 618–19

  and *IRemoteActivation* interface, 581–82

  and location transparency, 619–20

  vs. LPC model, 618

  and marshaling, 456–76

  as network protocol layer, 575, *575*

  and Object RPC, 576–77, 578

  overview, 617–20

  and PDUs, 586–89

  Prime application, 621–28

remoting, defined, 385

Remove method, collection objects, 227

RemQueryInterface2 method, *IRemUnknown2*
  interface, 600

RemQueryInterface method, *IRemUnknown*
  interface, 597, 598

RemRelease method, *IRemUnknown* interface,
  597, 599

RenameElement method, *IStorage* interface, *348*

ResolveOXID2 method, *IOXIDResolver*
  interface, 604

ResolveOXID method, *IOXIDResolver*
  interface, 602–3

resource dispensers, defined, 25

resource managers, defined, 25

<resource> tag, *248*

RetryRejectedCall method, *IMessageFilter*
  interface, 155–56

reusing code, 8–9

Revert method, *IStorage* interface, *348*

Revert method, *IStream* interface, *333*

RevertToSelf method, *IServerSecurity* interface, 570

RevokeInterfaceFromGlobal method,
  IGlobalInterfaceTable interface, 181

Revoke method, *IRunningObjectTable*
  interface, 381

roles, in MTS, 27

ROT. *See* Running Object Table (ROT)

RPCOLEMESSAGE structure, 470–75

RPCs. *See* Remote Procedure Calls (RPCs)

Running Object Table (ROT), 379–81

run-time errors. *See* exceptions

RuntimeException class, 255

S

SACLs. *See* system access control lists (SACLs)

SAFEARRAY data type, *96, 201*

safe arrays, 206–10

SAFEARRAY structure, 206–10

sandbox model, 142–43

SaveAllChanges method, *ICreateTypeLib2*
  interface, 317

Save method, *IPersistStreamInit* interface,
  331, 338

SCM. *See* Service Control Manager (SCM)

scripting languages
  overview, 242–43
  security issues, 244
scriptlets, 245–48
<scriptlet> tag, 247, *248*
<script> tag, 247, *248*
.sct files, 245, *245–46*
security
  COM model overview, 26–27, 528–32
  and DCOM Configuration utility, 532–50
  and Java applets, 142–43
  and registry, 532–50
  sandbox model, 142–43
  scripting, 244
  threading issues, 185–87
SECURITYBINDING structure, 594, 595
security blankets, 559
security descriptors, 528
security identifiers (SIDs), 528
Security Support Provider Interface (SSPI), 531
Security Support Providers (SSPs), 531.
    See also Windows NT LAN Manager
    Security Support Provider (NTLMSSP)
Seek method, *IStream* interface, *332*
self-extracting Setup files, *139*
self-registering components, 75–81
SendReceive method, *IRpcChannelBuffer*
    interface, 470, 473, 474, 475
ServerFillBuffer method, *IChannelHook*
    interface, 614
ServerGetSize method, *IChannelHook*
    interface, 614
ServerNotify method, *IChannelHook* interface,
    613, 614
Service Control Manager (SCM), 69, 411, 432,
    442, 459, 582–83

SetBindOptions method, *IBindCtx* interface, 363
SetBlanket method, *IClientSecurity* interface, 559,
    573, 574
SetClass method, *IStorage* interface, *348*
SetDocString method, *ICreateTypeLib2*
    interface, 305
SetElementTimes method, *IStorage* interface, *348*
SetErrorInfo function, 254
SetEvent Win32 API function, 394, 414, 419–20,
    448–49
SetFuncAndParamNames method,
    ICreateTypeInfo interface, 317
SetGuid method, *ICreateTypeInfo* interface,
    310, 312
SetGuid method, *ICreateTypeLib* interface, 304
SetImplTypeFlags method, *ICreateTypeInfo*
    interface, 313
SetName method, *ICreateTypeLib* interface, 304
SetPriorityClass function, 147
SetSize method, *IStream* interface, *332*
SetStateBits method, *IStorage* interface, *348*
SetThreadPriority function, 147
SetTypeFlags method, *ICreateTypeInfo* interface,
    310, 311
SetVersion method, *ICreateTypeLib2* interface,
    304, 305
SetWindowLong Win32 API function, 608
shared memory and custom marshaling, 431,
    432, 440
short data type, *95, 201, 486*
SIDs. *See* security identifiers (SIDs)
signed data types, *95, 201*
Simple Negotiation Mechanism (Snego), 532
simple objects, 113, *113*
SimplePing method, *IOXIDResolver* interface,
    605, 607
Simple Smart Pointer (SSP) template class, 106–7

single data type, *96, 201*

single-threaded apartment (STA) model

   interactions involving in-process components, 166–69

   vs. other apartment models, 148, 149, 183–85

   overview, 149–53

   when to use, 162–64

singletons

   building in COM+, 425

   ClientChannelHook example, 615

   defined, 424

sink objects

   C++ example, 279–83

   defined, 271, *272*

   Java example, 289–90

   multiple, 282–83

   Visual Basic example, 283–89

small data type, *486*

smartpointerclient.cpp file, 109, *109*

smart pointers, 105–9

Snego (Simple Negotiation Mechanism), 532

software

   and COM+ development philosophy, 6–11

   object-oriented programming, 7–8

   reusable components, 8–9

SOLE_AUTHENTICATION_INFO structure, 556, *557*

SOLE_AUTHENTICATION_LIST structure, 556, *557*

SOLE_AUTHENTICATION_SERVICE structure, 553–55

source code vs. binary data, 9

source interfaces

   defined, 271, *272*

   IDL notation, 273

   simple example, 272–73

SQL Server, 17

SSPI. *See* Security Support Provider Interface (SSPI)

SSPs. *See* Security Support Providers (SSPs)

STA. *See* single-threaded apartment (STA) model

standard interfaces, 29, 396.

   See also custom interfaces

standard marshaler. *See* proxy manager

standard marshaling

   architecture, 456–76, *458*

   vs. custom marshaling, 399–400, *400,* 431–35

   interfaces, 460–75

   IPSFactoryBuffer interface, 461–65

   IRpcChannelBuffer interface, 459

   IRpcProxyBuffer interface, 458, *458*

   IRpcStubBuffer interface, 459

   overview, 396–98, 455–56

   and proxy/stub DLLs, 396–98, 455, 459, 460

static_cast operator, 51

Stat method, *IStorage* interface, *348*

Stat method, *IStream* interface, *333*

STDOBJREF structure, 592–93

storage. *See* structured storage

stream objects. *See IPersistStream* interface; *IStream* interface

string binding, 622, 623–24

STRINGBINDING structure, 594–95

string class template, 104–5

string data type, *96, 201*

string names, 364. *See also* monikers

strings

   BASIC, 204–6

   as character arrays, 498–501

   converting interface pointers to, 476–79

structured storage

   IPropertySetStorage interface, 349–53

structured storage, *continued*

    IPropertyStorage interface, 349–53

    IStorage interface, 347–49

    IStream interface, 349

    overview, 346–47

stub, defined, 429

subscribers, 27–28

Sum method, *ISum* interface, 29–30, 33, 57

SumTransit structure, 449

symmetric multiprocessing (SMP), 3

system access control lists (SACLs), 528

T

tables. *See* Global Interface Table (GIT); Running
    Object Table (ROT); v-tables

TCP/IP protocol, tunneling, 584–85

template keyword, 103

templates, C++. *See also* Active Template Library
    (ATL)

    function vs. class, 103–4

    vs. macros, 102

    overview, 102–5

    and smart pointers, 105–9

    two types, 103–4

TerminateThread Win32 API function, 146

TestCancel method, *ICancelMethodCalls*
    interface, 522

testing

    ATL-based COM+ objects from Visual
      Basic, 117

    Visual Basic components from C++, 125

    Visual J++ components from C++, 141

threading models

    choosing, 162–64

    and free-threaded marshaler, 172–81

threading models, *continued*

    for in-process components, 165–87

    interactions among, 166–69

    multi-threaded model, 157–58

    overview, 148–49

    for remote components, 152–53

    security issues, 185–87

    single-threaded model, 149–53

threads. *See also* apartments; threading models

    as kernel objects, 146–47

    overview, 146–47

    and symmetric multiprocessing, 3

    synchronization issues, 147, 162–63

    ten commandments, 193–94

three-tier system architecture

    business logic tier, 18, *18,* 19

    client (presentation) tier, 18, *18,* 19

    data services tier, 18, *18,* 19–20

    Windows DNA, 18–20

tlbinf32.dll file, 326

.tlh files, 101

.tli files, 102

transactions

    atomicity of, 26

    and COM+ objects, 26

    consistency of, 26

    durability of, 26

    isolation of, 26

    overview, 24–26

    properties of, 26

trusted Java applets, 142–43

TRUSTEE structure, 543, *544*

tunneling TCP/IP protocol, 584–85

two-phase commit protocol, 25–26

TYPEFLAGS values, 310, *310–11,* 311, 312
TYPEKIND values, 305–6, *305*
TypeLib Information component, 326
type libraries
    creating at run time, 302–17
    creating using MIDL compiler, 93–96, 301
    embedding in components, 96, 101
    marshaling, 200–201, 398–99
    overview, 92–93
    registering, 96–100
    using, 92–93
    and Visual Basic, 92, *93,* 301, 326–27
Type Libraries.dsw workspace file, 99
type library identifiers (LIBIDs), 318
types. *See* data types; type libraries
type systems, C++ vs. COM+, 51

U
UDTs. *See* user-defined types (UDTs)
Unadvise method, *IConnectionPoint*
    interface, 276
unique pointers, 504–5
universally unique identifiers (UUIDs)
    defined, 33
    vs. globally unique identifiers (GUIDs), 34
unknown.h file, 44–45, 46
unknown.idl file, 33, 58
UnlockRegion method, *IStream* interface, *333*
unmarshaling interface pointers, 444–50
UnmarshalInterface method, *IMarshal* interface,
    436–37, 446, 450, 457
UnRegisterCategories method, 267
UnregisterServerEx function, 76, 77, 475
UnregisterServer function, 76, 77
UnRegisterTypeLib function, 97, 100, 406

unsigned data types, *95*
URL monikers, *359*
User Datagram Protocol (UDP), 575
user-defined types (UDTs), 210–12
users, defining in DCOM Configuration utility
    interactive, 548–49
    launching, 548
    specific, 549–50
UUIDs. *See* universally unique identifiers
    (UUIDs)

V
VARIANT Automation-compatible IDL type,
    201–4
VARIANT data type, *96, 201,* 227–28
variants, 201–4
VARIANT structure, 201–4
varying arrays, 495–96
vbclient.cpp file, 126, *126*
VBScript, 243, 245, *245–46*
virtual functions, 29–30. *See also* v-tables
Visual Basic
    and ActiveX Controls, 259–60, *260,* 298
    Automation-compatible data types, *201*
    building Automation clients, 240–42
    building client applications with scriptlet
        components, 248
    building clients, 122
    building components, 124–26
    building persistable objects in, 339–43
    and class moniker, 370, 377
    and *CoCreateInstanceEx* function, 118
    and COM+ error handling, 252–55
    and COM+ interfaces, 122–24
    COM+ programming basics, 118–26

Visual Basic, *continued*

component threading issues, 188–92

and connection points, 297–99

controlling persistence from, 343–44

GetObject function vs. COM+ *MkParseDisplayName* function, 366–67, 376

and *ICatInformation* interface, 268, 270

and *IDispatch* interface, 241

and IDL-defined data types, 95, *95–96*

and *ISum* interface, 31, 124–26

and Java moniker, 378–79

New keyword, 118, 241–42

and new moniker, 377, 378

and object-oriented programming, 7

passing arrays, 502–3

and *QueryInterface* method, 119–21

singleton implementation, 425–26

sink object example, 283–89

testing ATL-based COM+ objects from, 117

testing components from C++, 125

and type libraries, 92, *93*, 301, 326–27

Visual C++. *See also* C and C++ programming languages

ATL COM+ AppWizard, 112, *112*

ATL Object Wizard, 113–16, *113*

building COM+ objects using ATL, 116–17

smart pointer support, 107–9

Visual J++. *See also* Java

building COM+ client programs, 135–36

building COM+ components, 140–41

calling COM+ objects from Java applications, 127–28, *128*

COM+ directives, 129, *129*

@com comments, 128–29, *129*

defined, 126

Visual J++, *continued*

implementing sinks, 289–90

insidecom.java file, 131, *131–32*

isum.java file, *130*

packaging Java components, 138–40

testing components from C++, 141

and type libraries, 301

v-tables

defined, 29–30

and interface pointers, 44, 429

pointing to, 43–44, *43*

re-creating, 429

W

WaitForSingleObject Win32 API function, 394, 414, 419

Wait method, *ISynchronize* interface, 515

wchar_t data type, *95, 486*

Win32 API

CloseHandle function, 146

CreateProcess function, 146

CreateThread function, 146, 148, 157–58

DispatchMessage function, 150

ExitThread function, 146

FreeLibrary function, 63

GetCurrentThreadID function, 151, 521

GetExitCodeThread function, 146

GetMessage function, 150

GetProcAddress function, 63, 68

GetWindowLong function, 608

LoadLibrary function, 63, 68

as programmatic interface, 11

RegCloseKey function, 75

RegCreateKeyEx function, 75

RegDeleteKey function, 75

Win32 API, *continued*

   RegEnumKeyEx function, 75

   RegisterClass function, 150

   RegOpenKeyEx function, 75

   RegSetValueEx function, 75

   SetEvent function, 394, 414, 419–20, 448–49

   TerminateThread function, 146

   TRUSTEE structure, 543, 544

   WaitForSingleObject function, 394, 414, 419

window message queues. *See* message queues, in STA threading model

Windows 95, running DCOM Configuration utility, 530

Windows 98, running DCOM Configuration utility, 530

Windows Distributed interNet Applications Architecture. *See* Windows DNA

Windows DNA

   business logic tier, 18, *18,* 19

   client (presentation) tier, 18, *18,* 19

   data tier, 18, *18,* 19–20

   overview, 18

Windows NT LAN Manager Security Support Provider (NTLMSSP), 532

Windows Scripting Host, 244–45

window stations, 549

winerror.h file, 251

Win main start-up function, 404

wizards

   ATL COM+ AppWizard, 112, *112*

   ATL Object Wizard, 113–16, *113*

Write method, *ISequentialStream* interface, 332, 338, 439

X

XML (Extensible Markup Language), and scriptlets, 245–48

X/Open DTP XA standard, 24–25

Z

zip files, *139*

Guy Eddon

Although he maintains his original ambition to become a world-famous cello player, Guy has taken a sabbatical to learn about the wonderful world of software development. His first real project was a game, Danny's Rooms, which he wrote for the autistic son of his cello teacher. In 1992, Danny's Rooms won an award from the Johns Hopkins National Search for Computing to Assist Persons with Disabilities and was featured on a segment of the National Public Radio program *All Things Considered*. Guy's first article, about OS/2, was published in *Windows Developer's Journal*. He has also written for *Microsoft Systems Journal, Microsoft Interactive Developer,* and *Computer*. His first book, *RPC for NT,* was published in 1994 by R&D Publications. Since then, Guy and his father, Henry, have coauthored *Active Visual Basic 5.0* (1997), *Inside Distributed COM* (1998), and *Programming Components with Microsoft Visual Basic 6.0* (1998), all published by Microsoft Press.

Henry Eddon

Henry's involvement with computers dates back to the IBM 1132 series at Haifa University. There he created the first computerized student admissions record written in Fortran IV. He later graduated from Columbia University with a degree in mathematics and moved from the Commodore SuperPET to a HERO 1 robot and then to an original IBM PC. In 1984, Henry and an ophthalmologist friend created AMOS, an insurance billing and patient appointment–scheduling program that achieved speed by bypassing MS-DOS to access video memory directly. Henry has earned a Master Mechanic license from the National Institute for Automotive Service Excellence, written a 6800 Motorola assembler to enable programming of the HERO 1 robot in assembly language instead of machine code, and earned Certified Computing Professional (CCP) status from the Institute for Certification of Computing Professionals (ICCP). He is employed in the information services division of United Parcel Service.

The manuscript for this book was prepared and submitted to Microsoft Press in electronic form. Text files were prepared using Microsoft Word 97. Pages were composed by Microsoft Press using Adobe PageMaker 6.52 for Windows, with text in Galliard and display type in Helvetica bold. Composed pages were delivered to the printer as electronic prepress files.

Cover Graphic Designer
Girvin Strategic Branding and Design

Cover Illustrator
Glenn Mitsui

Principal Interior Graphic Artist
Rob Nance

Principal Compositor
Barbara Levy

Indexer
Julie Kawabata

Master
the building blocks of
32-bit and 64-bit
development

MICROSOFT® PROGRAMMING SERIES

Microsoft®

CD-ROM included

Programming
Applications
for Microsoft
Windows®
Fourth Edition

Over 200,000 copies of previous editions in print!

Jeffrey Richter

Master the critical building blocks of 32-bit and 64-bit Windows-based applications

U.S.A.   **$59.99**
U.K.   £56.49 [V.A.T. included]
Canada $89.99
ISBN 1-57231-996-8

Here's definitive instruction for advancing the next generation of Windows-based applications—faster, sleeker, and more potent than ever! This fully updated expansion of the best-selling *Advanced Windows* digs even deeper into the advanced features and state-of-the-art techniques you can exploit for more robust Windows development— including authoritative insights on the new Windows 2000 platform.

Microsoft®

mspress.microsoft.com

Petzold
for the
MFC programmer!

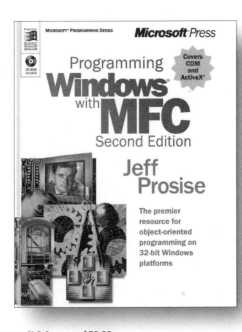

Expanding what's widely considered the definitive exposition of Microsoft's powerful C++ class library for the Windows API, PRO-GRAMMING WINDOWS® WITH MFC, Second Edition, fully updates the classic original with all-new coverage of COM, OLE, and ActiveX.® Author Jeff Prosise deftly builds your comprehension of underlying concepts and essential techniques for MFC programming with unparalleled expertise—once again delivering the consummate resource for rapid, object-oriented development on 32-bit Windows platforms.

U.S.A.	**$59.99**
U.K.	£56.99 [V.A.T. included]
Canada	$89.99
ISBN 1-57231-695-0	

Microsoft
mspress.microsoft.com

Learn how
COM+
can simplify your
development tasks

U.S.A. **$24.99**
U.K. £22.99
Canada $37.99
ISBN 0-7356-0666-8

Wouldn't it be great to have an enterprise application's infrastructure so that you could inherit what you need and spend your time writing your own business logic? COM+ is what you've been waiting for—an advanced development environment that provides prefabricated solutions to common enterprise application problems. UNDERSTANDING COM+ is a succinct, entertaining book that offers an overview of COM+ and key COM+ features, explains the role of COM+ in enterprise development, and describes the services it can provide for your components and clients. You'll learn how COM+ can streamline application development to help you get enterprise applications up and running and out the door.

mspress.microsoft.com

Here they are in one place—
practical,
detailed
explanations
of the Microsoft
networking APIs!

Microsoft has developed many exciting networking technologies, but until now no single source has described how to use them with older, and even some newer, application programming interfaces (APIs). NETWORK PROGRAMMING FOR MICROSOFT® WINDOWS® is the only book that provides definitive, hands-on coverage of how to use legacy networking APIs, such as NetBIOS, on 32-bit platforms, plus recent networking APIs such as Winsock 2 and Remote Access Service (RAS).

U.S.A.	**$49.99**
U.K.	£46.99 [V.A.T. included]
Canada	$74.99
ISBN 0-7356-0560-2	

mspress.microsoft.com

MICROSOFT LICENSE AGREEMENT

Book Companion CD

IMPORTANT—READ CAREFULLY: This Microsoft End-User License Agreement ("EULA") is a legal agreement between you (either an individual or an entity) and Microsoft Corporation for the Microsoft product identified above, which includes computer software and may include associated media, printed materials, and "on-line" or electronic documentation ("SOFTWARE PRODUCT"). Any component included within the SOFTWARE PRODUCT that is accompanied by a separate End-User License Agreement shall be governed by such agreement and not the terms set forth below. By installing, copying, or otherwise using the SOFTWARE PRODUCT, you agree to be bound by the terms of this EULA. If you do not agree to the terms of this EULA, you are not authorized to install, copy, or otherwise use the SOFTWARE PRODUCT; you may, however, return the SOFTWARE PRODUCT, along with all printed materials and other items that form a part of the Microsoft product that includes the SOFTWARE PRODUCT, to the place you obtained them for a full refund.

SOFTWARE PRODUCT LICENSE

The SOFTWARE PRODUCT is protected by United States copyright laws and international copyright treaties, as well as other intellectual property laws and treaties. The SOFTWARE PRODUCT is licensed, not sold.

1. GRANT OF LICENSE. This EULA grants you the following rights:

  a. Software Product. You may install and use one copy of the SOFTWARE PRODUCT on a single computer. The primary user of the computer on which the SOFTWARE PRODUCT is installed may make a second copy for his or her exclusive use on a portable computer.

  b. Storage/Network Use. You may also store or install a copy of the SOFTWARE PRODUCT on a storage device, such as a network server, used only to install or run the SOFTWARE PRODUCT on your other computers over an internal network; however, you must acquire and dedicate a license for each separate computer on which the SOFTWARE PRODUCT is installed or run from the storage device. A license for the SOFTWARE PRODUCT may not be shared or used concurrently on different computers.

  c. License Pak. If you have acquired this EULA in a Microsoft License Pak, you may make the number of additional copies of the computer software portion of the SOFTWARE PRODUCT authorized on the printed copy of this EULA, and you may use each copy in the manner specified above. You are also entitled to make a corresponding number of secondary copies for portable computer use as specified above.

  d. Sample Code. Solely with respect to portions, if any, of the SOFTWARE PRODUCT that are identified within the SOFTWARE PRODUCT as sample code (the "SAMPLE CODE"):

    i. Use and Modification. Microsoft grants you the right to use and modify the source code version of the SAMPLE CODE, *provided* you comply with subsection (d)(iii) below. You may not distribute the SAMPLE CODE, or any modified version of the SAMPLE CODE, in source code form.

    ii. Redistributable Files. Provided you comply with subsection (d)(iii) below, Microsoft grants you a nonexclusive, royalty-free right to reproduce and distribute the object code version of the SAMPLE CODE and of any modified SAMPLE CODE, other than SAMPLE CODE (or any modified version thereof) designated as not redistributable in the Readme file that forms a part of the SOFTWARE PRODUCT (the "Non-Redistributable Sample Code"). All SAMPLE CODE other than the Non-Redistributable Sample Code is collectively referred to as the "REDISTRIBUTABLES."

    iii. Redistribution Requirements. If you redistribute the REDISTRIBUTABLES, you agree to: (i) distribute the REDISTRIBUTABLES in object code form only in conjunction with and as a part of your software application product; (ii) not use Microsoft's name, logo, or trademarks to market your software application product; (iii) include a valid copyright notice on your software application product; (iv) indemnify, hold harmless, and defend Microsoft from and against any claims or lawsuits, including attorney's fees, that arise or result from the use or distribution of your software application product; and (v) not permit further distribution of the REDISTRIBUTABLES by your end user. Contact Microsoft for the applicable royalties due and other licensing terms for all other uses and/or distribution of the REDISTRIBUTABLES.

2. DESCRIPTION OF OTHER RIGHTS AND LIMITATIONS.

  • **Limitations on Reverse Engineering, Decompilation, and Disassembly.** You may not reverse engineer, decompile, or disassemble the SOFTWARE PRODUCT, except and only to the extent that such activity is expressly permitted by applicable law notwithstanding this limitation.

  • **Separation of Components.** The SOFTWARE PRODUCT is licensed as a single product. Its component parts may not be separated for use on more than one computer.

  • **Rental.** You may not rent, lease, or lend the SOFTWARE PRODUCT.

  • **Support Services.** Microsoft may, but is not obligated to, provide you with support services related to the SOFTWARE PRODUCT ("Support Services"). Use of Support Services is governed by the Microsoft policies and programs described in the user manual, in "on-line" documentation, and/or in other Microsoft-provided materials. Any supplemental software code provided to you as part of the Support Services shall be considered part of the SOFTWARE PRODUCT and subject to the terms and conditions of this EULA. With respect to technical information you provide to Microsoft as part of the Support Services, Microsoft may use such information for its business purposes, including for product support and development. Microsoft will not utilize such technical information in a form that personally identifies you.

- **Software Transfer.** You may permanently transfer all of your rights under this EULA, provided you retain no copies, you transfer all of the SOFTWARE PRODUCT (including all component parts, the media and printed materials, any upgrades, this EULA, and, if applicable, the Certificate of Authenticity), **and** the recipient agrees to the terms of this EULA.

- **Termination.** Without prejudice to any other rights, Microsoft may terminate this EULA if you fail to comply with the terms and conditions of this EULA. In such event, you must destroy all copies of the SOFTWARE PRODUCT and all of its component parts.

3. **COPYRIGHT.** All title and copyrights in and to the SOFTWARE PRODUCT (including but not limited to any images, photographs, animations, video, audio, music, text, SAMPLE CODE, REDISTRIBUTABLES, and "applets" incorporated into the SOFTWARE PRODUCT) and any copies of the SOFTWARE PRODUCT are owned by Microsoft or its suppliers. The SOFTWARE PRODUCT is protected by copyright laws and international treaty provisions. Therefore, you must treat the SOFTWARE PRODUCT like any other copyrighted material **except** that you may install the SOFTWARE PRODUCT on a single computer provided you keep the original solely for backup or archival purposes. You may not copy the printed materials accompanying the SOFTWARE PRODUCT.

4. **U.S. GOVERNMENT RESTRICTED RIGHTS.** The SOFTWARE PRODUCT and documentation are provided with RESTRICTED RIGHTS. Use, duplication, or disclosure by the Government is subject to restrictions as set forth in subparagraph (c)(1)(ii) of the Rights in Technical Data and Computer Software clause at DFARS 252.227-7013 or subparagraphs (c)(1) and (2) of the Commercial Computer Software—Restricted Rights at 48 CFR 52.227-19, as applicable. Manufacturer is Microsoft Corporation/One Microsoft Way/Redmond, WA 98052-6399.

5. **EXPORT RESTRICTIONS.** You agree that you will not export or re-export the SOFTWARE PRODUCT, any part thereof, or any process or service that is the direct product of the SOFTWARE PRODUCT (the foregoing collectively referred to as the "Restricted Components"), to any country, person, entity, or end user subject to U.S. export restrictions. You specifically agree not to export or re-export any of the Restricted Components (i) to any country to which the U.S. has embargoed or restricted the export of goods or services, which currently include, but are not necessarily limited to, Cuba, Iran, Iraq, Libya, North Korea, Sudan, and Syria, or to any national of any such country, wherever located, who intends to transmit or transport the Restricted Components back to such country; (ii) to any end user who you know or have reason to know will utilize the Restricted Components in the design, development, or production of nuclear, chemical, or biological weapons; or (iii) to any end user who has been prohibited from participating in U.S. export transactions by any federal agency of the U.S. government. You warrant and represent that neither the BXA nor any other U.S. federal agency has suspended, revoked, or denied your export privileges.

6. **NOTE ON JAVA SUPPORT.** THE SOFTWARE PRODUCT MAY CONTAIN SUPPORT FOR PROGRAMS WRITTEN IN JAVA. JAVA TECHNOLOGY IS NOT FAULT TOLERANT AND IS NOT DESIGNED, MANUFACTURED, OR INTENDED FOR USE OR RESALE AS ON-LINE CONTROL EQUIPMENT IN HAZARDOUS ENVIRONMENTS REQUIRING FAIL-SAFE PERFORMANCE, SUCH AS IN THE OPERATION OF NUCLEAR FACILITIES, AIRCRAFT NAVIGATION OR COMMUNICATION SYSTEMS, AIR TRAFFIC CONTROL, DIRECT LIFE SUPPORT MACHINES, OR WEAPONS SYSTEMS, IN WHICH THE FAILURE OF JAVA TECHNOLOGY COULD LEAD DIRECTLY TO DEATH, PERSONAL INJURY, OR SEVERE PHYSICAL OR ENVIRONMENTAL DAMAGE. SUN MICROSYSTEMS, INC. HAS CONTRACTUALLY OBLIGATED MICROSOFT TO MAKE THIS DISCLAIMER.

DISCLAIMER OF WARRANTY

NO WARRANTIES OR CONDITIONS. MICROSOFT EXPRESSLY DISCLAIMS ANY WARRANTY OR CONDITION FOR THE SOFTWARE PRODUCT. THE SOFTWARE PRODUCT AND ANY RELATED DOCUMENTATION ARE PROVIDED "AS IS" WITHOUT WARRANTY OR CONDITION OF ANY KIND, EITHER EXPRESS OR IMPLIED, INCLUDING, WITHOUT LIMITATION, THE IMPLIED WARRANTIES OF MERCHANTABILITY, FITNESS FOR A PARTICULAR PURPOSE, OR NONINFRINGEMENT. THE ENTIRE RISK ARISING OUT OF USE OR PERFORMANCE OF THE SOFTWARE PRODUCT REMAINS WITH YOU.

LIMITATION OF LIABILITY. TO THE MAXIMUM EXTENT PERMITTED BY APPLICABLE LAW, IN NO EVENT SHALL MICROSOFT OR ITS SUPPLIERS BE LIABLE FOR ANY SPECIAL, INCIDENTAL, INDIRECT, OR CONSEQUENTIAL DAMAGES WHATSOEVER (INCLUDING, WITHOUT LIMITATION, DAMAGES FOR LOSS OF BUSINESS PROFITS, BUSINESS INTERRUPTION, LOSS OF BUSINESS INFORMATION, OR ANY OTHER PECUNIARY LOSS) ARISING OUT OF THE USE OF OR INABILITY TO USE THE SOFTWARE PRODUCT OR THE PROVISION OF OR FAILURE TO PROVIDE SUPPORT SERVICES, EVEN IF MICROSOFT HAS BEEN ADVISED OF THE POSSIBILITY OF SUCH DAMAGES. IN ANY CASE, MICROSOFT'S ENTIRE LIABILITY UNDER ANY PROVISION OF THIS EULA SHALL BE LIMITED TO THE GREATER OF THE AMOUNT ACTUALLY PAID BY YOU FOR THE SOFTWARE PRODUCT OR US$5.00; PROVIDED, HOWEVER, IF YOU HAVE ENTERED INTO A MICROSOFT SUPPORT SERVICES AGREEMENT, MICROSOFT'S ENTIRE LIABILITY REGARDING SUPPORT SERVICES SHALL BE GOVERNED BY THE TERMS OF THAT AGREEMENT. BECAUSE SOME STATES AND JURISDICTIONS DO NOT ALLOW THE EXCLUSION OR LIMITATION OF LIABILITY, THE ABOVE LIMITATION MAY NOT APPLY TO YOU.

MISCELLANEOUS

This EULA is governed by the laws of the State of Washington USA, except and only to the extent that applicable law mandates governing law of a different jurisdiction.

Should you have any questions concerning this EULA, or if you desire to contact Microsoft for any reason, please contact the Microsoft subsidiary serving your country, or write: Microsoft Sales Information Center/One Microsoft Way/Redmond, WA 98052-6399.

Register Today!

Return this
Inside COM+ Base Services
registration card today

mspress.microsoft.com

0-7356-0728-1

Inside COM+ Base Services

_____ _____ _____
FIRST NAME   MIDDLE INITIAL   LAST NAME

_____
INSTITUTION OR COMPANY NAME

_____
ADDRESS

_____

_____   _____ _____
CITY   STATE   ZIP
                                             (   )
_____   _____
E-MAIL ADDRESS   PHONE NUMBER

U.S. and Canada addresses only. Fill in information above and mail postage-free.
Please mail only the bottom half of this page.

**For information about Microsoft Press®
products, visit our Web site at
mspress.microsoft.com**